Meta-Programming in Logic Programming

Logic Programming

Ehud Shapiro, editor

Koichi Furukawa, Fernando Pereira, and David H. D. Warren, associate editors

The Art of Prolog: Advanced Programming Techniques, Leon Sterling and Ehud Shapiro, 1986

Logic Programming: Proceedings of the Fourth International Conference, edited by Jean-Louis Lassez, 1987 (volumes 1 and 2)

Concurrent Prolog: Collected Papers, edited by Ehud Shapiro, 1987 (volumes 1 and 2)

Logic Programming: Proceedings of the Fifth International Conference and Symposium, edited by Robert A. Kowalski and Kenneth A. Bowen, 1988 (volumes 1 and 2)

Constraint Satisfaction in Logic Programming, Pascal Van Hentenryck, 1989

Logic-Based Knowledge Representation, edited by Peter Jackson, Hans Reichgelt, and Frank van Harmelen, 1989

Logic Programming: Proceedings of the Sixth International Conference, edited by Giorgio Levi and Maurizio Martelli, 1989

Meta-Programming in Logic Programming, edited by Harvey Abramson and M. H. Rogers, 1989

Meta-Programming in Logic Programming

edited by Harvey Abramson and M. H. Rogers

The MIT Press
Cambridge, Massachusetts
London, England

Library of Congress Cataloging-in-Publication Data

Meta-programming in logic programming / edited by Harvey Abramson
    and M.H. Rogers.
        p.   cm. — (Logic Programming)
      ISBN 0-262-51047-2
      1. Logic programming. I. Abramson, Harvey. II. Rogers, M. H.,
    1930–   . III. Title: Title: Meta-programming. IV. Series.
    QA76.63.M47 1989
    006.3—dc20
                                          89-35120
                                          CIP

MIT Press

0262510472

ABRAMSON
META PROGRAMMING

Contents

Contents

Series Foreword

The logic programming approach to computing investigates the use of logic as a programming language and explores computational models based on controlled deduction.

The field of logic programming has seen a tremendous growth in the last several years, both in depth and in scope. This growth is reflected in the number of articles, journals, theses, books, workshops, and conferences devoted to the subject. The MIT Press series in logic programming was created to accommodate this development and to nurture it. It is dedicated to the publication of high-quality textbooks, monographs, collections, and proceedings in logic programming.

Ehud Shapiro
The Weizmann Institute of Science
Rehovot, Israel

Foreword

A meta-program is any program which treats another program as data. The language in which the meta-program is written is usually called the meta-language, and the language of the program which is the data for the meta-program is called the object language. This is a wide ranging definition in that it includes such "familiar" meta-programs as compilers, editors, simulators, debuggers, program transformers, and so on. When the meta-language and object-language are identical, it also includes "meta-circular interpreters", i.e., interpreters for a language which are written in the language being interpreted.

Meta-programming is a subject therefore of considerable practical and theoretical interest, and has been for some time. There is an added dimension to this interest when it becomes easy to write, test, and consider the implications of meta-programs. Most of the meta-programs mentioned above, where the meta-language and object language are different, are complicated objects, hard to write, hard to maintain, and hard to understand. Consider, however, the following well known "vanilla" interpreter for logic programs and pure Prolog:

$$solve(empty) \leftarrow$$
$$solve(x \& y) \leftarrow solve(x) \land solve(y)$$
$$solve(x) \leftarrow clause(x, y) \land solve(y)$$

Although it is possible to write meta-circular interpreters in other programming languages, LISP for example, they are not quite as concise as this one.

This standard vanilla interpreter leads into many practical and theoretical issues. On the practical side, to take a few examples, more flavors are wanted in the sense of being able to provide a complete definition of real programming languages such as Prolog (with some admittedly unsavoury features) and to implement sophisticated knowledge based systems, including expert systems. On the theoretical side, the simple vanilla interpreter leads into tricky questions of representation and of soundness and correctness of the interpreter.

In order to address these practical and theoretical problems, $\mathcal{META}_{88}$, a Workshop on Meta-Programming in Logic Programming was held at the University of Bristol, 22-24 June, 1988. This book is the result of that workshop, containing all but a few of the original papers presented there, and quite often, with the advantage of the more relaxed form of book publication, in an expanded and deepened form. [1] We shall let the papers speak for themselves, the collection as a whole representing a fairly comprehensive view of what meta-programming is about within the discipline of logic programming.

---

[1] The papers which do not appear here have been published elsewhere. Alan Bundy's *The Use of Explicit Plans to Guide Inductive Proofs* appears in Proceedings of CADE9, edited by Luck, R. and Overbeek, R., Springer-Verlag, and Harvey Abramson's *Metarules and an Approach to Conjunction in Definite Clause Translation Grammars*, appears in Logic Programming: Proceedings of the Fifth International Conference and Symposium, edited by Robert K Kowalski and Kenneth A. Bowen, MIT Press.

The $\mathcal{META}_\circledR$Workshop was organized by Prof. J.W. Lloyd who also edited the original, provisional Proceedings. The members of the Program Committee were

- Harvey Abramson, University of Bristol

- P.M. Hill, University of Bristol

- J.W. Lloyd, University of Bristol

- S.G. Owen, Hewlett-Packard Research Labs, Bristol

- M.H. Rogers, University of Bristol

- J.C. Shepherdson, University of Bristol

Many thanks go to Peter Phillips, LaTeX hacker extraordinaire, for his efforts in bringing a host of varied papers to a uniform style.

Harvey Abramson
M.H. Rogers
April 1989

Meta-Programming in Logic Programming

Chapter 1

A Meta-Rule Treatment for English Wh-Constructions

Lynette Hirschman[1]

Paoli Research Center
Unisys Defense Systems

Abstract

This paper describes a general meta-rule treatment of English wh-constructions (relative clauses, and questions) in the context of a broad-coverage logic grammar that also includes an extensive meta-rule treatment of co-ordinate conjunction. Wh-constructions pose difficulties for parsing, due to their introduction of a dependency between the wh-word (e.g., *which*) and a corresponding *gap* in the following clause: *This is the book which I thought you told me to refer to ( ).* The gap can be arbitrarily far away from the wh-word, but it *must* occur within the clause, or the sentence is not well-formed, as in **The book which I read it.*

A meta-rule treatment has several advantages over an Extraposition Grammar-style treatment: a natural delimitation of the gap scope, the ability to translate/compile the grammar rules, and ease of integration with conjunction. Wh-constructions are handled by annotating those grammar rules that license a gap or realize a gap. These annotations are converted, via the meta-rule component, into parameterized rules. A set of paired input/output parameters pass the need for a gap from parent to child and left sibling to right sibling until the gap is realized; once the gap is realized, the parameter takes on a *no_gap* value, preventing further gaps from being realized. This 'change of state' in the paired parameters ensures that each gap is filled exactly once. The conjunction meta-rule operates on the parameterized wh-rules to link gaps within conjoined structures by unification, so that any gap within a conjoined structure is treated identically for all conjuncts.

[1] This work has been supported in part by DARPA under contract N00014-85-C-0012, administered by the Office of Naval Research; and in part by internal Unisys funding.

1.1   Introduction

Wh-constructions are one of the classically difficult parsing problems, because a correct treatment requires interaction of non-adjacent constituents, namely the wh-word, which introduces a constituent in clause-initial position, and the following construction which is missing a constituent (the *gap*). The gap can be arbitrarily far from the introducing wh-word (an *unbounded dependency*); in particular, it can appear within deeply embedded constructions, such as *the person that [I had hoped [Jane would tell [( ) to get the books]]]*, where there are three levels of embedded structure. It is possible, in principle, to write a rule for each case where a gap can appear. However, since the number of constructions which can accommodate a gap is very large (e.g., most complement types), this is both extremely labor-intensive and unmaintainable from the grammar writer's point of view.

It is also possible to write general rules for gap-realization, e.g., a noun phrase can be realized as a gap. If this approach is taken, then these rules must be carefully constrained to accept gaps only when inside a wh-construction; in addition, the wh-construction must contain exactly *one* gap. These restrictions involve complex and expensive search up and down the parse tree, to determine whether a gap is occurring inside a wh-construction.

In many ways, the wh-problem parallels the problem of co-ordinate conjunction that has also been a major obstacle for natural language systems. Both constructions involve gaps, both affect large portions of the grammar, and both require a major modification to the grammar and/or to the parsing mechanism to handle the linguistic phenomena.

There have been two basic approaches to conjunction and wh-constructions in the computational linguistics literature: modification of the parser (interpreter) and meta-rules. Of these, the first approach has been far more common. For conjunction, a number of variants on the 'interrupt' driven approach have been presented, both in conventional natural language processing systems [13, 12, 14], and in the context of logic grammars [4]. The same is true for logic grammar implementations of wh-constructions: the most generally used treatment is the interpreter-based treatment of Extraposition Grammar (XG) [10].

Meta-rules offer an appealing alternative to interpreter-based approaches, both for conjunction and for wh-expressions. Meta-rules are particularly well-suited to phenomena that range over a variety of syntactic structures, where the linguistic description would otherwise require regular changes to a large set of grammar rules. The use of meta-rules turns out to be efficient computationally. It also preserves compactness of the underlying grammar, so that the grammar is still maintainable from the point of view of the grammar-writer. Finally, the meta-rule approach avoids additional interpretive overhead and permits translation/compilation of grammar rules for efficient execution [5].

For conjunction, the meta-rule approach forms the basis for a comprehensive treatment of co-ordinate conjunction in Restriction Grammar [7]. Abramson has provided a generalization of this approach, formulating meta-rules as a specialized case of meta-programming [2]. Other researchers have also examined a meta-rule approach to related phenomena; Banks and Rayner, for example, have proposed a meta-treatment of the comparative [3].

For wh-constructions, we propose here an approach based on parameterization of the grammar rules. This is similar in spirit to the GPSG notion of 'slash categories' [6], but in the framework of logic grammar. The use of parameterized rules to pass gap information has previously been proposed in a logic grammar framework, specifically as *gap-threading* [10, 11]. Our approach differs from Pereira's in several ways, the most important of which is the use of meta-rules. The meta-rule approach provides a much cleaner user interface, making it possible for the grammar writer to use linguistically motivated annotations to indicate gap license and gap realization for the unparameterized BNF definitions in the grammar. The meta-rules process these annotations to generate parameterized grammar rules which, in turn, can be translated and compiled for efficient execution. The meta-rule treatment also has the property of combining seamlessly with a meta-rule treatment of co-ordinate conjunction.

1.2 Wh-Constructions: The Linguistic Issues

Wh-constructions are one instance of a class of problems referred to as *unbounded dependencies* – that is, constructions where the interdependent entities may be arbitrarily far apart. In the case of wh-constructions, we have a wh-expression which begins the clause (e.g., *who, what, which, whose book, how*, etc.) followed by a *gap* at some later point in the clause. The wh-expression may take the place of a noun phrase, an adjective phrase or an adverbial phrase. These may appear in the subject, object or sentence adjunct positions.

As the sentences of Figure 1.1 illustrate, there are a variety of wh-constructions, namely, relative clauses (including the zero-complementizer case, where an overt wh-word is absent, as in *the person I saw*), indirect questions (*I don't know what they mean*), wh-questions (*What do you want?*), and headless relatives (*You get what you deserve*). In addition to these basic types of wh-construction, there are also some constructions where the wh-expression is embedded inside a noun phrase (*this is the person whose mother I met*), with the wh-word *whose* modifying a noun phrase; the subsequent gap is filled by the noun phrase (*the person's mother*) of which the wh-word is a part. There are also wh-constructions embedded in prepositional phrases, as in *the person from whom I learned it* or *the door the key to which is missing*.

A wh-construction involves (1) a *wh-word* (e.g., *who*) contained in a clause-initial *wh-expression*; and (2) a *gap*: a constituent omitted in the clause following the wh-word, e.g., *the book which I bought ( )*. Relative clauses also have an antecedent for the relative pronoun (the wh-word); for questions, the wh-word marks the questioned item.

Wh = who; gap = subject NP
The person who () was here
Wh = who(m); gap = object NP
Who did you see ()?
Wh = that; gap = object NP
The time that I spent ()
Wh = that; gap = sentence adjunct adverbial
The time I visited them ()
Wh = who(m); gap = embedded object
The person who they told me they had tried to visit ()
Wh = who; gap = embedded subject
Who did they tell you () had visited them?
Wh = how; gap = sentence adjunct adverbial
Do you know how they did it ()?

Figure 1.1: Wh-constructions in English

To regularize a wh-construction, the wh-expression fills in the gap, and the wh-word is replaced by its antecedent (if in a relative clause).[1] For example, in the phrase *the movie which I saw ( )*, the wh-expression is *which* and the gap is after *saw*. Moving the wh-expression into the gap, we get *the movie [I saw which]*. Then, replacing *which* by its antecedent (*the movie*), we get: *the movie [I saw the movie]*. Similarly for questions, we get *what did you see ( )?* regularized as *did you see what?*. In some cases, however, the wh-word is not identical to the whole wh-expression, as in *the bird whose nest I found ( )*. Here, the wh-expression is *whose nest*, and the wh-word is *whose*. Again, we replace the gap (the object of *found*) by the wh-expression, to get *the bird [I found whose nest]*. Then we replace the wh-word by its antecedent, namely *the bird*: *the bird [I found the bird's nest]*, preserving the possessive marker from *whose*. Similarly in a question, we get: *which book did you read ( )* regularized as *did you read which book?*. To summarize, wh-expressions are introduced by a phrase containing a wh-word; following a wh-expression, there must be a gap, and this gap is understood as the wh-expression, after it has had the antecedent of the wh-word word filled in (if in a relative clause).

---

[1]The expression *replace by its antecedent* is used loosely here. What is really meant is replacing the relative pronoun by a pointer to the antecedent. This preserves co-referentiality of the relative pronoun and its antecedent, and avoids the dangers of copying quantifier and other modifier information.

The need for a gap can be captured very simply by associating with each grammar definition a set of paired input/output parameters. The input parameter signals whether or not a gap is need when the node is about to be constructed, at rule invocation time. The output parameter signals whether that need has been satisfied once the node is completed, at rule exit. Thus an assertion in a relative clause has as its input parameter the need for a gap (**need_gap**) and on exit, that need must have been satisfied (indicated by a **no_gap** output parameter). These parameters, once set, are simply passed along from parent to child, and sibling to sibling, via unification through linked input/output parameters.

However, an assertion may also occur as the main clause, where it is not licensed for a gap. This is illustrated in Figure 1.2 by the (simplified) definition for a sentence, as having two alternatives: an assertion or a question. The definition for *assertion* itself therefore must be neutral with respect to gaps, since that depends on where it is called from (relative clause or sentence). The parameters in the assertion definition simply pass along the information from parent to child and sibling to sibling. If the assertion is in a relative clause, then the need for a gap is passed along until some node (*nullwh* in Figure 1.2) realizes the gap (that is, accepts the empty string), at which point its output parameter is set to **no_gap**; this is passed along and finally, back up to assertion. If the assertion occurs as the main clause of a sentence, it has no need for a gap and in fact, cannot unify with the gap realization rule, which requires an input parameter of **need_gap**.

This mechanism enforces the constraint that only a node with the parameter pair (**need_gap/no_gap**) can dominate a gap. Any node whose input and output parameters are equal has not 'changed state' – that is, whatever it needed (or didn't need) on rule entry, it will still need at rule exit. Procedurally, any rule whose input and output parameters are equal cannot unify with the gap realization rule. The flow of information through the tree is illustrated in Figure 1.3.

1.3 The Framework: Restriction Grammar

The proposed solution is presented in the context of Restriction Grammar [8], which is the syntactic portion of the PUNDIT text processing system [9]. However, this solution is only dependent on a few general properties of Restriction Grammar, which it shares with other formalisms (e.g., Definite Clause Translation Grammars [1]). A Restriction Grammar is written in terms of context-free BNF definitions, augmented with constraints (*restrictions*) on the well-formedness of the resulting derivation tree. Constraints operate on the derivation tree, which is constructed automatically during parsing; restrictions traverse and examine this tree, to determine well-formedness.

One of the significant characteristics of Restriction Grammar is the *absence* of parameters. Context sensitivity is enforced by the restrictions, which obtain information from the derivation (parse) tree, rather than via parameter passing.

% Simplified BNF definitions before parameterization for
 wh-constructions:

```
sentence    ::= assertion; question.
rel_clause  ::= wh, assertion.
assertion   ::= subject, verb, object.
subject     ::= noun_phrase.
verb        ::= *v.                    % * indicates terminal lexical
 category
object      ::= noun_phrase; assertion;....

noun_phrase ::= lnr; *pro.
noun_phrase ::= nullwh.
lnr         ::= ln, *n, rn.     % noun with left, right adjuncts.
rn          ::= null; pp; rel_clause.

null        ::= % .     % empty string (for empty adjunct slots)
nullwh      ::= % .     % empty string for gap realization.

wh          ::= [who]; [which]; ....
```

% Parameterized BNF definitions for handling relative clause:
% Where parameters pass no information, input = output parameter.

```
sentence(X/X)       ::= assertion(no_gap/no_gap); question
(need_gap/no_gap).
rel_clause(X/X)     ::= wh(Y/Y), assertion(need_gap/no_gap).
assertion(In/Out)   ::= subject(In/Subj), verb(Subj/Verb), object
(Verb/Out).
subject(In/Out)     ::= noun_phrase(In/Out).
verb(In/In)         ::= *v.
object(In/Out)      ::= noun_phrase(In/Out); assertion(In/Out); ...

noun_phrase(In/In) ::= lnr(In/In); *pro.
noun_phrase(need_gap/no_gap)
                    ::= *nullwh.               % empty string
                                               %      for gap
lnr(In/In)          ::= ln(In/In), *n, rn(In/In).  % noun + left,
                                               % right adjuncts
rn(In/In)           ::= null(In/In); pp(In/In);
                            relative_clause(In/In).

null(In/In)         ::= % . % empty string (for empty adjunct slots)
nullwh(need_gap/no_gap)
                    ::= % . % empty string for gap realization.
wh(In/In) ::= [who]; [which]; ....
```

Figure 1.2: Simplified Rules with Parameters for Wh.

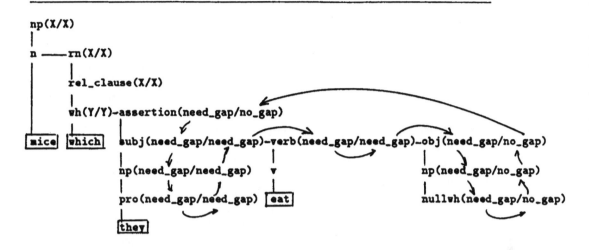

Figure 1.3: Flow of Information in *...mice which they eat.*

Restriction Grammar is implemented as a form of logic grammar which includes parameters not just for the word stream, as in DCG's, but also for the automatic construction of the derivation tree as well. In addition, each grammar rule is augmented with an associated regularization rule (indicated by a right hand arrow →), which incrementally constructs an *Intermediate Syntactic Representation (ISR)*. The ISR is an operator/operand notation that represents a canonical, regularized form of the parse tree. The regularization rule composes the ISRs of the daughter nodes in the derivation tree into the ISR of the current node, using lambda reduction. Computation of the ISR for wh-constructions is discussed in greater detail in section 6.

1.4   The Solution: Meta-Rules

Although parameterization is an elegant and efficient solution, it presents a major problem − it obscures the declarative aspect of the BNF rules, and correct parameterization of rules can be tedious and error prone, especially since there are some 40 object types in our current broad-coverage grammar of English.

The solution is to define a set of annotations to express the required linguistic constraints: gap introduction via wh-word, gap realization, and gap prohibition. Figure 1.4 shows a grammar using annotations defined as prefix operators applied to the node names in BNF definitions. Gap introduction is written as <<, gap realization as >>, and gap prohibition as <>. These are used, for example, to flag the need for a wh-word in a wh-expression, followed by the need to realize a gap:

```
rel_clause ::= <<wh, >>assertion.
```

Annotations can appear on either the left-hand side or the right-hand side of BNF definitions. By introducing the gap-requirement on the right-hand side of a BNF definition, we create a conditional gap requirement. For example, *assertion* requires a gap in the context of a relative clause, but not as the normal realization of a sentence (main clause) option. Thus we do not want to annotate the definition for *assertion*, but the call to *assertion* in *rel_clause*. However, the definition for *nullwh* is always a gap realization rule, hence it is annotated on the left-hand side (see Figure 1.4).

In certain cases, we need to define a special gap-requirement rule. For example, we define a special case for noun-phrase gap realization. This enables us to *block* transmission of gap parameters in all other options of noun phrase. To do this, we use the third annotation <> to set input parameter equal to output parameters. This annotation is also used to show that the verb can never license a gap. Similarly, the determiner (*det*) and pre-nominal adjective (*adjs*) rules cannot license a gap.

The remainder of the rules require no annotation; their parameters simply transmit whatever gap information is passed in. Figure 1.5 shows the parameterized definitions corresponding to the annotated definitions used in Figure 1.4.

1.5   The Meta-Rule Component

The meta-rule component for parameterization is implemented as a general procedure which adds parameters to each production in the grammar. At grammar read-in time, each rule is parsed and parameterized appropriately, depending on its annotation. The basic case is no annotation, in which case the following rules apply (*Label* is the left-hand side of the BNF definition; *Rule* is the right-hand side):

```
% Basic case:
wh_params(Label,Rule,NewLabel,NewRule) :-
    check_head_params(Label,InParam/OutParam,NewLabel),
    take_apart(Rule,NewRule,InParam,OutParam),!.

check_head_params(Label,Params,NewHead) :-
        insert_param(Head,Params,NewHead).
insert_param(Head,Params,NewHead) :-
        NewHead =..[Head,Params].

% Conjunction
take_apart((A,B),(NewA,NewB),InParam,OutParam) :- !,
```

```
% ANNOTATED SOURCE RULES

% Operator definitions
:- op(500,fx,[<<,>>,<>]).

% Relative clause requires  gap in assertion.
rel_clause  ::= <<wh, >>assertion.

assertion   ::= subject, verb, object.
subject     ::= noun_phrase.
<>verb      ::= *v.          % verb can't have gap.
object      ::= noun_phrase; assertion..

% Regular noun phrase rule.
% Parameters block gap
<>noun_phrase ::= lnr.
% Gap realization rule
>>noun_phrase ::= nullwh.

lnr         ::= ln, *n, rn. % lnr =
                            % left-adjunct + noun + right-adjunct

% Left noun adjunct rules
ln          ::=  det, adjs.
<>det       ::= *t; null.    % t = determiner
<>adjs      ::= null; *adj, adjs.

% Right noun adjunct rules
rn          ::= null; pp; rel_clause.
pp          ::= *prep, noun_phrase.

% Normal empty string rule
null        ::= % .
% Gap realization rule
>>nullwh    ::= %.

% Wh-word Rules
<<wh        ::= [which]; [who].
```

Figure 1.4: Illustration of Annotated Rules for Wh

```
% PARAMETERIZED VERSION OF ANNOTATED RULES

% Operator definitions
:- op(500,fx,[<<,>>,<>]).

% rel_clause          ::= <<wh, >>assertion.
rel_clause(In/In)    ::= wh(need_wh/no_wh),
                         assertion(need_gap/no_gap).

% Gap propagation rules, generated via Meta-Rule
assertion(In/Out)    ::=
        subject(In/Subj), verb(Subj/Verb), object(Verb/Out).
subject(In/Out)      ::= noun_phrase(In/Out).
verb(In/In)          ::= *v.                    % <>verb ::= *v.
object(In/Out)       ::= noun_phrase(In/Out);
                         assertion(In/Out).

%  Regular noun phrase rule.
%  Annotation blocks gap: <>noun_phrase ::= lnr.
noun_phrase(In/In) ::=        lnr(In/In).
% Gap realization rule: >>noun_phrase ::= nullwh.
noun_phrase(need_gap/no_gap)
                 ::= nullwh(need_gap/no_gap). % the empty string
lnr(In/Out)          ::= ln(In,Out1), *n, rn(Out1/Out).
% Left noun adjunct rules
ln(In/Out)           ::=  det(In/Out1), adjs(Out1/Out).
det(In/In)           ::= *t; null(In/In).    % <> det ::= *t; null.
adjs(In/In)          ::= null(In/In); *adj, adjs(In/In).
                                    % <>adjs ::= null; *adj,
                                    %                    adjs.
% Right noun adjunct rules
rn(In/Out)           ::= null(In/Out); pp(In/Out);
                         rel_clause(In/Out).
pp(In/Out)           ::= *prep, noun_phrase(In/Out).
% Normal empty string rule
null(In/In)          ::= % .
% Gap realization rule
nullwh(need_gap/no_gap) ::= %.
% Wh-word Rules
wh(need_wh/no_wh)  ::= [which];[who].  % <<wh ::= [which];[who].
```

Figure 1.5: Illustration of Parameterized Rules for Wh

```
    take_apart(A,NewA,InParam,OutParamA),
    take_apart(B,NewB,OutParamA,OutParam).
```

```
% Non-Terminal
take_apart(Def,NewDef,InParam,OutParam) :-
    insert_param(Def,InParam/OutParam,NewDef),!.
```

If there is a terminal symbol, indicated by *, there is clearly no gap, and input
and output parameters are equal; terminal symbols do not get parameterized:

```
% Terminal
take_apart(*Atom,*Atom,InParam,InParam) :- !.
```

Parameterization of embedded disjunction poses a problem, because there
is a possibility that different disjuncts could instantiate the *In/Out* parameters
differently. To catch this problem, each disjunct is computed separately, and a
routine *same_params* checks the results, to make sure that they are consistent,
before instantiating the parameters. If they are inconsistent, it issues a warning
message. Otherwise, it unifies the inputs of the disjunctions; likewise, it unifies the
outputs. It is always possible to avoid the warning message by splitting embedded
disjunctions into separate rules, as was done for the noun_phrase definition (see
Figure 1.4).

```
% Disjunction
take_apart((A;B),(NewA;NewB),InParam,OutParam) :-
    take_apart(A,NewA,InParamA,OutParamA),
    take_apart(B,NewB,InParamB,OutParamB),
    same_params((A;B),
        InParamA,InParamB,InParam,OutParamA,OutParamB,OutParam),!.
```

```
take_apart((A;B),_,_,_) :- !,
    print('$$$ Warning:  disjunct '),
    print(A), print(';'), print(B),
    print(' may not be parameterized correctly!').
```

There is also a special case for each annotation, for both the left-hand side
of the rule (*check_head_params/3*) and the right-hand side (*take_apart/4*). For
the case of the wh-word <<), the rule is shown below. In this case, the wh-word
functions independently of other nodes in the definition and so it does not hook
up to the input/output parameters.[2]

---

[2]In actuality, the wh-expression needs to pass some information about the wh-word
to the expression containing the gap, and this rule will be revised in section 6.

```
% << Needs wh-word
check_head_params(<<Head,(need_wh/no_wh),NewHead) :- !,
    insert_param(Head,(need_wh/no_wh),NewHead).

take_apart(<<Def,NewDef,InParam,InParam) :- !,
    insert_param(Def,(need_wh/no_wh),NewDef).
```

The gap-requirement annotation >> also disconnects the phrase containing the gap from its parent and siblings.

```
% >> Requires gap
check_head_params(>>Head,(need_gap/no_gap),NewHead) :- !,
    insert_param(Head,(need_gap/no_gap),NewHead).

take_apart(>>Def,NewDef,InParam,InParam) :-!,
    insert_param(Def,(need_gap/no_gap),NewDef).
```

Finally, the annotation <> enforces sameness of input and output, precluding realization of a gap:

```
% <> Rules out gap
check_head_params(<>Head,In/In,NewHead) :- !,
    insert_param(Head,In/In,NewHead).

take_apart(<>Def,NewDef,InParam,InParam) :- !,
    insert_param(Def,InParam/InParam,NewDef).
```

This small set of annotations is sufficient to describe the wh-constructions in English with one minor addition, needed to handle conjunction correctly (see section 7). Using this small set of annotations, the grammar writer can control the flow of gap information, without having a grammar cluttered with parameters. Unification is used to control generation of gaps only where required, so the technique is also efficient, avoiding extensive search to determine presence/absence of a gap.

1.6 Refinements

The treatment described above leaves open several issues. The first of these is the proper generation of a regularized syntax (*Intermediate Syntactic Representation*) for these constructions. It is clear that the compositional representation of a gap-containing expression can readily be described as a lambda expression. First, the wh-expression itself can be viewed as a lambda expression, which produces a *filler* when applied to the referent of the relative pronoun. Then, the gap-containing expression is a lambda expression, which when applied to the filler, produces a completed clause:

the book which I bought ( ):

```
=>      book1, lambda(Filler, [I bought Filler]),
                                  [lambda(Wh,[Wh]),book1]
=>      book1, lambda(Filler, [I bought Filler]), [book1]
=>      book1, [I bought book1].
```

Only wh-words in relative clauses have antecedents, namely the head noun to which the relative clause is attached. Wh-words in questions stand for the questioned element in the clause; in this case, we insert a dummy element **wh_gap** to mark the questioned element.

what did you buy ( )?

```
=>      lambda(Filler,[you buy Filler]), [lambda(Wh, [Wh]), wh\_gap]
=>      lambda(Filler,[you buy Filler]), [wh_gap]
=>      [you buy wh_gap]
```

This treatment extends very nicely to complex wh-expressions, such as *the person whose book I borrowed*, which can be represented as follows:

the person whose book I borrowed ( )

```
=>      person1,
         lambda(Filler,[I borrow Filler]), [lambda(Wh, [Wh 's book]),
 person1]
=>      person1, lambda(Filler, [I borrow Filler]), [person1 's book]
=>      person1, [I borrow person1's book]
```

This treatment has one unfortunate property: at the time that the lambda variable is generated for the relative clause, there is no way of knowing where it should be placed in the lambda expression, that is, where the associated gap in the assertion will be. For example, the lambda variable associated with a noun phrase gap could be realized as the subject or the object of the clause. Our solution is to pass the lambda variable along, embedded in the gap parameters, until the noun-phrase gap-realization rule rule is reached, at which point the lambda variable becomes the representation of the gap, shown in Figure 1.6.

We implement this by treating **need_gap** as a functor with an argument for the lambda variable. To avoid explicit mention of parameters in the source rules, we again use an annotation. Access to the lambda variable embedded in the need_gap parameter is given by the annotation **//lambdaVar(Var)**, where **//** is a binary operator.

Figure 1.6 shows several wh-constructions, with their associated ISR rules. The ISR rule appears on the right hand side of the arrow '->'. The node names within the ISR rule access the ISRs associated with the named node.

There are other complications in covering wh-constructions. One issue is that several different types of gap can occur, specifically noun phrase gaps, adverbial phrase gaps, and even adjective gaps:

> *The book that I bought* (np gap)
> *What did you buy?* (np gap)
> *The place I put it* (adverb gap)
> *Where did you get it?* (adverb gap)
> *The way I did it* (adverb gap)
> *How big is it?* (adjective gap)

In many cases, the wh-word signals the type of gap to be expected. This information is critical to determining what element should be realized as the gap. A simple way of handling this is to add a 'gap-type' argument to the information being passed in the parameters. Thus for *noun_phrase* to realize a gap, the gap type must be *np*; for an *adverb* to realize the gap, we must have gap type *adv*. This information is computed in the handling of the wh-expression and passed along to the gap-licensing construction. Thus the wh-expression does in fact have to communicate information to the construction dominating the gap. This is implemented by a slight complication to the meta-rule. The gap type information is accessed by the annotation **//type(GapType)** on the appropriate rule.

Finally, the semantics needs to know what the wh-word word was, so that it can distinguish between location expressions (*the place where I left it*) from temporal expressions (*the month I left*). Of course, there is not always an overt wh-word to indicate gap type: *the time I spent* (np gap) vs. *the time I visited* (adverb gap). All of these complications can be handled by embedding an additional parameter to carry the actual wh-word (if present) into the basic *need_gap* expression. This information is accessed by the annotation **//wh_word(WH)** and is used in constructing the final ISR.

1.7 Wh and Conjunction

A major complication occurs in the interaction between wh-constructions and conjunction. For example, with conjunction, it is not longer true that there is exactly one gap per wh-expression. Within a conjoined construction, the conjuncts must be identical with respect to gaps – if one conjunct has a gap, the other must have one as well, as in:

```
% ANNOTATED RULES with ISR

:- op(500,fx,[<<,>>,<>,><]).
:- op(400,xfy,//).

<>rn        ::=  null -> lambda(N, [N]);
                 pn -> lambda(N, [N, !pn]);
                 rel_clause
                      -> lambda(N, [N, [-rel_clause, [+rel_clause,
                                                       copy(N)]]]).
% +Def extracts the head of a list; -Def get the tail of the list.
rel_clause ::= <<wh, >>assertion//lambdaVar(Gap)
                      -> [wh, lambda(Gap, [assertion])].

assertion ::= subject, verb, object -> [verb, object, subject].
subject   ::=  noun_phrase -> noun_phrase.
<>verb    ::=  *v -> lambda(Obj, [lambda(Subj, [v, Subj, Obj])]).
object    ::=  noun_phrase -> noun_phrase; assertion -> assertion.
<>noun_phrase
          ::=  lnr -> lnr.
% gapped noun_phrase -- lambda variable is ISR.
>>noun_phrase//lambdaVar(Gap)
          ::=  nullwh -> Gap.
<<wh      ::=  [which];[who] -> lambda(Filler, [Filler]).


% PARAMETERIZED VERSION
rn(In/In) ::= null(In/In) -> lambda(N, [N]).
             pn(In/In) -> lambda(N, [N,!pn]);
             rel_clause(In/In)
                  -> lambda(N, [N, [-rel_clause, [+rel_clause,
                                                   copy(N)]]]).
% +Def extracts the head of a list; -Def gets the tail of the list.
rel_clause(In/In)
          ::= wh(need_wh/no_wh), assertion(need_gap(Gap)/no_gap)
                  -> [wh, lambda(Gap, [assertion])].
noun_phrase(In/In)
          ::= lnr(In/In) -> lnr.
noun_phrase(need_gap(Gap)/no_gap)
          ::= nullwh(need_gap(Gap)/no_gap) -> Gap.
% omitted defs for assertion, subject, verb, object.
wh(need_wh/no_wh)
          ::= [which];[who] -> lambda(Filler, [Filler]).
```

Figure 1.6: The ISR Rules for Wh-Constructions

or
>   *the books which I bought ( ) and you read ( )*

but not
>   *the letter that ( ) arrived yesterday and I sent ( ) on to you.*

>   **the books which I bought and you read them*

In an interpreter-based treatment of wh-constructions, the interpreter needs to make a special provision for 'resetting' its state to handle gaps over conjoined structure – that is, it must account for the fact that there may be two gaps if the wh-construction has scope over a conjoined structure. One advantage of a meta-rule treatment is that this interaction occurs in an extremely natural way: the meta-rules for wh-expressions are applied first; then the conjunction meta-rules simply copy the parameters of the first conjunct for the second conjunct. Since these are implemented as logical variables, the parameters of the two conjuncts are unified, and hence are guaranteed to have exactly the desired behavior.

The ability to factor syntax and semantics cleanly makes it possible to implement a simple meta-rule treatment of conjunction [7]. The basic idea is to use meta-rules to generate all possible conjoinings as explicit rules. Because there are no parameters in the rules, and because the ISR rules are compositional and cleanly factored from the BNF definitions, the meta-rules are very simple. Figure 1.7 shows the transformation of a (simplified) assertion definition into a conjoined assertion definition. The resultant rule is a disjunction; one branch allows a conjunction, followed by a recursive call to assertion; the other branch terminates after application of a restriction. Each branch has associated with it a separate regularization rule. The original meta-rules, though simple, are low-level operations, concerned with maintaining and updating a recorded database of rules. Recently, a general mechanism to support the statement of meta-rules has been proposed [2] this treatment would provide a more elegant statement of the meta-rules used to handle conjunction in Restriction Grammar.
  The current conjunction meta-rules will handle correctly the interaction of wh-expressions and conjunction. However, one minor problem is the preservation of a source form of the rules, for inspection and editing by the grammar-writer. This requires that conjunction operate on the source (unparameterized) form of the rules. By introduction of one addition annotation $><$, it is possible to apply conjunction to the source rule, which can then be parameterized via the wh meta-rule component. The $><$ annotation simply ensures that its operand receives the parameters associated with the left-hand side of the definition. Thus the conjunction meta-rule generates:

```
% Conjunction meta-rule (using '=>' as infix operator):
    (LHS ::= Body -> ISR) =>
    (LHS ::= Body,
        (*conj_wd, LHS  -> [conj_wd, ISR, LHS]
        ; {wconj_restr} -> ISR)).

% Example of meta-rule applied to assertion definition:

assertion ::= subject, verb, object -> [verb, subject, object].
        =>
assertion ::= subject, verb, object,
                (*conj_wd, assertion
                    -> [conj_wd, [verb, subject, object],
                                                    assertion]
                ; {w_conj_restr} -> [verb, subject, object]).
```

Figure 1.7: Generation of Conjunction via Meta-Rule

```
assertion ::= subject, verb, object,
                ( *conj_wd, ><assertion
                    -> [conj_wd, [verb, subject, object],
                                                    assertion]
                {w_conj_restr} -> [verb, subject, object]).
```

The introduction of the >< annotation requires a slight complication to the code for **take_apart**, but is very straight-forward. The result is the following parameterized definition for assertion:

```
assertion(In/Out) ::=
    subject(In/Subj), verb(Subj/Verb), object(Verb/Out),
        (*conj_wd, assertion(In/Out)
            -> [conj_wd, [verb, subject, object], assertion]
        ; {w_conj_restr} -> [verb, subject, object]).
```

Combining treatment of conjunction and wh-constructions, the system is able to parse sentences such as:

The disk which he repaired and she installed is working.

The disk which she repaired and installed has failed.
What disk did she repair and he install?
The disk which was installed but not repaired has been removed.
Which disks and drives are failing?
What does she believe they will repair and the engineer will maintain?

1.8   Conclusion

It is clear that meta-rules provide a powerful approach to a range of grammatical problems. In particular, meta-rules are very well-suited to the handling of phenomena that require a regular change to a large range of grammatical constructions. Although the parameterization approach outlined here for wh-constructions differs considerably from the meta-rule treatment of conjunction, they both share the property of enabling the grammar writer to capture a high-level generalization that applies to many rules in the grammar. Perhaps even more interesting is the fact that these meta-rule treatments appear to combine gracefully, in a way that does not appear to be readily available through the extended interpreter approach of Extraposition Grammar.

We plan to investigate other possible applications of parameterized grammar rules. These include the use of parameters to propagate feature information, and the use of parameters to 'compile' restrictions into unification of parameters, for greater efficiency and greater *locality* within subtrees. By using parameters instead of explicit constraints on tree-shape, it may be possible to save well-formed subtrees. The problem of putting together well-formed subtrees can then be captured via unification, rather than by constraints which must look outside the local subtree.

As we continue to develop meta-rule approaches to various grammatical phenomena, it will be important to abstract from the specifics outlined here and move towards a more general language for the statement of grammatical meta-rules. Just as grammar examples provide fertile ground for the application of meta-programming techniques, we expect meta-programming techniques to provide more elegant and efficient ways of capturing the meta-rules.

1.9   Acknowledgements

A number of people have made important contributions to this work. The basic grammatical insights come from Marcia Linebarger, the principal developer of our broad-coverage English grammar. The implementation of the ISR has been done by John Dowding, who also suggested the appropriate treatment of gaps and of complex wh-expressions. Deborah Dahl, Rebecca Passonneau and François Lang provided a number of helpful suggestions on the organization of the paper. I am also indebted to Dale Miller for interesting insights about the meta-programming aspects of the wh-problem.

References

[1] Harvey Abramson. Definite clause translation grammar. In *Proc. 1984 International Symposium on Logic Programming*, pages 233–241, Atlantic City, NJ, 1984.

[2] Harvey Abramson. Metarules and an approach to conjunction in definite clause translation grammars: some aspects of grammatical metaprogramming. In *Logic Programming: Proc. of the 5th International Conf. and Symposium*, pages 233–248, MIT Press, Cambridge, MA, 1988.

[3] Amelie Banks and Manny Rayner. Comparatives in logic grammars – two viewpoints. In *Proc. of the 2nd International Workshop on Natural Language Understanding*, Simon Fraser University, Vancouver, B.C, August, 1987.

[4] Veronica Dahl and Michael McCord. Treating co-ordination in logic grammars. *American Journal of Computational Linguistics*, 9(2):69–91, 1983.

[5] John Dowding and Lynette Hirschman. Dynamic translation for rule pruning in restriction grammar. In *Proceedings of the 2nd International Workshop On Natural Language Understanding and Logic Programming*, Vancouver, B.C., Canada, 1987.

[6] G. Gazdar. Unbounded dependencies and co-ordinate structure. *Linguistic Inquiry*, 12:155–184, 1981.

[7] Lynette Hirschman. Conjunction in meta-restriction grammar. *Journal of Logic Programming*, 4:299–328, 1986.

[8] Lynette Hirschman and Karl Puder. Restriction grammar: a prolog implementation. In D.H.D. Warren and M. VanCaneghem, editors, *Logic Programming and its Applications*, pages 244–261, Ablex Publishing Corp., Norwood, N.J., 1986.

[9] Martha S. Palmer, Deborah A. Dahl, Rebecca J. [Schiffman] Passonneau, Lynette Hirschman, Marcia Linebarger, and John Dowding. Recovering implicit information. In *Proceedings of the 24th Annual Meeting of the Association for Computational Linguistics*, Columbia University, New York, August 1986.

[10] F.C.N. Pereira. Extraposition grammars. *American Journal of Computational Linguistics*, 7:243–256, 1981.

[11] Fernando Pereira and Stuart Shieber. *Prolog and Natural-Language Analysis.* University of Chicago Press, Chicago, Illinois, 1987.

[12] C. Raze. A computational treatment of coordinate conjunctions. *American Journal of Computational Linguistics*, 1976. Microfiche 52.

[13] Naomi Sager. Syntactic analysis of natural language. In *Advances in Computers*, pages 153–188, Academic Press, New York, NY, 1967.

[14] William A. Woods. Progress in natural language understanding: an application to lunar geology. In *AFIPS Conference Proceedings*, 1973.

Appendix

Meta-Rules for Parameterization of BNF Definitions

```
% Do parameter generation at rule read-in time,
% to capture meta-rules.
% Pick up rule, add parameters, and record new rule.
Label ::= Rule :-
  wh_params(Label,Rule,ParamLabel,ParamRule),
  record(ParamLabel,(ParamLabel ::= ParamRule),_).

% Generate wh-parameters
wh_params(Label,Rule,NewLabel,NewRule) :-
  make_head_params(Label,InParam/OutParam,NewLabel),
  take_apart(Rule,NewRule,InParam,OutParam).

% Parameterize head of rule
%       Case 1 -- head cannot dominate gap; close off parameters
make_head_params(Head,InParam/InParam, NewHead) :-
  cant_pass_on(Head),!,
  insert_param(Head,InParam/InParam,NewHead).
%       Case 2 -- parameterize head.
make_head_params(Head,InParam/OutParam, NewHead) :-
  insert_param(Head,InParam/OutParam,NewHead).

% TAKE APART RULE BODY to insert params
% Semantics Rule
take_apart((A -> B), (NewA -> B), InParam,OutParam) :- !,
  take_apart(A,NewA,InParam,OutParam).
% Conjunction
take_apart((A,B),(NewA,NewB),InParam,OutParam) :- !,
```

```
  take_apart(A,NewA,InParam,OutParamA),
  take_apart(B,NewB,OutParamA,OutParam).
% Disjunction
take_apart((A;B),(NewA;NewB),InParam,OutParam) :-
  take_apart(A,NewA,InParamA,OutParamA),
  take_apart(B,NewB,InParamB,OutParamB),
  same_params(
(A;B),InParamA,InParamB,InParam,OutParamA,OutParamB,OutParam),!.
take_apart((A;B),_,_,_) :- !,
  print('$$$ Error:  disjunct '), print(A), print(';'), print(B),
  print(' cannot be parameterized correctly!').
% Literal
take_apart([Word|MoreWords],[Word|MoreWords],InParam,InParam) :- !.
% Restriction
take_apart({Restr},{Restr},InParam,InParam) :- !.
% Prune
take_apart(prune(Name,Defs),prune(Name,NewDefs),InParam,
                                           OutParam) :- !,
  take_apart(Defs,NewDefs,InParam,OutParam).
% Literal
take_apart(*Atom,*Atom,InParam,InParam) :- !.
% Empty node
take_apart(% , % , InParam,InParam) :- !.
% Non-Terminal
take_apart(Def,NewDef,InParam,OutParam) :-
  check_params(Def,InParam,OutParam),
  insert_param(Def,InParam/OutParam,NewDef),!.
take_apart(Def,Def,InParam,InParam).

% cant_pass_on sets two parameters equal in the head of the
% name rule;
%      this means that the automatically generated
%      nodes of this type
%      CANNOT contain a gap or a wh word.  These nodes have
 hand-generated
%      parameterized rules that permit gap or wh-words.
cant_pass_on(sa).
cant_pass_on(rn).
cant_pass_on(nstg).
cant_pass_on(thats).

insert_param(Head,X/Y,NewHead) :-
  Head =.. [Head|Args],
  NewHead =..[Head,X/Y|Args].
```

Chapter 2
Analysis of Meta-Programs

P.M. Hill [1]   J.W. Lloyd

University of Bristol

Abstract

This paper provides a theoretical foundation for meta-programming in Logic Programming. After introducing the two basic representation schemes, two standard meta-programs are studied and their correctness is proved. Meta-logical predicates similar to those provided in Prolog are defined. Deficiencies in the meta-programming facilities provided by Prolog are discussed and it is shown how these deficiencies can be remedied.

2.1 Introduction

A meta-program is a program which uses another program (the object program) as data. Meta-programming techniques underlie many of the applications of Logic Programming. For example, knowledge base systems consist of a number of knowledge bases (the object programs), which are manipulated by interpreters and assimilators (the meta-programs). Other important kinds of software, such as debuggers, compilers, and program transformers, are meta-programs.

There is now a vast literature on various aspects of meta-programming in Logic Programming. For example, papers concerned with the application of meta-programming to knowledge base systems include [1], [2], [4], [5], [9], [15], [17], [18], [23], [26], and [28]. The textbook of Sterling and Shapiro [25] contains a discussion of the programming techniques relevant to meta-programming. Only a few papers discuss the theoretical foundations of meta-programming. These include [3], [6], [7], [19], and [27]. Other aspects of meta-programming are discussed in [16], [21], [24], and [29]. A collection of recent papers on meta-programming is contained in [12]. There is a discussion in [10] of current research issues in meta-programming.

[1] supported by a WISE Fellowship, funded by Cable and Wireless plc.

However, in spite of the fact that meta-programming techniques are widely and successfully used, the foundations of meta-programming and the meta-programming facilities provided by most currently available Prolog systems are by no means satisfactory. For example, on the theoretical side, some important representation and semantic issues are normally glossed over. Furthermore, most currently available Prolog systems do not make a clear distinction between the object level and meta-level, do not provide explicit language facilities for representation of object level expressions at the meta-level, and do not provide important meta-programming software, such as partial evaluators.

The intention of this paper is to provide a theoretical foundation for meta-programming. It is part of a larger project, which also includes an investigation of appropriate language facilities for meta-programming and the application of meta-programming techniques.

We begin the motivation for this paper by pointing out an important and largely neglected representation issue in meta-programming. One of the best known meta-programs is the standard *solve* interpreter, which consists of the following definition for *solve*

$$solve(empty) \leftarrow$$
$$solve(x \& y) \leftarrow solve(x) \land solve(y)$$
$$solve(x) \leftarrow clause(x, y) \land solve(y)$$

together with a definition for *clause*, which is used to represent the object program. For example, if the object program contains the clause

$$p(x, y) \leftarrow q(x, z) \land r(z, y)$$

then there is a corresponding clause of the form

$$clause(p(x, y),\ q(x, z) \& r(z, y)) \leftarrow$$

appearing in the definition of *clause*.

This interpreter is sometimes called the *vanilla* interpreter [26]. Many important meta-programs are extensions of one kind or another of the vanilla interpreter. See, for example, [21], [26], and [25].

However, the declarative meaning of the vanilla interpreter is by no means clear. The problem is that the variables in the definition of *clause* and the variables in the definition of *solve* intuitively range over different domains. (Informally, the variables in *clause* range over elements of the domain of the intended interpretation (based on a pre-interpretation J, say) of the object program, while the variables in *solve* range over conjunctions of J-instances of atoms.) Thus the intended interpretation is simply not a model of the program. This is not just a minor mathematical oddity. In particular, the problem certainly cannot be solved by simply asserting that each kind of variable is just a "logical variable". What is at stake here is whether it is possible to give a simple and precise semantics to the vanilla interpreter and other meta-programs. Without such a semantics, it is impossible, for example, to prove their correctness or prove the correctness of transformations performed on them.

If the different kinds of variables are intended to range over different domains, then there is a clear solution. We should introduce types (also called sorts) into the language underlying the meta-program. We call this the *typed* representation. Then, for example, using an appropriately typed version of the vanilla interpreter, it is possible to prove its soundness and completeness for both the declarative and procedural semantics.

However, the typed representation introduces another problem related to the fact that an object level variable is represented by a meta-level *variable*. This leads to severe semantic problems with the meta-logical predicate *var* [25]. With this representation, there seems to be no way of giving a declarative semantics to *var*. To see the difficulty, consider the goals

$$\leftarrow var(x) \wedge solve(p(x))$$

and

$$\leftarrow solve(p(x)) \wedge var(x)$$

If the object program consists solely of the clause $p(a)\leftarrow$, then (using the "leftmost literal" computation rule) the first goal succeeds, while the second goal fails.

These considerations lead to another representation scheme in which object level expressions are represented by ground terms at the meta-level. In such a representation, an object level variable is represented by a meta-level constant, say. This kind of representation, which we call the *ground* representation, is a standard tool in mathematical logic and has been discussed occasionally in the Logic Programming literature [3], [6]. Using the ground representation, it is possible to give appropriate definitions for the meta-logical predicates of Prolog.

The purpose of this paper, then, is to undertake a systematic study of the typed and ground representations, to investigate their application to two standard meta-programs, and to give definitions for the meta-logical predicates of Prolog. As we will demonstrate, this work provides a better understanding of meta-programs, it provides a basis on which questions of correctness, transformation, and so on, can be studied, and it indicates the programming language features required to better support meta-programming.

We confine attention in this paper to the static aspects of meta-programming. The dynamic aspects of meta-programming, including the study of declarative counterparts for Prolog's *assert* and *retract*, are considered in detail in [7].

The outline of the paper is as follows. In the next section, we introduce the basic concepts on which the remainder of the paper depends. In section 3, we introduce the typed representation and prove the correctness of the vanilla interpreter. In section 4, we introduce the ground representation and prove the correctness of an interpreter useful for implementing co-routining. In section 5, we give the definitions, based on the ground representation, for the meta-logical predicates of Prolog. The final section contains a general discussion of Prolog's meta-programming facilities and gives future research directions.

2.2 Basic Concepts

In this section, we introduce various concepts which will be needed later.

Definition A *program statement* (resp., *program clause*) is a first order formula of the form $A \leftarrow W$, where A is an atom and W is a first order formula (resp., conjunction of literals). The formula W may be absent. Any variables in A and any free variables in W are assumed to be universally quantified at the front of the program statement. A is called the *head* and W the *body*.

Definition A *program* (resp., *normal program*) is a finite set of program statements (resp., program clauses).

Definition A *goal* (resp., *normal goal*) is a first-order formula of the form $\leftarrow W$, where W is a first order formula (resp., conjunction of literals). Any free variables in W are assumed to be universally quantified at the front of the goal.

Definition The *definition* of a predicate symbol p in a program P is the set of all program statements in P which have p in their head.

Definition Let J be a pre-interpretation of a first order language, V a variable assignment wrt J, and A an atom. Suppose A is $p(t_1, \ldots, t_n)$, and $d_1, \ldots, d_n$ in the domain of J are the term assignments of $t_1, \ldots, t_n$ wrt J and V. We call $A_{J,V} = p(d_1, \ldots, d_n)$ the *J-instance of A wrt V*.

Definition Let J be a pre-interpretation of a program P. The mapping T_P^J from the lattice of interpretations based on J to itself is defined as follows. Let I be an interpretation based on J. Then $T_P^J(I) = \{A_{J,V} : A \leftarrow W \in P, V$ is a variable assignment wrt J, and W is true wrt I and $V\}$.

Definition A program is *call-consistent* if no predicate symbol in the program depends negatively on itself.

The definition of call-consistency is due to Sato [22] and Kunen [8]. Clearly every stratified program is call-consistent. We will require the result that call-consistent programs have consistent completions [22], [8].

Definition A *quantifier-free* formula is a first order formula constructed from atoms and the connectives $\neg$, $\wedge$, and $\leftarrow$ only.

For the interpreter in section 4, we will be interested in returning computed answers, not just demonstrating derivability as in [3]. For this purpose, it is convenient to use the concept of a resultant from [13].

Definition A *resultant* is a first order formula of the form $Q_1 \leftarrow Q_2$, where Q_i is either absent or a conjunction of literals ($i = 1, 2$). Any variables in Q_1 or Q_2 are assumed to be universally quantified at the front of the resultant.

Note that a resultant is not a clause unless Q_1 is either absent or a single literal. A normal goal is a special case of a resultant in which Q_1 is absent.

We now adapt the definition in [11] of SLDNF-refutation, which is based on goals, to a definition based on resultants.

Definition Let $R = Q \leftarrow L_1 \wedge \cdots \wedge L_m \wedge \cdots \wedge L_p$ be a resultant and $C = A \leftarrow M_1 \wedge \cdots \wedge M_q$ a program clause. Then the resultant R' is *derived* from R and C if L_m is an atom, called the *selected* atom in R, and R' is $(Q \leftarrow L_1 \wedge \cdots \wedge L_{m-1} \wedge M_1 \wedge \cdots \wedge M_q \wedge L_{m+1} \wedge \cdots \wedge L_p)\theta$, where θ is an mgu of L_m and A.

We call a derivation step as above a *positive* derivation step to distinguish it from a *negative* derivation step in which a ground negative literal is selected.

Resultants contain all the information required for correct standardization apart. In each step of a derivation, it is, of course, necessary to choose an appropriate variant of the program clause. We do this here by simply renaming variables in the program clause so that the variant program clause does not have any variables in common with the current resultant. This differs from the way standardization apart is handled in [11], where it is required that the variant has no variables in common with any goal in the derivation up to that point. The use of resultants, rather than goals, in refutations allows us to handle standardization apart very neatly in the interpreter in section 4.

In [11], the definitions of SLDNF-refutation and finitely failed SLDNF-tree are defined mutually recursively. Since we propose to continue defining finitely failed SLDNF-trees for goals, rather than resultants,[1] the definition of finitely failed SLDNF-tree given in [11] is adopted here *verbatim* (except that here we employ the weaker form of standardization apart described above). The modified definition of SLDNF-refutation is as follows.

Definition Let P be a normal program and R a resultant. An *SLDNF-refutation of rank 0* of $P \cup \{R\}$ consists of a sequence $R_o = R, R_1, \ldots, R_n = Q \leftarrow$ of resultants and a sequence $C_1, \ldots, C_n$ of variants of program clauses of P such that each R_{i+1} is derived from R_i and C_{i+1}. We call R_n the *final resultant* of the refutation.

Definition Let P be a normal program and R a resultant. An *SLDNF-refutation of rank $k+1$* of $P \cup \{R\}$ consists of a sequence $R_o = R, R_1, \ldots,$ $R_n = Q \leftarrow$ of resultants and a sequence $C_1, \ldots, C_n$ of variants of program clauses

---

[1] One could define finitely failed SLDNF-trees for resultants, but such a definition is not needed here.

of P or ground negative literals, such that, each for each i, either

1. R_{i+1} is derived from R_i and C_{i+1}, where C_{i+1} is a variant of a program clause, or

2. R_i is $Q_1 \leftarrow L_1 \wedge \cdots \wedge L_m \wedge \cdots \wedge L_p$, the selected literal L_m in R_i is a ground negative literal $\neg A_m$, and there is a finitely failed SLDNF-tree of rank k for $P \cup \{\leftarrow A_m\}$. In this case, R_{i+1} is $Q_1 \leftarrow L_1 \wedge \cdots \wedge L_{m-1} \wedge L_{m+1} \wedge \cdots \wedge L_p$ and C_{i+1} is $\neg A_m$.

We call R_n the *final resultant* of the refutation.

Definition Let P be a normal program and R a resultant. An *SLDNF-refutation* of $P \cup \{R\}$ is an SLDNF-refutation of rank k for $P \cup \{R\}$, for some k.

Definition Let P be a normal program and $\leftarrow Q$ a normal goal. A *computed answer* for $P \cup \{\leftarrow Q\}$ is a substitution θ for the variables appearing in Q such that there is an SLDNF-refutation for $P \cup \{Q \leftarrow Q\}$ with final resultant $Q\theta \leftarrow$.

Note that the final resultant encapsulates most of the information about the result of the refutation. It does not include all, because it does not give the original goal $\leftarrow Q$ and the computed answer θ, but only the effect $Q\theta$ of applying θ to Q. But, given Q as well as the final resultant, θ can be recovered.

The only difference between the above definition of computed answer and the one in [11] is the way standardization apart is handled. All the results in [11] for SLDNF-resolution continue to hold for the above definition.

In this paper, we use typed (that is, many-sorted), as well as type-free, first order theories. The concepts of term, formula, first order language, pre-interpretation, and interpretation for a typed first order theory are defined in [11]. It is straightforward to define the other concepts of Logic Programming in the typed case. The development of the theory in [11] for the type-free case can be carried through with only minor changes for the typed case. In fact, we will require the typed versions of a number of the results in [11]. It will be always clear from the context when a reference to a result in [11] actually refers to the typed version of the result.

In particular, when a program P is based on a typed language, by *comp*(P) we mean the typed version of the completion of P. Thus the equality theory for *comp*(P) is given by the axioms 1 to 8 on page 145 of [11]. (Axioms 9, the domain closure axioms, are not required.)

Other terminology and notation not explained in the paper can be found in [11].

2.3   Typed Representation

In this section, we introduce the typed representation, which is a scheme for representing the quantifier-free formulas of a (type-free) language $\mathcal{L}$ in a typed language $\mathcal{L}'$.

$\mathcal{L}'$ has two types o and μ.[2] Given a constant a in $\mathcal{L}$, there is a corresponding constant a' of type o in $\mathcal{L}'$. Given a variable x in $\mathcal{L}$, there is a corresponding variable x' of type o in $\mathcal{L}'$. Given an n-ary function symbol f in $\mathcal{L}$, there is a corresponding n-ary function symbol f' of type $o \times \cdots \times o \to o$ in $\mathcal{L}'$. Given an n-ary predicate symbol p in $\mathcal{L}$, there is a corresponding n-ary function symbol p' of type $o \times \cdots \times o \to \mu$ in $\mathcal{L}'$. We assume that the mappings $a \to a'$, $x \to x'$, $f \to f'$, and $p \to p'$ are all injective. The language $\mathcal{L}'$ has a constant *empty* of type μ. In addition, $\mathcal{L}'$ contains the function symbols &, *if*, and *not* of type $\mu \times \mu \to \mu$, $\mu \times \mu \to \mu$, and $\mu \to \mu$, respectively. Finally, $\mathcal{L}'$ has two predicate symbols *solve* and *clause* of type μ.

If a is a constant, x is a variable, f is a function symbol, and p is a predicate symbol in $\mathcal{L}$, then we represent a by a', x by x', f by f', and p by p' in $\mathcal{L}'$. We define the representation of terms inductively. If $f(t_1, \ldots, t_n)$ is a term in $\mathcal{L}$, we represent $f(t_1, \ldots, t_n)$ by the term $f'(t'_1, \ldots, t'_n)$ of type o in $\mathcal{L}'$, where $t'_1, \ldots, t'_n$ are the representations of $t_1, \ldots, t_n$, respectively. If $p(t_1, \ldots, t_n)$ is an atom in $\mathcal{L}$, we represent $p(t_1, \ldots, t_n)$ by the term $p'(t'_1, \ldots, t'_n)$ of type μ in $\mathcal{L}'$. We also define the representation of quantifier-free formulas inductively. If the quantifier-free formulas F and G in $\mathcal{L}$ are represented by F' and G', respectively, then $\neg F$, $F \wedge G$, and $F \leftarrow G$ are represented by the terms $not(F')$, $F'\&G'$, and F' *if* G', respectively, of type μ in $\mathcal{L}'$.

The typed normal program $\mathbf{V}$, based on the language $\mathcal{L}'$, consists of the following definition for *solve*.

$$solve(empty) \leftarrow$$

$$\forall_\mu x, y \;\; solve(x \& y) \leftarrow$$
$$solve(x) \wedge$$
$$solve(y)$$

$$\forall_\mu x \;\; solve(not(x)) \leftarrow$$
$$\neg solve(x)$$

$$\forall_\mu x, y \;\; solve(x) \leftarrow$$
$$clause(x \; if \; y) \wedge$$
$$solve(y)$$

Given a normal program P, based on the language $\mathcal{L}$, the program $\mathbf{V}_P$ consists of the above program $\mathbf{V}$, together with a clause of the form

[2]o for object and μ for meta

$\forall_o x'_1, \ldots, x'_k \; clause(A' \; if \; Q') \leftarrow$

for every clause $A \leftarrow Q$, with variables $x_1, \ldots, x_k$, in P, and a clause of the form

$\forall_o x'_1, \ldots, x'_k \; clause(A' \; if \; empty) \leftarrow$

for every clause $A \leftarrow$, with variables $x_1, \ldots, x_k$, in P.

THEOREM 2.3.1. *Let P be a normal program and $\leftarrow Q$ a normal goal with variables $x_1, \ldots, x_k$. Let $\mathbf{V}_P$ be defined as above. Then the following hold.*

1. *$comp(P)$ is consistent iff $comp(\mathbf{V}_P)$ is consistent.*

2. *$\{x_1/t_1, \ldots, x_k/t_k\}$ is a correct answer for $comp(P) \cup \{\leftarrow Q\}$ iff $\{x'_1/t'_1, \ldots, x'_k/t'_k\}$ is a correct answer for $comp(\mathbf{V}_P) \cup \{\leftarrow solve(Q')\}$.*

3. *$\leftarrow Q$ is a logical consequence of $comp(P)$ iff $\leftarrow solve(Q')$ is a logical consequence of $comp(\mathbf{V}_P)$.*

Proof Let I be an interpretation based on a pre-interpretation J for $\mathcal{L}$ and suppose that I is a fixpoint of T_P^J. We construct from J and I a pre-interpretation J' for $\mathcal{L}'$ and an interpretation I' based on J' such that I' is a fixpoint of $T_{\mathbf{V}_P}^{J'}$.

Let I have the domain D. Then I' has domain $D_o = D$, where D_o is the domain of type o. We define D_μ to be the typed "Herbrand" universe constructed from $\{empty\} \cup \{p'(d_1, \ldots, d_n) : p$ is a predicate symbol of arity n in $\mathcal{L}$ and $d_1, \ldots, d_n \in D\}$ as the primitive terms and the function symbols $\&$, if, and not.

If a is a constant in $\mathcal{L}$, then a' is assigned the same element of D_o by I', as a is by I. If f is an n-ary function symbol in $\mathcal{L}$, then f' is assigned the same mapping from $D_o^n \rightarrow D_o$ by I', as f is by I. If p is an n-ary predicate symbol in $\mathcal{L}$, then I' assigns p' the mapping from D_o^n into D_μ defined by $(d_1, \ldots, d_n) \rightarrow p'(d_1, \ldots, d_n)$. The constant $empty$, the unary function symbol $\&$, and the binary function symbols not and if are given their free (Herbrand) interpretations on D_μ under I'. This defines the pre-interpretation J' on which I' is based.

Next we give assignments under I' for the predicate symbols $solve$ and $clause$. We first consider $solve$, whose assignment is defined inductively on the number of occurrences of $\&$ and not in its argument. For the base case, $solve(E)$ is assigned true under I' iff either $E = empty$ or $E = p'(d_1, \ldots, d_n)$ and $p(d_1, \ldots, d_n)$ is assigned true under I. For the inductive case, $solve(E)$ is assigned true under I' iff either $E = not(F)$, for some $F \in D_\mu$, and $solve(F)$ is assigned false under I' or $E = F \& G$, for some F and $G \in D_\mu$, and $solve(F)$ and $solve(G)$ are assigned true under I'.

The assignment under I' to $clause$ is as follows. If $E \in D_\mu$, $clause(E)$ is assigned true under I' iff either there is a clause $A \leftarrow Q$ in P and a variable assignment V' wrt J' such that $E = (A')_{J',V'} \; if \; (Q')_{J',V'}$ or there is a clause $A \leftarrow$ in P and a variable assignment V' wrt J' such that $E = (A')_{J',V'} \; if \; empty$. This completes the definition of I'.

The next step is to show that I' is a fixpoint of $T_{V_P}^{J'}$. First, we show that $I' \subseteq T_{V_P}^{J'}(I')$. If $clause(E) \in I'$, then it is clear that $clause(E) \in T_{V_P}^{J'}(I')$. Also $solve(empty) \in T_{V_P}^{J'}(I')$. If $solve(E\&F) \in I'$, then $solve(E)$ and $solve(F) \in I'$ and hence $solve(E\&F) \in T_{V_P}^{J'}(I')$. If $solve(not(E)) \in I'$, then $solve(E) \notin I'$ and hence $solve(not(E)) \in T_{V_P}^{J'}(I')$. Finally, suppose $solve(p'(d_1,\ldots,d_n)) \in I'$. Hence $p(d_1,\ldots,d_n) \in I$. Since $I \subseteq T_P^J(I)$, there exists a clause $A \leftarrow Q$ in P and a variable assignment V wrt J such that $p(d_1,\ldots,d_n) = A_{J,V}$ and Q is true wrt I and V. If Q is not empty, $solve(Q')$ is true wrt I' and V', where V' is a variable assignment wrt J' such that, for each variable x in $\mathcal{L}$, the assignment by V to x is equal to the assignment by V' to x'. Furthermore, $clause(A' \; if \; Q')$ is true wrt I' and V'. Hence $solve(p'(d_1,\ldots,d_n)) \in T_{V_P}^{J'}(I')$. The case when Q is empty is similar. This completes the proof that $I' \subseteq T_{V_P}^{J'}(I')$.

Next we show that $T_{V_P}^{J'}(I') \subseteq I'$. If $clause(E) \in T_{V_P}^{J'}(I')$, then it is clear that $clause(E) \in I'$. Clearly $solve(empty) \in T_{V_P}^{J'}(I')$ and $solve(empty) \in I'$, by definition. Suppose now that $solve(E\&F) \in T_{V_P}^{J'}(I')$. Hence $solve(E) \in I'$ and $solve(F) \in I'$ and so $solve(E\&F) \in I'$. If $solve(not(E)) \in T_{V_P}^{J'}(I')$, then $solve(E) \notin I'$ and hence $solve(not(E)) \in I'$. Finally, suppose $solve(p'(d_1,\ldots,d_n)) \in T_{V_P}^{J'}(I')$. Hence $clause(p'(d_1,\ldots,d_n) \; if \; E) \in I'$ and $solve(E) \in I'$, for some $E \in D_\mu$. By the definition of I', either there exists a clause $A \leftarrow Q$ in P and a variable assignment V' wrt J' such that $p'(d_1,\ldots,d_n) = (A')_{J',V'}$ and $E = (Q')_{J',V'}$ or there exists a clause $A \leftarrow$ in P and a variable assignment V' wrt J' such that $p'(d_1,\ldots,d_n) = (A')_{J',V'}$ and $E = empty$. In the first case, $solve((Q')_{J',V'}) \in I'$. Hence Q is true wrt I and V. where V is the variable assignment wrt J such that, for each variable x in $\mathcal{L}$, the assignment by V to x is equal to the assignment by V' to x'. Thus $p(d_1,\ldots,d_n) \in T_P^J(I)$. The other case is similar. Since $T_P^J(I) \subseteq I$, we have that $p(d_1,\ldots,d_n) \in I$. Hence $solve(p'(d_1,\ldots,d_n)) \in I'$. This completes the proof that I' is a fixpoint of $T_{V_P}^{J'}$.

Next suppose $I \cup \{d = d : d \in D\}$ is a (normal) model for $comp(P)$. Then $I' \cup \{d =_o d : d \in D_o\} \cup \{E =_\mu E : E \in D_\mu\}$ is a (normal) model for $comp(\mathbf{V}_P)$, by proposition 14.3 of [11] and the above argument.

Now we turn to the converse direction. Suppose that I' is an interpretation for $\mathcal{L}'$ based on a pre-interpretation J' such that I' is a fixpoint for $T_{V_P}^{J'}$. From J' and I', we construct a pre-interpretation J for $\mathcal{L}$ and an interpretation I based on J such that I is a fixpoint for T_P^J.

Suppose I' has domain D_o of type o and domain D_μ of type μ. We define the domain of I to be $D = D_o$. If a is a constant in $\mathcal{L}$, then I assigns a the same element as I' assigns a'. Similarly, if f is a function symbol in $\mathcal{L}$, then I assigns f the same mapping as I' assigns f'. Finally, if p is a n-ary predicate symbol in $\mathcal{L}$ and $d_1,\ldots,d_n \in D$, then I assigns $p(d_1,\ldots,d_n)$ to be true iff I' assigns $solve(p'(d_1,\ldots,d_n))$ to be true. This completes the definition of J and I. Next we show that I is a fixpoint of T_P^J.

First we show that $I \subseteq T_P^J(I)$. Let $p(d_1, \ldots, d_n) \in I$. By the definition of I, we have that $solve(p'(d_1, \ldots, d_n)) \in I'$. Since $I' \subseteq T_{V_P}^{J'}(I')$, we have that $clause(p'(d_1, \ldots, d_n) \, if \, E) \in I'$ and $solve(E) \in I'$, for some $E \in D_\mu$. Hence either there exists a clause $A \leftarrow L_1 \wedge \cdots \wedge L_k$ in P such that $p'(d_1, \ldots, d_n) = (A')_{J', V'}$ and $E = (L_1')_{J', V'} \& \cdots \& (L_k')_{J', V'}$, for some variable assignment V', or there exists a clause $A \leftarrow$ in P such that $p'(d_1, \ldots, d_n) = (A')_{J', V'}$ and $E = empty$, for some variable assignment V'. In the first case, $solve((L_1')_{J', V'} \& \cdots \& (L_k')_{J', V'}) \in I'$ and hence $solve((L_i')_{J', V'}) \in I'$, for $i = 1, \ldots, k$. For those L_i which are negative literals, say $\neg B_i$, we have that $solve((B_i')_{J', V'}) \notin I'$. By the definition of I, we have that $L_1 \wedge \cdots \wedge L_k$ is true wrt I and V, where V is the variable assignment wrt J such that, for each variable x in $\mathcal{L}$, the assignment by V to x is equal to the assignment by V' to x'. Hence $p(d_1, \ldots, d_n) \in T_P^J(I)$. The other case is similar.

Next we prove that $T_P^J(I) \subseteq I$. Suppose that $p(d_1, \ldots, d_n) \in T_P^J(I)$. Hence there exists a clause $A \leftarrow Q$ in P and a variable assignment V such that $p(d_1, \ldots, d_n) = A_{J, V}$ and Q is true wrt I and V. If Q is not empty, since $T_{V_P}^{J'}(I') \subseteq I'$, we have that $solve((Q')_{J', V'}) \in I'$, where V' is a variable assignment wrt J' such that, for each variable x in $\mathcal{L}$, the assignment by V to x is equal to the assignment by V' to x'. Since $clause(p'(d_1, \ldots, d_n) \, if \, (Q')_{J', V'}) \in I'$, we have that $solve(p'(d_1, \ldots, d_n)) \in T_{V_P}^{J'}(I')$ and so $solve(p'(d_1, \ldots, d_n)) \in I'$. Hence $p(d_1, \ldots, d_n) \in I$. The case when Q is empty is similar.

Next suppose that $I' \cup \{d =_o d : d \in D_o\} \cup \{E =_\mu E : E \in D_\mu\}$ is a (normal) model for $comp(\mathbf{V}_P)$. Then, using proposition 14.3 of [11] and the above argument, we have that $I \cup \{d = d : d \in D\}$ is a model for $comp(P)$.

Part (1) of the theorem now follows immediately. Parts (2) and (3) follow from the model-theoretic construction above. $\blacksquare$

COROLLARY 2.3.2.   *Under the conditions of theorem 2.3.1, the following hold.*

1. *If $\{x_1'/t_1', \ldots, x_k'/t_k'\}$ is a computed answer for $\mathbf{V}_P \cup \{\leftarrow solve(Q')\}$, then $\{x_1/t_1, \ldots, x_k/t_k\}$ is a correct answer for $comp(P) \cup \{\leftarrow Q\}$.*

2. *If $\mathbf{V}_P \cup \{\leftarrow solve(Q')\}$ has a finitely failed SLDNF-tree, then $\leftarrow Q$ is a logical consequence of $comp(P)$.*

Proof The corollary follows immediately from theorem 2.3.1, and theorems 15.4 and 15.6 of [11]. $\blacksquare$

Next we turn to the appropriate version of theorem 2.3.1 for SLDNF-resolution.

THEOREM 2.3.3. *Let* P *be a normal program and* $\leftarrow Q$ *a normal goal with variables* $x_1, \ldots, x_k$. *Let* $\mathbf{V}_P$ *be defined as above. Then the following hold.*

1. $\{x_1/t_1, \ldots, x_k/t_k\}$ *is a computed answer for* $P \cup \{\leftarrow Q\}$ *iff* $\{x'_1/t'_1, \ldots, x'_k/t'_k\}$ *is a computed answer for* $\mathbf{V}_P \cup \{\leftarrow solve(Q')\}$.

2. $P \cup \{\leftarrow Q\}$ *has a finitely failed SLDNF-tree iff* $\mathbf{V}_P \cup \{\leftarrow solve(Q')\}$ *has a finitely failed SLDNF-tree.*

Proof Let $\mathbf{A} = \{solve(x)\}$ and let $\mathbf{V}_P^*$ be a partial evaluation of $\mathbf{V}_P$ wrt $\mathbf{A}$ obtained by an unfolding of the fourth clause in the definition for *solve*. $\mathbf{V}_P^*$ contains a clause of the form

$$\forall_o x'_1, \ldots, x'_k \ solve(A') \leftarrow$$

for each clause in P of the form

$$\forall x_1, \ldots, x_k \ A \leftarrow$$

and it contains a clause of the form

$$\forall_o x'_1, \ldots, x'_k \ solve(A') \leftarrow M_1 \wedge \ldots \wedge M_n$$

for each clause in P of the form

$$\forall x_1, \ldots, x_k \ A \leftarrow L_1 \wedge \ldots \wedge L_n,$$

where $M_i = solve(L'_i)$, if L_i is a positive literal, and $M_i = \neg solve(A')$, if $L_i = \neg A$ is negative literal. $\mathbf{V}_P^*$ also contains the first three clauses for *solve* (and the definition for *clause*, which plays no further part in the proof). Since $\mathbf{A}$ is singular and $\mathbf{V}_P^* \cup \{\leftarrow solve(Q')\}$ is $\mathbf{A}$-closed, we see that $\mathbf{V}_P^* \cup \{\leftarrow solve(Q')\}$ has a computed answer θ iff $\mathbf{V}_P \cup \{\leftarrow solve(Q')\}$ does, and also $\mathbf{V}_P^* \cup \{\leftarrow solve(Q')\}$ has a finitely failed SLDNF-tree iff $\mathbf{V}_P \cup \{\leftarrow solve(Q')\}$ does, using theorem 4.3 in [13]. We can thus restrict further attention to $\mathbf{V}_P^*$.

The result now follows by comparing $\mathbf{V}_P^*$ and P. A refutation for $P \cup \{Q \leftarrow Q\}$ (resp., finitely failed tree for $P \cup \{\leftarrow Q\}$) clearly has a corresponding refutation for $\mathbf{V}_P^* \cup \{solve(Q') \leftarrow solve(Q')\}$ (resp., finitely failed tree for $\mathbf{V}_P^* \cup \{\leftarrow solve(Q')\}$). This gives the only-if halves of parts (1) and (2). In the converse direction, suppose first that we have a refutation for $\mathbf{V}_P^* \cup \{solve(Q') \leftarrow solve(Q')\}$. By the switching lemma (lemma 4.6 in [13]), we can obtain a new refutation in which all uses of the first three clauses in the definition of *solve* occur in the initial part of the refutation. This new refutation clearly has a corresponding refutation for $P \cup \{Q \leftarrow Q\}$, which gives the result for the if-half of part (1). Suppose next we have a finitely failed tree for $\mathbf{V}_P^* \cup \{\leftarrow solve(Q')\}$. By applying the persistence of failure lemma (lemma 4.10 in [13]), we can obtain a new finitely failed tree for $\mathbf{V}_P^* \cup \{\leftarrow solve(Q')\}$ in which all uses of the first three clauses in the definition of *solve* occur in an initial single branch of the tree.

This new finitely failed tree clearly has a corresponding finitely failed tree for $P \cup \{\leftarrow Q\}$, which gives the result for the if-half of part (2). ∎

We have confined attention to the vanilla interpreter, which is the simplest and most basic of this kind of interpreter. However, other interpreters which are extensions of the vanilla interpreter (see, for example, [26] and [25]) could be analysed by a similar approach.

2.4   Ground Representation

We now introduce the ground representation, which is similar to the typed representation except for the the representation of variables. The use of types, in the ground representation below, is by no means essential. In [7], we investigate a ground representation where the use of types is not required. The crucial aspect of a ground representation is in fact the representation of object level variables by ground terms at the meta-level.

$\mathcal{L}'$ has three types o, μ, and η. Given a constant a in $\mathcal{L}$, there is a corresponding constant a' of type o in $\mathcal{L}'$. Given a variable x in $\mathcal{L}$, there is a corresponding constant x' of type o in $\mathcal{L}'$.[3] Given an n-ary function symbol f in $\mathcal{L}$, there is a corresponding n-ary function symbol f' of type $o \times \cdots \times o \to o$ in $\mathcal{L}'$. Given an n-ary predicate symbol p in $\mathcal{L}$, there is a corresponding n-ary function symbol p' of type $o \times \cdots \times o \to \mu$ in $\mathcal{L}'$. We assume that the mappings $a \to a'$, $x \to x'$, $f \to f'$, and $p \to p'$ are all injective. The language $\mathcal{L}'$ has a constant *empty* of type μ. In addition, $\mathcal{L}'$ contains the function symbols &, *if*, *not*, *positive*, *negative*, and *resultant* of type $\mu \times \mu \to \mu$, $\mu \times \mu \to \mu$, $\mu \to \mu$, $\mu \to \eta$, $\mu \to \eta$, and $\mu \times \mu \times \mu \times \mu \to \eta$, respectively. Finally, $\mathcal{L}'$ includes the predicate symbols *solve*, *succeed*, *fail*, *select*, and *derive* of type $\mu \times \mu$, $\mu \times \mu$, μ, $\mu \times \mu \times \eta \times \mu \times \mu$, and $\eta \times \mu \times \mu$, respectively, plus some further predicate symbols specified below.

If a is a constant, x is a variable, f is a function symbol, and p is a predicate symbol in $\mathcal{L}$, then we represent a by a', x by x', f by f', and p by p' in $\mathcal{L}'$. We define the representation of terms inductively. If $f(t_1, \ldots, t_n)$ is a term in $\mathcal{L}$, we represent $f(t_1, \ldots, t_n)$ by the term $f'(t'_1, \ldots, t'_n)$ of type o in $\mathcal{L}'$, where $t'_1, \ldots, t'_n$ are the representations of $t_1, \ldots, t_n$, respectively. If $p(t_1, \ldots, t_n)$ is an atom in $\mathcal{L}$, we represent $p(t_1, \ldots, t_n)$ by the term $p'(t'_1, \ldots, t'_n)$ of type μ in $\mathcal{L}'$. We define the representation of quantifier-free formulas inductively. If the quantifier-free formulas F and G in $\mathcal{L}$ are represented by F' and G', then $\neg F$, $F \wedge G$, and $F \leftarrow G$ are represented by $not(F')$, $F' \& G'$, F' *if* G', respectively, of type μ in $\mathcal{L}'$.

We also employ $\leftarrow$ as a unary connective. Thus $F \leftarrow$ is equivalent to F and $\leftarrow G$ is equivalent to $\neg G$. We represent $F \leftarrow$ by F' *if empty* and $\leftarrow G$ by *empty if* G'.

---

[3]Note that this implies allowing infinitely many constants in $\mathcal{L}'$, as there are infinitely many variables in $\mathcal{L}$. In [7], we give an alternative representation for variables which avoids this.

We represent the empty resultant by *empty if empty*.

To reduce the number of special cases, we write $L'_i \& \cdots \& L'_m$, when $m < i$, as an alternative notation for *empty*, $L'_1 \& \cdots \& L'_{i-1} \& L'_{i+1} \& \cdots \& L'_n$, when $i \leq 1$, as an alternative notation for $L'_{i+1} \& \cdots \& L'_n$, $L'_1 \& \cdots \& L'_{i-1} \& L'_{i+1} \& \cdots \& L'_n$, when $i \geq n$, as an alternative notation for $L'_1 \& \cdots \& L'_{i-1}$, and $L'_1 \& \cdots \& L'_{i-1} \& L'_{i+1} \& \cdots \& L'_n$, when $n = 1$, as an alternative notation for *empty*.

We now present an interpreter useful for implementing co-routining. The interpreter captures the procedural semantics of normal programs and goals given by SLDNF-resolution and is a descendant of the "demo" interpreter first given in [3]. The main differences with [3] are that our interpreter handles negation and we (implicitly) obtain computed answers. The use of this kind of interpreter for implementing co-routining is discussed, for example, in [17] and [18].

The typed program **G**, based on the language $\mathcal{L}'$, consists of the following definition for *solve*,

$$\forall_\mu x, y \ \ solve(x, y) \leftarrow$$
$$succeed(x \ if \ x, y \ if \ empty)$$

and the following definitions for *succeed*, *fail*, and *head_formula*, together with definitions for *conjunction_of_literals* (see section 5) and *derive* (and predicate symbols upon which *derive* and *conjunction_of_literals* depend).

$$\forall_\mu x \ \ succeed(x \ if \ empty, x \ if \ empty) \leftarrow$$
$$head\_formula(x)$$

$$\forall_\mu l, r, s, u, v, w, x, y, z \ \ succeed(x \ if \ y, z) \leftarrow$$
$$select(y, l, positive(s), r, u) \ \wedge$$
$$clause(w) \ \wedge$$
$$derive(resultant(x, l, s, r), w, v) \ \wedge$$
$$succeed(v, z)$$

$$\forall_\mu l, r, s, u, x, y, z \ \ succeed(x \ if \ y, z) \leftarrow$$
$$select(y, l, negative(s), r, u) \ \wedge$$
$$fail(empty \ if \ s) \ \wedge$$
$$succeed(x \ if \ u, z)$$

$$\forall_\mu l, r, s, u, y \ \ fail(empty \ if \ y) \leftarrow$$
$$select(y, l, positive(s), r, u) \ \wedge$$
$$\forall_\mu w, z \ (fail(z) \leftarrow clause(w) \wedge derive(resultant(empty, l, s, r), w, z))$$

$$\forall_\mu l, r, s, u, y \ \ fail(empty \ if \ y) \leftarrow$$
$$select(y, l, negative(s), r, u) \ \wedge$$
$$succeed(empty \ if \ s, empty \ if \ empty)$$

$\forall_\mu l, r, s, u, y \ fail(empty \ if \ y) \leftarrow$
$\qquad select(y, l, negative(s), r, u) \wedge$
$\qquad fail(empty \ if \ s) \wedge$
$\qquad fail(empty \ if \ u)$

$head\_formula(empty) \leftarrow$

$\forall_\mu x \ head\_formula(x) \leftarrow$
$\qquad conjunction\_of\_literals(x)$

Given a normal program P, based on the underlying language $\mathcal{L}$, the program G_P consists of the above program **G**, together with definitions for *clause*, *select*, and predicate symbols upon which *select* depends.

We define *clause* as follows. There is a clause of the form

$clause(A' \ if \ Q') \leftarrow$

for every clause $A \leftarrow Q$ in P, and a clause of the form

$clause(A' \ if \ empty) \leftarrow$

for every clause $A \leftarrow$ in P.

Informally, the intended meanings of the predicate symbols in the program G_P are as follows. (The precise intended meanings are given in the proof of theorem 2.4.2.)

The predicate symbol *succeed* is intended to be true when the first argument represents a resultant R, the second argument represents a resultant $Q \leftarrow$ and there is an SLDNF-refutation of $P \cup \{R\}$ with final resultant $Q \leftarrow$.

The predicate symbol *fail* is intended to be true when the argument represents a normal goal $\leftarrow Q$ and $P \cup \{\leftarrow Q\}$ has a finitely failed SLDNF-tree.

The predicate symbol *head_formula* is intended to be true when the argument is *empty* or represents a conjunction of literals.

The predicate symbol *conjunction_of_literals* is intended to be true when the argument represents a conjunction of literals.

The predicate symbol *derive* is intended to be true when the first argument is of the form $resultant(E, F, G, H)$, where $E \ if \ F\&G\&H$ represents a resultant R and G represents an atom A, the second argument represents a clause C, and the third argument represents a resultant derived from R using selected atom A and a variant of C (where the variant and R are standardized apart).

The predicate symbol *select* is intended to be true when the first argument represents a conjunction of literals Q, the second argument represents the conjunction of literals to the left of the selected literal in Q, the third argument is of the form $positive(E)$ or $negative(E)$, where E represents the atom appearing in the selected literal (and where *positive* indicates that it is a positive literal and *negative* indicates that it is a ground negative literal), the fourth argument represents the conjunction of literals to the right of the selected literal in Q, and the fifth argument represents the conjunction of literals obtained from Q by deleting the selected literal.

The predicate symbol *clause* is intended to be true when the argument represents a clause in P.

It is anticipated that *select* would be user defined and *derive* would be system defined. We assume that the definitions of *select* and *derive* do not depend upon *succeed* or *fail*. The definitions of *select* and *derive* are not specified, but each must satisfy various conditions defined below.

Example The following is a version of *select* which (safely) implements the Prolog "leftmost literal" computation rule. (The definitions of *atom*, ... are given in section 5.)

$$\forall_\mu x \; select(x, empty, positive(x), empty, empty) \leftarrow$$
$$atom(x)$$

$$\forall_\mu x, y \; select(x \& y, empty, positive(x), y, y) \leftarrow$$
$$atom(x) \land$$
$$conjunction\_of\_literals(y)$$

$$\forall_\mu x \; select(not(x), empty, negative(x), empty, empty) \leftarrow$$
$$ground\_atom(x)$$

$$\forall_\mu x, y \; select(not(x) \& y, empty, negative(x), y, y) \leftarrow$$
$$ground\_atom(x) \land$$
$$conjunction\_of\_literals(y)$$

Let $\mathbf{G_1}$ be the program consisting solely of the definitions for *select* and *derive* (and predicate symbols upon which they depend). The next theorem gives a condition on $\mathbf{G_1}$ which is sufficient to ensure the consistency of $comp(\mathbf{G}_P)$.

THEOREM 2.4.1. *If $\mathbf{G_1}$ is call-consistent, then $comp(\mathbf{G}_P)$ is consistent.*

Proof Since $\mathbf{G_1}$ is call-consistent, it is clear that $\mathbf{G}_P$ is call-consistent. The result now follows, since, by [8] or [22], a call-consistent program has a consistent completion. ∎

Theorem 2.4.2 below is concerned with the declarative semantics of $\mathbf{G}_P$. To state the conditions on *select* and *derive* required by this theorem, we employ the (typed) Herbrand pre-interpretation J' for $\mathcal{L}'$. The domain D_o is the Herbrand universe constructed from the constants of the form a', where a is a constant in $\mathcal{L}$, from the constants of the form x', where x is a variable in $\mathcal{L}$, and from the function symbols f', where f is a function symbol in $\mathcal{L}$. The constants a' and

x' are assigned themselves in D_o. If f is an n-ary function symbol in $\mathcal{L}$, then J' assigns to f' the mapping from D_o^n into D_o defined by $(t_1, \ldots, t_n) \to f'(t_1, \ldots, t_n)$. The domain D_μ consists of the Herbrand universe constructed from $\{empty\} \cup \{p'(t_1, \ldots, t_n) : p$ is a predicate symbol of arity n in $\mathcal{L}$ and $t_1, \ldots, t_n \in D_o\}$ as primitive terms, and the function symbols $\&$, if, and not. If p is an n-ary predicate symbol in $\mathcal{L}$, then J' assigns to p' the mapping from D_o^n into D_μ defined by $(t_1, \ldots, t_n) \to p'(t_1, \ldots, t_n)$. The constant $empty$ is assigned itself on D_μ. Also J' assigns not the mapping from D_μ into D_μ defined by $E \to not(E)$, it assigns if the mapping from D_μ^2 into D_μ defined by $(E, F) \to E$ if F, and it assigns $\&$ the mapping from D_μ^2 into D_μ defined by $(E, F) \to E\&F$. The domain D_η consists of the Herbrand universe $\{positive(E) : E \in D_\mu\} \cup \{negative(E) : E \in D_\mu\}$ $\cup \{resultant(E, F, G, H) : E, F, G, H \in D_\mu\}$. Finally, J' assigns $positive$ the mapping from D_μ into D_η defined by $E \to positive(E)$, it assigns $negative$ the mapping from D_μ into D_η defined by $E \to negative(E)$, and it assigns $resultant$ the mapping from D_μ^4 into D_η defined by $(E, F, G, H) \to resultant(E, F, G, H)$.

A (typed) Herbrand interpretation for $\mathcal{L}'$ is, of course, an interpretation based on J'. Theorem 2.4.2 below requires that $\mathbf{G}_1$ has an Herbrand interpretation M_1 satisfying the following conditions:

(S1) If $select(E, F, G, H, K) \in M_1$, then $E = L_1' \& \cdots \& L_n'$ $(n \geq 1)$, where L_j are literals $(1 \leq j \leq n,)$, $F = L_1' \& \cdots \& L_{i-1}'$, $H = L_{i+1}' \& \cdots \& L_n'$, $K = L_1' \& \cdots \& L_{i-1}' \& L_{i+1}' \& \cdots \& L_n'$, and either $G = positive(L_i')$ and L_i is a positive literal or $G = negative(A')$ and $L_i = \neg A$ is a ground negative literal, for some i, $1 \leq i \leq n$.

(D1) If $derive(E, F, G) \in M_1$, then
$E = resultant(W', L_1' \& \cdots \& L_{i-1}', L_i', L_{i+1}' \& \cdots \& L_n')$
(resp., $E = resultant(empty, L_1' \& \cdots \& L_{i-1}', L_i', L_{i+1}' \& \cdots \& L_n')$), where
$n \geq 1$, W is a conjunction of literals, each L_j is a literal $(1 \leq j \leq n)$, and L_i is an atom for some i, $1 \leq i \leq n$, $F = C'$, where C is a clause, and $G = U'$, where U is a resultant which is derived from the resultant $W \leftarrow L_1 \wedge \cdots \wedge L_n$ (resp., $\leftarrow L_1 \wedge \cdots \wedge L_n$) and a (suitably standardized apart) variant of C using selected atom L_i.

Also, $derive(E, F, G_1) \in M_1$ and $derive(E, F, G_2) \in M_1$ implies $G_1 = G_2$.

In addition, if $R = W \leftarrow L_1 \wedge \cdots \wedge L_n$ (resp., $R = \leftarrow L_1 \wedge \cdots \wedge L_n$) $(n \geq 1)$ is a resultant, L_i is an atom for some i, $1 \leq i \leq n$, C is a clause, and there is a resultant derived from R and a (suitably standardized apart) variant of C using selected atom L_i, then there exists G in D_μ such that $derive(resultant(W', L_1' \& \cdots \& L_{i-1}', L_i', L_{i+1}' \& \cdots \& L_n'), C', G) \in M_1$ (resp., $derive(resultant(empty, L_1' \& \cdots \& L_{i-1}', L_i', L_{i+1}' \& \cdots \& L_n'), C', G) \in M_1$).

THEOREM 2.4.2. *Let P be a normal program, $\leftarrow Q$ a normal goal, and θ an answer for $P \cup \{\leftarrow Q\}$. Let $\mathbf{G}_P$ and $\mathbf{G}_1$ be defined as above. Suppose that $\mathbf{G}_1$ has an Herbrand interpretation M_1, which is a fixpoint of $T_{\mathbf{G}_1}^{J'}$ and satisfies S1 and D1. Then the following hold.*

1. *If $\{x/(Q\theta)'\}$ is a correct answer for $comp(\mathbf{G}_P) \cup \{\leftarrow succeed(Q'\ if\ Q', x\ if\ empty)\}$, then θ is a computed answer for $P \cup \{\leftarrow Q\}$.*

2. *If $fail(empty\ if\ Q')$ is a logical consequence of $comp(\mathbf{G}_P)$, then $P \cup \{\leftarrow Q\}$ has a finitely failed SLDNF-tree.*

Proof Let $R = W \leftarrow S$ or $R = \leftarrow S$ be a resultant, where $S = L_1 \wedge \cdots \wedge L_n$ $(n \geq 1)$, and suppose L_i is selected in R, for some i, $1 \leq i \leq n$. We say the selection step is *compatible* with M_1 if whenever L_i is a positive literal, $select(L_1' \& \cdots \& L_n', L_1' \& \cdots \& L_{i-1}', positive(L_i'), L_{i+1}' \& \cdots \& L_n', L_1' \& \cdots \& L_{i-1}' \& L_{i+1}' \& \cdots \& L_n') \in M_1$, and whenever $L_i = \neg A$ is a ground negative literal, $select\ (L_1' \& \cdots \& L_n', L_1' \& \cdots \& L_{i-1}', negative(A'), L_{i+1}' \& \cdots \& L_n', L_1' \& \cdots \& L_{i-1}' \& L_{i+1}' \& \cdots \& L_n') \in M_1$.

Suppose there is a resultant U derived from R by a positive derivation step using a clause C and selected positive literal L_i. We say the derivation step is *compatible* with M_1 if whenever $R = W \leftarrow S$, then $derive(resultant(W', L_1' \& \cdots \& L_{i-1}', L_i', L_{i+1}' \& \cdots \& L_n'), C', U') \in M_1$, and whenever $R = \leftarrow S$, then $derive(resultant(empty, L_1' \& \cdots \& L_{i-1}', L_i', L_{i+1}' \& \cdots \& L_n'), C', U') \in M_1$.

An SLDNF-refutation or finitely failed SLDNF-tree is *compatible* with M_1 if every selection step and positive derivation step is compatible with M_1.

We construct an Herbrand interpretation M for $\mathbf{G}_P$ which is a fixpoint of $T_{\mathbf{G}_P}^{J'}$ as follows. For *select* and *derive* (and predicate symbols upon which they depend), the assignments given by M are the same as those given by M_1.

We define $clause(E) \in M$ iff either $E = A'\ if\ S'$ and $A \leftarrow S$ is a clause in P or $E = A'\ if\ empty$ and $A \leftarrow$ is a clause in P. (Note that *select* may depend upon *clause*. In this case, the two possible assignments for *clause* coincide.)

We define $conjunction\_of\_literals(E) \in M$ iff $E = L_1' \& \cdots \& L_n'$ $(n \geq$ where each L_j is a literal $(1 \leq j \leq n)$.

We define $head\_formula(E) \in M$ iff either $E = empty$ or $E = L_1' \& \cdots \& L_n'$ $(n \geq 1)$, where each L_j is a literal $(1 \leq j \leq n)$.

The predicate symbols *atom* and *literal* are given the obvious assignments in M.

We define $succeed(E, F) \in M$ iff $E = R'$, R is a resultant, $F = S'$, and there is an SLDNF-refutation of $P \cup \{R\}$ with final resultant S such that the refutation is compatible with M_1.

We define $fail(E) \in M$ iff $E = G'$, where G is a normal goal, and there is a finitely failed SLDNF-tree for $P \cup \{G\}$ such that the tree is compatible with M_1.

We define $solve(E, F) \in M$ iff $succeed(E\ if\ E, F\ if\ empty) \in M$.

One can verify that M is indeed a fixpoint of $T_{G_P}^{J'}$. Then M, together with the appropriate identity relations assigned to $=_o$, $=_\mu$, and $=_\eta$, is a model for $comp(G_P)$, by theorem 17.2 of [11]. Parts (1) and (2) of the theorem now follow. ∎

The conditions required for theorem 2.4.2 to hold may appear to be formidable to check in practice. However, we intend that *derive* be a system predicate and the implementation guarantee that the definition for *derive* (and predicate symbols upon which it depends) has a fixpoint satisfying D1. Consequently, it is only necessary to check that the definition for *select* (and predicate symbols upon which it depends) has a fixpoint satisfying S1. (We are assuming here, as seems sensible, that the definition of *derive* does not depend on *select*.) We believe that the conditions on *select* will be easy to check in practice. For example, the definition of the "leftmost literal" computation rule given earlier clearly satisfies the conditions. Note also that, while the conditions on *select* ensure soundness, they do not guarantee any form of completeness. To take an extreme case, if *select* has the empty definition, then the conditions are satisfied. In this case, of course, G_P never computes anything of interest.

Example Let P be $p \leftarrow$, *select* have the empty definition, and *derive* have any definition with a fixpoint satisfying D1, as required by the theorem. Then the identity substitution ε is a computed answer for $P \cup \{\leftarrow p\}$, but $\{x/(p\varepsilon)'\}$ is not a correct answer for $comp(G_P) \cup \{\leftarrow succeed(p' \text{ if } p', x \text{ if } empty)\}$. Thus the converse of part (1) of theorem 2.4.2 does not hold.

A similar example shows that the converse of part (2) of theorem 2.4.2 does not hold.

COROLLARY 2.4.3. *Under the conditions of theorem 2.4.2, the following hold.*

1. *If $\{x/(Q\theta)'\}$ is a computed answer for $G_P \cup \{\leftarrow succeed(Q' \text{ if } Q', x \text{ if } empty)\}$, then θ is a computed answer for $P \cup \{\leftarrow Q\}$.*

2. *If the identity substitution is a computed answer for $G_P \cup \{\leftarrow fail(empty \text{ if } Q')\}$, then $P \cup \{\leftarrow Q\}$ has a finitely failed SLDNF-tree.*

3. *If $\{x/(Q\theta)'\}$ is a correct answer for $comp(G_P) \cup \{\leftarrow succeed(Q' \text{ if } Q', x \text{ if } empty)\}$, then θ is a correct answer for $comp(P) \cup \{\leftarrow Q\}$.*

4. *If $fail(empty \text{ if } Q')$ is a logical consequence of $comp(G_P)$, then $\leftarrow Q$ is a logical consequence of $comp(P)$.*

Proof The corollary follows immediately from theorem 2.4.2, and theorems 18.6 and 18.7 of [11]. ∎

Theorem 2.4.4 below shows that, given suitable conditions on $\mathbf{G}_1$, results similar to the converses of parts (1) and (2) of corollary 2.4.3 hold. The theorem requires that $\mathbf{G}_1$ satisfy the following condition:

(D2) For any resultant $R = W \leftarrow L_1 \wedge \cdots \wedge L_n$ (resp., $R = \leftarrow L_1 \wedge \cdots \wedge L_n$) and clause C, if there is a resultant V derived from R and a (suitably standardised apart) variant of C, using selected atom L_i, then
$\mathbf{G}_1 \cup \{\leftarrow derive(resultant(W', L_1' \& \cdots \& L_{i-1}', L_i', L_{i+1}' \& \cdots \& L_n'), C', x)\}$
(resp., $\mathbf{G}_1 \cup \{\leftarrow derive(resultant(empty, L_1' \& \cdots \& L_{i-1}', L_i', L_{i+1}' \& \cdots \& L_n')$,
$C', x)\}$) has a finite SLDNF-tree with a unique computed answer ϕ such that $x\phi = V_1'$, where V and V_1 are variants.

Otherwise,
$\mathbf{G}_1 \cup \{\leftarrow derive(resultant(W', L_1' \& \cdots \& L_{i-1}', L_i', L_{i+1}' \& \cdots \& L_n'), C', x)\}$
(resp., $\mathbf{G}_1 \cup \{\leftarrow derive(resultant(empty, L_1' \& \cdots \& L_{i-1}', L_i', L_{i+1}' \& \cdots \& L_n')$,
$C', x)\}$) has a finitely failed SLDNF-tree.

Let R be a safe computation rule. We make the assumption in theorem 2.4.4 below that R is "consistent over variants", in the sense that if G and H are normal goals which are variants, then $R(G) = R(H)$. For theorem 2.4.4, we require the following definition.

Definition Let R be a safe computation rule. Then we say that $\mathbf{G}_1$ is *R-complete* if

whenever Q is $L_1 \wedge \cdots \wedge L_n$ ($n \geq 1$) and $R(\leftarrow Q) = L_i$ for some i, $1 \leq i \leq n$, where L_i is a positive literal, then $\mathbf{G}_1 \cup \{\leftarrow select(L_1' \& \cdots \& L_n', w, x, y, z)\}$ has computed answer $\{w/L_1' \& \cdots \& L_{i-1}', x/positive(L_i'), y/L_{i+1}' \& \cdots \& L_n'$, $z/L_1' \& \cdots \& L_{i-1}' \& L_{i+1}' \& \cdots \& L_n'\}$, and

whenever Q is $L_1 \wedge \cdots \wedge L_n$ ($n \geq 1$) and $R(\leftarrow Q) = L_i$ for some i, $1 \leq i \leq n$, where $L_i = \neg A$ is a ground negative literal, then $\mathbf{G}_1 \cup \{\leftarrow select(L_1' \& \cdots \& L_n', w, x, y, z)\}$ has computed answer $\{w/L_1' \& \cdots \& L_{i-1}'$, $x/negative(A'), y/L_{i+1}' \& \cdots \& L_n', z/L_1' \& \cdots \& L_{i-1}' \& L_{i+1}' \& \cdots \& L_n'\}$.

THEOREM 2.4.4. *Let P be a normal program, $\leftarrow Q$ a normal goal, and R a safe computation rule. Let $\mathbf{G}_P$ and $\mathbf{G}_1$ be defined as above, where $\mathbf{G}_1$ satisfies D2 and is R-complete. Then the following hold.*

1. *If θ is an R-computed answer for $P \cup \{\leftarrow Q\}$, then $\{x/(Q\theta\xi)'\}$ is a computed answer for $\mathbf{G}_P \cup \{\leftarrow succeed(Q' \text{ if } Q', x \text{ if } empty)\}$, for some renaming substitution ξ for $Q\theta$.*

2. *If $P \cup \{\leftarrow Q\}$ has a finitely failed SLDNF-tree via R, then the identity substitution is a computed answer for $\mathbf{G}_P \cup \{\leftarrow fail(empty \text{ if } Q')\}$.*

Proof The proof proceeds by mutual induction on the rank of the refutation and finitely failed tree. In each of the base steps and induction steps, we proceed by induction on the length of a refutation and height of a finitely failed tree. ∎

For another example of the use of the ground representation, the reader is referred to sections 19 and 20 in [11], in which the soundness and completeness of a declarative error diagnoser is proved.

2.5   Meta-Logical Predicates

In this section, we give the definitions of a set of useful meta-logical predicate symbols. These definitions are all based on the ground representation. Note that some of the predicate symbols have a different meaning to the way they are used in Prolog. The intended interpretation for these predicate symbols is based on the Herbrand pre-interpretation for $\mathcal{L}'$, the language used in section 4, augmented by the predicate symbols, function symbols, and constants introduced in this section. We continue to denote the augmented language by $\mathcal{L}'$.

In this section, we assume that $\mathcal{L}$ contains the constants $a_1, \ldots, a_l$, the function symbols $f_1, \ldots, f_m$ of arity $k_1, \ldots, k_m$, respectively, and the predicate symbols $p_1, \ldots, p_n$ of arity $h_1, \ldots, h_n$, respectively. (Note that the arity of a predicate symbol may be 0.)

We begin with the predicate symbol *constant* of type o in $\mathcal{L}'$, which is intended to be true when its argument is the representation of a constant in $\mathcal{L}$. The definition of *constant* is as follows.

$$constant(a'_1) \leftarrow$$
$$\vdots$$
$$constant(a'_l) \leftarrow$$

The definition of the predicate symbol *nonvar* of type o, which is intended to be true when its argument is the representation of a non-variable term in $\mathcal{L}$, is as follows.

$$\forall_o x \; nonvar(x) \leftarrow$$
$$\quad constant(x)$$

$$\forall_o x_1, \ldots, x_{k_1} \; nonvar(f'_1(x_1, \ldots, x_{k_1})) \leftarrow$$
$$\vdots$$
$$\forall_o x_1, \ldots, x_{k_m} \; nonvar(f'_m(x_1, \ldots, x_{k_m})) \leftarrow$$

The definition of the predicate symbol *var* of type o, which is intended to be true when its argument is the representation of a variable in $\mathcal{L}$, is as follows.

$$\forall_o x \; var(x) \leftarrow$$
$$\quad \neg nonvar(x)$$

This definition provides a satisfactory declarative and procedural semantics for *var* which avoids the kind of problem referred to in the first section.

It is possible to identify two different kinds of use of *var* in Prolog. The first is the "meta-level" use which can be understood as above. This use of *var* is exemplified by the unification algorithm given on page 152 of [25]. The other use is the "control" use, which is exemplified by the program for *plus* given on page 147 of [25]. This control use of *var* is confusing because it appears necessary to give some kind of declarative semantics to the corresponding *var* atoms appearing in the program. In fact, no such declarative semantics is necessary or even possible (as was pointed out in section 1). It would be preferable to disallow this use of *var* and replace it by explicit control annotations, which achieve the same effect.

The next predicate symbol of type μ is *atom*, which is intended to be true when its argument is the representation of an atom in $\mathcal{L}$. The definition of *atom* is as follows.

$$\forall_o x_1, \ldots, x_{h_1} \;\; atom(p'_1(x_1, \ldots, x_{h_1})) \leftarrow$$
$$\vdots$$
$$\forall_o x_1, \ldots, x_{h_n} \;\; atom(p'_n(x_1, \ldots, x_{h_n})) \leftarrow$$

The predicate symbol *literal* of type μ is intended to be true when its argument is the representation of a literal in $\mathcal{L}$. Its definition is as follows.

$$\forall_\mu x \;\; literal(x) \leftarrow$$
$$\qquad atom(x)$$

$$\forall_\mu x \;\; literal(not(x)) \leftarrow$$
$$\qquad atom(x)$$

The predicate symbol *conjunction_of_literals* of type μ is intended to be true when its argument is the representation of a conjunction of literals in $\mathcal{L}$. Its definition is as follows.

$$\forall_\mu x \;\; conjunction\_of\_literals(x) \leftarrow$$
$$\qquad literal(x)$$

$$\forall_\mu x, y \;\; conjunction\_of\_literals(x \& y) \leftarrow$$
$$\qquad literal(x) \wedge$$
$$\qquad conjunction\_of\_literals(y)$$

There are two predicate symbols *ground_term* and *ground_atom*, which do the job of the system predicate *ground* in Prolog. First, *ground_term* of type o is intended to be true when its argument is the representation of a ground term in $\mathcal{L}$. The definition of *ground_term* is as follows.

$$\forall_o x \;\; ground\_term(x) \leftarrow$$

$$constant(x)$$

$$\forall_o x_1, \ldots, x_{k_1} \; ground\text{-}term(f'_1(x_1, \ldots, x_{k_1})) \leftarrow$$
$$ground\text{-}term(x_1) \land$$
$$\vdots$$
$$ground\text{-}term(x_{k_1})$$

$$\vdots$$

$$\forall_o x_1, \ldots, x_{k_m} \; ground\text{-}term(f'_m(x_1, \ldots, x_{k_m})) \leftarrow$$
$$ground\text{-}term(x_1) \land$$
$$\vdots$$
$$ground\text{-}term(x_{k_m})$$

The predicate symbol *ground_atom* of type μ is intended to be true when its argument is the representation of a ground atom in $\mathcal{L}$. Its definition is as follows.

$$\forall_o x_1, \ldots, x_{h_1} \; ground\text{-}atom(p'_1(x_1, \ldots, x_{h_1})) \leftarrow$$
$$ground\text{-}term(x_1) \land$$

$$ground\text{-}term(x_{h_1})$$

$$\forall_o x_1, \ldots, x_{h_n} \; ground\text{-}atom(p'_n(x_1, \ldots, x_{h_n})) \leftarrow$$
$$ground\text{-}term(x_1) \land$$

$$ground\text{-}term(x_{h_n})$$

Next we turn to the Prolog meta-logical predicates *functor* and *arg* [25]. In fact, we define variants of these predicates, called *function*, *f_arity*, *f_argument*, *predicate*, *p_arity*, and *p_argument*. The main difference between Prolog's *functor* and the version given here is that *functor* enables explicit access to the function symbol itself. With the ground representation employed so far, it is not possible to do this because a function symbol in $\mathcal{L}$ is represented by a function symbol in $\mathcal{L}'$, which must always appear in the context of a term. Direct access to the representation of a function symbol requires that we represent a function symbol in $\mathcal{L}$ by a constant in $\mathcal{L}'$. The ground representation then requires some slight modifications to enable the representation of terms, which could be carried out if required. However, most uses of *functor* in Prolog don't require direct access to the function symbol. Instead, having available the most general term constructed from that function symbol is equally effective. We follow that approach here.

The predicate symbol *function* has type $o \times o$. Its definition is as follows.

$$\forall_o x_1, \ldots, x_{k_1}, y_1, \ldots, y_{k_1} \ function(f_1'(x_1, \ldots, x_{k_1}), f_1'(y_1, \ldots, y_{k_1})) \leftarrow$$

$$\vdots$$

$$\forall_o x_1, \ldots, x_{k_m}, y_1, \ldots, y_{k_m} \ function(f_m'(x_1, \ldots, x_{k_m}), f_m'(y_1, \ldots, y_{k_m})) \leftarrow$$

The intended use of *function* is that the first argument is used to input the representation of a term and the second argument returns a term "template" with the same function symbol, but variables in the arguments.

For the predicate symbol f_arity, we require some way of referring to the arity of a function symbol. For this purpose, we introduce a constant 0 of type *natural_number* and a function symbol s of type *natural_number* $\rightarrow$ *natural_number*. We then employ the usual convention of denoting $s^n(0)$ by n. The predicate symbol f_arity has type $o \times$ *natural_number*. Its definition is as follows.

$$\forall_o x_1, \ldots, x_{k_1} \ f\_arity(f_1'(x_1, \ldots, x_{k_1}), k_1) \leftarrow$$

$$\vdots$$

$$\forall_o x_1, \ldots, x_{k_m} \ f\_arity(f_m'(x_1, \ldots, x_{k_m}), k_m) \leftarrow$$

The predicate symbol $f\_argument$ has type $o \times$ *natural_number* $\times o$. Its definition is as follows.

$$\forall_o x_1, \ldots, x_{k_1} \ f\_argument(f_1'(x_1, \ldots, x_{k_1}), 1, x_1) \leftarrow$$

$$\forall_o x_1, \ldots, x_{k_1} \ f\_argument(f_1'(x_1, \ldots, x_{k_1}), k_1, x_{k_1}) \leftarrow$$

$$\forall_o x_1, \ldots, x_{k_m} \ f\_argument(f_m'(x_1, \ldots, x_{k_m}), 1, x_1) \leftarrow$$

$$\vdots$$

$$\forall_o x_1, \ldots, x_{k_m} \ f\_argument(f_m'(x_1, \ldots, x_{k_m}), k_m, x_{k_m}) \leftarrow$$

The predicate symbols *predicate*, p_arity, and $p\_argument$ have type $\mu \times \mu$, $\mu \times$ *natural_number*, and $\mu \times$ *natural_number* $\times o$, respectively. Their definitions are as follows.

$$\forall_o x_1, \ldots, x_{h_1}, y_1, \ldots, y_{h_1} \ predicate(p_1'(x_1, \ldots, x_{h_1}), p_1'(y_1, \ldots, y_{h_1})) \leftarrow$$

$$\forall_o x_1, \ldots, x_{h_n}, y_1, \ldots, y_{h_n} \ predicate(p_n'(x_1, \ldots, x_{h_n}), p_n'(y_1, \ldots, y_{h_n})) \leftarrow$$

$$\forall_o x_1, \ldots, x_{h_1} \ \ p\_arity(p'_1(x_1, \ldots, x_{h_1}), h_1) \leftarrow$$

$$\forall_o x_1, \ldots, x_{h_n} \ \ p\_arity(p'_n(x_1, \ldots, x_{h_n}), h_n) \leftarrow$$

$$\forall_o x_1, \ldots, x_{h_1} \ \ p\_argument(p'_1(x_1, \ldots, x_{h_1}), 1, x_1) \leftarrow$$

$$\forall_o x_1, \ldots, x_{h_1} \ \ p\_argument(p'_1(x_1, \ldots, x_{h_1}), h_1, x_{h_1}) \leftarrow$$

$$\forall_o x_1, \ldots, x_{h_n} \ \ p\_argument(p'_n(x_1, \ldots, x_{h_n}), 1, x_1) \leftarrow$$
$$\vdots$$
$$\forall_o x_1, \ldots, x_{h_n} \ \ p\_argument(p'_n(x_1, \ldots, x_{h_n}), h_n, x_{h_n}) \leftarrow$$

Finally, we come to the Prolog predicate $==$. The ground representation makes $==$ unnecessary as it can be replaced by $=_o$ and $=_\mu$.

2.6 Discussion

The quality of a programming language depends mainly on two factors: its expressiveness and its semantics. A programming language which is highly expressive allows programmers to easily and quickly write their programs and, generally, to program at a conveniently high level. A programming language which has a simple and elegant mathematical semantics allows programmers to more easily prove their programs correct and to be assured of the correctness of program transformations, optimizations, and so on.

Prolog's success is undoubtably due to its very high expressiveness. In a wide variety of application areas, programmers are able to get the job done more easily and quickly in Prolog than in other languages. Prolog's importance and widespread use is well justified by these advantages. However, Prolog's semantics (and by Prolog, we mean the practical programming language as it is embodied in currently available Prolog systems, not the idealised pure subsets studied in [11], for example) is much less satisfactory. The problems with the semantics are numerous and well known: lack of occur check, unsafe negation, undisciplined use of cut, assert and retract, and so on. These so-called "impure" aspects of Prolog cause many practical Prolog programs to have no declarative semantics at all and to have unnecessarily complicated procedural semantics. This means that the verification, (systematic) construction, transformation, optimization, and debugging of many Prolog programs is practically impossible.

The solution to this problem is to take more seriously the central thesis of Logic Programming, which is that a program is a first order theory and that computation is deduction from the theory. This is the motivation for this paper. We have studied the meta-programming facilities of Prolog (other than *assert* and *retract*) with a view to making explicit the underlying theories and thus providing a satisfactory declarative and procedural semantics for meta-programs. (The predicates *assert* and *retract* are studied elsewhere; see, for example, [2], [3], [4], and [7].) It is clear that Prolog's meta-programming problems can be traced to the fact that it doesn't handle the representation requirements properly. The most obvious symptom of this is with *var*, which has no declarative semantics at all in Prolog. However, the results of this paper show that, once an appropriate representation is used, there are no theoretical impediments to obtaining a satisfactory declarative and procedural semantics for the meta-programming facilities of Prolog. Within the framework of the appropriate representation, a meta-program is a (typed) first order theory and the meta-logical predicates, such as *var*, have straightforward definitions, which provide simple and elegant declarative and procedural semantics.

With the most basic theoretical issues resolved, we now turn to implementation issues. First, meta-programming needs an adequate type system. The requirement of a type system for Prolog is evident from many other points of view as well, so nothing more need be said here. Second, the Prolog system should make the representation explicitly available to the programmer. In other words, some convenient notation should be available to refer to what we have denoted here by a', f', ... Third, there should be considerable effort put into providing an efficient implementation of the meta-logical predicates. We have in mind an implementation via a compilation process, whereby a meta-program written in the language of this paper and employing the meta-logical predicates defined here is compiled (safely!) into a lower-level program similar to what Prolog programmers currently write. For example, it should be possible to exploit the Prolog systems low level representation of variables, rather than directly use the definition of *var* given above, but do this in such a way as to preserve the declarative and procedural semantics of *var* given by this definition. From this perspective, one can regard current Prolog meta-programs as written in a low-level machine or assembler language and that we wish to allow programmers to program at a much higher level.

There are other issues which also need to be addressed. We have confined attention in this paper to providing representation schemes suitable for handling normal programs and goals. However, ultimately we want to be able represent (arbitrary) programs and goals [11]. This means we must have some way of representing formulas with quantifiers. For the ground representation, this can be handled by what appears to be a very straightforward extension of the framework and results of this paper. (See [11] for an application of this extension to a declarative error diagnoser.) However, for the typed representation, the representation of formulas with quantifiers takes us outside first order logic into some kind of higher order logic with λ-terms [14], [24]. This path is also worth following as a move to the greater expressiveness of higher order logics will probably be generally beneficial, not just for meta-programming.

This raises the related issue of the relative merits of the typed representation versus the ground representation. Although the typed representation is super-ficially attractive, explaining easily as it does the standard *solve* interpreter, it fails badly with meta-programs which make use of *var*. Since many practical meta-programs make heavy use of *var*, the ground representation is the more important of the two representations. Therefore, a serious implementation effort towards making the ground representation efficient would produce great benefits.

Recently there has been interest in the systematic construction of meta-programs. (See, for example, [17] and [26].) For example, if a programmer wanted to write an interpreter with two separate functions, it would be convenient if it were possible to write two separate interpreters, each with one of the functions, and then have the interpreters automatically combined into the required inter-preter. Indeed, it is possible that a calculus of operations on meta-programs could be the basis of a theory of expert system shells.

The interpreter **G** was designed to implement the definitions of SLDNF-refutations and finitely failed SLDNF-trees. Consider the following variant of this interpreter.

$$\forall_\mu x \ \ succeed(x \ if \ empty, x \ if \ empty) \leftarrow$$
$$\qquad head\_formula(x)$$

$$\forall_\mu l, r, s, u, v, w, x, y, z \ \ succeed(x \ if \ y, z) \leftarrow$$
$$\qquad select(y, l, positive(s), r, u) \wedge$$
$$\qquad clause(w) \wedge$$
$$\qquad derive(resultant(x, l, s, r), w, v) \wedge$$
$$\qquad succeed(v, z)$$

$$\forall_\mu l, r, s, u, x, y, z \ \ succeed(x \ if \ y, z) \leftarrow$$
$$\qquad select(y, l, negative(s), r, u) \wedge$$
$$\qquad \neg succeed(empty \ if \ s, empty \ if \ empty) \wedge$$
$$\qquad succeed(x \ if \ u, z)$$

The difference between **G** and the variant is that **G** handles negation with the predicate *fail* while the variant handles negation with $\neg succeed$. We conjecture that this variant interpreter captures the procedural semantics of stratified normal programs and normal goals given by SLS-resolution [20]. It would be interesting to prove analogous results for this variant to those obtained in this paper.

Partial evaluation is another topic which has recently attracted great interest. Its application to meta-programming is now well known. (See, for example, [5], [9], [13], [16], [17], [18], [21], [26], [28] and [29].) For the typed representation, the usefulness of partial evaluation is clear from the proof of theorem 2.3.3, in which partial evaluation is used to remove a layer of interpretation by eliminating the calls to *clause*. In the case of the vanilla interpreter, (a subprogram of) the partially evaluated version of V_P is actually "isomorphic" to P. However, the utility of partial evaluation for the ground representation is not so clear and needs further investigation.

Meta-programming is already of great importance and usefulness. By taking the representation and semantic issues seriously, we can put meta-programming on a much firmer theoretical basis, which will bring further benefits for the whole field of Logic Programming.

References

[1] D. Black and J. Manley. *A Logic-Based Architecture for Knowledge Management.* Technical Memo HPL-BRC-TM-86-037, Hewlett-Packard Bristol Research Centre, 1986.

[2] K.A. Bowen. Meta-level programming and knowledge representation. *New Generation Computing*, 3(3):359–383, 1985.

[3] K.A. Bowen and R.A. Kowalski. Amalgamating language and metalanguage in logic programming. In K.L. Clark and S.-A. Tarnlund, editors, *Logic Programming*, pages 153–172, Academic Press, London, 1982.

[4] K.A. Bowen and T. Weinberg. A meta-level extension of prolog. In *IEEE Symposium on Logic Programming*, pages 669–675, Boston, 1985.

[5] P. Coscia, P. Franceschi, G. Levi, G. Sardu, and L. Torre. Object level reflection of inference rules by partial evaluation. In P. Maes and D. Nardi, editors, *Meta Level Architectures and Reflection*, North-Holland, 1988.

[6] K. Eshghi. *Meta-Language in Logic Programming.* PhD thesis, Department of Computing, Imperial College, 1986.

[7] P.M. Hill and J.W. Lloyd. *Meta-Programming for Dynamic Knowledge Bases.* Technical Report CS-88-18, Department of Computer Science, University of Bristol, 1988.

[8] K. Kunen. *Signed Data Dependencies in Logic Programs.* Technical Report # 719, Computer Sciences Department, University of Wisconsin, 1987. To appear in The Journal of Logic Programming, 1988.

[9] G. Levi and G. Sardu. Partial evaluation of metaprograms in a "multiple worlds" logic language. In D. Bjorner, A.P. Ershov, and N.D. Jones, editors, *Workshop on Partial Evaluation and Mixed Computation*, pages 213–223, Gl. Avernaes, Denmark, October 1987.

[10] J.W. Lloyd. Directions for meta-programming. In *Proceedings of the International Conference on Fifth Generation Computer Systems*, pages 609–617, Tokyo, 1988.

[11] J.W. Lloyd. *Foundations of Logic Programming*. Springer-Verlag, second edition, 1987.

[12] J.W. Lloyd, editor. *Workshop on Meta-Programming in Logic Programming*, Bristol, June 1988.

[13] J.W. Lloyd and J.C. Shepherdson. *Partial Evaluation in Logic Programming*. Technical Report CS-87-09, Department of Computer Science, University of Bristol, 1987.

[14] D.A. Miller and G. Nadathur. *Higher-Order Logic Programming*. Technical Report MS-CIS-86-17, Department of Computer and Information Science, University of Pennsylvania, 1986.

[15] T. Miyachi, S. Kunifuji, II. Kitami, K. Furukawa, A. Takeuchi, and II. Yokota. *A Knowledge Assimilation Method for Logic Databases*. Technical Report TR-025, ICOT, 1983.

[16] G. Neumann. *Meta-Interpreter Directed Compilation of Logic Programs into Prolog*. Technical Report RC 12113, IBM T.J. Watson Research Center, 1986.

[17] S. Owen. *The Development of Explicit Interpreters and Transformers to Control Reasoning about Protein Toplogy*. Technical Memo IIPL-ISC-TM-88-015, IIewlett-Packard Bristol Research Centre, 1988.

[18] S. Owen and R. IIull. *The Use of Explicit Interpretation to Control Reasoning about Protein Toplogy*. Technical Memo, IIewlett-Packard Bristol Research Centre, 1988.

[19] L.M. Pereira and L.F. Monteira. The semantics of parallelism and co-routining in logic programming. In *Mathematical Logic in Computer Science*, pages 611–657, Colloquia Mathematica Societatis Janos Bolyai, Salgotarjan, IIungary, 1978.

[20] T. Przymusinski. On the declarative and procedural semantics of logic programming. 1987. Unpublished manuscript.

[21] S. Safra and E. Shapiro. Meta interpreters for real. In II.-J. Kugler, editor, *Information Processing 86*, pages 271–278, North IIolland, Dublin, 1986.

[22] T. Sato. *On Consistency of First Order Logic Programs*. Technical Report TR-87-12, Electrotechnical Laboratory, 1987.

[23] W.P. Sharpe, R. Hull, D.S. Black, J.C. Manley, and S.J.M. Zaba. *A Methodology and Architecture for Knowledge Base Management Systems*. Technical Memo HPL-BRC-TM-86-038, Hewlett-Packard Bristol Research Centre, 1986.

[24] J. Staples, P.R. Robinson, and R.A. Hagen. Qu-prolog - an extended prolog for symbolic computation. In *Proc. Eleventh Australian Computer Science Conference*, Brisbane, 1988.

[25] L. Sterling and E. Shapiro. *The Art of Prolog*. MIT Press, 1986.

[26] L.S. Sterling and R.D. Beer. *Meta-Interpreters for Expert System Construction*. Technical Report TR 86-122, Center for Automation and Intelligent Systems Research, Case Western Reserve University, 1986.

[27] V.S. Subrahmanian. Foundations of metalogic programming. In J.W. Lloyd, editor, *Workshop on Meta-Programming in Logic Programming*, pages 53–66, Bristol, June 1988.

[28] A. Takeuchi and K. Furukawa. Partial evaluation of Prolog programs and its application to meta programming. In H.-J. Kugler, editor, *Information Processing 86*, pages 415–420, North Holland, Dublin, 1986.

[29] R. Venken. A prolog meta-interpreter for partial evaluation and its application to source to source transformation and query optimization. In *ECAI-84: Advances in Artificial Intelligence*, pages 91–100, North-Holland, Pisa, 1984.

Chapter 3

Metalogic Programming and Direct Universal Computability [1]

Howard A. Blair

Syracuse University

Abstract

Direct universal computability by logic programs is defined. When the set of function symbols of L is infinite there are recursive subsets of the Herbrand universe and Herbrand base of L which are not computable by any logic program. The availability of an effective enumeration of the Herbrand universe U_L of L for inclusion in programs is shown to be *necessary* and sufficient for direct universal computability by logic programs with respect to L. We then show this result holds with respect to completions of normal programs as well.

3.1 Introduction

Nearly all programming languages in use are universal in the sense that every partial recursive function over a suitable subset of the syntactic input/output domain of the language is computable by some program in the language. This subset of the I/O domain is thought of as representing, for example, the natural numbers or the set of all finite length strings over a finite alphabet. Particular implementations of such languages impose practical limitations on this universality, of course. Programs can't exceed the memory capacity of machines, and sometimes in a machine independent way programming languages anticipate these practical limitations by formally imposing a limit on string lengths or integer magnitudes, e.g. PASCAL's <u>maxint</u>.

These practical limitations aside, still most universal programming languages really aren't universal in the sense that not every partial recursive function over

[1]Research sponsored in part by U.S. Air Force Contract F30602-85-C-0008

the entire syntactic input/output domain is computable by some program in the language. Rather, and to repeat, the computational universality of the language is only representable by *encoding* another suitable domain, over which the partial recursive functions can be defined within the syntactic input/output domain of the language.

This paper shows that when the input/output domain of any class of logic programs is taken to be the Herbrand universe of a language L with infinitely many function symbols, this class of logic programs must suffer this same deficiency. We then show that by admitting metalogic programs this deficiency is eliminated. In one sense this is obvious; if we have sufficiently many metalevel relations and/or functions available it is fairly clear that indeed every partial recursive function over the Herbrand universe is computable by including these relations within the programs. But the point here is to exhibit a single simple useful *necessary* and *sufficient* metalevel relation for achieving computational universality directly on the Herbrand universe.

Logic programming takes place over languages with infinite alphabets; we do not imagine that when we program there are only thirty-seven unary function symbols, binary function symbols, etc. up to at most twenty argument places and, should we exhaust the supply, we have to start encoding. But if we imagine a potentially infinite supply of function symbols then we must lose computational universality without encoding. The sparest requirements for recovering it are what this paper is about and they involve a single infinite axiom scheme to effectively enumerate the Herbrand universe. Whatever other deep and important reasons there are for developing metalogic programming, the *necessity* of this infinite axiom scheme or an equivalent construction, is itself a compelling foundational argument for developing it. [1]

That such a difficulty intuitively exists is obvious. For example, PROLOG's metalevel relation **functor** can be used to compute the predicate constant(X) which is true when the (ground) value of X is a constant, and false if the (ground) value of X is not a constant. Proving that no completion of a normal logic program can compute constant(X) is interesting. Note that this predicate *can* be computed by such a program if the language over which the program is expressed has only finitely many function symbols.

The inability to compute certain partial recursive functions over U_L, the Herbrand universe of a language L with infinitely many function symbols, is *not* due *merely* to the fact that the alphabet of a finite program is finite whereas the alphabet of L is not. For example the program whose only clause is $p(X, X) \leftarrow$ computes the equality relation over *all* of U_L (with of course the aid of an under-

---

[1] The author sketched this argument together with technical results in support of it as a panalist at the Workshop on Foundations of Deductive Databases and Logic Programming, Washington, D.C., August, 1986. It has not been developed in a paper prior to this one.

lying equality theory) and the normal and stratified program

$$q(X,Y) \leftarrow \neg p(X,Y)$$
$$p(X,X) \leftarrow$$

computes the 'not equals' relation over all of U_L. (See definition 4, below).

Definition and discussion of the terminology and apparatus of mathematical logic used in this paper, but not explicitly defined here, can be found in [Sh67], and similarly, definitions of terms from the foundations of logic programming that are not explicitly defined here can be found in [Ll84,87].

Plan of the paper: In section 3.2 direct universal computability by logic programs is defined with respect to a (first-order) language L. It is then proved in a model-theoretic fashion that when the set of function symbols of L is infinite, no (finite) logic program can compute the successor function associated with an effective enumeration of the Herbrand universe U_L of L, and hence the class of such programs is not directly computationally universal on U_L. Section 3.3 discusses how to provide a means for naming syntactic objects using the successor function (expressed as a relation) and in section 3.4 a very basic naming relation is used to encode partial recursive functions over U_L in the Herbrand universe of a restriction of L that has only finitely many function symbols. In this way the sufficiency of being able to compute the successor function over U_L to achieve direct computational universality over U_L is established. (This is straightforward; section 3.2 is harder.) Finally, in section 3.5, we extend the results of section 3.2 to normal programs, i.e. programs in which negation is allowed in clause bodies. Because of the vital role played by the equality theory component of completions of normal programs, which it does not play in proving ground atomic logical consequences of ordinary definite clause programs, extending the results of section 3.2 is not straightforward.

Throughout, *infinite* is used to mean *countably infinite*.

3.2   Direct Computational Universality

Let L be a countable first-order language with possibly infinitely many function symbols. U_M is the Herbrand universe of language M and B_M is the Herbrand base of M, for each language M. Constants are function symbols. We assume that L contains at least one constant, and that the sets of function and relation symbols of L are decidable. A set of formulas of language L is said to be *over L*.

DEFINITION 3.2.1. :   *A partial function* $\varphi : U_L^n \longrightarrow U_L$ *is directly computable by logic program P using* $(n+1)$-*ary relation symbol q if for all terms* $t_1, \ldots, t_n, t$ *of* U_L, *it holds that*

$$P \models q(t_1, \ldots, t_n, t) \quad \text{iff} \quad \varphi(t_1, \ldots, t_n) \text{ is defined and } \varphi(t_1, \ldots, t_n) = t.$$

(IIere, the symbol $\models$ as in $\Sigma \models A$, where Σ is a set of formulas, is used to mean that A is a logical consequence of Σ. The term '*directly*' is used in the preceding definition to emphasize that the partial recursive function to be computed is defined directly over the syntactic input/output domain of the program rather than being an encoding of a partial recursive function defined over some other domain, the nonnegative integers for example.

DEFINITION 3.2.2. :   *A class $\mathcal{F}$ of logic programs is directly universal with respect to language L if every partial recursive function defined over U_L is directly computable by some program in $\mathcal{F}$.*

THEOREM 3.2.1. :   *Let $\mathcal{F}$ be the class of all logic programs over L (with finitely many clauses). If L has infinitely many function symbols, then $\mathcal{F}$ is not directly universal.*

Proof:
  Suppose L has infinitely many function symbols, and let

$$E = <\, t^{(0)}, t^{(1)}, \ldots \,>$$

be a one-to-one effective enumeration of U_L. Such an enumeration can easily be constructed from the counting procedure in the elementary proof of the countability of L.

  Let $\mathbb{N}$ be the set of nonnegative integers and let $\underline{\text{next}}(t^{(n)}) = t^{(n+1)}$. (Upon reflection, it should be intuitively apparent that $\underline{\text{next}}$ is not directly computable by any logic program; we shall *prove* this.)

  Suppose $P \in \mathcal{F}$ using binary relation symbol q computes $\underline{\text{next}}$. A priori, in the absence of further argument, it may be that no function symbols occur in P. Let $L(P)$ be the smallest language over which P can be expressed. ($L(P)$ is the language whose function and relation symbols are the function and relation symbols occurring in P). Let L' be a language with finitely many function symbols and at least one constant such that $L(P)$ is a restriction of L' and L' is a restriction of L. Let $M_{P,L'}$ be the least IIerbrand model of P with respect to language L'. ($M_{P,L'}$ is the least fixed point of the familiar operator $\mathbf{T}_P$, but where $\mathbf{T}_P$ is defined on the power set of $B_{L'}$, not merely the power set of the IIerbrand base of $L(P)$).

  For each $n > 0$,

$$P \models q(t^{(n)}, t^{(n+1)}).$$

Suppose $t^{(n)} \in U_{L'}$. We shall show that $t^{(n+1)}$ must also be in $U_{L'}$.

$$M_{P,L'} \models \exists X\, q(t^{(n)}, X).$$

Thus for some $s \in U_{L'}$,

$$M_{P,L'} \models P \models q(t^{(n)}, s).$$

But then

$$P \models q(t^{(n)}, s).$$

Hence,

$$t^{(n+1)} = \underline{next}(t^{(n)}) = s.$$

Let $t^{(N)}$ be the first term in the enumeration E which is in $U_{L'}$. It follows by a straightforward induction argument that

$$\forall n \geq N : t^{(n)} \epsilon U_{L'}.$$

E is an enumeration of all of U_L, so $U_L - U_{L'}$ is finite, which is false; so we have a contradiction to the assumption that P computes $\underline{next}$. $\square$

Corollary 3.2.1: Let $\mathcal{F}$ be the class of all logic programs over L (with finitely many clauses). Let

$$E = < t^{(0)}, t^{(1)}, \ldots >$$

be a one-to-one effective enumeration of U_L. Let $\underline{next}(t^{(n)}) = t^{(n+1)}$, for each $n \epsilon \mathbf{N}$. If L has infinitely many function symbols, then no program in $\mathcal{F}$ computes $\underline{next}$.

$\square$

Next, the class of what is to count as a program is expanded to allow the inclusion of an infinite axiom scheme to compute $\underline{next}$.

DEFINITION **3.2.3.** : *A primitive metalogic program P over L is a logic program (with finitely many clauses) over L together with the axiom scheme*

$$\text{MAGIC:} \quad \underline{next}_E(t, t') \leftarrow$$

for each pair of terms t, t' in U_L such that t' is the immediate successor of t in the one-to-one effective enumeration E of U_L. It is assumed that $\underline{next}_E$ is a binary relation symbol of L. We also consider a logic program over L without axiom scheme(MAGIC) to be a degenerate case of a primitive metalogic program. If scheme(MAGIC) is included in P, then we say that P is nondegenerate.

3.3 What's in a Name?

A ubiquitous aspect of treatments of metalogic is the inclusion of a facility, such as for example Gödel numbering, to provide names in the syntax of the logic for each syntactic object in the logic's language.

Just to start with, observe that for a fixed language L (with at least two binary relation symbols) we can, if desired, *compute* names for every ground term of L using a primitive metalogic program. Consider the following program <u>Name</u> which consists of scheme(MAGIC) together with the clauses

$$\underline{\text{name}}(t^{(0)}, a) \;\;\leftarrow$$
$$\underline{\text{name}}(Y, s(N)) \;\;\leftarrow\;\; \underline{\text{next}}(X, Y) \;\&\; \underline{\text{name}}(X, N).$$

Then

$$P \models \underline{\text{name}}(t, s^n(a)) \;\;\text{iff}\;\; t \text{ is the } n\text{-th term in the enumeration } E.$$

The are at least two reasons for not just letting ground terms name themselves. It is convenient, as is illustrated on a theoretical level in the next section, to have names be terms in a restriction of L to a language with only finitely many function symbols. Secondly, we generally want to be able to name all (at least well-formed) syntactic objects of a logic within the logic, not just ground terms.

There are multiple ways of extending the very simple naming facility using program <u>Name</u> to a means of naming much more comprehensive sets of syntactic objects than just ground terms. One such way is illustrated by the following. Given language L name every symbol **u** of L, including variables, quantifiers, etc., with a new unary function symbol $\ulcorner \mathbf{u} \urcorner$. Then, using the results of the next section, we can construct a primitive metalogic program, <u>NAME</u> which enumerates all terms built from these new unary function symbols and a fixed constant, and also computes the successor function with respect to this latter enumeration. <u>NAME</u> thus enumerates the class of names of all strings of symbols of the language L, whether the strings themselves are well formed syntactic objects of L or not. Moreover the introduction of new symbols is not strictly necessary. Using a fixed binary function symbol to serve as a list constructor, the same effect can be achieved where the symbol names $\ulcorner \mathbf{u} \urcorner$ are replaced by, for example, what amounts to their Gödel numbers using a fixed unary function symbol, as in the program <u>Name</u>, above. In this manner, names are again terms in a restricted part of L using only finitely many function symbols. This is not an argument that one's naming facility should be constructed this way in practice. Rather, it is intended as a sketch of an argument to show that in theory primitive metalogic programs are sufficient for constructing robust naming facilities. Pairing names with what they name at the object level is done via *provability* and related predicates as in [BK82] and [BJ80].

3.4   Direct Universal Computability Revisited

Let <u>Name</u> be the primitive metalogic program used to name ground terms defined in section 3.2. The next theorem shows that scheme(MAGIC) is sufficient for realizing direct universal computability.

THEOREM 3.4.1. : *The family of all primitive metalogic programs over language L is directly universal over L. It is assumed that L contains infinitely many n-ary relation symbols, for each nonegative integer n.*

Proof:

Let $\varphi : U_L^k \longrightarrow U_L$ be a partial recursive function. Without loss of generality, we assume that the constant and unary function symbols a and s, respectively, are in L, as well as the binary relation symbols <u>next</u> and <u>name</u>.

Define $\rho : \{s^n(a) \mid n \,\epsilon\, \mathbb{N}\}^k \longrightarrow \{s^n(a) \mid n \,\epsilon\, \mathbb{N}\}$ by

$$\rho(s^n(a)) = s^m(a) \ \text{iff} \ \varphi(n) = m.$$

Let L' be the language whose relation symbols are those of L and whose function symbols are s and a. Thus $U_{L'} = \{s^n(a) \mid n \,\epsilon\, \mathbb{N}\}$. It is well-known that [cf. AN78, SS82, Ap87, Bl87] if L' has finitely many function symbols, then the class of all definite clause logic programs over L' computes every partial recursive function over $U_{L'}$. Thus, there is a logic program over L' which computes ρ using, say, relation symbol q.

Obtain the primitive metalogic program Q from P by adding to P the axioms and axiom scheme(MAGIC) (renaming relation symbols in P if necessary) of <u>Name</u> and the clause:

$$r(X_1, \dots, X_n, Y) \ \leftarrow \ \begin{aligned} &q(U_1, \dots, U_n, V) \ \& \\ &\underline{name}(X_1, U_1) \ \& \ \dots \ \& \ \underline{name}(X_n, U_n) \\ &\& \ \underline{name}(Y, V)\,. \end{aligned}$$

Then

$$Q \models r(t_1, \dots, t_n, t) \ \text{iff} \ \varphi(t_1, \dots t_n) \ \text{is defined and} \ \varphi(t_1, \dots t_n) = t.$$

(This construction amounts to the obvious encoding of the partial recursive function φ as a partial recursive function over a suitable restriction of L which does permit direct universal computability.)

□

Theorem 1 and theorem 2 together say that for a class of programs over a language L to be directly universal, it must be that some program in the class computes the relation $\underline{next}_E$, where E is an enumeration of U_L, and that scheme(MAGIC), which does compute $\underline{next}_E$, is not derivable from nonmetalogic programs.

3.5 Negation Doesn't Help

This section shows that completions of normal programs (programs with negation permitted in clause bodies) are not sufficient for computing the $\underline{next}_E$ function upon which scheme(MAGIC) is based. The proof given for theorem 1 implicitly depended on the fact that the equality theory component of program completions are not required for proving ground instances of relations from P. But, the axioms of the equality theory component of a completion of a normal program do play a vital role in proving ground instances of relations. Moreover these equality theories contain several infinite axiom schema (in addition to the infinite axiom scheme for occur-check) if the language L in which they are expressed has infinitely many function symbols. The proof given for theorem 1 is not straightforwardly adaptable to the case of normal programs because in general we lack least Herbrand models and because the set of ground atomic consequences of $comp_L(P)$ varies nonmonotonically as L varies as an extension of the language $L(P)$, the smallest language over which P is expressed.

By $comp_L(P)$ for a normal program P we mean the completion of P as defined in [Ll84], but with the equality theory extended to govern all function symbols of L, not just those in P. Moreover, $comp_L(P)$ contains all formulas $\forall X_1 \ldots \forall X_k \, \neg p(X_1, \ldots , X_k)$ for all relation symbols p of L which do not occur in heads of clauses in P.

DEFINITION 3.5.1. : *A partial function* $\varphi : U_L^n \longrightarrow U_L$ *is directly computable by normal program P using $(n+1)$-ary relation symbol q if for all terms $t_1, \ldots , t_n, t$ of U_L*

$$comp_L(P) \models q(t_1, \ldots , t_n, t) \quad iff \quad \varphi(t_1, \ldots , t_n) \text{ is defined and} \\ \varphi(t_1, \ldots , t_n) = t \,.$$

Note that definition 4 does generalize definition 1 since if P is a definite clause program,

$$P \models q(t_1, \ldots , t_n, t) \quad \text{iff} \quad comp_L(P) \models q(t_1, \ldots , t_n, t) \,.$$

DEFINITION 3.5.2. : *A class $\mathcal{F}$ of normal programs is directly universal with respect to language L if every partial recursive function defined over U_L is directly computable by some program in $\mathcal{F}$.*

THEOREM 3.5.1. : *Let $\mathcal{F}$ be the class of all normal programs over L (with finitely many clauses). If L has infinitely many function symbols, then $\mathcal{F}$ is not directly universal.*

Proof:
We first prove three technical lemmas.

LEMMA **3.5.1.** : *Suppose L has infinitely many function symbols of arity greater than 1, and suppose*

$$comp_L(P) \models p(t, f(r_1, \ldots, r_k))$$

where t and $f(r_1, \ldots, r_k))$ are in U_L and f is a nonconstant function symbol that does not occur in term t or in P. Then for all but a finite number of nonconstant function symbols g of L, there exist terms t' of U_L whose top-level function symbol is g such that

$$comp_L(P) \models p(t, t').$$

Proof of Lemma 1:

Suppose $comp_L(P) \models p(t, f(r_1, \ldots, r_k))$ as in the hypothesis of the lemma. By the completeness theorem there is a proof

$$\Pi \text{ of } p(t, f(r_1, \ldots, r_k))$$

which uses only finitely many of the formulas of L and, therefore, only finitely many function symbols of L.

Let Σ_0 be the set of axioms of $comp_L(P)$ used in Π. Then let

$$\Sigma_0 \cup \{\neg p(t, f(r_1, \ldots, r_k))\} = \Sigma$$

Then Σ is inconsistent.

Let g be a function symbol of arity greater than 1. We define the syntactical fg-compilation of terms of L (containing variables) in which g does not occur. Denote the fg-compilation of t by t^{fg}:

i) X^{fg} is X, for any variable X.

ii) $(f(u_1, \ldots, u_k))^{fg}$ is
$$\begin{cases} g(u_1^{fg}, \ldots u_k^{fg}, a, \ldots a) \\ \quad \text{if arity}(g) > \text{arity}(f) \\ g(u_1^{fg}, g(u_2^{fg}, \ldots g(g(u_m^{fg}, \ldots u_k^{fg}) \ldots)) \\ \quad \text{if arity}(g) < \text{arity}(f) \\ \quad \text{and } m = \text{arity}(f) - \text{arity}(g) + 1 \end{cases}$$

a is just some fixed constant.

iii) $(h(u_1, \ldots, u_m))^{fg}$ is $g(u_1^{fg}, \ldots, u_k^{fg})$ if h is not f.

fg-compilation is extended to sets of formulas Γ which do not contain any occurrence of g by defining Γ^{fg} to be the result of fg-compiling all occurrences of terms appearing as arguments to relation symbols in formulas in Γ. Note that fg-compilation is not defined if the arity of f is greater than 1, but g is unary.

Now, recall the set of formulas Σ given above. Σ is inconsistent iff Σ^{fg} is inconsistent; so Σ^{fg} is inconsistent. (Note that if arity$(f) = $ arity(g), then Σ^{fg} results by substituting all occurrences of f in formulas in Σ with g.)

Σ_0^{fg} is a set of axioms of $comp_L(P)$, since f does not occur in P, and the fg-compilation of any axiom of the equality theory component of $comp_L(P)$ that appears in Σ is itself such an axiom, since fg-compilation preserves variable and constant occurrences (note that f is not a constant) and is one-to-one.

Hence

$$\text{comp}_L(P) \models p(t, (f(r_1, \ldots, r_k))^{fg})$$

for all but a finite number of nonconstant function symbols g of arity greater than 1.

This completes the proof of lemma 1.

LEMMA 3.5.2. : *Suppose L has infinitely many unary function symbols and suppose $\text{comp}_L(P) \models p(t, f(r))$ where t and $f(r)$ are in U_L and f is a unary function symbol that does not occur in term t or in P. Then for all but a finite number of unary function symbols g of L, there exist terms t' of U_L whose top-level function symbol is g such that*

$$\text{comp}_L(P) \models p(t, t').$$

The proof of lemma 2 is just like the proof of lemma 1 after noting that fg-compilation is trivially extendable to the case where f and g are both unary.

LEMMA 3.5.3. : *Suppose $\text{comp}_L(P) \models p(t, e)$ where t, e are in U_L and e does not occur in t or in P. Suppose L contains infinitely many constants but only finitely many nonconstant function symbols. Then, for all but a finite number of constants e' of L,*

$$\text{comp}_L(P) \models p(t, e').$$

Proof of Lemma 3:

Proceed exactly as in the proof of lemma 1, but instead of applying fg-compilation, replace all occurrences of e in Σ (where Σ is constructed as in the previous proof) by a constant e' not appearing in Σ.

This completes the proof of lemma 3.

We can now conclude the proof of theorem 3. As in the proof of theorem 1, let E be a one-to-one effective enumeration of U_L, and suppose there is a normal program P that computes $\underline{\text{next}_E}$ using binary relation symbol q.

case 1: L contains infinitely many nonconstant function symbols of arity greater than 1.

Let t, t' be the first pair of terms in the enumeration E such that $\underline{\text{next}_E}(t) = t'$ and the top level function symbol of t' is f where f does not occur in either t or P and is not a constant. (There must be such a pair.)

By lemma 1, there are infinitely many distinct terms in U_L such that

$$\text{comp}_L(P) \models q(t, t'').$$

which contradicts that P computes $\underline{next}_F$.

case 2: L consains infinitely many unary function symbols. Then we proceed as in the previous case taking f to be unary and using lemma 2. **case 3:** L contains infinitely many constants and only finitely many function symbols. Let t be a term in U_L such that $\underline{next}_F(t) = e$, and e does not occur in t or in P. By lemma 3, there are infinitely many constants e' such that

$$\text{comp}_L(P) \models q(t, e').$$

which again contradicts that $\text{comp}_L(P)$ computes $\underline{next}_F$.

□

References

[AN78]   Andreka, II. and Nemeti, I. "The Generalised Completeness of IIorn Predicate Logic as a Programming Language". Acta Cybernetica, vol. 4, no. 1, 1978, pp. 3-10.

[Ap87]   Apt, K. R. "Introduction ot Logic Programming", to appear in *IIandbook of Theoretical Computer Science*, (J. van Leeuwen, Managing Editor).

[Bl87]   Blair, II. A., "Canonical Conservative Extensions of Logic Program Completions", in *Proc. 1987 Symposium on Logic Programming*, September, 1987, IEEE Computer Society Press. pp. 154-161.

[BJ80]   Boolos, G., & Jeffrey, R. *Computability and Logic*, Cambridge University Press, 1980.

[BK80]   Bowen, K. A. & Kowalski, R. A. "Amalgamating Language and Metalanguage in Logic Programming" in *Logic Programming*, K. L. Clark & S.-A. Tärnlund, Academic Press, 1982. pp. 153-172.

[Ll84]   Lloyd, J. W., *Foundations of Logic Programming*, Springer-Verlag, 1984. (Second edition, 1987).

[Sh67]   Shoenfield, J. *Mathematical Logic*. Addison-Wesley, Reading, Mass. 1967.

[SS82]   Sebelik, J. & Stepanek, P. "IIorn Clause Programs for Recursive Functions", in *Logic Programming*, K. L. Clark & S.-A. Tärnlund, (eds.) Academic Press, 1982. pp.324-340.

Chapter 4

A Simple Formulation of the Theory of Metalogic Programming

V.S. Subrahmanian

Syracuse University

Abstract

Metalevel inference techniques have been widely applied in logic programming and artificial intelligence. Essentially, given a language L, a metalevel statement S (w.r.t. L) is a statement *about* the syntactic objects of L. Despite the widespread use of metalogic in logic programming and AI, it was only recently that foundational studies on the semantics of metalogic as a programming language were undertaken, independently by Hill and Lloyd [23] and Subrahmanian [40]. We present here what we hope is a first step towards a comprehensive theory of metalevel inference in logic programming.

4.1 Introduction

Knowledge bases "store" knowledge. However, possessing knowledge is by itself not enough – we need to know how to reason *with* this knowledge, how to reason *about* this knowledge, how to reason *about* the knowledge of other individuals (or other knowledge bases), and how to cooperatively interact with other individuals (or knowledge bases) so as to pool available knowledge together and thus take better informed decisions.

It is commonly accepted that Knowledge is True Belief. Hence, we need to reason not only about knowledge, but also about beliefs. Everyday, we are faced with individuals who believe things that are incorrect. For instance, I may believe (incorrectly) that Toronto is the capital of Canada. Later, someone may present convincing evidence to me that Ottawa is the capital of Canada. Thus, I am forced to *revise* my belief.

So we are led to the questions:

1. How do we reason about knowledge and beliefs ?

2. Can we design a programming language to reason about knowledge and beliefs ?

3. Can we reason about the knowledge and beliefs of a particular reasoning agent (e.g. a human being) ?

4. How can two or more different reasoning agents *pool* their resources (i.e. knowledge and beliefs) together ?

The principal aim of this paper is to answer Question 2 above. We will then show (briefly) how the language thus designed enables us to achieve solutions to each of the other questions posed above.

In order to design an idealized programming language *IPL* of this nature, we need to identify the principal criteria that such a programming language should possess.

Reasoning about Knowledge and Belief. Our major desire is to talk of knowledge and beliefs. Hence, if p is a proposition, we need to be able to say things like "p is *known*" and that "p is *believed*" in our language *IPL* . Thus, we need in *IPL* , the ability to *refer to* formulas. If logic programming hopes to provide the right setting for artificial intelligence, logic programs must have this *referential ability*. This point was realized by Bowen and Kowalski [6] in their pioneering paper on amalgamating object language and metalanguage in logic programming. They realized, and this point is crucial, that the theory of metalogic as developed by logicians for several decades, itself serves this need. Thus, given a first order language L, all we need in the programming language *IPL* , is the ability to refer to formulas in L. And when L is itself rich enough to refer to syntactic objects in L, then L serves as its own meta-language. Bowen and Kowalski [6] claimed that classical first order logic is indeed rich enough to serve as its own metalanguage – a claim that is, in reality, quite well known to logicians for a long time [3].

Semantical Properties. Secondly, the language *IPL* should have a clear declarative semantics, i.e. the meaning of a program P in this language must be characterized elegantly in terms of model theory (and if possible, in other, non-operational ways).

Cooperative Reasoning. Thirdly, such a program P (which presumably reflects the views of a reasoning agent) must be able to talk about the knowledge and beliefs of *other* programs (i.e. beliefs of another reasoning agent). Moreover, P must be able to "take decisions" based on the knowledge (or lack theoreof) of a program P' (which presumably contains the knowledge of a different reasoning agent).

Belief Maintenance. Fourthly, just as human beings can change their beliefs, programs in such languages must have the ability to add and/or drop some of their beliefs.

We try to show here that the amalgamation of object language and metalanguage in logic programming satisfy the criteria listed above. In particular, we will:

1. briefly state the syntax of a metalogic program

2. given a naming mechanism that satisfies certain simple conditions, we will show that metalogic programs have a clear and elegant declarative semantics

3. briefly examine various alternative naming mechanisms which could be used to drive metalogic programming languages

4. show that metalogic programming can be used to reason about beliefs and knowledge

5. discuss the difference between metalogic programming with the object language and metalanguage completely separated, and with the object language included in the metalanguage.

6. show that reasoning agents (i.e. metalogic programs) can cooperate

7. show that knowledge bases can be updated (in our version of metalogic programming) by adding/deleting certain pieces of knowledge.

8. show that reasoning agents have the power of *introspection* (i.e. reasoning about themselves) by showing how to simulate the auto-epistemic logic of Moore [32] in metalogic.

9. show that metalogic can be used to write theorem provers for various propositional non-classical logics.

Our treatment of various issues described above are not meant to be exhaustive. Rather, I try to outline the basic ideas behind a system of metalogic programming that allows the expressive power needed to facilitate reasoning about knowledge and beliefs, cooperative reasoning, introspective reasoning, dynamic knowledge base maintenance, etc. I try to show that such things *can* be done cleanly, elegantly, and naturally within the framework of metalogic programming that we propose here. How these things *should* be done in order to gain the high degree of efficiency required of a working system is beyond the scope of this paper.

4.2   Syntax of Metalogic Programs

We assume that the language L has, in addition to the logical symbols and ",", "(",")", "⌈","⌉"the following mutually disjoint sets of symbols.

1. the set OV of *ordinary variable* symbols

2. the set SV of *scheme variable* symbols

3. the (finite) set $\mathcal{P}$ of predicate symbols

4. the (finite) set $\mathcal{F}$ of function symbols

Given a set Var of variable symbols, we use the notation $\Sigma(Var, \mathcal{F})$ to denote the terms generated by the set $\mathcal{F}$ of function symbols and some set Var of variable symbols.. Any member of $\Sigma(OV, \mathcal{F})$ is called an *ordinary term*, while any member of $\Sigma(SV, \mathcal{F})$ is called a *scheme term*. The set of atoms that can be constructed from a set $Term$ of terms and and a set $Pred$ of predicate symbols is denoted by $\Lambda(Term, Pred)$. Members of $\Lambda(\Sigma(OV, \mathcal{F}), \mathcal{P})$ will be called (ordinary) atoms in future.

DEFINITION 1. Any scheme variable is an *atomic pattern*. Any atom in $\Lambda(\Sigma(OV, \mathcal{F}), \mathcal{P})$ is an atomic pattern. Any atomic pattern is a pattern. If $A_0, A_1, \ldots, A_n$ are atomic patterns containing free occurrences of the variables $x_1, \ldots, x_k$ (and no others), then

$$(\forall x_1) \cdots (\forall x_k)(A_0 \Leftarrow A_1 \& \ldots \& A_n)$$

is a *pattern*.

Intuitively, a pattern is nothing but the usual notion of a clause in logic programming except that a scheme variable may occur in place of an atom.

We assume that L contains the unary predicate symbol *demo*, ternary predicate symbols *add_to* and *drop_from* and a binary predicate symbol *justification*. These symbols are called *reserved predicate symbols*. Any atom of the form $p(\vec{t})$ where p is an n-ary reserved predicate symbol, and $\vec{t}$ is an n-tuple of terms is called a *reserved* atom.

DEFINITION 2. If p is an n-ary predicate symbol, and $\wp_1, \ldots, \wp_n$ are patterns, then $p(\lceil \wp_1 \rceil, \ldots, \lceil \wp_n \rceil)$ is an *atomic schema* (or *scheme atom*). (This notation is really shorthand for $p(\lceil (\forall) \wp_1 \rceil, \ldots, \lceil (\forall) \wp_n \rceil)$ where the universally quantified variables are the *ordinary* variables of the $\wp_i$. If ℓ_0 is an atomic schema and $\mho_1, \ldots, \mho_k$ are either atoms or atomic schema, then

$$\ell_0 \Leftarrow \mho_1 \& \ldots \& \mho_k$$

is a *scheme clause* (sometimes referred to as an *axiom schema*).

Note that explicit quantification over scheme variables is not allowed, i.e. all occurrences of scheme variables are free occurrences. Intuitively, in a scheme clause, names of ordinary logic program clauses may occur as arguments to the predicate symbols. But ordinary atoms may not occur in the head of a scheme clause, though they may occur in the body.

EXAMPLE 1. Suppose X is an ordinary variable, and V_1, V_2 are scheme variables. Let p, q be unary predicate symbols. Then

$$p(\lceil q(a) \rceil) \Leftarrow q(b)$$

is a scheme clause. Similarly,

$$p(\lceil q(X) \rceil) \Leftarrow q(a)$$

is a scheme clause. Here X is an ordinary variable. Similarly,

$$p(\lceil V_1 \Leftarrow V_2 \rceil) \Leftarrow q(a)$$

is a scheme clause. Here, V_1, V_2 are scheme variables.

DEFINITION 3. Suppose $B_1, \ldots, B_n$ are (possibly reserved, possibly scheme) atoms, and A an atom that is not a reserved atom, then

$$A \Leftarrow B_1 \& \ldots \& B_n$$

is a *program clause*. (As usual, all ordinary variable symbols occurring in a program clause are assumed to be implicitly universally quantified.) A is called the *head* of the above program clause; $B_1 \& \ldots \& B_n$ is called the *body*.

DEFINITION 4. A *metalogic program* is a pair $\langle PC, SC \rangle$ where PC is a finite set of program clauses and SC is a finite set of scheme clauses such that no scheme clause has any reserved predicate symbol as the predicate symbol associated with its head.

Note that no reserved atom may occur in the head of a program clause or a scheme clause in a metalogic program though such atoms may occur in the body of a program clause and scheme clause.

4.3 Metaclosure = Program Clauses + Scheme

We assume the existence of a Godel Numbering (cf. Boolos and Jeffrey[3]) of the strings of L (all these strings may not be wffs, of course). We assume L contains the symbol "," as well as an infinite supply of variable symbols. If F is a formula, we use the notation $\lceil F \rceil$ to denote the Godel number of the wff F.

THEOREM 1. (**Fundamental Property of Godel Numberings**) (cf. Boolos and Jeffrey[3]) Suppose $\mathcal{G}$ is a Godel Numbering of a language L. Then $\mathcal{G}$ is a total recursive function. i.e. given a string s in L, the computation of $\mathcal{G}(s)$ always terminates, and given some Godel Number n, it is possible to find a string s in L such that $\mathcal{G}(s) = n$. □

We use the notations U, V (possibly subscripted) to denote scheme variables and $\mathbf{A}$ to denote scheme atoms (possibly subscripted). Throughout this paper, we use the notation T (possibly subscripted and/or superscripted) to denote a theory that is axiomatizable via a finite set of definite clauses.

DEFINITION 5. A *formula substitution* is a substitution of scheme variable free *closed* wffs of L for scheme variables. If a formula substitution σ is applied to a non-scheme formula F, then $F\sigma = F$. Composition of formula substitutions is similar to composition of ordinary substitutions.

DEFINITION 6. A *scheme-variable removing formula substitution* is a formula substitution $\{V_1/F_1, \ldots, V_k/F_k\}$ such that no scheme variable occurs in any F_i, $1 \leq i \leq k$. If F is a formula (possibly containing scheme variables) and σ is a scheme variable removing formula substitution such that every scheme variable occurring in F is in the domain of σ, then $F\sigma$ is a *formula instance* of F.

DEFINITION 7. Suppose $\mathbf{SF}$ is a formula containing scheme variables $V_1, \ldots, V_n$. An interpretation I is a model of $\mathbf{SF}$ iff I is a model of every formula instance of $\mathbf{SF}$.

DEFINITION 8. A *provability predicate* w.r.t. an interpretation I is a unary predicate symbol p in L such that the following axiom schemes (scheme clauses) (cf. Boolos and Jeffrey[3]) are true in I:

$$p(\lceil V \rceil) \Leftarrow V \tag{P1}$$
$$p(\lceil V \rceil) \Leftarrow p(\lceil V \Leftarrow U \rceil) \,\&\, p(\lceil U \rceil) \tag{P2}$$

Here, U, V are scheme variables of L^1.

DEFINITION 9. A *truth predicate* w.r.t. an interpretation I is a unary predicate symbol, t, in L such that the following axiom scheme is true in I:

$$t(\lceil V \rceil) \Leftrightarrow V \tag{T1}$$

DEFINITION 10. Suppose p_1, p_2 are provability predicates w.r.t. an interpretation I. Then $p_1 \preceq_I p_2$ iff $p_2(\lceil V \rceil)$ holds in I whenever $p_1(\lceil V \rceil)$ holds in I. The relations $p_1 \prec_I p_2$, $p_1 \succeq_I p_2$ and $p_1 \succ_I p_2$ are defined in the usual manner.

DEFINITION 11. Suppose p_1, p_2 are provability predicates w.r.t. all models of M. Then $p_1 \preceq p_2$ iff $p_1 \preceq_I p_2$ for all models I of M. The relations $\prec$, $\succ$ and $\succeq$ on provability predicates are defined in the usual way.

---

[1] Note that our notion of *provability predicate* is slightly weaker than that of [3] because we (implicitly) talk only of a provability predicate for the theory that is axiomatized by the empty set. By the Reduction Theorem for first order logic (cf. [37]), this allows us to discuss provability in any finitely axiomatizable theory. This point is discussed further at the end of this section.

DEFINITION 12. A predicate symbol p (resp. q) of L is an *assertional predicate* (resp. *retractional predicate*) w.r.t. an interpretation I iff I satisfies axiom schemes (A1)–(A2) (resp. (R1)–(R3)) below:

$$p(\lceil T \rceil, \lceil V \rceil, \lceil T \,\&\, V \rceil) \Leftarrow \qquad\qquad (A1)$$
$$p(\lceil T \rceil, \lceil V \rceil, \lceil V \,\&\, T \rceil) \Leftarrow \qquad\qquad (A2)$$
$$q(\lceil T \,\&\, V \rceil, \lceil V \rceil, \lceil T \rceil) \Leftarrow \qquad\qquad (R1)$$
$$q(\lceil V \,\&\, T \rceil, \lceil V \rceil, \lceil T \rceil) \Leftarrow \qquad\qquad (R2)$$
$$q(\lceil T_1 \,\&\, V \,\&\, T_2 \rceil, \lceil V \rceil, \lceil T_1 \,\&\, T_2 \rceil) \Leftarrow \qquad\qquad (R3)$$

The axiom schemes (P1)–(P2), (A1)–(A2),(R1)–(R3) are intended to axiomatize, respectively, the following predicate symbols:

$$demo, add\_to, drop\_form$$

The predicate symbol *justification* is intended to be the same as Pr of Boolos and Jeffrey[3] where it is not axiomatized. Recently, there has been considerable interest in justifying inferences in non-monotone reasoning systems (cf. Gargov[14], Brown and Shoham[10]).

DEFINITION 13. A binary predicate symbol j is said to be a *justification* predicate w.r.t. an interpretation I iff I satisfies the following axiom schemes:

$$j(\lceil V \rceil, \lceil V \rceil) \Leftarrow \qquad\qquad (J1)$$
$$j(\lceil V \rceil, \lceil J, J' \rceil) \Leftarrow j(\lceil V \Leftarrow U \rceil, \lceil J \rceil) \,\&\, j(\lceil U \rceil, \lceil J' \rceil) \qquad\qquad (J2)$$

(Note: The assumption that L contains "," is needed in this definition.)

Just as in the case of provability predicates, an ordering $\sqsubseteq_I$ can be defined on assertional, retractional, and justification predicate symbols w.r.t. an interpretation I. Given a metalogic program M, this definition can then be extended to be independent of I in the manner of Definition 11.

DEFINITION 14. The *metaclosure $C(M)$* of the metalogic program $M = \langle PC, SC \rangle$ is the (infinite) set of definite clauses obtained by adding to PC, the following clauses:

1. The clauses obtained from (P1)–(P2) replacing p by *demo* and applying all scheme-variable removing formula substitutions to (P1)–(P2).

2. The clauses obtained from (A1)–(A2) and (R1)–(R3) replacing p and q by *add_to* and *drop_from* respectively and replacing T by arbitrary finitely definite-clause axiomatizable theories and then applying all possible scheme variable removing formula substitutions to (A1),(R1)–(R3).

3. The clauses obtained from (J1) and (J2) with j replaced by *justification* and then applying all possible scheme variable removing formula substitutions to $(J1)$ and $(J2)$.

4. All clauses obtained by applying scheme variable removing substitutions to all scheme clauses in SC.

Note, therefore, that the metaclosure of a metalogic program is an infinitary logic program. Thus, the metaclosure of a metalogic program $M = \langle PC, SC \rangle$ is essentially PC, together with all appropriate formula instances of the axiom schemes (P1)–(P2), (A1)–(A2),(R1)–(R3),(J1),(J2) and the scheme clauses of SC. Our aim now is to show that we do not really need to consider the full metaclosure, but can just work with the metalogic program and the scheme (rather than with all *instances* of the axiom schemes). This leads to the equation Metaclosure = Program Clauses + Scheme. If M is a logic program, we use the notation $M + \mathbf{S}$ to denote $M \cup \{(P1),(P2),(A1),(A2),(R1),(R2),(R3),(J1),(J2)\}$. We now define a monotone operator Δ_M from interpretations to interpretations as follows:

DEFINITION 15. Let M be a metalogic program and A a ground atom in L.

1. (A not a reserved atom) Then $A \in \Delta_M(I)$ iff there is a ground instance (or a scheme variable free instance) of a clause in M of the form

$$A \Leftarrow B_1 \& \ldots \& B_n$$

such that $\{B_1, \ldots, B_n\} \subseteq I$.

2. ($A = demo(n)$) (**Reflection**) $demo(n) \in \Delta_M(I)$ iff either

   (a) $F \in I$ where $\lceil F \rceil = n$ or
   (b) $demo(m_1), demo(m_2) \in I$ where $m_1 = \lceil F \Leftarrow F' \rceil$ and $m_2 = \lceil F' \rceil$.

3. ($A = add\_to(n_1, n_2, n_3)$) $A \in \Delta_M(I)$ iff $n_1 = \lceil T \rceil$, $n_2 = \lceil F \rceil$ and $n_3 = \lceil T' \rceil$, for some finitely definite-clause axiomatizable theory T, some formula F and the theory $T' = T \& F$.

4. ($A = drop\_from(n_1, n_2, n_3)$) $A \in \Delta_M(I)$ iff $n_2 = \lceil F \rceil$ and one of the following cases apply:

   (a) $n_1 = \lceil T \& F \rceil$ and $n_3 = \lceil T \rceil$
   (b) $n_1 = \lceil F \& T \rceil$ and $n_3 = \lceil T \rceil$
   (c) $n_1 = \lceil T_1 \& F \& T_2 \rceil$ and $n_3 = \lceil T_1 \& T_2 \rceil$

5. ($A = justification(n_1, n_2)$) Suppose $n_1 = \lceil F \rceil$ where F is a wff. Then $A \in \Delta_M(I)$ iff there is some wff G and some integers m_1, m_2, m_3, m_4 such that $justification(m_1, m_2) \in I$ and $justification(m_3, m_4) \in I$ and

   (a) $m_1 = \lceil F \Leftarrow G \rceil$
   (b) $m_2 = \lceil J_1 \rceil$, i.e. m_2 names a string J

Strings of L   Names

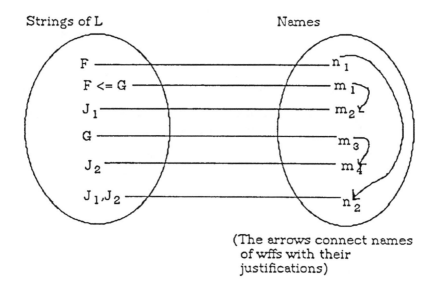

(The arrows connect names
of wffs with their
justifications)

Figure 4.1:

(c) $m_3 = G$

(d) $m_4 = \lceil J_2 \rceil$

(e) $n_2 = \lceil J_1, J_2 \rceil$

(See Figure 4.1 for a clear explanation of this case).

The proof of the following results are straightforward and closely parallel those for classical logic programming (cf. Lloyd [26]).

THEOREM 2. I is an Herbrand model of $M + S$ iff $\Delta_M(I) \subseteq I$. □

LEMMA 1. Δ_M is monotone for any metalogic program M. □

DEFINITION 16. (**Transfinite Upward and Downward Iterations**)
The transfinite upward and downward iterations of Δ are defined as follows:

$\Delta_M \uparrow 0 = \emptyset$ $\qquad\qquad\qquad\qquad$ $\Delta_M \downarrow 0 = B_L$

$\Delta_M \uparrow \alpha = \Delta_M(\Delta_M \uparrow (\alpha - 1))$ $\qquad$ $\Delta_M \downarrow \alpha = \Delta_M(\Delta_M \downarrow (\alpha - 1))$

$\Delta_M \uparrow \lambda = \cup_{\eta < \lambda} \Delta_M \uparrow \eta$ $\qquad\qquad$ $\Delta_M \downarrow \lambda = \cap_{\eta < \lambda} \Delta_M \downarrow \eta$

where α and λ are successor and limit ordinals, respectively.

The following theorem is an immediate consequence of the monotonicity of Δ_M and the Tarski Knaster fixed point theorem.

THEOREM 3. There is a least ordinal α, called the *closure ordinal* of Δ_M such that $\Delta_M \uparrow \alpha = lfp(\Delta_M)$. Thus, $\Delta_M \uparrow \alpha$ is the least Herbrand model of $M + S$.□

DEFINITION 17. The *restriction* of an interpretation I to a predicate symbol p is $\{p(\vec{t}) \mid p(\vec{t}) \in I\}$ and is denoted by $I|p$.

THEOREM 4. Suppose M is a metalogic program. Then $\Delta_M \uparrow \alpha \mid demo$ is the least (according to the $\preceq$ ordering) provability predicate for M.   □

THEOREM 5. Suppose M is a metalogic program. Then I is a model of the metaclosure $C(M)$ of M iff I is a model of $M + S$.   □

LEMMA 2. For all ordinals α, $\Delta_M \downarrow \alpha$ is a model of $C(M)$, and hence of $M + S$. □

DEFINITION 18. An Herbrand model I of $C(M)$ is *supported* iff for all $A \in B_M$ such that $A \in I$, one of the following two conditions holds:

1. (A not a reserved atom) Then there is a ground instance of a clause in M of the form $A \Leftarrow B_1 \& \ldots \& B_k$ such that $\{B_1, \ldots, B_k\} \subseteq I$ OR

2. (A a reserved atom) there is a formula instance of a scheme in S of the form $A \Leftarrow B_1 \& \ldots \& B_n$ such that $\{B_1, \ldots, B_n\} \subseteq I$.

THEOREM 6. I is a supported model of $C(M)$ iff $\Delta_M(I) = I$.   □

DEFINITION 19. A metalogic program M is *canonical* iff $\Delta_M \downarrow \omega$ is a fixed–point of Δ_M.

THEOREM 7. If M is a canonical metalogic program, then $\Delta_M \downarrow \omega$ is the greatest supported model of M.   □

Unfortunately, the operator Δ_M is not continuous. To see this, consider the following example supplied to me by Howard Blair.

EXAMPLE 2. Let M be the program:

$$p \Leftarrow demo(\lceil (\forall x)q(x) \rceil)$$

$$q(a) \Leftarrow$$

$$q(s(X)) \Leftarrow q(X)$$

Clearly, all atoms of the form $q(t)$ are in $\Delta_M \uparrow \omega$, but $p \notin \Delta_M \uparrow \omega$. But as we are only considering Herbrand interpretations, we now have that $\Delta_M \uparrow \omega$ satisfies $(\forall x)q(x)$. Hence, $demo(\lceil (\forall x)q(x) \rceil) \in \Delta_M \uparrow (\omega + 1)$ and it follows that $p \in \Delta_M \uparrow (\omega + 2)$.

If we consider this example briefly, we are struck by one fact. Though $(\forall x)q(x)$ is true in the least Herbrand model of M (and hence in all Herbrand models of M), it is not true in all models of M. In particular, we can pick a pre-structure J whose domain of discourse is the Herbrand Universe of M together with the additional objects $b, s(b), s(s(b)), \ldots$. J behaves exactly like an Herbrand pre-interpretation, except that there is no ground term in the language of M that names the objects $b, s(b), s(s(b)), \ldots$. Thus, the operator Δ_M^J (i.e. the relativization of Δ_M to the pre-structure J) is just like Δ_M for the first ω iterations. But in the ω'th iteration, we have a difference – $\Delta_M^J \uparrow \omega$ does not satisfy $(\forall x)q(x)$. And indeed, $\Delta_M^J \uparrow \omega = \Delta_M^J \uparrow (\omega + 1)$ is the least fixed-point of Δ_M^J, i.e. the closure ordinal of Δ_M^J is ω.

The real problem that the above example demonstrates is that our axiomatization of the *demo* relation is too weak to *uniquely* and correctly axiomatize the intuitive notion of provability. But this is not a problem with our approach alone. The axioms of provability given in Boolos and Jeffrey [3] also have some highly non-standard models. Anyway, the lesson we just learnt is worth noting:

> We cannot hope to axiomatize provability by restricting ourselves to Herbrand models. In particular, if we do wish to look at provability through the "eyes" of one pre-structure, then we must re-define our notion of satisfiability.

What, if anything, can be done to alter the situation ? The solution seems to be to replace the notion of satisfaction by a model-theoretic *forcing* technique, due originally to Abraham Robinson [35]. In model theoretic forcing, individual models can "refer" to other models. So suppose I is an Herbrand interpretation, and F a closed formula. We define the relation "I forces F w.r.t. M" , denoted $I \mapsto_M F$, as follows:

1. If F is a ground atomic formula, then $I \mapsto_M F$ iff F is satisfied by I

2. $I \mapsto_M F_1 \,\&\, F_2$ iff $I \mapsto_M F_1$ and $I \mapsto_M F_2$

3. $I \mapsto_M F_1 \vee F_2$ iff $I \mapsto_M F_1$ or $I \mapsto_M F_2$

4. $I \mapsto_M F_1 \Leftarrow F_2$ iff whenever $I \mapsto_M F_2$, it is also the case that $I \mapsto_M F_1$.

5. $I \mapsto_M (\forall x)F$ iff for every structure J for L and every variable assignment V w.r.t. J such that J, V is a model of M, $J, V \models F$.

6. $I \mapsto_M (\exists x)F$ iff for some variable assignment V w.r.t. I, $I, V \models F$.

(When M is clear from context, we will simply write $I \mapsto F$ instead of $I \mapsto_M F$).

The key part of this definition is (5) above which requires that an interpretation I forces a universally quantified formula iff that universally quantified formula is true in all models of M. The definition of $\mapsto_M$ is conceptually very similar to the *local forcing* relation defined by Marek [29]. *We must note here that an* *interpretation I could force a formula $(\forall x)F$ even though $(\forall x)F$ is false in I. It* now turns out that associated with any metalogic program M, we can define a mapping Ξ_M from interpretations to interpretations. $\Xi_M(I)$ is defined in exactly the same way as $\Delta_M(I)$ except that in each case of Definition 15, we require the following *additional* condition:

1. $I \mapsto B_1 \,\&\, \cdots \,\&\, B_n$ is added to Part (1) of Definition 15

2. $I \mapsto F$ in part (2a), and $I \mapsto demo(\lceil F \leftarrow F' \rceil)$ and $I \mapsto demo(\lceil F' \rceil)$ for part (2b) where $\lceil F \rceil = n$ of Definition 15

3. there is no change in parts (3) and (4) of Definition 15.

The upward and downward iterations of Ξ_M are defined in the same way as the iterations of Δ_M are defined. It can easily be seen now that Example 2 is no longer applicable to Ξ_M. We have the following theorem:

THEOREM 8. Suppose M is a metalogic program. Then:

1. $\Xi_M(I) \subseteq I$ iff I is an Herbrand model of $M + \mathbf{S}$ and I forces $M + \mathbf{S}$.

2. Ξ is monotone.

3. $lfp(\Xi_M) = \Xi_M \uparrow \omega$

4. for all I, $\Xi_M(I) \subseteq \Delta_M(I)$.

5. $\Xi_M \uparrow \omega \mapsto F$ iff $lfp(\Delta_M) \models F$ and $M \models F$.

Proof. (1)
Part One. Suppose I is an Herbrand model of $M + \mathbf{S}$ that forces $M + \mathbf{S}$ and $A \in \Xi_M(I)$. There are various possibilities:
Subcase 1. (A not a reserved atom) Then there is a free variable void[2] instance

$$A \Leftarrow B_1 \,\&\, \cdots \,\&\, B_m$$

of a clause in M such that $I \mapsto (\exists)(B_1 \,\&\, \cdots \,\&\, B_m)$. As I forces $M + \mathbf{S}$ and as $I \mapsto (\exists)(B_1 \,\&\, \cdots \,\&\, B_m)$ it follows that $A \in I$.
Subcase 2. ($A \equiv demo(n)$) Suppose $A \in \Xi_M(I)$ and let $n = \lceil F \rceil$. We proceed by induction on the complexity of F.
I. If F is a ground atom, then either
(a) I forces F, in which case $F \in I$ (by definition)
(b) $demo(\lceil F \Leftarrow F' \rceil)$ is forced by I and $demo(\lceil F' \rceil)$ is forced by I. If F' (resp. $F \Leftarrow F'$) is of the form $(\forall x)F''$, then as I forces $M + \mathbf{S}$, it follows that $I \models F'$. And it then follows, as I forces $\mathbf{S}$, and I is a model of $M + \mathbf{S}$ that $demo(\lceil F \rceil) \in I$.

---

[2]A formula ψ is said to be *free variable void* iff there are no occurrences of free ordinary variables in ψ.

II. The cases when $F = F_1 \& F_2$, $F = F_1 \vee F_2$ and $F = (\exists x)F$ are straightforward.
III. If $F \equiv (\forall x)F'$, then as $\Xi_M(I)$ forces F, and hence, each model of $M + \mathbf{S}$ makes F' true. (by definition). As I is a model of $M + \mathbf{S}$, it follows that $I \models F$. As I is a model of $\mathbf{S}$ which contains the axiom scheme:

$$demo(\lceil V \rceil) \Leftarrow V$$

it follows that $I \models demo(\lceil F \rceil)$.
Subcase 3. The other cases follow in a straightforward manner. We have thus shown at this stage that if I is an Herbrand model of $M + \mathbf{S}$ that forces $M + \mathbf{S}$ then $\Xi_M(I) \subseteq I$. We now need to show the converse.
Part Two. Suppose now that $\Xi_M(I) \subseteq I$. Further, suppose that

$$A \Leftarrow B_1 \& \cdots \& B_m$$

is an instance of a clause in $M + \mathbf{S}$ that contains no free occurrences of any variable symbol and such that $I \mapsto (\exists)(B_1 \& \cdots \& B_m)$. Then $A \in \Xi_M(I)$, and hence $A \in I$ as $\Xi_M(I) \subseteq I$. Hence, $I \mapsto (A \Leftarrow B_1 \& \cdots \& B_m)$. By a similar argument, it is easy to show that $\Xi_M(I) \subseteq I$ imples that I is a model of $M + \mathbf{S}$. This completes the proof of part (1) of the theorem..
(2) To see that Ξ is monotone is straightforward.
(3) It is easy to see that the monotonicity property of (2) above requires only that we show that $lfp(\Xi_M) \subseteq \Xi_M \uparrow \omega$. And for this, we show only that $\Xi_M \uparrow \omega$ is a fixed-point of Ξ_M. Suppose it is not. Then, by monotonicity of Ξ_M, there is some $A \in \Xi_M \uparrow (\omega + 1) - \Xi_M \uparrow \omega$, i.e. there is some clause in $M + \mathbf{S}$ of the form:

$$A \leftarrow B_1 \& \cdots \& B_k$$

such that $\Xi_M \uparrow \omega \mapsto (\exists)(B_1 \& \cdots \& B_k)$. By definition, then there is an instance

$$(B_1 \& \cdots \& B_k)\theta$$

containing no free occurrences of variable symbols such that

$$\Xi_M \uparrow \omega \mapsto (B_1 \& \cdots \& B_k)\theta$$

But then, by definition of $\Xi_M \uparrow \omega$, for each $1 \leq i \leq k$, there is an $\alpha(i) < \omega$ such that

$$\Xi_M \uparrow \alpha(i) \mapsto B_i\theta$$

Then $\alpha = 1 + max\{\alpha(1), \ldots, \alpha(k)\}$ is an integer and

$$A \in \Xi_M \uparrow (\alpha + 1) \subseteq \Xi_M \uparrow \omega$$

A Contradiction. This completes part (3) of the proof.
(4) Immediate from the definition of Ξ_M.

(5) Suppose $\Xi_M \uparrow \omega \mapsto F$. Then as $\Xi_M(I) \subseteq \Delta_M(I)$ for all I, it follows that $\Xi_M \uparrow \omega \subseteq lfp(\Delta_M)$. Hence, it follows immediately by a straightforward induction on the structure of F that $lfp(\Delta_M) \models F$. If some $I \models M$ is such that $I \not\models F$, then F is not forced by $\Xi_M \uparrow \alpha$ for all α. Hence, when $\Xi_M \uparrow \omega \mapsto F$, it follows that every model I of M makes F true. At this point, we have proved one half of the *iff* statement.

The converse is more tricky. Suppose α is the closure ordinal of Δ_M and $\Delta_M \uparrow \alpha \models F$ and $M \models F$. We proceed by transfinite induction on α.

Base Case. $(\alpha = 1)$ Then F is a free variable void instance of a unit clause in $M + \mathbf{S}$ and clearly F is forced by $\Xi_M \uparrow 1$.

Inductive Case. (Part One. $\alpha+1$) We now proceed by induction on the complexity of F.

I. If F is an atomic formula, then $F \Leftarrow B_1 \& \cdots \& B_k$ is an instance of a clause in M containing no free occurrences of variable symbols such that $\Delta_M \uparrow \alpha$ makes $B_1 \& \cdots \& B_k$ true. By the Induction Hypothsis (on α), it follows that $\Xi_M \uparrow \omega$ forces $B_1 \& \cdots \& B_k$. Hence, $\Xi_M \uparrow (\omega + 1)$ forces F. But $\Xi_M \uparrow (\omega + 1) = \Xi_M \uparrow \omega$. Hence $\Xi_M \uparrow \omega$ forces F.

II. The case when F is of the form $F_1 \vee F_2$, $F_1 \Leftarrow F_2$ and $F_1 \& F_2$ are similar.

III. Suppose now that F is $(\forall x)F'$ (where F' may contain free occurrences of x). If $\Delta_M \uparrow (\alpha+1)$ models $(\forall x)F'$ and $M \models (\forall x)F'$, then we know that If $\Delta_M \uparrow (\alpha+1)$ models $demo(\lceil(\forall x)F'\rceil)$ (as $(\alpha + 1)$ is the closure ordinal of Δ_M). Hence, either $\Delta_M \uparrow \alpha$ models $(\forall x)F'$ in which case the result follows immediately from the induction hypothesis (on α) or there exists a formula F'' such that $\Delta_M \uparrow \alpha$ makes $demo(\lceil(\forall x)F' \Leftarrow F''\rceil)$ and $demo(\lceil F''\rceil)$ both true. By the Induction Hypothesis on α, we know then that $\Xi_M \uparrow \omega$ forces both $demo(\lceil(\forall x)F' \Leftarrow F''\rceil)$ and $demo(\lceil F''\rceil)$. Thus, $\Xi_M \uparrow (\omega + 1) = \Xi_M \uparrow \omega$ forces $demo(\lceil(\forall x)F'\rceil)$.

(Part Two. α a limit ordinal) This case is straightforward. $\square$

Connection with Binary Demo. The proposal of Bowen and Kowalski [6] includes the development of binary and ternary versions of *demo*. (In fact, Bowen and Kowalski do not speak of a unary *demo*). However, for finitely axiomatizable theories, our definition coincides with theirs by virtue of the well-known Reduction Theorem [37]. Thus, if **Demo** (note the boldface and the capital D) represents the binary provability predicate of Bowen and Kowalski [6], and T is any finitely axiomatizable theory (not necessarily finitely definite clause axiomatizable), the following relationship holds:

$$\mathbf{Demo}(\lceil T \rceil, \lceil F \rceil) \Leftrightarrow demo(\lceil F \Leftarrow T \rceil)$$

Our reason for changing the notation of Bowen and Kowalski is that it provides an easy way of accessing well-known results in the literature on provability predicates, notably those described by Boolos and Jeffrey[3] (cf. also Tarski[42, 43] and Lob[28]). It seems reasonable to claim that the results of this section substantiate the following claim made by Bowen and Kowalski that Nait Abdallah disputes:

"... the usual theory for Horn-clause program generalizes to the amalgamation universe" [6, p. 13]. The reason the Bowen–Kowalski claim seems reasonable is that the proofs of all the theorems established in this section proceed along lines analogous to the proofs of the corresponding theorems in the classical setting[26]. (For the theorems on supported models, the appropriate reference is Apt, Blair and Walker[1].) The only theorem in classical logic programming that does not carry over immediately to the setting of metalogic programming is the result on the continuity of T_P.

4.4   Unification in Meta

The introduction of strange kinds of variables (i.e. scheme variables), strange symbols ("⌈" ,"⌉" , etc.) causes an immediate concern. Do various properties that are usually decidable in the classical case still continue to be decidable ? In classical logic programming the familiar mechanical proof procedures have two key components – unification and resolution. The decidability of unification contributes to the completeness of resolution. We are forced to ask ourselves the questions:

1. What do we mean by unification in metalogic ?

2. Is this notion of unification decidable ?

The purpose of this section is to explain a solution to these two issues. We first introduce the concept of *meta-unification*, which is the counterpart (in metalogic) of ordinary first order unification. We then present an algorithm to decide meta-unifiability. Before proceeding, I present a few simple motivating examples to illustrate the strange problems that crop up in metalogic.

EXAMPLE 3.   Suppose M is the program:

$$p(X) \Leftarrow q(a)$$

$$q(a) \Leftarrow$$

Then S contains:

$$demo(\lceil V \rceil) \Leftarrow V$$

Consider now the query $demo(\lceil (\forall Z)p(Z) \rceil)$. The first point to note is that this is an acceptable query ! After all, $demo(\lceil (\forall Z)p(Z) \rceil)$. is just an atom – nothing more. Clearly, we desire that $demo(\lceil (\forall Z)p(Z) \rceil)$ and $demo(\lceil V \rceil)$ should meta-unify. (Note that we are not yet defining meta-unification; we are just saying that our definition for meta-unification should permit these two scheme atoms to unify).

In classical unification, we do not, typically, have quantifiers in the expressions we are seeking to unify. In meta-unification, we have to consider this additional complication.

EXAMPLE 4. Consider the atoms $p(\lceil V \rceil)$ and $p(a)$. Here V is a scheme variable. The first is a scheme atom, the second an ordinary atom. Then if for some formula F, it is the case that $\lceil F \rceil = a$, i.e. the name of F is a, then $p(\lceil V \rceil)$ and $p(a)$ should be allowed to meta-unify. Thus, these two expressions can meta-unify *iff* a is the Godel Number of some formula. On the other hand, consider $\lceil p(X) \rceil$ and $\lceil p(a) \rceil$. These two expressions should meta-unify in the obvious way via the substitution X/a.

The above examples show us two important differences between ordinary unification (cf. Lassez, Maher and Mariott[25]) and meta-unification.

1. We may wish to unify closed formulas in meta-unification.

2. The naming function plays a direct role in any notion of meta-unifiability.

DEFINITION 20. (Meta-Unifiability)

1. Two ordinary terms are meta-unifiable iff they are unifiable.

2. Suppose $E_1 \equiv p(t_1)$ where t_1 is an ordinary term and $E_2 \equiv p(\lceil F_2 \rceil)$ where F_2 is an ordinary formula. Then E_1 and E_2 are meta-unifiable iff some ground instance of t_1 is the name of F_2, i.e. t_1 has some ground instance t_2 such that t_2 is the Godel Number of F_2.

3. Suppose $E_1 \equiv p(\lceil t_1 \rceil)$ and $E_2 \equiv p(\lceil t_2 \rceil)$ are atoms containing no scheme variables. Then E_1, E_2 are meta-unifiable iff t_1 and t_2 are meta-unifable.

4. If V is a scheme variable and F is any formula, then V and F are meta-unifiable.

5. Suppose $E_1 \equiv \kappa(\lceil \wp_1 \rceil)$ and $E_2 \equiv \kappa(\lceil \wp_2 \rceil)$. Then E_1 and E_2 are meta-unifiable iff $\wp_1$ and $\wp_2$ are meta-unifiable. Here κ may be either a predicate symbol or a function symbol.

6. if $\wp_1$ and $\wp_2$ are unifiable clauses, then $\wp_1$ and $\wp_2$ are meta-unifiable and $\lceil \wp_1 \rceil$ and $\lceil \wp_2 \rceil$ are meta-unifiable.

In all of cases 2,3,5 above, the extension to k-ary predicates is defined in the obvious way.

THEOREM 9. Given any two syntactic expressions E_1, E_2, the problem: *Are E_1 and E_2 meta-unifiable ?* is decidable.

Proof. Given E_1, E_2, we first need to know which condition in the definition of meta-unifiability applies to E_1, E_2. This problem is clearly decidable. Now we show that each of the conditions defines a decidable condition.

(1) Condition 1 is decidable by the decidability of classical unification.

(2) Condition 2 may be decided as follows. Compute the Godel Number of F_2. By the Fundamental Property of Godel Numberings, this computation terminates, yielding an integer $gn(F)$. Check now if $gn(F)$ is an instance of t_1. This check is also guaranteed to terminate by well known results on classical unification. If yes, then E_1 and E_2 are meta-unifiable, else they are not meta-unifiable.

(3) Condition 3 is clearly decidable as t_1, t_2 are just ordinary terms.

(4) Immediate.

(5) In this case, the meta-unifiability of $\wp_1$ and $\wp_2$ may be assumed to be decidable by the induction hypothesis.

(6) Immediate.

This completes the proof.   □

4.5   Proof Theory for Meta

Metalogic programs look very much like classical logic programs. Hence, one may suspect (and hope) that the proof theory for metalogic programs is not very much more complex than the proof theory for classical logic programs. As we shall show in this section, this hope is fairly realistic.

Typically, the builders of the so-called "meta-interpreters" for logic programming (cf. [38]) have been using proof procedures which bear a distinct resemblance to SLD-Resolution. These interpreters were built, and used, for a long time without paying any regard to soundness and completeness issues. This situation has been rectified by Hill and Lloyd [23] who prove soundness and completeness theorems for what I call *naive*[3] metalogic programming (i.e. completely separating object language and metalanguage. More will be discussed about naive metalogic programming in a later section). And similar theorems were established in [40] for metalogic programming with the amalgamation. This provides a semantical basis for languages like MetaProlog [7].

DEFINITION 21.   A *query* is a conjunction of atomic schemes. All variables occurring in a query are assumed to be implicitly existentially quantified.

DEFINITION 22.   (Meta-Resolvents) Suppose $Q \equiv (\exists)(A_1 \& \ldots \& A_n)$ is a query and C a clause (or axiom schema) such that C and Q have no variables (ordinary or scheme) in common. Then a *meta-resolvent* of C and Q on A_i is:

1. Suppose A_i is an (scheme) atom in Q and A is the head of the (scheme) clause C, and A_i and A are meta-unifiable (via meta-unifier σ). If B is

[3]I do not intend the word naive in a derogatory sense.

the body of C, then $(\exists)(A_1 \& \ldots \& A_{i-1} \& B \& A_{i+1} \& \ldots \& A_n)\sigma$ is a meta-resolvent of Q and C on A_i.

2. If (1) above does not apply, then Q and C have no meta-resolvent on A_i.

DEFINITION 23. A *meta-deduction* from the query Q_1 is a sequence

$$\langle Q_1, C_1, \kappa_1 \rangle, \ldots, \langle Q_i, C_i, \kappa_i \rangle, \ldots$$

where Q_{i+1} is a meta-resolvent of Q_i and C_i via meta-unifier κ. (Note that C_i may either be a program clause or an axiom schema or a variant of one of these).

DEFINITION 24. A *meta-refutation* of the query Q_1 is a finite meta-deduction from Q_1 of the form

$$\langle Q_1, C_1, \kappa_1 \rangle, \ldots, \langle Q_n, C_n, \kappa_n \rangle$$

such that the meta-resolvent of Q_n and C_n is the empty query.

THEOREM 10. (Soundness) Suppose M is a metalogic program, and Q a scheme variable free query. If there is a meta-refutation of the query Q from M then $C(M) \models Q$.

Proof. By induction on the length of the meta-refutation.   □

DEFINITION 25. A metalogic program M is *decently behaved* iff:

1. all occurrences (in program clause bodies) of reserved atoms having *demo* as their predicate symbol have the form $demo(n)$ or $demo(\lceil V \rceil)$ or $demo(\lceil V \Leftarrow T \rceil)$ where V is a formula variable, T is a conjunction (possibly empty) of atoms, and V occurs in the head of the program clause under consideration.

2. all occurrences (in program clause bodies) of reserved atoms having *add_to* as their predicate symbol either have the first and second arguments ground or are of the form $add\_to(\lceil T \rceil, \lceil V \rceil, \lceil U \rceil)$ where T is as defined earlier and V occurs in the head of the clause under consideration. (A similar condition applies to *drop_from*).

3. all occurrences (in program clause bodies) of reserved atoms having *justification* as their predicate symbol have at least one argument containing no formula variables.

THEOREM 11. Suppose M is decently behaved and A is a variable free atom. Then

$$demo(\lceil A \rceil) \in lfp(\Delta_M) \Leftrightarrow C(M) \models A$$

DEFINITION 26. A query Q is said to be *decently behaved* w.r.t. a metalogic program M iff M is decently behaved AND there is no meta-deduction

$$\langle Q_1, C_1, \sigma_1 \rangle, \ldots, \langle Q_i, C_i, \sigma_i \rangle$$

from Q such that

1. there is an occurrence of a reserved atom of the form $add\_to(t1, t2, t3)$ or $drop\_from(t1, t2, t3)$ in some Q_i such that either $t1$ or $t2$ is a formula variable OR

2. there is an occurrence in some Q_i of a reserved atom of the form $demo(\lceil V \Leftarrow T \rceil)$ where V is a formula variable OR

3. there is an occurrence in some Q_i of a reserved atom of the form $demo(\lceil \mathbf{V} \Leftarrow U \rceil)$ where U is a formula variable OR

4. there is an occurrence of a reserved symbol of the form

$$justification\,(\lceil V \rceil, \lceil U \rceil)$$

where both U and V contain formula variables.

5. there is any atom in any Q_i having a non-reserved predicate symbol that contains an occurrence of a formula variable.

LEMMA 3. Suppose A is a ground atom that is decently behaved w.r.t. the metalogic program M such that $C(M) \models A$. Then there is a meta–refutation of A from M.

Proof. As $C(M) \models A$, it follows that $\Xi_M \uparrow \omega \mapsto A$ and hence there is some $n < \omega$ such that $\Xi_M \uparrow n \mapsto A$. The proof now follows by a straightforward induction on n. □

THEOREM 12. (**Completeness**) Suppose M is a metalogic program and Q a query that is decently–behaved w.r.t. M. If $C(M) \models Q$, then there is a meta–refutation of Q from M.

Proof. Immediate from Lemma 3. □.

4.6 Naming – A Discussion

Throughout[4] the previous sections, we have assumed the existence of a decent naming mechanism. While the existence of such naming mechanisms is well-known (in principle, anyway), it is hard to implement in practice. This is because

---

[4] A large part of this section is well-known to logicians. No claim of anything new is being made here. The point of this section is just to acquaint logic programming researchers with well-known work on naming done for centuries by philosophers and logicians.

we need a set N_0 of names for the syntactic entities of our object language, then we need a set N_1 of names for the objects in N_0, and a set N_2 of names for the objects in N_1 and so on. Thus, even for languages that are propositional, one may need infinitely many names.

Hill and Lloyd [23] develop a mechanism for naming (it is essentially a simple case of the well-known quotational device used by logicians [44, 2, 18]). However, as we shall show later, their method is applicable only to *naive* metalogic programming, i.e. it fails to provide names for objects in $N_1, N_2, \cdots$.

Essentially, the role of metalogic is to allow one to talk about the syntactic objects of some object language (called O, say). Thus, we have a metalanguage M that is powerful enough to discuss the properties of O. There are three ways in which M and O can interact:

1. M and O can be completely separated.

2. O is included in M.

3. O and M have some "common part" .

4.6.1   Completely Separate M and O

What do we mean when we say that M and O are *completely separate* ? How can one talk about O in M unless the syntactic objects in O can be represented in M ? Clearly, this is not possible.

But what we can insist on is that whenever some syntactic object o of O appears in a wff F of M, then o's name rather than o itself appears in F. Thus, for instance, if our naming device is *quotation*, i.e. the name of o is 'o', (here the pair of mated quotes forms a single symbol of M), then what we require is that any occurrence of o in M be quoted.

It is well-known that nested quotes cause horrible problems. Borrowing from Belnap and Grover[2, p.23], the expression

$$("\,`\alpha' = " = `\alpha')$$

"is ambiguous as to whether the rightmost occurrence of 'α' is to be taken as the main sign" . The upshot of *completely separating* M and O is that we can insist that the only things that can be quoted in M are syntactic objects of O. This completely removes the ambiguity in the above example. An inductive definition of such quotable syntactic expressions is developed by Belnap and Grover [2].

The approach of Hill and Lloyd [23] is essentially to completely separate M and O, and the naming device they use is essentially just quotation of quote-free object language expressions.

In some ways, this proposal is restrictive. Self-reference and the introspective power of a reasoning agent is lost in this approach. For instance, in this approach, the Liar is not expressible.

This sentence is false.

The above sentence is not expressible when M and O are completely separate. For, if n is the name (in M) of the above sentence then the above sentence is the same as:

'n' is false.

But this contains a quoted name. Any name itself is a quoted expression, and hence this sentence contains nested quotes and therefore can clearly not be in M.

4.6.2 *O* Included in *M*

The picture changes here. When M and O are completely separate, the following essential properties hold:

1. nested quotes were not allowed.

2. in particular, syntactic objects of M could not be named in M.

3. lastly, whenever a syntactic object o of O appeared in a wff F of M, o had to be quoted.

When all these conditions are dropped, then we say that O is included in M. Clearly, this gives rise to much greater expressiveness. For example, the sentence

This sentence is false.

can now be expressed in M without any problem. In addition, a reasoning agent has the power of full introspection. Thus, a reasoning agent can express the sentence:

I can prove that I can prove p.

by saying:

$demo(\lceil demo(\lceil p \rceil) \rceil)$.

(Here, we use the pair $\lceil, \rceil$ as quotation symbols).

We believe that when Bowen and Kowalski [6] wrote their pioneering paper, what they had in mind was that O be included in M. This is clear from the section in their paper on self-reference. And indeed, the design of the programming language MetaProlog permits nested *demo*'s.

From the above example, it is clear that the expressive power of the language obtained by only requiring that O be contained in M is much greater than that obtained when O and M are required to be completely separate. And it is this proposal that we will be principally concerned with in this paper.

The third proposal, viz. when M and O overlap, is very complicated and is beyond the scope of this paper.

4.7 Reasoning About Knowledge and Belief

Reasoning about knowledge and belief is an important area of artificial intelligence. There are many reasons why reasoning about knowledge and belief is necessary. Suppose we have a distributed system $(P_i)_{i \in \mathcal{A}}$ of processes. An individual process P_i may be regarded as a reasoning agent, which has an associated knowledge base KB_i. But the very nature of distributed processes makes it necessary for a particular process to chart its course of action based on the actions (or lack theoreof) of other processes in the system. Thus, knowledge bases $(KB_i)_{i \in \mathcal{A}}$, need to:

1. discuss the knowledge of other processes

2. access the knowledge of other processes

3. simulate the reasoning process of the other processes

Our purpose here is only to show that metalogic programs as described in the paper provide a sufficiently powerful formalism for these goals to be achieved. To show this, we will only show how the logic of knowledge of Halpern and Moses [21] can be represented as a metalogic program. The argument that such a logic is one of many reasonable ways of modelling distributed processes is presented by Halpern and Moses [21].

Let $TAUT$ be any logic program that acts as a theorem prover for propositional logic, such that there is a predicate symbol *taut* in $TAUT$ such that $taut(\lceil F \rceil)$ holds iff F is a propositional tautology. That such a program $TAUT$ exists is easy to verify and follows directly from the decidability of propositional logic and well-known results of Blair [4]. The following program now is an interpreter for the logic of knowledge given by Halpern and Moses [21, p.464]. Here, we associate an operator K_i with a reasoning agent i.

$S5_i$ Axioms

$$tr(\lceil V \rceil) \Leftarrow taut(\lceil V \rceil)$$
$$tr(\lceil K_i(V_1 \rightarrow V_2) \rightarrow (K_i V_1 \rightarrow K_i V_2) \rceil) \Leftarrow$$
$$tr(\lceil K_i V_1 \rightarrow V_1 \rceil) \Leftarrow$$
$$tr(\lceil K_i V_1 \rightarrow K_i K_i V_1 \rceil) \Leftarrow$$
$$tr(\lceil \neg K_i V_1 \rightarrow K_i \neg K_i V_1 \rceil) \Leftarrow$$
$$tr(\lceil V_1 \rceil) \Leftarrow tr(\lceil V_2 \rightarrow V_1 \rceil) \ \& \ tr(\lceil V_1 \rceil)$$

Here, K_i is a modal operator that says that "Reasoning agent i knows $\cdots$." V_1, V_2 above are used as scheme variables. The above program, together with the program $TAUT$, forms an interpreter for the modal logic $S5_i$ of knowledge of Halpern and Moses. Now, suppose we have n reasoning agents, i.e. $1 \leq i \leq n$. This is the typical situation in reasoning about distributed processes because we always have only finitely many processes at a given time. The axioms for the system of *implicit knowledge* based on n reasoning agents is defined by taking the set of axioms $S5_i$ for each $1 \leq i \leq n$ together with the following axioms for each $1 \leq i \leq n$:

$S5I_i$ Axioms

$tr(\lceil K_i V \rightarrow IV \rceil) \Leftarrow$
(This defines a family of axioms, one for each $1 \leq i \leq n$)
$tr(\lceil IV \rightarrow V \rceil) \Leftarrow$
$tr(\lceil IV \rightarrow IIV \rceil) \Leftarrow$
$tr(\lceil \neg IV \rightarrow I\neg IV \rceil) \Leftarrow$
$tr(\lceil (IV_1 \ \& \ I(V_1 \rightarrow V_2) \rightarrow IV_2 \rceil) \Leftarrow$

When we have n reasoning agents, the system $S5I^n$ is essentially the system of logic axiomatized by

$$ TAUT \cup \left(\bigcup_{i=1}^{n} (S5I_i \cup S5_i) \right). $$

The message logic MLI^n (Fagin and Vardi[13]) for n reasoning agents is obtained from $S5I^n$ by adding the axiom:

$$ tr(\lceil I\neg V \rightarrow (K_1 \neg V \ \lor \ldots \lor \ K_n \neg V)\rceil) \Leftarrow $$

The argument that such logics provide the appropriate formalism for reasoning about distributed processes is described by Fagin and Vardi [13] following on the earlier work of Halpern and Moses [21, 19]. Further work on how metalogic programming can be used in reasoning about distributed processes is necessary.

4.8 Naive vs. Amalgamated Metalogic

The designer of a programming language needs to make a trade-off between *efficiency* and *expressive power*. Expressive power allows the programmer greater latitude in programming. But this often comes at the expense of efficiency. A splendid example when this happens is full first order logic. Resolution-based interpreters for full first order logic are terribly inefficient. But when we restrict the latitude a programmer has by forcing him to write only definite clause programs (i.e. we sacrifice expressiveness), then we gain efficiency – for definite clauses have a sound, complete, and reasonably efficient interpreter, viz. an SLD-Resolution Theorem prover.

I call a metalogic programming language *naive* if it satisfies the requirement that the object language O and the metalanguage M are completely separate (in the sense of Section 6.1). In particular, such languages do not, in general, provide names for the syntactic objects of the metalanguage M.

It follows from comments of Belnap and Grover [2], that there are many uses for naive metalogic programming. After all, when does one really need to reason about metalanguage in practice ? When Belnap and Grover wrote their article, there were not many applications where one really needed to fully amalgamate object language and metalanguage. But since then, the field of distributed knowledge has rapidly grown, and the logics of knowledge and belief have been shown to be of considerable importance in both AI and distributed computing. In particular, it has been argued by various researcher like Moore [32] and Konolige [24] that reasoning agents must be able to *reflect* upon their own knowledge and beliefs. In order to do this, one needs to be able to name the syntactic objects of our metalanguage. Thus, amalgamated metalogic programming has many advantages, the principal ones being:

1. providing introspective reasoning facilities.

2. allowing nested names and hence greater expressiveness.

On the other hand, *naive* metalogic programming also has many advantages. First and foremost is its essential simplicity. This makes it very easy for programmers to understand naive metalogic programming – an important consideration in the design of a programming language. Secondly, it does possess some expressive power that our formulation does not. For instance, Hill and Lloyd[23] prove soundness and completeness theorems for processing normal queries (of certain kinds) to normal (naive) metalogic programs. But our semantical results apply only to pure (amalgamated) metalogic programs, and indeed the completeness theorems apply only to a subset of pure (amalgamated) metalogic programs.

Thus, we feel that there is a *split* in the logic programming community on the issue of what metalogic programming should look like. *And the discussion contained here and in Section 6 explain precisely why this split is natural.* This split is just a simple consequence of the fact that metalogic plays different roles in different contexts, and that the relationship between object language and metalanguage may be any of the three relationships mentioned in Section 6.

4.9   Cooperative Reasoning in Meta

Human beings often get together and cooperatively solve problems. A similar goal is addressed by researchers in distributed databases, where each database has some information, but needs additional information from some other databases in order to solve a given problem. Thus, if we have two expert systems E_1, E_2 (for the time being we do not worry about the language and/or form in which these expert systems are expressed), then it is quite possible that E_1 and E_2 may be able to solve a problem jointly, though neither of them may, by themselves, be able to solve the problem.

Thus, given a problem *Prob*, E_1 may wish to "ask" E_2 for its help in the solution of the problem. In order to do so, the *language in which E_1 is written must be expressive enough to* express the request for help. We believe that the proposal for metalogic programming developed in this proposal is expressive enough for this purpose. To emphasize this point, we show how the Three Wise Men puzzle (a well-known example of cooperative reasoning) is solved in our framework.

EXAMPLE 5. (**McCarthy's Three Wise Men Puzzle**) Essentially, the Three Wise Men puzzle involves three wise men $1, 2, 3$ (it is crucial that the three men be wise) each of whom is wearing a hat whose colour is either black or white. At least one of these is white. Each of the wise men is then asked (successively) if he knows the colour of the hat he is wearing. As the men are wise, they draw "correct" conclusions, and also are capable of drawing conclusions if they exists, i.e. they are "perfect" reasoning agents. The following is *common knowledge.*

1. each wise man knows that at least one of the three hats is white

2. each wise man knows that the other two wise men can draw perfect deductions, (and as he himself is wise, he can simulate the reasoning processes of the other two)

The above information can be encoded in the form of two tables (see Figure 4.2).

Both these tables are known to all three wise men. Nait Abdallah[34, p.12,pps 18–20] shows how his formalism can be used to solve this problem under the *additional assumption* that all three hats are white. We show how it can be solved with the first–order Bowen–Kowalski framework itself whatever the colours of the hats, i.e. we do not need the restriction that all three hats be white. We now give a set of sentences in metalogic that simulates the behaviour of the three wise men, and expresses their knowledge of the tables of Appendix I. (We use **theory1, theory2, theory3** to denote the knowledge of the wise men $1, 2, 3$ respectively). The predicate symbol *view* is used to denote the hats seen by a wise man – thus, $view(I, Color_1, Color_2)$ is used to denote the colours of hats as seen by the I'th wise man. Thus, $view(2, w, b)$ means that the second wise man sees that the first wise man is wearing a white hat, and that the third is wearing a black one. We assume below that in addition to the clauses listed for **theoryi**, there is an additional clause of the form $view(i, Colour_1, Colour_2)$ for each $1 \leq i \leq 3$ in **theoryi**.

	H1	H2	H3
C1	w	w	w
C2	w	w	b
C3	w	b	w
C4	w	b	b
C5	b	w	w
C6	b	w	b
C7	b	b	w

Hat Configurations

	1	2	3
C1	n	n	y
C2	n	y	-
C3	n	n	y
C4	y	-	-
C5	n	n	y
C6	n	y	y
C7	n	n	y

Answers of Wise Men

Figure 4.2:

theory1

$$knows(1, hat(1), w) \;\Leftarrow\; demo(\lceil view(1, b, b) \Leftarrow \textbf{theory1} \rceil)$$

theory2

$$
\begin{aligned}
knows(2, hat(2), w) \;\Leftarrow\;& demo(\lceil view(2, w, b) \Leftarrow \textbf{theory2} \rceil) \;\& \\
& demo(\lceil \neg knows(1, hat(1), X) \Leftarrow \\
& \quad comp(\textbf{theory1} \,\&\, \textbf{theory2}) \rceil). \\
knows(2, hat(2), w) \;\Leftarrow\;& demo(\lceil view(2, b, b) \Leftarrow \textbf{theory2} \rceil)
\end{aligned}
$$

theory3

$$
\begin{aligned}
knows(3, hat(3), w) \;\Leftarrow\;& demo(\lceil view(3, b, b) \Leftarrow \textbf{theory3} \rceil) \\
knows(3, hat(3), w) \;\Leftarrow\;& demo(\lceil view(3, w, b) \Leftarrow \textbf{theory3} \rceil) \;\& \\
& demo(\lceil \neg knows(1, hat(1), X) \Leftarrow \\
& \quad comp(\textbf{theory1} \,\&\, \textbf{theory3}) \rceil) \;\& \\
& demo(\lceil \neg knows(2, hat(2), Y) \Leftarrow \\
& \quad comp(\textbf{theory2} \,\&\, \textbf{theory3}) \rceil) \\
knows(3, hat(3), w) \;\Leftarrow\;& demo(\lceil view(3, b, w) \Leftarrow \textbf{theory3} \rceil) \;\& \\
& demo(\lceil \neg knows(1, hat(1), X) \Leftarrow \\
& \quad comp(\textbf{theory1} \,\&\, \textbf{theory3}) \rceil) \;\& \\
& demo(\lceil \neg knows(2, hat(2), Y) \Leftarrow \\
& \quad comp(\textbf{theory2} \,\&\, \textbf{theory3}) \rceil). \\
knows(3, hat(3), w) \;\Leftarrow\;& demo(\lceil view(3, w, w) \Leftarrow \textbf{theory3} \rceil) \;\& \\
& demo(\lceil \neg knows(1, hat(1), X) \Leftarrow \\
& \quad comp(\textbf{theory1} \,\&\, \textbf{theory3}) \rceil) \;\& \\
& demo(\lceil \neg knows(2, hat(2), Y) \Leftarrow \\
& \quad comp(\textbf{theory2} \,\&\, \textbf{theory3}) \rceil).
\end{aligned}
$$

4.10 Dynamic Knowledge Bases

Two of the most notorious features of Prolog are the *assert* and *retract* facilities. There is wide-spread agreement that some such method for dynamically modifying knowledge bases is needed. I concur with this view. There are two primary considerations to be considered when we design assertional and retractional facilities.

1. The commutativity of & must be preserved.

2. At any given point in the execution of a query, we must know from which theory we are trying to prove a particular subgoal.

Earlier, we presented axiom schemas that an assertional and retractional predicate must satisfy. Let us see how these work. Suppose we have a metalogic program M and the query:

$$add\_to(\lceil P \rceil, \lceil (\forall X)q(X) \Leftarrow p(X) \rceil, \lceil V \rceil) \ \& \ demo(\lceil q(a) \Leftarrow V \rceil)$$

This query asks whether $q(a)$ is true in the theory obtained by adding the clause $q(X) \Leftarrow p(X)$ to M. Note that the ordering of the two atomic subgoals in the query make no difference to the declarative meaning of this query. Consider now the Prolog queries

$$assert(q(X) \Leftarrow p(X)) \ \& \ q(X) \qquad\qquad\qquad (Q1)$$
$$q(X) \ \& \ assert(q(X) \Leftarrow p(X)) \qquad\qquad\qquad (Q2)$$

In some sense, (Q1) and (Q2) above show how the metalogic query above would be represented in Prolog. Unfortunately, (Q1) and (Q2) mean two different things. This is because the formula

$$assert(q(X) \Leftarrow p(X))$$

contains free occurrences of the variable symbol X. On the other hand, in the metalogic version of this query,

$$add\_to(\lceil P \rceil, \lceil (\forall X)q(X) \Leftarrow p(X) \rceil, \lceil V \rceil)$$

does not contain any free occurrences of X. Suppose $q(a), p(b)$ are logical consequences of P. Then, from (Q1), we could conclude the answer $X = b$. But from (Q2), the answer $X = b$ would never be returned. On the other hand, the metalogic version of (Q1),(Q2) will yield both the answers $X = a$ and $X = b$ irrespective of the ordering of the atomic subgoals. And in fact, the following result is easy to prove:

PROPOSITION 1. Suppose M is any metalogic program such that no scheme atom in M contains any free occurrences of ordinary variables and suppose $Q \equiv A_1 \& A_2$ is any query (possibly containing add_to and $drop\_from$) that satisfies the same condition. Then:

1. $C(M) \models A_1 \ \& \ A_2$ iff $C(M) \models A_2 \ \& \ A_1$.

2. there is a meta-refutation of A_1 & A_2 from the metalogic program M iff there is a meta-refutation of A_2 & A_1 from M.

□

This formalism is different from ordinary Prolog. This is a natural consequence of requiring that any occurrence of a syntactic expression (term or formula) from the object language O that occurs in the metalanguage M (i.e. in a scheme atom) contain no free occurrences of variable symbols. Thus, for instance, the Prolog goals

$$(\exists X)(assert(p(X) \Leftarrow q(X)) \& q(X)) \qquad (Q3)$$
$$(\exists X)(q(X) \& assert(p(X) \Leftarrow q(X))) \qquad (Q4)$$

cause different clauses to be added to the underlying program P. If $q(a)$ is the only atom that succeeds from P, then the first query causes the clause $(\forall X)p(X) \Leftarrow q(X)$ to be added to P, while the second query causes $p(a) \Leftarrow q(a)$ to be added to P. Thus, the & symbol behaves in a non-commutative fashion.

For some reason, the logic programming community finds the semantics of *retract* a much knottier problem than that of *assert*. In my opinion, this view is largely incorrect. The general principle that must guide our study of modifying knowledge bases is:

> Given a goal G and a subgoal G', it must always be clear which theory T (resp. T') we are seeking to prove G (resp. G') from. Knowledge Bases KB need not and should not be modified during the query answering process. Every subgoal G_i of the initial goal G must be solved relative to some knowledge base KB_i that can be named by KB. Asserts and retracts are just intended as a means of specifying a *new* Knowledge Base from which to prove one or more subgoal. As long as this intended *new* Knowledge Base is clearly specified (by an appropriate naming device), no problems arise.

In ordinary Prolog, the usual (operational) meaning ascribed to the query Q_0 below is:

$$A_1 \& \cdots \& A_i \& retract(Clause) \& A_{i+1} \& \cdots \& A_k$$

is:

1. solve the query $(A_1 \& \cdots \& A_i)$ and let θ be the computed answer substitution.

2. delete the (variants of) clause C in the current knowledge base (CURRKB) thus constructing a new knowledge base (NEWKB).

3. solve the query $(A_{i+1} \& \cdots \& A_k)\theta$ from NEWKB.

The three requirements listed above destroy the commutativity of $\&$. However, it is our thesis that the metalogic query below intuitively satisfies all the three requirements above without destroying the commutativity of AND.

$demo(\ulcorner A_1 \& \cdots \& A_i \Leftarrow CURRKB \urcorner)$ &
$drop\_from(\ulcorner CURRKB \urcorner, \ulcorner Clause \urcorner, \ulcorner NEWKB \urcorner)$ &
$demo(\ulcorner A_{i+1} \& \cdots \& A_k \Leftarrow NEWKB \urcorner)$.

A similar way of transforming Prolog queries containing *asserts* to metalogic queries containing *add_to* is easy to describe.

4.11 Introspection

Introspection is the ability of a reasoning agent ot reason about itself. Thus, when a reasoning agent asks itself "Is everything I believe true ?" , then the agent is asking an introspective question.

Introspection is an important phenomenon in human (and machine !) reasoning. For instance, if in distributed systems, a process is to draw sensible conclusions, it must *know what it does not know*. Only than can it ask another process for the required knowledge. We do such things every day. We realize we do not know anything about taxation, say, and consult a tax expert. The realization of knowing what we do not know is as important a part of human reasoning as knowing what we do know.

EXAMPLE 6. (Knight-Knave Islands) The knight-knave island scenario was introduced by Smullyan [39] who used it to illustrate various aspects of an agent reasoning about his/her own beliefs. The setting is as follows: a reasoning agent R is on an island, whose inhabitants are partitioned into two categories – compulsive liars (who always lie) and extraordinarily honest people (who always tell the truth). Our aim will be to show how many of Smullyan's problems are naturally represented in the form of metalogic programs. Let n be a particular native of this island. If p is a propostion, then we use $Bel(\ulcorner p \urcorner)$ to denote that "R believes p"

Accurate Reasoners. We say that R is *accurate* if R never believes any false proposition. Thus, accuracy can be represented as:

$$accurate_R \Leftarrow demo(\ulcorner Bel(\ulcorner V \urcorner) \rightarrow V \urcorner)$$

This says that R is accurate iff it can be shown that every belief of R is true.

Type 1 Reasoners. R is said to be a *type 1* reasoner iff he has a complete knowledge of propositional logic, i.e. he believes all the tautologies of propositional logic, and his beliefs are closed under modus ponens, i.e. if he believes p and $p \rightarrow q$, then he believes q. Thus, type 1-ness can be represented as:

$$type1_R \Leftarrow demo(\lceil taut(\lceil V \rceil) \rightarrow Bel(\lceil V \rceil) \rceil) \;\&\; mp_R$$

$$mp_R \Leftarrow demo(\lceil (Bel(\lceil V_1 \rightarrow V_2 \rceil) \;\&\; Bel(\lceil V_1 \rceil)) \rightarrow Bel(\lceil V_2 \rceil) \rceil)$$

Conceited Reasoners. R is *conceited* iff he believes that everything he believes is true, i.e. R believes that $Bel(p)$ implies p. This is formalized as:

$$conceited_R \Leftarrow demo(\lceil Bel(\lceil (Bel(\lceil V \rceil) \rightarrow V) \rceil) \rceil)$$

Peculiar Reasoners. R is *peculiar* iff for some proposition p such that he believes p and does not believe p. This can be expressed as:

$$peculiar_R \Leftarrow Bel(\lceil V \rceil) \;\&\; Bel(\lceil \neg V \rceil)$$

There are various other properties about introspective reasoners (e.g. Smullyan's [39] type 2, type 3, type 4 reasoners, normal reasoners, etc.) that can all be easily formulated in terms of metalogic programming. Thus, it gives us the power to reason about reasoning agents – even peculiar reasoning agents. In particular, note that peculiar reasoning agents who are not type 1 reasoning agents may, in general, be paraconsistent reasoning agents (cf. da Costa [11], Blair and Subrahmanian [5]).

Auto-Epistemic Logics. Another important proposal for introspective reasoning is auto-epistemic logic proposed by Moore [32]. Auto-epistemic logic is ordinary propositional logic augmented with a new logical symbol – the modal operator K. Auto-epistemic logic is widely used as a non-monotonic reasoning mechanism. Recently, Gelfond and Lifschitz [15] have used it to develop a declarative semantics for general logic programs that extends the stratified and locally stratified semantics. There is an operator Φ_T associated with a theory T which maps sets I of propositions to sets of propositions as follows:

$$\Phi_T(I) = Cn(I \cup \{K\psi \mid \psi \in T\} \cup \{\neg K\psi \mid \psi \notin T\}).$$

A theory T is an *expansion* of I iff $\Phi_T(I) = T$. A theory T is *stable* iff:

(St 1) T is closed under propositional consequence.

(St 2) $\psi \in T$ implies $K\psi \in T$.

(St 3) $\psi \notin T$ implies $\neg K\psi \in T$.

In metalogic, we can easily reason about auto-epistemic theories. For instance, we can code the stability conditions as the following metalogic program:

$$st1(\ulcorner T\urcorner) \Leftarrow demo(\ulcorner taut(\ulcorner V\urcorner) \rightarrow in(\ulcorner V\urcorner, \ulcorner T\urcorner)\urcorner).$$
$$st2(\ulcorner T\urcorner) \Leftarrow demo(\ulcorner in(\ulcorner V\urcorner, \ulcorner T\urcorner) \rightarrow in(\ulcorner KV\urcorner, \ulcorner T\urcorner)\urcorner)$$
$$st3(\ulcorner T\urcorner) \Leftarrow demo(\ulcorner notin(\ulcorner V\urcorner, \ulcorner T\urcorner) \rightarrow in(\ulcorner \neg KV\urcorner, \ulcorner T\urcorner)\urcorner)$$
$$stable(\ulcorner T\urcorner) \Leftarrow st1(\ulcorner T\urcorner) \,\&\, st2(\ulcorner T\urcorner) \,\&\, st3(\ulcorner T\urcorner).$$

As long as our theories T are propositional, the above metalogic program, together with appropriate (easily defined) axioms for the predicate symbols *in* and *notin*, correctly define the stability property.

This is one example of how metalogic programming can be used to express (and thus study) properties of auto-epistemic logics. Various other properties of non-classical logics like default logics, temporal logics, etc. can all be naturally expressed.

4.12   Simulating Non-Classical Logics in Meta

It is easy to write theorem provers for various non-classical logics in the form of metalogic programs. We give two such examples below, viz. a theorem prover intuitionistic logic and a theorem prover for propositional $S5$.

EXAMPLE 7. (Theorem Prover for Intuitionistic Logic) Dale Miller and his co-workers [30, 31] have shown how a simple interpreter for an intuitionistic logic can be written in λProlog – a higher order logic programming language developed at the University of Pennsylvania. Our aim below is to show that this interpreter can be written in metalogic itself and that it is not necessary to use higher order logic to formalize provability in the intuitionistic logic Miller considers. *I do not intend to claim here that metalogic is, in any sense, better than higher-order logic.* However, it appears to me (and I am not the only one in this respect, cf. Goguen [17]) that higher order logics are best avoided, in part, due to the fact that unification is undecidable, and because for the most part, there is no formalization of higher order logic that is both sound and complete [3]. As L is generated by finitely many function and predicate symbols, L can be expanded to a language L' containing (new) binary predicate symbols *pred*, *func* and unary predicate symbols *term*, *atom*. From the results of Blair [4], there exist programs PRED, FUNC, TERM, ATOM in L' such that

1. PRED $\models pred(\ulcorner r\urcorner, n)$ iff r is an n-ary predicate symbol of L'

2. FUNC $\models func(\ulcorner f\urcorner, n)$ iff f is an n-ary function symbol of L'

3. TERM $\models term(\ulcorner t\urcorner)$ iff t is a term in L'

4. ATOM $\models atom(\lceil a \rceil)$ iff a is an atom in L'

From these programs, it is easy to define a program INST[5] containing a binary predicate symbol *inst* such that INST $\models inst(\lceil C1 \rceil, \lceil C2 \rceil)$ iff $C2$ is an instance of $C1$. A predicate symbol *member* (with the obvious meaning) can also be easily defined. The proof rules for the intuitionistic logic considered by Miller and Nadathur[31] can now be coded as the following metalogic program.

$$
\begin{aligned}
intptr(\lceil C1 \rceil, \lceil \exists x.G \rceil) \quad &\Leftarrow \quad inst(\lceil G \rceil, \lceil G' \rceil) \,\&\\
&\qquad intptr(\lceil C1 \rceil, \lceil G' \rceil).\\
intptr(\lceil C1 \rceil, \lceil G_1 \,\&\, G_2 \rceil) \quad &\Leftarrow \quad intptr(\lceil C1 \rceil, \lceil G_1 \rceil) \,\&\\
&\qquad intptr(\lceil C1 \rceil, \lceil G_2 \rceil).\\
intptr(\lceil C1 \rceil, \lceil G_1 \vee G_2 \rceil) \quad &\Leftarrow \quad intptr(\lceil C1 \rceil, \lceil G_1 \rceil).\\
intptr(\lceil C1 \rceil, \lceil G_1 \vee G_2 \rceil) \quad &\Leftarrow \quad intptr(\lceil C1 \rceil, \lceil G_2 \rceil).\\
intptr(\lceil C1 \rceil, \lceil D \Rightarrow G \rceil) \quad &\Leftarrow \quad intptr(\lceil C1 \,\&\, D \rceil, \lceil G \rceil).\\
intptr(\lceil C1 \rceil, \lceil A \rceil) \quad &\Leftarrow \quad inst(\lceil C1 \rceil, \lceil C2 \rceil) \,\&\\
&\qquad member(\lceil A \rceil, \lceil A2 \rceil).\\
intptr(\lceil C1 \rceil, \lceil A \rceil) \quad &\Leftarrow \quad inst(\lceil C1 \rceil, \lceil C2 \rceil) \,\&\\
&\qquad member(\lceil G \Rightarrow A \rceil, \lceil C2 \rceil) \,\&\\
&\qquad intptr(\lceil C1 \rceil, \lceil G \rceil).
\end{aligned}
$$

I must emphasize that no claim of efficiency is being made as far as the above interpreter is concerned. I strongly suspect that the theorem prover (written in λProlog) for intuitionistic logic that has been developed by Dale Miller and his associates is efficient. I only wish to point out that such theorem provers *can* be written in metalogic itself.

EXAMPLE 8. (**Theorem Prover for the Modal Logic** $S5$) Given below is a metalogic theorem prover for the propositional modal logic $S5$ as axiomatized in Chellas [12, p. 14].

$$
\begin{aligned}
&s5thm(\lceil \Box A \rightarrow A \rceil) \Leftarrow\\
&s5thm(\lceil \Diamond A \rightarrow \Box \Diamond A \rceil) \Leftarrow\\
&s5thm(\lceil \Box(A \rightarrow B) \rightarrow (\Box A \rightarrow \Box B) \rceil) \Leftarrow\\
&s5thm(\lceil \Diamond A \rightarrow \neg \Box \neg A \rceil) \Leftarrow\\
&s5thm(\lceil \neg \Box \neg A \rightarrow \Diamond A \rceil) \Leftarrow\\
&s5thm(\lceil A \rceil) \Leftarrow taut(\lceil A \rceil)
\end{aligned}
$$

[5] This program would essentially be similar to the definition of the predicate symbol *match* of Bowen[7].

$s5thm(\lceil \Box A \rceil) \Leftarrow s5thm(\lceil A \rceil)$

$s5thm(\lceil B \rceil) \Leftarrow s5thm(\lceil A \rceil) \ \& \ s5thm(\lceil A \to B \rceil)$

Theorem provers for various other non-classical logics that have a proof theoretic axiomatization may be encoded in metalogic in an easy way.

4.13   Conclusions

My intention in writing this paper was three-fold:

1. first, to develop a theoretical basis for metalogic programming and lay to rest various misconceptions (cf. [33, 34]) in the logic programming community about what metalogic is all about.

2. to take the first steps towards a comparative evaluation of naive and amalgamated metalogic programming.

3. to take the first (albeit, small) steps towards showing that various useful forms of reasoning (e.g. cooperative reasoning, dynamic knowledge base maintenance, reasoning about knowledge and beliefs, introspective reasoning, etc.) can all be captured within the framework of Meta.

As I have pointed out repeatedly throughout this paper, many of the topics discussed here have been treated only superficially. I have tried to discuss more about what *can* be done in Meta rather than *how* to do it in Meta. This leaves open the major problem of how to efficiently implement various proposals outlined in this paper.

The issue of what happens when the object language O and the metalanguage M overlap is one that has not been addressed either here or by Hill and Lloyd [23]. I believe that any attempt to capture the advantages of both these proposals (i.e. that of keeping O and M completely separate, and that of O being included in M) will inevitably lead to O and M overlapping. Thus, this is perhaps the most important issue to address in the next few years.

Other important directions for metalogic programming have been outlined by John Lloyd [27].

Acknowledgements

This work was supported by U.S. Air Force Contract F30602-85-C-0008. I thank Howard Blair and Sanjay Manchanda for pointing out some errors in an early version of the manuscript.

References

[1] K.R. Apt, II. A. Blair and A. Walker. (1988) *Towards a Theory of Declarative Knowledge*, in: Foundations of Logic Programming and Deductive Databases, ed. Jack Minker, Morgan Kauffman.

[2] N. D. Belnap and D. Grover. (1972) *Quantifying in and Out of Quotes*, in: Truth, Syntax and Modality, ed. II. Leblanc, North Holland.

[3] G. Boolos and R. Jeffrey. (1980) *Computability and Logic*, Cambridge University Press.

[4] II. A. Blair. (1987) *Canonical Conservative Extension of Logic Program Completions*, Proc. 4th IEEE Symposium on Logic Programming, pps 154–161, Computer Society Press.

[5] II. A. Blair and V.S. Subrahmanian. (1987) *Paraconsistent Logic Programming*, to appear in Theoretical Computer Science. Preliminary verion in Lecture Notes in Computer Science, Vol. 287, Springer Verlag.

[6] K. A. Bowen and R.A. Kowalski. (1982) *Amalgamating Language and Metalanguage in Logic Programming*, in Logic Programming, eds. K.L. Clark, S.-A. Tarnlund, pps 153–172, Academic Press.

[7] K.A. Bowen. (1985) *Metalevel Programming and Knowledge Representation*, New Generation Computing, 3, 4, pps 359–383.

[8] K.A. Bowen and T. Weinberg. (1985) *A Metalevel Extension of Prolog*, in Proc. 2nd IEEE Symp. on Logic Programming, pps 669–675, Boston, Computer Society Press.

[9] K.A. Bowen. (1986) *Quantification and Naming: Language Foundations*, manuscript.

[10] A.L. Brown and Y. Shoham. (1987) *New Results in Semantical Non-Monotonic Reasoning*, draft manuscript.

[11] N. C. A. da Costa. (1974) *On the Theory of Inconsistent Formal Systems*, Notre Dame Journal of Formal Logic, 15, pps 497–510.

[12] B. F. Chellas. (1980) Modal Logic: An Introduction, Cambridge University Press.

[13] R. Fagin and M. Vardi. (1986) *Knowledge and Implicit Knowledge in a Distributed Environment: Preliminary Report*, in: Proc. of the Conference on Theoretical Aspects of Reasoning About Knowledge, pps 187–206, Morgan Kaufmann.

[14] G. Gargov. (1987) *New Semantics for Some Many-Valued Logics*, Journal of Non-Classical Logic, 4, 1, pps 37–56.

[15] M. Gelfond and V. Lifschitz. (1988) *The Stable Model Semantics for Logic Programming*, Proc. 5th International Conference/Symposium on Logic Programming, MIT Press.

[16] W. Goldfarb. (1981) *The Undecidability of the Second-Order Unification Problem*, Theoretical Computer Science, 13, pps 225–230.

[17] J.A. Goguen. (1988) *Higher Order Functions Considered Unnecessary for Higher Order Programming*, draft manuscript.

[18] D. Grover. (1972) *Propositional Quantification and Quotation Contexts*, in: Truth, Syntax and Modality, ed. II. Leblanc, North Holland.

[19] J. Y. Halpern and Y. Moses. (1984) *Knowledge and Common Knowledge in a Distributed Environment*, Proc. 3rd ACM Symp. on Principles of Distributed Computing, pps 50–61.

[20] J. Y. Halpern. (1987) *Reasoning About Knowledge: An Overview*, in Proc. of the Conference on Theoretical Aspects of Reasoning About Knowledge, pps 1–17, Morgan Kaufmann.

[21] J. Y. Halpern and Y. Moses. (1985) *Towards a Theory of Knowledge and Ignorance: Preliminary Report*, in: Logics and Models of Concurrent Systems, ed. K. R. Apt, Springer Verlag.

[22] L. Henkin. (1960) *On Mathematical Induction*, American Math. Monthly, 67, pps 323–338.

[23] P. M. Hill and J. W. Lloyd. (1988) *Analysis of Meta-Programs*, Tech. Report CS-88-08, University of Bristol, U.K.

[24] K. Konolige. (1988) *On the Relationship Between Default and Autoepistemic Logic*, Artificial Intelligence, 35, pps 343–382.

[25] J.-L. Lassez, M.J. Maher and K. Mariott. (1988) *Unification Revisited*, in: Foundations of Logic Programming and Deductive Databases, ed. Jack Minker, Morgan Kauffman.

[26] J.W. Lloyd. (1984) *Foundations of Logic Programming*, Springer.

[27] J. W. Lloyd. (1988) *Directions for Meta-Programming*, Tech. Report CS-88-10, University of Bristol, UK.

[28] M. Lob. (1955) *Solution of a Problem of Leon Henkin*, Journal of Symbolic Logic, 20.

[29] W. Marek. (1988) *A Natural Semantics for Modal Logic Over Databases*, Theoretical Computer Science, 56, pps 187–209.

[30] D. Miller. (1986) *A Theory of Modules for Logic Programming*, Proc. 3rd IEEE Symp. on Logic Programming, pps 106–114, Computer Society Press.

[31] D. Miller and G. Nadathur. (1987) *A Logic Programming Approach to Manipulating Formulas and Programs*, Proc. 4th IEEE Symp. on Logic Programming, pps 379–388, Computer Society Press.

[32] R. C. Moore. (1985) *Semantical Considerations on Non-Monotonic Logic*, Artificial Intelligence, 25, pps 75–94.

[33] M.A. Nait Abdallah. (1986) *Ions and Local Definitions in Logic Programming*, in Proc. Symp. on Theoretical Aspects of Computer Science, Lecture Notes in Computer Science, Vol. 210, pps 60–72.

[34] M.A. Nait Abdallah. (1987) *Logic Programming with Ions*, Proc. 14th Intl. Coll. on Automata, Languages and Programming, Lecture Notes in Computer Science, Vol. 267, pps 11–20.

[35] A. Robinson. (1971) *Forcing in Model Theory*, Proc. Symp. Mat. Instituto Nazionale i Alta Matematica 5, pps 64–80.

[36] A. Robinson. (1975) *Model Theory and Algebra: A Tribute to Abraham Robinson*, Springer.

[37] J. Shoenfield. (1967) *Mathematical Logic*, Addison Wesley.

[38] L. Sterling and E. Shapiro. *The Art of Prolog*, MIT Press.

[39] R. M. Smullyan. (1986) *Logicians Who Reason About Themselves*, Proc. of the Conference on Theoretical Aspects of Reasoning About Knowledge, pps 341–352, Morgan Kaufmann.

[40] V.S. Subrahmanian. (1988) *Foundations of Metalogic Programming*, in: Proc. of the Workshop on Meta-Programming in Logic Programming, ed. John W. Lloyd, Bristol, UK.

[41] V.S. Subrahmanian. (1988) *Quotational Devices and Supervaluations in Metalogic Programming*, in preparation.

[42] A. Tarski. (1956) *The Concept of Truth in Formalized Languages*, in A.Tarski: Logic, Semantics and Metamathematics, Oxford Univ. Press.

[43] A. Tarski, A. Mostowski and R. Robinson. (1953) *Undecidable Theories*, North Holland.

[44] D. O. Wray. (1987) *Logic in Quotes*, J. of Philosophical Logic, 16, pps 77–110.

Chapter 5

A Classification of
Meta-level Architectures

Frank van Harmelen

Department of Artificial Intelligence
University of Edinburgh
80 South Bridge
Edinburgh EH1 1HN
frankh%uk.ac.ed.aiva@nss.cs.ucl.ac.uk

Abstract

The goal of this paper is to categorise the meta-level systems in the literature on the basis of their crucial architectural features, concentrating on the relation between meta-level and object-level interpreter. We will discuss the communication between these two components and we will distinguish a number of typical architectures. After that we will discuss a number of other, independent properties by which these systems can be distinguished, although they are of secondary importance. Subsequently, we will compare the different types of architectures, and on the basis of this comparison we argue in favour of one particular type of meta-level system, the so called *bi-lingual meta-level inference systems*.

5.1 Introduction

The use of meta-level architectures as the basis for building reasoning systems has become widely accepted. The past 10 years have seen the advent of many different systems that in one way or another claim to be a meta-level architecture. The main benefits of meta-level architectures are twofold: meta-level architectures allow the separation of domain knowledge (*what* does the system know), from control knowledge (*how* does the system use its knowledge), and they allow the explicit representation of this control knowledge, as opposed to implicitly building this knowledge into the implementation of the system, or mixing it with the domain knowledge. This separate and explicit representation of control knowledge has a number of advantages, as argued by numerous authors:

- A system with explicitly and separately represented control knowledge is more modular, and therefore easier to develop, debug and modify ([7], [4] and [1]).

- It becomes possible to use the same domain knowledge for multiple purposes ([4]).

- The system can generate explanations of its own behaviour on the basis of the explicit control knowledge ([23])

- Finally, the separation of control knowledge from domain knowledge allows domain knowledge to be purely declarative in nature. While formulating domain knowledge we do not have to worry about efficiency, only about the "representational adequacy" (in the words of McCarthy). In the control knowledge on the other hand, the efficiency of the problem solving process is the most prominent aspect ("computational adequacy").

Many systems described in the literature provide ways of explicitly representing meta-knowledge, and of controlling the inference process. The systems that were used as the basis for the following categorisation are (in chronological order) GOLUX [13], FOL [25], TEIRESIAS [7], PRESS [20], NEOMYCIN [5], the Prolog systems by [10] [11] and by [2], MLA [12], 3-LISP [19], S.1 [8], BB1 [14], KRS [16], PDP-0 [15] and Socrates [6]. Where relevant, we will briefly describe some features of these systems.

The goal of this paper is to develop a classification of this multitude of different architectures, based on their essential features. Perhaps surprisingly, the diversity of meta-level systems found in the literature can be classified into a limited number of typical architectures. The advantage of such a classification is that it will allow us to compare the meta-level systems at a high level, using only their essential architectural properties, and abstracting away from incidental features.

5.2   Classification of meta-level architectures

The essential characteristic of meta-level architectures is, of course, that they consist of two levels, the object-level and the meta-level. Each layer can be seen as an individual system with a representation language and an interpreter for expressions in that language. The purpose of the object-level is to perform reasoning in the application domain of the system, while the goal of the meta-level is to control the behaviour of the object-level[1]. The system as a whole can at any moment

---

[1]Notice that we restrict our interest in meta-level architectures to those where the meta-level is used to control the search at the object-level. Meta-level architectures

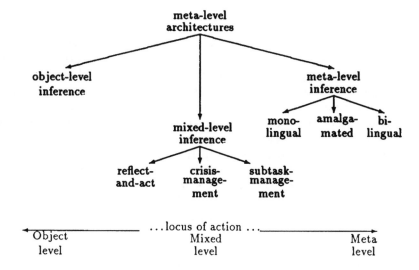

Figure 5.1: Classification of meta-level systems

be active at one of the two levels; either it is interpreting object-level expressions (using the object-level interpreter), or it is interpreting meta-level expressions (using the meta-level interpreter). This leads us to the notion of the *locus of action* (using a phrase coined in [24]): the place in the system which is active at any one point in time. This locus of action can then be either the object-level or the meta-level. It is exactly this locus of action that will form the basis for our main classification of meta-level architectures. We will distinguish a spectrum of systems, with at one end of the spectrum systems where the locus of action is almost all the time at the object-level, and where meta-level activity takes places only occasionally. At the other end of the spectrum we will see systems where the converse is true: almost all (or sometimes: all) system activity takes place at the meta-level, and (almost) no activity takes place at the object-level. The systems in the middle of this spectrum exhibit equal amounts of object-level and meta-level activity. This classification, plus further subdivisions, is shown in figure 5.1 and we will discuss each of the types of system in this classification in the following subsections.

can be used for many purposes, such as extending the set of results computable at the object-level, to perform meta-theoretic reasoning concerning consistency and redundancy, learning etc, but these other uses of meta-level architectures are not our primary interest in this paper.

5.2.1 Object-level inference systems

On one extreme of the classification shown in figure 5.1 are the systems where
the main activity is at the object-level. In fact, these systems do not have a
proper meta-level interpreter (ie. an interpreter for meta-level expressions), but
only an object-level interpreter that takes the meta-level expressions into account
during its computational cycle in order to adjust its behaviour. As a result,
the object-level interpreter executes two types of instructions: firstly, the object-
level expressions it is supposed to interpret, and secondly the meta-level expressions that affect its behaviour. Typically, the object-level interpreter performs a
fixed computational cycle, and the meta-level expressions concern certain fixed
points within this cycle. Systems in this category are the Prolog system by Gal-
laire/Lasserre and GOLUX.

For instance in the Prolog system developed by Gallaire and Lasserre, a number of meta-predicates can be defined that handle both clause selection and conjunct ordering. These predicates are then used in an interpreter-loop to determine
the behaviour of the system. A fixed vocabulary of meta-predicates is available
that can express a variety of properties of the object-level propositions that compete for execution. These properties include among others the number of literals
in a clause, the presence of a particular literal in a clause, the value of any ancestor
of a clause, and the invocation depth of the clause. The object-level propositions
that are present in the knowledge base can be specified in the meta-rules by their
position in the knowledge base, or by a (partial) specification of their contents.
In the Prolog syntax that is used in the system, a clause like

```
order(p(X,Y), [N1, N2, N3, ..., Ni]) :-
       C1, C2, C3, ..., Ck.
```

states that for the resolution of literals that are an instantiation of `p(X,Y)` the
clauses numbered `N1, N2, ..., Ni` will be used in that order, provided the conditions `C1, ..., Ck` are met. Notice that the variables `X,Y, N1, N2, ..., Ni`
can be used in the conditions `Ci`. An example of this would be

```
order(p(X), [1, 2, 3]) :- cond1(X).
order(p(X), [1, 3, 2]) :- cond2(X).
order(p(X), [3, 1, 2]) :- cond3(X).
```

This specifies a different order for the clauses for `p(X)` for different conditions on
the argument `X`.

An example of content directed conflict resolution is

```
before(p(_), Clause1, Clause2) :-
       length(Clause1,_,N), length(Clause2,_,M),
       N < M.
```

which states that for the resolution of literals of the form p(_) shorter clauses will be used before longer clauses. Replacing p(_) with either a variable or a more specific term (e.g. p([])) would enlarge or reduce the scope of this heuristic. This enables the formulation of both domain dependent and domain independent strategies.

The system also provides a mechanism for conjunct ordering. In earlier work along the same lines [10], further facilities were proposed to

- assign priority numbers to competing clauses,

- block backtracking over specified clauses (corresponding to dynamic cut introduction)

- inhibit the execution of literals until they reach some degree of instantiation.

The important point for the classification of meta-level systems is that all the meta-predicates are annotations that are used by a predefined and unchangeable interpreter. In other words, the behaviour of the interpreter (in this case the Prolog interpreter) is parametrised over the definition of meta-level annotations as described above, but cannot be redefined to any further extent. For instance, it would be impossible to specify a forward chaining interpreter in the Gallaire-Lasserre systems, since the hardwired object-level interpreter presumes a backward chaining control regime. It is important to realise that the use and meaning of all the meta-level predicates are fixed by the system by the way they are used in the predefined and hardwired object-level interpreter. It is not possible to extend this set. Thus, object-level inference systems provide only a limited amount of flexibility, and cannot be redefined beyond the scope of the annotations that the object-level interpreter takes into account.

5.2.2 Mixed-level inference systems

In the middle of figure 5.1 we find systems where the computation takes place at both the meta- and the object-level. Object-level and meta-level computations are interleaved, and some mechanism is provided for switching between the two. The computation at the object-level is monitored by the meta-level. We can further subdivide this category of systems in the middle of the spectrum on the basis of the criterion that is used for switching between object- and meta-level, as shown in figure 5.1.

Reflect-and-act systems

Sometimes the meta-level is called very frequently, before or after every object-level step. This organisation has been called a *reflect-and-act* loop, since the object-level "acts", the meta-level "reflects" on the object-level actions and these

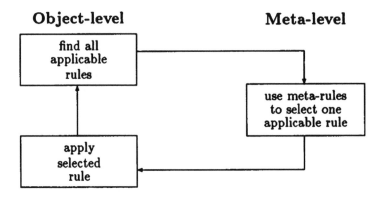

Figure 5.2: Flow of control in reflect-and-act systems

two together are chained together in a continuous loop. Systems with this architecture are the production rule system TEIRESIAS and the blackboard system BB1.

The flow of control in such reflect-and-act systems can be described as in figure 5.2. The object-level interpreter finds the set of all applicable object-level rules and passes this *conflict-resolution set* on to the meta-level interpreter. The meta-level interpreter uses its control knowledge to select one of these applicable rules, which is then handed down again to the object-level interpreter, which applies this rule. In a system like TEIRESIAS the control knowledge for conflict resolution is written down in meta-rules such as:

```
if $rule1 mentions the $current-goal
and $rule2 does not mention the $current-goal
then $rule1 should be used before $rule2
```

Crisis-management systems

Sometimes the meta-level is called only if a *crisis* or an impasse occurs in the object-level computation, for example when too many or not enough steps are possible at the object-level. PDP-0 for instance, is a program that models the behaviour of human problem solvers in the domain of thermodynamics. When the system is given a problem to solve, it selects a problem solving strategy on the basis of characteristics of the input problem. This strategy will be executed by the object-level problem solver. When the program comes to a dead end, for example because none of the known strategies is applicable, or because of the unexpected failure of an applied strategy, this will be noticed by a supervising

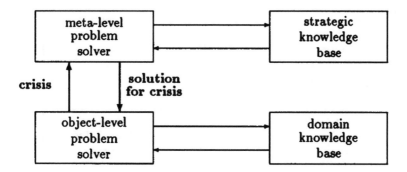

Figure 5.3: Flow of control in crisis-management systems

component. The supervisor will then ask the meta-problem solver to propose an adjustment of the current goal-tree, in order to solve the impasse.

The flow of control in crisis-management systems is summarised in figure 5.3. The object level interpreter uses the domain knowledge to solve a particular problem, and only hands over control to the meta-level interpreter if some kind of crisis occurs which prevents the object-level computation from continuing. The meta-level interpreter then uses its strategic (meta-level) knowledge base to try and solve this crisis. If some kind of solution has been found it is handed down to the object-level interpreter which can then proceed with the computation. Different kinds of crises can occur. One example of a crisis is when no object-level rules can be found that apply to the current subgoal. The meta-level interpreter then has to find a different subgoal for the continuation of the object-level computation. In this way we could implement user-directed backtracking, rather than the built-in standard behaviour of a system like Prolog. Another example of a crisis is when more than one object-level rule applies to the current subgoal. The object-level interpreter then turns to the meta-level for conflict resolution. In this way a reflect-and-act system can be simulated in an efficient way by a crisis-management system (efficient since the meta-level is only called if there is indeed more than one applicable object-level rule, rather than in every loop, as in reflect-and-act systems).

Subtask-management systems

Yet another approach is where the meta-level knowledge is used to partition the object-level task into a number of *subtasks*. In such a system, the meta-level interpreter decides on a task to be done, and this task will then be executed by the object-level interpreter. After completion of this object-level task (be it successful or not), the meta-level decides on the next subtask for the object-level. This approach is taken in S.1, NEOMYCIN and MLA.

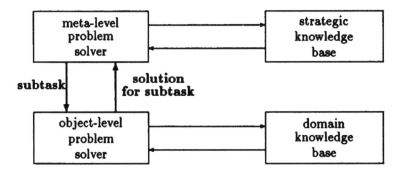

Figure 5.4: Flow of control in subtask-management systems

The flow of control in subtask-management systems is described in figure 5.4. The meta-level interpreter first decides upon a subtask to be solved by the object-level interpreter. The object-level interpreter then tries to solve this subtask, and only returns to the meta-level when it has either found a solution or when it has established that it cannot solve the subtask. On the basis of this result the meta-level interpreter can then try to find a new subgoal to be solved. Subtasks are like conventional subroutines in that they can call each other, resulting in a stack-based scheduling of tasks. Subtasks can be either very simple knowledge base partitions that try to solve a particular subgoal, or they can have a more elaborate structure. The subtask concept from NEOMYCIN is a good illustration. Subtasks in NEOMYCIN consist of:

- The focus: this is the argument with which the task is called. This often represents the object to which the task is applied.

- Three sets of meta-rules: the DOBEFORE, DODURING and DOAFTER rules that represent the prologue of the task, the main body and the epilogue respectively.

- The goal that is recorded to show that the task has been accomplished. This can be seen as the result of the task if it exits successfully.

- The end-condition that may abort the task when it becomes true.

As can be seen from figures 5.3 and 5.4 the architectures for crisis- and subtask-management systems are very similar. The main differences are in the the kind of data that is passed between the object- and the meta-level, and in the place where the computation starts: the systems communicate either in terms of crises and their solutions or in terms of subtasks and their solutions; furthermore, crisis-management systems initiate their computation at the object-level, while subtask-management systems start their computation at the meta-level.

5.2.3   Meta-level inference systems

On the right side of the spectrum in figure 5.1 we see systems where the computation mainly takes place at the meta-level. In these systems the behaviour of the object-level is fully specified at the meta-level. Using this description of the object-level, the meta-level can completely simulate the object-level inference process. This means that there is no longer a need for an explicit object-level interpreter. As a result, the object-level interpreter is no longer present in the system, and its behaviour is completely simulated by the execution of its specification at the meta-level. Systems from this category are PRESS, 3-LISP, KRS, the amalgamated Prolog system by Bowen and Kowalski, and Socrates.

As an example of meta-level inference systems we consider PRESS. This system performs symbolic algebraic manipulations. One of the main features of PRESS is that the system proceeds in its problem solving process by trying to prove theorems at the meta-level, producing object-level proofs as a side effect. The key idea of meta-level inference is that strategies are considered to be at the meta-level of the domain. That is, the strategies are axioms of a meta-theory. For example, consider the following meta-level axiom from PRESS

```
singleocc(X, L=R) &
position(X,L,P)   &
isolate(P, L=R, Ans) ->
solve(L=R, X, Ans).
```

This can be considered procedurally as a strategy to solve an equation: to solve an equation L=R in X giving answer Ans, satisfy the subgoals on the left. However, it also has a declarative meaning in the meta-theory. The declarative meaning is

> "If L=R contains exactly one occurrence of X, and the position of this occurrence in tt L is P, and if the result of isolating X in L=R is Ans, then Ans is a solution to the equation L=R, with X as the unknown."

Note that this description refers to properties such as position and number of occurrences of X. These are meta-theoretic syntactic features. A meta-level axiom as the above would get used by a typical call to the `solve`-procedure of PRESS, as in for example:

```
?- solve(log(e,x+a)+log(e,x-a),x,Ans).
```

The inference of PRESS occurs at the meta-level. Some of the meta-level predicates are of the form

New is the result of applying Rule to Old.

To satisfy such a predicate, the rule **Rule** is applied to the expression **Old** to produce **New**. As a result of this, an algebraic transformation has occurred at the object-level, the expression Old has been transformed into New: the object-level strategies are executed by performing inferences in the meta-theory. Thus, search at the object-level is replaced by search at the meta-level. This works well because, as described in [18], the meta-level search space is much better behaved than the object-level space. In particular, the branching rate of the meta-level space is much lower, and most wrong choices lead to dead ends rapidly. The use of meta-level inference moves the search process from the object-level to the meta-level, and thereby transforms an ill-behaved search space to a better behaved one. If the meta-level space is still too complex, it is possible to axiomatise the control of this level, i.e. to produce a meta-meta-level. This process can in theory be continued until the control process of the highest level becomes trivial. This usually happens very early, so only two levels are needed.

The important difference between meta-level inference systems and object-level inference systems as discussed above is that the meta-level predicates of a system like PRESS are interpreted by an independent meta-level interpreter. The set of meta-level predicates (as singleocc, isolate etc) is therefore fully extendible and redefinable, unlike the meta-level predicates in object-level inference systems, which are a fixed set.

The problem of choosing between the various strategies that are axiomatised at the meta-level and that are applicable at a point in the problem solving process now depends on the proof procedure that is used for the meta-level interpreter. The systems mentioned here use different techniques for this task. PRESS relies on the built in, fixed behaviour of a Prolog interpreter for this task. The system described in [21] is a re-implementation of PRESS. It does allow reasoning about the selection of strategies, rather than using a hardwired interpreter.

An important subdivision of meta-level inference systems can be made on the basis of the relation between the object-level language L and the meta-level language M used by the system. On the one hand, there are the systems that we will call *monolingual*. In these systems M and L are the same language, and no syntactic distinction is made between object-level and meta-level expressions. Examples of these systems are 3-LISP and the Gallaire/Lasserre system. In these systems LISP and Prolog is used for both M and L. On the other hand there are the *bilingual* systems that support two strictly separate languages L and M. In order to provide upwards and downwards communication between L and M, the languages are related via a naming convention which translates sentences, sets of sentences and other linguistic entities of L into variable free terms of M. This choice between monolingual and bilingual systems has a profound effect on the structure of meta-level interpreters. Taking a Prolog system as an example, we can program a simple meta-level Prolog interpreter in Prolog as follows:

```
solve([]).
solve([G|Gs]) :-
    clause(G, B),
```

```
    append(B, Gs, NewGs),
    solve(NewGs).
```

This is a monolingual meta-level interpreter which relies on the mixing of object-level terms and meta-level terms for the communication between the two levels. Object-level predicates are regarded as meta-level function symbols, but variables at both levels are represented as Prolog variables, thereby not making a distinction between object-level variables (ranging over object-level terms) and meta-level variables (ranging over object-level formulas). As a result, the built-in unification algorithm of Prolog can be used at both levels. A bilingual version of the same Prolog interpreter in Prolog would look like

```
solve([], []).
solve([G|Gs], S) :-
    clause(G, C),
    rename_vars(C, [G|Gs], C1),
    head(C1, H1),
    unify(G, H1, S1),
    body(C1, B1),
    append(B1, Gs, NewGs),
    instantiate(NewGs, S1, NewGsPlusS1),
    solve(NewGsPlusS1, S2),
    compose(S1, S2, S).
```

This version of the Prolog meta-interpreter in Prolog allows for a separate representation of object- and meta-level variables. Only meta-level variables are represented by Prolog variables, and object-level variables correspond to particular kinds of variable free meta-level terms. As a result, an object-level formula such as $\forall x \forall y\ f(x,y)$ can be represented as the ground meta-level term `all(var(1),all(var(2),f(var(1),var(2))))`. Simpler naming relations are also possible, such as the standard quoting relation, where each object-level term is represented by a single meta-level atom: `"∀x ∀y f(x,y)"`. This is the naming relation used in Socrates. A third approach is presented in [2], and consists of *amalgamating* L and M. In this approach L and M are in fact the same language, but the naming convention is employed as above, so that each object-level expression has a variable free term as its name associated with it. (Since this variable free term is itself again a syntactically correct object-level expression, since $L=M$, it again must have another variable free term as its name, ad infinitum).

This concludes our classification of meta-level architectures according to their locus of action. This distinction corresponds roughly to a distinction made by Silver [18] between *object-level driven* and *meta-level driven* systems. Systems at the left end of the spectrum shown in figure 5.1 are object-level driven, since their main computation takes place at the object-level, and systems at the right end of the spectrum are meta-level driven.

5.3   Other properties of meta-level architectures

In this section we will discuss some more properties of meta-level architectures
that can be used to further classify them, beyond the classification on the basis
of the locus of action as described in the previous section. Some of the properties
discussed in this section are found implicitly in the literature. The aim of this
section is to sharpen these criteria, and to make them explicit. Figure 5.5 at the
end of this section will summarise the position of all the systems mentioned above
with respect to all of these properties.

5.3.1   Linguistic relation between levels

The distinction between monolingual, bilingual and amalgamated systems used to
subdivide meta-level inference systems in the previous section can in fact be used
more generally, to apply also to object-level inference and mixed-level inference
systems.

Object-level inference systems can have their meta-level instructions to the
object-level interpreter expressed in a language that is either the same as or
different from the object-level language. The Gallaire/Lasserre system relies on
the two languages being the same, whereas GOLUX separates the two languages,
providing an explicit *quoting mechanism* to give meta-level names to object-level
expressions (using this mechanism, the ground terms at the meta-level that are
used as the names of object-level expressions are always atomic constants).

The distinction between monolingual, bilingual and amalgamated systems
also applies to mixed-level systems. TEIRESIAS is a bilingual system: although
both object-level and meta-level language are production rule languages, they are
quite different languages, properly separated; the languages are of the same type,
namely production rule languages, but they are not identical. This is similar to
GOLUX, where both meta-level and object-level language are of the same type
(first order predicate calculus), but are in fact separate languages. The same re-
mark holds for MLA. NEOMYCIN and S.1 are also bilingual systems. but in both
these systems the meta-level language is not only different from the object-level
language, but also of a different type: Both NEOMYCIN and S.1 use production
rules at the object-level, but use some special purpose language at the meta-level:
the task-language in NEOMYCIN and so called control-blocks in S.1.

5.3.2   Declarative or procedural meta-language

The control knowledge of the meta-level can be either expressed in a *declarative*
or a *procedural* language. Expressions in a procedural language can only be
understood in terms of the *behaviour* of the meta-level interpreter, the actions
it takes, the order in which it does things etc., whereas a declarative language
states true facts that can be understood without reference to the behaviour of
the meta-level interpreter. For example, the meta-level expressions of GOLUX are

purely declarative descriptions of properties of object-level proof trees, whereas something like the control knowledge of s.1 is purely procedural in nature, talking about the order in which to perform actions, sequences and loops of instructions etc. Yet other systems (such as PRESS) have a meta-level language that has both a declarative and a procedural reading.

5.3.3 Partial specifications

An important property of some of the systems mentioned above is that they allow the *partial specification* of meta-level knowledge. Such systems (like GOLUX, Gallaire/Lasserre, MLA, 3-LISP, KRS and Bowen/Kowalski) provide a *default specification* of the behaviour of the system that can be totally or partially overwritten by the user to modify the systems default behaviour. In some of these systems the default definition is explicitly available for inspection in the system (3-LISP, KRS, Bowen/Kowalski), whereas the other systems (GOLUX, Gallaire/Lasserre, MLA) only contain an implicit definition of their default behaviour.

5.3.4 Completeness and strictness

As mentioned in the introduction, one of the main purposes of having a meta-level architecture at all is to allow the object-level to be purely declarative, without having to worry about procedural aspects. Thus, for any given query, the object-level (implicitly) specifies a set of answers[2]. It is the task of the meta-level interpreter to determine which of these possible answers is going to be actually computed, and in which order. Furthermore, in some systems, it is possible for the meta-level to extend the set of answers derivable from the object-level theory, using meta-theoretic devices like *reflection principles* [9], implemented for instance in FOL [25]. We call a meta-level architecture *complete* if it computes *all* the results derivable from the object-level theory (i.e. the meta-level does not *suppress* any object-level results). We call a meta-level system *strict* if it computes *only* results derivable from the object-level theory (i.e. the meta-level does not *extend* the object-level results). Notice that it is possible for a meta-level architecture to be both *incomplete* and *unstrict*, namely if the meta-level suppresses some of the object-level results, but also computes extra ones. We use the term *exact* when a meta-level system is both complete and strict: an exact system computes all and only those results derivable from the declarative object-level theory.

With these definitions it is clear that completeness of a meta-level system is not always a desirable property. The whole point of a meta-level architecture is often to prune parts of the object-level search space, thereby suppressing certain object-level results because they are too expensive to compute. [22] used the term

---

[2]This is most clear is the object-level consists of a logical theory plus a set of logical inference rules, but similar notions exist for other declarative representation languages

"positive heuristic" in connection with the concept of completeness: a positive heuristic is

> "a heuristic that prefers certain object-level computations over others, but that does not prohibit certain computations altogether."

In other words, a system that only allows positive heuristics is automatically complete. Whether strictness of a meta-level system in the above sense is always a desirable property is less clear. In the context of using meta-level systems for control, we probably do not want to extend the results of the object-level theory, but one possible use of a meta-level architecture (although not our interest here) is exactly to try and extend the results of the object-level theory (FOL is an example of this).

A system like the Gallaire/Lasserre Prolog system is one of the few systems mentioned above that is complete: its only concern is the ordering of clauses and literals, thereby affecting only the order in which the object-level computation takes place, but not its ultimate outcome[3]. A system like GOLUX is not complete: for instance we can force proofs in GOLUX to be deterministic, thereby pruning alternative solutions. However, GOLUX is strict in the above sense: no new object-level results can be introduced through meta-level computation. This is not true in meta-level inference systems like KRS and 3-LISP: since their meta-levels completely specify the object-level computation, it is well possible to extend the object-level behaviour in order to produce extra results.

This concludes our discussion of different properties to distinguish meta-level architectures. The table in figure 5.5 summarises the position of all the systems mentioned above on these properties.

5.4 Comparison of the different architectures

In this section we will compare the architectures discussed above, and we will conclude that the one based on meta-level inference is most promising. The other approaches all have major problems associated with them. Meta-level inference does not suffer from these problems, while it offers several advantages.

The most obvious problem is associated with the object-level-inference systems. The meta-level does not have a separate place in the architecture of these systems, and is not stated as explicitly as would be necessary in order to achieve the advantages of a meta-level architecture (better explanation, re-usability and ease of development and debugging). The main structure of the control strategy of these systems is only implicit in the system. Although possibly available for inspection, it is never available for modification, and only a restricted number of aspects of the control strategy can be changed. For instance in the Gallaire/Lasserre

[3]Strictly speaking, this is only true for those versions of their system that do not allow dynamic cut-introduction. This corresponds to dynamically removing object-level backtrack-points, thereby potentially suppressing certain object-level results.

System	Architect. type	linguistic relation	declarative/ procedural	partial spec.	strict & complete
TEIRESIAS	reflect-act	bi-ling.	decl.	yes	C– ; S+
S.1	task-man.	bi-ling.	proc.	?	C– ; S+
BB1	reflect-act	bi-ling.	proc.	yes	C– ; S+
MLA	task-man.	bi-ling.	decl.	yes	C– ; S+
KRS	meta-inf.	mono-ling.	$-^1$	yes	C– ; S–
NEOMYCIN	task-man.	bi-ling.	proc.	$-^2$	C– ; S+
PRESS	meta-inf.	bi-ling.	decl.&proc.	$-^2$	– ; S+
GOLUX	object-inf.	bi-ling.	decl.	yes	C– ; S+
PDP-0	crisis-man.	?	?	$-^2$	?
Gallaire	object-inf.	mono-ling.	decl.&proc.	yes	$C+^4$; $S-^3$
Bowen	meta-inf.	amalgam.	decl.&proc.	yes	C– ; S+
3-LISP	meta-inf.	mono-ling.	proc.	yes	C– ; $S-^3$
Socrates	meta-inf.	bi-ling.	decl.&proc.	no	C– ; S–

Legend:

?	=	unknown, cannot be determined from available literature.
$-^n$	=	not applicable, see note n.
C+/–	=	completeness enforced/not enforced.
S+/–	=	strictness enforced/not enforced.

Notes:

1. It is unclear how the object-oriented paradigm relates to the distinction declarative vs. procedural.

2. The possibility of partial specifications does not occur in this system since it is a program built for a particular task, containing a full specification of one appropriate control regime.

3. The system can be made unstrict because the confusion between object-level and meta-level language (monolingual) allows the meta-level predicates to introduce arbitrary bindings for the object-level variables.

4. The system is only complete without the facility of dynamic cut-introduction.

Figure 5.5: Properties of meta-level systems

system, it is possible to change the clause- and literal-selection strategies, but the fact that the system is chronologically backtracking and backward chaining is hardwired.

The mixed level systems do not suffer from this problem, but they have other problems associated with them, which can best be discussed using the subcategories from section 2:

A problem that is associated with both the crisis-management systems and the reflect-and-act systems is that the search in the solution space is still performed at the object-level. As a result, the meta-level knowledge is only used as a preference criterion over the separate object-level search space, whereas in systems that are more meta-level driven the meta-level knowledge is used to completely specify the whole structure of the search space of the system. This means that no full advantage is taken from the fact that the meta-level search space is better behaved than the object-level search space.

A problem associated with the task-management systems is what could be called the black-box effect: after the meta-level has decided on a task to be performed by the object-level, the object-level is no longer under the control of the meta-level, and again no full benefit is gained from the differences between meta-level and object-level search.

None of the mixed-level inference systems makes all the control knowledge in the system explicit: reflect-and-act systems only deal with conflict resolution strategies, crisis-management systems know how to solve impasses in the computation and subtask-management systems represent the selection of goals and subgoals, but none of them contains a full description of the object-level computation.

Meta-level inference systems do not suffer from these problems. In meta-level inference systems, the meta-knowledge is not just used as preference criteria over the separate object-level search space, but it is used to completely specify the whole structure of the search space. Meta-level inference systems perform their search in the meta-level search space and thereby gain the full benefit of the nicer properties of the meta-level search space. Furthermore, meta-level inference systems contain a full specification of the inference strategy of the system, thereby allowing the user to change any part of this strategy, and not just only a few predefined aspects of it.

This leaves us with the choice between the different subtypes of meta-level inference systems: monolingual, bilingual and amalgamated systems. A number of reasons can be given why it is important for the meta-level language to be separated from the object-level languages, thus ruling out both the mono-lingual and the amalgamated systems. First of all, there is an epistemological reason. [17] and [3] argue that different domains require different representation languages. Since the object-level and the meta-level deal with widely different domains (the object-level deals with the application domain of the system, while the meta-level deals with the issue of controlling the object-level), it follows that these two levels of the system do indeed need different representation languages to suit their different needs.

A second argument concerns the modularity of the system. One of the advantages of separating control knowledge from domain knowledge is that the two can be changed independently. However, this ability to vary the two levels independently would be greatly reduced if control knowledge and domain knowledge were represented together in one and the same language.

The third argument is one about explanation. As argued in [23], the explanations given by reasoning systems should not only include *what* the system is doing, but also *why* it is doing a particular action and not another one. In order to enable the system to include control knowledge explicitly in its explanations, it is important that control knowledge can be syntactically distinguished from domain knowledge.

A further problem associated with the amalgamated approach is the recursive application of the naming convention. Each ground term in the meta-level language that is the name of an object-level formula is itself again an object-level formula (since the two languages are the same), and thus has some ground term as its name, etc. This introduces the possibility of self-referential sentences, which is necessary for introspection, or for incompleteness proof à la Gödel (the self-referential capability is used in exactly this way in [2]). However, if we are not interested in these aspects of meta-level reasoning this added complexity is not needed, and we can get away with the much simpler construction of separate languages.

Thus having narrowed our choice down to bi-lingual meta-level inference system, we still have to discuss the best position on the other properties of meta-level systems described in the previous section: the possibility of partial specifications, a declarative versus a procedural meta-level language, and enforcing strictness and completeness on the meta-level.

The possibility of writing only partial specifications of the control strategy of the system is obviously attractive for the development of a system. We can gradually refine the control strategy of the system, without overcommitting ourselves at any point, postponing decisions until we understand enough of the domain. However, a high price needs to be paid for this possibility, resulting in a severe restriction of the system's architecture. In order for the system to be able to "fill in the gaps" of the partial specification of the control regime by the user, it is necessary that this partial specification is of a particular format, so that it is possible for the system to identify which parts of the control regime are underspecified, and need to be filled in with default values. This restricts the possible range of control regimes that can be formulated by the user.

Concerning the issues of strictness and completeness we can say the following: For reasons discusses before, we would not want to enforce completeness on a meta-level architecture, since often the whole point of having a meta-level is to be able to avoid the expensive computation of certain object-level results. Whether strictness, not allowing the meta-level to extend the set of results that can be computed by the meta-level, is a desirable property, is less clear in general, and depends on the purpose for which the architecture will be used.

5.5 Conclusion

We have categorised the meta-level systems described in the literature, and have distinguished the following types:

- object-level inference systems

- mixed-level inference systems, which can be divided into

    - reflect-and-act systems
    - crisis-management systems
    - subtask-management systems

- meta-level inference systems, which can be divided into

    - mono-lingual systems
    - bi-lingual systems
    - algamated systems

Furthermore, a number of secondary properties of meta-level architectures were identified:

- Is the meta-level language declarative or procedural.

- Does the system allow partial specifications of the control regime.

- Does the system enforce strictness and completeness of the control regime.

We have compared these systems, and have argued in favour of bi-lingual, meta-level inference systems.

Acknowledgements

I am grateful to Han Reichgelt and Fausto Giunchiglia for comments on earlier versions of this paper. The work reported here was made possible by the Alvey/SERC grant "A flexible toolkit for expert systems", grant no. GR/D/17151. The author is currently supported on grant no. GR/D/44270.

References

[1] L. Aiello and G. Levi. The uses of metaknowledge in AI systems. In *Proceedings of the Sixth European Conference on Artificial Intelligence, ECAI '84*, pages 707–717, Pisa, September 1984.

[2] K.A. Bowen and R.A. Kowalski. Amalgamating language and metalanguage in logic programming. In K. Clark and S. Tarnlund, editors, *Logic Programming*, pages 153–172, Academic Press, 1982.

[3] B. Chandrasekaran. Towards a functional architecture for intelligence based on generic information processing tasks. In *Proceedings of the Tenth IJCAI*, pages 1183–1192, International Joint Conference on Artificial Intelligence, Milan, August 1987.

[4] W. Clancey. The epistemology of rule-based expert systems: a framework for explanation. *Artificial Intelligence*, 20:215–51, 1983.

[5] W. Clancey and C. Bock. *MRS/NEOMYCIN: Representing Metacontrol in Predicate Calculus*. Technical Report No. IIPP-82-31, Stanford Heuristic Programming Project, 1982.

[6] R. Corlett, N. Davies, R. Khan, II. Reichgelt, and F. van Harmelen. The architecture of socrates. In P. Jackson, II. Reichgelt, and F. van Harmelen, editors, *Logic-Based Knowledge Representation*, MIT Press, 1989.

[7] R. Davis. Meta-rules: reasoning about control. *Artificial Intelligence*, 15:179–222, 1980.

[8] L. Erman, A. Scott, and P. London. Separating and integrating control in a rule-based tool. In *Proceedings of the IEEE workshop on principles of knowledge based systems*, pages 37–43, Denver, Colorado, December 1984.

[9] S. Feferman. Transfinite recursive progressions of axiomatic theories. *The Journal of Symbolic Logic*, 27(3):259–316, September 1962.

[10] M. Gallaire and C. Lasserre. Controlling knowledge deduction in a declarative approach. In *Proceedings of the Sixth IJCAI*, pages S1–S6, International Joint Conference on Artificial Intelligence, Tokyo, August 1979.

[11] M. Gallaire and C. Lasserre. Meta-level control for logic programs. In K. Clark and S. Tarnlund, editors, *Logic Programming*, pages 173–188, Academic Press, 1982.

[12] M. Genesereth and D. Smith. An overview of Meta-Level Architecture. In *Proceedings of AAAI-83*, pages 119–124, American Association for Artificial Intelligence, 1983.

[13] P. Hayes. Computation and deduction. In *Proceedings of the Symposium on the Mathematical Foundations of Computer Science*, pages 105–117, Czechoslovakian Academy of Sciences, 1973.

[14] B. Hayes-Roth. A blackboard architecture for control. *Artificial Intelligence*, 26:251–321, 1985.

[15] W.N.H. Jansweijer, J.J. Elshout, and B.J. Wielinga. The expertise of novice problem solvers. In *Proceedings of the Seventh European Conference on Artificial Intelligence, ECAI '86*, pages 576–585, Brighton, July 1986.

[16] P. Maes. Introspection in knowledge representation. In *Proceedings of the Seventh European Conference on Artificial Intelligence, ECAI '86*, pages 256–269, Brighton, July 1986.

[17] H. Reichgelt and F. van Harmelen. Criteria for choosing representation languages and control regimes for expert systems. *The Knowledge Engineering Review*, 1(4):2–17, December 1986.

[18] B. Silver. *Meta-level Inference. Studies in Computer Science and Artificial Intelligence*, North Holland Publishers, 1986.

[19] B. Smith. Reflection and semantics in LISP. In *Proceedings of POPL'84*, pages 23–35, Salt Lake City, Utah, January 1984.

[20] L. Sterling, A. Bundy, L. Byrd, R. O'Keefe, and B. Silver. Solving symbolic equations with PRESS. In J. Calmet, editor, *Computer Algebra*, Springer Verlag, 1982.

[21] T. Takewaki, A. Takeuchi, S. Kunifuji, and K. Furukawa. *Application of Partial Evaluation to the Algebraic Manipulation System and its Evaluation.* Technical Report TR-148, Tokyo, ICOT Research Centre, December 1985.

[22] L. Wallen. *Towards the Provision of a Natural Mechanism for Expressing Domain Specific Global Strategies in General Purpose Theorem-Provers.* Technical Report DAI Research Paper No. 202, Department of Artificial Intelligence, University of Edinburgh, 1983.

[23] D. Warner Hasling. Abstract explanations of strategy in a diagnostic consultation system. In *Proceedings of AAAI-83*, pages 157–161, American Association for Artificial Intelligence, Washington D.C., August 1983.

[24] B. Welham. Declaratively programmable interpreters and meta-level inferences. In P. Maes and D. Nardi, editors, *Meta-level architectures and reflection*, North Holland Publishers, 1987.

[25] R. Weyhrauch. Prolegomena to a theory of mechanised formal reasoning. *Artificial Intelligence*, 13:133–170, 1980.

Chapter 6

Reflection in Constructive and Non-constructive Automated Reasoning [1]

Fausto Giunchiglia   *Alan Smaill*

University of Edinburgh

Abstract

This paper describes the logical properties of various versions of reflection, and compares examples of its use in two automated reasoning systems, one in the FOL system [Wey80], the other in the NuPRL system [CAB*86]. It is suggested that this approach is capable of increasing the meta-reasoning capabilities of automated systems and aiding in the modelling of human reasoning processes.

6.1 Introduction

Recently researchers in Artificial Intelligence (AI) and Computer Science (CS) have devoted much attention to systems with reflective capabilities, *ie* to systems where parts are able to refer to other parts of the system or even to themselves (in AI, [MN88] contains a number of papers and a good bibliography on the topic, but see also [BK82, Smi83]; in CS, see [KC86]). On the other hand the idea of building systems with self-referential capabilities is not novel and has been successfully exploited by logicians at least since the thirties when Gödel proved his famous incompleteness theorems. As a result, the same word (*"reflection"*) is used with meanings which, even if based on similar underlying ideas, are substantially different.

We feel that reflection is important not only for its intrinsic logical interest but also because it allows the extensibility of the meta-reasoning capabilities of automated reasoning systems. While meta-level inference has been employed successfully in the past, for example in [SBB*82], it has not generally been the practice to make the means of this reasoning itself the object of interest[1]. It seems

---

[1] Financial support has been provided by SERC grant GR/E/44598 and SERC/Alvey grant GR/D/44270.
[1] For an exception see [Sil83]

important to develop the means to reason about meta-level objects, say tactics, in the same way that is possible for object-level structures. One way of achieving this is to use a declarative metatheory, and reflection provides us with just this.

In Logic Programming it is very useful to carry out what is essentially metareasoning and object-level reasoning in a single framework: the problem is finding a convincing semantics for such a hybrid system. Our approach is not to try to justify some part of this existing practice, but to see how various kinds of reflection can help to to get the semantics right in the context of theorem proving systems.

The goal of this paper is to describe the logical properties of reflection and the various forms that it can take, and then to give examples of reflective reasoning in two automated reasoning systems, one in the FOL system [Wey80] (developed in an AI context), the other in the NuPRL system [CAB*86] (developed in a CS context). Thus the second section, which is a brief history of how the ideas underlying reflection developed in the logicians' community, sets the background for the understanding of the two implementations. We feel that a sound analysis of the potential of the two implementations, and more generally of reflection, must be based on a clarification of the terminology based on a historical analysis of the ideas and their evolution. Sections three and four discuss two issues in reflection (truthfulness, and conservative/non-conservative versions) which are relevant to the comparisons of the two implementations. Then section five fixes the terminology used in the rest of the paper while sections six and seven are the examples of reflective reasoning in FOL and NuPRL respectively. Finally, section eight compares the two implementations.

6.2   Logical background

When Gödel set about proving his theorem [God31] about Peano Arithmetic, his plan involved encoding certain meta-statements as statements in the object language. Thus predicates of the syntax and proof theory of the object theory (such as being a well-formed formula, one formula following from another by some rule of inference, or being the conclusion of a proof) were represented by object-level predicates (as it happened, as predicates of natural numbers, but any moderately complicated object theory would suffice). The formulae and proofs were themselves encoded as numbers via a Gödel numbering. The encoding was chosen in such a way that certain properties would be provable; for example, if sub(X,Y,Z) is a function intended to yield (the code of) the result of substituting the term (whose code is) Z for the variable (whose code is) Y in the formula (whose code is) X, then the following fact holds:

$$\vdash sub(\lceil \phi(v) \rceil, \lceil v \rceil, \lceil t \rceil) = \lceil \phi(t) \rceil$$

for all formulae ϕ, variables v and terms t where $\lceil \ \rceil$ represents encoding [God31]. Similarly, proofs were encoded (as sequences of formulae) to satisfy properties such as the *provable closure* under the rules of inference, *eg*

$$\vdash Prov(\lceil \phi \rceil) \& Prov(\lceil \phi \to \psi \rceil) \to Prov(\lceil \psi \rceil).$$

where *Prov* is the predicate that indicates the provability of an (encoded) formula. The object of the exercise was double. First of all he could prove the incompleteness of any theory in which this encoding could be performed (first incompleteness theorem), since it is possible to concoct a proposition which encodes its own unprovability, at which point it is easy to show that such a proposition is neither provable nor disprovable. Secondly he could prove that a consistent theory could not prove its consistency, in other words, that a theory that could prove its consistency was inconsistent (second incompleteness theorem).

Given that we cannot have completeness for theories of the sort described above, there are still stratagems that can be employed to soften the blow of Gödel's theorem. This was the direction taken by Turing and Feferman. The idea underlying both approaches was to build new theories by extending old ones with unprovable axioms (for instance a consistency statement) such that, at each step, the new theory should be different from the old one (no consistent theory can prove its consistency).

Turing (in [Tur39]) saw that this operation of adding a true but unprovable sentence to a theory could be iterated through the transfinite. So he started from a given recursively enumerable axiom system A_0 (where some arithmetical sentence expressing the consistency of A_0 could be represented) and at each step producing a new recursively enumerable axiom system A_α as follows:

- A_0 is given;

- $A_{\alpha+1} = A_\alpha \cup \{Cons_{A_\alpha}\}$ where $Cons_{A_\alpha}$ is some arithmetical sentence expressing the consistency of A_α

- If α is a limit ordinal, $A_\alpha = \bigcup_{l<\alpha} A_l$

He showed that this operation could be carried out in such a way as to give a form of completeness for Π_1 formulae. More precisely, for any true proposition of arithmetic with only universal prenex quantifiers, there will occur at some point in the sequence of progressively enlarged theories a theory in which the proposition is provable.

Feferman extended Turing's work by considering different ways of extending incomplete theories to form progressions of theories indexed by constructive ordinals. He introduced (we think) the phrase *reflection principle* to describe a type of process whereby incomplete theories may be extended by certain axioms *which express a certain trust in the original system of axioms*. In [Fef62, p274] Feferman gives the following definition of a reflection principle:

By a **reflection principle** *we understand a description of a procedure for adding to any set of axioms A certain new axioms whose validity follows from the*

*validity of the axioms A and which formally express, within the language of A,
evident consequences of the assumption that all the theorems of A are valid.*

In other words, given a set of axioms Γ a reflection principle would allow us to
find routinely a set of propositions Δ so that not only would $\Gamma \cup \Delta$ be consistent
(provided Γ is consistent) but where Δ expresses in some way that the statements
of Γ are valid. (For a discussion of Feferman's use of "valid" in this context, see
later.) This seems to be the first appearance of the term "reflection principle";
since then the term "reflection" has been used in diverse ways, some far from the
original motivation. One of the goals of this paper is to try to establish a clear
usage for the terms.

We can see that the process considered by Turing of adding the formal consistency statement to a theory is a reflection principle as Feferman describes it:
the added sentence is taken to be the sentence which encodes the statement "the
theory is consistent". The added proposition can be seen in the metatheory to be
valid if the theory is valid; and the added sentence expresses formally precisely
the assumption that all of the theorems of A are valid.

Feferman considered a number of reflection principles. The first version he
considered (in [Fef62]), already found in Turing, was to obtain A_{k+1} as the union
of A_k and all the sentences of the form $Prov_{A_k}(\lceil \phi \rceil) \rightarrow \phi$. Turing had conjec-
tured that a class of true sentences wider than that obtained from the addition of
formalised consistency statements could be obtained from this principle. As Feferman proved, this process turned out to be globally equivalent to that proposed
by Turing. He gave also a version in which the added propositions take the form

$$Prov_{A_k}(\lceil \phi(\check{x}) \rceil) \rightarrow \phi(x)$$

for all formulae ϕ with one free variable where the symbol $\check{x}$ indicates that x is
to be disquoted. Feferman showed that such a principle could yield a form of
completeness as above for *all* propositions of arithmetic. The iteration is carried
out using the constructive ordinals, and involves complex arguments about paths
through these ordinals. The theory is not constructive[2].

6.3 Feferman's validity: truthfulness of reflection

The predicates such as *Prov* which are used in the formulation of Feferman's
principles are object level predicates that encode predicates that occur naturally at
the meta level. The predicate is given uniformly for any recursively defined object
theory (up to the details of the encoding, but it is known that the interesting
properties of these predicates are independent of such details). *What sort of*

---

[2]Even if not explicitly stated so far, all the results obtained by Feferman apply not
only to a formalised theory of arithmetic (such as PA) but also to all the theories which
are at least as strong as PA (such as extensions of PA itself) and, more generally, to all
the systems where PA is relatively interpretable [TMR68].

relationships might we want to hold between properties of a formal theory and metastatements about the theory, either made in a separate metatheory or encoded in the theory itself?

For an object theory, often the only criterion of acceptability is taken to be its consistency. For a metatheory, the situation is different. A metalanguage can be set up with appropriate predicates so that it can be readily applied as the metalanguage of some particular language; but the notions of metalanguage and metatheory don't make sense on their own. A metalanguage is a metalanguage relative to an object language, a metatheory is a metatheory of a particular object theory. In such a meta/object theory pair, we are interested not only in the consistency of the two theories, but also in the relation between the properties of the object theory and the assertions of the metatheory. For example, we could not want to include in a metatheory of the pure first-order propositional calculus a proposition like $Axiom(\lceil p \& \neg p \rceil)$.

This issue is (we think) closely related to the notion of validity invoked by Feferman. The notion of validity Feferman is invoking is clearly not the usual first-order notion of validity, since no theory with an axiom which is not a truth of logic is valid in the sense of being true in every first-order model. Feferman *refers to some preferred model or class of models*. Thus, for the case of arithmetic, the added propositions should have the property that they are true in the standard model for arithmetic, provided that the original theory is true in the standard model of arithmetic. The formalised consistency proposition has this property. On the other hand, adding the negation of the formalised consistency statement to the theory, while it would not cause the loss of consistency, does not satisfy the desired condition. We suggest that an extension of a given theory A be called *truthful* if *the validity of the added (meta-)axioms follows from the validity of the axioms of the original theory and formally expresses evident consequences of the assumption that all the theorems of A are valid (taking validity as meaning true in some preferred model or class of models).* The concept of truthfulness can also be generalised to the case when object theory and meta theory are separated by requiring that all the axioms of the metatheory satisfy the condition above. For example, ideally we would have $Axiom(\lceil \phi \rceil)$ in the metatheory if ϕ is an axiom of the corresponding theory.

Unfortunately, even if we want truthfulness, inside a single theory we cannot have certain versions of it. We might for example want an object-level predicate P with the property that $\vdash P(\lceil \phi \rceil) \leftrightarrow \phi$ (such a predicate is known as the *truth predicate*). Tarski showed that this is impossible (for arithmetic). [Tar36] .

6.4 Conservative or non-conservative reflection?

The reflection principles used by Feferman generally extend a theory by the addition of some unprovable statements. A reflection principle in Feferman's sense allows us to exploit at the object level the results of an argument in the metatheory *which could not be obtained by any argument that remains within the object theory.* Although Feferman uses the term reflection principle only in the case where a strengthening of the object theory is involved, these ideas can also be useful where no strengthening is concerned [Smo85]. The *Prov* predicate can be constructed in a definitional extension of the object theory, so that there is no strengthening of the theory required. Some facts are known to hold in such a definitional extension. For instance it is known (Löb's theorem) [Lob55] that:

$$\vdash Prov(\ulcorner \phi \urcorner) \rightarrow \phi \quad \text{iff} \quad \vdash \phi$$

Moreover, the *Prov* predicate has pleasant properties. If we index the predicate to show the theory T relative to which the formalisation is made, it can be shown to satisfy the following:

$$
\begin{aligned}
T \vdash \phi & \Rightarrow \quad T \vdash Prov_T(\ulcorner \phi \urcorner) \\
T \vdash Prov_T(\ulcorner \phi \urcorner) \wedge Prov_T(\ulcorner \phi \rightarrow \psi \urcorner) & \rightarrow \quad Prov_T(\ulcorner \psi \urcorner) \\
T \vdash Prov_T(\ulcorner \phi \urcorner) & \rightarrow \quad Prov_T(\ulcorner Prov_T(\ulcorner \phi \urcorner) \urcorner)
\end{aligned}
$$

(Here $\Rightarrow$ is the meta-connective.) These are known as the *(Löb) derivability conditions*. It seems that the term reflection has been extended to cover this notion as well, so that the *Prov* predicate is described (say) as reflecting down the proof theory from the meta to the object theory. This is an extension of the use of Feferman. We suggest that *reflection principle* be reserved for the use that Feferman describes involving a genuine enlargement of a theory, using *reflection* for the more general notion.

   Although reflection principles are by definition not provable, weakened versions of them may be. When this is the case, we can work simply in the original theory extended by definitions and not worry about problems of the consistency of the extended theory. For example, in Heyting Arithmetic (HA) [Tro73] the following fact holds:

$$HA \vdash Prov_n(\ulcorner \phi \urcorner) \rightarrow \phi$$

where the natural number n indicates a restriction to derivations containing formulae of logical complexity less than or equal to n (classical analogues are also available). The above fact holds for each n. Following Troelstra [Tro73] let's call these principles (both in the case of intuitionistic and classical logic) *partial reflection principles*. They are *partial* in that the full provability predicate is restricted to $Prov_n$. Thus, without leaving the original theory, we can show $\vdash \phi$ by showing $\vdash Prov_n(\ulcorner \phi \urcorner)$ for an appropriate n.

   The full reflection principle seems more interesting, and more problematic. For AI it opens up real possibilities of treatment of introspection and self-consciousness. The sort of problems that arise concern the question of having multiple theories, progressively enlarged by some reflection principle (so keeping close to Feferman's ideas), and implementing the relation between these theories. This involves at least looking at the relation between two theories, either a meta/object pair, or a sequence (finite or infinite or transfinite) of theories. For partial reflection the choice seems to be open to work in a single theory or in an explicit object/meta pair. The advantage of working in a single theory seems to be *the assurance of foundational soundness*. Another issue is that in a single theory approach *there is no need to implement the relation between theories* (which might be computationally expensive). On the other hand, *working in a single theory might make the meta-arguments too cumbersome*.

6.5   Some terminology

In this paper the word *reflection* has been used to describe the procedure of extending a given theory in a certain formal system so as to allow the expression of properties of the (same or another) formal system [3]. By *reflection principle* is meant any form of reflection where this extension takes the form of added (meta-)axioms which are **not** provable in a conservative extension of the theory considered, and where the additional statements can be justified in terms of their truthfulness. If the requirement of truthfulness is dropped, we will speak of an *enlarged reflection principle*. By *partial reflection* is meant any form of reflection where the extension to the theory takes the form of a definitional extension. The same terminology will also be used when the theory is extended by an inference rule, *eg*:

$$\frac{Prov(\lceil \phi \rceil)}{\phi}$$

On the other hand, in the AI community, the ideas underlying reflection are applied to situations where the antecedent of the inference rule is stated in one theory and the succedent in another (usually called the object theory OT). In this two-theory framework a further difference in the statement of reflection is that the operation of *coding* is substituted with the operation of *naming*. Thus the new version of the reflection principle (as it is for instance in both [Wey80, BK82]) is:

$$\frac{\vdash_{MT} Prov(``\phi")}{\vdash_{OT} \phi}$$

where "ϕ" is *the name* of ϕ. In the case that we have both this inference and its converse, the situation is close to that described by the Tarski truth definition [Tar36], as is expected since the meta-theory is simply a theory of the object-level syntax and proof theory. The difference is that here we are interested not in semantic correspondence but in inference *between* theories.

The authors of [BK82] start from an object theory OT, describe an associated metatheory MT and then "amalgamate" the two theories, resulting, it is claimed,

---

[3]In this paper no attempt is made to classify all the different uses of self-referential capabilities present in the AI literature and which are not related to some precisely defined formal system.

in a conservative extension of the original theory. Another example of this two-theory framework is implemented in [Wey80]. Here there are no constraints on how *Prov* is defined and the user is able to define his own *Prov* predicate. In the following we will use the words partial reflection and (enlarged) reflection principle also in the case of two theories. No systematic analysis of these sorts of reflection involving inference *between* theories appears to have been carried out.

In [Smi86] the author speaks of reflection *upwards* from the object to its representation and of reflection *downwards* from the representation to the object [4]. The same idea is also found in [BK82]. This kind of terminology has proved useful to describe reflection in a two-theory framework. Thus we also say that we have *reflection down* when we have the inference rule:

$$\frac{\vdash_{MT} Prov(\text{``}\phi\text{''})}{\vdash_{OT} \phi}$$

and we say that we have *reflection up* when we have the inference rule:

$$\frac{\vdash_{OT} \phi}{\vdash_{MT} Prov(\text{``}\phi\text{''})}$$

Note that, when OT is the same theory as MT, reflection up could be proved as a derived inference rule and reflection down is the (enlarged) reflection principle. More generally reflection down is the two-theory (enlarged) reflection principle.

6.6 Reflection in the FOL system

6.6.1 Non-constructive Theorem-Proving

The FOL system is a proof checker using sorted first order classical logic. It allows the user to define multiple theories, name them, switch from one to another, each theory with its own (multisorted) language, preferred model (simply model from now on) and axioms. Inside each theory the user can define how certain constants are interpreted in the model. For instance the numeral ONE in a theory about natural numbers can be "attached" (that is "interpreted") in the model as the number "1". Analogously, in a metatheory, the function $mkequal$ (which can be used to form the term $mkequal(\text{``}x1\text{''}, \text{``}x2\text{''})$ can be attached in the model to a function $mkequa$ which, given two objects, returns the assertion of their equality. Thus $mkequal(\text{``}x1\text{''}, \text{``}x2\text{''})$, where "x1" is the name of (the element, belonging to the domain of the model) $x1$, "x2" is the name of (the element, belonging to the domain of the model) $x2$, is the name of (the element, belonging to the domain of the model) $x1 = x2$ [5].

---

[4]The author actually uses the word *introspection* to mean reflection and gives the word *reflection* another meaning. Such a distinction is not relevant here and thus not discussed.

[5]This brief description of the FOL system is very rough and in many ways imprecise. See [Wey77, Wey80] for a full account.

6.6.2 Reflection

The implementation of the FOL reflection principle will be described using a very simple example. Let's consider the following situation: a metatheory (of name META) whose language contains the sorts $INDVAR$ and WFF, a unary predicate $THEOREM$ (which in the FOL reflection principle plays the role of the formalised provability predicate $Prov$), an individual variable x of sort $INDVAR$, a function $mkequal$ as above which takes two terms of sort $INDVAR$ and returns an object of sort WFF and an axiom (of name M) which says that any object is equal to itself. In FOL terms:

```
NAMECONTEXT META;

DECLARE SORT INDVAR WFF;
DECLARE PREDCONST THEOREM 1;
DECLARE FUNCONST mkequal(INDVAR,INDVAR)=WFF;
DECLARE INDVAR x [INDVAR];

AXIOM M: forall x.THEOREM(mkequal(x,x));
```

Let's suppose that the function $mkequal$ is interpreted as above.

```
ATTACH mkequal TO mkequa;
```

Now let's suppose we have an object theory (of name OT) whose language contains only an individual variable Y. Here we will describe how the reflection principle can be used from OT to assert as a theorem that $Y = Y$. In FOL terms:

```
MAKECONTEXT OT;
SWITCHCONTEXT OT;
DECLARE INDVAR Y;

REFLECT M Y;
```

The process associated with the last command can be divided in six steps each being performed either in OT or in $META$.

STEP 1: Being in OT the word $REFLECT$ is parsed. The next argument *must be* the name of a fact in $META$. Thus FOL automatically switches context and goes to META.

STEP 2: In $META$, M is parsed and the axiom $\forall x.THEOREM(mkequal(x,x))$ is returned. The variable x in M must be instantiated to a constant in $META$ which will be the name of a symbol of the language of OT. Since the sort of x is $INDVAR$ then the symbol of the language of OT must have syntactic type $Indvar$ (it must be an individual variable). Since in $META$ there are no constants of sort $INDVAR$, FOL must introduce a newly created one. But before extending the language of $META$ first FOL switches back to OT to parse the individual variable (to avoid extra work in case of error).

STEP 3: Being in OT, Y is parsed. In general as many items must be parsed as there are quantified variables in the fact in META. Since no more arguments are needed ";" is parsed and then it is switched back to $META$.

STEP 4: Being in $META$, now a new constant (for instance) I of sort $INDVAR$ is created and added to the language of $META$. I is then defined as the name in $META$ of Y [6]. Finally a universal elimination is performed on M obtaining $THEOREM(mkequal(I,I))$.

STEP 5: Still being in $META$, $THEOREM(mkequal(I,I))$ is evaluated in META's model. $THEOREM$ has no interpretation. $mkequal(I,I)$ evaluates to $Y = Y$, namely $mkequal(I,I)$ turns out to be the name of $Y = Y$. Thus the result is something which could be written as $THEOREM("Y = Y")$ where "$Y = Y$" should be read as *the name of* $Y = Y$.

STEP 6: At this point the reflection principle can be applied. Thus FOL forgets everything in $META$ (in this case, deletes I from the language and Y from the domain of interpretation), switches back to OT and, if there have been no errors (as it is in this example), instantiates what the argument of $THEOREM$ is name of ($Y = Y$ in this case) as a theorem of OT.

6.6.3 Some comments

It can be easily seen how the guarantee of truthfulness of the object-theory/metatheory relation is missing and the user is free to choose his own theory and metatheory. In particular the user can choose the axioms which describe the meaning of the predicate $THEOREM$. No provability conditions are hardwired in the metatheory. The FOL reflection principle is by default an enlarged reflection principle, it is up to the user whether or not make it truthful. This has been left out on purpose. In fact *it is an issue whether truthfulness is a wanted property*. While this might be the case for theories about mathematics and related sciences, in general this is not the case in AI applications. For instance, in human reasoning this is usually not the case and also in more traditional data base applications truthfulness is a very strong requirement.

The FOL "$REFLECT$" command does actually much more than simply performing the reflection principle. There is an initial stage of building up the relation between names and objects while the (enlarged) reflection principle, as defined above, is performed only in the last (sixth) step. Note that there is no reflection up but only reflection down.

---

[6] The operation performed here amounts to taking an element of the language of OT (Y) as the object, belonging to the domain of interpretation of $META$, which is the interpretation of I. This operation has various epistemological consequences which would need a lot of discussions. Since out of the goals of this paper, this issue is not further discussed (but see [Tar36]).

In the FOL reflection principle the link *name-object* is present explicitly. This idea is also employed in [Smi86] (where this is stated as a very important requirement). This approach substantially differs from the logicians' approach where the reflection principle works correctly simply because of the properties carried by the various predicates (such as *Prov*) and terms (such as $\lceil\phi\rceil$) in the definitional extension of Peano Arithmetic (see section 6.2).

Another major difference (from the logicians' reflection) is that the FOL reflection principle is stated using terms belonging to two different languages. Of course in some cases *OT* could be the same theory as *MT* (this case has been hinted in [Wey80] and called *self-reflection*) even if the overall structure of the FOL system suggests as more natural the use of distinct theories. The two-theory approach has major consequences. For instance, in the formulation of the reflection principle using names rather than codes follows from this fact. *In this two-theory framework naming is the natural counterpart of the logicians' coding.* The possibility of creating self-referential statements arises when successive inferences pass forward and backward between theories. On the other hand naming is *not* coding and the way the reflection principle is used changes. For instance, when formalising the proof of Gödel's theorem in FOL, it becomes necessary to manipulate simultaneously distinct naming and coding operations.

The FOL reflection principle together with a declarative metatheory separate from the object theory allows results to be exported from one theory to the other. This fact has already been exploited in the past in various cases (see for instance [Wey82]). At present we are studying the possibility of applying the FOL reflection principle to control search in theorem proving. The idea would be to have an explicit and declarative representation in the metatheory of overall (as opposed to local) strategies (or sense of direction) that a theorem prover would use while trying to prove a goal. These general strategies, called *proof plans* in [Bun88], possibly constructed out of simpler sub proof plans (see [Bun88] but also end of section 6.7.2 in this paper for more details) would be represented as sets of first order formulas. This would allow us to perform any kind of formula manipulation on this explicit representation and thus to improve the "quality" of the represented proof plan (*eg* making it more efficient, more general and so on) but at the same time would allow it to be "*run*" via the reflection principle so that it effectively drives the search in the object theory.

6.7 Reflection in the NuPRL System

6.7.1 Constructive Theorem-Proving

The NuPRL system was developed by Constable ([CAB*86]) as a theorem-proving system for a higher-order constructive logic based on Martin-Löf's type theory ([Mar79]). In the system, proofs are constructed top-down in a sequent calculus, and simultaneously with such construction an associated algorithm is constructed in the form of a term of the NuPRL language. This term is known as the *extract term* of a given proof, and it represents computational content that may be associated with the statement that has been proved. This close relationship between proof in constructive logic and algorithm is suggested by Heyting's semantics for intuitionistic logic. Evaluation of the extract term for given parameters then results in the execution of a program in the following way.

In a typical case, we are interested in a statement of the form

$$\forall x\!:\!A\ \exists y\!:\!B\ \Phi(x,y)$$

where A and B are types. If we find a constructive proof of this statement, we will also obtain an extract term of the form $\lambda x.\tau(x)$ with the property that we can prove

$$\forall x\!:\!A\ \Phi(x,\tau(x)).$$

Evaluating $(\lambda x.\tau(x))(a)$ for some a in A computes some output b for each input a.

If we regard $\forall x : A\ \exists y : B\ \Phi(x,y)$ as a specification of a relation we want to hold between some input x and output y, the extract term we find thus gives us an algorithm that provably satisfies this specification. The language of NuPRL contains, apart from the usual types expected in a computer language, dependent function and product types, quotient and set types, and arbitrary recursive types, making it highly expressive.

This approach allows us to treat the problems of synthesis and transformation of programs using techniques from theorem proving and proof transformation. It is a possible kernel of a system to aid the development of correct software, but many problems remain to be overcome.

At Edinburgh we now have two versions of the system. One uses the functional programming language ML and the other Prolog to implement the application of the object-level proof rules. Both allow the user to write tactics that can combine patterns of these object-level inference rules and control the search for proof. Even with the increase in flexibility that these tactics bring, experience shows that using this method to synthesise life-size algorithms (*eg* a unification algorithm) remains difficult.

It seems that for this approach to succeed the meta-reasoning capabilities of the system will need to be enhanced. Not only are tactics needed in a form that will execute combinations of proof steps at the object-level, we also want to reason about them, or more accurately about their specifications. If we had a *declarative meta-language* (and the Prolog tactics are not yet this) it would become possible to do this, and to synthesise, verify, transform and learn such tactics. Knoblock and Constable have suggested an approach using reflection that promises well [KC86].

6.7.2 Reflection

We shall restrict attention to a *partial reflection* approach, though a full reflection approach is also possible. The suggestion is to use the NuPRL system as its own metalanguage, so allowing proofs in the metatheory of NuPRL to be constructed uniformly with proofs in the object theory. This can be done by adding definitions inside the system *without modifying the underlying code*. This represent a *single theory conservative version of partial reflection*. Object-level proofs can then be used to synthesise algorithms, proofs containing meta-terms can be used to synthesise meta-operations, in particular tactics. Following Alan Bundy, we shall call a *method*[Bun88] a specification of a tactic in a definitional extension of NuPRL .

The idea is to introduce the types *type, term, sequent, proof, proof_of, refine, rule* and so on, together with appropriate axiom. We cannot have a type of all types, but the type structure of NuPRL is already stratified over so-called *universes*, so we can define the type "type" to be, say, the third universe level $U3$. This means that we will have available only the metatheory of proofs using the second universe level (the choice of 3 is arbitrary - this corresponds to picking some particular value for n in the partial reflection principle of section 6.4.)

Sequents are represented as pairs of the form $(list\_of\_hypotheses, conclusion)$, written $hyps >> concl$. Partial proofs are represented as trees of sequents; the type *proof* will have such trees where each non-terminal node is made of a sequent together with an inference rule and the subproofs associated with the subgoals of the inference rule.

We have partial proofs of arbitrary sequents, in the form of proof trees with the given sequent as the root of the tree (though the top-level sequent (the *goal*) of a NuPRL proof has no hypotheses). Such a proof tree for a sequent σ will have the type $proof\_of(\sigma)$, which can be given as a subtype of the type *proof*, namely

$$\{p : proof | goal(p) = \sigma \ in \ sequent\}.$$

The children of a node in the proof tree are related to the node by a refinement function. The refinement function has the type

$$refine : \{s : sequent \# r : rule | applies(s, r)\} \rightarrow sequent \ list.$$

Thus the refinement function defines the "immediate successor" relation in the proof tree in terms of applications of the primitive inference rules.

With this machinery we can specify tactics by means of assertions of the form

$$\forall \sigma : sequent \ (precon(\sigma) \rightarrow \exists p : proof\_of(\sigma) \ postcon(p);$$

where $precon(\sigma)$ will define the conditions under which the tactic is applicable, and $postcon(p)$ will give a description of the effects of the tactic. For example, take $precon(\sigma)$ to assert that (σ) is a (constructive) propositional tautology, and *postcon*(*p*) to assert that *p* is a *complete* proof. Proving this assertion constructively amounts to finding an algorithm that returns a proof given a tautology; the extract term of the proof of the above statement will be a tactic that does just that.

We also want to be able to consider how, given a number of methods (*ie* specifications of tactics) of the above form, they can be combined to form more powerful methods; we want to be able to do this not simply by chaining tactics together, but also conditionally and recursively. This can be done in the present context by specifying the overall method, and allowing in its proof that the assertions associated with the methods that have already been realised may be introduced as lemmas. If this is successful, the extract term of the resulting proof will be a tactic composed from these other tactics, possibly using conditional and recursive forms. Automating this process of proving assertions of this form from lemmas of a similar form would amount to making a planning system for the construction of methods.

There are still a number of difficulties in the way of this programme. We want to allow that tactics can fail (though we may want to insist that if so they fail finitely); we can cope here by taking a more general format to specify our tactics. We want to be able to execute the tactics as tactics in the system itself: but tactics synthesised in this way will be written in NuPRL, not in Prolog or ML. Short of reimplementing NuPRL in NuPRL, the answer would seem to involve working on the routines that apply inference rules to the proof tree, so that they will accept this alternative syntax.

6.7.3 Some Comments

Using partial reflection, it is possible to automate reasoning about part of the object-level proof theory of NuPRL inside NuPRL itself, allowing us to gain the same benefits at the meta-level that NuPRL gives us at the object-level in being able to construct objects that provably satisfy their specification. So far no mention has been made even of a partial reflection principle, though such a principle should be provable in this context. If we had a constructive proof of the partial reflection principle, and so had its extract term, this would allow us to obtain the extract term of a given theorem by applying the extract term of the partial reflection principle to the extract term of the abstract proof. This step would be important in synthesis proofs, where the goal is to obtain some algorithm and not simply to be assured of its existence. For verification proofs, the step would not be necessary, since an abstract proof of the correctness of an algorithm would carry the same assurance as an object-level proof.

The logic of NuPRL is higher-order and constructive; this is not important for the purposes of reflection, as long as it is expressive enough to allow encoding. In fact, the coding is easier in NuPRL than in say arithmetic since we can use the type-constructors of the language in the encoding rather the meagre resources of arithmetical syntax. On the other hand, the lack of a clear separation between the logic and the syntax of the system complicates the task. We are using a single-theory, conservative version of reflection here, though Knoblock and Constable also propose a non-conservative version using a tower of extensions to the theory. Although a conservative approach cannot give a real reflection principle, it allows a single system to simulate a large amount of metareasoning, and gives us the assurance that our system remains consistent.

Since the theory inside which the user works in the NuPRL system is fixed, this could allow us to hardwire in the system a truthful reflected metatheory, say for some fixed fragment of the type theory. The user would then be able to extend the meta-level reasoning ability of the system by constructing objects in this metatheory which would then be available for use in subsequent operation of the system.

6.8 Final considerations

Even if both FOL and NuPRL were originally built (we think) in order to formalise mathematics there is a slight difference in emphasis, maybe deriving from the different backgrounds (AI and CS) the two systems come from. Thus FOL is based on classical first order logic (formal system of natural deduction), makes use of metatheories and leaves the user free to choose his own theory, while NuPRL is based on constructive higher order logic (formal system of sequent calculus) and originally was concerned to develop a control regime at the meta-level rather than a declarative meta-theory.

As a consequence, even if both systems can be used in similar if not identical ways to exploit the potentialities of a declarative metatheory and the various forms of reflection, the two systems turn out to have different characteristics. In our experience, FOL turns out to be easier to use when trying to formalise the kind of (informal) metareasoning which goes on in any book of mathematical logic and which allows the mathematician to justify his operations, while NuPRL is better suited to the task of program verification/ synthesis (where the choice of a constructive logic is determinant),and for the formalisation of object-level constructive mathematics. Thus FOL is currently being used to formalise the metatheory of Gödel's proof of the first incompleteness theorem, while NuPRL can be used to formalise various induction proofs in the context of program verification and synthesis [B*88].

This difference propagates down to the two uses of metatheoretic arguments and of reflection. In NuPRL the control of the object-level inference has always been a major issue and led (originally) to the use of ML as the metalanguage while in FOL the emphasis on performing metareasoning (per se) led to the use from the start of a declarative metalanguage. On the other hand when thinking of giving NuPRL a declarative metalanguage it is useful to work with partial reflection, while for the FOL the choice has been for a two-theory enlarged reflection principle.

Acknowledgements

Both authors thank Alan Bundy and all the people working inside and around the Mathematical Reasoning Group at the Department of Artificial Intelligence of the University of Edinburgh for the many discussions and the fun we had together. The first author also thanks Richard Weyhrauch for the great time had and the huge number of things learned when working at the FOL project at the Computer Science Department of Stanford University.

References

[B*88]   A. Bundy et al. Proving properties of logic programs: a progress report. In L. Clarke, editor, *Proceedings of UK IT 88*, pages 131–134, The Information Engineering Directorate, Swansea, Wales, 1988. Also available as DAI Research Paper No. 361.

[BK82]   K.A. Bowen and R.A. Kowalski. Amalgamating language and meta-language in logic programming. In S. Tarlund, editor, *Logic Programming*, pages 153–173, Academic Press, New York, 1982.

[Bun88]   A. Bundy. The use of explicit plans to guide inductive proofs. In *9th Conference on Automated Deduction*, pages 111–120, Springer-Verlag, 1988. Longer version available as DAI Research Paper No. 349.

[CAB*86] R.L. Constable, S.F. Allen, II.M. Bromley, et al. *Implementing Mathematics with the Nuprl Proof Development System*. Prentice Hall, 1986.

[Fef62]   Solomon Feferman. Transfinite recursive progressions of axiomatic theories. *Journal of Symbolic Logic*, 27:259–316, 1962.

[God31]   K Gödel. Über formal unentscheidbare Sätze der Principia Mathematica und verwandter Systeme I. *Monatsh. Math. Phys.*, 38:173–98, 1931. English translation in [Ileijenoort 67].

[Ilei67]   J van Ileijenoort. *From Frege to Gödel: a source book in Mathematical Logic, 1879-1931*. Ilarvard University Press, Cambridge, Mass, 1967.

[KC86]   T. B. Knoblock and R.L. Constable. Formalized metareasoning in type theory. In *Proceedings of LICS*, pages 237–248, IEEE, 1986.

[Lob55]   M.II. Löb. Solution of a problem of Leon Henkin. *Journal of Symbolic Logic*, 20:115–118, 1955.

[Mar79]   Per Martin-Löf. Constructive mathematics and computer program-
           ming. In *6th International Congress for Logic, Methodology and Phi-
           losophy of Science*, pages 153–175, Hannover, August 1979. Published
           by North Holland, Amsterdam. 1982.

[MN88]   P. Maes and D. Nardi. *Meta-level Architectures and Reflection.* North
           Holland, 1988.

[SBB*82]   L. Sterling, A. Bundy, L. Byrd, R. O'Keefe, and B. Silver. Solving sym-
           bolic equations with PRESS. In J. Calmet, editor, *Computer Algebra,
           Lecture Notes in Computer Science No. 144.*, pages 109–116, Springer
           Verlag, 1982. Also available from Edinburgh as Research Paper 171.

[Sil83]   B. Silver. Learning equation solving methods from examples. In A.
           Bundy, editor, *Proceedings of the Eighth IJCAI*, pages 429–431, Inter-
           national Joint Conference on Artificial Intelligence, 1983. Also available
           from Edinburgh as Research Paper 184.

[Smi83]   B.C. Smith. Reflection and semantics in LISP. In *Proc. 11th ACM
           POPL*, pages 23–35, 1983.

[Smi86]   B.C. Smith. Varieties of self-reference. In J. Halpern, editor, *Procs. of
           the Conference on Theoretical Aspects of Reasoning about Knowledge*,
           Morgan Kaufman, 1986.

[Smo85]   C. Smorynski. *Self-Reference and Modal Logic.* Springer-Verlag, Berlin,
           1985.

[Tar36]   A. Tarski. Der Wahrheitsbegriff in den formalisierten Sprachen. *Studia
           Philosophica*, 1:261–405, 1936. English translation in [Tarski 56].

[Tar56]   A. Tarski. *Logic, Semantics, Metamathematics.* Oxford University
           Press, 1956.

[TMR68]   A. Tarski, A. Mostowski, and R.M. Robinson. *Undecidable theories.*
           North-Holland, 1968.

[Tro73]   A.S. Troelstra. Metamathematical investigations of intuitionistic arith-
           metic and analysis. *Lecture notes in mathematics*, 344, 1973.

[Tur39]   A.M Turing. Systems of logic based on ordinals. *Proceedings of the
           London Mathematical Society*, 45:161–228, 1939.

[Wey77]   R.W. Weyhrauch. *A Users Manual for FOL.* Technical Report STAN-
           CS-77-432, Computer Science Department, Stanford University, 1977.

[Wey80]   R.W. Weyhrauch. Prolegomena to a theory of Mechanized Formal Rea-
          soning. *Artificial Intelligence. Special Issue on Non-monotonic Logic*,
          13(1), 1980.

[Wey82]   R.W. Weyhrauch. An example of FOL using Metatheory. Formalizing
          reasoning systems and introducing derived inference rules. In *Proc. 6th
          Conference on Automatic Deduction*, 1982.

Chapter 7

Processing Techniques for Discontinuous Grammars

Verónica Dahl   Pierre Massicotte

Simon Fraser University

Abstract

In this article we discuss metaprogramming for discontinuous grammars—i.e., logic grammars in which productions can skip over unidentified strings of constituents called skips, and reposition them without analysing them. We present an interpreter for a specific discontinuous grammar family in which skips are not allowed to move (the *static discontinuity* family), and we give an economical methodology for constructing and processing their parse history for the purpose of enforcing constraints which can be expressed in terms of node domination relationships.

7.1 Introduction

Discontinuous grammars were devised by V. Dahl in 1981, as a generalization of extraposition grammars [22]. They are basically metamorphosis grammars [6] with the added flexibility that unidentified strings of constituents can be referred to (usually through a pseudo-symbol *skip(X)*, where X stands for the skipped substring), to be repositioned, copied or deleted at any position.

More formally, a discontinuous grammar is a quintuple (V_N, V_T, κ, s, P), where V_T and V_N are the terminal and nonterminal vocabularies respectively, whose union is called V, $s \in V_N$ and is the starting symbol, κ is the set of skip symbols, with κ and V non intersecting, and P is a set of productions of the form

$$nt, \alpha_0, skip(X_1), \alpha_1, \ldots, skip(X_n), \alpha_n \to \beta_0, skip(X_1'), \beta_1, \ldots, skip(X_m'), \beta_m$$

where $nt \in V_N$; the α_i and $\beta_i \in V*$; the $skip(X_i)$ and $skip(X_i') \in \kappa$; $n, m \geq 0$. The usefulness of this formalism has been studied in [9, 23, 13].

In [8], the author proposed a linguistically interesting class of Discontinuous Grammars, where skips are not allowed to move. This feature, called *static discontinuity*, is at the origin of two systems, developed in V. Dahl's research group, using Government-Binding theory [5]: a machine-error message generator from conceptual graphs, and a grammar of Spanish with clitic treatment. Material related to our adaptation of Government-Binding theory is covered in [2], and other material related to these applications, in [3, 1, 4]. A subclass of Static Discontinuity grammars was studied in [24]. The metaprograms shown in this paper are, however, different from those used in these various articles.

The only other approaches, to our knowledge, to capture Government-Binding theory within logic programming are those of Randy Sharp, which uses strictly logic programming [26], that of Ed Stabler, based on restricting logic grammars through constraints on logical derivations in the parser [28, 27], and that of Mark Johnson, based on program transformation and coroutining of the principles of Government-Binding theory [18, 17].

This article examines central metaprogramming issues for Discontinuous grammars and, in particular, Static Discontinuity grammars. We first present a brief history of Discontinuous grammar processors, and we outline a unification-focused approach to constraining them. We next discuss in more detail some techniques for processing Static Discontinuity grammars, for which we present both a concise interpreter (eleven clauses) and a particularly economic methodology for implementing constraints of a typical linguistic type: those which can be expressed in terms of node domination in a parse tree. We then present our concluding remarks.

7.2 Discontinuous grammar processors

7.2.1 History

The first processor for discontinuous grammars was a compiler devised by V. Dahl and later coded by Michael McCord during their joint work on the treatment of a linguistic problem: coordination. This compiler, which we call **synal**, was described in detail in [13]. It is very concise but inefficient, since it determines what strings to skip by sequentially trying strings of length 0, 1, 2, etc., and backtracking upon failure.

This compiler motivated Harvey Abramson to propose a more efficient but less encompassing **synal** version, also studied in [13] This second version limits the formalism to rules with only one skip string, which can only be followed by a single terminal, and which must rewrite at the rightmost position of the right hand side. In other words, rules have the following form, with α and β strings in $V*$, and $nt \in V_N$:

$$nt, \alpha, skip(X), [terminal] \rightarrow \beta, skip(X).$$

This is very restrictive, but still more flexible than metamorphosis grammars, and the implementation is an interesting application of message passing.

A third implementation was proposed by Fred Popowich [23]. This is a shift-reduce parser which operates in a bottom-up manner and can therefore afford to allow terminals as well as non-terminals to be the leading symbol of a rule.

Further work on discontinuous grammars [15] introduced a modular constraining mechanism to the basic compiler, *synal*. This addition mechanizes the dynamic blocking of movement rules whenever a statically specified constraint on movement is about to be violated. A constraint is expressed in a single clause which characterizes a domain in the parsing derivation under which no element can move. However, because such domains are typically characterized in terms of hierarchy, whereas the parsing derivation of a discontinuous grammar is typically a graph, this implementation resorted to an artifice which is not very elegant; and a further artifice was needed to avoid loops. Moreover, the constraint format was not well-suited for the typical constraints of Government-Binding theory [5], in which we had become increasingly interested.

In order to solve these three problems, as well as to improve on synal—which does not work for generation and which exhibits too much backtracking—V. Dahl then developed a more efficiently implementable family of discontinuous grammars, where only explicit constituents around the skips are allowed to move, while the skips themselves stay where they are [8, 11, 12]. This *static discontinuity* feature allows the parsing derivation to be shaped as a tree rather than a graph, thus providing a more direct means for describing the typically hierarchical constraints of linguistic theories. Section 7.3 describes this formalism and some considerations on metaprogramming for it.

7.2.2   Constraining Discontinuous Grammars—a unification-focused approa ch

Unification-focused graph representation

In [20], we introduce a representation and processing scheme for graphs in which important instances of traversal are replaced largely by unification. It can be used for type checking from a graph representing semantic types and their relationships of inclusion. We can also exploit it for constraining discontinuous grammars in a more efficient manner than that described in [15]. This graph methodology evolved from an old technique for reducing semantic agreement to syntactic matching presented for natural language applications in [10]. It can be summarized as follows:

- each node is associated to an incomplete representation of the path(s) to which it belongs. For instance, if the graph has an arc from node 1 to node 3 and another from node 3 to node 8, the incomplete path representations associated to the nodes are:

for node 8: [1,3,8|X]

for node 3: [1,3|Y]

for node 1: [1|Z]

This association is generated by a small compiler that transforms a graph description in terms of a relation "parent(X,Y)" (the list of parents of node X is Y) into a convenient representation that uses difference lists. For the above example, the path from the root to each node is unique and therefore explicitly represented. In general, procedures for calculating the subpaths that are not unique are included in the representation.

- associating an incomplete path with a given node is largely done through unification.

- comparing nodes for domination is also largely done through unification. For instance, if the graph represents semantic type inclusions (i.e., there is an arc from node N_1 to node N_2 if the type represented by N_2 is a subset of the type represented by N_1), we can check whether a node (say, node 8) in the above graph, represents a subtype of another node (say, node 3) without traversing the graph. We simply need to check whether there exists a path from the root to node 3 that is a prefix to a path from the root to node 8. This in turn reduces to unification of the difference lists representing their associated paths (the difference list for an incomplete path P is an expression P\X, where X is P's tail variable).

prefix(Xs\Ys,Xs\Zs) :- nonvar(Ys).[1]

- for checking that type 8 is a subtype of type 3, we would issue the call:

?- prefix([1,3|Y]\Y,[1,3,8|X]\X).

Exploiting the methodology for discontinuous grammars

We can use this graph representation scheme to keep a dynamically constructed parsing record for discontinuous grammars. As a derivation proceeds, each node introduced is associated with its partial path representation as described above. When a discontinuous rule needs to check on whether it is about to violate a movement constraint, the relevant hierarchical relationships between the nodes can be efficiently tested through unification-focused procedures such as the **prefix**

---

[1]This is a simple but destructive definition, in that it has the side effect of converting the supertype's path into the subtype's one. Copies could be made before the call, or, as we have done elsewhere [19, 20], the definition could be expressed in terms of appending difference lists. For the specific purpose of processing discontinuous grammars, however, we shall see that we can safely use the destructive version.

one above. Moved constituents can be related to their corresponding hierarchies easily, through their associated paths.

It is not our purpose here to further describe this graph methodology, or to detail its adaptation into the constraint-enforcing scheme just sketched. We are presently more interested in the static discontinuity formalism, which we next discuss, than in the general discontinuous grammar one. But we hope this section has given enough insight on a fairly general representation scheme well suited for efficiently processing discontinuous grammars with constraints. We shall return to the subject of constraints and of incomplete path representation in the context of Static Discontinuity grammars, for which we will describe them in more detail.

7.3   Processing static discontinuity grammars

7.3.1   Definition

A **static discontinuity grammar** (SDG) is a logic grammar $G = (V_N, V_T, P, s)$ where V_N, V_T and s have their usual meanings, and P is a set of productions, each of one of the two following forms:

- Type-1 productions:

$$nt \rightarrow \beta.$$

- Type-2 productions:

$$nt_1 \rightarrow \beta_1$$
$$nt_2 \rightarrow \beta_2$$

$$nt_n \rightarrow \beta_n$$

where nt_i are non terminals, and β_i are sequences of terminals and non-terminals (Prolog calls may be included too, but in this article we shall disregard them). Rules of the second form (discontinuous rules) as can be seen, consist of various context-free like rules. They can be used to rewrite strings of the form:

$$nt'_1 \, s_1 \, nt'_2 \, s_2 \, \ldots \, nt'_n$$

into:

$$(\beta_1 \, s_1 \, \beta_2 \, s_2 \, \ldots \, \beta_n) \, \theta$$

where nt_i unifies with nt'_i with a most general unifier θ and s_i are strings of terminals and non terminals.

Because the strings s_i are not moved, the corresponding part of the derivation can be depicted by drawing an arc from nt'_i to β_i for every i. Graphically:

$$\dots \; nt'_1 \; s_1 \; nt'_2 \; s_2 \; \dots \; nt'_n \; \dots$$

$$\beta_1 \, \theta \quad \beta_2 \, \theta \qquad \beta_n \, \theta$$

Notice that, although the parsing depiction remains a tree, context-sensitive and transformational power are expressively present in the sharing of the substitution θ by all symbols concerned, and in the fact that subrules provide context to each other.

Different strategies for applying the subrules of a discontinuous rule determine specific variants of the SDG formalism: subrules can be seen as a set or a list, they can be applied in parallel (i.e., only when a completely matching string is found in a parsing state) or in successive steps that keep track of the substitutions to propagate and of the unapplied subrules, etc. The next section presents an interpreter that uses the latter strategy, while providing a parallel flavour whenever possible. The implementation of another subclass of Static Discontinuity Grammars is discussed in [24]. Scattered context grammars [16] can be considered a non-logical grammar antecedent of SDGs, in which grammar symbols have no arguments and subrules must apply simultaneously. They describe a subset of context-sensitive languages, whereas in SDGs full context-sensitive and transformational power is preserved.

The complete definition of SDGs includes primitives for describing constraints which will be dynamically enforced. These are described in Section 7.3.3.

7.3.2 A short interpreter

Interpreters are not the most efficient implementations for grammar formalisms, but they are very useful for testing various parsing strategies. We now present one of the versions we have been experimenting with, consisting of eleven Prolog rules which interpret discontinuous productions in SDGs by applying each applicable subrule as soon as possible. It can be viewed as a pseudo-parallel interpreter, in that if all subrules are immediately applicable, they will be applied at once, achieving a parallel effect.

The main procedure is **parse(String, State, Pending_subrules)**, where **String** is the list of words of a presumed sentence in the language defined by the input grammar, **State** is the current parsing state, and **Pending_subrules** is a list of pending subrules from a type-2 production. The first call must initialize **State** to a list containing the initial symbol, and **Pending_subrules** to [ ].

Type-1 productions are stored in the form:

$$\text{rule(Head,Body\_list).}$$

and type-2 productions, in the form:

rule(Head$_1$,Body_list$_1$,[[Head$_2$ |Body_list$_2$],...,[H ead$_n$ |Body_list$_n$]]).

The grammar must have stopping clauses before recursive ones, to avoid looping.

The first rule for **parse** is the terminating one; the second recognizes a terminal symbol; the third applies an applicable pending subrule left from a previous partial application of a type-2 production. The fourth rule applies a matching type-2 production by applying its first subrule and concatenating all others into the **Pending_subrules** list. The rest of the metaprogram is obvious from its comments.

Notice that different strategies can be easily adopted through small changes to this interpreter. For instance, the **getsubrule** predicate, which presently chooses subrules in order unless otherwise provoked through backtracking, can be changed to randomly choose any subrule, or to choose them in a predefined order.

```
parse([],[],[]).
parse([T1|T],[T1|S],P) :- parse(T,S,P).
parse(S,G,P) :-
        getsubrule(P,[H|B],P1),           /* if any subrule can be applied, */
        break(G,F,H,L),                         /* apply it */
        concat(F,B,F1),
        concat(F1,L,G1),
        parse(S,G1,P1).
parse(S,[H|G],P) :-
        rule(H,B,Sr),                     /* apply a type-2 rule, append waiting */
        concat(B,G,G1),                        /* subrules on the pending list */
        concat(Sr,P,P1),
        parse(S,G1,P1).
parse(S,[H|G],P) :-
        rule(H,B),                                       /* apply a type-1 rule */
        concat(B,G,G1),
        parse(S,G1,P).
```

```
/* getsubrule(List of pending rules, Subrule chosen, Newlist of pending rules) */
getsubrule([R|P],R,P).                  /* gets a subrule out of the pending list */
getsubrule([R1|P],R,[R1|P1]) :- getsubrule(P,R,P1).
```

```
break([H|L],[],H,L).
break([H1|L],[H1|F],H,L1) :- break(L,F,H,L1).
```

```
concat([],Y,Y).
concat([X|R],Y,[X|Z]) :- concat(R,Y,Z).
```

7.3.3   Incorporating constraints

As we said before, many linguistic constraints on movement of constituents are expressed in terms of node domination in a tree hierarchy. This section discusses a unification-focused scheme for implementing such constraints in Static Discontinuity Grammars. For simplicity, we now assume the simultaneous interpretation of the subrules in a discontinuous rule (i.e., a completely matching string must be present in the parsing state before the rule can apply). Under this assumption, let us begin with some useful definitions.

Some definitions

- Given a static discontinuity grammar G defined as in Section 7.3.1, we define a **rewrite relation** between sentential forms (elements of $V*$) as follows:

$$\delta_1 \, nt' \, \delta_2 \;\Rightarrow\; (\delta_1 \, \beta \, \delta_2) \, \theta$$

for the first type of production, where θ is the mgu of nt and nt', and δ_1 and $\delta_2 \in V*$. For the second type of production, we have:

$$\delta_1 \, nt'_1 \, s_1 \, nt'_2 \, s_2 \, \cdots \, nt'_n \, \delta_2 \;\Rightarrow\; (\delta_1 \, \beta_1 \, s_1 \, \beta_2 \, s_2 \, \cdots \, \beta_n \, \delta_2) \, \theta$$

where θ is the mgu of the nt_i and nt'_i, and where δ_1 and $\delta_2 \in V*$.

The language described by G is defined by:

$$L(G) = \{ w \in V_T* \mid s \stackrel{*}{\Rightarrow} w \}$$

- Given a static discontinuity grammar G and a sentence t in $L(G)$, we define a *parsing tree* for t as a tree whose nodes belong to V, whose root is the starting symbol s, and the rest of the tree is constructed by using the rewriting relation, as follows:

$$\text{if } s = s_1 \Rightarrow s_2 \Rightarrow \cdots \Rightarrow s_n = t$$

then for every transition

$$s_i = \delta_1 \, nt' \, \delta_2 \;\Rightarrow\; s_j = (\delta_1 \, \beta \, \delta_2) \, \theta_i$$

obtained through a type-1 production $nt \rightarrow \beta$, there is an arc from nt' to each of the symbols in $\beta\theta_i$; and for every transition

$$s_i = \delta_1 \, nt'_1 \, s_1 \, nt'_2 \, s_2 \, \cdots \, nt'_n \, \delta_2 \;\Rightarrow\; s_j = (\delta_1 \, \beta_1 \, s_1 \, \beta_2 \, s_2 \, \cdots \, \beta_n \, \delta_2) \theta_i$$

obtained through a type-2 production $[nt_1 \rightarrow \beta_1, \ldots, nt_n \rightarrow \beta_n]$, there is an arc from nt_i' to each of the symbols in $\beta_i \theta_i$.

The contextual symbols in $\delta_1, \delta_2, s_1, s_2, \ldots, s_{n-1}$ also become affected by θ_i in the tree, although no explicit tree expansion shows it. This affectation can be thought of as substitution propagation.

- For each node n in a parsing tree T, we define an **incomplete path** for n as the expression

$$[s, n_2, n_3, \ldots, n_j, n \mid V]$$

where s is the starting symbol, $\Gamma(s) = n_2, \Gamma(n_2) = n_3, \ldots$, and $\Gamma(n_j) = n$; and V is a variable, called the **tail variable** of the path.

- We say a node n_1 **dominates** a node n in a parse tree if n_1 is different from n and belongs to n's incomplete path.

It is easy to see that a node n_1 dominates a node n in a parse tree $\Leftrightarrow$ there exists a mgu of their respective incomplete paths, p_1 and p, and in the unified expression n_1 precedes n.

Keeping a parse history

In order to enforce linguistic or other constraints on movement rules, we need to keep a parse history that we can examine. Typically this is done through constructing the parse tree incrementally as each rule applies. In SDG, we only need to know, for each leaf node at any given moment of the parse, its associated incomplete path. With this information alone, we can always reconstruct the tree so far, and, as we have seen, this notation lends itself to very efficient comparisons between nodes. It is moreover very easy to build an incomplete path incrementally: when adding a new arc from n_i to n_j, we simply unify the tail variable in n_i with $n_j \backslash Z$, where Z is a new variable.

We next illustrate constraint enforcement metaprogramming ideas with the example of a crucial constraint of Government-Binding theory.

Implementing a linguistic constraint: subjacency

What is subjacency Subjacency can in general be viewed as the interdiction for a production to move any constituent X to a position outside a domain n_1 in the situation:

$$[_{n_1} \ldots [_{n_2} \ldots X \ldots] \ldots]$$

where both n_1 and n_2 are bounding nodes.

The concept of a *bounding node* is a language-dependent one: in English, *sentence* and *noun-phrase* are bounding nodes; the bounding nodes for Italian

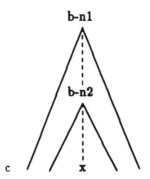

Figure 7.1: A parse tree

are *sentence-bar* and *noun-phrase*[2], etc... We shall assume that a given grammar input to our metaprocessor identifies its bounding nodes by the notation: $b-Node$, where "$-$" is a binary operator in infix notation.

It is outside the scope of this paper to linguistically motivate this constraint, let us merely say that it filters out ungrammatical sentences such as "Who do you wonder why John likes?". Some more details can be found for instance in [12, 7]. A full description of Government-Binding theory is given in [5].

Implementing subjacency   For explanatory purposes, let us consider the following discontinuous rule:

$$[c \rightarrow x, x \rightarrow d]$$

which can be seen as a static depiction of the movement of a constituent x into c's present position. If the parse tree at the point in which this rule can apply has the form where $n1$ does not dominate c, the rule would be attempting to move x outside of $n1$, and in this case subjacency should block the rule's application. All that a processor needs to check, therefore, in order to block the rule, is whether there exist two bounding nodes in x's path, $n1$ and $n2$, such that

dominates(N2,X), dominates(N1,N2), not(dominates(N1,C)).

Using the definition of node domination given in the previous section, and the obvious fact that $n1$ precedes n in the unified expression if the tail variable of the path for $n1$ is no longer a variable after unification, we can define node domination as follows:

----

[2]These constituents are respectively called "s", "n double bar" and "s bar" in Government-Binding theory. It is not our purpose here to explain their significance.

```
dominates(N1,N) :-
       path(N1,Pathn1),
       path(N,Pathn),
       prefix(Pathn1,Pathn).
```

```
prefix(Path\T1,Path\T) :- nonvar(T1).
```

(In practice, no path-calculating predicate is needed: the (difference-list expression of the) path for each leaf node can be carried together with the node itself).

However, this definition would fail for the first two calls to **dominates**, because the first argument is unknown. We define instead a procedure **dangerous(Px,Pn1)**, which partially identifies the situation depicted in Figure 7.1 — i.e., all of it minus the non-domination of c by $n1$. This procedure uses the incomplete path of X (Px) to recognize whether X is in a potentially dangerous path, and if so, yields the difference list $Pn1\backslash Tn1$ for the path Pn1 associated to the bounding node $N1$ of the dangerous situation, for further checking. In other words, this procedure succeeds if a node x with path Px is dominated by a bounding node $n2$, which in turn is dominated by another node $n1$ with path $Pn1$:

```
dangerous(Px,Pn1) :- dang(Px,Pn1,[]).
```

```
dang(X,_,_) :- var(X), !, fail.
dang([b-N1|Px],[b-N1|Tn1]\Tn1,[]) :- dang(Px,_,foundn1).
dang([b-N2|Px],_,foundn1).
dang([N|Px],_,foundn1) :- dang(Px,_,foundn1).
dang([N|Px],[N|Pn1]\Tn1,[]) :- dang(Px,Pn1\Tn1,[]).
```

The auxiliary predicate uses a flag in its last argument, to indicate whether a first bounding node $N1$ has been found. Its first clause fails if the tail variable of the path for X has been reached. The second clause recognizes $N1$, stores it as the last (known) element of the path for $N1$ and examines the rest of the path for X through a recursive call. The third clause recognizes a second bounding node $N2$ and stops. The fourth and fifth clauses respectively skip or store a node, according to whether we are past an $N1$ node or not.

We can now use this procedure to define the rule blocking condition, given the difference list representations of the paths for c and for x (respectively, the first and second arguments) :

```
block(Pc,Px\Tx) :-
       dangerous(Px,Pn1),
       not(dominates(Pn1,Pc)).
```

```
dominates(X\T1,X\T) :- nonvar(T1).
```

where **not** is the usual negation-by-failure (this, by the way, makes the use of a destructive definition for **dominates** inocuous: its arguments will come out intact after the check).

In short, subjacency can be implemented, using our approach, by an eight-clause procedure, which recursively examines the relevant subpath for X once, and performs one further check through unification.

Clearly, other constraints than subjacency can easily exploit this methodology whenever they can be expressed in terms of node domination relationships, as is often the case.

7.4 Conclusion, extensions

We have discussed metaprogramming issues for the Discontinuous grammar formalism in a general way, and presented a very concise interpreter for Static Discontinuity grammars in particular, as a basis for experimenting with different strategies—and therefore, producing different subclasses of the Static Discontinuity grammar family. We have also discussed how to constrain statically described movement of constituents is a very economic fashion, using unification-geared tree representation and processing schemes. These techniques can, of course, materialize in different ways. In a forthcoming article, we examine their integration within a particular application.

Our discussion, modulo appropriate strategy, is valid both for parsing and for generation. Similarly, although we center the discussion on logic grammars, both the static discontinuity framework and our metaprogramming schemes for it can apply to *logic programming* proper as well as to logic grammars. In this context, introduced by V. Dahl in 1986, it gives rise to Discontinuous Logic Programming [14], in which strings of atoms in a proof state can be skipped while expanding other explicit, discontinuous atoms in that state, all with shared substitutions. In other words, various Horn-clause like rules:

$$h1 :- b1.$$
$$h2 :- b2.$$
$$\vdots$$
$$hn :- bn.$$

can be grouped to provide context to each other through shared substitutions. Applied to a proof state

$$\ldots h1' \ldots h2' \ldots hn' \ldots$$

for instance, where hi matches hi' with substitution θ, we can obtain the proof state:

$$(\ldots b1 \ldots b2 \ldots bn \ldots)\theta$$

in which each hi' has been replaced by the body bi of the matching subrule[3]

The same idea was followed up in [25], where it can be found renamed as DISLOG.

The work of Monteiro [21] can be considered an antecedent of it, within the area of concurrent programming and with a fixed parallel strategy for applying the subrules. Rewriting the interpreter presented in Section 7.3.2 for discontinuous logic is, in fact, a very straightforward operation, yielding an even shorter processor—with one clause less.

Acknowledgements

We would like to thank Harvey Abramson for his help in finding a name for the Static Discontinuity Grammar formalism; he , Fred Popowich and the anonymous referees for useful comments on this article's first draft; and all the people who, as either members of or visitors to V. Dahl's research group, have contributed in one way or another to the development and testing of various processing schemes and applications for Static Discontinuity grammars: Michel Boyer, Charles Brown, Sharon Hamilton, Diane Massam, Brenda Orser, T. Pattabhiraman and Patrick Saint-Dizier. One of these applications was supported by an SUR research contract from IBM Canada, others, by NSERC grant 06-4244. The metaprograms presented here, however, are V.Dahl's sole responsibility, and were developed under NSERC grant 06-4244.

Endorsement

It is the authors' wish that no agency should ever derive military benefit from the publication of this paper. Authors who cite this work in support of their own are requested to qualify similarly the availability of these results.

References

[1] C. Brown. *Generating Spanish Clitics using Static Discontinuity Grammar.* PhD thesis, Simon Fraser University, 1987.

[2] C. Brown, V Dahl, D. Massam, P. Massicotte, and T. Pattabhiraman. *Tailoring Government and Binding Theory for Use in Natural Language Translation.* Technical Report LCCR 86-4, Simon Fraser University, 1986.

---

[3]Whether subrules actually apply simultaneously on the same proof state or not is, of course, a matter of strategy, but it is useful for explanatory purposes to view them in concerted action.

[3] C. Brown, T. Pattabhiraman, M. Boyer, D. Massam, and V. Dahl. *Tailoring Conceptual Graphs for Use in NL Translation.* Technical Report LCCR 86-14, Simon Fraser University, 1986.

[4] C. Brown, T. Pattabhiraman, and P. Massicotte. *Towards a Theory of Natural Language Generation: The Connection between Syntax and Semantics. Natural Language Understanding and Logic Programming II*, North-Holland, 1988.

[5] N. Chomsky. *Lectures on Government and Binding, the Pisa Lectures.* Foris Publications, Holland, second (revised) edition, 1982.

[6] A. Colmerauer. *Metamorphosis Grammars*, pages 133–189. Volume 63 of *Lecture Notes in Computer Science*, Springer-Verlag, 1978.

[7] V. Dahl. *Discontinuous Grammars.* Technical Report CSS/LCCR TR88-26, Simon Fraser University, 1988.

[8] V. Dahl. Gramaticas discontinuas: una herramienta computacional con aplicaciones en la teoria de reccion y ligamiento. *Revista Argentina de Lingüistica*, 2(2), 1986.

[9] V. Dahl. More on gapping grammars. In *Proceedings International Conference on V Generation Compute r Systems*, Tokyo, 1984.

[10] V. Dahl. On database systems development through logic. *ACM Transactions on Database Systems*, 7(1):102–123, March 1982.

[11] V. Dahl. Representing linguistic knowledge through logic programming. In *Fifth International Conference/Symposium on Logic Programming*, Seattle, August 1988.

[12] V. Dahl. Static discontinuity grammars for government and binding theory. In *Proc. Workshop 'Informatique et langue naturelle', Université de Nantes*, 1988.

[13] V. Dahl and II. Abramson. On gapping grammars. In *Proceedings, Second International Logic Programming Conference, Uppsala, Sweden*, pages 77–88, Universitet Uppsala, 1984.

[14] V. Dahl, C. Brown, and S. Hamilton. *Static Discontinuity Grammars and Logic Programming.* Technical Report LCCR 86-17, Simon Fraser University, 1986.

[15] V. Dahl and P. Saint-Dizier. *Constrained Discontinuous Grammars—A linguistically motivated tool for processing language.* Technical Report LCCR 86-11, Simon Fraser University, 1986.

[16] S. Greibach and J. Hopcroft. Scattered context grammars. *Journal of Computer and System Sciences*, (3):233–247, 1969.

[17] M. Johnson. *Move-α and the Unfold-Fold Transformation*. Technical Report, Brain and Cognitive Sciences, M.I.T., 1988.

[18] M. Johnson. *The Use of Knowledge of Language*. Technical Report, Brain and Cognitive Sciences, M.I.T., 1987.

[19] P. Massicotte. *Generating Conceptual Graphs from F-Structures*. Master's thesis, Simon Fraser University, 1988.

[20] P. Massicotte and V. Dahl. Handling concept-type hierarchies through logic programming. In *Proc. Third Annual Workshop on Conceptual Graphs*, 1988.

[21] L. Monteiro. *Distributed Logic: A Logical System for Specifying Concurrency* . Technical Report 5/81, Centro de Informatica, Universidade Nova de Lisboa, 1981.

[22] F.C.N. Pereira. Extraposition grammars. *American Journal for Computational Linguistics*, 7, 1981.

[23] F.P. Popowich. Unrestricted gapping grammars. *Computational Intelligence*, 2, 1986.

[24] P. Saint-Dizier. *Contextual Discontinuous Grammars. Natural Language Understanding and Logic Programming II*, North-Holland, 1988.

[25] P. Saint-Dizier. *Dislog: Programming in Logic with Discontinuities*. Technical Report LCCR 87-13, Simon Fraser University, 1987.

[26] R. Sharp. *A Model of Grammar Based on Principles of Government and Binding*. Master's thesis, University of British Columbia, 1985.

[27] E.P. Stabler, Jr. *Parsing with Explicit Representations of Syntactic Constraints . Natural Language Understanding and Logic Programming II*, North-Holland, 1988.

[28] E.P. Stabler, Jr. Restricting logic grammars with government-binding theory. *Journal of Computational Linguistics*, To appear, 1987.

N. B. In early reports, or early drafts of them, the Static Discontinuity grammar formalism was either unnamed (as in [8]) or was loosely and inappropriately called Constrained Discontinuous Grammars (as in [14, 1]). To avoid confusion, the misnaming in these reports was corrected by the authors once a suitable name was coined, since Constrained Discontinuous Grammars is in fact a different, existing formalism ([15]), which simply augments general Discontinuous Grammars with constraints, and does not possess the Static Discontinuity feature. Its constraints, as described in 7.2.1, have served as ancestors of SDG constraints, but are in fact quite different, since, among other things, the latter exploit the feature of unmovable skips for achieving power that cannot be attained in Constrained Discontinuous Grammars.

Chapter 8

Semantically Constrained Parsing and Logic Programming

Seiki Akama†   Akira Ishikawa‡

†*Fujitsu Ltd., 3-9-18 Shin-Yokohama,*
Yokohama, 222, Japan.
‡*Sophia University,*
Dept of English Language and Studies,
7 Kioi-cho, Chiyoda-ku
Tokyo, 102, Japan.

Abstract

In a parsing process, the parser often needs semantic information to solve word sense ambiguity. A parser which can be augmented by explicit semantic constraints while retaining the modularity of syntax has significance in developing a functional grammatical theory as advocated by Kay (1979). This paper presents a meta-interpreter approach to explicitly introducing semantic constraints in a syntactic parser based on Lexical Functional Grammar. The problem of lexical ambiguity during parsing is shown to be solvable by means of lexical information encoded in constraining equations of the grammar. The generality of this approach in comparison with Stabler (1987)'s syntactic constraints based on G-B theory is discussed.

8.1 Introduction

We will propose a way of explicitly incorporating semantic constraints into syntactic parsing. The formalism, which we call semantically constrained parsing, is a meta-interpreter approach to achieving modularity and communication in the specification of a parser. It is an application of meta-programming in logic programming.

Research on natural language processing in Prolog has centered around syntax rather than semantics. Such frameworks as DCG, EXG, etc. established a natural relationship between parsing and deduction in logic. Their interest, however, was focused on the syntactic aspects of logic programming. On the other hand, the semantic aspects of logic programming such as inference, and problem solving have not been given due attention.

It is, however, often difficult to incorporate semantic information systematically into syntactic parsing. As a result, the standard organization of a natural language understanding system is hierarchical, resorting to sequential processing, say, from syntax to semantics. The difficulty lies not only in such problems as efficiency and power, but also in achieving the independence of the parser from the semantic component. Even current researches in this field do not seem to come up to these requirements. Hirst (1987) deals with the problem of lexical disambiguation in a system which uses syntactic and semantic rules in tandem. One of the chief objects of the system is to provide a semantics suitable for various applications of natural language processing. Thus, the system's semantic interpreter, called ABSITY, produces as output computationally tractable semantic objects based on frames in a way which guarantees the extendability of the system, i.e. by maintaining the compositionality of semantics. While the basic design features listed by Hirst for the semantic component of natural language understanding systems (p.26) seem very sound to the present authors, his mechanism for lexical disambiguation, called Polaroid Words, leaves much to be desired to achieve full interaction between syntax and semantics. As is noted by Hirst, Polaroid Words cannot make use of syntactic information during disambiguation processes, although certain types of lexical ambiguities are known to be easily resolved by referring to the syntactic categories of the associated but discontinuously occurring lexical items (keep quite, keep the diary, keep staring, etc. p.79). This lack of communication between syntax and semantics also entails the system's inability to handle passive sentences (p.114).

We should note that the trouble is not necessarily with the lack of relevant information encodable in Polaroid Words. Word Expert Semantics (Small,1980) illustrates an extreme case in which each word is a multi-purpose procedure endowed with all the levels of information. As criticized by Hirst, this approach fails to take advantage of syntactic generalizations as a separate level of analysis, thus being antithetical to the modular approaches. What is required is not the convergence of every sort of information in single units, but an efficient and powerful mechanism for communication among different levels of information. The modular organization of a natural language understanding system cannot be viable unless the different modules can work in tandem. In this respect, Polaroid Words fail to come up to this requirement in that they insulate lexical semantics from the syntactic module.

Communication across module boundaries becomes even more vital when the system is extended to incorporate new modules for treating a new set of phenomena, e.g. discourse semantics. It is usually the case that a separate level of phenomena requires several independent modules each dealing with a different sort of information. Carter (1987) shows an anaphora-resolution system (SPAR) consisting of five components (Boguraev's analyzer, the structure matcher, the Anaphor Resolution rules, the inference mechanism, and the generator), some of which must have access to the more general sources of linguistic knowledge like grammar rules and a lexicon. However, the current SPAR system can be taken to be intentionally keeping the number of components to a minimum by subscribing to a shallow processing approach which avoids operations using extra-linguistic knowledge as much as possible. Also, communication between the components is kept to a minimum by ordering them hierarchically instead of working all of them at the same time in an interactive fashion. A good case might be made for this organization of the SPAR system because of the nature of the problem in question. But, it is at least noticeable that the system is not flexible enough to be able to adopt a different mode of utilizing its components. As noted by Carter himself, the problem of quantified phrases calls for not only greater use of the inference mechanism, but also a proper incorporation of a pragmatics component. Such an incremental expansion of the system does not seem to be expected.

As we have seen, a natural language understanding (NLU) system tends to be bound by a specific set of phenomena. As the result, its overall organization is often so rigidly fixed that its incremental sophistication is not conceivable. As Kay (1979) argues, an NLU system must be based on a functional grammatical theory, by which he means a theory which regards a language as a system for encoding and transmitting ideas and is prepared to take into account any function which concerns the process of encoding and transmitting ideas. Such a functional perspective expects NLU systems to be receptive to incremental changes.

The idea of semantically constrained parsing directly concerns these considerations of modularity and communication. First, we propose a meta-interpreter approach to introducing semantic constraints explicitly into syntactic parsing processes. The organization of the meta-interpreter is such that any sort of syntactic component can be linked with any sort of semantic component. This arrangement reflects the design feature of full modularity. More concretely, it is motivated by the presence of a number of promising syntactic theories such as GB, HPSG, and LFG, which have aroused the serious interest of computational linguists. In semantically constrained parsing, the syntactic component is supposed to make purely syntactic contributions to the whole parsing process. As a result, a syntactic component based on theory A can be replaced by another based on theory B without changing the other components orchestrated by the meta-interpreter if the basic nature of information to be contributed by the new component is the same as that of the old one. Similarly, any type of semantic theory can be interfaced with the meta-interpreter.

Second, the number of modules to be incorporated into semantically constrained parsing is not restricted to any fixed number. This means that we can expand the system to incorporate not only semantic modules but also those dealing with pragmatic information. It is one of the major advantages of the meta-interpreter approach that we can directly register rule-like knowledge in a module and use it from another module. By contrast, standard devices for interfacing two modules such as Hirst's Polaroid Words tend to be severely restricted in this regard and capable of using only lexical knowledge.

Third, semantically constrained parsing also addresses the issue of efficiency. Since constraints are directly encodable in the form of rules, they can be used as demons. In other words, they are checked only when there is a need to. If the checking task is relegated to a relatively isolated level of mechanism, it should become an independent process which is obligatorily undergone in every instance of the relevant operations. In our meta-interpreter approach, every constraint can be used as a demon, thus making for efficiency.

This paper is organized in the following way. In section 8.2, we will discuss the motivations of our approach. Section 8.3 deals with the theoretical relevance of linguistic frameworks to the modularity and communication of semantically constrained parsing. In section 8.4, we will present the formal mechanism of our meta-interpreter.

8.2   Semantic constraints and meta-programming

We will illustrate our idea of semantically constrained parsing by taking the problem of lexical ambiguity as an example. During parsing, the parser often encounter lexical ambiguities which cannot be resolved in terms of syntactic information alone. Some cases are simple enough to be solved in an ad hoc way. The following example from Nida et al. (1969) shows such a case.

(1)   a.   The horse runs.   (hasiru)
       b.   The water runs.   (nagareru)
       c.   The tap runs.   (moreru)
       d.   His nose runs.   ((hana ga) deru)
       e.   The motor runs.   (mawaru)
       f.   The business runs.   (eigyousuru)
       g.   The vine runs.   (nobiru)

These different senses of runs correspond to different Japanese verbs as shown in the parentheses. In this case, the lexical ambiguity is encountered when runs is being parsed. If parsing is left-to-right, we have sufficient information for its disambiguation at this point. So, an ad hoc introduction of a feature to be shared by the head noun of the subject noun phrase and the corresponding sense of runs is enough to solve this case.

However, the more usual cases of lexical ambiguity need more context for disambiguation. Consider the following example, also taken from Nida et al. (1969).

	subject	verb	1st object	2nd object	modifier
1.	human	charge	human	sum of money	for+object/ action
2.	human/ machine	charge	battery/gun/ hole/etc.		with+explosive/ dynamite
3.	human	charge	human		socially accept- able act(to-inf/ with+noun)
4.	human	charge	merchandize		to+human
5.	moving object/ human	charge	object/human		
6.	human	charge	human		with+evil act

Table 8.1: Semantic Contexts

(2) a. He charged the man ten cents for the pencil.
      (seikyuusita)
    b. He charged the battery. (zyuudensita)
    c. He charged them to do their duty. (meizita)
    d. He charged it to the man's account at the store.
      (tukenisita)
    e. He charged into the enemy. (totugekisita)
    f. He charged the man with murder. (kokusosita)

Each of the six different senses of charged can be distinguished from the others by its semantic context, as given in table 8.1.

As is clear from the table, the ambiguity of charged cannot be resolved by the semantic information of the subject alone except perhaps with sense 5. We need a combination of semantic information from different parts of the sentence to deal with this kind of lexical ambiguity. The ad hoc way of introducing a specific feature for each sense of the word is not feasible in this case. We have to respect the compositionality of semantic representation if we are to give a principled solution to this problem.

Moreover, it is not desirable to arrange for semantic processing to come after all syntactic parsing has finished. Such a parser would not be able to use semantic information during syntactic parsing to narrow down the candidates of a syntactic parse as human speakers do. Again, some systems might opt for such a hierarchical organization in the interests of efficiency. As we argued above, the resultant systems will lack inter-modular communication, which makes the inclusion of further modules extremely difficult.

Bowen and Kowalski (1982) introduces the meta-predicate 'demo' into Prolog to achieve the so-called amalgamated logic programming, strengthening its expressive power with a meta-level control mechanism. With 'demo' defining the provability relation of the object language, the resulting language becomes more flexible in solving various problems in AI. The reason is that object- and meta-level problems are interchangeable by the linking rule called reflection principle. For example, (3) shows a meta-interpreter for pure Prolog.

(3)   demo(true) ←
       demo(P & Q) ← demo(P) & demo(Q)
       demo(P) ← clause(P,Q) & demo(Q)

Meta-programming allows us to constrain a proof process explicitly. Stabler (1987) shows how to intorduce syntactic constraints explicitly into a syntactic parser by using this idea of meta-programming. In our semantically constrained parsing, the idea of a meta-interpreter is further extended to cover semantic constraints. Our fundamental thesis is that semantic constraints act as meta-knowledge vis-a-vis syntactic parsing. Syntactically unsolvable problems such as word sense disambiguation can be solved by appealing to semantic meta-knowledge. For example, semantically constrained parsing uses constraints introduced by lexical items such as the ones for charge in Table 8.1. The checking of such constraints can occur at arbitrary points during parsing. This is because in our meta- interpreter approach, constraint-checking for a particular syntactic constituent can be placed at an arbitrarily chosen stage of syntactic parsing. It should also be noted that we can use lexical information directly as semantic constraints. As we argued in section 8.1, it is one of the major advantages of semantically constrained parsing in Prolog that constraints are encodable in the lexicon in the form of rules to be directly employable in parsing processes. Thus our meta-interpreter for semantically constrained parsing makes for modularity and communication in the parser.

The scope of the present paper overlaps Wilks' preferential semantics with respect to the mechanism for ordering preferences. Some readers might be unduly struck by the flavor of Katz-Fodor- type semantics in our exposition. We have chosen this example in order to illustrate our meta-interpreter approach to semantic problems in general. The difference between the previous two semantic theories and our approach should be sought in the fact that ours is a solution to the problem of lexical disambiguation by means of a meta-programming control mechanism. Although in this paper, we do not address other semantic issues such as semantic representation of sentences, quantifier scope, intensional context, etc., we believe that it will become clear in this exposition that many of them can be given a solution in this framework if we provide relevant modules for them. As to semantic representation, the reader is asked to assume that the parser builds Montague-type logical forms (cf. Akama (1986), Akama & Kawamori (1988)). But, in this paper, nothing depends on particular forms that the semantic representations of sentences take.

8.3 Lexical Functional Grammar

We will use Lexical Functional Grammar (LFG) as the grammatical framework for syntactic parsing in this paper. LFG is a linguistic theory in the tradition of generative grammar. It is regarded as one of the so-called unification grammars which are attracting the interest of many computational linguists (cf. Shieber (1986)). Although our semantically constrained parsing is independent of any particular grammatical framework as we have already noted, LFG presents interesting problems as to how we should deal with constraints. Again, it is one of the major advantages of our meta-interpreter approach that it can incorporate any serious linguistic framework as its syntactic component.

Before going to the problem of constraints just mentioned, let us briefly review the organization of LFG (cf. Bresnan (1982), Kaplan & Bresnan (1982), Ishikawa (1985)). LFG assigns two levels of representation to a sentence. One is called the c- structure(constituent structure) of the sentence, which is a Chomskian tree representing its structural organization in terms of syntactic categories except that each node of the tree is associated with a set of annotations bearing information on the f-structure corresponding to the node. The other level of representation is called the f-structure (functional structure) of the sentence, which is a set of attribute-value pairs showing the grammatical relations involved in the sentence. There are three well-formedness conditions on f-structures. A sentence is grammatical when its f-structure is well-formed, i.e. satisfying all three well-formed conditions.

The well-formed conditions are as follows:

Uniqueness every attribute in a f-structure must have exactly one value.

Coherence every attribute belonging to class GF must be mentioned in the semantic form, which is the value of PRED of the f-structure, where class $GF = \{SUBJ, OBJ, OBJ2, OBL, XCOMP, COMP\}$.

Completeness every attribute mentioned in the semantic form which is the value of PRED of the f-structure must have a value in the f-structure.

Using LFG has certain consequences on the treatment of constraints. First, semantic constraints for lexical disambiguation can refer to the f-structure constituents of a sentence rather than to its semantic representation itself. In other

words, the f-structure of the sentence becomes a level for interfacing different levels
of modules. F-structure is more convenient for this purpose than semantic representations because being a kind of syntactic representation,it retains the features
of linguistic expressions. In general, it is easier to formulate semantic constraints
operating on syntactic constituents than ones operating on semantic constituents
since semantic representations may not reflect surface syntactic constituent structure at all. Moreover, since semantic representations vary considerably among
different semantic theories, adopting one particular theory entails corresponding
changes in the lexicon. This is antithetical to our thesis of maintaining modularity and communication. By contrast, as conventional dictionaries testify, information in terms of syntactic constituents is more theory-neutral (cf. Longman
Dictionary of Contemporary English). The level of grammatical functions such
as SUBJ, OBJ, etc. which is reflected in the f-structure provides a suitable level
of generalization for encoding linguistic information, whether lexical, semantic or
pragmatic.

Second, the well-formedness conditions for f-structures represent a different
class of constraints from semantic constraints for lexical disambiguation. They
are close to what Stabler (1987) calls global constraints in that they are effective
throughout the parsing process. On the other hand, the semantic constraints are
similar to what Stabler calls local constraints since they can be dropped as soon
as they are satisfied. This difference presents a problem of efficiency if constraint-
checking is given the same treatment of control to these two classes constraints.
Our solution to this problem shows the flexibility of the control mechanism of
semantically constrained parsing.

8.4   Formalizing a meta-interpreter for semantically con-
strained parsing

We have noted that the syntactic component carries the three well-formedness
conditions for f-structure. LFG also has another class of constraints called constraining equations which impose local restrictions on the well-formedness of f-
structures. Unlike Stabler's local constraints, constraining equations mostly come
from lexical items. In this respect, they resemble the semantic constraints discussed in this paper. So, these two kinds of constraints are treated in the same
way.

In order to be able to incorporate all these kinds of constraints, we use a new
predicate 'constraint'. The modified meta-interpreter using this predicate is as
follows.

(4) demo(true) ←
    demo(P & Q) ← demo(P) & demo(Q)
    demo(P) ← clause(P,Q) & demo(Q) & constraint(P')

constraint(P') ← constraint(clause(P',Q'))
               & constraint(Q')
constraint(P') ← C
constraint(P' & Q') ← constraint(P') & constraint(Q')

Here P' denotes the name of P, and C a set of constraints associated with P. In short, *constraint*(P') acts as a meta- interpreter of the next lower level. *constraint*(P'), involving a function (denoted by the prime) which converts P into its name P', is represented by C. C, in its turn, represents a conjunction of rules acting as constraints associated with P. This meta-interpreter is easily presentable as a top-down parser in a simple form of constrained parsing. We use a definite clause grammar (DCG) by Pereira & Warren (1980) for our parser.

(5) demo(Theory,true,L,L) ←
demo(Theory,P & Q,L0,L) ←
          demo(Theory,P,L0,L1) & demo(Theory,Q,L1,L)
demo(Theory,P,L0,L) ←
        member(clause(P,Q),Theory)
        & demo(Theory,Q,L0,L1)
        & constraint(P',L1,L)

constraint(P',L0,L) ←
        constraint(clause(P',Q'),L0,L1)
        & constraint(Q',L1,L)
constraint(P' & Q',L0,L) *leftarrow*
        constraint(P',L0,L1)
        & constraint(Q',L1,L)
constraint(P',L0,L) ← solve(P',L0,L)

Theory denotes a knowledgebase. $L, L0$ and $L1$ stand for lists whose members are constraints. When two of these occur in the same predicate, the left one corresponds to the input list, and the right one the output list. P' indicates the set of constraints associated with category P. *Solve* passes constraint P' to the evaluation process. If the relevant information for checking it is not yet available, the constraint is added to the constraint list. If P' is satisfied, no incrementation of the constraint list occurs. If P' fails, the current process is killed and backtracking takes place. This formulation implies that any constraint can be framed in the knowledgebase to be applied to certain computaion at appropriate times.

Let us consider how we can deal with the various constraints in question. As to syntactic parsing, we use a DCG parser with an explicit routine for solving equations, following Yasukawa (1984). The c-structure rules look as follows.

(6) a. s(F_S,Old,New) →
        np(F_NP,Old,Old1),

equate([subj,F_S],F_NP,Old1,Old2)
vp(F_VP,Old2,Old3),
equate(F_S,F_VP,Old3,New)

b. np(F_NP,Old,New) →
        det(F_DET,Old,Old1),
        equate(F_NP,F_DET,Old1,Old2),
        n(F_N,Old2,Old3),
        equate(F_NP,F_N,Old3,New)

F_S, F_NP, etc. are f-structures for node S, node NP, etc. *Old*, *Old1*, *Old2*, *Old3*, and *New* are differential lists. *Equate* is one of the procedures in the f-structure inducing algorithm. The whole set of c-structure rules is part of the Theory in (5). For the sake of efficiency, the three well-formedness conditions are treated as global constraints. Following Stabler (1987), we provide an independent procedure for them.

(7) demo(P) ←
        demo(Theory,P,[],L), empty(L),
        P=..[Cat,F_str,A,B],
        global_constraints(F_str)

global_constraints(F) ←
        uniqueness(F),
        coherence(F),
        completeness(F)

Semantic constraints are introduced in lexical items in the form of constraining equations. The lexical entry for the third sense of charge in Table 8.1 corresponds to the following clauses when the modifying part is a to-infinitive.

(8) verb(F_V,3,[charged—X],X) ←
        equate([pred,F_V],
        sem_form(charge3([subj,obj,xcomp]))),
        equate([tense,F_V],past)

prime(verb(F_V,3[charged—X],X) ←
        c_equate(sem_cat(subj,F_V),human),
        c_equate(sem_cat(obj,F_V),human),
        c_equate(sem_cat(xcomp,F_V),legal)

In (8), the second argument of *verb* is the index for the sense of the verb. *Sem_form* stands for semantic form. *Prime* relates the verb to its constraining equations. *Sem_cat* retrieves the semantic category (semantic role) of the attribute (1st argument) in the f-structure (2nd argument). Lexical entries such as in (8) are all part of the Theory.

8.5   Conclusion

We have proposed a meta-programming approach to achieving modularity and communication in natural language parsing. Our formalism called semantically constrained parsing gives a full control of various constraints involved in parsing. We have dealt with the problem of lexical ambiguity, using LFG as our grammatical framework.

It is also suggested in this paper that the distinction made in Stabler (1987) between global and local constraints might be given a more general interpretation such that local constraints deal with declarative knowledge, and global constraints procedural knowledge. One result is that constraints can be directly connected with the rules in the knowledgebase. While Stabler's formulation was largely dependent on the G-B framework, semantically constrained parsing is general enough to be applicable to any syntactic theory.

It should also be pointed out that the current formulation of semantically constrained parsing is extendable to incorporate further levels of information such as pragmatics (cf. Akama (1986)).

References

Akama, S.(1986) Methodology and Verifiability in Montague Grammar. Proc. of COLING '86, 88-90.

Akama, S. and M. Kawamori. (1988) Data Semantics in Logic Programming Framework. in Natural Language Understanding and Logic Programming II. edited by V. Dahl and P. Saint-Dizier. North Holland, Amsterdam, 135-51.

Bowen, K.A. and R. Kowalski.(1982) Amalgamating language and metalanguage in logic programming. in Logic Progrmming, edited by K.L. Clark and S.-A. Tarnlund. NY:Academic Press. 153-72.

Bresnan, J.(1982) The Mental Representation of Grammatical Relations. Cambridge, Mass: MIT Press.

Carter, D. (1987) Interpreting Anaphoras in Natural Language Texts. Chicester: Ellis Horwood Ltd.

Hirst, G.(1987) Semantic Interpretation and the Resolution of Ambiguity. Cambridge: Cambridge Univ. Press.

Ishikawa, A. (1985) Complex Predicates and Lexical Operations in Japanese. Ph.D. Thesis, Stanford.

Kay, M. (1979) Functional Grammar. Proc. of the 5th Ann. Mtg. of the Berkeley Linguistic Society.

Kaplan, R. and J. Bresnan. (1982) Lexical Functional Grammar: A Formal System for Grammatical Representation, in The Mental Representation of Grammatical Relations, edited by J. Bresnan. Cambridge, Mass.:MIT Press.

Nida, E.A., C.R. Taber & N.S. Brannen(1969) The Theory and Practice of Translation. Leiden: E.J. Brill.

Pereira, F.C.N. and D.II.D. Warren.(1980) Definite clause grammars for language analysis–a survey of the formalism and a comparison with augmented transition networks. Artificial Intelligence 13, 3(May 1980), 231-78.

Shieber, S.(1986) An Introduction to Unification-Based Aproaches to Grammar. CSLI. Stanford.

Small,S.L.(1980) Word Expert Parsing: A theory of distributed word-based natural language understanding. Doctroal Diss., Univ. of Maryland.

Stabler, E.P., Jr. (1986) Restricting logic grammars. Proc. of the 5th Nat. Conf. on Artificial Intelligence, AAAI-86, 1048-52.

Stabler, E.P., Jr. (1987) Parsing with Explicit Representation of Syntactic Constraints. Proc. of Second International Workshop on Natural Language Understanding and Logic Programming. Simon Fraser University, Vancouver, B.C., Canada. 17-19 August.

Yasukawa, II. (1984) LFG System in Prolog. Proc. of Coling '84, 358-61.

Chapter 9

Negation as Failure:
Proofs, Inference Rules and Meta-interpreters[1]

Albert Bruffaerts   Eric Henin

Philips Research Laboratory Brussels

Abstract

The paper presents sets of inference rules to build natural deduction proofs able to justify both successes and failures of query evaluation based on an extension of SLDNF-resolution. The proofs are done wrt a weaker form of Clark's Completed Data Base and are compatible with 2- or 3-valued semantics and classical or intuitionistic derivability. The paper also presents a Prolog meta-interpreter which produces proof trees representing those natural deduction proofs. The external behaviour of the meta-interpreter presented here is similar to that of Prolog. Other behaviours, perhaps more adequate in the context of expert system explanation facilities, may be programmed quite easily.

9.1   Introduction

Explanations are an essential part of expert systems and their systematic generation is an active research area [5, 14, 16, 21, 23]. In the framework of logic-based knowledge representation formalisms, derivation trees built by the query evaluation process form the raw material from which explanations are generated [9, 20, 22]. Currently, *how* explanations justify system answers by tracing rule applications, *why* explanations justify system questions by displaying a stack of goals, and *why-not* explanations justify system failures by enumerating failure branches of the evaluation tree.

When negation as failure is allowed in rules and queries, the fact that successes and failures of query evaluation are not handled uniformly is annoying since failure

[1]This work was partially funded by the European Economic Community under Project P316 of the ESPRIT programme.

of a query is equivalent to success of its negation. Besides, enumerating failure branches is not as convincing as traversing a proof tree because completion axioms do not appear explicitly.

This paper presents sets of inference rules such that natural deduction proofs can be built to justify both successes and failures of query evaluation based on an extension of SLDNF-resolution. The proofs are done relatively to a theory which is a weaker form of Clark's Completed Knowledge Base [6].[1] The proofs are compatible with 2- or 3-valued semantics and classical or intuitionistic derivability.

The paper also presents a Prolog meta-interpreter which produces proof trees which are a computer representation of natural deduction proofs based on the proposed inference systems. The external behaviour of the meta-interpreter presented here is similar to that of Prolog: (1) it enumerates all the proofs of successes, but only one proof of failure, and (2) no variables are instantiated on failure. Other behaviours, perhaps more adequate in the context of expert system explanation facilities, may be programmed quite easily.

We argue in [4] that actual proof trees are important for logic-based representation formalisms, even if it is now recognized that a mere trace of the inferences drawn during the problem solving phase of the expert system only describes the system behaviour and does not justify it. Indeed, nothing prevents from tracing inferences drawn during an explanation phase of the expert system. Hence, one can imagine that part of the knowledge base is dedicated to the so-called deep explanations by encoding how general concepts and principles of some causal model of the application domain apply to the solution previously computed by the expert system.

The structure of the paper is as follows. Section 9.2 defines the language and the meta-language used throughout the paper. Section 9.3 presents the inference systems, while Section 9.4 shows the Prolog meta-interpreters. An example of proof built by the meta-interpreter is shown in the Appendix.

This paper is an extensively rewritten version of [3] where our approach is compared with related works published in the literature. The novelties of this paper are:

- equations are allowed in rule bodies and queries,

- a weaker completed theory is used,

- an extension of SLDNF-resolution is used,

- compatibility with 2- or 3-valued semantics and classical or intuitionistic derivability has been consciously pursued.

---

[1] Clark's actual terminology is Completed Data Base, but in the context of this paper, we prefer the term Completed Knowledge Base.

9.2   Notations

First, let us define some Prolog syntactic entities which are restricted forms of first-order logic formulae:

rule	= atom '<-' rule_body.
query	= rule_body.
rule_body	= disjunct { ';' disjunct }.
disjunct	= conjunct { ',' conjunct }.
conjunct	= positive_literal | '(' rule_body ')' | 'not' conjunct.
positive_literal	= 'true' | equation | atom.[2]

Sections 9.3.1 and 9.3.2 suppose *definite* rules and queries, i.e. rules and queries written without the 'not' operator, while section 9.3.3 deals with *normal* rules and queries, i.e. rules and queries possibly written with the 'not' operator. These notions of "definite" and "normal" are not the classical ones [13], since disjunctions, equations and nesting are allowed in queries and rule bodies; nevertheless the main distinction, the presence or absence of negation, is preserved.

Throughout this paper, Greek letters (possibly with subscript or accent) are used to denote meta-variables ranging over specific Prolog syntactic entities with the following conventions:

ϵ, η, ν range over variables (e.g. X, Y),
ϕ ranges over function symbols (e.g. f, g),
π ranges over predicate symbols (e.g. p, q),
τ ranges over terms (e.g. f(a,g(Y))),
β ranges over rule bodies.

The meta-language also uses the notion of list, functional dependency, total substitution, universal and existential closure, and syntactic identity with the following conventions:

$\vec{\epsilon}$ denotes a list of variables $\epsilon_1, \ldots, \epsilon_n$,
$\vec{\tau}$ denotes a list of terms $\tau_1, \ldots, \tau_n$,
$\vec{\tau_1} = \vec{\tau_2}$ denotes the conjunction of equations $\tau_{11} = \tau_{21} \wedge \ldots \wedge \tau_{1n} = \tau_{2n}$,
$\tau[\vec{\epsilon}]$ denotes a term τ where variables $\vec{\epsilon}$ are the *only possibly*
          occurring variables[3],
$\beta[\vec{\epsilon}]$ denotes a rule body β with the same dependency,
$\vec{\tau}[\vec{\epsilon}]$ denotes a list of terms $\tau_1[\vec{\epsilon}], \ldots, \tau_n[\vec{\epsilon}]$ with the same dependency,
$\{\vec{\epsilon}/\vec{\tau}\}$ denotes the simultaneous total substitution of each variable ϵ_i
          by the corresponding term τ_i,
          such a total substitution may be applied to any term or formula,
Θ denotes a substitution,

---

[2]Equations and 'true' are not considered as atoms.

$\forall^* \cdot \beta$ denotes the universal closure of β,

$\exists^* \cdot \beta$ denotes the existential closure of β,

$\equiv$ denotes syntactic identity.

9.3 Theoretical framework

9.3.1 Success as provability

The theory of successful SLD-derivations is usually done for definite rules and queries [13]. A definite knowledge base KB contains a collection of definite *rules* of the form:

$$\pi(\vec{\tau}[\vec{\epsilon}]) \mathrel{<\text{-}} \beta[\vec{\epsilon}, \vec{\nu}], \tag{9.1}$$

where $\vec{\epsilon}$ denotes all the variables occurring in the rule head and $\vec{\nu}$ denotes all the variables occurring only in the rule body. The predicate symbol π is neither '=' nor 'true' and the rule body β possibly contains equations (positive literals of the form $\tau_1 = \tau_2$), arbitrarily nested disjunctions and conjunctions, but no negation[4].

The logical reading of such a rule assumes all the variables to be universally quantified:

$$\forall \vec{\epsilon}, \vec{\nu} \ \cdot \ \pi(\vec{\tau}[\vec{\epsilon}]) \leftarrow \beta[\vec{\epsilon}, \vec{\nu}], \tag{9.2}$$

which is logically equivalent to:

$$\forall \vec{\epsilon} \ \cdot \ \pi(\vec{\tau}[\vec{\epsilon}]) \leftarrow \exists \vec{\nu} \ \cdot \ \beta[\vec{\epsilon}, \vec{\nu}]. \tag{9.3}$$

A relation π may be defined by a set of rules of the form (9.1).

We can associate with KB, a first-order theory $\mathcal{S}[\text{KB}]$ whose axioms consist of the logical counterparts of the KB rules. But since equations may occur in queries and rule bodies, the theoretical foundations for definite knowledge bases are extensions of the results in [13] developed by Jaffar et al. [10]. In fact, a theory of equality is needed to constrain the interpretation of the binary predicate symbol '=' in a way compatible with the unification algorithm used during the query evaluation process. In the case of successful queries, the only requirement on the equality theory and its corresponding unification algorithm is that two unifiable terms must be equal according to the theory. Since we intend to use Robinson's unification algorithm to evaluate the equations, the standard equality theory ($\mathcal{SET}$) is adequate; indeed, by definition of a most general unifier (mgu), it is true that:

$$\begin{aligned}&\text{if } \tau_1 \text{ and } \tau_2 \text{ are unifiable with mgu } \Theta\\&\text{then } \mathcal{SET} \models \forall^* \cdot \tau_1 \Theta = \tau_2 \Theta,\end{aligned} \tag{9.4}$$

---

[3]Thus, $\tau[\mathtt{X,Y}]$ may denote terms like $\mathtt{f(a,b)}$, $\mathtt{g(X)}$ or $\mathtt{h(Y,X,d)}$, but not terms like $\mathtt{f(Z,W)}$, $\mathtt{g(U)}$ or $\mathtt{h(X,Y,Z)}$.

[4]Facts are written: $\pi(\vec{\tau}[\vec{\epsilon}]) \mathrel{<\text{-}} \mathbf{true}$.

where $\mathcal{SET}$ contains the following axioms[5]:

$$\forall x \; \cdot \; x = x$$
$$\forall x, y \; \cdot \; x = y \supset y = x$$
$$\forall x, y, z \; \cdot \; x = y \wedge y = z \supset x = z$$
$$\forall x_1, y_1, \ldots, x_n, y_n \; \cdot \; x_1 = y_1 \wedge \ldots \wedge x_n = y_n$$
$$\supset \phi(x_1, \ldots, x_n) = \phi(y_1, \ldots, y_n)$$
where ϕ is a function symbol of arity n
$$\forall x_1, y_1, \ldots, x_n, y_n \; \cdot \; x_1 = y_1 \wedge \ldots \wedge x_n = y_n$$
$$\supset (\pi(x_1, \ldots, x_n) \rightarrow \pi(y_1, \ldots, y_n))$$
where π is a predicate symbol of arity n.

Those axioms simply state that equality is an equivalence relation and that equal terms may be substituted.

A definite *query* is a rule body

$$\beta,$$

possibly containing equations, arbitrarily nested disjunctions and conjunctions, but no negation. The logical interpretation of a query is a request to verify whether its existential closure is a logical consequence of $\mathcal{S}[\text{KB}] \cup \mathcal{SET}$:

$$\mathcal{S}[\text{KB}] \cup \mathcal{SET} \models \exists^* \cdot \beta.$$

More precisely, a query is interpreted as a request for finding a substitution Θ of its variables which makes the universal closure of $\beta\Theta$ a logical consequence of $\mathcal{S}[\text{KB}] \cup \mathcal{SET}$:

$$\mathcal{S}[\text{KB}] \cup \mathcal{SET} \models \forall^* \cdot \beta\Theta. \tag{9.5}$$

SLD-resolution, extended with rules for handling disjunctions, equations and nesting, is a non-deterministic decision procedure finding a most general substitution Θ to establish the truth of assertion (9.5). The soundness and completeness of SLD-resolution in the context of an equality theory is studied in [10].

Since natural deduction proofs are desired, we present an inference system in which we can build a proof that a successful query is a theorem of the theory associated with the knowledge base. According to the goals pursued, various inference systems may be considered. If one is interested in theoretical foundations, the set of inference rules will be drawn from the tradition of mathematical logic (see [18]). Guided by the objective of constructing natural deduction proofs which would serve as the basis for explanations in expert systems, we propose an inference system $(\vdash_S)$ which contains the following inference rules to justify successful SLD-derivations:

---

[5]Note that a second implication symbol ($\supset$) is used simultaneously with the one introduced previously ($\rightarrow$). In the current context of 2-valued models, they must be considered identical. Later in the paper, in the context of 3-valued semantics, they will be given different meanings.

$$\frac{\forall^* \cdot \beta_i}{\forall^* \cdot \beta_1 \vee \beta_2}$$

$$\text{where } 1 \leq i \leq 2 \tag{9.6}$$

$$\frac{\forall^* \cdot \beta_i \quad (1 \leq i \leq 2)}{\forall^* \cdot \beta_1 \wedge \beta_2} \tag{9.7}$$

$$\frac{}{\mathit{true}} \tag{9.8}$$

$$\frac{}{\forall^* \cdot \tau_1 = \tau_2}$$

$$\text{where } \tau_1 \equiv \tau_2 \tag{9.9}$$

$$\frac{\forall \vec{\epsilon} \cdot \pi(\vec{\tau}\,'[\vec{\epsilon}]) \leftarrow \exists \vec{\nu} \quad \beta[\vec{\epsilon}, \vec{\nu}] \quad (\text{variant of } \mathcal{S}[\text{KB}] \text{ axiom})}{\forall^* \cdot \beta\{\vec{\epsilon}/\vec{\tau_1}\}\{\vec{\nu}\,'/\vec{\tau_2}\}}$$
$$\overline{\forall \vec{\eta} \quad \pi(\vec{\tau}\,[\vec{\eta}])}$$

$$\text{where } \vec{\tau}\,'\{\vec{\epsilon}/\vec{\tau_1}\} \equiv \vec{\tau} \text{ and } \vec{\epsilon}, \vec{\nu}, \vec{\eta} \text{ are disjoint and } \vec{\nu}\,' \subseteq \vec{\nu}. \tag{9.10}$$

The inference system $\vdash_S$ is such that the $\mathcal{SET}$ axioms do not occur in the proofs. In fact, it does not prove equation solvability, which was not considered interesting from an explanation point of view; this is possible because inference rule (9.9) incorporates the property of most general unifiers (9.4).

Inference rules (9.6) – (9.10) are sufficient to justify any successful SLD-derivation in the context of definite rules and queries. In other words, any query β to which corresponds a successful SLD-derivation with answer Θ is a theorem of $\mathcal{S}[\text{KB}]$:

$$\mathcal{S}[\text{KB}] \vdash_S \forall^* \cdot \beta\Theta.$$

Besides, it is obvious that $(\mathcal{S}[\text{KB}], \vdash_S)$ is sound wrt $(\mathcal{S}[\text{KB}] \cup \mathcal{SET}, \models)$, which means that each theorem proved with these inference rules from $\mathcal{S}[\text{KB}]$ is a logical consequence of $\mathcal{S}[\text{KB}] \cup \mathcal{SET}$. In the context of definite rules and queries, $\vdash_S$ is also complete wrt to $\models$, since SLD-resolution is complete.

9.3.2   Finite failure as provable falsity

In the theoretical framework of the previous section, finite failure of the evaluation of a query β may only be interpreted at the meta-level as:

$$\mathcal{S}[\text{KB}] \cup \mathcal{SET} \not\models \exists^* \cdot \beta.$$

This interpretation justifies the absence of proof with respect to $S[KB]$ and $\vdash_S$ in case of failure. However, one may associate with the knowledge base KB some "completed" theory $C[KB]$ such that failure of the evaluation of a query β may be interpreted as the fact that the negation of its existential closure is a logical consequence of this theory:

$$C[KB] \models \neg \exists^* \cdot \beta,$$

or equivalently,

$$C[KB] \models \forall^* \cdot \neg \beta.$$

Essentially, there are two possible frameworks for defining such a theory: Clark's *Completed Knowledge Base* (CKB) [6, 13], and Reiter's *Closed World Assumption* (CWA) [15]. Shepherdson compares both approaches in [17]. Roughly speaking, CKB transforms the set of if-rules defining a predicate into a unique logical equivalence, while CWA supposes that KB contains only the positive knowledge but is complete so that any positive ground literal not implied by $S[KB] \cup SET$ is considered false.

For our purpose of constructing proofs explaining failures, CWA is impractical. Indeed, CWA associates with the knowledge base KB a complete theory whose axioms, in general, cannot be recursively enumerated [1]. Besides, all the negative axioms would be difficult to explain since it is the absence of proof for the positive counterpart which justifies them. The theoretical merit of CWA is that it depends only on the logical contents of KB and not on the way rules are written; it may also be considered as an operational weakness.

CKB, on the contrary, associates with the knowledge base KB a theory whose axioms are a straightforward syntactic transformation of the KB rules. They are thus easy to explain. Besides, CKB gives, in some way, a direction to logical implication, and therefore allows some "programming."

For all those reasons, we have chosen to associate with the knowledge base KB the theory defined by Clark's approach. However, we do not use the classical presentation based on logical equivalence; instead, with each predicate π, we associate a failure axiom which, added to the rules defining π, yields a set of axioms equivalent to Clark's completed definition of π, at least for 2-valued models. The advantages of this presentation are multiple:

- it is incremental rather than destructive; instead of replacing $S[KB]$ by a new theory, one simply adds axioms to it so that the assertion $C[KB] \models S[KB]$ is trivially true;

- in the context of knowledge base characterizations which are based on 3-valued semantics (see section 9.3.3), it defines a weaker theory than Clark's approach;

- it simplifies theoretical developments by eliminating the equivalence connective [18].

The failure axiom associated with a predicate π is defined as follows. Assume predicate π is defined by p rules like:

$$\pi(\vec{\tau_i}[\vec{\epsilon_i}]) \text{ <- } \beta_i[\vec{\epsilon_i}] \quad (1 \leq i \leq p),$$

where $\vec{\epsilon_i}$ denotes all the variables occurring in the i-th rule. These KB rules, instead of being read as (9.2) or (9.3), may be read as:

$$\forall \vec{\eta} \cdot \pi(\vec{\eta}) \leftarrow \exists \vec{\epsilon_i} \cdot \vec{\eta} = \vec{\tau_i}[\vec{\epsilon_i}] \wedge \beta_i[\vec{\epsilon_i}] \quad (1 \leq i \leq p),$$

where $\vec{\eta}$ are variables not occurring in $\vec{\epsilon_i}$ ($1 \leq i \leq p$). First, we reduce the various rules defining predicate π to a unique axiom:

$$\forall \vec{\eta} \cdot \pi(\vec{\eta}) \leftarrow \bigvee_{i=1}^{p} (\exists \vec{\epsilon_i} \quad \vec{\eta} = \vec{\tau_i}[\vec{\epsilon_i}] \wedge \beta_i[\vec{\epsilon_i}]),$$

logically equivalent to:

$$\forall \vec{\eta} \cdot \pi(\vec{\eta}) \leftarrow \exists \vec{\epsilon} \cdot \bigvee_{i=1}^{p} (\vec{\eta} = \vec{\tau_i}[\vec{\epsilon}] \wedge \beta_i[\vec{\epsilon}]),$$

where $\vec{\epsilon}$ is the union of the $\vec{\epsilon_i}$ ($1 \leq i \leq p$). Since the disjunction in the previous formula has the form of an acceptable rule body, we can rewrite it as:

$$\forall \vec{\eta} \cdot \pi(\vec{\eta}) \leftarrow \exists \vec{\epsilon} \cdot \beta'[\vec{\eta}, \vec{\epsilon}].$$

Once the rules defining π have been reduced to a unique success axiom, it is easy to define the corresponding failure axiom:

$$\forall \vec{\eta} \cdot \neg \pi(\vec{\eta}) \leftarrow \forall \vec{\epsilon} \cdot \neg \beta'[\vec{\eta}, \vec{\epsilon}]. \tag{9.11}$$

If there is no KB rule for predicate π, its failure axiom is:

$$\forall \vec{\eta} \cdot \neg \pi(\vec{\eta}) \leftarrow true. \tag{9.12}$$

However, it is not sufficient to complete the theory $\mathcal{S}[\text{KB}]$; the accompanying equality theory $\mathcal{SET}$ must also be completed. Jaffar et al. [10] show that, in order to interpret failure as falsity, the equality theory E used for success has to be completed in a theory E* such that:

$$\text{E} \models \tau_1 = \tau_2 \quad \text{iff} \quad \text{E*} \models \tau_1 = \tau_2.$$

Besides, E* must be unification-complete, which means that two terms are unifiable if and only if they are equal wrt E*. In general, unification-completeness does not guarantee the existence of a unique most general unifier, so that a new concept of general failure must be used instead of the classical finite failure of [13].

Since we have restricted ourselves in this paper to Robinson's unification algorithm, we have fixed E to be $\mathcal{SET}$ so that E* is its natural completion, Clark's equality theory ($\mathcal{CET}$), which enforces free interpretation of terms in all models: two syntactically different ground terms always denote different objects. $\mathcal{CET}$ is unification-complete, and moreover, guarantees the existence of a unique most general unifier; therefore, the concept of finite failure is sufficient. $\mathcal{CET}$ is made of the axioms of $\mathcal{SET}$ completed by the following ones:

$$\forall^*\forall x \cdot \neg x = \tau$$
where $x \not\equiv \tau$ and x actually occurs in τ
$$\forall x_1,\ldots,x_n,y_1,\ldots,y_m \cdot \neg \phi_1(x_1,\ldots,x_n) = \phi_2(y_1,\ldots,y_m)$$
where $\phi_1 \not\equiv \phi_2$ and $n,m \geq 0$
$$\forall x_1,y_1,\ldots,x_n,y_n \cdot \neg x_1 = y_1 \vee \ldots \vee \neg x_n = y_n$$
$$\supset \neg \phi(x_1,\ldots,x_n) = \phi(y_1,\ldots,y_n)$$
where ϕ is a function symbol of arity n.

Let us call $\mathcal{F}[KB]$ the theory made of the failure axioms corresponding to all KB predicates. It is trivial to see that $C[KB] = S[KB] \cup \mathcal{F}[KB] \cup \mathcal{CET}$ is equivalent to the usual definition of Clark's completed knowledge base for 2-valued models and classical derivability, since in this context, contraposition of implications is valid.

Whenever, for a query β, there exists a finitely failed SLD-tree, i.e. a finite SLD-tree every branch of which fails, it is a result of [19] that:

$$C[KB] \models \forall^* \cdot \neg \beta. \tag{9.13}$$

As the basis of an explanation facility for expert systems, we are interested in natural deduction proofs of (9.13). Therefore, we propose a set of inference rules ($\vdash_F$) which, by mimicking the SLD-resolution process, justifies any finitely failed SLD-tree by a proof. The set of inference rules is followed by some comments.

$$\frac{\forall^* \cdot \neg \beta_i \quad (1 \leq i \leq 2)}{\forall^* \cdot \neg (\beta_1 \vee \beta_2)} \tag{9.14}$$

$$\frac{\forall^* \cdot \neg ((\beta_1 \wedge \beta) \vee (\beta_2 \wedge \beta))}{\forall^* \cdot \neg ((\beta_1 \vee \beta_2) \wedge \beta)} \tag{9.15}$$

$$\frac{\forall^* \cdot \neg (\beta_1 \wedge (\beta_2 \wedge \beta))}{\forall^* \cdot \neg ((\beta_1 \wedge \beta_2) \wedge \beta)} \tag{9.16}$$

$$\frac{\forall^* \cdot \neg \beta}{\forall^* \cdot \neg (true \wedge \beta)} \tag{9.17}$$

$$\frac{\forall^* \cdot \neg \, \tau_1 = \tau_2}{\forall^* \cdot \neg \, (\tau_1 = \tau_2 \, \wedge \, \beta)} \tag{9.18}$$

$$\frac{\forall^* \cdot \neg \, \beta\Theta}{\forall^* \cdot \neg \, (\tau_1 = \tau_2 \, \wedge \, \beta)}$$

where Θ is mgu of τ_1 and τ_2 $\tag{9.19}$

$$\frac{\forall \vec{\eta} \cdot \neg \, \pi(\vec{\eta}) \leftarrow \forall \vec{\epsilon} \cdot \neg \, \beta'[\vec{\eta}, \vec{\epsilon}] \quad \text{(variant of } \mathcal{F}[\text{KB}] \text{ axiom)}}{\forall \vec{\nu} \cdot \neg \, (\pi(\vec{\tau}[\vec{\nu}]) \, \wedge \, \beta[\vec{\nu}])}$$
with middle line $\forall^* \cdot \neg \, (\beta'\{\vec{\eta}/\vec{\tau}\} \, \wedge \, \beta)$

where $\vec{\nu}, \vec{\eta}, \vec{\epsilon}$ are disjoint $\tag{9.20}$

$$\frac{\forall \vec{\eta} \cdot \neg \, \pi(\vec{\eta}) \leftarrow \textit{true} \quad \textbf{(variant of } \mathcal{F}[\text{KB}] \textbf{ axiom)}}{\forall \vec{\nu} \cdot \neg \, (\pi(\vec{\tau}[\vec{\nu}]) \, \wedge \, \beta[\vec{\nu}])}$$

where $\vec{\nu}, \vec{\eta}$ are disjoint $\tag{9.21}$

$$\frac{\forall^* \cdot \neg \, (\beta_2 \, \wedge \, \beta_1)}{\forall^* \cdot \neg \, (\beta_1 \, \wedge \, \beta_2)} \tag{9.22}$$

$$\frac{}{\forall^* \cdot \neg \, \tau_1 = \tau_2}$$

where τ_1 and τ_2 are not unifiable $\tag{9.23}$

$$\frac{\forall \vec{\eta} \cdot \neg \, \pi(\vec{\eta}) \leftarrow \forall \vec{\epsilon} \quad \neg \, \beta'[\vec{\eta}, \vec{\epsilon}] \quad \text{(variant of } \mathcal{F}[\text{KB}] \text{ axiom)}}{\forall \vec{\nu} \cdot \neg \, \pi(\vec{\tau}[\vec{\nu}])}$$
with middle line $\forall^* \cdot \neg \, \beta\{\vec{\eta}/\vec{\tau}\}$

where $\vec{\nu}, \vec{\eta}, \vec{\epsilon}$ are disjoint $\tag{9.24}$

$$\frac{\forall \vec{\eta} \cdot \neg \, \pi(\vec{\eta}) \leftarrow \textit{true} \quad \text{(variant of } \mathcal{F}[\text{KB}] \text{ axiom)}}{\forall \vec{\nu} \cdot \neg \, \pi(\vec{\tau}[\vec{\nu}])}$$

where $\vec{\nu}, \vec{\eta}$ are disjoint. $\tag{9.25}$

Some remarks about the inference rules:

1. Rule (9.14) handles isolated disjunctions: a disjunction fails if both disjuncts fail.

2. Rules (9.15) – (9.21) handle conjunctions in the Prolog-like manner, from left to right, possibly propagating variable bindings.

(a) Rules (9.15) – (9.16) handle conjunctions whose first conjunct is not a literal, using distributivity of conjunction over disjunction and associativity of conjunction to justify a left-to-right computation rule.

(b) Rules (9.17) – (9.21) handle conjunctions whose first conjunct is a positive literal.

    i. The literal *true* is handled by rule (9.17).

    ii. When the first conjunct is an equation, either the equation is unsolvable and the conjunction is proved false (9.18), or the equation is solvable and the proof goes on with the additional variable bindings required by the most general solution of the equation (9.19). The latter rule incorporates the following result of [18] about equations and most general unifiers:

$$\text{if } \tau_1 \text{ and } \tau_2 \text{ are unifiable with mgu } \{\vec{\nu}/\vec{\tau}\}$$
$$\text{given by the usual unification algorithm}$$
$$\text{then } \mathcal{CET} \models \forall^* \cdot \tau_1 = \tau_2 \supset \vec{\nu} = \vec{\tau}$$
$$\text{and } \mathcal{CET} \models \forall^* \cdot \tau_1 = \tau_2 \wedge \beta \leftrightarrow \tau_1 = \tau_2 \wedge \beta\{\vec{\nu}/\vec{\tau}\}.$$

    iii. According to rule (9.20), when the first conjunct is an atom defined by KB rules, it is substituted by the instantiated body of its failure axiom, and the proof proceeds; according to rule (9.21), when the first conjunct is an atom which is not defined by KB rules, the conjunction is proved false.

3. Rule (9.22) allows proofs of conjunction falsity for finitely failed SLD-tree built via an arbitrary computation rule.

4. Rules (9.23) – (9.25) handle isolated positive literals:

(a) Rule (9.23) incorporates the classical result that:

$$\text{if } \tau_1 \text{ and } \tau_2 \text{ are not unifiable,}$$
$$\text{then } \mathcal{CET} \models \forall^* \cdot \neg \tau_1 = \tau_2.$$

(b) the failure of an atom is justified by the failure of the instantiated body of its failure axiom (9.24) or by the absence of KB definition (9.25).

The inference system $\models_F$ is such that only axioms from $\mathcal{F}[KB]$ are used in proofs. This is possible because, in the context of definite rules and queries, negative information can only be deduced from failure axioms. Besides, we drop proofs of equation solvability or unsolvability due to their lack of interest from an explanation point of view.

Thus, inference rules (9.14) – (9.25) are sufficient to justify any finitely failed SLD-tree in the context of definites rules and queries. In other words, for any query β to which corresponds a finitely failed SLD-tree, the following assertion is true:

$$\mathcal{F}[\text{KB}] \vdash_F \forall^* \quad \neg \beta.$$

Besides, it is obvious that $(\mathcal{F}[\text{KB}], \vdash_F)$ is sound wrt $(\mathcal{C}[\text{KB}], \models)$, which means that each theorem proved with the preceding inference rules from $\mathcal{F}[\text{KB}]$ is a logical consequence of $\mathcal{C}[\text{KB}]$. In the context of definite rules and queries, $\vdash_F$ is also complete wrt to $\models$, since SLD-resolution is complete for failure.

9.3.3 Provable negation as finite failure

This section, contrarily to the previous ones, deals with normal rules and queries, i.e. with rules and queries possibly containing negations. The standard way to evaluate normal queries wrt normal rules is by extending SLD-resolution with the following negation-as-failure rules:

not β succeeds if β fails and β is ground;
not β fails if β succeeds and β is ground;
not β flounders otherwise.

This extended SLD-resolution is usually called SLDNF-resolution [13]. We use here slightly different negation-as-failure rules by relaxing the groundness constraint:

not β succeeds with the identity substitution as answer if β fails;
not β fails if β succeeds with answer Θ and Θ is a renaming substitution;
not β flounders otherwise.

This variation, hereafter called SLDNF'-resolution, was already suggested by Kunen [12]. It can evaluate more queries than classical SLDNF-resolution, while requiring the same computational machinery. It is also more symmetric in the sense that whenever a query β fails, not β succeeds and conversely; the constraint of groundness destroys this symmetry for non-ground queries. Besides, it allows extensions of the knowledge base language with quantifiers and sets and it is actually closer to the behaviour of some Prolog systems [7].

Other rules have been proposed, as in [18], where an SLDNFS'-resolution encompasses SLDNF'-resolution. However, their interest is theoretical rather than practical since they are not computable.

The theoretical foundations of this section are mainly found in [18, 19]. The basic result for our purposes is that SLDNF'-resolution is sound for normal rules and queries wrt $(\mathcal{C}[\text{KB}], \models)$. In other words, for any query β to which corresponds a successful SLDNF'-derivation with answer Θ,

$$\mathcal{C}[\text{KB}] \models \forall^* \cdot \beta\Theta,$$

and for any query β to which corresponds a finitely failed SLDNF'-tree,

$$\mathcal{C}[\text{KB}] \models \forall^* \cdot \neg \beta.$$

The ability to make natural deduction proofs must now be extended to success and failure of normal queries wrt normal rules. Because the negation-as-failure rules transform failure in success and vice versa, the whole set of inference rules $\vdash_S \cup \vdash_F$ is needed.[6] However, it is not sufficient: a new set of inference rules ($\vdash_N$) is required to handle the failure of negations occurring in conjunctions and in isolation.

$$\frac{\forall^* \cdot \beta_1}{\forall^* \cdot \neg(\neg \beta_1 \wedge \beta_2)} \tag{9.26}$$

$$\frac{\forall^* \cdot \neg \beta_2}{\forall^* \cdot \neg(\neg \beta_1 \wedge \beta_2)} \tag{9.27}$$

$$\frac{\forall^* \cdot \beta}{\forall^* \cdot \neg\neg\beta} \tag{9.28}$$

The set of inference rules $\vdash_{NF'} = \vdash_S \cup \vdash_F \cup \vdash_N$ is sufficient to justify any successful SLDNF'-derivation and any finitely failed SLDNF'-tree in the context of normal rules and queries. In other words, for any query β to which corresponds a successful SLDNF'-derivation with answer Θ,

$$\mathcal{S}[\text{KB}] \cup \mathcal{F}[\text{KB}] \vdash_{NF'} \forall^* \cdot \beta\Theta,$$

and for any query β to which corresponds a finitely failed SLDNF'-tree,

$$\mathcal{S}[\text{KB}] \cup \mathcal{F}[\text{KB}] \vdash_{NF'} \forall^* \cdot \neg \beta.$$

The interest of these results could have been questioned by the fact that $\mathcal{C}[\text{KB}]$ may be inconsistent. Happily enough, $\mathcal{C}[\text{KB}]$ is consistent for any semi-strict knowledge base [12]. Besides, if one leaves 2-valued semantics of logic for 3-valued semantics à la Kleene, $\mathcal{C}[\text{KB}]$ is consistent for any normal knowledge base [11, 8]. In such a framework, the truth tables of the logical connectives are defined as:

$\neg$	t	f	u
	f	t	u

$\wedge$	t	f	u
t	t	f	u
f	f	f	f
u	u	f	u

$\vee$	t	f	u
t	t	t	t
f	t	f	u
u	t	u	u

$\supset$	t	f	u
t	t	f	u
f	t	t	t
u	t	u	u

$\rightarrow$	t	f	u
t	t	f	f
f	t	t	t
u	t	t	t

[6] Although these inference rules were developed for definite rules and queries, they are also sound for normal rules and queries.

One may also prefer intuitionistic derivability to classical derivability [18]. It is therefore rather interesting to observe that $(\mathcal{S}[\mathrm{KB}]\cup\mathcal{F}[\mathrm{KB}], \vdash_{NF'})$ is compatible with those various declarative characterizations of the knowledge base. Indeed, the results used here are valid in all frameworks and every inference rule of $\vdash_{NF'}$ is sound wrt 2- or 3-valued semantics and classical or intuitionistic derivability [18]. In summary, we have the following soundness relationship:

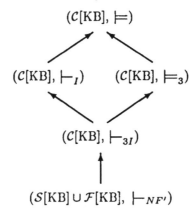

where $\models$, $\vdash_I$, $\models_3$, $\vdash_{3I}$ denote respectively the logical consequence relation in 2-valued models, the intuitionistic derivability relation for 2-valued semantics, the logical consequence relation in 3-valued models, the intuitionistic derivability relation of Shepherdson, which is compatible with 3-valued semantics.

9.4   The meta-interpreters

9.4.1   Success

The interpreter `prove_success` of Figure 9.1 evaluates a query according to the computation and search rules of Prolog (left-to-right, depth-first) and builds the corresponding proof tree according to the inference system $\vdash_S$. A *proof tree* for a formula is a tree (a) whose root node is an inference rule instance which has the formula as conclusion, and (b) whose subtrees are proof trees for the premises of the inference rule instance of the root node. The nodes of the proof tree built by the interpreter thus correspond to instances of inference rules (9.6) – (9.10) actually used to derive the query.

To each inference rule corresponds a Prolog clause of the interpreter. All Prolog variables remaining uninstantiated in the collected proof tree have to be interpreted as universally quantified. If there are several possible answers or proof trees for a successful query, they are enumerated by backtracking, just as in Prolog. KB rules defining a predicate are delivered, one at a time, by procedure `kb_axiom` which returns two copies of each rule: the first one is used to obtain the

```
prove_success( (P;Q), (P;Q) <= [Proof] )                        9.6
:- !,
   ( prove_success( P, Proof )
   ; prove_success( Q, Proof )
   ).

prove_success( (P,Q), (P,Q) <= [ProofP, ProofQ] )              9.7
:- !, prove_success( P, ProofP ),
   prove_success( Q, ProofQ ).

prove_success( true, true <= tautology )                       9.8
:- !.

prove_success( T1 = T2, T1 = T2 <= unification )               9.9
:- !, T1 = T2.

prove_success( P,  P <= [Axiom <= kb_axiom, PrBody] )          9.10
:- kb_axiom( P, (P <- Body), Axiom ),
   prove_success( Body, PrBody ).
```

Figure 9.1: Interpreter – Proof tree – Success

substitutions appearing in inference rule (9.10), the second one is used to keep an uninstantiated version of the rule as first premise of this inference rule.

As Prolog, this interpreter is sound wrt SLD-resolution. Every successful query can thus be interpreted as a theorem of $S[\mathrm{KB}]$. But, also as Prolog, due to its depth-first search rule, it is incomplete: it can enter infinite loops so that not all queries $\beta[\vec{\nu}]$ verifying assertion (9.5) can be successfully evaluated.

9.4.2   Failure

The interpreter **prove_failure** of Figure 9.2 builds a proof tree in case of failure of a query evaluation, according to the inference system $\vdash_F$. The nodes of the proof tree are instances of inference rules (9.14) – (9.25).

As in the case of success, the computation rule is that of Prolog: conjuncts are selected in left-to-right order so that inference rule (9.22) expressing the commutativity of the conjunction is not implemented in the interpreter. It is fairly easy to convince oneself that this interpreter, as Prolog, builds only one proof of the failure of a query. This is a property of the interpreter, since more than one proof can be obtained by using the inference rules $\vdash_F$. Strictly speaking, the presence of the inference rule expressing the commutativity of the conjunction makes inference rule (9.17) unnecessary from a theoretical point of view; it is however required in the interpreter in order to reproduce the left-to-right computation rule

```
prove_failure( (P ; Q), not (P ; Q) <= [ProofP, ProofQ] )              9.14
:- !, prove_failure( P, ProofP ),
   prove_failure( Q, ProofQ ).

prove_failure( ((P1 ; P2), Q), not ((P1 ; P2), Q) <= [Proof] )         9.15
:- !, prove_failure( (P1, Q ; P2, Q), Proof ).

prove_failure( ((P1, P2), Q), not ((P1, P2), Q) <= [Proof] )           9.16
:- !, prove_failure( (P1, (P2, Q)), Proof ).

prove_failure( (true, Q), not (true, Q) <=  [ProofQ] )                 9.17
:- !, prove_failure( Q, ProofQ ).

prove_failure( (T1 = T2, Q), not (T1 = T2, Q) <= [Proof] )             9.18
:- prove_failure( T1 = T2, Proof), !.

prove_failure( (T1 = T2, Q), not (T1 = T2, Q) <= [ProofQ] )            9.19
:- !, copy_term( (T1 = T2, Q), (T1P = T2P, QP) ),
   T1P = T2P,
   prove_failure( QP, ProofQ ).

prove_failure( (P,Q), not (P,Q) <= [Axiom2 <= fkb_axiom|Premise] )
:- !, failure_axiom( P, Axiom1, Axiom2 ),
   ( Axiom1 = (not P <- not Body)                                      9.20
     -> prove_failure( (Body, Q), Proof ),
        Premise = [Proof]
   ; Premise = []                                                     9.21
   ).

prove_failure( T1 = T2, not (T1 = T2) <= unification )                 9.23
:- !, \+ (T1 = T2).

prove_failure( P, not P <= [Axiom2 <= fkb_axiom|Premise] )
:- failure_axiom( P, Axiom1, Axiom2 ),
   ( Axiom1 = (not P <- not Body)                                     9.24
     -> prove_failure( Body, Proof ),
        Premise = [Proof]
   ; Premise = []                                                    9.25
   ).
```

Figure 9.2: Interpreter – Proof tree – Failure

of Prolog.

All the variables occurring in the proof tree must be universally quantified except those occurring only in the body of a failure axiom which must be quantified as shown in formula (9.11).

The procedure `prove_failure` never instantiates variables in its first argument representing the goal to be proved false; therefore, in the first clause of `prove_failure`, there is no risk of accidental instantiation of variables in Q through instantiation of corresponding variables in P during the proof of failure of *(P;Q)*.

In the clause corresponding to inference rule (9.19), the equation is first copied to keep an uninstantiated version in the proof tree. For the same reasons as procedure `kb_axiom`, procedure `failure_axiom` returns two copies of the failure axiom corresponding to a predicate.

The interpreter `prove_failure` succeeds only on failing queries; together with the interpreter `prove_success` it forms a full-fledged query evaluator which is sound wrt SLD-resolution in the context of definite rules and queries. When it terminates reporting either the success or the failure of a query, the answer may always be logically interpreted as a theorem of $\mathcal{C}[\text{KB}]$. Again, as a Prolog interpreter, it is not complete; every query satisfying assertion (9.5) or (9.13) is not necessarily evaluable by the query evaluator due to potential loops which yield infinite branches in the evaluation tree.

9.4.3 Negation

The implementation of the negation-as-failure rules to handle normal rules and queries requires adding some clauses to each part of the query evaluator. The clause of Figure 9.3, which implements the first negation-as-failure rule, must be added to the interpreter `prove_success`.

The clauses of Figure 9.4 must be added to the interpreter `prove_failure`. Again, although the inference rules $\vdash_{NF'}$ would allow more than one proof, the interpreter builds only one proof in case of failure of a negation. As shown in the first clause of Figure 9.4, inference rule (9.26) is applied when the first conjunct not β_1 fails, that is when β_1 succeeds with a renaming substitution; in this case, only the first proof built for this success is computed, this reproduces the operational behaviour of Prolog. Inference rule (9.27) is only applied when the first conjunct not β_1 succeeds (that is, when β_1 fails).

Procedure `variant` tests whether its two arguments are variants.

9.5 Conclusion

We have described inference systems which enable the construction of natural deduction proofs justifying successes and failures of query evaluation based on an extension of SLDNF-resolution. These proofs, based on a weaker form of Clark's

```
prove_success( (not P), Proof )
:- !, prove_failure( P, Proof ).
```

Figure 9.3: Interpreter – Proof tree – Negation

```
prove_failure( (not P, Q), not (not P, Q) <= [Proof] )
:- !, copy_term( P, P2 ),
   ( prove_success( P2, Proof ) ◄─────────────────────── 9.26
     -> ( variant( P, P2 ) -> true ; floundering )
   ; prove_failure( Q, Proof ) ◄─────────────────────── 9.27
   ).

prove_failure( (not P), not (not P) <= [Proof] ) ◄─────── 9.28
:- !, copy_term( P, P2 ),
   ( prove_success( P2, Proof )
     -> ( variant( P, P2 ) -> true ; floundering ) ).
```

Figure 9.4: Interpreter – Proof tree – Negation

Completed Knowledge Base, are compatible with various declarative knowledge base characterizations using 2- or 3-valued semantics and/or classical or intuitionistic derivability.

We have also described a Prolog meta-interpreter which builds proof trees which are a representation of natural deduction proofs. This meta-interpreter emulates the external behaviour of Prolog, but other behaviours may be programmed quite easily.

In a more detailed account of our work [2], we show how to allow nondeterministic Prolog evaluable literals in the KB rules, how to simplify completed definitions, and how to shorten the obtained proof trees by using derived inference rules. These proofs provide a sound foundation on which an expert system explanation facility may be developed.

References

[1] K.R. Apt, II. Blair and A. Walker, Towards a Theory of Declarative Knowledge, in: *Foundations of Deductive Databases and Logic Programming*, J. Minker (Ed.), Morgan Kaufmann Publishers, 1988, 89-148.

[2] A. Bruffaerts and E. Henin, Proof Trees for Negation as Failure or Yet Another Prolog Meta-Interpreter, Research Report, Philips Research Laboratory Brussels, January 1988.

[3] A. Bruffaerts and E. Henin, Proof Trees for Negation as Failure: Yet Another Prolog Meta-Interpreter, in: *Proceedings of the 5th International Conference and Symposium on Logic Programming*, R.A. Kowalski and K.A. Bowen (Eds), The M.I.T. Press, August 1988, 343-358.

[4] A. Bruffaerts and E. Henin, Some Claims about Effective Explanation Generation in Expert Systems, in: *Proceedings of the AAAI'88 Workshop on Explanation*, M.R. Wick (Ed.), CS Dept of University of Minnesota, August 1988, 83-86.

[5] W.J. Clancey, The Epistemology of a Rule-Based Expert System – a Framework for Explanation, *Artificial Intelligence*, **20**, 1983, 215-251.

[6] K.L. Clark, Negation as Failure, in: *Logic and Databases*, H. Gallaire and J. Minker (Eds), Plenum Press, New-York, 1978, 293-322.

[7] K.L. Clark, F.G. McCabe and S. Gregory, IC-Prolog Language Features, in: *Logic Programming*, K.L. Clark and S.-A. Tärnlund (Eds), Academic Press, New York, 1982, 253-266.

[8] M. Fitting, A Kripke-Kleene Semantics for Logic Programs, *Journal of Logic Programming*, **2**, 1985, 295-312.

[9] P. Hammond, micro-Prolog for Expert Systems, in: *micro-Prolog: Programming in Logic*, K.L. Clark and F.G. McCabe (Eds), Prentice-Hall International Series in Computer Science, 1984, 294-315.

[10] J. Jaffar, J.-L. Lassez and M. Maher, A Theory of Complete Logic Programs with Equality, *Journal of Logic Programming*, **3**, 1984, 211-223.

[11] K. Kunen, Negation in Logic Programming, *Journal of Logic Programming*, **4**, 1987, 289-308.

[12] K. Kunen, Signed Data Dependencies in Logic Programs, Computer Sciences Technical Report #719, University of Wisconsin, Madison, October 1987.

[13] J.W. Lloyd, *Foundations of Logic Programming*, Second, Extended Edition, Springer-Verlag, 1987.

[14] R. Neches, W.R. Swartout and J. Moore, Explainable (and Maintainable) Expert Systems, Proc. of the Ninth Int. Joint Conf. on Artificial Intelligence, Los Angeles, California, August 1985, 382-389.

[15] R. Reiter, On Closed World Data Bases, in: *Logic and Databases*, H. Gallaire and J. Minker (Eds), Plenum Press, New-York, 1978, 55-76.

[16] M.-C. Rousset and B. Safar, Negative and Positive Explanations in Expert Systems, *Applied Artificial Intelligence*, **1**, 1987, 25-38.

[17] J.C. Shepherdson, Negation as Failure: A Comparison of Clark's Completed Data Base and Reiter's Closed World Assumption, *Journal of Logic Programming*, **1**, 1984, 51-79.

[18] J.C. Shepherdson, A Sound and Complete Semantics for a Version of Negation as Failure, revised version of Report No. PM-88-03 School of Mathematics, University of Bristol, 1988, to appear in *Theoretical Computer Science*.

[19] J.C. Shepherdson, SLDNF-resolution with Equality, Report No. PM-88-05, School of Mathematics, University of Bristol, 1988.

[20] L. Sterling and M. Lalee, An explanation Shell for Expert Systems, Tech. Report TR-125-85, Center for Automation and Intelligent Systems Research, CWRU, Cleveland, USA, 1985.

[21] W.R. Swartout, XPLAIN: A System for Creating and Explaining Expert Consulting Programs, *Artificial Intelligence*, **21**, 1983, 285-325.

[22] A. Walker, M. McCord, J.F. Sowa, W.G. Wilson, *Knowledge Systems and Prolog*, Addison-Wesley, 1987.

[23] J.L. Weiner, BLAH, A System Which Explains Its Reasoning, *Artificial Intelligence*, **15**, 1980, 19-48.

Appendix: Example

In order to illustrate the behaviour of the interpreter `prove_failure` of Figure 9.2, we present here an example of a proof for a query which fails. The proof tree delivered by the interpreter has been post-processed so that the proof is presented in readable form. Appropriate quantification has been introduced for the variables remaining uninstantiated in the proof tree.

Assuming the following knowledge base which is borrowed from [20]:

```
pastry(Dish) <- type(Dish, cake).
pastry(Dish) <- type(Dish, bread).

type(d1, cake) <- true.    size(d1, big) <- true.
type(d2, cake) <- true.    size(d2, big) <- true.
```

the proof of failure of the query `pastry(d1), size(d1,small)` is:

```
By (9.20)  forall [A],
           not pastry(A) <- forall [B,C],
                            not ( [A] = [B], type(B, cake)
                                ; [A] = [C], type(C, bread))   [fkb axiom]
           forall [A,B],
           not (([d1] = [A], type(A, cake)   [d1] = [B], type(B, bread)),
                size(d1, small))
           => not (pastry(d1), size(d1, small))

By (9.15)  forall [A,B],
           not ( ([d1] = [A], type(A, cake)), size(d1, small)
               ; ([d1] = [B], type(B, bread)), size(d1, small) )
           => forall [A,B],
              not (( [d1] = [A], type(A, cake)
                   ; [d1] = [B], type(B, bread) ),
                   size(d1, small))

By (9.14)  forall [A],
           not (([d1] = [A], type(A, cake)), size(d1, small))
           forall [B],
           not (([d1] = [B], type(B, bread)), size(d1, small))
           => forall [A,B],
              not ( ([d1] = [A], type(A, cake)), size(d1, small)
                  ; ([d1] = [B], type(B, bread)), size(d1, small) )

By (9.16)  forall [A],
           not ([d1] = [A], type(A, cake), size(d1, small))
           => forall [A],
              not (([d1] = [A], type(A, cake)), size(d1, small))

By (9.19)  not (type(d1, cake), size(d1, small))
           => forall [A],
              not ([d1] = [A], type(A, cake), size(d1, small))

By (9.20)  forall [A,B],
           not type(A, B) <- not ( [A,B] = [d1,cake], true
                                 ; [A,B] = [d2,cake], true )   [fkb axiom]
           not (( [d1,cake] = [d1,cake], true
                ; [d1,cake] = [d2,cake], true ),
                size(d1, small))
           => not (type(d1, cake), size(d1, small))

By (9.15)  not ( ([d1,cake] = [d1,cake], true), size(d1, small)
               ; ([d1,cake] = [d2,cake], true), size(d1, small) )
           => not (( [d1,cake] = [d1,cake], true
                   ; [d1,cake] = [d2,cake], true ),
                   size(d1, small))
```

By (9.14) `not ((([d1,cake] = [d1,cake], true), size(d1, small))`
           `not ((([d1,cake] = [d2,cake], true), size(d1, small))`
           `=> not ( ([d1,cake] = [d1,cake], true), size(d1, small)`
           `       ; ([d1,cake] = [d2,cake], true), size(d1, small) )`

By (9.16) `not ([d1,cake] = [d1,cake], true, size(d1, small))`
           `=> not (([d1,cake] = [d1,cake], true), size(d1, small))`

By (9.19) `not (true, size(d1, small))`
           `=> not ([d1,cake] = [d1,cake], true, size(d1, small))`

By (9.17) `not size(d1, small)`
           `=> not (true, size(d1, small))`

By (9.24) `forall [A,B],`
           `not size(A, B) <- not ( [A,B] = [d1,big], true`
           `                      ; [A,B] = [d2,big], true )    [fkb axiom]`
           `not ( [d1,small] = [d1,big], true`
           `    ; [d1,small] = [d2,big], true )`
           `=> not size(d1, small)`

By (9.14) `not ([d1,small] = [d1,big], true)`
           `not ([d1,small] = [d2,big], true)`
           `=> not ( [d1,small] = [d1,big], true`
           `       ; [d1,small] = [d2,big], true )`

By (9.18) `not [d1,small] = [d1,big]`
           `=> not ([d1,small] = [d1,big], true)`

By (9.23) `=> not [d1,small] = [d1,big]    [by unification]`

By (9.18) `not [d1,small] = [d2,big]`
           `=> not ([d1,small] = [d2,big], true)`

By (9.23) `=> not [d1,small] = [d2,big]    [by unification]`

By (9.16) `not ([d1,cake] = [d2,cake], true, size(d1, small))`
           `=> not (([d1,cake] = [d2,cake], true), size(d1, small))`

By (9.18) `not [d1,cake] = [d2,cake]`
           `=> not ([d1,cake] = [d2,cake], true, size(d1, small))`

By (9.23) `=> not [d1,cake] = [d2,cake]    [by unification]`

By (9.16) `forall [B],`
           `not ([d1] = [B], type(B, bread), size(d1, small))`
           `=> forall [B],`
           `   not (([d1] = [B], type(B, bread)), size(d1, small))`

Chapter 10

An Integrated Interpreter for Explaining Prolog's Successes and Failures

L. Ümit Yalçinalp   *Leon Sterling*

Case Western Reserve University

Abstract

We describe a Prolog meta-interpreter which is capable of explaining Prolog's successes and failures, and enforcing a depth bound to prevent infinite computation. The program is interesting on two accounts. It is the first program which explains both successes and failures in a single meta-interpreter. Also, its development has been according to a new methodology for meta-programming which makes seemingly complicated meta-interpreters simple to understand.

Keywords: meta-interpreters, explanation systems, program composition, program enhancement

10.1 Introduction

To demonstrate that Prolog is a good language for writing rule-based expert systems, researchers have incorporated explanations within Prolog. The first account of how to extend Prolog to include explanations was given by Clark and McCabe [2]. Their approach was to modify the Prolog program constituting the knowledge base. An extra argument was added to each predicate to represent the proof tree of the predicate. Explanation of a goal was than an appropriate description of the proof tree computed when solving the goal.

Clark and McCabe's work was extended in the construction of the APES (Augmented Prolog for Expert Systems) expert system shell in micro-Prolog described by Hammond in [3]. A simple explanation capability was given extra features, such as a query-the-user [6] facility for conducting an interactive dialogue and a facility for explaining failures. Underlying APES is an appropriate interpreter.

In fact, explanations are an excellent application of meta-programming. An interpreter for explanation can be very cleanly expressed as a collection of meta-interpreters. The capabilities of APES are shown how to be written in principle in a homogeneous manner in the paper by Sterling and Lalee [10]. Similar interpreters are described by Niblett in [5] and Walker in [12].

A major weakness in the systems reported above is explaining failure. In [1, 3, 10], and [12] the interpreter for explaining failure is distinct from the interpreter for explaining success. The user must know in advance whether the goal is going to succeed or fail. If this is not known, the goal must be executed twice. Further, the treatment of failure is ad-hoc. APES explains the left-most failure, Walker chooses to explain the longest failure branch. Sterling and Lalee's interpreter [10] presents some unspecified collection of failure branches to the user. In the absence of knowing the user's intentions, we claim that it is best reproduce Prolog's behaviour.

This paper describes an integrated meta-interpreter for explaining Prolog computations. The guiding principles are integration and faithfully following Prolog. It obviates the need for separate interpreters, and mirrors the behaviour of Prolog during failure.

Besides being a technical solution to integrating successes and failures in one interpreter, this paper is an example of developing meta-programs using a methodology for meta-programming being developed by the COMPOSERS logic programming group at Case Western Reserve University. The methodology is based on enhancing and composing meta-interpreters. The rationale underlying the methodology is outlined in [4]. The underlying techniques are described in [9].

The paper is organized as follows. The next section gives our model for Prolog computations, a basic meta-interpreter reflecting that model, and three extensions, failure, findall, and query-the-user, that are simple to express in the meta-interpreter. The following section uses terminology for describing how complicated meta-interpreteres can be built from simpler pieces. It follows the treatment of [9] in describing meta-interpreters. It describes the component pieces and enhancements that we make. Finally a sample run is given followed by conclusions.

10.2   Modelling the Execution of Prolog

A good explanation system for Prolog programs should accurately mirror one's underlying model of Prolog's execution. Our view of a Prolog computation is the depth-first traversal of the search tree defined by a given query and program. Leaves of the tree are either success nodes or failure nodes. Detailed definitions of the search tree, success and failure can be found in [11]. Each time a success node is found, the computation returns the solution to the user, then waits for the user to request more solutions. This continues until the user is satisfied or there are no more solutions. If no (more) success branches are found failure is reported. An explanation system for Prolog should behave identically, but provide an explanation of the behaviour of the program instead of a 'yes' or 'no' answer.

Our basic approach to building an explanation system is to develop an appropriate meta-interpreter as described in this section. The first subsection explains what needs to be made explicit in the meta-interpreter, specifically the distinction between forward and backward failures. The following subsection introduces the basic meta-interpreter, while the third subsection shows three extensions of the basic interpreter.

10.2.1 Forward and Backward Failures

Before defining the execution model of Prolog in Prolog itself, we examine how the failures are *actually* generated. Failures in a Prolog execution can occur in two different ways.

- The first type of failure occurs at any branch of the search tree when a leaf node fails to unify (at the forward attempt to satisfy this node). Either there is no clause with the name of the predicate, or the goal does not unify with the existing clauses in the database which have the same name. This type of failure will be referred to as a *forward failure*. It can be identified immediately during Prolog execution and be represented explicitly in the search tree.

- The second type of failure occurs during *backtracking* to generate alternative/more branches to solve a specified goal. Failures during backtracking generate alternate paths. The leaf nodes of those new paths might still be success or failure nodes which can be captured explicitly. Therefore, these failures will eventually generate more solutions or exhaust the search space. The effect of these failures is therefore *implicit* and we would like to have this effect in a system simulating the Prolog behaviour. We will call these failures *backward failures* since they occur in the opposite direction in the execution, namely during backtracking on predicates which have been investigated before.

10.2.2 A Prolog Meta-Interpreter

These observations underly the Prolog interpreter *solve_goal/2* shown in Figure 10.1. Our intent is to capture Prolog's execution fully so that an explicit search tree of this execution can be generated effectively. The interpreter should be fail-safe so that no information is lost and the failures are detected or imposed

```
solve_goal(Goal,Result):-
    solve_branch(Goal,Result),
    filter_failure(Result,Goal).
solve_goal(Goal,no).

solve_branch(true,yes) .
solve_branch((A,B),Result) :-
    solve_branch(A,Result1),
    solve_conj(Result1,B,Result).
solve_branch(A,R) :- sys(A),(A → R = yes ; R = no).
solve_branch(A,no) :- not clause(A,B).
solve_branch(A,Result) :-
    clause(A,B), solve_goal(B,Result).

solve_conj(yes,B,Result) :- solve_branch(B,Result).
solve_conj(no,B,no).

filter_failure(yes,Goal).
filter_failure(no,Goal) :- fail.
```

Figure 10.1: Basic Interpreter

by the interpreter. How information from the search tree is collected is described in Section 3.

The relation *solve_goal(Goal,Result)* is true if *Result* is the result, either *yes* or *no*, of solving *Goal*. The main work of *solve_goal* is done by *solve_branch* which traverses a branch of the search tree returning *yes* if it is a success branch, and *no* if it is a failure branch. The five clauses of *solve_branch* represent five mutually exclusive cases, solving an empty goal, a conjunctive goal, a system goal, finding a failure branch and succesfully reducing a clause. Cuts may be necessary to enforce that the clauses are mutually exclusive in some Prologs.

Forward failures are captured explicitly, then, as failure branches in the tree. Getting a negative result does not ensure that there will not be (a) solution(s) in the search tree, however. Solutions might exist in the other branches which have not been investigated yet. Therefore, the interpreter should investigate alternate branches in the search tree. This is handled by forcing *solve_branch* to backtrack if *Result* is negative. This is done by *filter_failure* which filters the failures occurring during the execution until a solution is found. Otherwise, the *solve_branch* eventually fails due to backward failures by traversing the whole search tree for this goal.

To capture the result of an execution correctly, *solve_goal* should be *fail-safe*. Therefore, a negative result should be returned if the search tree is exhausted.

This is accomplished by the presence of the second clause for *solve_goal*. In this manner, this interpreter exactly imitates execution model of Prolog by explicitly defining this behaviour and it is fail-safe at the top level.

10.2.3 Extending the Meta-Interpreter

The Prolog interpreter that is given in Figure 10.1 can be extended in various ways. This is achieved by adding the appropriate clause for *solve_branch*. In this section, we give three specific examples: negation-as-failure, finding all results to a particular goal and a query-the-user facility.

The basic interpreter can be extended immediately to model negation as failure as follows:

```
solve_branch(not Goal,Not_Result) :-
    solve_goal(Goal,Result),!,
    invert(Result,Not_Result).

invert(yes,no).
invert(no,yes).
```

As can be seen easily,the behaviour of negation-as-failure is fully captured within a *single* meta-interpreter by a suitable abstraction of Prolog's execution. If a solution exists for a goal, it will be returned by *solve_goal*, which therefore indicates that the negation of this goal fails. Otherwise, if a goal fails in all possible branches of the search tree defining the goal, that indicates that the negation of the goal succeeds. It is certainly more *powerful* than separating the behaviour of Prolog to capture proof trees and failure trees by using different interpreters. Here, the behaviour is captured by *one traversal of the search tree*.

Another immediate extension to the interpreter in Figure 10.1 is to find all the solutions of a goal using *findall*. This extension can be illustrated with the following code:

```
solve_branch(findall(X,Goal,Solutions),yes) :-
    findall(R-X,solve_goal(Goal,R),Set_Sols),
    eliminate(Set_Sols,Solutions).
```

Here, all solutions of a goal will be obtained by *solve_goal* until a 'no' result is obtained for *solve_goal*. Trying to solve *solve_goal* further will result in failure. Therefore all solutions of a goal and a 'no' solution is accumulated by Prolog's findall for each term in a list of solutions given by *Set_Sols*. The predicate *eliminate* gets rid of the failure results if a solution exists from the *Set_Sols* to obtain the actual solution set for *findall*.

The interpreter in Figure 10.1 can also be extended to include facilities for querying the user about a particular predicate. We follow the approach in [10] is adopted. We assume that some predicates can be asked to the user if they can not

be solved otherwise. These predicates will be called *askable* and they are expected
to be previously defined before execution. A desirable feature of a query-the-user
facility is to minimize the number of questions asked. This requires keeping track
of user defined facts. The user defined facts might affect the behaviour of the
interpreter in two ways:

- If the predicate under investigation has been asserted previously, it is already
  known to be true. Therefore, it will be treated as a fact, a ground goal.

- If the predicate is a definition of a mutually exclusive concept (e.g. 'brand'
  of beer, 'type' of flower) and an existing fact related to such a definition
  will imply that the current predicate evaluated will be *known to be false*.
  For example, if a previous fact has been asserted to the database showing
  that a dish is type of meat, then the dish type can not be dessert, i.e. it is
  known to be false.

Otherwise, the user is asked about the predicate as shown below.

% *after the last clause for solve_goal*

```
solve_branch(A,Result) :-
    askable(A),
    investigate(A,Result).

investigate(Goal,yes):-
    known_to_be_true(Goal),!.
investigate(Goal,no) :-
    known_to_be_false(Goal),!.
investigate(Goal,Result) :-
    query_user(Goal,Result).
```

With those extensions, the basic interpreter incorporates *not, findall,* and
query-the-user facility correctly. This interpreter generates the same search tree
that a Prolog interpreter generates for finding a solution to a goal. In the next
section, we will show how this interpreter will be enhanced to become a useful
backbone of a Prolog explanation system.

10.3   Enhancing the Prolog Interpreter

The previous section introduced a meta-interpreter that mimics the Prolog's behaviour. Extra capabilities were then added. In this section, we will explore how
this interpreter can be *enhanced* to serve as an explanation system for Prolog.
    Recent research on meta-interpreters has shown how to develop a meta-inter-
preter with a particular behaviour by extensions to a basic interpreter [8, 9]. The

complicated meta-interpreter is built as separate pieces which are then composed [8, 9] into a single meta-interpreter which has the composite functionality of all the interpreters that were used. Details about composition and the terminology we use can be found in [9]. In this paper, we apply composition to build the meta-interpreter for explanation.

Deriving new programs from existing ones is carried out by a sequence of operations which preserve or extend the meaning of the existing programs, namely *modulation, enhancement* and *mutation* [9].

A program is called a modulant of another if it can be derived from the other by a sequence of unfold and abstraction transformations. That is, we can introduce a new clause to the program to group clauses together to reflect an abstraction. None of the examples in this paper use modulation.

An enhancement of a program performs the same computation as the original, but does something extra. Examples are computing an extra argument or producing a side effect such as writing to screen. The underlying computation is not changed, however.

A mutation of a program, in contrast, has a modified computation with respect to the original. It is usually accomplished by adding extra clauses to the program that alter the declarative meaning.

Our intent is to now to *change* our interpreter without essentially altering its declarative meaning. It should be able to provide an explanation mechanism for its own behaviour, which is the same as Prolog's behaviour. The basic interpreter should be modified to provide:

- **proof trees for showing success and failure branches.** If the search tree is kept correctly, then it is easy to provide an explanation depending on the model. The model is the same as Prolog's execution model, therefore we should be able to provide explanations depending on the proof trees generated by the interpreter.

- **answers to why questions.** The interpreter has the capability of querying the user, but does not have any means for justifying the reason(s) why a question was asked. Therefore, a history of the execution should be provided.

Previous research has shown that the capabilities of proof trees and rule histories for why explanations are given by straightforward **enhancements** of the basic interpreter. As illustrated in [9], we can compose interpreters that generate a proof tree for our computation with one that carries a context of the rule history, and one which can compute the depth of the tree. Related examples can be found in the same study.

We use the same approach for enhancing our interpreter. Three additional arguments, namely *Proof, History* and *Depth* have to be included in our interpreter. Each is built as a separate enhancement. To illustrate we show the enhanced clause of *solve_branch* for each.

Proof: We can easily collect the branches of the search tree with an additional argument to our interpreter. It should be noted that the collected proof tree that should be returned depends on the *Result* of the computation at a particular branch. If a goal has a solution, only the proof tree that has generated the successful result should be returned and the failure branches that have been generated so far should be discarded.

Collecting successful branches as a proof tree is straightforward and well-known and described in [11] for example. The enhanced clause of *solve_branch* is

```
solve_branch(A,Result,A-ProofB) :-
    clause(A,B),
    solve_goal(B,Result,ProofB).
```

Otherwise, the branches of the search tree which result in failure should be 'kept' until a solution is encountered. If a goal fails, all the failure branches showing the failure should be provided. Referring to the interpreter in Figure 10.1, it is clear that "a storing mechanism" is needed for keeping the branches in addition to this interpreter. An immediate enhancement will be then to produce a side effect to keep the failure branches, which can be handled by *filter_failure*. If a solution is found by *solve_goal*, then existing failure branches for this goal should be collected and discarded. The *filter_failure* goal collects those branches by using the uninstantiated copy of the goal, *Goal_Copy*, as shown in Figure 10.2. If no solution is found at all, all the failure branches should be collected. This can be handled by the last clause of *solve_goal*. The discussed effects are reflected in *solve_goal* as follows:

```
solve_goal(Goal,Result,Proof):-
    copy_goal(Goal,Goal_Copy),
    solve_branch(Goal,Result,Proof),
    filter_failure(Result,Goal,Goal_Copy,Proof).
solve_goal(Goal,no,fail(Goal,Neg_Proof)) :-
    collect_neg(Goal,Neg_Proof).
```

The proof for successes and forward failures are distinguished from backward failures by creating different structures as seen in the complete program in Figure 10.2. Indeed the distinction we drew between forward and backward failures was precisely to allow us to carry the meaning of the branches to allow the correct explanation.

History: The history, or the collection of ancestors of a goal, is needed only when the user requests justification of the reasons that a question was asked. Following the same approach as in [10], the history might be presented to the user for justification. As the user needs justification *why* a question was asked, the History argument might be presented to show the computation at each level. Therefore, adding an argument to carry a goal's history to the interpreter will enhance its behaviour. An example of such an enhancement is below:

```
solve_branch(A,Result,History) :-
    clause(A,B),
    solve_goal(B,Result,[rule(A,B)|History]).
```

Depth: A useful extension to our interpreter is to keep track of the depth of the current computation. An example of such an interpreter can be found in [7]. It is straightforward to enhance our interpreter by including an extra argument that computes the depth. This enhancement is useful to impose a depth bound cut-off for a solution. In this manner, the user can be informed whether a possible *overflow* has occurred during execution. This could be handled by indicating overflow as the *Result*. The mutated version will require changes in handling the conjunction of clauses, namely *solve_conj*, to stop the solution if a 'no' or an 'overflow' occurs. An example of such an enhancement is follows:

```
solve_branch(A,Result,Depth) :-
    Depth > 0,
    clause(A,B),
    New_Depth is Depth - 1,
    solve_goal(B,Result,New_Depth).
```

In fact clause order can be exploited to check whether the depth is zero before trying any of the other clauses. This approach is taken in the full interpreter. The resulting enhanced interpreter is presented in Figure 10.2. This interpreter can return the proof for success and failure, stops whenever the computation exceeds a limit, and carries the ancestors of a solution as a context for querying the user. It is used for running Prolog programs. We let the code speak for itself.

10.4   A Sample Run

The interpreter that was constructed in the previous sections is used as the basis of a shell for executing Prolog goals. We call this shell the *Explain* shell. Just like the command level in Prolog, the user can execute goals at the top level and the result of the execution is similar to Prolog's. In order to differentiate this shell, the command level prompt is changed to '# > 'as shown in Figure 10.3.

Figure 10.3 is an actual run of the Explain shell on a small rule based system given in [10] and [11]. It demonstrates some of its features.

The Explain shell can be used just like Prolog. However, the result of goal execution can be requested by the user for *explanation* in this shell. Therefore, the shell waits for the user prompt after every execution. This level is indicated by a "#1 >" prompt. At this instance, the user can ask for another solution or how

```
solve_goal(Goal,Result,Proof,History,Depth):-
    copy_goal(Goal,Goal_Copy),
    solve_branch(Goal,Result,Proof,History,Depth),
    filter_failure(Result,Goal,Goal_Copy,Proof).
solve_goal(Goal,no,fail(Goal,Proof_Set),History,Depth):-
    collect_neg(Goal,Proof_Set).

solve_branch(true,yes,fact,Hist,D) :- !.
solve_branch(Goal,overflow,overflow,History,0) :- !.
solve_branch(not Goal,Not_Result,Proof,History,Depth) :-
    solve_goal(Goal,Result,Goal_Proof,History,Depth),!,
    invert(Result,Not_Result,Goal,Goal_Proof,Proof).
solve_branch((A,B),Result,(ProofA,ProofB),Hist,D):-
    solve_branch(A,Result1,ProofA,Hist,D),
    solve_conj(Result1,B,Result,ProofB,Hist,D).
solve_branch(findall(X,Goal,Solutions),yes,Proof,Hist,D) :-
    findall(R-(X,P),solve_goal(Goal,R,P,Hist,D),Set_Sols),
    eliminate(Set_Sols,Solutions,Proof).
solve_branch(A,Result,sys,Hist,D) :- sys(A),(A → R = yes ; R = no).
solve_branch(A,no,not_clause-A,Hist,D) :- not clause(A,B),
    not is_askable(A),!.
solve_branch(A,Result,A-ProofB,Hist,D) :- clause(A,B), D1 is D-1,
    solve_goal(B,Result,ProofB,[rule(A,B)|Hist],D1).
solve_branch(A,Result,Proof,Hist,D) :-
    is_askable(A),
    investigate(A,Result,Proof,Hist).

solve_conj(yes,B,Result,Proof,Hist,D) :- solve_branch(B,Result,Proof,Hist,D).
solve_conj(overflow,B,overflow,unsearched,Hist,D).
solve_conj(no,B,no,unsearched,Hist,D).

invert(no,yes,Goal,Proof,not Goal-succeeds_dueto_all_fail-Proof).
invert(yes,no,Goal,Proof,not Goal-fails_due_success-Proof).

filter_failure(yes,Goal,Goal_Copy,Proof) :-
    collect_neg(Goal_Copy,Failures).
filter_failure(overflow,Goal,Goal_Copy,Proof).
filter_failure(no,Goal,Goal_Copy,Proof) :- store_neg(Goal,Proof),!,fail.

eliminate([yes-(X,Proof)|Ss],[X|Xs],[Proof|Proofs]) :-
    eliminate(Ss, Xs, Proofs).
eliminate([no-(X,Proof)], [], []).
```

Figure 10.2: Extended and Enhanced Interpreter

```
#> place_in_oven(brownies,P).
Is brownies type of cake ? yes.
Is brownies size of small ? yes.
Goal = place_in_oven(brownies,top)
1# yes ? > another.
1# no ? > whynot.
```
The goal place_in_oven(brownies,_887) fails.
Here is/are the reason(s) :

1 According to the rule :
  IF
    brownies is (a) pastry AND
    brownies is size of small
  THEN place_in_oven(brownies,top) is true...
  BUT this rule could not be proven because of the following 2 reason(s):
    1 brownies is (a) pastry fails because
    there is NO OTHER alternative solution for brownies is type of cake
    2
    According to the rule :
    IF
      brownies is type of bread
    THEN brownies is (a) pastry is true...
    BUT this rule could not be proven because
      brownies is type of bread is known to be false
⋮

4 According to the rule :
  IF
    brownies is (a) slow_cooker
  THEN place_in_oven(brownies,low) is true...
  BUT this rule could not be proven because
    According to the rule :
    IF
      brownies is type of milk_pudding
    THEN brownies is (a) slow_cooker is true...
    BUT this rule could not be proven because
      brownies is type of milk_pudding is known to be false
```
1 # no ? > next.
# > exit.
```

Figure 10.3: A sample run of a small expert system

the result is found, if the goal has succeeded. The answers given by the user are indicated by `typewriter` font in Figure 10.3. The form of 'how' explanations is exactly as in [10] and can be inferred from the format in Figure 10.3. If there is no solution, or there is no alternative solution for a solved goal, the user might wish the system to explain why a solution does not exist. This explanation is provided by parsing the branches of the search tree that have been created and collected by the *Proof* argument in the interpreter. Note that a *whynot* explanation is given both when there is no solution or when the subsequent attempt to generate an alternative solution fails. Since the search tree is kept for a goal explictly, there is no difference in explainining the behaviour of the shell, neither for both of the failure cases nor how a solution is found.

In Figure 10.3, a solution is found but the request for an alternate solution fails since such a solution does not exist. The failure branches are explained to the user in the illustrated manner. For each explanation branch, a number is provided to show the appropriate nesting. Each investigated rule in the tree is presented following the reasons why this rule could not succeed.

The Explain Shell has been tested by using small expert systems. The additional time required for obtaining missing information by querying the user, parsing the search tree and presenting the explanations changes the run time with respect to the complexity of the request. We found that explanations of whynot branches usually double the execution time due to the number of branches involved in an unsuccessful computation.

10.5   Conclusion

We have presented a new interpreter which is capable of explaining both Prolog's successes and failures. This interpreter is successively built up from a basic interpreter which has Prolog's execution model and generates the same search tree. This interpreter is further extended to encorporate additional features such as negation-as-failure, findall and query-the-user facility and enhanced to provide the exact search tree of the execution, the history and the depth of the solutions by applying program composition techniques. The resulting interpreter is the basis of an explanation shell.

What we find significant about the work is how easy it was to build a single integrated interpreter once we had a good basic language for talking about Prolog's execution model and how to construct meta-interpreters. This is in contrast to the research reported in [10] where the language was not fully developed and separate interpreters resulted. The ease of development suggests that the language for describing meta-interpreters and the associated methodology are helpful. We look forward to applying the language and methodology in future work.

Acknowledgements

This work was supported by NSF grant 1R187-03911, and facilities provided through the Center for Automation and Intelligent Systems Research. We also appreciate the contributions of the other members of the COMPOSERS group, in particular Arun Lakhotia.

References

[1] Bruffaerts A. and Henin E. *Proof Trees for Negation as failure: Yet Another Prolog Meta Interpreter*, Proceedings of the 5th International Conference and Symposium in Logic Programming, pp. 343-358, The MIT Press, 1988.

[2] Clark, K.L. and McCabe, F.G. *PROLOG: a language for implementing expert systems*, in Machine Intelligence 10 (eds. Hayes, Michie and Pao), pp. 455-470, Ellis-Horwood, 1982.

[3] Hammond, P. *micro-PROLOG for Expert Systems* in micro-PROLOG: Programming in Logic, Prentice Hall International, 1984.

[4] Lakhotia A. and Sterling L.S. Logic Program Development by Stepwise Enhancement, Tech. Report CES-88-22, Dept. of Computer Engineering and Science, Case Western Reserve University, 1988.

[5] Niblett, T. *YAPES - Yet Another Prolog Expert System*, Tech Report, TIRM-84-008, The Turing Institute, Glasgow, UK, 1984.

[6] Sergot, M.J. *A Query-the-User Facility for Logic Programming*, Integrated Interactive Computer Systems, Ed. P. Degano and E. Sandewall, North Holland, 1983.

[7] Shapiro E.Y. *Algorithmic Program Debugging* MIT Press, 1983.

[8] Sterling, L.S. and Beer, R.D. *Meta-Interpreters for Expert System Construction*, J. of Logic Programming, 1989 (to appear), also CAISR TR 151-86, Case Western Reserve University, 1986.

[9] Sterling L.S. and Lakhotia A. *Composing Prolog Meta Interpreters*, Proceedings of the 5th International Conference and Symposium in Logic Programming, pp. 386-403, The MIT Press, 1988.

[10] Sterling, L.S. and Lalee, M. *An Explanation Shell for Expert Systems*, Computational Intelligence, pp. 136-141, 1986.

[11] Sterling, L.S. and Shapiro, E.Y. *The Art of Prolog*, MIT Press, 1986.

[12] Walker, A., McCord, M., Sowa J., and Wilson W. *Knowledge Systems and Prolog*, Addison-Wesley, 1987.

Chapter 11

Tracing Requirements for Multi-layered Meta-programming

Andrew Bowles   *Paul Wilk*

*Department of Artificial Intelligence and
Artificial Intelligence Applications Institute,
University of Edinburgh*

Abstract

This paper discusses the requirements for a programming methodology often used in Artificial Intelligence (AI) which we call Multi-layered Meta-programming. In this methodology, rather than implementing a solution in some base language, layers of high level languages are rapidly designed and implemented through experimental AI programming. The approach has the special characteristic that any one of the levels in the hierarchy may have to be modified at any time during development. Often the only way to unravel the complexities of a design change or identifying a bug in these many layered systems is through applying conventional debugging strategies; which are inadequate for the task. So, in this work we discuss alternative approaches to the problem and give our views on what we perceive to be the implementation requirements for multi-layered tracing and debugging. These requirements have been formed from hard experience gained through having to apply ad-hoc debugging strategies. The hooks for a multi-view tracer are described which have been tested in the ongoing development of applications to develop and test the instrumentation of a Parlog interpreter written in Prolog.

11.1   Introduction

A programming methodology often used in Artificial Intelligence (AI), as well as in other fields, is *stratified* or *layered* design. When faced with a problem, rather than implementing a solution directly in some base language, a new, more appropriate, higher level language is designed in which to express a solution, and this is implemented in the base language. This methodology can have several iterations yielding as a final solution a hierarchy of different languages each more appropriate to expressing the solution than the language below. The resulting solution is easier to comprehend, modify and re-use.

This approach is of course not new; it is the methodology supported by languages which encourage the use of procedural abstraction and abstract data types. What is different in AI is the extent to which the language levels are different from the ones below. A typical example of the use of abstract data types is implementing a set as a list which is in turn implemented as a chain of pointers. Each of these levels in the hierarchy use the same language constructs and control structure as the one below and can be viewed simply as enhancements to the abstract machine with which you are programming. The sort of hierarchies used in AI, however, can have completely new abstract machines at each level which only inherit various convenient primitive operations, such as unification, rather than the control structure of the underlying language.

There is the problem of how to implement such hierarchies of languages. One possible solution is to implement the system bottom up and only move up a level when you are satisfied with the correctness of the current level. This approach is not appropriate to AI because in AI the design will typically change as the programmer gains a greater understanding of the overall problem; it is necessary to be able modify any part of the hierarchy at any time. Also, having to wait for a complete implementation of a lower level before beginning to program a higher level is not appropriate to the rapid prototyping development methodology, used in AI, where the emphasis is on developing solutions to problems quickly so that implementation experiments may be carried out at minimum cost.

The 'concurrent' implementation of the hierarchy, however, leads to other programming problems caused by the conceptual complexities of dealing with several different languages in one stratified program. To find a bug that is potentially anywhere in the hierarchy it would seem inefficient to pick some arbitrary level at which to apply conventional debugging strategies and hope for the best. Since we cannot rely on the absolute correctness of any level in the hierarchy a debugging strategy will have to support controlled moves between the different levels. In the general case the ability to debug all levels simultaneously seems to be required.

We believe the above discussion motivates the need for tracers which can provide different levels of trace corresponding to the different language levels in the program, and which enable the user to switch between these different traces interactively.

In this paper we show the need for a system hook with which to build such multi-view tracers. The paper is organised as follows. Firstly, we describe the built in tracers typically provided in current Prolog environments. Secondly, we show how a multi-view tracer might work. Next, since current systems do not support tracer building directly we show the techniques used in building tracers.

These techniques can be incorporated into the system level as a 'hook' from which to hang different tracers. We then consider the implications of a system hook for building our multi-view trace and conclude that, really, a system hook needs to be incorporated at every level in a language hierarchy. We have implemented a simple multi-view trace based on this.

11.2 Built-in Tracers in Prolog environments

Tracers are designed around a 'story' of Prolog execution[Pain & Bundy 87]. A story is an account of the workings of a Prolog system used to explain and predict a program's behaviour. Ideally a story should cover all the mechanisms in a system; a user should not need to resort to different stories to explain all the details of a program. A tracer does not necessarily use all the details that a story might provide; all that is needed is an explanation of the control flow of Prolog execution. The way this is usually described is in terms of ports. A port is an entry or exit place of the control flow into or out of a predicate invocation. A tracer simply produces some behaviour, such as printing a message, whenever execution passes through a port. You can treat ports as the 'significant events' in the execution of a Prolog program just as function call and return are the significant events in Lisp execution. The standard trace of execution is expressed in terms of a four-port model [Byrd 80], where the ports are named call, fail, succeed (or exit) and redo. There are other alternatives, such as three and seven port models [Clark & McCabe 84, Plummer 86].

Typically, all Prolog implementations provide the programmer with a tracer. The usual execution models used are based on the four-port model, from the original DEC10 Prolog system [Bowen 81], with surprisingly few variations. A noteable exception is the Transparent Prolog Machine [Eisenstadt & Brayshaw 86]. The tracer typically provides a set of commands that enables the output to be controlled interactively. For example, the skip command suppresses all trace output until program execution next passes through a port of the current predicate invocation.

The built in tracer is usually the only one that the system supports directly; there is no way in which a user may switch to using a different tracer which might provide a more useful output. Tracers are treated as an integral part of the system and are not available for user inspection and alteration.

Built in tracers do, however, provide some facilities for 'programming' so that a more desirable trace output can be generated. Firstly, spy points can be placed on specific predicates so that only these predicates are mentioned in the trace output. In some systems, such as [Int86], extra conditions can be placed on spy points so that only invocations of spied predicates that satisfy these conditions are mentioned. Secondly, the trace messages are produced using the print system predicate, and so they may be pretty printed using the portray facility. The TPM system provides facilities for altering the trace display[Brayshaw & Eisenstadt 88] but it is unclear how powerful these facilities are.

11.3   A Multi-view Trace

We presented the need for multi-view tracers in the introduction. Here we illustrate what features a multi-view trace might provide by using a concrete example of a language hierarchy used in Edinburgh as part of research into evaluating different CCND logic languages and their appropriateness to various AI programming techniques [Trehan & Wilk 88, Pinto 87]. There are three different language levels, illustrated in Figure 11.1.

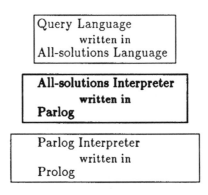

Figure 11.1: Example of a language hierarchy

In this language hierarchy it is valid to trace on any of the three program and language combinations (boxes in Figure 11.1) that the hierarchy contains depending on the circumstances. Each of these traces are different views of the execution of the same overall program. For example, when explaining the workings of the all solutions language a trace of the execution of an example query executed by the all solutions interpreter is required. Similarly, if the implementation of the Parlog interpreter is to be debugged, a trace of the Prolog system executing the Parlog interpreter is required. When using a multi-view trace we require the ability to see all these different levels.

The execution model used by each view is dependent on the language level the view is tracing. Also the commands defined by each view for controlling its own output interactively will use some control language most appropriate to the execution model, and so the commands will typically change between each view. Each view must provide its own facilities for querying the user and interpreting any answers in its own terms, though clearly every view cannot be querying the user simultaneously. Thus the different views are largely independent of each other because each displays a different execution model, but they must communicate to some extent to ensure the correct interpretation of control commands.

11.4 Implementing Tracers

Tracers can be imagined to work using the following model. During an object level program's execution, messages are passed to the tracer as significant events such as procedure calls and returns occur. The tracer interprets these messages in some suitable way and produces appropriate behaviour. The tracer cannot affect the execution of the object program by binding variables, though it can using side effects or by forcing fails. Also, the monitoring tool doesn't necessarily run concurrently with the program; the messages can be buffered and interpreted at any time.

There are two possible ways of implementing such a scheme. Both involve adding extra code to the system but in different places. The following two sections briefly describe each alternative.

11.4.1 Adding Code to the program

The trace code, which performs the output and querying operations, can be added to the program at the places where 'significant events' occur. This technique will be familiar to anyone who has inserted print statements into their programs to display the values of variables. Using operations such as Prolog's assert and retract the extra trace code can be added and removed automatically rather than by editing code directly. The Edinburgh Prolog toolkit contains two tools, namely the advice package and a run time mode checker that perform this type of operation, but both change the code quite drastically [Bowles 88, Bowles & Wilk 88]. The technique of adding extra code to a program is known as *code wrapping*. Code wrapping has problems:

- The code that a user sees in a listing does not correspond to that in the editor. This might cause some confusion.

- Since the code in the clause is altered, assert and retract do not work as normal on a wrapped predicate. Similarly, system predicates cannot be wrapped.

- Several code wrapping tools cannot be used in combination since each has no knowledge of what other extra code might already be in wrapped around predicates in the database.

However certain uses of code wrapping, those that simply add code rather than alter it, seem reasonable when implementing rudimentary traces. For example, if you are only interested in the details of one particular procedure, building a tracer by adding a few print statements around the uses of that procedure seems the most straight forward method, especially as the overheads of running a full tracer are avoided. Notice that such uses of code wrapping assume that printing primitives are available in the language. The query language in the example above is a language which might not have these facilities.

11.4.2   Adding Code to the Interpreter

The alternative to code wrapping is to supplement the interpreter that executes the program with the extra trace code.

```
% Standard pure Prolog interpreter.
interp(true).
interp((G1,G2))     interp(G1), interp(G2).
interp(G) :- before(G), clause(G,B), interp(B), after(G).

% before/1 models the call and fail ports.
before(G) :- write('call '), write(G), nl.
before(G) :- write('fail '), write(G), nl, fail.

% after/1 models the succeed and redo ports.
after(G) :- write('succeed '), write(G), nl.
after(G) :- write('redo '), write(G), nl, fail.
```

Figure 11.2: Pure Prolog tracer for four port box execution model

To illustrate, Figure 11.2 shows the usual pure Prolog interpreter modified to convert it to produce a standard four port trace during program execution. Clearly, more complex trace code is needed to provide an interactive tracer with the usual facilities provided in a built-in tracer.

Both of the above alternatives share the following problem. To produce a behaviour in terms of some execution model of a program the ports must be explicit in the program. It is impossible to implement a seven port box model trace for Prolog [Plummer 86], where the extra ports show details of the attempts at finding a clause head to match against, by either code wrapping or by supplementing the simple interpreter given above because the details of the attempted head matches are not explicit in either the program or the interpreter.

We concentrate on building tracers by supplementing interpreters rather than by using code wrapping because, for the exhaustive traces that are typically required for a language, it is more applicable.

11.5   A trace hook in a Prolog system

As mentioned earlier, the main problem with built-in tracers is that they form an integral part of the Prolog system and can only be programmed in limited ways. Therefore they do not form a good basis on which to implement a multi-view trace as described above.

```
interp(true).
interp((G1,G2)) :- interp(G1), interp(G2).
interp(G) :- before(G), clause(G,B), interp(B), after(G).

before(G) :- tracehook(call,G).
before(G) :- tracehook(fail,G), fail.

after(G) :- tracehook(succeed,G).
after(G) :- tracehook(redo,G), fail.

% tracehook/1 calls the (user defined) trace code.
% The fail is needed to avoid unwanted instantiations.
tracehook(Port,Message) :- tracecode(Port,Message), fail.
tracehook(Port,Message).
```

Figure 11.3: A tracer with a programmable trace hook

We believe that there is a need for a trace 'hook' in Prolog environments to allow user defined tracers to be implemented. The tracer in Figure 11.2 can be extended to illustrate how a system hook could be added to many Prolog systems. Figure 11.3 shows the tracer with appropriate modifications. Imagine this to be the interpreter of the Prolog system (or a model of the execution of the compiled code), except that the predicate tracecode/2 is a normal user predicate and clauses for it can be asserted and retracted under user control. Figure 11.4 shows trace code which implements the same tracer as Figure 11.2.

A trace hook such as this allows a separation of concerns between writing an interpreter for a language and writing the tracer for it. The interface (that is a set of ports) provided by the trace hook can be decided at an early stage

```
tracecode(Port,Message) :-
    write(Port), write(' '), write(Message), nl.
```

Figure 11.4: Example code to implement a four-port execution model

in implementation since it is dependent on the language not on that language's implementation. Given the trace hook interface, the trace builder is free to implement any tracer that is needed without having to go back into the system level, or to re-implement an entire interpreter. The process would be even easier if the built-in trace were provided in the Prolog library so that the programmer could make use of any useful predicates that it defines.

11.6   Implementing a multi-view tracer

Of course, this tracer will be for Prolog. In a multi-view tracer we wish to be able to build tracers for every language in the hierarchy, not just for Prolog; which would be the bottom level. Following on from our earlier point concerning the need for events to be explicit, to be able to trace them, it seems unlikely that we will be able to implement a tracer targeted at a different language in terms of the significant events (that is ports) of the underlying Prolog execution, and so the Prolog trace hook does not seem adequate for implementing a full multi-view tracer.

This suggests the need for each level in a language hierarchy to have its own trace hook. As illustrated, implementing a trace hook is a simple matter of altering an interpreter by adding code at the places where significant events occur. Figure 11.5 shows part of a simple Parlog interpreter written in Prolog with a three port tracer hook. These ports show the successful and suspended Parlog reductions. Figure 11.6 shows some example trace code to implement a simple Parlog trace.

In all our examples Prolog has been used to illustrate the implementation of a trace hook. As we have described them so far, a trace hook at one language level is implemented by adding code to the interpreter for that language written in the language of the next lower level in the hierarchy. To implement a trace hook on the all solutions language in our example, so that, say, explanation facilities can be implemented, it is necessary to add a trace hook call to the all solutions interpreter in Parlog, and write the explanation code also in Parlog.

Clearly, it would be better to have all the trace code for the entire hierarchy written in the same language, in this case Prolog. This would maximise the reuseability of the trace code. This requires each interpreter in the hierarchy to be able to 'drop down' into Prolog. The same effect can be achieved by ensuring each language in the hierarchy can drop down into the one below. Whether this is possible, or desirable, in all languages is not clear.

We have implemented a simple multi-view tracer for our example hierarchy using the techniques described.

```
% Parlog interpreter in Prolog giving a Parlog trace hook with ports
% showing attempted reduction, successful reduction and suspension. The
% interpreter does not detect deadlock nor deal with negation
parloginterp(Goal) :-
   makequeue(Goal,Queue), solve(Queue).

solve(Queue) :- isemptyqueue(Queue).
solve(Queue) :-                           % mapqueue applies each item
   mapqueue(trytoreduce,Queue,NewQueue),  % in Queue to trytoreduce
   solve(NewQueue).                       % and merges the results to
                                          % make NewQueue

trytoreduce(Goal,Body) :-
   tracehook(attemptreduce,Goal),
   maketemplate(Goal,Template),
   parlogclause(Template,Guard,Body),     % pick up a clause.
   checkmodes(Goal,Template),             % unify Goal to Template.
   parloginterp(Guard),
   tracehook(succeedreduce,Body).
trytoreduce(Goal,Body) :-
   tracehook(suspend,Goal).

tracehook(Port,Message) :- tracecode(Port,Message), fail.
tracehook(Port,Message).
```

Figure 11.5: The top level predicates in a Parlog interpreter with a tracer hook

11.7 Summary and Further Issues

We have illustrated the usefulness of trace hooks so that user defined tracers may
be easily constructed. A multi-view tracer has been used to illustrate this point.
We believe a multi-view tracer is a useful tool when developing layered programs
using a 'concurrent' development methodology and that designing such a tracer
and its trace hooks is a good first step during implementation. This should be
investigated further in real programming situations, perhaps using languages other
than Prolog as a base.

If a language interpreter has a trace hook then various tools other than tracers
can also be implemented:

- Tools which check some property of a program dynamically. For example,
  one way to catch possible infinite loops is to have a depth bound on the
  number of recursions. A tool to spot potential infinite recursions would

```
tracecode(attemptreduce,Goal) :-
   write('try reduce '), write(Goal), nl.
tracecode(succeedreduce,Body) :-
   write('reduced to '), write(Body), nl.
tracecode(suspend,Goal) :-
   write(suspended), nl.
```

Figure 11.6: Example code for a Parlog trace which displays attempted reductions

ensure that this limit has not been reached at every procedure call.

- Tools which gather statistics about a running program. To check that hashing on the first argument is effective, an instrumentation tool which records the percentage of procedure calls which have their first argument instantiated could be used.

We have concentrated on language hierarchies built out of interpreters. The programming task at each level other than the topmost level is to construct an interpreter for the language of the level above in terms of the language of the level below. In general, a level might also consist of a compiler or make use of conventional procedural and data abstraction techniques. These levels will also need to support a trace hook system.

Acknowledgements

The authors would like to thank Rajiv Trehan. The first author is supported by the British Science and Engineering Research Council under a Research Studentship.

References

[Bowen 81]   *DECSystem-10 Prolog User's Manual.* Department of Artificial Intelligence, University of Edinburgh, 1981. Available as Occasional Paper No 27.

[Bowles & Wilk 88]   A. W. Bowles and P. F. Wilk. *Some Design Principles for Prolog Support Environments.* Technical Report AIAI-TR-35, Artificial Intelligence Applications Institute, University of Edinburgh, 1988.

[Bowles 88]   A. W. Bowles. *Enhancing Prolog Programming Environments.* Project Report AIAI-PR-16, Artificial Intelligence Applications Institute, University of Edinburgh, 1988. Also, Dept. Artificial Intelligence, University of Edinburgh, MSc Thesis 1987.

[Brayshaw & Eisenstadt 88] M. Brayshaw and M. Eisenstadt. *Adding Data and Procedure Abstraction to the Transparent Prolog Machine.* Technical Report 31, HCRL, Open University, 1988. Submitted to 5th Int. Logic Programming Conf. Seattle.

[Byrd 80] L. Byrd. Understanding the Control Flow of Prolog Programs. In S. Tarnlund, editor, *Logic Programming Workshop 80*, pages 127–138, Debrecen, Hungary, 1980.

[Clark & McCabe 84] K. L. Clark and F. G. McCabe. *micro-Prolog: Programming in Logic.* Prentice Hall, 1984.

[Eisenstadt & Brayshaw 86] M. Eisenstadt and M. Brayshaw. *The Transparent Prolog Machine TPM.* Technical Report 21, Human Cognition Research Laboratory, The Open University, 1986. Also in Journal of Logic Programming,1988.

[Int86] *IF/Prolog version 3.1.0 Reference Manual.* InterFace GmbH, Munich, 1986.

[Pain & Bundy 87] H. Pain and A. Bundy. What stories should we tell novice Prolog programmers? In R. Hawley, editor, *Artificial Intelligence Programming Environments*, chapter 6, pages 119–130, Ellis Horwood, 1987.

[Pinto 87] H. Pinto. *Implementing Meta-Interpreters and Compilers for Parallel Logic Languages in Prolog.* Project Report AIAI-PR-14, Artificial Intelligence Applications Institute, University of Edinburgh, 1987.

[Plummer 86] D. Plummer. *SODA: Screen Oriented Debugging Aid.* Software Report 3, Department of Artificial Intelligence, University of Edinburgh, 1986.

[Trehan & Wilk 88] R. Trehan and P. F. Wilk. *A Parallel Chart Parser for the Committed Choice Non-Deterministic (CCND) Logic Languages.* Technical Report AIAI-TR-36, Artificial Intelligence Applications Institute, University of Edinburgh, 1988. Also: Department of Artificial Intelligence, University of Edinburgh, Research Paper-366. To be presented at: 5th Int. Logic Programming Conf. Seattle.

Chapter 12

The Compilation of Forward Checking Regimes through Meta-Interpretation and Transformation

Danny De Schreye   *Maurice Bruynooghe*

Department of Computer Science
Katholieke Universiteit Leuven

Abstract

We present a technique for the transformation of declarative generate-and-test programs into equivalent programs (computing the same sets of answer substitutions) following a forward checking control regime. The technique is composed of an initial transformation on the logic component of the program in order to add information regarding the domains of variables. Then, abstract meta-interpretation is used to simulate and explore the computational flow that the transformed program would have under a forward checking control rule. Finally, from the trace of this meta-interpretation a new program is synthesized.

12.1 Introduction

Pure Horn clause logic programming takes a special place among programming languages. It is not merely a complete programming language, with the full capabilities of any Turing machine, but it can also be considered as a general purpose theorem prover. A problem domain can be specified in terms of Horn clauses and the system can be asked to deduce answers to queries concerning the domain.

Initially, this second use for the language was strongly promoted and the declarativity of pure logic programming was considered as its highest asset. However, the standard depth-first, left-to-right computation rule of Prolog is not sufficiently powerful to support the specificational approach. Following the *Algorithm = Logic + Control* equation of Kowalski [Kowalski '79], different methods were designed to allow special control rules to be added to declarative logic programs, in order to improve the efficiency of the theorem provers search. These methods can be classified into three main groups.

A first one promotes the use of meta-interpreters to guide the computation (e.g. [Gallaire,Laserre '82], [Pereira '84], [Safra,Shapiro '86]). The main advantage of this approach is that there are practically no limitations to the type of control rules that can be enforced on the initial program. A major drawback is that the overhead caused by the additional layer of interpretation significantly reduces the ultimate gain in efficiency. So, in practice, the main use for this method lies in rapid prototyping and in the exploration of large search spaces with more advanced control rules (e.g. constraint satisfaction problems).

A second approach to the separation of logic and control is the introduction of Prolog-variants, including special language features for the specification of control rules (e.g. [Clark et al '82], [Colmerauer '82], [Genesereth,Ginsberg '85], [Naish '85]). Here, the theorem prover is no longer restricted to the depth-first, left-to-right control rule, but will select a goal and clause for further resolution based on the control declarations of the programmer and on the computational status of the programs execution.

In a third method, the control of programs is changed through transformation (e.g. [Burstall,Darlington '77], [Gregory '80], [Narain '86], [Sato,Tamaki '84], [Gallagher '86], [Bruynooghe et al '86]). This method has the advantage of producing the most efficient programs, because the actual selection of a goal and clause are no longer determined at run-time. On the other hand, the synthesis step involved is usually much more complicated and hard to automate. The main reason is that with this method, the information on the actual combinations of goals that will occur at run-time is not available. Thus, it is no longer a simple matter of using the computation rule to select among goals. The type of actions that will have to be taken at run-time must now be predicted at compile-time, using only the source code and the computation rule. This is the reason why several new transformation methods are based on:

- an preliminary phase of meta-interpretation, to gather information on the type of computation that may be expected under the new control rule.

- abstract interpretation; since the information gathered through meta-interpretation should not describe the execution of one single concrete query, but of all possible queries of interest.

In [Gallagher '86], [Gallagher,Codish '87], [Bruynooghe et al '86], [De Schreye,Bruynooghe '88] and [De Schreye,Bruynooghe '89], hybrid methods based on meta-interpretation, abstract interpretation and program synthesis were proposed. The first two aim at the specialization of pairs consisting of a program and a meta-interpreter, the others at the compilation of coroutining regimes for generate-and-test programs. In both cases, the synthesis results in a meta-program, in which the predicates of the initial program obtain the status of both functors and predicates.

In this paper, we describe an extension and application of the hybrid transformation scheme proposed in [Bruynooghe et al '86]. Where this method was originally developed to enforce coroutining on generate-and-test programs using *instantiation based computation rules* (see [De Schreye,Bruynooghe '89]), we here extend it to support transformations leading to more sophisticated control structures. For constraint satisfaction problems, the efficiency of a coroutining regime cannot compete with some of the more advanced control algorithms, such as forward checking, looking ahead and intelligent backtracking. The enforcement of these control structures on logic programs has been studied both through meta-interpretation and by means of Prolog-variants [Van Hentenryck '87]. Here we will demonstrate, how the transformation technique in [Bruynooghe et al '86] can be extended to enforce a forward checking behavior on a given generate-and-test program as well.

Our method can be split up into two components. Informally stated, the first one is dealing with some initial considerations on the specification of the logic component for a given search problem, the second with enforcing a new control rule on the logical specification. The paper is organized accordingly. The second section introduces a first step in the transformation scheme. It presents a uniform way of specifying generate-and-test programs that allow the generation of solutions starting from predefined domains. In the third section we recall some basic facts and features of the transformation method presented in [Bruynooghe et al '86]. Section four describes how forward checking can be imposed on the domain version of the program. This is a direct application of the compilation of control presented in [Bruynooghe et al '86]. We end with a discussion on potential extensions of the method.

12.2   Specification of the logic component

Here, we illustrate how a minimal module with special library predicates can be provided, so that programs generating values from predefined domains can be described in a declarative way and so that they are ready to be used as input for a second transformation step, focussing on control. In our solution, special care has been taken of the selection of an appropriate representation for domains. For this specific application, this representation must allow both the generator and test predicates to update the contents of the domain. Furthermore, these updates should remain completely transparent to the user. The programmer should only be confronted with the problem of specifying a correct generate-and-test program for the problem at hand. The management of domains is left to the implementation of the library. In this sense, this initial step can also be regarded as a first transformation. Adding the semantics of the library predicates converts the logic component from a general generate-and-test specification to a program with domain-generation.

The solution we suggest, consists of two extra predicates:

- *create_dom/3* : allows the programmer to specify the domain from which a given variable should be selected. Its arguments are

  1. arg1: an atom uniquely identifying the domain (this is only essential when variables are generated from different domains during one program),

  2. arg2: either a predicate which can be called to compute the domain, or true,

  3. arg3: either a variable occurring in arg2 that will contain the domain after successful termination of a call to arg2, or a term (the - fixed - domain),

- *select_from_dom/2* : assigns an arbitrary value from the domain identified by its first argument to the variable in its second argument.

As an example for the entire technique, both in this section and the next, we discuss the N_queens problem. With the library predicates described above, a declarative generate-and-test program, with integrated domains, is:

Queens(_n, _q):-
          create_dom(queens, Gendom(_d, _n), _d),
          Gen(_n, _q), Safe(_q).

Gendom(nil, 0) .
Gendom([_n|_d], _n):-
          _n > 0, _m is _n -1, Gendom(_d , _m).

Gen(0, nil).
Gen(_n, [_h|_t]):-
          _n > 0, _m is _n - 1,*select_from_dom***(queens, _h),**
          Gen(_m , _t).

Safe(nil).
Safe([_x]).
Safe([_x, _y|_z]):-
          N_attack(_x, 1, [_y|_z]), Safe([_y|_z]).

N_attack(_x, _t,nil) .
N_attack(_x, _t, [_y|_z]):-

Test(_x, _t, _y), _s is _t + 1, N_attack(_x, _s, _z).

Test(_x, _t, _y):-
    diff(_y , _x + 0), diff(_y , _x + _t), diff(_y , _x - _t).

Observe that the program merely differs from a classical N_queens generate-and-test version through its calls to the two library predicates. No further references to domains are made and the programmer is not confronted with any considerations regarding their use throughout the computation.

The way in which they will be used is made explicit by the definitions for the library predicates:

create_dom(_id, _proc, _d1):-
    call(_proc), real_create(_d1, _d2),
    retractall(dom(_id, _)), assert(dom(_id, _d2)), !.

real_create(nil , nil).
real_create([_h|_t], [(_h,_)|_t1]):-
    real_create(_t , _t1) .

select_from_dom(_id, (_n , _d)) :-
    dom(_id, _d), member((_n,1), _d).

member(_x , [_x|_t]) .
member(_x , [_y|_t]):-
    member(_x , _t) .

The predicate *create_dom* starts by building the domain (which we assume to be a list of values) using the procedure _proc. It proceeds by converting the domain into a special representation. This is performed by the predicate real_create/2, which constructs a new list where each member is a couple consisting of a domain value and an associated free variable. At runtime, these variables will be allowed to obtain either the value 0 (meaning that this value is no longer selectable for the corresponding domain variable) or 1 (indicating that the domain variable has now obtained this value). The procedure terminates by asserting this new representation for the domain. The non-deterministic procedure *select_from_dom* starts by recollecting a copy of the asserted domain. It does not associate a simple domain value to its second argument, as might be expected by the programmer. Instead, it instantiates the second argument to a couple, consisting of a selectable domain value (the next member of the domain that does not have a 0 associated to it) and the domain itself. This make the domains available for possible updates in the test predicates if (later on) a forward checking control regime is imposed.

The program which we obtained is certainly no more efficient than any other generate-and-test program for N_queens. On the contrary, due to the more complicated data structures, this program is rather slow. However, its form is very suitable for transformation towards a forward checking regime. As a final preparation of this transformation, it must be specified which calls in the testing part require a forward checking behavior and how this forward testing should be performed. This is done through a third library predicate:

- *forward/1* : declares that the call arg1 (which is assumed to be a call to a builtin test predicate) should be executed in a forward checking manner.

In our example, all calls to diff/2 should be replaced by corresponding calls to forward(diff/2). Also a forward version of the builtin diff/2 should be provided. An example of how this could be done is listed below.

```
forward(diff( (_a, _), ( _b , _) + _t )):-
    ground(_a), ground(_b), !, _a ≠ _b + _t .
forward(diff( (_a, _d1), (_b, _) + _t )):-
    ground(_b), !, _s is _b + _t, fordiff( _d1, _s).
forward(diff ( (_a, _), (_b, _d2) + _t)):-
    ground(_a), _s is _a - _t, fordiff( _d2, _s).
forward(diff( (_a, _d1), (_b, _d2) - _t)):-
    forward(diff( (_b, _d2), (_a, _d1) + _t)).


fordiff( nil , _ ).
fordiff( [(_x,_y)|_tail], _s):-
    (_x = _s , !, _y = 0 ; fordiff( _tail, _s) ).
```

As an example of how these predicates will be used, suppose that (as in the 3-Queens problem) the initial value for the domain is [3,2,1]. The predicate real_create/2 converts the representation of the domain to [(3, _), (2, _), (1, _)]. Since the second library predicate *select_from_dom/2* instantiates its second argument to a term of type (_n, _dom), calls to forward(diff/2) will allways be of the type:
?- forward(diff((_n1, [(3, _), (2, _), (1, _)], (_n2, [(3, _), (2, _), (1, _)]+_t)).
If the program above is executed following the standard computation rule, then _n1, _n2 and _t will all be ground (integers) at the time of the call to forward(diff/2). This implies that under the standard computation rule only the first and the fourth clause for forward(diff/2) will be used. In particular, the clauses for fordiff/2 will never be activated. However, in section 12.4 we will specify and compile a computation rule such that at the time of any call to forward(diff/2) either _n1 or _n2 is uninstantiated. Assume that _n1 = 3, _n2 is free and _t = 1. Due to the call to ground/1, the query above can only succeed with the third clause for forward(diff/2) and it gives rise to a new call:

?- fordiff([(3, _), (2, _), (1, _)] , 2).

This call instantiates the second argument of the second member in the list to 0, indicating that the domain value 2 is no longer selectable for the corresponding domain variable.

12.3 Compiling control

The remainder of our technique is a direct application of the hybrid transformation method described in [Bruynooghe et al '86]. Therefore, it seems appropriate to recall some facts from that paper.

Suppose that a highly declarative - but inefficient - Horn clause program is given, together with a special computation rule for this program. The method aims at synthesizing a new Horn clause program from these two, which has the same computational behavior (same branchings and unifications) under the standard computation rule as the old program under the special rule.

In order to obtain this, first, the behavior of the old program under the special rule has to be explored. Furthermore, we are not interested in its behavior for a specific query, but for an entire class of queries for which we want the transformation to be correct.

This part of the technique is achieved through abstract meta-interpretation. A general abstract meta-interpreter was built, which allows a user to specify the query patterns of interest and offers him the possibility of selecting, from each state obtained during the computation, the abstract subgoal that should be further expanded. One abstract resolution step is performed with the selected subgoal and a new state is achieved.

If a selected subgoal is not in need of coroutining (if it behaves sufficiently efficient under the standard computation rule), this information can be specified as well. In this case, the abstract interpretation module computes all abstract output patterns for the goal and applies the resulting abstract substitutions to the remaining goals in the state to obtain all descendent states.

As an easy example, consider the following clauses for the Permutation-sort program.

Sort(_x, _y):- Perm(_x, _y), Ord(_y) .

Perm(nil,nil).
Perm([_x|_y],[_u|_v]):- Del(_u,[_x|_y], _w), Perm(_w, _v) .

Del(_x,[_x|_y], _y).
Del(_x,[_y|_u],[_y|_v]):- Del(_x, _u, _v) .

Ord(nil).
Ord([_x]).

Ord($[\_x, \_y | \_z]$):- $\_x \leq \_y$, Ord($[\_y | \_z]$) .

For this program, a interesting class of queries can be specified through the abstract pattern Sort(G, V_1), where G is a notation for any ground term and $V_i, i \in \aleph_0$, is a notation for a free variable. With a special computation rule which differs only from the standard computation rule in its eagerness to expand subgoals of type Ord(G) and Ord($[G, G | V_i]$), we get the abstract trace described in Fig.1. At each resolution step, the resulting abstract substitution is denoted as a label on the arc. In the trace, each goal of type Del($V_i, [G | G], V_j$) was completely (and abstractly) solved using the standard computation rule.

In a second phase, a new program is synthesized that will perform the same computations at run time as the ones displayed in the abstract trace. The basic principle for this step is that a transition such as:

state S_2 : $Perm(G, V_1), Ord(V_1)$

leads to

state S_4 : $Del(V_2, [G | G], V_4), Perm(V_4, V_3), Ord([V_2 | V_3])$,

with abstract substitution $G := [G | G]$ and $V_1 := [V_2 | V_4]$, can be synthesized with the new clause:

Perm($[\_x | \_y], [\_u | \_v]$), Ord($[\_u | \_v]$):-
    Del($\_u, [\_x | \_y], \_w$), Perm($\_w, \_v$), Ord($[\_u | \_v]$).

However, since this is not a Horn clause, meta-predicates are required. A finite set of new predicates are assigned to the states in the trace and Horn clauses of the type:

P(Perm($[\_x | \_y], [\_u | \_v]$), Ord($[\_u | \_v]$)):-
    Q(Del($\_u, [\_x | \_y], \_w$), Perm($\_w, \_v$), Ord($[\_u | \_v]$)).

are derived. Observe that the predicates of the old program now occur as functors in the new one. This is only an illustration of the easiest case. In many transformation sessions, states occur with a continuously changing number of subgoals. In such examples it is necessary to gather the predicates of the old program into lists and to represent them as members of a list-argument in the predicates of the new program. This may be thought of as a list of predicate calls of a same type that will have to be processed in sequence. Examples of such lists are presented in the N_queens transformation of section 12.4.

If the selected goal was completely solved using the standard computation rule, we generate clauses of the type:

Q(Del($\_u, [\_x | \_y], \_w$), Perm($\_w, \_v$), Ord($[\_u | \_v]$)):-
    Del($\_u, [\_x | \_y], \_w$),

R(Perm($\_w$, $\_v$), Ord($[\_u|\_v]$)).

where the solved subgoal is repeated in the body of the new clause.

With this method and using a powerful partial evaluator based on the information gathered in the abstract interpretation, we obtain the new program:

Sort_new(nil,nil).
Sort_new($[\_x|\_y]$,$[\_u|\_v]$):-
    Del($\_u$, $[\_x|\_y]$, $\_w$),
    P(Perm($\_w$, $\_v$), Ord($[\_u|\_v]$)).

P(Perm($[\_x|\_y]$,$[\_u|\_v]$), Ord($[\_z, \_u|\_v]$)):-
    Del($\_u$, $[\_x|\_y]$, $\_w$),
    $\_z \leq \_u$,
    P(Perm($\_w$, $\_v$), Ord($[\_u|\_v]$)).
P(Perm(nil,nil), Ord($[\_z]$)).

Up till now, the method was designed to enforce a coroutining behavior based on an instanstiation based selection of the subgoals. In the next section, we show how it can also be used to enforce more advanced control rules.

For more details on the method we refer to [Bruynooghe et al '86], on correctness and completeness to [De Schreye,Bruynooghe '89], on the modules for abstract interpretation to [De Schreye,Bruynooghe '88] and on the scheme for partial evaluation to [De Schreye,Bruynooghe '87].

12.4 Synthesis of a forward checking program

What remains to be done is the specification of the class of queries of interest and of a forward checking control rule for the N_queens problem. The method described in the previous section can then be activated to generate a new program.

In the example, the queries of interest are '?- Queens($\_n$, $\_q$)', with $\_n$ ground and $\_q$ a free variable. With the notation of section 12.3: '?- Queens(G, V_1)'.

Precisely as for Permutation_sort, the control rule should again coincide with the standard computation rule, except for its eagerness to expand or solve subgoals of certain types. Using one additional constant, **Dm**, in our abstract notation to denote lists of (partially instantiated) couples - the domains -, these subgoals are:

- Safe($[(G, Dm), (V_i, Dm)|V_j]$) : expand,

- N_attack($((G, Dm), G, [(V_i, Dm)|V_j]$) : expand,

- Test($(G, Dm), G, (V_i, Dm)$) : solve.

The special symbol **Dm** is not needed within the transformation, but is merely used to reduce the size of the terms. With this computation rule, the abstract trace is built. A segment of that trace is drawn is Fig.2. In order to make a further reduction in the size of the picture, we have only drawn a segment of one branch of the abstract trace tree. Also, both the subgoals that are completely solved using the standard computation rule (e.g. Test((G, Dm, G, (V_{10}, Dm)), V_{12} is G) and the abstract substitutions (e.g. $V_{12} := G$) are represented as labels on the arcs. The selected subgoals are denoted in italic (e.g. *Queens*(G, V_1)).

Observe how in an initial phase of the interpretion (1) a call to *select_from_dom* is completely solved (both dom(G, V_6) and Member((V_5, G), Dm) are executed following the stardard computation rule). The position of the first queens is determined. Later on (2), for the second call select_from_dom(G, V_7), dom(G, V_{11}) is still completely solved but the call to Member((V_{10}, G), Dm) is suspended. It means that we generate the shape of the domain for the second queen, but we postpone the action of assigning it a position (V_{10} remains uninstantiated). Instead, we wait until a call to Test((G, Dm), G, (V_{10}, Dm)) eliminates certain values from the domain Dm of V_{10}, through the assignment of zero's to certain uninstantiated variables in Dm (see fordiff/2). Then we select a value for V_{10} from the remaining domain values.

Starting from this trace tree, the synthesis algorithm of [De Schreye,Bruynooghe '89] generates the following new program:

```
Queens_new(_n, _q):-
      Create_dom(queens, Gendom(_d, _n), _d),
      Q_Gen(Gen(_n, _q),[Safe(_q)],nil,nil).

Q_Gen(Gen(_n,[_h|_t]), _s1, _s2, _n_att):-
      _n > 0,
      Q_Sum_Test([Gen(_m, _t)], _s1,[Select_from_dom(queens, _h)],
      _m is _n - 1, _s2,nil,nil,nil,nil,_n_att,nil).
Q_Gen(Gen(0,nil),nil,[_s],nil):-
      Q_Safe2(_s).
Q_Gen(Gen(0,nil),nil,[_s],[_h_att|_t_att]):-
      Q_N_attack2([_h_att|_t_att], _s).

Q_Sum_Test([_gen], _s1,[_sel], _m is _k - _1,
_s2,nil,nil,nil,nil, _n_att,nil):-
      _m is _k - _1,
      Q_Select_from_dom(_gen, _s1, _sel, _s2, _n_att).
Q_Sum_Test(nil,nil,nil, _m is _k + _1,[_h_s|_t_s],[_gen],[_mem],[_n_att1],
[Test((_a , _doma), _k,(_b , _domb))],[_h_att2|_t_att2], _n_att3):-
      _m is _k + _1,
      Test((_a , _doma), _k,(_b , _domb)),
      Q_N_attack1(_gen, _mem,[_h_att2|_t_att2],
      nil,[_h_s|_t_s],[_n_att1|_n_att3]).
```

Q_Sum_Test(nil,nil,nil, _m is _k + _1,[_s],[_gen],[_mem],[_n_att1],
[Test((_a , _doma), _k,(_b , _domb))],nil, _n_att2):-
    _m is _k + _1,
    Test((_a , _doma), _k,(_b , _domb)),
    Q_Safe1(_gen, _mem, _s,[_n_att1|_n_att2]).
Q_Sum_Test(nil,[_s],nil, _m is _k + _1,nil,[_gen],[_mem],[_n_att1],
    [Test((_a , _doma), _k,(_b , _domb))],nil, _n_att2):-
    _m is _k + _1,
    Test((_a , _doma), _k,(_b , _domb)),
    Q_Member(_gen, _mem, _s,[_n_att1|_n_att2]).

Q_Select_from_dom(_gen,nil,Select_from_dom(_id, (_a , _dom)),
[_h_s|_t_s],[_h_att|_t_att]):-
    dom(_id, _dom),
    Q_N_attack1(_gen,Member((_a , 1), _dom),
    [_h_att||_t_att],nil,[_h_s|_t_s],nil).
Q_Select_from_dom(_gen,nil,Select_from_dom(_id, (_a , _dom)),[_s],nil):-
    dom(_id, _dom),
    Q_Safe1(_gen,Member((_a , 1), _dom), _s,nil).
Q_Select_from_dom(_gen,[_s],Select_from_dom(_id, (_a , _dom)),nil,nil):-
    dom(_id, _dom),
    Q_Member(_gen,Member((_a , 1), _dom), _s,nil).

Q_Member(_gen,Member(_a , _doma), _s, _n_att):-
    Member(_a , _doma),
    Q_Gen(_gen,nil,[_s], _n_att).

Q_Safe1(_gen, _mem,Safe([(_a,_doma), (_b,_domb)|_other]), _n_att):-
    Q_N_attack1(_gen, _mem,[N_attack((_a , _doma),1,[(_b,_domb)|_other])],
    [Safe([(_b,_domb)|_other])],nil, _n_att).

Q_N_attack1(_gen, _mem,[N_attack((_a,_doma), _n, [(_b,_domb)|_other])
|_t_att1], _s1, _s2, _n_att2):-
    Q_Sum_Test(nil, _s1,nil, _m is _n + 1, _s2,[_gen],[_mem],[N_attack((_a , _doma),
    _m, _other)], [Test((_a , _doma), _n,(_b , _domb))], _t_att1, _n_att2).

Q_N_attack2([N_attack(_, _,nil)], _s):-
    Q_Safe2(_s).

Q_N_attack2([N_attack(_, _, nil), _n_att|_t_att], _s):-
    Q_N_attack2([_n_att|_t_att], _s).

Q_Safe2(Safe([_x])).

In this program, one new predicate is generated to represent all the states
in the trace from which a same type of subgoal (same predicate and same in-

stantiation pattern) was selected. The names of the new predicates were selected accordingly. Each clause reexpresses a unification which was also present in one of the clauses of old program (and for that same selected subgoal). In addition, each new clause has a number of arguments containing a bookkeeping on the remaining types of goals that may be present if the computation selects this clause. The final call in the body of each clause expresses which is the next action (subgoal selection) that has to be performed. Observe that all goals that were solved using the standard computation rule in the abstract trace are repeated as calls in the body of the new clauses. This implies that the definitions for these predicates have to be copied from the old program to the new one.

Because the program is a result of an automated synthesis, it is particularly well suited to be optimized through partial evaluation. In [De Schreye,Bruynooghe '87] we proposed a scheme for the partial evaluation of programs of this type. It stresses the importance of the detection of an initialization step in the programs execution. To the abstract trace of Fig.2, we can associate a flowchart containing the sequences of clauses from the old program that were consecutively expanded or solved. The initial subsequences of this flowchart which have only been passed through a finite number of times are classified as initialization. For N_queens, this leads to the following two initialization clauses:

Queens_new(_n, [(_a, _dom)]):-
    create_dom(queens, Gendom(_d, _n), _d),
    _n > 0,
    0 is _n - 1,
    dom(queens, _dom),
    Member((_a, 1), _dom).

Queens_new(_n, [(_a, _doma), (_b, _domb)|_tq]):-
    create_dom(queens, Gendom(_d, _n), _d),
    _n > 0,
    _m is _n - 1,
    dom(queens, _doma),
    Member((_a, 1), _doma),
    _m > 0,
    _k is _m - 1,
    dom(queens, _domb),
    Q_Sum_Test(nil,[Safe([(_b, _domb)|_tq])]),nil, _p is 1 + 1,nil,
    [Gen(_k, _tq)],[Member((_b, 1), _domb)],[N_attack((_a, _doma), _p, _tq)],
    [Test((_a, _dom),1,(_b, _domb))],nil,nil).

The main advantage of this step is that a number of clauses (Queens_new, second clause for Q_Gen, second and third clause for Q_select_from_dom) may be eliminated from the program, since they are only activated during the initialization. The remainder of the partial evaluation phase is quite similar to the method of [Gallagher,Codish '87]. All loops in the flowchart with the clauses expanded from the old program are cut in such a way that a minimal number of clause sequences are obtained. The main difference with [Gallagher,Codish '87] is that we do not cut on branching points, but only on those nodes of the flowchart were multiple paths produce a call to the same predicate. This leads to a final set of clauses (in addition to the initialization and the clauses for Test, Member, create_dom, and Gendom):

Q_Sum_Test(nil,nil,nil, _k is _m + _n,[_hs|_ts],[_gen],[_mem],[_N_att1],[Test((_a , _doma), _m,(_b , _domb))],[N_attack((_c,_domc), _p, [(_d, _domd)|_other])|_t_att2], _n_att3):-
 _k is _m + _n,
 Test((_a , _doma), _m,(_b , _domb)),
 Q_Sum_Test(nil,nil,nil, _q is _p + 1,[_hs|_ts],[_gen],[_mem],[N_attack((_c , _domc), _q, _other)], [Test((_c , _domc), _p,(_d , _domd))], _t_att2,[_N_att1|_n_att3]).
Q_Sum_Test(nil,nil,nil, _k is _m + _n,[Safe([(_a, _doma), (_b,_domb)|_other])], [_gen],[_mem],[_n_att1],[Test((_c , _domc), _m,(_d , _domd))],nil, _n_att2):-
 _k is _m + _n,
 Test((_c , _domc), _m,(_d , _domd)),
 Q_Sum_Test(nil,[Safe([(_b,_domb)|_other])],nil, _q is 1 + 1,
 nil,[_gen],[_mem], [N_attack((_a , _doma), _q, _other)],[Test((_a ,
 _doma),1,(_b , _domb))],nil,[_n_att1|_n_att2]).
Q_Sum_Test(nil,[_s],nil, _k is _m + _n,nil,[Gen(_p,[(_a, _doma)|_t])],
[Member(_x, _domx)], [N_attack((_b , _domb), _r,[(_c,_domc)|_other])],
[Test((_d , _domd), _m,(_e , _dome))],nil, _n_att):-
 _k is _m + _n,
 Test((_d , _domd), _m,(_e , _dome)),
 Member(_x, _domx),
 _p > 0,
 _q is _p - 1,
 dom(queens, _doma),
 Q_Sum_Test(nil,nil,nil, _t is _r + 1,[_s],[Gen(_q, _t)],[Member((_a , 1), _doma)],
 [N_attack((_b , _domb), _t, _other)],[Test((_b , _domb), _r,(_c , _domc))], _n_att,nil).
Q_Sum_Test(nil,[_s],nil, _k is _m + _n,nil,[Gen(0,nil)],[Member(_x, _domx)],
[_n_att1], [Test((_b , _domb), _m,(_c , _domc))],nil, _n_att2):-
 _k is _m + _n,
 Test((_b , _domb), _m,(_c , _domc)),
 Member(_x, _domx),
 Q_N_attack2([_n_att1|_n_att2], _s).

Q_N_attack2([N_attack(_, _,nil)], Safe([_x])).
Q_N_attack2([N_attack(_, _, nil), _n_att|_t_att], _s):-
 Q_N_attack2([_n_att|_t_att], _s).

12.5 Discussion

The transformation method of [Bruynooghe et al '86] was developed to compile instantiation based computation rules for given declarative generate-and-test programs. Forward checking is not a computation rule. Our contribution in this paper is to provide an initial transformation on the logic component of such generate-and-test programs, so that forward checking for the original program can be achieved through executing the second program under an instantiation based computation rule.

The specification of that computation rule can easily be automated. A test which is declared as forward checkable in the second program should be eager for activation as soon as all but one of the domain variables in its arguments have obtained a value and all of the domain variables have obtained a description of the domain.

The applicability of the method is not restricted to forward checking. Other control regimes used for constraint satisfaction problems (e.g. looking ahead) can equally well be compiled with the same method.

In some respects the method compares favourably to the technique of [Van Hentenryck '87]. It does not require a special Prolog variant. In [Van Hentenryck '87] the domain-manipulation predicates are implemented as builtins, where as our method uses a library of such predicates. Secondly, in the technique of [Van Hentenryck '87] the forward checking control is provided at run time (it uses a variant of MU-Prolog), where as in our method, it is compiled. Correspondences are that in both techniques the problem is split up into augmenting the original specification with domain manipulation and controling the extended specification. A drawback of the method presented here, is that our implementation of the domain is not as efficient as the one used in [Van Hentenryck '87], which is closely related to techniques used in linear programming.

Our plans for further work in this field are to investigate whether similar solutions can be found using representations for the domains which are more efficient than the lists of couples we have used here. We also want to replace the initial phase of adding the library predicates by an actual transformation of the old program. In this transformation, domains should be integrated as additional arguments into the predicates of the old program. We hope that this will not only eliminate the need for 'assert' in our method, but that we can also support a more efficient generation of values from the domain (e.g. in many application - among which N_queens - two domain variables are not allowed to obtain the same value).

12.6   References

[Bruynooghe et al '86] Bruynooghe M., De Schreye D. and Krekels B., Compiling Control, Proc.Third International Symposium on Logic Programming, 1986, pp. 70-78, revised version in J.Logic Programming, 1988.

[Burstall,Darlington '77] Burstall R.M. and Darlington J., A transformation system for developing recursive programs, JACM, 24, 1977, pp. 44-67.

[Clark et al '82] Clark K.I., McCabe F.G., Gregory S., IC-Prolog language features, Logic programming, ed. Clark/Tarnlund, 1982, pp. 254-266.

[Colmerauer '82] Colmerauer A., Prolog II, manuel de reference et modele theoretique, Marseille, 1982.

[De Schreye,Bruynooghe '87] De Schreye D., Bruynooghe M., On the transformation of logic programs with instantiation based computation rules, Technical report CW55, dept. computer science, K.U.Leuven, Belgium, 1987.

[De Schreye,Bruynooghe '88] De Schreye D., Bruynooghe M., An application of abstract interpretation in source level program transformation, Proc. of the International Workshop on Programming Language Implementation and Logic Programming, 1988, Orleans.

[De Schreye,Bruynooghe '89] De Schreye D., Bruynooghe M., On the transformation of logic programs with instantiation based computation rules, J.Symbolic Computation, to appear.

[Gallagher '86] Gallagher J., Transforming logic programs by specializing interpreters, Proc. 7th European conference on Artificial Intelligence, 1986, pp. 109-122.

[Gallagher,Codish '87] Gallagher J., Codish M., Specialisation of Prolog and FCP programs using abstract interpretation, in Proceedings of the workshop on partial evaluation and mixed computation, 1987, Denmark.

[Gallaire,Laserre '82] Gallaire H. and Laserre C., A control meta language for logic programming, in *Logic Programming*, eds. Clark L. and Tarnlund S.A., Academic Press, 1982, pp. 173-185.

[Genesereth,Ginsberg '85] Genesereth M.R. and Ginsberg M.L., Logic Programming, CACM 28(9), Sept. 1985, pp. 933-941.

[Gregory '80] Gregory S., Towards the compilation of annotated logic programs, Res.Report DOC80/16, June 1980, Imperial College.

[Kowalski '79] Kowalski R.A., Algorithm = logic + control, CACM 22(7), July 1979, pp. 424-436.

[Naish '85] Naish L., Automating control for logic programs, J. Logic Programming 2, 1985, pp. 167-183.

[Narain '86] Narain S., A technique for doing lazy evaluation in Logic, J.Logic Programming 3 (3), 1986, pp. 259-276.

[Pereira '84] Pereira L.M., Logic control with logic, in Implementations of Prolog, ed. Cambell, Ellis, Horwood, 1984, pp.177-193.

[Safra,Shapiro '86] Safra S., Shapiro E., Meta-interpreters for real, in Proceedings of IFIP, 1986.

[Sato,Tamaki '84] Sato T., Tamaki H., Transformational logic program synthesis, FGCS '84, Tokyo, 1984.

[Van Hentenryck '87] Van Hentenryck P., Consistency techniques in logic programming, Ph.D. thesis FUNDP, Namur, Belgium, 1987.

Chapter 13

Using Safe Approximations of Fixed Points for Analysis of Logic Programs

Michael Codish   John Gallagher   Ehud Shapiro

The Weizmann Institute of Science

Abstract

In this paper we apply the result that when using abstract interpretation for program analysis, we do not necessarily need to compute an abstract least fixed point, or indeed any fixed point of the abstract semantic function. Any meaning which is a safe approximation of the least fixed point can give useful information. In particular, the sequence of meanings obtained by applying the semantic function iteratively to the top element of the domain yields safe approximations, since this sequence approaches the greatest fixed point from above. The framework of the technique is first defined, and its advantages and disadvantages discussed.

Two applications of the technique for the parallel logic programming language Flat Concurrent Prolog (FCP) are presented. The mode analysis application is based on a collecting semantics for SLD derivations, and has been incorporated in a compiler for FCP. The suspension analysis application is the first attempt, to our knowledge, to apply abstract interpretation to analyse reactive aspects of a parallel programming language.

13.1   Introduction

Abstract interpretation of a program computes an abstract program meaning, which can be computed finitely, but which yields approximate information about the behaviour of the program. A systematic treatment of abstract interpretation

in the framework of logic programming can be found in [9], [3] or [7]; we summarise
here the main points of the theory of abstract interpretation.

Cousot and Cousot [4] describe in their seminal paper on abstract interpretation several ways of approximating the fixed points of abstract semantic functions.
They note that if the least fixed point is unreachable then some upper bound of
the least fixed point may be computed instead, since this will also fulfill the correctness requirements. They show that descending sequences starting from an
upper bound can be used to approximate the abstract meaning.

However, applications of abstract interpretation to analysis of logic programs
[2], [16], [9], [5] have concentrated on computing a least fixed point abstract meaning, although Bruynooghe [3] notes that any fixed point will also do as an abstract
meaning. In this paper we present applications of abstract interpretation which
exploit the fact that not only any fixed point but also any upper bound of the
least fixed point will do. In the next section we present the definitions and main
results which are needed, and we discuss the notion of "safe approximation". In
Section 13.3 we briefly discuss the semantics of Flat Concurrent Prolog. Sections
13.4 and 13.5 contain examples of applications, mode analysis and suspension
analysis of Flat Concurrent Prolog programs. For each example, a method for
computing a sequence of increasingly precise safe approximations is defined, based
on an abstract domain and semantic function.

13.2   Abstraction and Approximation of Program Meaning

Program Meanings and Collecting Semantics

Assume that the standard meaning of logic programs can be formulated as a
mapping:

$$[\![\cdot]\!]_{std} : Prog \to Calls \to 2\ Values$$

That is, given a program from *Prog* and an initial call from *Calls*, the set of
results the program may compute is a set of elements from *Values*. The meaning
of a program P is defined as the least fixed point of some continuous iteration
function:

$$\mathcal{F}_P : (Calls \to 2\ Values) \to (Calls \to 2\ Values)$$

$$[\![P]\!]_{std} = lfp(\mathcal{F}_P)$$

The purpose of static analysis is to derive information about possible runtime behaviours of a program. Furthermore, it should derive information about
possible behaviours at specific points in the program. A typical analysis may
derive all possible values of a certain variable or all ways in which a program part
may be called. The formal treatment of static analysis requires a semantics in
which it is possible to reason about sets of computations and to associate program
points with denotations (i.e. elements of 2 *Values*).

Collecting Semantics:

Program points are associated with denotations using *environments*. An environment is a set of pairs of the form $\langle p, v \rangle$ where p is a program point and $v \in 2\ Values$ is a denotation. The set of all such pairs $\langle p, v \rangle$ is denoted by Env. We construct a function:

$$[\cdot]_{env} : Prog \rightarrow Calls \rightarrow 2\ Env$$

such that for a program P and an initial call c, $[P]_{env}(c)$ yields an environment recording program points encountered during a computation with their associated denotations.

Collecting semantics is then obtained by lifting $[\cdot]_{env}$ to account for sets of computations:

$$[\cdot]_{coll} : Prog \rightarrow 2\ Calls \rightarrow 2\ Env$$

$$[P]_{coll}(C) = \bigcup_{c \in C} [P]_{env}(c)$$

Note that by choosing the initial set of calls to be a singleton, we can simulate the standard semantics by taking the denotation at some program point designated as final.

In this paper we will use entities similar to *minimal function graphs* [10], [25] to represent environments. In this approach denotations are associated with program points using a partial function from program points to denotations. This function is minimal in the sense that for a given set of initial calls it only assigns denotations to program points that arise in computations of those initial calls. In the applications we shall see the structure of minimal function graphs in more detail.

As with the standard semantics, the meaning of a program P with the collecting semantics is defined as the least fixed point of some continuous iteration function:

$$\mathcal{F}_P : (2\ Calls \rightarrow 2\ Env) \rightarrow (2\ Calls \rightarrow 2\ Env)$$

If the set of initial calls $c \in 2\ Calls$ is fixed, we obtain a continuous function, $\mathcal{F}_{P,c} : 2\ Env \rightarrow 2\ Env$, whose least fixed point is the set of program points and associated denotations for any computation starting with an element of c. In this paper we define semantics by giving this function $\mathcal{F}_{P,c}$.

Abstract Interpretation and Safe Approximation

DEFINITION **13.2.1.** *abstract interpretation*
   Given a cpo $(Val, \sqsubseteq_{con})$ and a meaning function

$$[\cdot]_{con} : Prog \rightarrow Val$$

which we call the concrete domain and semantics, an abstract interpretation is defined by:

- *A cpo $(AVal, \sqsubseteq_{abs})$ (which we call the abstract domain).*

- *A pair of monotonic abstraction and concretisation functions $\alpha : Val \rightarrow AVal$ and $\gamma : AVal \rightarrow Val$ such that for any $x \in Val$ and $\chi \in AVal$, $x \sqsubseteq_{con} \gamma(\alpha(x))$ and $\chi = \alpha(\gamma(\chi))$.*

- *A mapping h which maps each subsidiary function $f : Val\ n \rightarrow Val$ in the definition of $[\![\cdot]\!]_{con}$ to an abstract function $f' = h(f)$, $f' : AVal\ n \rightarrow AVal$ such that for every $\bar{\chi} \in AVal\ n$, $f(\bar{\gamma}(\bar{\chi})) \sqsubseteq_{con} \gamma(f'(\bar{\chi}))$ where $\bar{\gamma}$ is the pointwise extension of γ to $AVal\ n$.*

Replacing each f in $[\![\cdot]\!]_{con}$ by $h(f)$ gives an abstract meaning function:

$$[\![\cdot]\!]_{abs} : Prog \rightarrow AVal$$

We sometimes say that $[\![\cdot]\!]_{abs}$ is an abstraction of $[\![\cdot]\!]_{con}$ and then refer to the implicitly defined α, γ and h.

In general, the abstract meaning of a program is less precise than the concrete meaning. An important property of abstract interpretation is that of *safety*. The abstract meaning of a program will always be a *safe approximation* of the concrete meaning.

DEFINITION **13.2.2**. *safe approximation*
   Given two meaning functions:

$$[\![\cdot]\!]_1 : Prog \rightarrow Val_1 \quad \text{and} \quad [\![\cdot]\!]_2 : Prog \rightarrow Val_2$$

and a monotonic mapping $\gamma : Val_2 \rightarrow Val_1$ we say that $[\![\cdot]\!]_2$ is a safe approximation of $[\![\cdot]\!]_1$ iff for all programs P, $\quad [\![P]\!]_1 \sqsubseteq_1 \gamma([\![P]\!]_2)$

PROPOSITION **13.2.3**. *If $[\![\cdot]\!]_1$ is an abstraction of $[\![\cdot]\!]_2$, then $[\![\cdot]\!]_1$ is a safe approximation of $[\![\cdot]\!]_2$.*

PROOF.
   Standard (see for example [4]).   □

This is the central result of abstract interpretation. It means that we may form abstractions of the collecting semantics which yield sound information about the runtime behaviour of programs. The safety condition states that concrete meaning of a program is "smaller than" ($\sqsubseteq_{con}$) the concretisation of the abstract meaning of the program. Moreover, abstract interpretation may terminate where the concrete interpretation does not.

When the concrete semantics is the collecting semantics, the notion of "smaller than" is set inclusion; that is, abstract interpretation may yield a larger set of possible values than actually occur in concrete computations.

The theory of abstract interpretation shows that abstract interpretations are safe approximations. In this paper we exploit the fact that there are other ways of constructing safe approximations to the collecting semantics.

Safe Approximation of Fixed Points

Program analysis based on abstract interpretation involves computation of least fixed points. We demonstrate that program analysis based on safe approximations does not necessarily require the computation of a least fixed point, albeit at the price of accuracy.

Recall that the least fixed point of a continuous function f on a lattice $(\mathcal{D}, \sqsubseteq)$ may be computed as the limit of the ascending Kleene sequence

$$\bot, f(\bot), \ldots, f\ n(\bot), \ldots$$

where $\bot$ is the least element of the lattice. Likewise, if $\top$ is the top element of the lattice, the decreasing Kleene sequence

$$\top, f(\top), \ldots, f\ n(\top), \ldots$$

approaches the greatest fixed point from above.

OBSERVATION 13.2.4. *For any n, m and continuous function f*

$$\bot \sqsubseteq f\ n(\bot) \sqsubseteq \mathit{lfp}(f) \sqsubseteq \mathit{gfp}(f) \sqsubseteq f\ m(\top) \sqsubseteq \top$$

PROPOSITION 13.2.5. *Let $[\![\cdot]\!]_{con} : Prog \rightarrow Val$ and $[\![\cdot]\!]_{abs} : Prog \rightarrow AVal$ be semantic functions over domains $(Val, \sqsubseteq_{con})$ and $(AVal, \sqsubseteq_{abs})$ respectively such that:*

- $[\![\cdot]\!]_{abs}$ *is an abstraction of $[\![\cdot]\!]_{con}$, and $\gamma : AVal \rightarrow Val$ is the corresponding concretisation function.*

- *For $P \in Prog$, $\mathcal{F}_P : Val \rightarrow Val$ and $\mathcal{AF}_P : AVal \rightarrow AVal$ are continuous functions such that $[\![P]\!]_{con} = \mathit{lfp}(\mathcal{F}_P)$ and $[\![P]\!]_{abs} = \mathit{lfp}(\mathcal{AF}_P)$.*

and for $0 \leq j \leq \omega$ let $[\![\cdot]\!] \downarrow j_{abs} : Prog \rightarrow AVal$ be the function defined by $[\![P]\!] \downarrow j_{abs} = \mathcal{AF}_P\ j(\top)$, for every $P \in Prog$.

Then for all j, $[\![\cdot]\!] \downarrow j_{abs}$ is a safe approximation of $[\![\cdot]\!]_{con}$.

PROOF.

For every $0 \leq j \leq \omega$ and $P \in Prog$, $lfp(\mathcal{F}_P) \sqsubseteq_{con} \gamma(lfp(\mathcal{AF}_P)) \sqsubseteq_{con}$ $\gamma(\mathcal{AF}\ j_P(\top))$ (from Observation 13.2.4, monotonicity of γ and the fact that $[\![\cdot]\!]_{abs}$ is an abstraction of $[\![\cdot]\!]_{con}$). $\square$

Application to Program Analysis

The result above suggests program analysis algorithms which construct a decreasing sequence of abstract program meanings. A descending Kleene sequence may be constructed, using the abstract semantic function starting with the greatest abstract meaning. Any member of this sequence, being a safe approximation of the concrete meaning, can be used for program analysis.

One advantage is that useful non-optimal results may be obtained quickly before the fixed point is reached. By contrast, if the abstract meaning is computed using an increasing sequence, the fixed point must be reached in order to ensure a safe result. Another possible advantage is that the sequence may converge towards the greatest fixed point faster than the the usual increasing sequence converges to the least fixed point. (This is the case in the mode analysis example below.) The disadvantage is that sometimes the greatest fixed point may not be precise enough to be useful.

13.3   Flat Concurrent Prolog

In this section we present SLD derivations for (definite clause) logic programs, and an informal presentation of collecting semantics for the parallel logic programming language, Flat Concurrent Prolog (FCP). The terminology used here, where not defined, follows Lloyd [14].

SLD Computation Trees

DEFINITION 13.3.1.   *Given a logic program P and initial goal G, the full SLD computation tree is defined as follows:*

1. *The root of the computation tree is labelled by G.*

2. *Each non-leaf node of the computation tree is labelled by a goal $\leftarrow A_1, ..., A_n$ and each leaf node is labelled by the empty goal (called true) or fail.*

3. *An internal node labelled by $\leftarrow H_1, ..., H_k$ has a successor labelled G iff G is obtained by resolving $\leftarrow H_1, ..., H_k$ on some literal H_j with some program clause C. fail is a successor iff $\leftarrow H_1, ..., H_k$ cannot be resolved with any clause.*

In a full SLD computation tree all literals in a goal are resolved upon. This should be distinguished from the SLD-tree for $P \cup \{G\}$ via R, as defined by Lloyd, where a computation rule R is used which selects one literal from each goal.

Flat Concurrent Prolog

The language FCP is described in [19]. The main feature to be noted in this context is presence of *read-only variables*, which are annotated by '?' ('X?'); other variables are called *writable*. Read-only variables are used to synchronise dataflow during program execution. Operationally, an attempt to bind a read-only variable $(X?)$ to a nonvariable term during unification does not succeed but rather suspends until a binding is made to a writable occurrence of the variable (X). Here we define the unification of a set of terms to succeed or fail and indicate suspension by annotating the resulting substitution. An attempt to bind a read-only variable, $X?$ to a non variable term T is recorded in the unifying substitution to indicate the requirement that X be bound to T via a writable occurrence. For example, the terms $T_1 = f(X?)$ and $T_2 = f(a)$ unify with substitution $(X? \mapsto a)$ indicating that the unification succeeds and the restriction that X is previously bound to a.

DEFINITION **13.3.2.** *read-only variables and substitutions*

- *Let Var be a set of variables, called writable variables. Let Var? = $\{X? \mid X \in Var\}$ and $Var_? = Var \cup Var?$. Var? is called the set of read-only variables. Let Θ denote the set of substitutions on $Var_?$. We say that $\theta \in \Theta$ is admissible if $dom(\theta) \cap Var? = \emptyset$ and inadmissible if $dom(\theta) \cap Var? \neq \emptyset$.*

- *Let E be an expression; $vars(E)$, $r\_vars(E)$ and $w\_vars(E)$ denote respectively the sets of variables, read-only variables and writable variables occurring in E.*

- *The restriction $\sigma \upharpoonright V$ of a substitution σ to a set of variables $V \subseteq Var_?$ is defined as usual (see for example [6]). This definition extends naturally to sets of substitutions.*

Collecting Semantics of FCP

The semantics of concurrent languages usually contains some notion of *behaviours*, which consist of (possibly infinite) sequences of events, together with some suspension information. In [8] a fully abstract semantics for FCP is given. Program behaviours are described by sets of entities of the form (c, S) where c is a sequence of substitutions (events) and S indicates termination (tt), failure (ff) or suspension. In the case of suspension S is a substitution which does not release from suspension. We consider a concrete semantics for FCP similar to that described above except that S is a *ready set* (i.e. a set of actions the program may take after c).

Rather than give a full presentation of the concrete collecting semantics in this paper, we define below a function $\text{-o}\cdot\text{o-}$, which gives an operational definition of the meaning of a program P as a mapping from goals to sets of behaviours. We then sketch the collecting semantics obtained according to the outline in Section 2.1.

The dependencies of a program on its environment are expressed in the semantics using inadmissible substitutions. An inadmissible substitution in a behaviour (c, S) of a program specifies conditions on the program's environment. For example, an inadmissible substitution, θ, in the sequence c specifies that the environment provided the bindings for each of the read only variables in the domain of θ.

DEFINITION 13.3.3. *Let P be a program. For every goal G let*

$$
\text{-o}P\text{o-}(G) = \left\{ \langle \bar{\theta}_1\hat{}\cdots\hat{}\bar{\theta}_m, S\rangle \left|
\begin{array}{l}
G\rightarrow \theta_1 G_1 \rightarrow \theta_2 \ldots \rightarrow \theta_m G_m \\
\text{is an SLD derivation,} \\
\forall(1 \leq j \leq m)\ r\_vars(dom(\theta_j)) \subseteq V_{j-1}, \\
\text{and } \bar{\theta}_j = \theta_j \restriction V_{j-1}, \\
S = \left\{
\begin{array}{ll}
\{tt\} & G_m = true \\
\{ff\} & G_m = false \\
\bar{S} & \text{otherwise}
\end{array}
\right.
\end{array}
\right. \right\}
$$

where

For $1 \leq j \leq m$, $V_j = vars(G\theta_1 \ldots \theta_j)$ and

$$
\bar{S} = \left\{ \theta \restriction V_m \left|
\begin{array}{l}
G\rightarrow \theta_1 G_1 \rightarrow \theta_2 \ldots \rightarrow \theta_m G_m \rightarrow \theta G_{m+1} \\
\text{is an SLD derivation,} \\
r\_vars(dom(\theta)) \subseteq V_m)
\end{array}
\right. \right\}
$$

The restrictions on the read-only variables in the definition are to ensure that a derivation for a goal G does not claim to receive bindings from the environment to variables not accessible to the environment.

The elements in $\text{-o}P\text{o-}(G)$ are called behaviours and may be visualised as *brooms* [17], in which a sequence $\theta_1 \ldots \theta_m$ forms the broom stick, and the set S forms the brush attached to θ_m.

Let *Goals* be the set of goals and $\mathcal{B}$ be the set of behaviours. The above operational semantics is a function $\text{-o}\cdot\text{o-} : Prog \rightarrow Goals \rightarrow 2\,\mathcal{B}$. The collecting semantics for FCP is constructed following the outline in Section 2.1. The collecting points in the program are instances of the literals in the clause bodies; that is, elements of *Goals*. Adapting the idea of *minimal function graph* semantics [10] to represent an environment as a partial function from program points to sets of behaviours the collecting semantics is specified as a function:

$$[\cdot]_{FCPcoll} : Prog \rightarrow 2 \ Goals \rightarrow (Goals \rightarrow 2 \ \mathcal{B}).$$

We assume that for each program P there is a function

$$\mathcal{FCP}_P : (2 \ Goals \rightarrow (Goals \rightarrow 2 \ \mathcal{B})) \rightarrow (2 \ Goals \rightarrow (Goals \rightarrow 2 \ \mathcal{B}))$$

whose least fixed point is the collecting semantics for P in the above sense. Similarly, given a set of initial goals c, there is a function

$$\mathcal{FCP}_{P,c} : (Goals \rightarrow 2 \ \mathcal{B}) \rightarrow (Goals \rightarrow 2 \ \mathcal{B})$$

whose least fixed point is the minimal function graph for the goals c.

The elementary operations on sequences of substitutions are computationally complex and the actual order of events is not important for many kinds of analysis including those presented in this paper. For the analysis of suspension in Section 13.5, we consider abstract entities of the form $\langle \theta, S \rangle$ to represent all of the concrete entities $\langle \theta_1 \hat{} \cdots \hat{} \theta_m, S \rangle$ such that $\theta_1 \ldots \theta_m = \theta$. For the mode analysis described in Section 13.4 the suspension information S is also abstracted away.

These applications are used to demonstrate that safe approximations of least fixed points can yield useful information. In each case the application is based on safe approximation of a semantics for FCP which may itself be viewed as an abstraction of $\mathcal{FCP}_P$ or $\mathcal{FCP}_{P,c}$.

13.4 Application: Argument Modes in FCP

As the first example the problem of inferring argument modes for FCP programs is considered. An algorithm was developed by Taylor [21],[22], and incorporated into an FCP compiler. By presenting it in the framework of abstract interpretation we are able to show that Taylor's algorithm is sound.

The analysis method is developed in the following stages. We first define collecting semantics for SLD computations. Given a logic program P and a set of goals G, a function $\mathcal{SLD}_{P,G}$ is defined whose least fixed point is a set of calls and answer pairs. We argue that this is an abstraction of the concrete collecting semantics of FCP outlined in the previous section. Then the function $\mathcal{MGC}_{P,G}$ in which answer pairs are not considered is defined as an abstraction of $\mathcal{SLD}_{P,G}$. The function $\mathcal{AMGC}_{P,G}$ is yet another abstraction in which terms are abstracted to be variables or non-variables. The mode analysis algorithm is obtained by computing any one of the sequence of values $\mathcal{AMGC}_{P,G} \ n(\top) \ (0 \leq n \leq \omega)$, where $\top$ is the top element of the domain of $\mathcal{AMGC}_{P,G}$. The following diagram illustrates the development of the mode analysis algorithm.

$$\mathcal{FCP} \longrightarrow \ \alpha_1 \mathcal{SLD} \longrightarrow \ \alpha_2 \mathcal{MGC} \longrightarrow \ \alpha_3 \mathcal{AMGC}$$

Naturally, we could have presented directly $\mathcal{AMGC}$ as an abstraction of $\mathcal{FCP}$; the intermediate stages are given for explanatory purposes, and to suggest other abstractions for different applications.

Calls and Partial Answers for SLD Computations

DEFINITION **13.4.1.** *Let* $\leftarrow G_1, \ldots, G_n$ *be a goal at a node in a (full) SLD computation tree* T. *Then* G_j *is a* call *in* T *if some successor node is obtained by resolving upon* G_j.

Let G *be an atom and* $G \rightarrow \theta_1 G_1 \rightarrow \theta_2 \ldots \rightarrow \theta_m G_m$ *be an SLD-derivation of* $P \cup \{\leftarrow G\}$; *then* $\langle G, G\theta_1 \ldots \theta_m \rangle$ *is an* answer pair. *If* $G_m = true$ *then* $\langle G, G\theta_1 \ldots \theta_m \rangle$ *is called a* call-answer pair, *otherwise it is called a* partial answer pair.

Note that the set of partial answers includes pairs obtained from any SLD derivation, regardless of whether the derivation eventually yields an answer, a failure or divergence. Partial answers have been used by other authors for program analysis and transformation [23], [18], [24].

Each call G in a full SLD computation tree for P is associated with the set of answer pairs $\langle G, A \rangle$ defined by the SLD-derivations of $P \cup \{\leftarrow G\}$.

The expression $rename(E)$ denotes a copy of the expression E which is identical up to renaming of variables. We do not want to distinguish calls or answer pairs which are variants; therefore we use the notion of the canonical form of an expression [16]. The *canonical form* $|E|$ of an expression E is obtained by renaming the variables in a standard way.

DEFINITION **13.4.2.** *canonical form*

Let E *be an expression and let* $X_1, \ldots, X_m$ *be the sequence of distinct variables occurring in* E, *in order of first occurrence. Let* $Z_1, Z_2, \ldots$ *be an infinite sequence of variables, called the* canonical variables, *which do not occur except in canonical terms. Then the canonical form of* E *is defined by* $\|E\| = E\{X_1/Z_1, \ldots, X_m/Z_m\}$.

The definition of canonical form extends naturally to sets of expressions. The definition also extends to expressions containing read-only variables, where it is necessary to rename read-only variables by read-only variables.

DEFINITION **13.4.3.** *Let* P *be a program,* $Atoms_?$ *be the set of atoms constructed from the signature of* P *and the set of variables* $Var_?$, *and* $Pairs_?$ *be the set* $\{\langle G, A \rangle \mid G, A \in Atoms_?, A \text{ is an instance of } G\}$. *Then* $AP_? = |Atoms_?| \cup \|Pairs_?\|$ *and* $(2^{AP_?}, \subseteq)$ *is a complete lattice.*

Collecting Semantics of SLD Computations

The collecting semantics for SLD computations will be formed by expressing the meaning of a program with a set of initial calls as a set of calls and answer pairs. The collecting points in the program are the points before and after each goal in the clause bodies. We associate with each point before a goal a set of calls to that goal, and with each point after a goal a set of answer pairs for the goal. In this way we collect the set of all possible states of the variables in the program at runtime. In [7] we defined a continuous function over the set of calls and call-answer pairs, whose least fixed point gives the meaning of a Prolog program and goal. In this paper a more general function will be defined, whose least fixed point includes all calls in the full SLD computation tree.

An ordering on substitutions is defined as in Eder [6], with a corresponding supremum of a set of substitutions. These definitions are:

DEFINITION 13.4.4. *Let θ and σ be substitutions; $\theta \leq \sigma$ iff there exists a substitution ρ such that $\theta \circ \rho = \sigma$. Given a set of substitutions S, a supremum of S is a least substitution θ such that $\rho \leq \theta$, for all $\rho \in S$. We write $supremum(S)$ for the set of suprema of S.*

DEFINITION 13.4.5. $\Pi(G, S)$

Let S be a set of canonical partial answer pairs, and let $G = \leftarrow G_1, \ldots, G_n$ be a goal and $\{H_1, \ldots, H_k\} \subseteq \{G_1, \ldots, G_n\}$, such that $\forall j \ (1 \leq j \leq k) \ \exists A_j$ $\langle \|H_j\|, A_j \rangle \in S$. Then $\theta \in supremum(\{mgu(H_j, rename(A_j)) \mid 1 \leq j \leq n\})$ is called a partial answer substitution for G over S, where for all i and j, $vars(G_1, \ldots, G_n) \cap vars(rename(A_j)) = \emptyset$ and for $i \neq j$, $vars(rename(A_i)) \cap vars(rename(A_j)) = \emptyset$.

The set of partial answer substitutions of goal G over S is denoted $\Pi(G, S)$.

Note that ϵ (the empty substitution) is a partial answer substitution for $G_1, \ldots, G_n$ since the *supremum* of $\emptyset$ is ϵ.

We now define the semantic function, which is motivated by the following considerations. Let G be a call and $H \leftarrow B_1, \ldots, B_n$ be a clause and let $mgu(G, H) = \theta$. Let S be a set of partial answers; the following calls and partial answers can be derived:

- $\|B_j \theta \rho\|$ is a call, where ρ is a partial answer substitution for $(B_1, \ldots, B_{j-1}, B_{j+1}, \ldots, B_n)\theta$ over S.

- $\|\langle G, G\theta\sigma \rangle\|$ is a partial answer, where σ is a partial answer substitution for $(B_1, \ldots, B_n)\theta$ over S.

These are all the calls and partial answers which can be derived in the full SLD tree. A particular computation rule gives a subset of these calls and partial answers.

DEFINITION 13.4.6. $\mathcal{SLD}_{P,G} : 2\ AP_? \rightarrow 2\ AP_?$

Let P be a program and $G \in 2\ AP_?$ be a set of initial (canonical) calls. Then

$$\mathcal{SLD}_{P,G}(X) =$$

$$G \bigcup \left\{ \|(B_j \theta \rho)\| \,\middle|\, \begin{array}{l} C' \in X, C = rename(C'),\ H \leftarrow B_1, \ldots, B_m \in P, \\ vars(C) \cap vars(H, B_1, \ldots, B_m) = \emptyset, \\ mgu(C, H) = \theta, \\ \rho \in \Pi((B_1, .., B_{j-1}, B_{j+1}, .., B_m)\theta, X), \\ vars(ran(\rho)) \cap vars(C, H, B_1, \ldots, B_n) = \emptyset \end{array} \right\}$$

$$\bigcup \left\{ \|\langle C, (C\theta\rho)\rangle\| \,\middle|\, \begin{array}{l} C' \in X, C = rename(C'),\ H \leftarrow B_1, \ldots, B_m \in P, \\ vars(C) \cap vars(H, B_1, \ldots, B_m) = \emptyset, \\ mgu(C, H) = \theta, \\ \rho \in \Pi((B_1, \ldots, B_m)\theta, X), \\ vars(ran(\rho)) \cap vars(C, H, B_1, \ldots, B_n) = \emptyset \end{array} \right\}$$

A proof of continuity of this function is not included here; a very similar proof may be found in [7]. The least fixed point of this function contains all the calls and corresponding partial answers which are in the full SLD tree for P and G. If G is a singleton goal $\{G_1\}$, construction of the least fixed point using the ascending Kleene sequence $\emptyset, \mathcal{SLD}_{P,G}(\emptyset), \mathcal{SLD}_{P,G}\ 2(\emptyset), \ldots$ mirrors the top-down construction of the full SLD tree for P and G_1, using additional memo-tables for storing the partial answers to previously computed calls. A descending Kleene sequence does not have an obvious computational analogy, but abstractions of it may be used for program analysis as shown in the mode analysis example below.

As we mentioned earlier, our approach to collecting semantics is similar to the definition of minimal function graphs for collecting semantics of functional languages. In [10] the meaning of a functional program (with some given initial calls) is a partial function defined only for values in the domain for which the program function is actually called during the computation of the initial calls. If the program function is called and returns a value, this is represented by a pair in the minimal function graph, similar to our answer pairs. If the program diverges for some value v, the minimal function graph contains a pair $\langle v, \bot \rangle$. We represent this by a call for which there exists no corresponding call-answer pair (though there may exist partial answer pairs). Minimal function graphs are also used in a slightly different way as a framework for abstract interpretation of logic programs in [25].

SLD Computations as Abstractions of FCP Computations

As we discussed in Section 13.3, the meaning of an FCP program P with a goal G is a set of *behaviours*. A behaviour is a pair $\langle c, S \rangle$ where c is a sequence of substitutions and S is a ready set giving suspension information.

We assumed in Section 13.3 the existence of a function $\mathcal{FCP}_{P,G} : (Goals \rightarrow 2\ \mathcal{B}) \rightarrow (Goals \rightarrow 2\ \mathcal{B})$, where $\mathcal{B}$ is the set of behaviours, for each program P and set of calls G. We assert that $\mathcal{SLD}_{P,G}$ is an abstraction of $\mathcal{FCP}_{P,G}$. To justify this informally, consider a concretisation function $\gamma : AP_? \rightarrow (Goals \rightarrow 2\ \mathcal{B})$ defined such that $\gamma(\langle G, G\theta \rangle) = \{G \mapsto \{\theta_1\hat{}\ldots\hat{}\theta_m, S)G\theta\rangle \in AP_?$ represents a set of behaviours for G. Since the concept of synchronisation is not present in SLD computations, some of the behaviours in $\gamma(\langle G, G\theta \rangle)$ may not correspond to feasible FCP computations for G; in particular, a sequence $\theta_1\hat{}\ldots\hat{}\theta_m$ may include a resolution step which suspends in FCP.

Given an FCP program P and an FCP goal G, suppose that the least fixed point of $\mathcal{SLD}_{P,G}$ is a set of calls and answer pairs, say M. We argue that M represents (under a concretisation function based on γ above) a superset of $lfp(\mathcal{FCP}_{P,G})$.

Argument Modes

The basis of the mode analysis is the following definition of the *mode of an argument* of a predicate. Arguments are either input or output. The definition expresses the fact that an argument has mode input if no call instantiates a variable in that argument position in the call.

DEFINITION 13.4.7. *Let P be a program and C be a set of calls. Then for program predicate $p(t_1, \ldots, t_n)$ the j th argument has mode input with respect to C, if for all $p(s_1, \ldots, s_n) \in C$, the set K is empty, where*

$$K = \left\{ s_j \left| \begin{array}{l} H \leftarrow B \in P, \\ mgu(p(s_1, .., s_n), H)) = \theta, \\ s_j \in Var_?\ s_j\theta \notin Var_? \end{array} \right. \right\}$$

Otherwise, argument j has mode output with respect to C.

The correct modes for the arguments are obtained where C is the set of all calls which occur in the computation. Since this set is in general infinite, a mode analysis algorithm has to construct an approximation to the set of all calls which can be represented finitely.

LEMMA 13.4.8. *If S_1, S_2 are sets of calls where $S_1 \subseteq S_2$ then the input modes with respect to S_2 are a subset of the input modes with respect to S_1.*

PROOF.   Straightforward from the definition of modes.   □

This result means that a safe approximation (representing a superset) of the
set of calls may result in the derivation of less input modes.

Using the properties of read-only variables, the definition of modes can be
refined since in FCP no call is allowed to instantiate a read-only variable with a
non-variable.

DEFINITION **13.4.9.** *Let P be an FCP program and let $C \subseteq Atoms_?$ be a set of
FCP calls. Then for a program predicate $p(t_1, \ldots, t_n)$ the argument j has mode
input with respect to C, if for all $p(s_1, \ldots, s_n) \in C$, the set K is empty, where*

$$K = \left\{ s_j \left| \begin{array}{l} H \leftarrow B \in P, \\ mgu(p(s_1, .., s_n), H)) = \theta, \\ s_j \in Var, \ s_j\theta \notin Var_? \end{array} \right. \right\}$$

Otherwise, argument j has mode output with respect to C.

Most General Calls Semantics

The function $\mathcal{SLD}_{P,G}$ derives all calls which occur in the full SLD tree. We now
define an abstraction $\mathcal{MGC}_{P,G}$ of the semantics given by the $\mathcal{SLD}_{P,G}$ function,
in which partial answers are not considered, and a set of more general calls is
obtained. We start by defining a concretisation function mapping sets of atoms
to sets of atoms and pairs.

DEFINITION **13.4.10.** *Let the concretisation function $\gamma : 2 \, \|Atoms_?\| \rightarrow 2 \, AP_?$
and the ordering $\sqsubseteq$ on 2 $Atoms_?$ be respectively defined by:*

- $\gamma(X) = \{c \mid x \in X, \ c \text{ is an instance of } x\} \cup Pairs_?$

- $X_1 \sqsubseteq X_2 \text{ iff } \gamma(X_1) \subseteq \gamma(X_2)$

Given a program P and a set of initial calls G, the least fixed point of the
abstract semantic function $\mathcal{MGC}_{P,G}$ is a set of calls; the difference from $\mathcal{SLD}_{P,G}$ is
that partial answers are not used in the computation. The effect of using partial
answers in $\mathcal{SLD}_{P,G}$ is to generate calls which are instances of the calls generated
without using partial answers. Thus by ignoring the partial answers we derive
a more general set of calls produced by the computation. The concretisation
function γ defined above includes the whole set of partial answers in its result for
formal purposes, to ensure that $\mathcal{MGC}_{P,G}$ is an abstraction of $\mathcal{SLD}_{P,G}$.

Given program P and a set of canonical calls $G \in 2 \, \|Atoms_?\|$ the least fixed
point of the function $\mathcal{MGC}_{P,G} : 2 \, \|Atoms_?\| \rightarrow 2 \, \|Atoms_?\|$ is a set of calls.

DEFINITION 13.4.11. $\mathcal{MGC}_{P,G} : 2\,\|Atoms_?\| \to 2\,\|Atoms_?\|$

Given program P and a set of canonical calls $G \in 2\,\|Atoms_?\|$ the function $\mathcal{MGC}_{P,G}$ is defined as follows:

$$\mathcal{MGC}_{P,G}(X) = G \bigcup \left\{ \|(B_j\theta)\| \,\middle|\, \begin{array}{l} C' \in X,\ C = rename(C'), \\ H \leftarrow B_1,\ldots,B_m \in P, \\ vars(C) \cap vars(H, B_1,\ldots,B_m) = \emptyset, \\ mgu(C,H) = \theta \end{array} \right\}$$

PROPOSITION 13.4.12. *Given a program P, a set of initial calls G, and $X \in 2\,\|Atoms_?\|$ then $\mathcal{SCD}_{P,G}(\gamma(X)) \subseteq \gamma(\mathcal{MGC}_{P,G}(X))$.*

PROOF. Let $x \in \mathcal{SCD}_{P,G}(\gamma(X))$. We show that $x \in \gamma(\mathcal{MGC}_{P,G}(X))$. From the definition of $\mathcal{SCD}_{P,G}$ there are three cases for x.

(i) If $x \in \|Pairs_?\|$, then this is obvious since $\|Pairs_?\| \subseteq \gamma(y)$ for all y.

(ii) If $x \in \|Atoms_?\|$ and $x \in G$ then $x \in \mathcal{MGC}_{P,G}(X)$ and hence also $x \in \gamma(\mathcal{MGC}_{P,G}(X))$.

(iii) Finally, if $x \in \|Atoms_?\|$ and $x = y\theta\rho$ where $h \leftarrow \ldots, y, \ldots$ is a clause and there exists $\|w\| \in \gamma(X)$ such that $mgu(w,h) = \theta$, then there exists $\|z\| \in X$ such that $w = z\sigma$. In this case $mgu(z,h) = \sigma\theta$, hence $y\sigma\theta \in \mathcal{MGC}_{P,G}(X)$. Renaming ensures that σ does not affect the variables of y. Hence $y\theta\rho(= x)$ is an instance of $y\sigma\theta$ and therefore $x \in \gamma(\mathcal{MGC}_{P,G}(X))$.

□

COROLLARY. $\mathcal{MGC}_{P,G}$ *is an abstraction of $\mathcal{SCD}_{P,G}$, and it follows (by Proposition 13.2.3) that $lfp(\mathcal{SCD}_{P,G}) \subseteq \gamma(lfp(\mathcal{MGC}_{P,G}))$, that is, that $\mathcal{MGC}_{P,G}$ is a safe approximation of $\mathcal{SCD}_{P,G}$.*

Abstraction of FCP Atoms

We next develop an abstraction of the $\mathcal{MGC}$ semantics of FCP programs, which will be called $\mathcal{AMGC}$. The lattice $2\,Atoms_?$ has infinite height. In order to ensure that the analysis terminates in a finite number of iterations, we define the function $\mathcal{AMGC}_{P,G}$ over a lattice of finite height, in which we use an abstract constant *nonvar* to represent all non-variable terms.

DEFINITION 13.4.13. *Given a program P and a set of writable and read-only variables, the set of abstract atoms $AA_?$ is the set of atoms $p(\beta_1,\ldots,\beta_n)$ where p is a predicate in P and the arguments β_j are either variables or the term nonvar.*

DEFINITION **13.4.14.** $\gamma : 2^{\|AA_?\|} \to 2^{\|Atoms_?\|}$

Let the monotonic concretisation function be defined as follows:

$$\gamma(X) = \left\{ p(t_1, \ldots, t_n) \;\middle|\; \begin{array}{l} p(\beta_1, \ldots, \beta_n) \in X, \\ ((t_j \text{ is not a variable and } \beta_j = nonvar) \vee \\ (t_j \text{ is an instance of } \beta_j \text{ and } \beta_j \neq nonvar)) \end{array} \right\}$$

The abstract ordering on $AA_?$ *is defined as before, such that* $X_1 \sqsubseteq X_2$ *iff* $\gamma(X_1) \sqsubseteq \gamma(X_2)$.

When performing mode analysis, a set of abstract calls is computed. Modes are derived directly from the set of abstract calls rather than from the corresponding set of concrete FCP calls. We now define argument modes with respect to a set of abstract calls and show that they are correct with respect to the concrete calls.

DEFINITION **13.4.15.**   *The j th argument of program predicate $p(x_1, \ldots, x_n)$ is input with respect to a set $C \subseteq AA_?$ of abstract FCP calls, iff there does not exist a call $p(\beta_1, \ldots, \beta_n) \in C$, where β_j is a writable variable.*

PROPOSITION **13.4.16.**   *Given a program P and a set $S \subseteq AA_?$, then the set of input argument modes with respect to S is a subset of the set of input argument modes derived with respect to $\gamma(S)$.*

PROOF.

Suppose argument j of predicate p is input with respect to S. Then there does not exist $p(\beta_1, \ldots, \beta_n) \in S$ such that β_j is a writable variable. By definition of γ there does not exist $p(s_1, \ldots, s_n) \in \gamma(S)$ such that s_j is a writable variable. Hence argument j of p is input with respect to $\gamma(S)$.   □

Note that the modes derived from S and $\gamma(S)$ are not in general identical since definition of modes with respect to abstract calls does not take into account the clauses which match a call, whereas this is taken into account in the definition of modes with respect to concrete calls.

Two abstract atoms $p(\alpha_1, \ldots, \alpha_n)$ and $p(\beta_1, \ldots, \beta_n)$ may be unified by the usual *mgu* algorithm. However we cannot use *mgu* directly to unify an abstract atom with a concrete atom (say the head of a clause) since *nonvar* should unify with any term, although it is non-variable. Therefore we define the following function δ to convert concrete atoms to abstract atoms.

DEFINITION **13.4.17.** $\delta : Atoms_? \to AA_?$

Let $p(t_1, \ldots, t_n) \in Atoms_?$. Then $\delta(p(t_1, \ldots, t_n)) = p(\beta_1, \ldots, \beta_n)$ where $\beta_j = nonvar$ if t_j is non-variable and $\beta_j = t_j$ otherwise.

We note that for all $T \in Atoms_?, T \in \gamma(\{\delta(T)\})$.

We make the following claim, which is used to establish the safety of the mode analysis algorithm.

CLAIM.   Let $T_1, T_2 \in Atoms_?$ and let $mgu(T_1, T_2) = \theta$. Let $\beta_1, \beta_2 \in AA_?$ be atoms such that $T_1 \in \gamma(\{\beta_1\})$ and $T_2 \in \gamma(\{\beta_2\})$. Then $mgu(\beta_1, \beta_2) = \sigma(\neq fail)$ and for all $S \in Atoms_?$ $S\theta \in \gamma(\{\delta(S)\sigma\})$.

We can now define the abstract function to be used for mode analysis. We modify the function $\mathcal{MGC}$ by using δ to convert body and head atoms to abstract atoms before applying mgu.

DEFINITION 13.4.18. $\mathcal{AMGC}_{P,G} : 2 \, AA_? \rightarrow 2 \, AA_?$

Let P be an FCP program and $G \subseteq 2 \, AA_?$ be a set of abstract FCP calls. Then we define the function $\mathcal{AMGC}_{P,G}$ as follows:

$$\mathcal{AMGC}_{P,G}(X) = G \; \bigcup \; \left\{ \|(\delta(B_j))\theta\| \; \middle| \; \begin{array}{l} C \in X, \, H \leftarrow B_1, \ldots, B_m \in P, \\ mgu(rename(C), \delta(H)) = \theta, \\ vars(rename(C)) \cap \\ vars(H, B_1, \ldots, B_n) = \emptyset \end{array} \right\}$$

We sometimes refer to $\mathcal{AMGC}$ rather than $\mathcal{AMGC}_{P,G}$ where there is no ambiguity.

Given a program P and a goal G, the least fixed point of $\mathcal{AMGC}$ is the abstract meaning of P with G. We now show that the abstract meaning is a safe approximation of the concrete meaning.

PROPOSITION 13.4.19.   Let P be an FCP program and $G \subseteq 2 \, AA_?$ be a set of canonical abstract FCP calls. Then $\mathcal{MGC}_{P,\gamma(G)}(\gamma(X)) \subseteq \gamma(\mathcal{AMGC}_{P,G}(X))$.

PROOF.   Let $x \in \mathcal{MGC}_{P,\gamma(G)}(\gamma(X))$. We show that $x \in \gamma(\mathcal{AMGC}_{P,G}(X))$. From the definition of $\mathcal{MGC}_{P,\gamma(G)}$ there are two cases for x.

(i) If $x \in \gamma(G)$ then $x \in \gamma(\mathcal{AMGC}_{P,G}(X))$ since $G \subseteq \mathcal{AMGC}_{P,G}(X)$.

(ii) Secondly suppose $x = y\theta$, where there exists $\|w\| \in \gamma(X)$ and $h \leftarrow \ldots, y, \ldots$ such that $mgu(w, h) = \theta$. Therefore there exists $\|z\| \in X$ such that $w \in \gamma(\{z\})$. By the Claim above $mgu(z, \delta(h)) = \sigma$ and $y\theta \in \gamma(\{\delta(y\sigma)\})$. Hence $y\theta \in \gamma(\mathcal{AMGC}_{P,G}(X))$.

$\square$

COROLLARY. $\mathcal{AMGC}$ is an abstraction of $\mathcal{MGC}$ and it follows (by Proposition 13.2.3) that $lfp(\mathcal{MGC}_{P,\gamma(G)}) \subseteq \gamma(lfp(\mathcal{AMGC}_{P,G}))$.

An Algorithm For Mode Analysis

As shown in Section 13.2, we can safely approximate the least fixed point of the abstract semantic function $\mathcal{AMGC}$ by a decreasing sequence of values

$$\top, \mathcal{AMGC}(\top), \mathcal{AMGC}\,2(\top), \ldots$$

Modes may safely be deduced from any of these sets. In fact, in the case of FCP programs this turns out to be a much more practical way of inferring modes than by trying to reach the least fixed point by an ascending sequence, since most of the mode information may be deduced in one iteration.

As top element we take the set of abstract FCP calls consisting of the set $\top$ defined by:

$$\top = \left\{ \|p(X_1, \ldots, X_n)\| \,\middle|\, \begin{array}{l} p \text{ is a program predicate}, \\ X_1, \ldots, X_n \text{ distinct writable variables} \end{array} \right\}$$

This is the top element of the lattice $2\ AA_?$ since for all $S \in 2\ AA_?, \gamma(\top) \supseteq \gamma(S)$.

Modes are deduced from a set of calls according to Definition 13.4.18 by assigning output mode to any argument of a predicate where at least one writable variable occurs in a call to that predicate, and input mode otherwise.

EXAMPLE 1. *Given the following FCP program:*

```
p(X,Y) :- q(X,Y).
q(X,Y) :- r(X,Y).
r(X,Y) :- s(X,Y).
```

Let p(X?,Y) be the initial call. The sequence of sets of calls deduced by $\mathcal{AMGC}$ is as follows:

1.   {p(X,Y),q(X,Y),r(X,Y),s(X,Y)}
2.   {p(X?,Y),q(X,Y),r(X,Y),s(X,Y)}
3.   {p(X?,Y),q(X?,Y),r(X,Y),s(X,Y)}
4.   {p(X?,Y),q(X?,Y),r(X?,Y),s(X,Y)}
5. · {p(X?,Y),q(X?,Y),r(X?,Y),s(X?,Y)}

The last set is the fixed point, and from it we can deduce that the first argument of each predicate is input. Modes derived from sets 1 to 4 are also correct, but less precise. From the second set we can deduce that the first argument of p(X,Y) is input, from the third that the first argument of q(X,Y) is input, and so on. If we had approximated the set of calls by an ascending sequence, then it would have been necessary to reach the fixed point in order to be sure that no input modes had been falsely inferred. By approaching a fixed point from above, however, we infer correct modes at each intermediate stage.

P	$\mathcal{AMGC}$ 1(T)	$\mathcal{AMGC}$ 2(T)	$\mathcal{AMGC}$ 3(T)	$\mathcal{AMGC}$ 4(T)	$\mathcal{AMGC}$ 5(T)
debugger	44	**46**			
lint	129	156	160	161	**162**
graphics	85	**87**			
assembler	**49**				
tokenizer	22	**24**			
parser	50	61	67	**68**	
encoder	229	**232**			
simulator	222	233	**234**		
preprocessor	302	358	376	**383**	

Table 13.1: **Number of Input Arguments Derived After Successive Iterations of** $\mathcal{AMGC}$

In this artificial example one mode was deduced on each iteration. In practice there is a lot more information in the clauses, in the form of read-only annotations and non-variable terms, and most of the modes may be deduced in the first couple of iterations. Table 13.1 shows results from experiments with sizable test programs including an FCP parser and tokenizer, a debugger and graphics programs (and a given initial goal for each program). It was found that on average over 85% of the input modes contained in the greatest fixed point (shown in bold type in Table 13.1) were discovered after one iteration, even though as many as six iterations were required to detect the fixed point. For this reason the mode analysis algorithm incorporated in the FCP compiler [22] stops after the first iteration, yielding a non-optimal but safe result. Further iterations could be performed if more optimisation is required.

Greater precision could be obtained by allowing the abstract term *nonvar* to occur at any level in terms, rather than just at argument level. It would also be possible to give a more accurate definition of modes, in which separate modes for each clause were derived from a set of calls, rather than one mode for each argument position.

13.5   Application: Deadlock and Suspension in FCP

The previous example considered an abstraction for which we could ignore the concurrent aspects of the language FCP. For many applications sufficient approximations to the desired information can be found when abstracting details such as the order in which events occur or the ways in which parallel components interact. Another important aspect of parallel programs is branching information. Two FCP programs may differ only in the way that they suspend at different program points. For example both of the programs:

```
p(X,Y) :- X? = a | true.              p(X,Y) :- q(X?).
p(X,Y) :- Y? = a | true.              p(X,Y) :- q(Y?).

                                      q(a).
```

will suspend with the goal $\leftarrow$p(X,Y) until the environment provides one of the substitutions $(X \mapsto a)$ or $(Y \mapsto a)$. The difference between the two programs is that if the environment provides the substitution $(X \mapsto a)$ then the left program will not remain suspended while the right one might.

Branching information can indicate the "degree of suspension" at a program point either by describing the set of possible next choices available (*ready sets*), or by describing the set of events the program cannot participate in (*failure sets*).

In the previous section FCP computations were abstracted collecting the composed effect of the sequences but ignoring the order of the events and the branching information. This section describes an analysis which detects suspension and deadlock possibilities of a program. It is described as an abstraction of a semantics which collects the branching information of a program and the composed substitutions (ignoring as before the order of events).

Inadmissible substitutions indicate dependencies on the environment to provide certain bindings. If a computation for a goal G is at a point in which all of its alternative next reductions involve inadmissible substitutions then we say that the computation is *suspended*. A special case of suspension is that of *deadlock*. The environment of a program can only provide substitutions to variables that occur in the goal G. Deadlock situations arise when a computation depends on bindings to variables which are not accessible to the environment.

We will define a semantic function $\mathcal{S}_{P,c}$. This function will collect branching information for a program P and a set of initial calls c. The branching information collected by $\mathcal{S}_{P,c}$ will then be used to reason about possible suspensions and deadlocks of P and some goal G from c. As in the previous example, safe approximations to the least fixed point can be used.

A Semantics for the Analysis of Suspension

The collecting semantics for analysis of suspension is specified for each program P and initial set of calls c as the least fixed point of a continuous function $\mathcal{S}_{P,c} : 2\ Env \rightarrow 2\ Env$.

Again we adapt the idea of minimal function graphs to represent an environment as a partial function from program points to sets of values. For the FCP collecting semantics, program points were associated with sets of behaviours (i.e. elements of $2\ \mathcal{B}$); for this application, program points will be associated with sets of *suspensions* in which the order of events is ignored. The set of suspensions is denoted by $\mathcal{SUSP}$. Our approach is compositional, namely the meaning of a goal is defined in terms of the composition of the meanings of the literals in the bodies of the clauses for that goal.

The least fixed point of $S_{P,c}$ can be represented as a partial function, $\chi :$ *Atoms* $\rightarrow 2$ *SUSP* which associates with every goal G which is encountered in a computation for one of the initial goals in c a set of suspensions $\chi(G) \in 2$ *SUSP* such that $\rightarrow\!\!P\!\!\!\not\!\rightarrow(G) \subseteq \gamma(\chi(G))$. The least fixed point can then be approximated as shown in the previous sections.

DEFINITION 13.5.1. (*Atoms* $\rightarrow 2$ *SUSP*, $\sqsubseteq$)

- Let Θ denote the set of read-only substitutions and $\mathbf{P}(\Theta) = \{tt\} \cup 2 \Theta \cup \{ff\}$.

  SUSP $= \{\langle\theta, S\rangle \mid \theta \in \Theta,\ S \in \mathbf{P}(\Theta)\}$.

- Let *Atoms* $\rightarrow 2$ *SUSP* denote the set of partial functions from *Atoms* to subsets of *SUSP*.

- For $\chi_1, \chi_2 :$ *Atoms* $\rightarrow 2$ *SUSP* we define $\chi_1 \sqsubseteq \chi_2$ iff $\forall a \in dom(\chi_1),\ \chi_1(a) \subseteq \chi_2(a)$

- Let $\bot :$ *Atoms* $\rightarrow 2$ *SUSP* denote the partial function which is undefined for every $a \in$ *Atoms*

- (*Atoms* $\rightarrow 2$ *SUSP*, $\sqsubseteq$) is a complete lattice.

The semantic function $S_{P,c} :$ (*Atoms* $\rightarrow 2$ *SUSP*) $\rightarrow$ (*Atoms* $\rightarrow 2$ *SUSP*) for a program P and an initial set of calls (unit goals) c will be motivated by the following considerations:

1. $S_{P,c}(\bot) :$ (*Atoms* $\rightarrow 2$ *SUSP*) is the partial function which maps each initial goal $G \in c$ to $\{\langle\epsilon, ready(G, P)\rangle\}$ and is undefined for any $G \notin c$ where $ready(G, P)$ denotes the ready set of a (unit) goal G with a program P.

2. If χ is an environment, (i.e. a partial function *Atoms* $\rightarrow 2$ *SUSP*) then $S_{P,c}(\chi)$ is an environment such that:

   Let $G \in dom(\chi)$, $H \leftarrow B_1, \ldots, B_n$ be a renamed clause and $mgu(G, H) = \theta$.

   - If $B_i\theta \notin dom(\chi)$ then $S_{P,c}(\chi)(B_i\theta) = \{\langle\epsilon, ready(B_i\theta, P)\rangle\}$.
   - $S_{P,c}(\chi)(G) = \chi(G) \cup X$ where $\langle\sigma, S\rangle \in X$ if $\langle\varphi, \tilde{S}\rangle$ is in the *composition* of $\chi(B_1\theta), \ldots, \chi(B_n\theta)$, and $\langle\sigma, S\rangle$ is the *restriction* of $\langle\theta\varphi, \tilde{S}\rangle$ to the variables in G.

DEFINITION **13.5.2.** *composition*

- Let θ and φ be substitutions. We define the *difference*, $diff(\theta, \varphi)$, between θ and φ to be the most general unifier of the set of equations $\{X\theta = X\varphi\theta \mid X \in dom(\varphi)\}$ [12].

- Let θ and φ be substitutions. The *merge* of θ and φ is defined as follows:

$$merge(\theta, \varphi) = \{\theta\, diff(\theta, \varphi), \varphi\, diff(\varphi, \theta)\}$$

Note that this definition is similar to the definition given by Eder [6] for *supremum*. However when considering substitutions with read-only variables the order of the arguments is significant. For example let $\theta = (X \mapsto f(a))$ and $\varphi = (X? \mapsto f(Y))$, then $diff(\theta, \varphi) = diff(\varphi, \theta) = (Y \mapsto a)$, and $merge(\theta, \varphi) = \{(X \mapsto f(a), Y \mapsto a), (X? \mapsto f(a), Y \mapsto a)\}$.

- Let $X, Y \subseteq \mathcal{SUSP}$. The composition $X\|Y$ is defined as follows:

$$X\|Y = \left\{ \langle\theta, S\rangle \;\middle|\; \begin{array}{l} \langle\theta, S\rangle \in \langle\theta_1, S_1\rangle\|\langle\theta_2, S_2\rangle, \\ \langle\theta_1, S_1\rangle \in X, \langle\theta_2, S_2\rangle \in Y \end{array} \right\}$$

where

$$\langle\theta_1, S_1\rangle\|\langle\theta_2, S_2\rangle = \left\{ \langle\theta, S\rangle \;\middle|\; \begin{array}{l} \text{if } merge(\theta_1, \theta_2) = \{fail\} \\ \quad \text{then } \langle\theta, S\rangle \in \{\langle\theta_1, \{ff\}\rangle, \langle\theta_2, \{ff\}\rangle\} \\ \text{else } \theta \in merge(\theta_1, \theta_2) \text{ and} \\ \quad S = \\ \quad \text{if } S_1 = S_2 = \{tt\} \text{ then } \{tt\} \text{ else} \\ \qquad ((S_1 \cup S_2) \cap \{ff\}) \cup \\ \qquad \{diff(\theta, \varphi) \mid \varphi \in (S_1 \cup S_2) \setminus \{tt, ff\} \end{array} \right\}$$

DEFINITION **13.5.3.** *ready set*

Let P be a (renamed) program and $G \in Atoms$ be a goal, then

$$ready(G, P) = \begin{array}{l} \{\theta \mid mgu(G, H) = \theta, (H \leftarrow B_1 \ldots B_n) \in P\} \;\cup \\ \{tt \mid G = true\} \;\cup \\ \{ff \mid \not\exists mgu(G, H), (H \leftarrow B_1 \ldots B_n) \in P\} \end{array}$$

DEFINITION **13.5.4.** $S_{P,c} : (Atoms \rightarrow 2^{\mathcal{SUSP}}) \rightarrow (Atoms \rightarrow 2^{\mathcal{SUSP}})$

Let P be a program and c be a set of initial goals then,

$$S_{P,c}(\chi) =$$

$$\{G \mapsto \{\langle\epsilon, ready(G, P)\rangle\} \mid G \in c, G \notin dom(\chi)\} \;\bigcup$$

$$\left\{ B \mapsto \{\langle \epsilon, ready(B,P)\rangle\} \;\middle|\; \begin{array}{l} H \leftarrow B_1, \ldots, B_n \text{ is a renamed clause,} \\ G \in dom(\chi), \; mgu(G,H) = \theta, \\ B \in \{B_1\theta, \ldots, B_n\theta\}, \; B \notin dom(\chi) \end{array} \right\} \cup$$

$$\left\{ G \mapsto \chi(G) \cup X \;\middle|\; \begin{array}{l} H \leftarrow B_1, \ldots, B_n \text{ is a renamed clause,} \\ G \in dom(\chi), \; mgu(H,G) = \theta, \\ X = \left\{ \langle \sigma, S \rangle \;\middle|\; \begin{array}{l} \langle \varphi, \tilde{S} \rangle \in \chi(B_1\theta) \| \cdots \| \chi(B_n\theta), \\ \sigma = \theta\varphi \restriction vars(G), \\ S = \{\tilde{\theta} \in \tilde{S} \mid r\_vars(dom(\tilde{\theta})) \\ \quad \subseteq vars(G\sigma)\} \restriction vars(G\sigma) \end{array} \right\} \end{array} \right\}$$

We state without proof the following claim:

CLAIM.

- $S_{P,c} : (Atoms \to 2\,\mathcal{SUSP}) \to (Atoms \to 2\,\mathcal{SUSP})$ is continuous.

- $S_{P,c}$ is an abstraction of $\mathcal{FCP}_{P,c}$.

Examples

We now demonstrate how safe approximations $S_{P,c}\,j(\top)$ of $lfp(S_{P,c})$ may provide useful information about the suspension and deadlock possibilities of a program P.

NOTATION.

- For a set of variables V,

$$\mathcal{SUSP}_V = \{\langle \theta, S \rangle \in \mathcal{SUSP} \mid dom(\theta) \subseteq V, \; \forall \varphi \in S \; dom(\varphi) \subseteq V\theta\}.$$

- Let φ be a substitution and V be a set of variables; $(G, \mathcal{SUSP}_V\,\varphi)$ denotes the set

$$\left\{ (G, \langle \varphi\theta \restriction vars(G), S \rangle) \;\middle|\; \begin{array}{l} \langle \theta, S \rangle \in \mathcal{SUSP}_V, \\ \forall \sigma \in S \; dom(\sigma) \subseteq vars(G\varphi\theta) \end{array} \right\}$$

In the following examples we sometimes describe an environment $\chi : Atoms \to 2\,\mathcal{SUSP}$ by listing elements of the form (G, e) where $e \in \chi(G)$.

EXAMPLE 2. *Consider the following program P:*

```
h(Y) :- p(X), q(X,Y).
p(X) :- X=a | true.
q(X,Y) :- X?=a | p(Y).
```

with the initial set of goals $c = \{\leftarrow h(Y)\}$.

$\mathcal{S}_{P,c}\ 0(\top):$

$\quad (h(Y), \mathcal{SUSP}_{\{Y\}})$

$\quad (p(X), \mathcal{SUSP}_{\{X\}})$

$\quad (q(X, Y), \mathcal{SUSP}_{\{X,Y\}})$

$\mathcal{S}_{P,c}\ 1(\top):$

$\quad (h(Y), \mathcal{SUSP}_{\{Y\}})$

$\quad (p(X), \langle \epsilon, \{(X \mapsto a)\}\rangle)$
$\quad (p(X), \langle (X \mapsto a), \{tt\}\rangle)$

$\quad (q(X, Y), \langle \epsilon, \{(X? \mapsto a)\}\rangle)$
$\quad (q(X, Y), \mathcal{SUSP}_{\{X,Y\}}\ (X? \mapsto a))$

$\mathcal{S}_{P,c}\ 2(\top):$

$\quad (h(Y), \langle \epsilon, \{\epsilon\}\rangle)$
$\quad (h(Y), \mathcal{SUSP}_{\{Y\}})$

$\quad (p(X), \langle \epsilon, \{(X \mapsto a)\}\rangle)$
$\quad (p(X), \langle (X \mapsto a), \{tt\}\rangle)$

$\quad (q(X, Y), \langle \epsilon, \{(X? \mapsto a)\}\rangle)$
$\quad (q(X, Y), \langle (X? \mapsto a), \{(Y \mapsto a)\}\rangle)$
$\quad (q(X, Y), \langle (X? \mapsto a, Y \mapsto a), \{tt\}\rangle)$

$\mathcal{S}_{P,c}\ 3(\top):$

$\quad (h(Y)\ \langle \epsilon, \{\epsilon\}\rangle)$
$\quad (h(Y)\ \langle \epsilon, \{(Y \mapsto a)\}\rangle)$
$\quad (h(Y), \langle (Y \mapsto a), \{\epsilon\}\rangle)$
$\quad (h(Y), \langle (Y \mapsto a), \{tt\}\rangle)$

$\quad (p(X), \langle \epsilon, \{(X \mapsto a)\}\rangle)$
$\quad (p(X), \langle (X \mapsto a), \{tt\}\rangle)$

$\quad (q(X, Y), \langle \epsilon, \{(X? \mapsto a)\}\rangle)$
$\quad (q(X, Y), \langle (X? \mapsto a), \{(Y \mapsto a)\}\rangle)$
$\quad (q(X, Y), \langle (X? \mapsto a, Y \mapsto a), \{tt\}\rangle)$

The entities in the above series of approximations can be used to analyse the suspension and deadlock possibilities of P. For example, $\mathcal{S}_{P,c}\ 0(\top)$ indicates possibility of deadlock for all goals (because $(G, \langle \epsilon, \emptyset \rangle) \in \mathcal{SUSP}_{vars(G)}$ for all G). From $\mathcal{S}_{P,c}\ 1(\top)$ we can determine that the goal $p(X)$ does not suspend; however $q(X, Y)$ may suspend on X or on Y and $h(Y)$ may suspend on Y. From $\mathcal{S}_{P,c}\ 2(\top)$ we know furthermore that $q(X, Y)$ may suspend only on X.

This example is clearly finite and for some finite j, $\mathcal{S}\ j_{P,c}(\top)$ is a fixed point. In general we may consider a further abstraction of the domain such as a depth bound on the terms, which places a finite upper bound on the height of the domain lattice.

Safe Approximation from Below

The definitions of abstract interpretation and safe approximation presented in Section 13.2 are adequate for applications which approximate program meaning *from above*. That is, applications for which the concretisation of the abstract meaning of a program is "larger than" ($\sqsupseteq_{con}$) its concrete meaning. However, for some applications it is appropriate to approximate program meaning *from below*;

that is, safe approximations will represent meanings which are "smaller than" the concrete meanings. For such applications a more general definition of abstract interpretation is required. We shall not present such a definition here, however the following example demonstrates that such applications can be useful.

For any FCP program P, calculation of $\mathcal{FCP}_P\ 2(\bot)$ provides a useful static check on P, since it may indicate erroneous clauses in P^1. Consider an example taken from [13]:

EXAMPLE 3. *Let P be the following (erroneous) procedure taken from a quicksort program and let $c = Atoms$. The variable XS? in the first clause is misspelled, and should be Xs?.*

```
partition([X|Xs],Y,[X|Ls],Rs) :-
        X =< Y | partition(XS?,Y?,Ls,Rs).
partition([X|Xs],Y,Ls,[X|Rs]) :-
        X > Y | partition(Xs?,Y?,Ls,Rs).
partition([],Y,[],[]).
```

- The environment $\mathcal{FCP}_{P,c}\ 1(\bot)$ contains an entity

  $$(partition(XS?,Y?,Ls,Rs),\langle\epsilon,ready(partition(XS?,Y?,Ls,Rs),P)\rangle)$$

  and each substitution in $ready(partition(XS?,Y?,Ls,Rs),P)$ contains a binding to the read-only variable XS?.

- The environment $\mathcal{FCP}\ 2_{P,c}(\bot)$ contains an entity

  $$(partition(Z,U,V,W),\langle(Z\mapsto[X|Xs],V\mapsto[X|Ls]),\emptyset\rangle)$$

  which corresponds to the reduction of the goal partition(Z,U,V,W) using the first clause. The restriction of $\mathcal{FCP}_{P,c}\ 1(\bot)(partition(XS?,Y?,Ls,Rs))$ to the variables in the head of the first clause results in an empty ready set which indicates deadlock.

- Since $\mathcal{FCP}_{P,c}\ 2(\bot)\subseteq lfp(FCP_{P,c})$ any deadlock indicated in $\mathcal{FCP}_{P,c}\ 2(\bot)$ will also be indicated in $lfp(FCP_{P,c})$.

---

[1]Although we have not included a definition of $\mathcal{FCP}_P$ in this paper, we note that for an initial set of calls c, $\mathcal{FCP}_{P,c}\ 1(\bot) = S_{P,c}\ 1(\bot)$ and $\mathcal{FCP}_{P,c}\ 2(\bot) = S_{P,c}\ 2(\bot)$.

13.6 Discussion

The use of abstract interpretation for analysis of logic programs is now well-established. Although theoretical results have shown that safe approximations can be constructed by a descending Kleene sequence, to our knowledge this has not been previously applied in practical algorithms for analysis of logic programs.

Although we did not define explicitly the concrete collecting semantics of FCP, we gave the type of the semantic function and defined the concrete domain of interpretation to contain sets of behaviours of the form (c, S), where c is a sequence of substitutions and S is a ready set. We then assumed a function $\mathcal{FCP}_P$ whose least fixed point was the concrete collecting meaning of P. Both of the applications described in the paper were developed by defining successive abstractions of the concrete semantics. The function $\mathcal{S}_{P,c}$ developed for the suspension analysis abstracted away the order of substitutions, but retained the suspension information in the ready sets. The $\mathcal{SCD}_{P,G}$ function which was used in the development of the mode analysis algorithm abstracted away the ready set as well.

Our suspension analysis application is the first attempt, to our knowledge, to apply abstract interpretation to analyse reactive aspects of a parallel programming language. We expect such analyses to be useful in the justification of semantics-based program transformations of parallel programs.

The $\mathcal{SCD}_{P,G}$ function is of interest in its own right. The notion of a partial answer is a generalisation of the notion of an answer or success pattern, which is used in semantics of Prolog by several authors [11], [15], [3], [7]. Partial answers appear to play an increasingly important role in logic program semantics [23], [18], [24]. The $\mathcal{SCD}_{P,G}$ function which is based on partial answers includes partial, failing and diverging computations in the meaning of a program as well as successful computations.

It is a matter for further study to decide exactly when the technique of approximating the abstract meaning by a decreasing sequence is useful. Clearly the greatest fixed point of the abstract semantic function should be a fairly precise approximation to the least fixed point, and the iteration should converge to this from above relatively quickly compared to the ascending sequence. For the mode analysis of FCP this was the case; the reason is that typically a lot of information is available in the body literals compared to the information propagated by the initial goal, due to the read-only annotations. However an attempt to formulate Prolog mode analysis in this framework indicated that the results would not be precise enough. We suspect that type inference for logic programs (for instance, as formulated by Yardeni and Shapiro [26]) is another kind of analysis for which this technique might be useful.

Our last example demonstrates that applications in which safe approximations represent subsets of the concrete program meaning may be useful for program analysis. Such applications will typically check "existential properties", i.e. will check if there exists a program point (or set of program points) which satisfies some property. In this example the analysis tries to establish the property "there exists a deadlocked computation". An approximation from below (e.g. $\mathcal{FCP}_P\ 2(\perp)$) suffices to establish this. Instead of $\mathcal{FCP}_P$ we could use any abstract function whose least fixed point is less than $\mathit{lfp}(\mathcal{FCP}_P)$.

Acknowledgements

We would like to thank Steve Taylor, whose work on the global analysis of FCP programs was the starting point for this paper. We would also like to thank Eyal Yardeni for valuable discussions on the topics of abstract interpretation and semantics of logic programs. This is a revised and extended version of a paper presented at the Meta88 Workshop on Metaprogramming in Logic Programming, Bristol, June 1988.

References

[1] S. Abramsky and C. Hankin (eds.); *Abstract Interpretation of Declarative Languages*, Ellis Horwood 1987.

[2] M. Bruynooghe, G. Janssens, A. Callebaut, B. Demoen; Abstract Interpretation: Towards the Global Optimisation of Prolog Programs; Proceedings of IEEE Symposium on Logic Programming, San Francisco 1987.

[3] M. Bruynooghe; A Framework for the Abstract Interpretation of Prolog; Report CW 62, Dept. of Computer Science, Katholieke Universiteit Leuven, Belgium, October 1987.

[4] P. Cousot, R. Cousot; Abstract Interpretation: A Unified Lattice Model for Static Analysis of Programs by Construction or Approximation of Fixpoints; Proceedings of Principles of Programming Languages 1977.

[5] S.K. Debray; Global Optimizations of Logic Programs; Ph.D. Thesis, State University of New York at Stony Brook; December 1986.

[6] E. Eder; Properties of Substitutions and Unifications; *J. Symbolic Computation* 1985 1, 31-46.

[7] J. Gallagher, M. Codish, E. Shapiro; Specialisation of Prolog and FCP Programs Using Abstract Interpretation; *New Generation Computing*, 6 (1988) 159-186.

[8] R. Gerth, M. Codish, Y. Lichtenstein, E. Shapiro; Fully Abstract Denotational Semantics for Flat Concurrent Prolog; Proceedings, Logic In Computer Science, Edinburgh, IEEE (1988).

[9] N.D. Jones, II. Söndergaard; A Semantics-Based Framework for the Abstract Interpretation of Prolog; Chapter 6 in [1].

[10] N.D. Jones, A. Mycroft; Dataflow Analysis of Applicative Programs using Minimal Function Graphs; Proceedings of Principles of Programming Languages 1986.

[11] T. Kanamori, T. Kawamura; Analyzing Success Patterns of Logic Programs by Abstract IIybrid Interpretation; ICOT Technical Report, 1987.

[12] J.-L. Lassez, M.J. Maher, K. Mariott; Unification Revisited; in *Foundations of Deductive Databases and Logic Programming*, J. Minker (Ed.), Morgan Kauffmann, 1987.

[13] Y. Lichtenstein, E. Shapiro; Concurrent Algorithmic Debugging ; Weizmann Institute Technical Report, Dept of Computer Science, CS87-20., (December, 1987).

[14] J.W. Lloyd; *Foundations of Logic Programming, 2nd Edition*; Springer-Verlag, 1987.

[15] H. Mannila, E. Ukkonen; Flow Analysis of Prolog Programs; Proceedings of IEEE Symposium on Logic Programming, San Francisco 1987.

[16] C.S. Mellish; Abstract Interpretation of Prolog Programs; Proc. 3rd ICLP, LNCS 225; Springer-Verlag; 1986; also Chapter 8 in [1].

[17] A. Pnueli; Linear and Branching Structures in the Semantics and Logics of Reactive Systems; Proc. 12th ICALP, Nafpilon, Greece, LNCS-194, Springer-Verlag; July 1985.

[18] G.A. Ringwood; Pattern-directed, Markovian, linear, guarded definite clause resolution; Dept. of Computing, Imperial College, London (1987), (unpublished).

[19] E. Shapiro, Concurrent Prolog: A Progress Report, *IEEE Computer*, August 1986. Also appears as Chapter 5 in [20].

[20] E. Shapiro (ed.), *Concurrent Prolog: Collected Papers*; Vol. 1 and 2, MIT Press 1987.

[21] S. Taylor, E. Shapiro; Compiling Concurrent Logic Programs into Decision Graphs; Weizmann Institute Technical Report, Dept of Computer Science, CS87-12. (July 1987).

[22] S. Taylor; Parallel Logic Programming Techniques; Ph.D. Thesis, Department of Computer Science, Weizmann Institute of Science (submitted).

[23] P. Vasey; Qualified answers and their application to transformation; Proc. 3rd ICLP, LNCS 225; Springer-Verlag, (ed.) E. Shapiro; 1986.

[24] M.II. van Emden; Conditional Answers for Polymorphic Type Inference; Proceedings of the 5th International Conference and Symposium on Logic Programming, (eds.) R. Kowalski and K. Bowen; MIT Press 1988.

[25] W. Winsborough; A Minimal Function Graph Semantics for Logic Programs; Technical Report 711, Computer Sciences Dept., University of Wisconsin-Madison, August 1987.

[26] E. Yardeni, E. Shapiro; A Type System For Logic Programs; Weizmann Institute Technical Report, Dept of Computer Science, CS87-05., (March 1987). Also appears as Chapter 28 in [20].

Chapter 14

Type Inference by Program Transformation and Partial Evaluation

Thom W. Frühwirth

Technical University of Vienna
Institut für Angewandte Informatik
Paniglgasse 16/E181-2
A-1040 Wien Austria
thom@tuhold.uucp

Abstract

In this paper we give an overview of the type inference method developed for a polymorphic type system in Prolog [Frühwirth-1,2,4,5]. The type language is a subset of pure Prolog. In the type system, operations on types including negation are provided [Frühwirth-4]. The partial evaluation of each operation is defined by equality preserving rewrite rules. Type inference is achieved by applying a special operation, namely projection, to procedures. We define a non-redundant standard form for types. Standardization is achieved by simply applying the rewrite rules for each type operation. We further define rewrite rules for usual partial evaluation to derive more precise types.

14.1 Introduction

It is generally agreed that type information aids

- debugging to detect type inconsistencies as in [Johnson/Walz] for the functional language ML,

- program verification [Kanamori/Horiuchi],

- program documentation,

- optimized compiling [Tamaki/Sato], [Hentenryck/Dincbas], [Bruynooghe et al] and [Weiss/Schonberg] for the set-oriented language SETL.

If we consider Prolog as an untyped language, types have to be inferred from the program. To describe the resulting types, a type expression sublanguage (short: type language) is necessary. The type language is a subset of the programming language Prolog itself, thus making it particularly easy to deduce, reason about and utilize type information. Current research [Walker et al] in addition suggests that type information provides constructive negation. Our type representation is easily transformable to other representations like type expressions [Bruynooghe et al], regular trees [Mishra], polymorphic types [Mycroft/O'Keefe] or rewriting expressions [Zobel]. We provide a simple yet powerful type inference technique for full Prolog using Prolog resulting in Prolog. The inferred type procedures can be used to check the consistency of the program and in some cases even to generate instances of the type. Other approaches

- restrict Prolog,

- restrict types to be regular or non-recursive,

- employ a type sublanguage different from Prolog,

- do not remove redundancy in types,

- do not provide operations on types.

We define useful operations on types - this is not covered in this overview, see [Frühwirth-4,5]. These include type operations for negation, intersection and union of types as well as boolean operations for the comparison of types. A special operation called projection is utilized to infer types for an arbitrary subterm of a clause or procedure. The semantics of the operations is given by rewrite rules.

14.2 Preliminaries

We first define the logic programming languages for which our results apply. Then we clarify what we mean by types, operations on types and type inference.

14.2.1 Full Prolog

Full Prolog is any sequential Prolog implementation. Any system predicate is allowed. We assume the semantics described in [Lloyd]. In the examples discussed here we follow the syntax of Edinburgh Prolog. A Prolog *term* is either a constant, a variable, a function-symbol or a predicate-symbol applied to arguments. Arguments themselves are terms. The number of arguments (arity) is fixed for each function- and predicate- symbol. In most Prolog implementations function-

and predicate-symbols are not distinguished syntactically, but by context. A Prolog *program* is a finite set of procedures. A procedure defines a *predicate*. A *procedure* is a sequence (not set as in pure Prolog) of clauses. A *clause* consists of a *head* and a (possibly empty) body. The *body* consists of *subgoals* connected by *conjunctions* or *disjunctions*. A clause with an empty body is called *fact* (unit clause), any other clause *rule* . A fact is equivalent to a rule with the (empty) body *true*. A rule is *recursive* if a subgoal, directly or indirectly, calls the predicate associated with the rule.

14.2.2   Types in Prolog

The *type* of a predicate is defined by the type of its arguments. An n-ary predicate $p(a_1, a_2, \ldots, a_n)$ with n distinct variables a_i is said to be in *general form* [Kanamori/Horiuchi]. The form p/n is short for $p(A_1, A_2, \ldots, A_n)$ where the A_i's are distinct variables. Let $H_{p/n}$ be the Herbrand Universe (set of all ground terms) implied by p/n. Given n sets T_i (possibly infinite) of ground terms, then the tuples $(T_1 \times T_2 \times \ldots T_n)$ define the type of a predicate p/n if the sets T_i enumerate the ground instances of all terms occurring as argument A_i when the call to p/n succeeds. Variables are considered to stand for an arbitrary term of the Herbrand Universe. So the type inference mechanism proposed does not deal with mode information. For the handling of variables in projection (composition lemma), see there. A type predicate is a unary relation which is true and only true for every term in the set t_i. We may say that type predicates check whether a given term is in the domain of an argument A_i defined by the set T_i. E.g., for the predicate $p/2$ defined by the facts $\{p(1,a), p(2,b), p(3,c)\}$ the type is given as $(type\, p(X,Y) \leftarrow p_1(X), p_2(Y))$. The type predicate $p_1/1$ for the first argument is defined by the facts $\{p_1(1), p_1(2), p_1(3)\}$, $p_2/1$ by $\{p_2(a), p_2(b), p_2(c)\}$. The type of $p/2$ allows any combination of terms, thus $\{p(1,a), p(1,b), p(1,c), p(2,a), \ldots, p(3,c)\}$. Note that the predicates $p_1/1$ and $p_2/1$ define the smallest independent type for $p/2$.

The type of an argument may also be defined indirectly by the types of its subterms. Given $\{q(f(1,a)), q(f(2,b)), q(f(3,c))\}$ a valid type may be

$$\{q_1(f(1,a)), q_1(f(2,b)), q_1(f(3,c))\},$$

as well as

$$(q_1'(f(X,Y)) \leftarrow q_{1_1}(X), q_{1_2}(Y)),$$

where q_{1_1} and q_{1_2} define the obvious types. Of course the type of q_1 for q/1 is more precise than the type q_1'.

14.2.3   Operations on Types

There are three classes of operations on types. All operations take types as their arguments. The first class, type operations, yields a type as result. We define any of this operations on types in terms of the basic type operations negation and intersection. Note the analogy to relational algebra [Date]; Prolog implementations for the operations of relational algebra have been given in [Frühwirth-3]. Second, boolean operations provide comparison of types. Last, numeric operations measure properties of types and terms with integer values.

Program transformation (source-to-source transformation) is a meta-programming technique which maps one program into another program in the same language. Partial evaluation is a program transformation, which preserves the semantics of the program. Partial evaluation of operations on types is achieved by equality preserving rewrite rules of the form $(A \rightarrow B \text{ if } C)$. A and B are type expression, i.e., type goals or clauses of a type procedure. C is a precondition on the rule. The Prolog term A is replaced with the term B if conditions C are fulfilled. The rewrite rules preserve equality, that means that the types A and B have the same domain. A term is rewritten by repeatedly applying the rewrite rules to its components. Only the first matching rule with satisfied precondition is applied, so the rewriting process is deterministic. The transitive closure of the rewriting rules yields the initial type in standard form . If no more rewriting rule can be applied, the resulting type expression is the initial type expression in standard form.

14.2.4 Type Inference

Finding out the type of a procedure from its definition is called type inference. The object is to find as small a type assignment as feasible. The problem of finding the smallest type assignment is unsolvable. It is undecidable whether for a given set of parameters a procedure will succeed. Another problem is that types are often infinite sets [Kluzniak]. To solve the constraints implied by the definition, type unification is employed. This technique was first formulated by [Milner] for the functional language ML. Another method is type inference by dataflow analysis. A method first introduced for imperative programs is abstract interpretation [Bruynooghe et al]. We may think of it as having an abstract meta-interpreter producing conditions fulfilled by a query instead of successful instances of the query. Because of the termination problems with recursive structures, both methods must impose a depth-restriction on terms [Bruynooghe et al], [Kluzniak]. Instead of abstractly interpreting a goal our method 'abstractly compiles' the predicate it calls clausewise. As the transformed program is simpler than the original program, problems like recursions can be easier handled in the transformed program.

14.3 Type Language

The type language is defined. A standard form for types is introduced. In the following, we use the terms 'type' and 'type predicate' interchangeably.

14.3.1 Type Language and Type Predicates

The type language is a subset of pure Prolog like in [Kanamori/Horiuchi] and [Yardeni/Shapiro]. Hence the order of subgoals in a clause and of clauses in a procedure is not relevant. The subgoals of each clause are restricted to call type predicates (including itself). The only arguments allowed in the subgoals are the variables in the single argument of the head or in the arguments of a comparison. Therefore a type clause has no local variables.

Definition A *type program* consists of type procedures defining type predicates. The clauses of a type program satisfy the following conditions:

1. Every head is unary. There are special predefined unary predicates (basic types) which cannot be a head.

2. The body is a conjunction, disjunction or negation of subgoals.

3. A subgoal is either

    (a) a conjunction, disjunction or negation of subgoals or

    (b) a unary type predicate or

    (c) one of the nullary predicates 'true' and 'fail' or one of the binary predicates '=' and '= / ='.

4. Every variable in a clause occurs at most once in each of its literals. Every variable in the body occurs either in the head argument or in the argument of the predicates '=' and '= / ='.

Definition *Basic types* are predefined types which partition the ground terms in the Herbrand Universe into disjoint equivalence classes. For every ground term is exactly of one basic type. Basic types are disjoint. A proper set of basic types is {*integer/1, real/1, atom/1, compound/1*} [BSI]. We use these basic types in our examples. According to the definition of basic types we do not regard the type *integer* as subset of the type *real*. Note that the domain defined by a basic type can never be defined by a derived type predicate without that type. E.g. to define integers recursively, an increment function would be needed, which is not in the type language. For a theoretical discussion of this issue see [Blair].

Definition The universal type denoted by *any_term/1* defines the set of all ground terms in the Herbrand Universe. A call to *any_term/1* always succeeds. The union of all basic types yields the universal type.

```
% This type enumerates the seasons

season(spring).
season(summer).
season(autumn).
season(winter).

% The type for clauses

is_clause(C):- atom(C); compound(C).
% The type list defines a wellformed list

list([]).
list([X|L]):- list(L).
```

Figure 14.1: Derived type predicates

Definition The empty type denoted by *no_term/1* defines the empty set of terms. A call to *no_term/1* always fails. The intersection of any two different basic types yields the empty type. In practice, the empty type never comes into play, as type clauses containing it are removed. Such a type clause may indicate an ill-typed clause.

Definition A derived type predicate (figure 14.1) is a type predicate defined by a type procedure. A derived type cannot be a basic type and vice versa.

14.3.2 Standard Form

The purpose of type standardization is a non-redundant simplified representation of a type. Uniqueness is not enforced to avoid combinatorical explosion in the number of clauses. Different derived types for the same domain may have different standard types (figure 14.3). The standard type language is a superset of regular unary logic (RUL) proposed by [Yardeni/Shapiro]. Standardization is achieved by applying the rewriting rules given for each operation on types.

Definition A *standard type* (figure 14.2) is a derived type. The clauses of a standard type procedure satisfy the following conditions:

1. Non-redundancy. Every ground term in the domain of the type predicate is derivable exactly once.

2. The body is a conjunction of subgoals.

```
% The standard type for is_clause

is_clause(C):- atom(C).
is_clause(C):- compound(C).

% Now the standard type of lists

list([]).
list([X|L]):- any_term(X), list(L).

% Standard types of system predicates

type X=Y:- any_term(X), any_term(Y).
type X>Y:- numeric(X), numeric(Y).
type assert(C):- is_clause(C).
type functor(C,F,N):- is_clause(C), atom(F),integer(N).
```

Figure 14.2: Some standard types

3. A subgoal is either

   (a) a unary predicate or
   (b) the binary inequality predicate '$\neq$'.

4. Every variable in the single argument of the head is the single argument of exactly one subgoal in the body. If the single argument of the head is a variable, this variable is typed by a basic type.

5. Each recursive rule is directly recursive.

Unfolding of recursive rules as with *list/1* and different folding of clauses into subtypes as with *color'/1* allow different standard forms for the same domain. Nevertheless the definition guarantees that there is a non- redundant, unique standard form (up to renaming) for every type procedure and that types having the same standard form are identical.

14.4 Projection

We now describe how to compute the type for an arbitrary subterm of a procedure. This is done by applying type projection to arbitrary procedures. First, we say which subterm we want to type in a clause or procedure by giving the position of the subterm in the procedure head. Second, to derive a type for that position,

```
% Here is another standard type for lists

list'([]).
list'([X]).
list'([X,Y|L]):- any_term(X), any_term(Y), list'(L).
```

Figure 14.3: Different standard types for the same domain

we must type the variables at the position in the head. If a variable is contained in a subgoal, it is typed by this subgoal. To be exact, it is typed by the type of the position of the variable in the subgoal.

14.4.1 Position of a Term

We identify a subterm in a literal by its position in the literal ([Sterling/Shapiro], p.364). Independently a similar notion, that of a selector, is introduced in a recent paper of [Bruynooghe/Janssens]. The position is given as a list of indices and defined recursively by:

- $T[] = T$

- $f(T_1, \ldots, T_i, \ldots, T_n)[i, p_1, \ldots, p_r] = T_i[p_1, \ldots, p_r]$ where f is an arbitrary functor

For example the variable X has position $[1,1]$ in the term $list([X|L])$. Within a constant only the identity position $[]$ exists, within a variable potentially every position exists, but cannot be evaluated. The composition of two positions is again a position:

$$T[p_1, \ldots, p_r][q_1, \ldots, q_s] = T[p_1, \ldots, p_r, q_1, \ldots, q_s].$$

Composition Lemma Let $T[p_1, \ldots, p_r] = T_1$ and $T[p_1, \ldots, p_r][q_1, \ldots, q_s] = T_2$, then T_2 is also a subterm of T_1, as $T_1[q_1, \ldots, q_s] = T_2$. If we want to find the position of the subterm $T[p_1, \ldots, p_r, q_1, \ldots, q_s]$ in another Term S, but $T[p_1, \ldots, p_r]$ is a variable and has position $[t_1, \ldots, t_t]$ in S, $T[p_1, \ldots, p_r] = S[t_1, \ldots, t_t]$, then $T[p_1, \ldots, p_r, q_1, \ldots, q_s]$ has position $[t_1, \ldots, t_t, q_1, \ldots, q_s]$ in S.

14.4.2 Type Inference by the Projection Algorithm

Type projection is a program transformation technique. The algorithm simply transforms every literal of a procedure into literals of its type procedure (figure 14.4).

```
% Lets go for append/3

append([],L,L).
append([X|L1],L2,[X|L3]):- append(L1,L2,L3).

% Type projections for the arguments of append/3

append1([]).
append1([X|L1]):- append1(L1).

append2(L).
append2(L2):- append2(L2). % redundant recursion

append3(L).
append3([X|L3]):- append3(L3).
```

Figure 14.4: Types derived by type projection

Given a procedure P and a subterm position $[p_1, \ldots, p_r]$, the procedure P consists of clauses $(H_i \leftarrow B_i)$ with subgoals SG_{i_j}. The type procedure for $P[p_1, \ldots, p_r]$ consists of clauses $(TH_i \leftarrow TB_i)$. Let $H_i[p_1, \ldots, p_r] = A_i$ and Vs_i be the (possibly empty) set of free variables in the term A_i. If $H_i[p_1, \ldots, p_n]$ with $n < r$ is a variable, then introduce a new variable A_i with $H_i[p_1, \ldots, p_r] = A_i$ and apply the composition lemma given in section 14.4.1. If the position does not exist in a term, the subterm has the empty type. Type projection transforms each clause $(H_i \leftarrow B_i)$ into the corresponding type clause $(TH_i \leftarrow TB_i)$, where

1. the argument of TH_i is $H_i[p_1, \ldots, p_r]$, and

2. in TB_i every subgoal SG_{i_j} of B_i is replaced by a conjunction of type predicates of SG_{i_j}. For every variable occurring in $H_i[p_1, \ldots, p_r]$ also occurring in SG_{i_j} at position $[p_1, \ldots, p_s]$ the type predicate of $SG_{i_j}[p_1, \ldots, p_s]$ with the single argument V is in this conjunction. If SG_{i_j} contains no variable of $H_i[p_1, \ldots, p_r]$ replace it by 'true'.

The type identifier (functor of the type procedure) assumed here is the functor of the procedure extended by the position typed.

14.5 Standardization

Standardization provides a non-redundant, unique representation (up to renaming) of types generated by projection. We divide the standardization process into four steps according to the four conditions - preprocessing, type intersection, type union, postprocessing. Standardization has a strong resemblance to partial evaluation (specialized for pure Prolog with only unary predicates) as defined in [Tamaki/Sato-2] and [Venken]. We employ unfolding in a breadth first manner to guarantee earliest possible termination of the algorithm.

The Algorithm At every stage of the algorithm: Immediately remove clauses which contain a subgoal identical to their head to avoid redundant recursion; immediately remove the subgoal 'true' in conjunctions.

14.5.1   Preprocessing

1. Standardize all types called by the type procedure to be standardized.

2. Unfold disjunctions by replacing them by a set of clauses, one for each or-branch (see [Lloyd] for more details).

14.5.2   Type Intersection

Removing redundancy within clauses syntactically means to replace all subgoals containing the same variable by a single subgoal. Type intersection is analogous to the unification of type expressions in [Zobel] and performed by repeatedly unfolding (and folding for recursive rules) the subgoals. Each clause is processed in the following way:

1. if there is no subgoal for a variable V of the head, then insert $any\_term(V)$

2. if there is exactly one subgoal then exit

3. if there is more than one subgoal for a variable V of the head, then replace them by a call to the type resulting from the intersection of these subgoals.

Termination If both types are basic, termination is straightforward. Else r and s are unfolded (or copied if basic types). For every resulting conjunction the standardization algorithm is recursively applied. For every variable in a conjunction typed more than once, those types are intersected. Repeated unfolding of a non-recursive derived type will result in conjunctions of basic types or 'true' in the end. Thus the algorithm terminates when at least one non-recursive type is in the intersection. If both types are recursive, repeated unfolding will result in the reoccurrence of a type. If the same variable is typed as in the starting type, the type is removed as redundant recursion. Else the unfolding will go on, till both types in the intersection are re-occurring, then they will be folded and the algorithm terminates.

```
% The standard form of the types of append/3

append1([]).
append1([X|L1]):- any_term(X), append1(L1).

append2(L):- any_term(L).

append3(L):- any_term(L).
```

Figure 14.5: Standard type predicates for *append/3*

14.5.3 Type Union

To remove redundancy the clauses are checked pairwise for common i.e. redundant solutions. We remove redundancy by computing the union of the subtypes defined by the clauses. The redundancy check is performed by intersecting the bodies of the clauses over the most general unifier implied by their heads.

Program 14.5 shows the standard type predicates for *append/3*.

14.6 Extended Type Projection

Type projection can be extended by partial evaluation and negation handling. Extended type projection results in more precise types.

14.6.1 Partial Evaluation

The idea is to call goals which are sufficiently bound [Venken], so that only terms of its solution are in the corresponding type. A goal is safely callable in the process of partial evaluation, if it is sufficiently bound so that the set of solutions is finite (in practice: sufficiently small) and if the predicate called by the goal is

1. free of side-effects (unlike *!/0*, *assert/1*, *read/1*,...),

2. not dependent on the state of computation (unlike *var/1*, *clause/2*, *random/2*, *time/1*,...).

The predicate *safely_callable/1* (figure 14.6) checks if a predicate is safely callable. The system predicate *bound/1* (synonym for *nonvar/1*) checks if a term is bound (not a free variable). The system predicate *ground/1* succeeds for any ground term.

With partial evaluation, aliasing can be covered resulting in more precise types. (Nevertheless, aliasing is better handled by introducing polymorphic types, see [Frühwirth-5]). Aliasing is the effect that in a call two terms contained in the

```
safely_callable(X=Y).
safely_callable(X==Y).
safely_callable(X>Y):- bound(X), bound(Y).
safely_callable(call(C)):- safely_callable(C).
safely_callable(functor(C,F,N)):- bound(C).
safely_callable(functor(C,F,N)):- bound(F), bound(N).
```

Figure 14.6: Some safely callable system predicates

```
type X=X:- any_term(X).
type X==X:-any_term(X).
type X<=X:- numeric(X).
type X<=Y:- numeric(X), numeric(Y).
type assert(C):- is_clause(C).
type functor(F,F,0):- atom(F).
type functor(C,F,N):- compound(C), atom(F), integer(N).
```

Figure 14.7: Extended types for system predicates

arguments may be unified. A predicate is aliasing if its procedure includes a clause where a variable appears more than once in the head. Some system predicates are aliasing (figure 14.7).

14.6.2 Negation of Goals

With type negation the types of a class of negated goals can be inferred. But note that in most cases the negated goal succeeds not only for all instances not in the type of the goal, but also for most instances in the type of the goal. In this case the only type derivable is the universal type, so the negation could simply be ignored. Nevertheless if the procedures called by a negated goal satisfy the definition of a type procedure, we can utilize all type information inherent in the negation. First we standardize the subgoals of the negated call. The resulting negation is removed by program transformation. The only negative information necessary is the negated unification operator $\neq /2$; therefore it was introduced in the type language (figure 14.8).

14.7 Discussion

Our work may be seen as extension of [Zobel], although the approaches are completely different. [Zobel] removes some but not all redundancy with simplifi-

```
% not(integer(X)) is replaced by

not_integer(X):- real(X).
not_integer(X):- atom(X).
not_integer(X):- string(X).
not_integer(X):- compound(X).

% not(list(X)) is replaced by

not_list(X):- X =/= [], X =/= [_|_].
not_list([X|L]):- not_list(L).
```

Figure 14.8: Negated types of integer and list

cation; recursion causes some minor problems. [Tamaki/Sato], [Kluzniak] concentrate on the inference process, thus a type language is not defined and operations on types are not covered. The depth of terms is restricted. So their types are non-recursive in [Bruynooghe et al], [Kluzniak], [Tamaki/Sato]. In [Kanamori/Horiuchi], [Mishra] types are inferred from pure Prolog predicates. [Bruynooghe et al] does not allow repeating functors in types, he provides intersection and a restriction-operation (merging) on type graphs. Merging may be seen as a special kind of union. All types must be taken from a predefined set of disjoint types in [Kanamori/Horiuchi]. [Kluzniak] uses a data-flow-oriented approach in Ground Prolog to synthesize types. [Mishra] provides a distribution operation. [Tamaki/Sato] describes the derivation of success sets in pure Prolog and their application. Our type system can be characterized in the following way:

- type language which is a subset of pure Prolog

- types are fully recursive and non-regular

- a non-redundant standard form for types is defined

- a rich set of operations on types including negation

- type inference by type projection in full Prolog

- projection types any subterm of a clause or procedure

- usual partial evaluation by rewrite rules makes type inference more precise

But we also like to mention the deficiencies of the approach as presented here:

- type declarations and type checking are not handled

- type inference by projection cannot utilize the type information contained in local variables of a clause like most other approaches to type inference do, therefore may be less precise

- aliasing is not covered in full generality like in [Kluzniak] and [Bruynooghe], again type information is lost

These problems are overcome in [Frühwirth-5], mainly by extending the type system sketched in this paper with polymorphic types.

14.8   Further Work

Further work [Frühwirth-5] defines a powerful polymorphic type systems based on the approach presented in this paper. Another interesting area is the application of the type system to aid debugging and program verification.

Acknowledgements   I would like to thank anonymous referees as well as Gerhard Fleischanderl, Franz Reichl, Andi Falkner for comments on earlier versions of the paper. I am grateful to Andrea Walter and Georg Gottlob for their support.

References

[Ait-Kaci/Nasr]   Ait-Kaci H and Nasr R, Logic and Inheritance, 13th ACM Symp. on Principles of Programming Languages, St. Petersburg Beach Florida, 1986

[Blair]   Blair H A, Metalogic Programming and Direct Universal Computability, Workshop on Meta-Programming in Logic Programming, Bristol U.K., June 22-24 1988

[Bruynooghe et al]   Bruynooghe M, Janssens G, Callebaut A and Demoen B, Abstract Interpretation: Towards the Global Optimization of Prolog Programs, 1987 Symposium on Logic Programming, San Fransisco California, 1987

[Bruynooghe/Janssens]   Bruynooghe M and Janssens G, An Instance of Abstract Interpretation: Integrating Type and Mode Inferencing, Extended Abstract, Dept. of Computer Science, Katholieke Universiteit Leuven, 1988

[BSI]   Scowen R S (Ed), Chung P, Dodd T, North N and Rubinstein M, Prolog Built-In Predicates Draft 4 PS/201, British Standards Institution, Teddington Middlesex, 1987

[Chan/Wallace]   Chan W and Wallace M, A Treatment of Negation during Partial Evaluation, Workshop on Meta-Programming in Logic Programming, Bristol U.K., June 22-24 1988

[Date]   Date C J, An Introduction to Database Systems, Third Edition, Addison-Wesley, Reading Massachusetts, February 1982

[Frühwirth-1]   Frühwirth Thom W, Type Inference by Program Transformation and Partial Evaluation, Workshop on Meta-Programming in Logic Programming, Bristol U.K., June 22-24 1988

[Frühwirth-2]   Frühwirth Thom W, Type Inference by Program Transformation and Partial Evaluation, IEEE Int. Conf. on Computer Languages 88, Miami Beach Florida, October 9-13 1988

[Frühwirth-3]   Frühwirth Thom W, Prolog, Logik und Datenbanken, Master Thesis (in german), Technical University of Vienna, Institut fuer Praktische Informatik, Vienna Austria, May 1986

[Frühwirth-4]   Frühwirth Thom W, A Type Language for Prolog and its Application to Type Inference, Computational Intelligence 88, Milan Italy, September 26-30 1988

[Frühwirth-5]   Frühwirth Thom W, A Polymorphic Type System for Prolog, Ph.D. Thesis, Technical University of Vienna, Vienna Austria, January 1989

[Johnson/Walz]   Johnson G F and Walz J A, A Maximum-Flow Approach to Anomaly Isolation in Unification-Based Incremental Type Inference, 13th ACM Symp. on Principles of Programming Languages, St. Petersburg Beach Florida, 1986

[Kanamori/Horiuchi]   Kanamori T and Horiuchi K, Type Inference in Prolog and its Application, 9th Int. Joint Conf. on Artificial Intelligence, Los Angeles California, 1985

[Kluzniak]   Kluzniak F, Type Synthesis for Ground Prolog, 4th Int. Conf. on Logic Programming, Melbourne Australia, 1987

[Lloyd]   Lloyd J W, Foundations of Logic Programming, Second, extended Edition, Springer Verlag, Berlin Germany,1987

[Milner]   Milner R, A Theory of Type Polymorphism in Programming, Journal on Computer and System Sciences Vol 17 No 3, 1978, pp 348-375

[Mishra]   Mishra P, Towards a Theory of Types in Prolog, 1984 Symposium on Logic Programming, Atlantic City New Jersey, 1984

[Mycroft/O'Keefe]   Mycroft A and O'Keefe R A, A Polymorphic Type System for Prolog, Artificial Intelligence, Vol 23, No 3, August 1984, pp 295-307

[Sterling/Shapiro]   Sterling L and Shapiro E, The Art of Prolog, MIT Press, Cambridge Massachusetts, 1986

[Tamaki/Sato]   Tamaki II and Sato T, Enumeration of Success Patterns in Logic Programs, Theoretical Computer Science 34, pp 227-240, North-Holland, 1984

[Tamaki/Sato-2]   Tamaki II and Sato T, Unfold/Fold Transformation of Logic Programs, 2nd Int. Conf. on Logic Programming, Upsalla Sweden, 1984

[Hentenryck]   Van Hentenryck P, A Theoretical Framework for Consistency Techniques in Logic Programming, 10th Int. Joint Conf. on Artificial Intelligence, Milan Italy, 1987

[Hentenryck/Dincbas]   Van Hentenryck P and Dincbas M, Domains in Logic Programming, National Conf. on Artificial Intelligence, Philadelphia, 1986

[Venken]   Venken R, A Prolog Meta-Interpreter for Partial Evaluation and its Application to Source to Source Transformation and Query-Optimization, in T.O'Shea (ed), Advances in Artificial Intelligence, ECCAI, Elsevier Science Publisher, Holland, 1985

[Walker et al]   Walker A , Foo N, Rao A, Taylor A, Deduced Relevant Types and Constructive Negation in Logic Programming, Report RC 13407, IBM T.J. Watson Research Center, New York, 1988

[Wegner/Cardelli]   Wegner P and Cardelli L, On Understanding Types, Data Abstraction, and Polymorphism, Computing Surveys, Vol 17, No 4, December 1985

[Weiss/Schonberg]	Weiss G and Schonberg E, Typefinding Recursive Structures: A Data-Flow Analysis in the Presence of Infinite Type Sets, 1986 Int. Conf. on Computer Languages, Miami Florida, 1986
[Yardeni/Shapiro]	Yardeni E and Shapiro E, A Type System for Logic Programs, in Concurrent Prolog: Collected papers, Shapiro E (ed), Vol 2, MIT Press, Cambridge Massachusetts, 1987, pp 211-244
[Zobel]	Zobel J, Derivation of Polymorphic Types for Prolog Programs, 4th Int. Conf. on Logic Programming, Melbourne Australia, 1987

Appendix

We show the result of applying our method for type inference, namely projection and subsequent standardization, to examples taken from other papers on type inference.

```
- Permuting Recursion [ZOBEL]

p(a,b).
p(X,Y):-p(Y,X).

% Projecting the arguments

p1(a).
p1(X):-p2(X).

p2(b).
p2(X):-p1(X).

% Result of standardization

p1(a).  p2(a).
p1(b).  p2(b).

- Mutual Recursion [ZOBEL]

even([]).
even([X|L]):-odd(L).

odd([X]).
```

```
odd([X,Y|L]):-even([Y|L]).
```

% Projection and standardization of arguments

```
even1([]).
even1([X|L]):-any_term(X), odd1(L).
```

```
odd1([X]) :- any_term(X).
odd1([X,Y|L]):- any_term(X), any_term(Y), odd1(L).
```

- Checking, if the elements of a list are sorted [ZOBEL]

```
sorted([]).
sorted([X]).
sorted([X,Y|L]):- XsY,sorted([Y|L]).
```

% Projection on the argument
% and on the positions needed by the argument

```
sorted1([]).
sorted1([X]).
sorted1([X,Y|L]):- numeric(X), numeric(Y), sorted11(Y),sorted12(L).
```

```
sorted11(X).
sorted11(X):- numeric(X).
```

```
sorted12([]).
sorted12([Y|L]):- numeric(Y), sorted11(Y),sorted12(L).
```

% Standardization

```
sorted1([]).
sorted1([X]).
sorted1([X,Y|L]):- numeric(X), numeric(Y), sorted12(L).
```

```
sorted12([]).
sorted12([Y|L]):- numeric(Y), sorted12(L).
```

- Generate a two lists of natural numbers,
  one odd, one even [KLUZNIAK]

```
gen(N,[],[]).
gen(N,[N|L1],[s(N)|L2]):- gen(s(s(N)),L1,L2).
```

```
% Project and standardize the arguments

gen1(N):- any_term(N).
gen2([]).
gen2([N|L1]):- any_term(N), gen2(L1).

gen3([]).
gen3([s(N)|L2]):- any_term(N), gen3(L2).

- Parser for regular expression by (a,b,emp) [TAMAKI/SATO]

exp(X,Z):- term(X,Y), exp_(Y,Z).
exp_(['+'|X],Z):- term(X,Y), exp_(Y,Z).
exp_(X,X).

term(X,Z):- factor(X,Y), term_(Y,Z).
term_(X,Z):- factor(X,Y), term_(Y,Z).
term_(X,X).

factor(['('|X],Z):- exp(X,[')'|Y]), factor_(Y,Z).
factor([a|X],Z):- factor_(X,Z).
factor([b|X],Z):- factor_(X,Z).
factor([emp|X],Z):- factor_(X,Z).
factor_(['*'|X],Z):- factor_(X,Z).
factor_(X,X).

% Type of first argument of exp/2

exp1(X):- term1(X).
exp_1(['+'|X],Z):- term1(X).
exp_1(X).

term1(X):- factor1(X).
term_1(X):- factor1(X).
term_1(X).

factor1(['('|X]):- exp1(X).
factor1([a|X]):- factor_1(X).
factor1([b|X]):- factor_1(X).
factor1([emp|X]):- factor_1(X).

factor_1(['*'|X]):- factor_1(X).
```

```
factor_1(X).

% Towards standard type of first argument of exp/2

exp1(X):- term1(X).
exp_1(X):- any_term(X).
term1(X):- factor1(X).
term_1(X):- any_term(X).
factor1(['('|X]):- exp1(X).
factor1([a|X]):- factor_1(X).
factor1([b|X]):- factor_1(X).
factor1([emp|X]):- factor_1(X).

factor_1(X):- any_term(X).

% Standard type of first argument of exp/2

exp1(['('|X]):- exp1(X).
exp1([a|X]):- any_term(X).
exp1([b|X]):- any_term(X).
exp1([emp|X]):- any_term(X).
```

Chapter 15

Complete Sets of Frontiers in Logic-based Program Transformation

Mantis H.M. Cheng   *Maarten H. van Emden*

Paul A. Strooper

Department of Computer Science, University of Victoria, Victoria, B.C., V8W 2Y2 Canada.

Abstract

Logic-based program transformation allows us to convert logic programs that are obviously correct (and as such can be considered as specifications), but often inefficient, into more efficient ones in such a way that correctness of answers is preserved. However, existing methods either do not guarantee completeness, or else introduce redundancy. We present a method for using sets of "partial derivation trees" to obtain a specialized version of a program for a particular query, guaranteeing completeness and avoiding redundancy. An example of specializing a meta interpreter for a particular program is given.

15.1 Introduction

The "fold" and "unfold" transformations were introduced by Burstall and Darlington [1] to make functional programs more efficient. What they had in mind was a system of "computer-aided programming" where a specification in functional form is transformed by means of a computer program into a functional program of acceptable efficiency. Independently of each other, Clark [2] and Hogger [5] have shown that these transformations also apply to logic programs. They pointed out that in this context they have an additional advantage: the transformed version is a logical consequence of the original. As a result, any answer obtainable from the transformed program is also an answer obtainable from the specification. The properties of logical consequence guarantee correctness with respect to the specification. But this correctness is only what is usually called *partial* correctness: it is not always clear whether all answers obtainable from the specification can also be obtained from the result of the transformation. When this is the case, we say that the transformed program is *complete* with respect to the specification.

In this paper we are only concerned with the "unfold" transformation, also called "partial evaluation" or "symbolic execution". As such, it appeals more directly to programming intuition: the transformed program is the result of replacing procedure calls by the appropriately instantiated bodies of their definitions. This sometimes allows more efficient execution of the transformed program.

But partial evaluation is only useful if we know it yields a complete result, otherwise we cannot discard the inefficient specification. Tamaki and Sato [12] show that certain transformations on clauses, including unfolding, preserve completeness. To make the results of Tamaki and Sato applicable to our purpose, it is necessary to eliminate from the program those clauses which are redundant with respect to the desired query. Although this can be achieved by means of a dependency analysis done after the transformations, we found it possible to combine the unfold transformation with a dependency analysis to achieve the desired result in a single operation, which is to build what we call a "complete set of frontiers".

In doing so, we take as starting point the idea of Vasey [15], who shows that the result of unfolding can be regarded as a "qualified answer". We obtain the desired completeness by considering frontiers of "conditional answers" (our preferred terminology for Vasey's qualified answers) in a suitable derivation tree. As a first approximation, our completeness is based on the fact that in the derivation tree no computation can "escape" the frontier. This observation is only an approximation, because in all but a few trivial cases one has to consider more than a single derivation tree with frontier. We characterize when enough frontiers have been found. These are then a set of clauses obtained by unfolding which is complete with respect to the specification.

Using a different criterion for completeness, Lloyd and Shepherdson [8] independently found a result similar to our frontier theorem.

15.2   The frontier theorem

From now on, we assume without loss of generality that each query posed to a logic program consists of a single goal. If this were not the case, and we would have a query of the form $?G_1, \ldots, G_n$ for $n > 1$, we can add the clause $G(X_1, \ldots, X_m) \leftarrow G_1, \ldots, G_n$ to the program and replace the query by $?G(X_1, \ldots, X_m)$. Here G stands for any predicate symbol not appearing elsewhere in the program, and $X_1, \ldots, X_m$ are the variables occurring in $G_1, \ldots, G_n$.

A *derivation tree* for a query Q is a tree with Q at the root. Each node in the tree is a query consisting of a conjunction of atomic formulae, called the *goals* of the query. If the query is not empty, it has a *selected goal*. A node N, consisting of the query $?G_1, \ldots, G_n$ with selected goal G_i has a child for each clause whose head unifies with G_i. If G_i unifies with the head of the clause $A \leftarrow B_1, \ldots, B_m$ with most general unifier θ, then the corresponding child consists of the query $?(G_1, \ldots, G_{i-1}, B_1, \ldots, B_m, G_{i+1}, \ldots, G_n)\theta$.

A *derivation* is a path starting from the root in the derivation tree which is either infinite or ends in a leaf node of the derivation tree. A *successful* derivation is a derivation ending in an empty query, denoted by □. A *failed* derivation is a derivation ending in a non-empty query with no children. It follows from the definition that this only happens if the selected goal does not unify with the head of any clause of the program. A *partial derivation* is a path starting from the root in the derivation tree. It can end in a non-leaf node of the derivation tree.

It should be noted that Prolog finds its answers by constructing a particular type of derivation tree, the *Prolog derivation tree*. This derivation tree is obtained by always selecting the leftmost goal in each query, and by ordering the children of a node in the same way as the corresponding clauses in the program. A successful response by Prolog corresponds to a successful derivation in the Prolog derivation tree, the answer substitution being the composition of all substitutions made in that derivation.

Starting with a program P, if there exists a successful derivation of the query $?G$, with θ being the composition of all substitutions in the derivation, then we say that $G\theta$ is an *(unconditional) answer* to the query. In this case the answer is a logical consequence of the program P, which we write as:

$$P \models \forall G\theta$$

where the universal quantification is over all variables in $G\theta$.

If, starting from the query $?G$, we have derived a non-empty query $?G_1, \ldots, G_n$, with θ being the composition of all substitutions so far, then the clause $G\theta \leftarrow G_1, \ldots, G_n$ is a *conditional* answer to the query. Again, as can easily be shown from the soundness of resolution, we have:

$$P \models \forall (G\theta \leftarrow G_1, \ldots, G_n)$$

where the universal quantification is over all variables occurring in the clause $G\theta \leftarrow G_1, \ldots, G_n$.

DEFINITION 15.1 (Partial derivation tree). *A partial derivation tree is a finite initial subtree of a derivation tree in which it is possible for non-empty leaf queries not to have a selected goal.*

In a partial derivation tree there are three types of leaves: empty queries, failed queries (these have a selected goal, but no children nodes) and non-empty queries with no selected goal. For each empty query, there is a corresponding unconditional answer. Each non-empty query with no selected goal has a corresponding conditional answer.

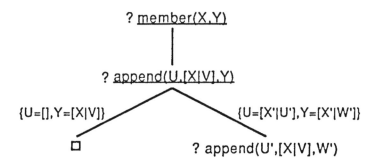

Figure 15.1: Partial derivation tree for member.

For example, consider the following program, defining the membership relation using the append relation:

```
% member( E, L ): element E is a member of list L.
% example: member( 3, [1,2,3,4,5] )
member( E, L ) <- append( U, [E|V], L );

% append( U, V, W ): list W is list V appended to list U.
% example: append( [1,2], [3,4,5], [1,2,3,4,5] )
append( [], V, V );
append( [X|U], V, [X|W] ) <- append( U, V, W );
```

A partial derivation tree for the query ?member(X,Y) is shown in Figure 15.1 (the selected goals are underlined).

DEFINITION 15.2 (Frontier). *The frontier of a partial derivation tree is the set of all unconditional and conditional answers corresponding to the leaf nodes.*

The frontier for the partial derivation tree in Figure 15.1 consists of the clauses

```
member( X, [X|V] );
member( X, [X'|W'] ) <- append( U', [X|V], W' );
```

where the first clause is the unconditional answer corresponding to the left branch of the partial derivation tree. The second clause is the conditional answer corresponding to the right branch.

The frontier of a partial derivation tree consists of clauses, and as such, we can regard it as a logic program. We would like to replace our original program by a frontier, but if we do that, the resulting program will not be complete. To obtain completeness, we have to consider a suitable set of frontiers, giving rise to a logic program by including the clauses in all of the frontiers. We formalize this idea by defining a *complete set of frontiers*.

In the following discussion, $L(F)$ denotes the set of goals appearing in the bodies of the clauses of a frontier F. Similarly, for a set of frontiers S, $L(S)$ denotes the union of the $L(F)$ for every frontier F in S. For a frontier F, $R(F)$ denotes the root of the partial derivation tree having F as a frontier. Finally, the goal G_1 is an *instance* of the goal G_2, if there exists a substitution θ such that $G_1 = G_2\theta$.

DEFINITION 15.3 (Complete set of frontiers). *A set of frontiers S for a query Q is complete iff the following three conditions hold:*

1. *each frontier F in S is non-trivial, that is, at least the root itself has a selected goal.*

2. *there is a frontier F in S such that Q is an instance of $R(F)$.*

3. *for each goal G in $L(S)$, there is a frontier F in S such that G is an instance of $R(F)$.*

The frontier for the partial derivation tree in Figure 15.1 is not complete by itself. The goal append(U',[X|V],W') is not an instance of the root of the partial derivation tree. If we add the frontier obtained by unfolding this goal once, which is

```
append( [], [X|V], [X|V] );
append( [X'|U'], [X|V], [X'|W'] ) <- append( U', [X|V], W' );
```

then we obtain a complete set of frontiers. Note that this is a version of the append program specialized for the purpose of the member program.

Any program P has at least one complete set of frontiers. For example, if we construct a frontier for the most general form of every predicate symbol appearing in P, then we have a complete set of frontiers (note that a frontier can be empty, which takes care of undefined calls in P). In fact, if we consider the frontiers in which we only select the root and do not select goals for any of the queries appearing at depth 1 in the partial derivation tree, then we obtain our original program as a complete set of frontiers.

The complete sets of frontiers given above are not very useful. The following algorithm suggests a more general way to obtain a complete set of frontiers S for a query Q and a program P.

1. Start with the frontier of any partial derivation tree for the query Q as the only element in S.

2. Select any goal, G, occurring in $L(S)$, but which is not an instance of $R(F)$ for any frontier F in S. Add the frontier of any partial derivation tree for

G to the set, after removing any frontier F for which $R(F)$ is an instance of G (since the answers in such a frontier will also be included in the frontier of G).

3. If no such goal exists, then S is a complete set of frontiers for Q in P.

Although we can select any goal which is not an instance of a derivation tree already constructed, it is often more efficient to choose the *most general form* of all the occurrences of any such goals with the same predicate symbol. The intuition behind a complete set of frontiers is that they are expanded versions of the original program specialized to the query. The following result formalizes this idea.

LEMMA **15.1.** *Let S be a complete set of frontiers for a query Q and a program P. If the goal G is an instance of $R(F)$ for a frontier F in S, and if there is a successful derivation D of G in P, then there is a successful derivation D' of G in S. Moreover, if θ_1 and θ_2 are the compositions of all substitutions in D and D' respectively, then $G\theta_1$ is an instance of $G\theta_2$.*

A proof of this lemma is presented in the appendix.

THEOREM **15.1** (Frontier Theorem). *If P is a program, Q a query, and S a complete set of frontiers for Q, then*

$$[Q] \cap \text{ success set of } P = [Q] \cap \text{ success set of } S$$

where $[Q]$ is the set of all ground instances of Q.

Proof   By the correctness of SLD-resolution we know that

$$\text{success set of } P \supseteq \text{success set of } S$$

and hence we also have

$$[Q] \cap \text{ success set of } P \supseteq [Q] \cap \text{ success set of } S.$$

Conversely, if $G \in [Q] \cap$ success set of P, then $G \in [Q]$ and by the definition of a complete set of frontiers we know that G is an instance of $R(F)$ for a frontier F in S. Thus we can apply the previous lemma (G is a ground goal, so the substitutions that take place during the derivation do not concern us here) to conclude that $G \in$ success set of S, and hence

$$[Q] \cap \text{ success set of } P \subseteq [Q] \cap \text{ success set of } S$$

and the proof is completed.   ∎

It should be noted that the frontier theorem is valid for frontiers of any derivation tree, not just the Prolog derivation tree. In this way, selection methods other than Prolog's can be "compiled into" the frontier.

In the next section, we give a detailed example of how the frontier theorem can be used. To illustrate the ideas involved we give a small example here, similar to one in [3]. Consider the following program to transpose a matrix:

```
% A matrix is represented as a list of rows, for example
% [[1,2,3],[4,5,6]].
% transpose( M1, M2 ): matrix M2 is the transpose of matrix M1.
% Example: transpose( [[1,2,3],[4,5,6]], [[1,4],[2,5],[3,6]] )
transpose( M, [] ) <- nullrows( M );
transpose( M, [R|Rs] ) <-
        colMat( R, M1, M ) & transpose( M1, Rs );

% colMat( C, M, CM ): matrix CM has column C as its first
%        column; the remainder of its columns constitute
%        matrix M.
% Example: colMat( [1,4], [[2,3],[5,6]], [[1,2,3],[4,5,6]] )
colMat( [], [], [] );
colMat( [X|Y], [Xs|Ys], [[X|Xs] | T] ) <- colMat( Y, Ys, T );

% nullRows( M ): matrix M only has empty rows in it.
% Example: nullRows( [[],[],[]] )
nullRows( [] );
nullRows( [[] | Rows] ) <- nullRows( Rows );
```

Suppose we know a matrix has two rows; then we obtain a specialized program by calculating a complete set of frontiers for the query ?transpose([R1,R2],T). The frontier of the partial derivation tree in Figure 15.2 consists of the clauses

```
T1: transpose( [[],[]], [] );
T2: transpose( [[X|Xs],[X'|Xs']], [[X,X'] | Rs] ) <-
            transpose( [Xs,Xs'], Rs );
```

where T1 is the unconditional answer corresponding to the derivation ending with the empty query. T2 is the conditional answer corresponding to right branch of the partial derivation tree. Since the only goal appearing in the body of the clauses is an instance of the root of the derivation tree, we know that this is a complete set of frontiers. Therefore, we have derived a specialized program to transform $n \times 2$ matrices.

15.3 Example: specializing a meta-interpreter

Meta programming is a powerful technique in logic programming. An example is a meta-interpreter allowing the programmer to separate the control and the data component of the program. A major problem with meta programming is the

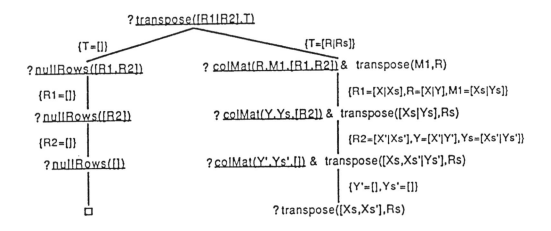

Figure 15.2: Partial derivation tree for transpose.

inherent lack of efficiency. Partial evaluation can be used to solve this efficiency problem [3, 11, 10]. In this section we show how we can use partial derivation trees to perform this task. The frontier theorem guarantees us that the resulting program is both correct and complete.

The application we will use is dataflow programming. Consider the dataflow network shown in Figure 15.3, which finds the sequence of Fibonacci numbers (this type of network was proposed in [6]). To keep the exposition simple, we consider an example with only two nodes; more interesting examples of dataflow programming are shown in [16]. Each node represents a processor, each arc a communication channel. Data flows through the arcs in the direction associated with it. Each processor computes independently of the others, and is activated as soon as enough data is available in its input channels.

The add node adds the two numbers on its input channels, and puts the result on its output channel. The shift node needs two numbers on its input channel; it copies one of these to each of its output channels. It removes only the first number from its input channel during the computation. The initial state of the network is shown in Figure 15.3; the channel between add and shift contains a 0 and a 1, the others are empty.

To represent the network in logic (see [13]), we first translate the nodes into a logic program. The definitions for the nodes in the network are

```
add( [X|Xs], [Y|Ys], [Z|Zs] ) <-
```

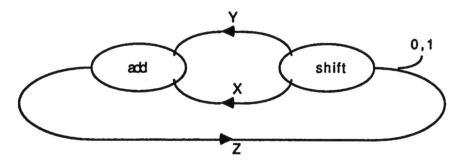

Figure 15.3: Dataflow network for the Fibonacci problem.

```
sum( X, Y, Z ) & add( Xs, Ys, Zs );

shift( [X1,X2|Xs], [X1|Ys], [X2|Zs] ) <-
     shift( [X2|Xs], Ys, Zs );
```

The relation sum(X, Y, Z) holds if Z = X + Y. To solve the Fibonacci problem, we have to specify how the nodes in the network are connected, and what the initial state of the network is. This is done by the condition in

```
fib( [0,1|Z] ) <- shift( [0,1|Z], X, Y ) & add( X, Y, Z );
```

The connections are represented by shared variables between the nodes, where the variables represent the stream of data flowing through a particular channel. The initial state is the difference between the arguments of two nodes that are connected. If we now ask the query ?fib(F) we would like F to be instantiated to the stream of Fibonacci numbers (note that we have an infinite derivation, so that in fact we never obtain a successful answer substitution; so what we want is F to be instantiated during this infinite computation).

Unfortunately, when we run this query on the standard Prolog interpreter, F only gets instantiated to a stream of uninstantiated variables. This is because the AND-control required to solve this problem is more complex than the one provided by Prolog, which attempts to prove a goal completely before proving the next goal in a query. One solution to this problem is to transform this program so that the AND-control is replaced by OR-control [14], which is easy to provide in Prolog. In this example we demonstrate the alternative of building a meta-interpreter providing the required AND-control.

In this problem, it is sufficient to treat the goals in a query as a queue rather than a stack; as in the meta-interpreter:

```
% prove( L ): the list of goals L can be proven.
prove( [] );
prove( [Goal | Goals] ) <-
```

```
            clause( Goal, Body ) &
            append( Goals, Body, NewGoals ) &
            prove( NewGoals );

    % append( U, V, W ): list W is list V appended to list U.
    % example: append( [1,2], [3,4,5], [1,2,3,4,5] )
    append( [], L, L );
    append( [X|Xs], L, [X|NL] ) <- append( Xs, L, NL );
```

More complex dataflow networks require a meta-interpreter based on the "freeze" concept [4].

Now that we are using a meta-interpreter, we have to specify the clauses of our program through the clause predicate. The clauses for the add and shift relation are

```
    % clause( H, B ) asserts that there is a clause with head H and
    %                body B in the program.
    clause( add([X|Xs],[Y|Ys],[Z|Zs]),[add(Xs,Ys,Zs)] ) <-
            sum( X, Y, Z );
    clause( shift([X1,X2|Xs],[X1|Ys],[X2|Zs]),
            [shift([X2|Xs],Ys,Zs)] );
```

Note that the sum predicate is moved outside the body as defined by the clause predicate. There are two reasons for this. First, it is a built-in predicate, which cannot be handled by our meta-interpreter as it stands. Moreover, we do not want it to be placed on the queue of goals to be executed. Instead, we want to execute it whenever we use the add clause. This is to make sure that the appropriate values get instantiated for the other clauses. As it turns out, this is not necessary in this case, as the shift clause does not require that the first two variables are instantiated before it can execute.

We also have to change the clause defining the actual fib predicate to

```
    fib( [0,1|Z] ) <- prove( [shift([0,1|Z],X,Y),add(X,Y,Z)] );
```

If we now ask the query ?fib(F) to Prolog, it will instantiate F to the stream of Fibonacci numbers.

Although the above program solves the Fibonacci problem, the meta-interpreter makes it inefficient. We will now eliminate the overhead of the meta-interpreter by using unfolding to obtain a complete set of frontiers. We are interested in the query ?fib(F). So we first create a frontier for this goal. By taking the partial derivation tree with only one level, we obtain the frontier with the clause

```
    fib( [0,1|Z] ) <- prove( [shift([0,1|Z],X,Y),add(X,Y,Z)] );
```

which is the original clause defining fib. The goal

```
prove( [shift([0 1 | Z],X,Y),add(X,Y,Z)] )
```

is not an instance of the root of the initial partial derivation tree, and so we have to create a frontier for it. We use the query ?prove([shift(U,V,W),add(X,Y,Z)]) with a more general goal as the root of the partial derivation tree. This has the advantage that any goal with the same predicates is an instance of this goal, so we do not have to create any new frontiers when such a goal appears in a frontier. By taking the appropriate partial derivation tree, we obtain the frontier with the single clause

```
prove( [shift([U1,U2|Us],[U1|Vs],[U2|Ws]),add(X,Y,Z)] ) <-
        prove( [add(X,Y,Z),shift([U2|Us],Vs,Ws)] );
```

in it. The goal

```
prove( [add(X,Y,Z),shift([U2|Us],Vs,Ws)] )
```

is not an instance of any of the roots of the partial derivation trees created thus far. Again, using the query ?prove([add(X,Y,Z),shift(U,V,W)]) with a more general goal, we can obtain the frontier with the clause

```
prove( [add([X|Xs],[Y|Ys],[Z|Zs]),shift(U,V,W)] ) <-
        sum( X, Y, Z ) & prove( [add(Xs,Ys,Zs),shift(U,V,W)] );
```

in it.

Now we have a complete set of frontiers (note that the sum predicate is built-in, and we assume the definitions for built-in predicates are included in any set of frontiers). Hence, the program

```
fib( [0,1|Z] ) <- prove( [shift([0,1|Z],X,Y),add(X,Y,Z)] );
prove( [shift([U1,U2|Us],[U1|Vs],[U2|Ws]),add(X,Y,Z)] ) <-
        prove( [add(X,Y,Z),shift([U2|Us],Vs,Ws)] );
prove( [add([X|Xs],[Y|Ys],[Z|Zs]),shift(U,V,W)] ) <-
        sum( X, Y, Z ) & prove( [shift(U,V,W),add(Xs,Ys,Zs)] );
```

is equivalent to the original program. If we ask the query ?fib(F) it will instantiate F to the stream of Fibonacci numbers.

Alternatively, we can obtain the frontier

```
prove( [shift([U1,U2|Us],[U1|Vs],[U2|Ws]),
        add([X|Xs],[Y|Ys],[Z|Zs])] ) <-
        sum( X, Y, Z ) &
        prove( [shift([U2|Us],Vs,Ws),add(X,Y,Z)] );
```

for the query ?prove([shift(U,V,W),add(X,Y,Z)]) by considering a larger partial derivation tree. That way we obtain the program

```
fib( [0,1|Z] ) <- prove( [shift([0,1|Z],X,Y),add(X,Y,Z)] );
prove( [shift([U1,U2|Us],[U1|Vs],[U2|Ws]),
        add([X|Xs],[Y|Ys],[Z|Zs])] ) <-
        sum( X, Y, Z ) &
        prove( [shift([U2|Us],Vs,Ws),add(X,Y,Z)] );
```

which is equivalent to the original one, and is even more efficient than the previous version since an additional level of the meta-interpreter has been removed.

15.4 Concluding remarks

We have extended the state of the art in logic-based program transformation by combining a completeness-preserving unfold operation with specialization to a particular query. However, in doing so, we have not included other important program transformations, such as folding, the use of functionality, and the use of various other properties of predicates. Of course, these other transformations can be applied to the complete set of frontiers generated by our method in such a way that Sato and Tamaki's results guarantee completeness. In another iteration a set of frontiers can be generated which is complete and nonredundant with respect to the query of interest.

It would be more natural to apply the other transformations as soon as applicable, that is, to include them into the algorithm for generating complete sets of frontiers. This is in fact done in the program transformation system implemented by Strooper [9]. Under guidance of the user, this system builds a frontier for a specified query. The user determines interactively whether the current SLD-derivation should be extended, in this way exerting full control over the choice of frontier, while avoiding the error-prone operations such as performing substitutions and recording the resulting frontier. As soon as the frontier is completed, the user specifies any of the transformation rules other than unfold to be applied to the frontier. The resulting set of frontiers is then tested for completeness and new frontiers are generated, as described in this paper.

As shown in [9], the implemented system has considerable practical potential. Future work is needed to analyze its correctness and completeness properties.

15.5 Acknowledgements

We gratefully acknowledge contributions to research facilities from the Natural Sciences and Engineering Research Council of Canada and from the Advanced Systems Institute of British Columbia. Thanks to an anonymous referee for the careful analysis and suggestions on our proofs; to Rajiv Bagai for his careful reading of an earlier version.

References

[1] R. Burstall and J. Darlington. A transformation system for developing recursive programs. *Journal of the ACM*, 24(1):44–67, 1977.

[2] K.L. Clark. Negation as failure. In II. Gallaire and J. Minker, editors, *Logic and Data Bases*, pages 293–322, Plenum Press, 1978.

[3] J. Gallagher. Transforming logic programs by specializing interpreters. In *Proc. of ECAI 86*, pages 109–122, 1986.

[4] F. Giannesini, II. Kanoui, R. Pasero, and M. van Caneghem. *Prolog*. Addison-Wesley, 1986.

[5] C.J. Ilogger. Derivation of logic programs. *Journal of the ACM*, 28(2):372–392, 1981.

[6] G. Kahn and D.B. MacQueen. Coroutines and networks of parallel processes. In *Information Processing 77*, pages 993–998, 1977.

[7] J.W. Lloyd. *Foundations of Logic Programming*. Springer-Verlag, Berlin, 1984.

[8] J.W. Lloyd and J.C. Shepherdson. *Partial Evaluation in Logic*. Technical Report CS-87-09, Bristol University, 1987.

[9] P.A. Strooper. *A Transformation System for Logic Programs*. Master's thesis, University of Waterloo, Waterloo, Ontario, December 1987.

[10] A. Takeuchi. Affinity between meta interpreters and partial evaluation. In *Information Processing 86*, pages 279–282, 1986.

[11] A. Takeuchi and K. Furukawa. *Partial Evaluation of Prolog Programs and its Application to Meta Programming*. Technical Report TR-126, ICOT, 1985.

[12] II. Tamaki and T. Sato. *A Transformation System for Logic Programs which Preserve Equivalence*. Technical Report TR-018, ICOT, 1983.

[13] M.II. van Emden and G.J. de Lucena Filho. Predicate logic as a language for parallel programming. In K.L. Clark and S.-A. Tärnlund, editors, *Logic Programming*, pages 189–198, Academic Press, London, 1982.

[14] M.II. van Emden and K. Yukawa. Logic programming with equations. *Journal of Logic Programming*, 4(4):265–288, 1987.

[15] P. Vasey. Qualified answers and their application to transformation. In *Proc. of the Third International Logic Programming Conference*, pages 425–432, 1986.

[16] W.W. Wadge and E.A. Ashcroft. *Lucid, the Dataflow Programming Language*. Academic Press, London, 1985.

Appendix: proof of lemma 15.1

Before we can prove lemma 15.1, we have to prove another lemma consisting of two parts. The first part is a more general form of the lifting lemma ([7, page 43]) which deals with partial derivations as well as successful derivations.

LEMMA **15.2.** *Given a program P, a goal G and a substitution θ. If there exists a (possibly incomplete) derivation D in P starting from $G\theta$ and ending in $G_1, ..., G_m$ with mgu's $\theta_1, ..., \theta_n$ appearing along the way, such that none of the variables of the variants of the clauses used in the derivation appear in $G\theta$ or G (this is a stronger requirement than the usual standardizing apart [7, page 36]). Then:*

1. *There exists a derivation D' in P starting with G, in which the same goals are selected as in the corresponding nodes in D, and the same clauses from P are used to resolve these goals. If $\theta'_1, ..., \theta'_n$ are the mgu's along the way and $G'_1, ..., G'_{m'}$ are the final goals then $m = m'$ and there exists a substitution δ such that $\theta\theta_1...\theta_n = \theta'_1...\theta'_n\delta$ and $(G'_1...G'_m)\delta = G_1...G_m$.*

2. *A variant of the (un)conditional answer $G\theta'_1...\theta'_n \leftarrow G'_1, ..., G'_m$ can be used in a one step resolution of $G\theta$, such that $G\theta\theta_1...\theta_n \leftarrow G_1...G_m$ is an instance of the resulting (un)conditional answer.*

Using this lemma we can prove lemma 15.1.

LEMMA **15.1.** *Let S be a complete set of frontiers for a query Q and a program P. If the goal G is an instance of $R(F)$ for a frontier F in S, and if there is a successful derivation D of G in P, then there is a successful derivation D' of G in S. Moreover, if θ_1 and θ_2 are the compositions of all substitutions in D and D' respectively, then $G\theta_1$ is an instance of $G\theta_2$.*

Proof   The proof will be by induction on the length of D. Let θ be the substitution such that $G = R(F)\theta$, and let T be the partial derivation tree corresponding to F.

We can use the switching lemma [7, page 45] repeatedly to obtain a successful derivation D'' of G in P in which the goals are selected in the same way as the corresponding path in T. By the previous lemma, which we can use since $G = R(F)\theta$, the corresponding path must exist in the frontier and we either obtain an empty query within the frontier, or we cross it with some remaining goals. For the queries beyond the frontier of T we always select the leftmost goal in D''. Then D'' is of the same length as D, and if θ_3 is the composition of all substitutions in D'', then $G\theta_3$ and $G\theta_1$ are variants.

There are two cases to consider:

1. We reach success within the frontier (this includes the base case where the length of D'' is 1). Since G is $R(F)\theta$, we can use the previous lemma and conclude that F (and hence S) contains an unconditional answer of the form $R(F)\theta'$, which unifies with G. Thus we can use this unconditional answer to obtain a succesful derivation of G in S. Moreover, if θ_2 is the mgu of G and $R(F)\theta'$ then we can also use the lemma to conclude that $G\theta_3$ (and hence also $G\theta_1$) is an instance of $G\theta_2$.

2. We cross the frontier at a point with the remaining subgoals $G'_1, ..., G'_n$. By the previous lemma, the corresponding query in D'' contains the goals $G_1, ..., G_n$ and there exists a substitution δ so that $G_1...G_n = (G'_1...G'_n)\delta$. This means that the frontier contains the conditional answer $R(F)\theta' \leftarrow G'_1, ..., G'_n$, which can be used to resolve G in S to obtain the goals $(G'_1, ..., G'_n)\gamma$, assuming γ is the mgu of G and $R(F)\theta'$ (without loss of generality, we can assume we need not use a variant here). Moreover, $G\alpha \leftarrow G_1...G_n$ is an instance of $(G \leftarrow G'_1...G'_n)\gamma$, where α is the composition of the substitutions in D'' before $G_1...G_n$ is reached.

   We always select the leftmost goal in D'' from $G_1...G_n$ on. Hence, it must contain a succesful derivation D_1 of G_1, say with α_1 being the composition of the substitutions. Now G_1 is an instance of $G'_1\gamma$, and G'_1 appears in the frontier of S, so G'_1, and hence G_1, must be the instance of a root of a frontier of S. Since D_1 is also shorter than D, we can use the induction hypothesis to conclude that there is a successful derivation of G_1 in S. But G_1 is an instance of $G'_1\gamma$, and so there is a derivation D'_1 of $G'_1\gamma$ in S. Moreover, if γ_1 is the composition of the substitutions in D'_1, then $G_1\alpha_1$ is an instance of $G'_1\gamma\gamma_1$.

   Similarly, D'' must contain a succesful derivation D_i of $G_i\alpha_1...\alpha_{i-1}$, with α_i being the composition of the substitutions. By the induction hypothesis, there must exist derivations D'_i of $G'_i\gamma\gamma_1...\gamma_{i-1}$ in S such that $G_i\alpha_1...\alpha_i$ is an instance of $G'_i\gamma\gamma_1...\gamma_i$, where γ_i is the composition of the substitutions in D'_i.

   So we obtain a successful derivation of G in S by first using the rule $R(F)\gamma' \leftarrow G'_1...G'_n$, and then using the derivations $D'_1, ..., D'_n$. Moreover, $G\alpha\alpha_1...\alpha_n$ is an instance of $G\gamma\gamma_1...\gamma_n$. ∎

Chapter 16

A Treatment of Negation during Partial Evaluation

David Chan†   Mark Wallace‡

†*Hewlett-Packard Laboratories*
Filton Road
Stoke Gifford
Bristol BS12 6QZ
‡*ECRC*
Arabellastr. 17
8000 Munchen 81
West Germany
mark%ecrcvax.UUCP@@Germany.CSNET
mcvax!unido!ecrcvax!mark

Abstract

Partial evaluation using SLDNF-resolution provides only limited treatment of negated subgoals. For logic programming systems that support coroutining, however, a partial evaluation that expands negated subgoals or eliminates the negation can produce very important improvements in the runtime efficiency. This paper describes two techniques for interpreting negation and introduces a meta-interpreter that integrates both techniques automatically selecting the technique most applicable to a given occurrence of negation. The output of the meta-interpreter is a partial evaluation in which negated subgoals are expanded as far as possible.

16.1   Introduction

The scope for partial evaluation of normal programs is limited when negated goals are treated using negation as failure. This is because in many cases negated goals in the bodies of program clauses cannot be expanded.

Negation as failure cannot be applied to a negated subgoal until it is ground. The variables appearing in negated subgoals are instantiated at runtime either by other goals within the program, or by the top-level input to the program. At partial evaluation time it may not be possible to instantiate all the variables. In some cases a goal whose execution is required to instantiate a variable in the negated subgoal may not be expanded during the partial evaluation. In other cases the top-level input required to instantiate the variable may not be supplied at partial evaluation time: the partial evaluation may be with respect to a non-ground input atom rather than a ground one. Whatever the cause, the effect is that no expansion of the negated subgoal is possible because its arguments never become instantiated at partial evaluation time.

Now we consider the expansion of a negated subgoal using negation as failure. At partial evaluation time one or more of the predicates involved in its complete expansion may not be fully defined, and therefore the negated subgoal cannot be evaluated to completion. In a literal sense, there is no well-defined notion of a "partially expanded" negated goal when negation as failure is used - it either succeeds or it fails. In this case again the effect is that any expansion of the negated subgoal is not possible during partial evaluation.

Because these restrictions are quite severe, we present an alternative partial evaluation of negative goals which allows their partial evaluation although the negated goal may not be ground. Furthermore the partial evaluation can still go ahead even if the negated goal depends upon predicates not yet available for expansion.

Rather than proposing an extended notion of partial evaluation, we present our treatment of negation in terms of an enhanced meta-interpreter, where negation is treated by certain rules in the interpreter. In cases where these rules can be expanded at partial evaluation time, the corresponding occurrences of negation are eliminated from the partially evaluated program, but we do not require all such occurrences to be eliminated. The runtime system may treat the remaining occurrences of negation in another way - for example using negation as failure.

16.1.1   Restrictions on Partial Evaluation of Negated Goals

In [Lloyd 87] a partial evaluation of an atom A in a program P) is defined in terms of an SLDNF-tree T for $P \cup \{\leftarrow A\}$. Each SLDNF-tree is defined via a *safe* selection rule. A safe rule only selects negative literals which are ground, and having selected a ground negative literal $\neg G$, it cannot select any of the other literals before the attempted proof of $\leftarrow G$ is complete.

A node (or goal) G_i is chosen from each non-failing branch of T. For G_i, θ_i is the set of substitutions, restricted to variables in A, arising in the SDLNF-derivation of $P \cup \{\leftarrow A\}$ up to $\leftarrow G_i$. The partial evaluation of A in P is the set of resultants $A\theta_i \leftarrow G_i$.

The first restriction on the partial evaluation of a negative goal $\leftarrow \neg s(X)$, is that if any predicate on which s depends is not available for expansion then $\neg s(X)$ cannot be expanded either. Since there are no nodes in the SLDNF-tree corresponding to subgoals in the evaluation of a negated literal, such literals cannot be anything other than fully evaluated. For example consider the program P_1:

$$p(X) \leftarrow r(X) \wedge \neg s(X)$$
$$r(X) \leftarrow rsub(X)$$
$$s(X) \leftarrow ssub(X)$$
$$sub(a) \leftarrow$$
$$sub(b) \leftarrow$$

The partial evaluations of the goal $p(x)$ in the program P_1 are:

$$p(X) \leftarrow rsub(X) \wedge \neg s(X)$$
$$p(X) \leftarrow \neg s(a)$$
$$p(a) \leftarrow$$

Because the node $\neg s(X)$ has no subnodes in the SLDNF-tree for $P_1 \cup \{\leftarrow p(X)\}$, the following is *not* a partial evaluation of $p(X)$ in P_1:

$$p(X) \leftarrow \neg ssub(a)$$

This implies a limitation on the partial evaluation of normal programs if specific predicates cannot be expanded. In the previous example, if $ssub$ cannot be expanded during partial evaluation, then the "best" possible partial evaluation of $p(X)$ in P_1 is

$$p(X) \leftarrow \neg s(a)$$

whereas a more optimised transformation of the procedure for p would indeed be

$$p(X) \leftarrow \neg ssub(a).$$

The second restriction on the expansion of negative goals $\leftarrow \neg s_1(X) \wedge \neg s_2(X)$ is that until one negative goal has been completely expanded, the other cannot be expanded at all. Even if negative goals could be partially expanded therefore, this restriction specifically prevents a partial evaluation of $p(X)$ in the program P_2

$$p(X) \leftarrow r(X) \wedge \neg s1(X) \wedge \neg s2(X)$$
$$r(a) \leftarrow$$
$$s1(X) \leftarrow s1sub(X)$$
$$s2(X) \leftarrow s2sub(X)$$

from yielding the set of resultants $p(a) \leftarrow \neg s1sub(a) \wedge \neg s2sub(a)$ because this would require the subgoal $\leftarrow \neg s2(a)$ to be selected before the attempted proof of $\leftarrow s1(a)$ was complete.

The third restriction on the expansion of the negative goal $\leftarrow \neg s(X)$ is that it cannot be expanded at all until it is ground. This means that if the predicate r cannot be expanded in the partial evaluation of $p(X)$ in the following program P_3, then no partial evaluation is possible at all.

$$p(X) \leftarrow r(X) \wedge \neg s(X)$$
$$s(X) \leftarrow \neg ssub(X)$$
$$ssub(a) \leftarrow$$

In fact the resultant $p(a) \leftarrow r(a)$ could yield considerable efficiency benefits at runtime.

16.1.2   Advantages of Expanding Negated Goals

The main advantage of expanding negated goals at partial evaluation time is the potential for increased efficiency at runtime of the partially evaluated program. This most obviously results from the chance to cut off certain branches from the SLDNF-tree for certain goals against the program. Also instantiations made during partial evaluation enable failure to be detected earlier at runtime, as well as accelerating unification.

However in this section we introduce a further advantage which applies particularly if the runtime logic programming system supports coroutining eg. [Clark 80,Naish 86a,Meier 88]. Consider the program P_4

$$p(X) \leftarrow \neg member(a, X) \wedge check_types(X)$$
$$member(X, [X|\_]) \leftarrow$$
$$member(X, [\_|T]) \leftarrow member(X, T)$$
$$check_types([X|T]) \leftarrow type(X) \wedge check_types(T)$$
$$check_types([]) \leftarrow$$
$$\cdots$$

Suppose the predicate *type* cannot be expanded during partial evaluation. Partially evaluating $p([X1, X2, X3, X4])$ in P_4 yields at best P_{4a}:

$$p([X1, X2, X3, X4]) \leftarrow$$
$$\neg member(a, [X1, X2, X3, X4]) \wedge$$
$$type(X1) \wedge type(X2) \wedge type(X3) \wedge type(X4)$$

At runtime suppose the goal $\leftarrow p([A, B, C, D])$ is invoked with A, B, C and D all variable, and the instantiation is only effected by evaluating *type*. This means that at runtime, using negation as failure with a sound computation rule, the negated goal $\neg member(a, [A, B, C, D])$ can only be selected after evaluating all four goals $\leftarrow type(A)$, $\leftarrow type(B)$, $\leftarrow type(C)$ and $\leftarrow type(D)$. An improved runtime performance could be obtained by splitting the negated goal into independent parts yielding P_{4b}:

$$p([X1, X2, X3, X4]) \leftarrow$$
$$\neg tmp(X1) \wedge \neg tmp(X2) \wedge \neg tmp(X3) \wedge \neg tmp(X4) \wedge$$
$$type(X1) \wedge type(X2) \wedge type(X3) \wedge type(X4)$$
$$tmp(a) \leftarrow$$

Assuming the negated goals were selected as soon as possible, the runtime behaviour of this version will be much better, since $\leftarrow tmp(Xi)$ is selected immediately after $\leftarrow type(Xi)$. Such a runtime behaviour is indeed provided in Nu-Prolog [Naish 86b], for example.

The reason that P_{4b} is better than P_{4a} is because by splitting the negated goal $\leftarrow \neg member(\ldots)$ into four independent negated goals, the partial evaluation P_{4b} offers much more opportunity for "coroutining" in the runtime system. Essentially the partial evaluation splits the negated *member* goal into pieces so that $\leftarrow \neg member(\ldots)$ is effectively coroutined with $\leftarrow check_types(dots)$.

In fact in Nu-Prolog the built-in predicate $\sim=$ (not equals) provides the required runtime behaviour, and no extra predicate *tmp* need be introduced:

$$p([X1, X2, X3, X4]) \leftarrow$$
$$(a \sim= X1) \wedge (a \sim= X2) \wedge$$
$$(a \sim= X3) \wedge (a \sim= X4) \wedge$$
$$type(X1) \wedge type(X2) \wedge type(X3) \wedge type(X4)$$

A similar transformation would benefit the *CHIP* logic programming system. In this system finite domains can be associated with variables, and inequalities on such variables can be used to restrict the domains yielding major performance improvements [vanHentenryck 87]. If A, B, C and D were domain variables, then the procedure

$$p([X1, X2, X3, X4]) \leftarrow$$
$$(a \sim= X1) \wedge (a \sim= X2) \wedge (a \sim= X3) \wedge (asim = X4)$$

could yield a much better performance for the subgoal $\leftarrow p([A, B, C, D])$ than

$$p([X1, X2, X3, X4]) \leftarrow$$
$$\neg member(a, [X1, X2, X3, X4])$$

16.1.3 Contents

Since partial evaluation cannot provide the best possible optimisation of certain normal programs because of the limitations of SLDNF resolution, an extension to SLDNF resolution could be suggested. However such a solution could imply that logic programming systems would have to support such an extension at runtime. We therefore propose to treat negation specially in the context of partial evaluation.

In the next section we present two techniques for eliminating negation in normal logic programs. The following section describes a meta-interpreter that implements both these techniques. Where the negation cannot be totally eliminated, it generates a runtime negation which is handled using standard negation as failure. In conclusion we point out some of the benefits such an integration of the techniques facilitates in generating improved partial evaluations.

16.2 Two Techniques for Eliminating Negation from Normal Logic Programs

16.2.1 Definitions

A *normal program clause* has a head which is an atom, and a body which is a set of literals, which may be positive or negative:

$$A \leftarrow Lit_1, Lit_2, \ldots, Lit_N$$

Each Lit_i may be a positive or a negative literal. A *normal goal clause* has an empty head. A *normal clause* is a normal program clause or a normal goal clause. When it is clear from the context we shall just call them *clauses*. We use *program* to mean a set of normal program clauses. We use a bold **X** to abbreviate a whole sequence of variables $X_1, \ldots, X_n$. The atom $p(X_1, \ldots, X_n)$ can therefore be abbreviated to $p(\mathbf{X})$.

16.2.2 Evaluating Non-Ground Negative Subgoals — Constructive Negation

The evaluation of non-ground negative subgoals is based on constructive negation. SLD resolution extended with constructive negation is formalized in terms of SLD-CNF resolution. Here we outline the procedure: the interested reader is referred to [Chan 88] for more details.

Let G be the goal $L_1, \ldots, L_m$ and the selected literal L_i be $\neg Q$. We derive lemmas for it by a subrefutation with $\leftarrow Q$ as the goal.

1. If there are no answers, then the single derived resolvent is

$$L_1, \ldots, L_{i-1}, L_{i+1}, \ldots, L_m$$

2. If there are n (normalized) answers $A_1, \ldots, A_n$ such that

$$Q \equiv A_1 \vee \ldots \vee A_n$$

a derived goal is then

$$L_1, \ldots, L_{i-1}, B_{j_1}, \ldots, B_{j_k j}, L_{i+1}, \ldots, L_m$$

where the $B_{j_1}, \ldots, B_{j_k j}$ is the NA_j in

$$NA_1 \vee \ldots \vee NA_p \equiv \neg(A_1 \vee \ldots \vee A_n)$$

If the answers are equivalent to *true* then the goal G fails.

Normalized Answers

Let $G_0 = \leftarrow Q = \leftarrow (L_1, \ldots, L_k)$, and the composition of unifiers (restricted to variables in Q) from the root to the terminal goal is θ. If the last goal is the empty clause, the pre-normalized form of an answer is

$$X_1 = X_1\theta \wedge \ldots \wedge X_m = X_m\theta$$

If the last goal is $\leftarrow IE_1, \ldots, IE_n$, the pre-normalized form of an answer is

$$X_1 = X_1\theta \wedge \ldots \wedge X_m = X_m\theta \wedge IE_1, \ldots, IE_n$$

where $X_1, \ldots, X_m$ are variables in Q that are bound by θ. (The computation rule selects only valid or unsatisfiable inequality, as a consequence a terminal goal can either be the empty clause or a conjunction of satisfiable inequalities.) The normal form of an answer to the query Q is the result of the following two step transformation. Non-goal variables are variables that are not in Q. We assume that there is an infinite number of constants and functions.

1. Redundant Variables and Equations are removed.

    If Y is a non-goal variable which is equated to a variable in $X_1, \ldots, X_m$, say X, then all occurrences of Y are replaced by X. All redundant equations are also removed.

2. Irrelevant inequalities are removed from the answer.

    An inequality is considered to be irrelevant if it contains a non-goal variable not in the equality part. Locally quantified variables do not count and are standardized apart.

Negation of Answers

Negating the disjunction $A_1 \vee \ldots \vee A_k$ can be done by negating each individual A_i and then recombining the components. One needs to be careful of the implicit quantification of variables when negating an answer containing variables. The procedure is based on the following lemma.

Lemma 16.1: Negating a $\exists$ quantified conjunction with an equation
Let the 3 quantified conjunction with an equation be $\exists \mathbf{X}, \mathbf{Y}(U = s, Q)$, where $\mathbf{X}$
are the variables in s and $\mathbf{Y}$ are the variables in Q that are not in $\mathbf{X}, U$ it is a
theorem of the equality theory that

$$\forall U(\neg \exists \mathbf{X}, \mathbf{Y}(U = s, Q) \equiv \forall X(U \neq s) \vee \exists X(U = s, \neg \exists Y Q))$$

A normalized answer is of the form $X_1 = r1 \wedge \ldots \wedge X_m = r_m \wedge IE_1 \wedge \ldots \wedge IE_n$.
Its negation generates $m + n$ components. The first m components from negating
the equality part is

$$\forall Y_1, \ldots, Y_{nv_1}(X_1 \neq r_1)$$
$$X_1 = r_1, \forall Y_{nv_1+1}, \ldots, Y_{nv_2}(X_2 \neq r_2)$$
$$\vdots$$
$$X_1 = r_1, \ldots, X_{m-1} = r_{m-1} \forall Y_{nv_{m-1}+1}, \ldots, Y_{nv_m}(X_m \neq r_m)$$

where $Y_1, \ldots, Y_{nv_1}$ are non-goal variables in $X_1 \neq r_1$, $Y_{nv_1+1}, \ldots, Y_{nv_2}$ are non-
goal variables in $X_2 \neq r_2$ that are not in $Y_1, \ldots, Y_{nv_1}$ etc.

If IE_1 is $s_1 \neq t_1$ then the next component is $X_1 \neq r_1 \wedge \ldots X_m \neq r_m \wedge s_1 = t_1$.
It is the same even if IE_1 is of the form $\forall(s1 \neq t1)$. After negation, the explicit
quantified variables turn into implicitly existential quantified ones. In the previous
case, all the variables in the inequality are quantified outside the inequality and
negating it does not involve any change of quantification. (If they contained a
variable that is not in the equality part, they would have been removed in the
normalization procedure [See above].) The next components are generated in the
similar way.

Applying this procedure, we can indeed get as the partial evaluation of $p(X)$
in program P_3 the resultant $p(a) \leftarrow r(a)$.

Forall Quantified Inequalities

The forall quantified inequalities can be treated directly in SEPIA [Meier 88] or
by using the anonymous variable in Mu-Prolog. For instance, $\forall Y(X \sim= f(Y))$
can be implemented in Mu-Prolog as $X \sim= f(\_)$. If a forall quantified variable
appears more than once in the inequality, we can transform it to one where they
appear only once. For instance, $\forall Y(X \sim= f(Y, Y))$ is equivalent to $\forall U, V(X \neq
f(U, V), U = V)$ which can be implemented in Mu-Prolog as $X \sim= f(\_, \_)$ or
$X = f(U, V), U \sim= V$.

Negating Qualified Answers

In the context of partial evaluation where certain predicates are not available
for expansion, we need to extend the notion of an answer to include arbitrary
predicates. Following [Vasey 86], we call them qualified answers. The extension
can be done as follows.

Let the subgoal to partial evaluate be $\neg Q$, and let a terminal goal for Q, $\leftarrow R$, be of the form

$$IE_1, \ldots, IE_{n_r}, M'_1, \ldots, M'_{n_d}$$

where IE are the satisfiable inequalities that are not selected and M' are the subgoals that are not expanded. A pre-normalized qualified answer for Q is of the form

$$\mathbf{X} = \mathbf{X}\theta, IE_1, \ldots, IE_{n_r}, M'_1, \ldots, M'_{n_d}$$

The first step of normalization is as before (see above). The second step is modified to remove only inequalities that contain a non-goal variable not in the equality part nor in $M'_1, \ldots, M'_{n_d}$. A normalized qualified answer for Q is then of the form

$$E_1, \ldots, E_{n_e}, L_1, \ldots, L_{n_a}, M_1, \ldots, M_{n_c}, L_{n_a+1}, \ldots, L_{n_b}, M_{n_c+1}, \ldots, M_{n_d}$$

where the E's are the equalities, the L's are the inequalities, the M's are other subgoals that are not expanded. We have renamed them as substitutions could have been made in the normalization process. The inequalities from $n_a + 1$ to n_b and M_{n_c+1} to M_{n_d} are those that contain a variable not in E nor in Q.

If Q has n normalized qualified answers, $QA_1, \ldots, QA_n$ then it can be shown that the completed database implies the following equivalence:

$$\forall (Q \equiv \exists QA_1 \vee \ldots \vee QA_n)$$

In other words, the answer to $\neg Q$ can be derived by negating the right-hand side. This can be done by negating each normalized answer and recombining the components. The negation of a normalized qualified answer,

$$E_1, \ldots, E_{n_e}, L_1, \ldots, L_{n_a}, M_1, \ldots, M_{n_c}, L_{n_a+1}, \ldots, L_{n_b}, M_{n_c+1}, \ldots, M_{n_d}$$

can proceed essentially as above. In fact, the procedure is exactly the same up to L_{n_a+1}. As the negation of $(L_{n_a+1}, \ldots, L_{n_b}, M_1, \ldots, M_{n_c})$ cannot be further simplified, the last disjunct is

$$E_1, \ldots, E_{n_e}, L_1, \ldots, L_{n_a}, M_1, \ldots, M_{n_c}, (L_{n_a+1}, \ldots, L_{n_b}, M_1, \ldots, M_{n_c})$$

For program P_1, we can indeed obtain $p(a) \leftarrow \neg ssub(a)$ as the partial evaluation of $p(X)$. The answer to $s(a)$ is just $ssub(a)$. Both E and L is empty and therefore its negation is just $\neg ssub(a)$. Similarly for program P_2, if $s1sub$ and $s2sub$ are not available for expansion, we can nonetheless expand $\neg s1(X)$ and $\neg s2(X)$ to get the partial evaluation $p(a) \leftarrow \neg s1sub(a) \wedge \neg s2sub(a)$.

16.2.3 Transformation of Negated Goals

Another technique for eliminating negation from logic programs is via program transformation. A set of sound transformations is proposed in [Sato 84]. However, the transformations cannot be automatically generated. In this section we describe a very simple and effective set of transformations which can be generated and performed automatically.

The completion of a procedure p has the form:

$$p(\mathbf{X}) \equiv \exists \mathbf{Y_1}.B_1[\mathbf{X}, \mathbf{Y_1}] \vee \ldots \vee \exists \mathbf{Y_N}.B_N[\mathbf{X}, \mathbf{Y_N}]$$

The negation of p is therefore equivalent to the negation of the right-hand side:

$$\neg p(\mathbf{X}) \equiv \forall \mathbf{Y_1}.\neg B_1[\mathbf{X}, \mathbf{Y_1}] \wedge \ldots \wedge \forall \mathbf{Y_N}.\neg B_N[\mathbf{X}, \mathbf{Y_N}]$$

In [Wallace 87] an implementation of negation is described in which the goal $\leftarrow \neg p(X)$ is dealt with by evaluating the right-hand side of the negated completion directly.

In the context of program transformation, however, we rather seek a transformed program whose syntax is unextended. We must therefore remove the universal quantifiers from the right-hand side. Lloyd and Topor describe a transformation which can indeed map goals which contain universal quantifiers into normal clauses again [Lloyd 84]. One could therefore imagine using their transformation to give a procedure for not_p by mapping the right-hand side of the negated completion to a set of normal clauses. The transformation eliminates universally quantified variables by introducing a new procedure. In practice, the result of such a direct application of their transformation is effectively the same procedure!

$$not_p(X) \leftarrow \neg p(X)$$

However, for procedures with no local variables, the completion has a more restricted form, such that negating the right-hand side need not result in an unmanageable formula.

Firstly, the clauses are split into disjoint sets so that no two clauses have unifiable heads. In the following $\mathbf{T}$ represents a sequence of terms. Given the procedure

$$p(\mathbf{T_1}) \leftarrow Body_1$$
$$p(\mathbf{T_2}) \leftarrow Body_2$$
$$\ldots$$
$$p(\mathbf{T_n}) \leftarrow Body_n$$

if any two heads $p(\mathbf{T_i})$ and $p(\mathbf{T_j})$ are unifiable, then the clauses $p(\mathbf{T_i}) \leftarrow Body_i$ and $p(\mathbf{T_j}) \leftarrow Body_j$ are in the same set. (In consequence, there might also be clauses with non-unifiable heads in the same set). All the clauses in a set are then combined into a single new clause by replacing substitutions in the head with equalities in the body where necessary, and forming a single body with disjunctions. For example, the procedure

$$p(f(a, 1)) \leftarrow Body_1$$
$$p(f(a, X)) \leftarrow Body_2$$
$$p(f(b, e)) \leftarrow Body_3$$
$$p(a) \leftarrow Body_4$$

would map to three exclusive clauses:

$$p(f(a, X)) \leftarrow (X = 1 \wedge Body_1) \vee Body_2$$
$$p(f(b, 3)) \leftarrow Body_3$$
$$p(a) \leftarrow Body_4$$

In the completion, therefore, the equalities are mutually exclusive:

$$p(\mathbf{X}) \equiv \exists \mathbf{Y_1}.(\mathbf{X} = \mathbf{Y_1} \wedge B_1[\mathbf{X}, \mathbf{Y_1}]) \vee \ldots \vee \exists \mathbf{Y_N}.(\mathbf{X} = \mathbf{Y_N} \wedge B_N[\mathbf{X}, \mathbf{Y_N}])$$

The result of negating the completion is:

$$\neg p(\mathbf{X}) \equiv \neg \exists \mathbf{Y_1}.(\mathbf{X} = \mathbf{Y_1} \wedge B_1[\mathbf{X}, \mathbf{Y_1}]) \wedge \ldots \wedge \neg \exists \mathbf{Y_N}.(\mathbf{X} = \mathbf{Y_N} \wedge B_N[\mathbf{X}, \mathbf{Y_N}])$$

Using lemma 16.1, we have

$$(\neg \exists \mathbf{Y}.(\mathbf{X} = \mathbf{Y} \wedge B[\mathbf{X}, \mathbf{Y}])) \equiv (\forall \mathbf{Z}.\neg \mathbf{X} = \mathbf{Z} \vee \exists \mathbf{Y}.(\mathbf{X} = \mathbf{Y} \wedge \neg B[\mathbf{X}, \mathbf{Y}]))$$

Thus, we can generate normal program clauses for the negation of p, which we can rename not_p:

$$not\_p(X) \leftarrow \mathbf{X} = \mathbf{Y_1} \wedge \neg B_1[\mathbf{X}, \mathbf{Y_1}]$$
$$\ldots$$
$$not\_p(X) \leftarrow \mathbf{X} = \mathbf{Y_N} \wedge \neg B_N[\mathbf{X}, \mathbf{Y_N}]$$
$$not\_p(X) \leftarrow \forall \mathbf{Y_1}.\mathbf{X} \sim= \mathbf{Y_1} \wedge \ldots \wedge \forall \mathbf{Y_N}.\mathbf{X} \sim= \mathbf{Y_N}$$

(The equalities can also be executed immediately, pushing the unification into the clause heads.) The universally quantified formulae in the last clause each govern a single inequality. These can be removed by the method described in [Lloyd 84], which results in the introduction of a new procedure:

$$not\_p(\mathbf{X}) \leftarrow \neg unify\_p\_head(\mathbf{X})$$
$$unify\_p\_head(\mathbf{Y_1})$$
$$\ldots$$
$$unify\_p\_head(\mathbf{Y_N})$$

The negation can be avoided if the universally quantified inequalities are handled by the logic programming system at runtime (see Section 16.3.1 below). It remains only to interpret the negation of each body B_i. However, since no quantifiers appear, the transformation defined in [Lloyd 84] will not introduce any new procedures. The result is an elimination of all the universal quantifiers which apper due to non-ground compound structures in the head of a clause.

Thus, our previous example yields:

$$not\_p(Y) \leftarrow (\forall X.Y \sim= f(a, X)) \wedge Y \sim= f(b, 3) \wedge Y \sim= a$$
$$not\_p(f(a, X)) \leftarrow (X \sim= 1 \vee \neg Body_1) \wedge \neg Body_2$$
$$not\_p(f(b, 3)) \leftarrow \neg Body_3$$
$$not\_p(a) \leftarrow \neg Body_4$$

The two most common examples of recursive predicates with no local variables are *member* and *append*. The transformation of *member* to *not_member* also appears in [Sato 84]:

$$not\_member(X, Y) \leftarrow \forall A, H, T.(X, Y) \sim= (A, [H|T])$$
$$not\_member(X, Y) \leftarrow X = A \wedge Y = [H|T] \wedge not(A = H \vee member(A, T))$$

On interpreting the negation in the body this becomes:

$$not\_member(A, [H|T]) \leftarrow A \sim= H \wedge not\_member(A, T)$$
$$not\_member(X, Y) \leftarrow \forall A, H, T.(X, Y) \sim= (A, [HT])$$

The predicate *append* yields:

$$not\_append([H|X], Y, [H|Z]) \leftarrow not\_append(X, Y, Z)$$
$$not\_append(A, B, C) \leftarrow \forall H, X, Y, Z.(A, B, C) \sim= ([H|X], Y, [H|Z]) \wedge$$
$$\forall Y.(A, B, C) \sim= ([], Y, Y)$$

If further functional dependencies can be identified, they can also be used to eliminate local variables. A frequent case is the appearance of a local variable to represent the result of a calculation in the clause body:

$$length([], 0) \leftarrow$$
$$length([H|T], N) \leftarrow N > 0 \wedge M \text{ is } N - 1 \wedge length(T, M)$$

For the built-in predicate *is*, a variable on the left-hand side is functionally dependent on those appearing on the right. The negated completion of *length* is

$$length(X, N) \equiv$$
$$(X, N) \sim= ([], 0) \wedge \neg \exists H, T, L.((H, X) = ([H|T], L) \wedge N > 0 \wedge$$
$$\exists M.((M \text{ is } L - 1)length(T, M)))$$

Using the lemma, the transformation yields

$$not\_length(X, N) \leftarrow (X, N) \sim= ([], 0) \wedge \forall H, T, L.(X, N) \sim= ([HT], L)$$
$$not\_length([H|T], N) \leftarrow \neg N > 0$$
$$not\_length([H|T], N) \leftarrow M \text{ is } N - 1 \wedge not\_length(T, M)$$

The use of functional dependencies was also suggested in [Naish 86b]. In that reference only functional dependencies between input arguments and output arguments in the head of a procedure were considered. The transformation reduced negation to inequalities only for negated goals with the input arguments instantiated. Furthermore, the functional dependencies had to be given by the user.

16.3   A Meta-Interpreter Handling Negation and its Partial Evaluation

16.3.1   An Overview of the Meta-Interpreter

We present a meta-interpreter written in a logic programming language in which $\sim=$ is a built-in predicate, whose computation rule chooses the leftmost literal goal first, but does not select $\sim=$ until either its arguments cannot be unified, or they are identical. A more sophisticated version of this predicate is also used, in which certain variables may be universally quantitied (See 16.2.2).

$$\forall s \sim= t$$

succeeds if its arguments cannot be unified, and fails if they can be unified only instantiating universally quantified variables. Such a built-in predicate is indeed supported in SEPIA [Meier 88] and Nu-Prolog [Naish 86a].

The meta-interpreter offers a number of alternatives for the handling of negated goals. Which alternative is used in the meta-interpretation of a particular occurrence of negation in a particular program depends upon which predicates are available for expansion (if a partial evaluation is being performed), the syntax of the program itself (for example whether the predicate in the negated goal is recursive), and the instantiation of the variables when the negated goal is selected.

The meta-interpreter employs SLD resolution extended in two ways. Firstly, the interpreter supports qualified answers, as defined in [Vasey 86]. This admits answers which are true under certain conditions — specifically if a certain unexpanded goal is satisfied. For example, a qualified answer to the query $p(X)$ in the program

$$p(X) \leftarrow q(X), r(X)$$
$$q(a) \leftarrow$$
$$\ldots$$

when r is not to be expanded is $X = a, r(a)$. The extension needed here is described in Section 16.2.2.

The meta-interpreter uses a selection function that only selects goals whose predicates are available for expansion. Furthermore, the selection function does not select goals matching an ancestor. This does not prevent all possible loops, but is a practical restriction in the context of partial evaluation. Goals that cannot be selected for the above reasons will appear as qualifications in answers returned by the meta-interpreter.

The second extension is, of course, for the handling of negated goals. When a negated goal $\leftarrow \neg B$ is selected, the meta-interpreter calls itself recursively on the positive part, $\leftarrow B$. The complete set of (qualified) answers is then negated to yield the answers to $\neg B$. In some cases, the negation of B can only be eliminated by introducing the predicate not_B.

For example, consider the program P_4 of section 1.2 above:

$$p(X) \leftarrow \neg member(a, X) \wedge check\_types(X)$$
$$member(X, [X|\_]) \leftarrow$$
$$member(X, [\_|T]) \leftarrow member(X, T)$$
$$check\_types([X|T]) \leftarrow type(X) \wedge check\_types(T)$$
$$check\_types([]) \leftarrow$$
$$\ldots$$

If the first input is $\leftarrow p([X1, X2, X3])$, the meta-interpreter selects the goal $\leftarrow \neg member(a, [X2, X2, X3])$ and calls itself recursively on the input $\leftarrow member(a, [X1, X2, X3])$. The evaluation yields the three answers $X1 = a, X2 = a, X3 = a$.

It is implied by the completed database that

$$member(a, [X1, X2, X3]) \equiv X1 = a \vee X2 = a \vee X3 = a$$

The answer to $\neg member(a, [X1, X2, X3])$ which we get by negating the answer to $member(a, [X1, X2, X3])$ is therefore

$$\neg member(a, [X1, X2, X3]) \equiv X1 \sim= a \vee X2 \sim= a \vee X3 \sim= a$$

The other goal $\leftarrow check\_types([X1, X2, X3])$ is expanded using standard SLD-resolution. The goals of the form $A \sim= B$ remain satisfiable and are never selected in this computation. Thus the meta-interpretation yields the following partial evaluation:

$$p([X1, X2, X3]) \leftarrow$$
$$X1 \sim= a \wedge X2 \sim= a \wedge X3 \sim= a \wedge type(X1) \wedge type(X2) \wedge type(X3)$$

Under a different input $\leftarrow p(X)$, the meta-interpreter selects the goal $\leftarrow \neg member(a, X)$ and calls itself recursively with the input $\leftarrow member(a, X)$. One answer is $X = [a|T]$. The search for the next answer generates a new subgoal $\leftarrow member(a, T)$. Since this matches an ancestor it cannot be selected, so the normalized qualified answer is: $X = [H|T], member(a, T)$.

It is implied by the completed database that

$$member(a, X) \equiv (\exists T.X = [a|T]) \vee (\exists H, T.X = [H|T] \wedge member(a, T))$$

The qualified answers to $\neg member(a, X)$ are $X \sim= [\_|\_]$ and $X = [H|T], a \sim= H, \neg member(a, T)$.

The negation can be eliminated by introducing a new predicate not_member_a defined as follows:

$$not\_member\_a(X) \leftarrow X \sim= [\_|\_]$$
$$not\_member\_a([H|T]) \leftarrow a \sim= H \wedge not\_member\_a(T)$$

The original goal $\leftarrow \neg member(a, X)$ is now expanded using this procedure, but the embedded call to *not_member_a* cannot be selected because it matches an ancester. Similarly, the expansion of the second goal $\leftarrow check\_types(X)$ is blocked because the embedded call to *check_types* also matches an ancestor. The result of partial evaluation in this case is thus:

$$p([]) \leftarrow$$
$$p([H|T]) \leftarrow a \sim= H \wedge not\_member\_a(T) \wedge type(H) \wedge check\_types(T)$$

If, as in this case, any predicate appears in a qualified answer, then it must also be available when the qualified answers are themselves evaluated. The runtime program, then, must include both the procedure for *check_types*, and the new procedure for *not_member_a*.

16.3.2 Recursive Calls to the Meta-Interpreter

In this section we explain how a new procedure *not_B* is created from the set of qualified answers to an atomic goal $\leftarrow B$. First we note two problems with the requirement for the meta-interpreter to call itself recursively.

When the selected goal is a negative literal $\leftarrow \neg B$, the meta-interpreter calls itself recursively on the positive part $\leftarrow B$. If B depends negatively on itself, then an infinite loop can arise. It would be possible to add B as an ancestor in the recursive call to the meta-interpreter. Otherwise, the meta-interpreter could simply be restricted to operate only on stratified programs [Apt 86].

The second problem is that the same negation could be treated repeatedly during partial evaluation. This is avoided by distinguishing compile time negations from runtime negations. A compile time negation is one that appers in the original program. When the meta-interpreter selects a negated literal $\leftarrow \neg B$ which appears in the original program, it calls itself on the positive part $\leftarrow B$, and all embedded negations are dealt with recursively. A new procedure *not_B* is generated, and used to evaluate $\leftarrow \neg B$. In some cases the generated procedure for *not_B* will itself contain negations, $\neg C$. Negations appearing in such generated procedures are termed runtime negations.

When $\leftarrow \neg B$ is expanded by the meta-interpreter using *not_B* the runtime negation $\leftarrow \neg C$ may be selected, but the meta-interpreter should not call itself recursively on $\leftarrow C$ because the runtime negation has already been fully treated during the expansion of $\leftarrow B$.

Suppose the set of resultants from the evaluation of B is

$$B\theta_1 \leftarrow Body_1$$
$$B\theta_2 \leftarrow Body_2$$
$$\ldots$$
$$B\theta_n \leftarrow Body_n$$

The resultants are split into disjoint sets so that no two resultants have unifiable heads, as described in Section 2.3 above.

Consider, for example, the negative goal $\leftarrow \neg p(X, b)$ in the program P_5:

$$p(f(X), a) \leftarrow Body1$$
$$p(f(X), b) \leftarrow Body2$$
$$p(f(2), b) \leftarrow Body3$$
$$p(a, b) \leftarrow Body4$$

The resultants from the evaluation of $\leftarrow p(X, b)$ are:

$$p(f(X), b) \leftarrow Body2$$
$$p(f(2), b) \leftarrow Body3$$
$$p(a, b) \leftarrow Body4$$

These resultants form two sets whose heads are not unifiable. Each set forms a single new resultant, yielding:

$$p(f(X), b) \leftarrow Body2 \vee (X = 2 \wedge Body3)$$
$$p(a, b) \leftarrow Body4$$

These new resultants are treated as a complete procedure for $p(X, b)$. A completion is formed, but not as in [Clark 77] with all the arguments in the left-hand side variable. Rather the left-hand side is the positive atom $p(X, b)$ itself. The completion is thus:

$$p(X, b) \equiv \exists Y.(X = f(Y) \wedge (Body2 \vee (Y = 2 \wedge Body3))) \vee X = a \wedge Body4$$

This completion is then negated using the method defined in Section 16.2.3 above, yielding the procedure:

$$not\_b\_p(X, b) \leftarrow \forall Y.X \sim= f(Y) \wedge X \sim= a$$
$$not\_b\_p(f(Y), b) \leftarrow \neg(Body2 \vee (Y = 2 \wedge Body3))$$
$$not\_b\_p(a, b) \leftarrow \neg Body4$$

Next the negation is pushed through each procedure body. The method here is based on that described in Section 16.2.2.4. In general, negation cannot be eliminated and the result will contain some explicitly quantified negative subgoal.

Consider the evaluation of $\leftarrow q(X)$ against the following program:

$$q(X) \leftarrow m(X) \wedge \neg r(X)$$
$$r(X) \leftarrow s(X, Y) \wedge t(Y)$$
$$s(f(U), U) \leftarrow$$
$$s(g(U), h(U, V)) \leftarrow$$

The predicates m and t are not available for expansion.

The evaluation of the goal $\leftarrow r(X)$ yields the following resultants:

$$r(f(U)) \leftarrow t(U)$$
$$r(g(U)) \leftarrow t(h(U, V))$$

The completion is thus

$$r(X) \equiv \exists U.(X = f(U) \wedge t(U)) \vee (X = g(U) \wedge \exists V.t(h(U, V)))$$

The negated procedure *not_r* is thus:

$$not\_r(X) \leftarrow \forall U.(X \sim= f(U)) \wedge X \sim= b$$
$$not\_r(f(U)) \leftarrow \neg t(U)$$
$$not\_r(g(U)) \leftarrow \neg \exists V.t(h(U, V))$$

No further simplification of this procedure possible.

The explicitly quantified subgoal $\neg \exists V.t(h(U, V))$ can be handled directly in runtime using constructive negation or if the target system uses negation as failure, the extended program clauses can be converted back to normal program clauses as described in [Lloyd 84]. For the negated, existentially quantified subgoal a new predicate is introduced.

The result is thus:

$$not\_r(X) \leftarrow \forall U.(X \sim= f(U)) \wedge X \sim= b$$
$$not\_r(f(U)) \leftarrow \neg t(U)$$
$$not\_r(g(U)) \leftarrow \neg exists\_t(U)$$
$$exists\_t(U) \leftarrow t(h(U, V))$$

The resultants returned by the original goal $\leftarrow q(X)$ are therefore:

$$q(X) \leftarrow m(X) \wedge \forall U.(X \sim= f(U)) \wedge X \sim= b$$
$$q(f(U)) \leftarrow m(f(U)) \wedge \neg t(U)$$
$$q(g(U)) \leftarrow m(g(U)) \wedge \neg exists\_t(U)$$

16.4 Conclusion

The partial evaluation of negative subgoals is uniquely important for logic programming systems that handle coroutining. A negative goal can only be selected for evaluation after all its arguments are instantiated. By eliminating the negation, or at least splitting it into smaller pieces, the partial evaluation effectively removes this restriction on its selection, and enables the runtime evaluation of the negative subgoal to be coroutined with the rest of the program.

In this paper we have described a practical approach to partial evaluation that improves the handling of negated subgoals. Two quite separate techniques for eliminating negation are embedded in a simple meta- interpreter. This results in a powerful algorithm that can eliminate negation in many situations and when negation cannot be eliminated, the meta-interpreter can still expand negated subgoals and produce an improved runtime program.

Acknowledgements

The authors are indebted to Herve Gallaire and Jean-Marie Nicolas for encouraging their collaboration, and to all at ECRC for keeping going a constant flow of ideas.

References

[Apt 86]   Apt, K.R., Blair, H. and Walker, A. Towards a Theory of Declarative Knowledge. In Foundations of Deductive Databases and Logic Programming (Preprints of Workshop). Univ. of Maryland, Washington D.C., August, 1986.

[Chan 88]   Chan, D. Constructive Negation Based on the Completed Database. In Proc Fifth Int. Conf. Symp. On Logic Programming. IEEE, Seattle, Washington, August, 1988.

[Clark 77]   Clark, K.L. Negation As Failure. In Gallaire, H. and Minker J. (editor), Logic and Databases, pages 293-322. Plenum Press, New York and London, 1977.

[Clark 80]   Clark, K.L. and McCabe, F.G. IC-Prolog: Aspects of its Implementation. In Tarnlund, S-A. (editor), Proc. Logic Programming Workshop, pages 190-197. Debrecen, Hungary, July, 1980.

[Lloyd 84]   Lloyd, J.W. and Topor, R.W. Making Prolog More Expressive. Technical Report 84/8, Dept. of Comp. Sci., Univ. of Melbourne, 1984.

[Lloyd 87]   Lloyd, J.W. and Shepherdson, J.C. Partial Evaluation in Logic Programming. Technical Report CS-87-09, Univ. of Bristol, Dec, 1987.

[Meier 88]   Meier, M., Dufresne, P., de Villeneuve, D. SEPIA. Technical Report TR-LP-36, ECRC, Arabella str. 17,800 Muenchen, 81, May, 1988.

[Naish 86a]   Naish, L. Negation and Quantifiers in NU-Prolog. In Shapiro E. (editor), Proc Third International Conference on Logic Programming, pages 624-634. Imperial College, London, UK, July, 1986.

[Naish 86b]   Naish, L. Negation and Control in Prolog. Springer-Verlag, 1986.

[Sato 84]   Sato, T. and Tamaki, H. Transformational Logic Program Synthesis. In Int. Conf. on Fifth Generation Computer Systems. Nov, 1984.

[vanIIentenryck 87] van IIentenryck, P. and Dincbas, M. Forward Checking in Logic Programming. In Proc. 4th Int. Conf. on Logic Programming, pages 229-256. Melbourne, Australia, May, 1987.

[Vasey 86]   Vasey, P. Qualified Answers and Their Application to Transformation. In Shapiro, E. (editor), Proc Third International Conference on Logic Programming, pages 425-432. Imperial College, London, UK, July, 1986.

[Wallace 87]   Wallace, M.G. Negation by Constraints: A Sound And Efficient Implementation of Negation in Deductive Databases. In Proc. 1987 Symposium on Logic Programming, pages 253-263. The Computer Society of the IEEE, IIyatt on Union Square, San Francisco, California, September, 1987.

Chapter 17

Issues in the Partial Evaluation of Meta-Interpreters

Stephen Owen

Hewlett-Packard Laboratories
Filton Road
Stoke Gifford
Bristol BS12 6QZ
England
sgo@hplb.lb.hp.co.uk

Abstract

We consider the specialisation of four meta-interpreters with respect to a particular object theory. We attempt to see specialisation in terms of partial evaluation (P.E.), comparing the results of P.E. with those produced by hand-written transformers. We see that simple P.E., as embodied in existing logic programming systems, is unable to specialise the interpreters successfully. However, we see that an extended P.E. framework, together with numerous enhancements, is able to emulate the hand-written transformers. We conclude that P.E. systems will have to incorporate the enhancements if they are to be able to specialise realistic meta-interpreters, as opposed to the simple ones which have treated in the literature so far.

17.1 Introduction

In this paper we discuss the use of partial evaluation to specialise meta-interpreters with respect to a particular object theory — the topological rules theory for proteins [8]. The interpreters were developed in order to control reasoning over the rules theory (see [7, 6]). The aim of specialising the interpreters with respect to the object theory is to remove the overhead which is associated with explicit interpretation [9], and thus to improve the overall performance of the system.

For each of the interpreters reported in [6], a corresponding transformer was written (by hand) which, when applied to an object theory, produces a new theory, which has the same (or nearly the same) search behaviour as the old theory, but which involves no explicit interpretation. The hand transformers were found, generally, to remove the overhead of explicit interpretation (see [6] for details). Partial evaluation (P.E.) has been proposed as a technique which can transform object theories with respect to interpreters automatically ([9, 3, 10]); that is, P.E. takes as input the interpreter and the object theory, and returns as output an amalgamated theory, which has the same search behaviour as the old interpreter/object theory pair, but contains no explicit interpretation (i.e. calls to *solve, member* etc, the principal predicates of the interpreter).

In this paper we examine whether P.E., as reported in the literature, is able to automatically transform the interpreters described in [7] with respect to the topological rules theory. In particular, we will see whether P.E. (in some form) is able to emulate the hand-written transformers. The hand transformers were written before the author knew about P.E.. The investigation reported here was motivated by a desire to test the claims ([9]) that such transformation can be achieved through P.E..

17.1.1   Partial evaluation in Prolog

We assume a basic knowledge of P.E. in pure Prolog (see [10], for example). The general form of a node in the P.E. tree for a goal G is

$$G^\theta : \quad (<susp>, <todo>)$$

where $<todo>$ is a conjunction of goals which have not been P.E.'d yet, $<susp>$ is a conjunction of suspended goals (often non-logicals) which have been produced by the goals which have already been P.E.'d, and θ is the substitution entailed by P.E. so far (initially, there is a single node $G : (nil, G)$); when $<todo>$ becomes empty, $<susp>$ forms the body of a new clause whose head is G^θ. Given a node as above, P.E. can proceed in two ways:

Single goal selection The first goal, H, from $<todo>$ is chosen, and P.E. is called recursively on it to produce a list of new specialised clauses matching H. The P.E. system then has three options:

1. to **unfold** the clauses into the node, producing a new node for each (the bodies of the new clauses are appended to the end of $<susp>$);

2. to maintain the new clauses separately, and to move the goal H to the end of *susp* (the predicate of H and the heads of the new clauses are renamed with a unique name, to distinguish this call from other specialised calls to the same predicate) — we call this option **auxiliary call creation.**

3. to replace the call with a disjunction, each disjunct consisting of the instantiation entailed by a clause, together with the body of the clause ([2] suggests this option). This is not significantly different from 2, and so we will not consider in separately in the following sections.

Single goal selection leads to an execution strategy similar to Prolog's — goals are selected from the left, and P.E. is completed on a chosen goal before any work is done on the rest of <*todo*>; this facilitates dealing with non-logicals (see [3] and below).

Folding transformation An initial segment, <*init*>, of <*todo*> is chosen, a new (uniquely named) predicate, p', is constructed, with arguments corresponding to the *external variables* of <*init*> (i.e. those shared with G^θ, <*susp*> or the rest of <*todo*>), and a single defining clause

$$p'(<extvars>) :- <init> .$$

This clause is then **folded** into the node, replacing <*init*> with $p'(<extvars>)$ (the latter is added to the end of <*susp*>), and a recursive call to P.E. on $p'(<extvars>)$ is initiated. The clauses produced from this are maintained separately.

Existing Prolog P.E. systems (such as [3, 11]) do not allow folding transformations. This, in itself, would prevent them from being effective on the interpreters discussed in this paper.

As presented above, it looks as if the P.E. system has to decide immediately whether to P.E. the goal at the front of <*todo*> or use a folding transformation. But after a single goal has been P.E.'d, we can decide not to follow either 1 or 2 above, but to revert to a folding transformation instead. The work done on the single goal will not have been wasted, since the first call on the new P.E. process for $p'(<extvars>)$ will be a call to P.E. on the same single goal; hence the clauses already produced can be re-used (following [3], we assume that the P.E. system stores the results of all P.E. calls, and re-uses them where possible).

In following sections, we will encounter the trade-offs which exist between the various possibilities open to P.E. — for example, unfolding may propagate variable bindings which enable P.E. to continue successfully on the rest of the subgoals, but may also lead to an explosion in code size; a folding transformation, by preventing immediate branching, may prevent repetition of suspended conditions in the new program, and hence lead to a smaller, faster program.

17.1.2 Theoretical issues — negation

Lloyd and Sheperdson [4] formally define, and prove properties of, P.E. in which single goal selection and unfolding are the only options (apart from suspension). Auxiliary call creation, and the folding transformation turn out to be very useful.

We therefore propose that Lloyd and Sheperdson's definition of P.E. be extended to allow these options. This complicates the formal definition of P.E. (the definition is made recursive — we do not go into the details here), but we conjecture that the results of [4] can be extended to the new definition.

Our interpreters use negation. Hence we require a P.E. system which can handle negation. Most Prolog P.E. systems do not. [4] defines P.E. for normal programs, i.e. ones which may include negation. However, Lloyd and Sheperdson's definition forces negated goals to be either totally evaluated, or not evaluated at all (see [4]). We will see that genuine *partial* evaluation of negated goals is important for P.E.'ing our interpreters. We propose that Lloyd and Sheperdson's (extended) definition of P.E. for normal programs be (further) extended in the following way: a negated goal, *not G*, may be selected during P.E. (whether or not it contains variables); P.E. is called on *G*; the new clauses produced are not unfolded (this would be unsound), but are maintained separately via auxiliary call creation. This rule will allow genuine P.E. of negations. Again, we conjecture that the results of [4] will extend to the new definition.

17.2 Partial evaluation of meta-interpreters

In the literature on P.E.'ing interpreters, it is standard to P.E. with respect to the set

$$S = \{solve(<theory>, p_1(X_1, \ldots X_{s_1})), \ldots solve(<theory>, p_r(X_1, \ldots X_{s_r}))\},$$

where $p_1, \ldots p_r$ are the predicates defined in $<theory>$, with arities $s_1, \ldots s_r$ respectively, and $<theory>$ is the object theory. It is also standard to suspend subgoals of the form $solve(<theory>, <goal>)$, where $<goal>$ is atomic, but not where $<goal>$ is a negation or a conjunction. This ensures that the program produced satisfies the **closure** condition, from [4], which is a condition for completeness of P.E.. It is also necessary for "pushing down of meta-arguments" (PDMA), replacing instances of $solve(<theory>, <goal>)$ in the new program by $<goal>$. Denote the interpreter together with the object theory by P, the P.E. of P w.r.t. S by P', and the result of PDMA on P' by P''. We sketch a proof of the procedural soundness and completeness of this process, assuming the soundness and completeness of the interpreter; we show

$$refute(P'' \cup \{\leftarrow G\}, \theta) \text{ iff } refute(P \cup \{\leftarrow solve(<theory>, G)\}, \theta),$$

for any object goal G, where $refute(C \cup \{G\}, \theta)$ means that the goal G has computed answer θ w.r.t. the set of clauses C, and $\overline{G}$ stands for goal produced by replacing each atom A in G by $solve(<theory>, A)$[1], assuming

$$refute(P \cup \{\leftarrow \overline{G}\}, \theta) \text{ iff } refute(P \cup \{\leftarrow solve(<theory>, G)\}, \theta).$$

[1] For simplicity of presentation, we ignore the representation of object clauses in the interpreter.

The latter condition is implied by the procedural soundness and completeness of the interpreter.

For any object goal G, it is easy to prove that

$$refute(P'' \cup \{\leftarrow G\}, \theta) \text{ iff } refute(P' \cup \{\leftarrow \overline{G}\}, \theta),$$

assuming that all occurrences of $solve(<theory>, A)$ in P' have A an atom. This justifies the PDMA step. Furthermore, the P.E. theorems of [4] allows us to conclude

$$refute(P' \cup \{\leftarrow \overline{G}\}, \theta) \text{ iff } refute(P \cup \{\leftarrow \overline{G}\}, \theta),$$

since $P' \cup \{\overline{G}\}$ is closed w.r.t. S^2. The desired result follows, given our assumption.

We could remove the need for the assumption about the interpreter if we P.E.'d w.r.t. $\{solve(<theory>, X)\}$ instead of S. However, we would get extra clauses as a result and would need *ad hoc* arguments to show that the extra clauses could effectively be ignored to allow PDMA to proceed (i.e. different arguments for each interpreter). On the other hand, our proof method only works if the conditions for PDMA are met.

In the following sections, we describe in detail the P.E. of four of the interpreters from [7]. As we proceed, we will accumulate requirements and recommendations for a P.E. system for full Prolog. Each requirement is labelled (by R_n, for some n) as it is used, and discussed at the end of the section.

The descriptions of the P.E. process for the interpreters are necessarily detailed. Furthermore, there is not enough space to include illustrations of the process. The reader may find it helpful to follow the process on a piece of paper, as we describe it.

17.3 Prevention of resatisfaction

Figure 17.1 shows a simple interpreter which prevents the attempted resatisfaction of uniquely solvable goals. We consider the partial evaluation of this interpreter with respect to the topological rules theory. Thus, we P.E. with respect to the set

$$\{solve(rules, p_1(X_1, \ldots X_{n_1})), \ldots solve(rules, p_r(X_1, \ldots X_{n_r}))\},$$

where $p_1, \ldots p_r$ are the predicates defined in rules, with arities $n_1, \ldots n_r$ respectively. We consider the process for a typical binary predicate $p(X, Y)$, with defining clauses $p(X^i, Y^i) :- <body_i>$, for $i = 1, \ldots, n$, where X^i and Y^i are (possibly) instantiated forms of X and Y.

---

[2]The theorems of [4] contain an unnecessary restriction — that the set P.E.'d w.r.t. be singular — which is violated by S. However the results can be simply generalised, replacing "singular" by "independent", where a set is independent if its elements are pairwise non-subsuming. S is independent.

```
1.   solve(_, true).
2.   solve(Theory, not Goal) :−
             not solve(Theory, Goal).
3.   solve(_, Goal) :−
             system(Goal),
             call(Goal).
4.   solve(Theory, (Goal, Rest)) :−
             solve(Theory, Goal),
             solve(Theory, Rest).
5.   solve(Theory, Goal) :−
             uniqueSoln(Theory, Goal),
             member(Theory, (Goal :− SubGoals)),
             solve(Theory, SubGoals), !.
6.   solve(Theory, Goal) :−
             not uniqueSoln(Theory, Goal),
             member(Theory, (Goal :− SubGoals)),
             solve(Theory, SubGoals).
```

Figure 17.1: Preventing resatisfaction

The call $solve(rules, p(X, Y))$ matches with clauses 3, 5 and 6 from Figure 17.1. Clause 3 leads to failure since the goal $system(p(X, Y))$ fails. The goal $uniqueSoln(rules, p(X, Y))$, arising from clause 5, will P.E. to a single clause, the body of which contains calls to *ground* on X and/or Y in some Boolean combination. The *ground* calls are suspended since the binding state of X and Y is not known at P.E. time (R_1). The predicate p may have more than one functionality, which would lead, initially, to more than one clause for $uniqueSoln(rules, p(X, Y)$; but all such clauses have the same head, and so their bodies can be merged in a disjunction (R_2).

The goal $uniqueSoln(rules, p(X, Y))$ thus leads to just one new clause, which is unfolded into the suspended goal list from clause 5.

The goal $not\ uniqueSoln(rules, p(X, Y))$, from clause 6, will, using the rule for negations, P.E. to the negation of the same groundness condition on X and Y (it may be possible to simplify the condition, replacing a negation of a disjunction by a conjunction of negations).

Thus we still have two branches to the P.E. tree for $solve(rules, p(X, Y))$. On each branch, the head of <todo> is now $member(rules, (p(X, Y) :− SubGoals))$. This will P.E. to a list of unit clauses, one for each defining clause for p. The P.E. system has three options — 1) auxiliary call creation, 2) unfolding, and 3) a folding transformation:

1. This turns out to be a bad move, since *SubGoals* is unbound in the next goal to be P.E.'d, *solve(rules, SubGoals)*. This goal cannot be suspended without violating the closedness condition; hence it has to be P.E'd, which leads either to an explosion of new clauses or to most of the explicit interpretation left in the new theory.

2. In general, this would not be possible, since there are suspended meta-logicals on the branch (R_3), and the clauses from *member* would bind variables. In fact, clauses from *rules* do not often bind variables in the head, so, in most cases, unfolding would be possible. If this is done, each new branch has a goal *solve(rules, <body>)*, for a particular clause body, and half of them also have cuts. The *solve* subgoals each P.E. (via clauses 2 and 4) to a single clause, with a conjunction of possibly negated *solve* calls to atomic goals as body; these *solve* calls are suspended since they match the standard suspension condition. For each branch, the single new clause is unfolded. For half of the branches, P.E. is complete; for the other half, a cut remains, which is suspended (since we cannot be sure that the preceding suspended goals on the branch will succeed (R_4)), completing P.E. for these branches as well. PDMA then produces $2 \cdot n$ new clauses for p. The new procedure runs slower than the $n + 2$ clauses produced by the hand transformer — the groundness checks are repeated, on backtracking, for each of the $2 \cdot n$ new clauses, whereas they are checked at most twice in the other version. Hence the new theory would, in general, be larger and slower than the hand-transformed version, with this option.

3. The best choice for a folding transformation is to create a new predicate definition,

$$p'(X, Y) \ :-$$
$$member(rules, (p(X, Y) \ :- \ SubGoals)),$$
$$solve(rules, SubGoals),$$

and fold this with each of the two branches (note that only *external* variables are included as arguments to p'). This choice is the best because (a) the cut left on the first branch would be suspended anyway, and so would not cause branching, and (b) it allows one new procedure to be used for both branches. The P.E. system would benefit from being able to make such reasoned choices of transformation. Now the call $p'(X, Y)$ is P.E.'d, branching with the clauses previously obtained for the *member* goal, and reducing the *solve* goal on each branch (as above) to possibly negated atomic calls to *solve*. After PDMA, the new procedure for p has the form

$$p(X, Y) \ :- \ <cond>, p'(X, Y), !.$$
$$p(X, Y) \ :- \ <cond'>, p'(X, Y).$$
$$p'(X^i, Y^i) \ :- \ <body_i> . \quad (\text{for } i = 1, \ldots n),$$

i.e. $n + 2$ clauses, which is identical to that produced by the hand transformer.

The above indicates the power that the folding transformation can have, reducing the size and increasing the speed of the resulting theory. Existing P.E. systems would be forced to choose 1 or 2.

Special purpose rules

R_1: **Suspension of** $ground(X)$ It is standard for Prolog P.E. systems to suspend meta-logical goals, such as $ground(X)$, unless X is ground at P.E. time, in which case the goal should succeed.

R_2: **Merging clauses with identical heads** This obvious rule can avoid fruitless branching in the P.E. space.

R_3: **Back-unification over built-ins** [5] points out that variable bindings cannot be validly propagated backwards over non-logical predicates. In our terms, we cannot allow unfolding to instantiate variables leftwards past suspended cuts or groundness conditions. The P.E. system described in [3] contains this rule. However, as [11] points out, unfolding is valid if the bindings concerned are added just after the suspended conditions as explicit equalities.

R_4: **Cuts** Again, it is standard for full Prolog P.E. systems to suspend cuts, in most cases. We will see below that it is important to be able to evaluate cuts at P.E. time, in certain cases.

17.4 Lemma generation

Figure 17.2 shows an interpreter which saves and re-uses lemmas for uniquely satisfiable goals[3]. Note that $uniqueSoln(Theory, Goal, Goal1)$ now has three arguments — the third is a possibly more general goal than $Goal$ which is also uniquely satisfiable. For discussion of the design of the interpreter, see [6, 7]. For our present purposes it is significant that $uniqueSoln$ now binds an argument and is (possibly) resatisfiable (in Figure 17.1, it is just a check).

The initial stages of P.E.'ing the goal $solve(rules, p(X, Y))$ are similar to before, except that three branches are produced, from clauses 5, 6 and 7. On the branch from clause 5, P.E.'ing the $uniqueSoln$ call may lead to more than one clause, which cannot be merged, having different heads. We can either branch by unfolding these clauses, or create a specialised predicate (a folding transformation is pointless since $uniqueSoln$ is the first call). Almost all Prolog P.E. systems

---

[3]We have omitted clauses 1-4, which are as in Figure 17.1.

```
5.  solve(Theory, Goal)  :-
            uniqueSoln(Theory, Goal, Goal₁),
            lemma(Goal₁), !,
            Goal₁ = Goal.
6.  solve(Theory, Goal)  :-
            uniqueSoln(Theory, Goal, _), !,
            member(Theory, (Goal :- SubGoals)),
            solve(Theory, SubGoals),
            add_lemma(Goal), !.
7.  solve(Theory, Goal)  :-
            not uniqueSoln(Theory, Goal, _),
            member(Theory, (Goal :- SubGoals)),
            solve(Theory, SubGoals).
```

Figure 17.2: Lemma interpreter

would unfold here, since the instantiations on the new branches could lead to further specialisation. In this case, it is better not to unfold, since all the remaining goals on the branch are suspended anyway (the *lemma* goal is suspended since *lemma* is a dynamic predicate (R_5), the cut is suspended, and the equality is suspended since we cannot pass bindings backwards over a cut (R_3)). More generally, even if further P.E. is possible, the *differences* in the bindings produced by the various clauses for *uniqueSoln* may not affect the result of P.E.. In such cases, unfolding would give no benefit and would lead to a larger theory. The problem is, of course, that we do not immediately know whether the differences in the bindings will be significant or not. The following are possible courses of action:

- consider both possibilities (i.e. unfolding and auxiliary call creation) separately, and compare the results. But, when nested, this rule could lead to explosion in the P.E. space;

- perform a cheap look-ahead to capture cases, such as the present one, in which it is clear that no further specialistion will take place. But this would not cope with another example of this problem discussed in section 17.5;

- use a "least commitment" strategy, in which both possibilities are explored together: the bindings from the new clauses are maintained explicitly, and, at each stage, it is checked whether P.E. deviates for any of the bindings; if so, unfolding takes place; if there is no deviation for any of the remaining goals on the branch, an auxiliary call is used instead. This appears the most promising possibility. But it is also the most radical, and requires considerable flexibility in the structure of the P.E. system (R_6).

We assume that unfolding is prevented in this case. Hence, clause 5 leads to just one principal clause, with an auxiliary procedure consisting of the clauses from *uniqueSoln*.

The *uniqueSoln* call on the branch from clause 6 *is* used as a check, since its third argument is a local variable. The P.E. system should recognize this, and allow merging of the clauses produced by P.E.'ing the *uniqueSoln* call into one (R_7) — not doing so would lead to a large space increase, on branching. This clause is then unfolded. The cut is suspended. The *member* call leads to a set of unit clauses, as before. Unfolding these clauses is not possible, because it would increase the scope of the suspended cut (R_8). Auxiliary call creation would be unsatisfactory, as discussed in Section 17.3 — the [3] system would be forced to do this, which would prevent successful P.E. of the interpreter. However, a folding transformation solves the problem: the same procedure p' as used in the last Section (and for the same reasons) is created, folded into the branch and suspended. The goal $p'(X, Y)$ is then P.E.'d separately, leading to n clauses as before. The *add_lemma* call P.E.'s to an *assert* call, which is suspended (R_9); the last call, a cut, is also suspended. Hence, clause 6 leads to one principal new clause, with an auxiliary procedure containing n clauses.

On the branch arising from clause 7, the *not uniqueSoln* goal will P.E. to a single Boolean combination of *ground*ness conditions. We could unfold the clauses arising from *member* (as long as they do not bind variables — R_5), but it is better (in terms of both size and efficiency) to apply the same folding transformation as that used on the branch from clause 6. Thus, clause 7 leads to just one new clause.

PDMA can now be applied to produce a new procedure of the following form:

$$p(X, Y) \;:- \; aux(X, Y, Z), \; lemma(Z), \; !, \; Z = p(X, Y).$$
$$p(X, Y) \;:- \; <cond>, \; !, \; p'(X, Y), \; assert(lemma(p(X, Y))), \; !.$$
$$p(X, Y) \;:- \; <cond'>, \; p'(X, Y).$$

where *aux* may have several simple defining clauses and p' has the same clauses as in the last section.

The new procedure is similar to that produced by the hand transformer, but not quite as efficient, since the *uniqueSoln* conditions are re-checked on backtracking. This is avoided if the interpreter was first rewritten in the following way: clauses 5 and 6 are merged to produce a clause with one *uniqueSoln* subgoal, followed by a disjunction of the remainder of the individual clause bodies. The validity (in the presence of cuts) and control of such transformations is problematic, however.

Special purpose rules

5. $solve(Theory, Goal, Control) :-$
   $set\_control(Goal, Control, NewControl),$
   $select\_clause(Theory, Goal, NewControl, SubGoals),$
   $solve(Theory, SubGoals, NewControl).$

6. $select\_clause(Theory, Goal, Control, SubGoals) :-$
   $member(Theory, (Goal :- SubGoals), Id),$
   $check\_global\_constraints(Theory, Control, Id).$
   $check\_local\_constraints(Theory, Goal, Id),$

7. $set\_control(q(X, Y), \_, sameSheet) :-$
   $ground(X),$
   $ground(Y),$
   $inSameSheet(X, Y), !.$

8. $set\_control(\_, C, C).$

Figure 17.3: Clause selection interpreter

R_5: **Dynamic predicates** The rule that calls to dynamic predicates be suspended is proposed in [3].

R_6: **Delaying unfold/auxiliary call decision** This is a potentially valuable capability for a P.E. system. Existing Prolog P.E. systems do not allow this flexibility.

R_7: **Extension of clause merging** Clauses whose heads only differ in argument positions which are local variables in the call can be merged.

R_8: **Cuts** If a branch contains a suspended cut, we cannot branch (i.e. unfold with more than one clause) on any subsequent goal in the branch. Similar, but stronger, restrictions apply to *assert* and *retract*: if there is a suspended goal which could ever lead to a call to *assert* or *retract*, subsequent branching is not allowed. [3] and [11], which both describe full Prolog P.E. systems, do not mention either of these restrictions; without them, P.E. is unsound.

R_9: **Suspend assert and retract** Calls to assert and retract must be suspended, like most other side-effecting calls.

17.5 Clause Selection

Figure 17.3 shows an interpreter which blocks certain resolutions which are either doomed to failure or redundant (see [6] for detailed discussion of this strategy). A 3-place *member* is used, which includes the unique clause identifier. *solve* has an extra argument: this is used to pass down control information which is used to block resolutions with certain clauses; a top-level call to the interpreter will have this argument instantiated to the constant *no_control*. Thus, we P.E. the interpreter with respect to the set

$$\{solve(rules, p_1(X_1, \ldots X_{n_1}), C), \ldots solve(rules, p_r(X_1, \ldots X_{n_r}), C)\}.$$

Note that clause 7, for *set_control*, applies to just one object-level predicate (which we call *q* here). As before, when P.E.'ing $solve(rules, p(X, Y), C)$, clause 4, which handles built-ins, leads to failure, leaving one branch, from clause 5. The first subgoal on the branch is *set_control*. We consider the cases $p = q$ and $p \neq q$ separately:

$\underline{p \neq q}$ Only clause 8 matches the *set_control* goal, and leads to a single unit clause, which is unfolded into the branch. We then P.E. the *select_clause* goal. The *member* subgoal P.E.'s to the usual set of unit clauses. A folding transformation is pointless, creating an auxiliary call leads to similar problems to those discussed above; hence the clauses arising from *member* are unfolded. On each of the n branches resulting, the next subgoal is of the form

$$check\_global\_constraints(rules, C, <id>),$$

where $<id>$ is a particular identifier. The definition of *check_global_constraints* is

$$check\_global\_constraints(rules, C, Id) :-$$
$$C \neq sameSheet, !.$$
$$check\_global\_constraints(rules, C, Id) :-$$
$$Id \neq 80,$$
$$Id \neq 82.$$

(80 and 82 are the identifiers of particular clauses in *rules*). If the second clause fails (which depends on $<id>$), one clause results from which the cut can be removed since $\neq$ is non-resatisfiable (R_{10}). If the second clause succeeds, the first clause can be ignored, since (a) its only cut is at the end of its body and (b) *check_global_constraints* is a check (i.e. does not bind variables), which can be established by mode analysis (R_{11}, R_{12}). Hence, in either case, the *check_global_constraints* call leads to a single clause without cuts, which is unfolded into the branch for *select_clause* (clauses containing cuts cannot in general be unfolded (R_{13}))

The next subgoal on each branch for

$$select\_clause, check\_local\_constraints(rules, p(X', Y'), <id>),$$

where X' and Y' are instantiated forms of X and Y, P.E.'s in a similar way, leading to one clause with (possibly) some suspended conditions in its body, but no cuts, which is unfolded. Thus P.E.'ing *select_clause* leads to n clauses which do not contain cuts. These are unfolded into the single branch arising from the original *solve* goal. The remaining *solve* subgoal on each of the branches reduces in the usual way to a conjunction of possibly negated *solve* calls to atomic goals which are suspended. Hence, in this case, n clauses are produced from $solve(rules, p(X, Y), C)$. After PDMA, we have n clauses of the form:

$$p(X^i, Y^i, C) \; :- \; (<cond_i>), <body_i>$$

for $i = 1, \ldots, n$ (some clauses have no $<cond_i>$).

$p = q$ In this case the *set_control* call P.E.'s to two clauses, the first of which contains a cut (which cannot be removed). Although it is unsound to unfold clauses containing cuts, in general, it is sound in this case since (a) there is only one active branch for *solve* and (b) *set_control* is the first subgoal in the body (R_{14}). Whether or not unfolding is a good idea is another matter — we are in a similar situation to that discussed in section 17.4. We assume that we adopt the third proposed solution to the problem: that is, we delay the decision, and P.E. the rest of the branch, at each stage checking whether the alternative bindings make any difference to P.E.. It turns out that, for *rules*, the bindings do not make any difference, so an auxiliary call is created for *set_control*. Unfolding with the n clauses from *select_clause* would lead to the *set_control* conditions being checked unnecessarily often.

Hence, a folding transformation is used. The result, in this case, is of the form:

$$p(X, Y, C) \; :- \; aux(X, Y, C, C'), p''(X, Y, C').$$
$$p''(X, Y, C) \; :- \; <cond>, <body_i> . \quad \text{(for } i = 1, \ldots, n),$$

where *aux* has two simple defining clauses, i.e. $n + 3$ clauses altogether. This result is significantly different from the hand transformer, which used *assert* and *retract* to implement global control, and thus avoided having extra arguments. However, in terms of size and efficiency, the result of P.E. is no worse, and is much cleaner.

Special purpose rules

R_{10} If P.E.'ing a goal results in a single clause whose body starts with a non-resatisfiable conjunction followed by a cut, the cut can be removed.

R_{11} Suppose a goal which is a check P.E.'s to a set of clauses which contains a unit clause; then (a) all subsequent clauses can be ignored (b) so can all previous clauses, as long as none of them contain non-terminal cuts. We also require that none of the clauses produced could ever call *assert* or *retract*. (This, and the above, rule, while useful, are not vital for the current interpreter).

R_{12}: **Mode analysis** Several of the other rules require mode analysis to determine, for example, that a particular argument will always be called as a free variable.

R_{13}, R_{14} Unfolding with clauses containing cuts is not allowed, in general. [3] includes this restriction. However there is an exception: if (a) there are no suspended calls on the branch, and (b) there is only one branch from the most recent call to P.E., unfolding of clauses containing cuts is allowed. This is a generalisation of a rule from [3].

17.6   Goal ordering

Figure 17.4 shows an interpreter which allows flexible goal ordering. Again, we will not discuss the design of the interpreter (see [6] for details). Once again, we consider P.E. of $solve(rules, p(X, Y))$ for a typical predicate p. Suppose that $<body_i>$ has n_i subgoals, for each i. There is just one matching clause, 2, for $solve(rules, p(X, Y))$. On the resulting branch, the first subgoal, $p(X, Y) \neq true$, reduces to $true$.

The next $select$ subgoal leads to a single unit clause without cuts, which is unfolded, since the cut in clause 7 can be evaluated immediately, pruning the other branches (R_{15}). The next call is $reduce(solve, rules, p(X, Y), SubGoals)$. Most of the P.E. happens within this call (we describe this below); for each branch which results, the remaining two subgoals can be evaluated totally to $true$.

$reduce(solve, rules, p(X, Y), Subgoals)$ will match with one clause, leading to subgoals

$$(member(rules, (p(X, Y) :- SubGoals)) , solve(rules, SubGoals)).$$

The first of these leads to n branches as usual; for each branch, a single subgoal, $solve(rules, <body_i>)$, remains. We consider the hardest case, when $<body_i>$ contains more than one subgoal. The $solve$ goal leads to a P.E. call on a $select$ goal; this matches with all four clauses for $select$, but the first one, 7, fails immediately. We consider the other three in turn:

Clause 8   The first call on the first new branch is $uniqs(rules, <body_i>, Uniqs)$. $uniqs$ returns the sublist of $<body_i>$ which is uniquely satisfiable. Simple P.E. could lead to a clause for each sublist of $<body_i>$, consisting of suspended groundness conditions, i.e. 2^{n_i} clauses[4]. Each such clause will have a different head, and so none can be merged. However, most of the clauses produced could never lead to success since they will have *inconsistent* groundness conditions. That is, while the condition $(ground(X), not\ ground(X))$ is not evaluable, and thus is suspended

---

[4]The number produced may be less than this, because some subgoals in $<body_i>$ may be uniquely satisfiable unconditionally.

```
 1.  solve(Theory, true).
 2.  solve(Theory, Goals)  :−
              Goals ≠ true,
              select(Theory, Goals, Goal, Left, Right, Flag),
              reduce(Flag, Theory, Goal, SubGoals),
              combine(SubGoals, Left, Right, NewGoals),
              solve(Theory, NewGoals).

 3.  reduce(expand, Theory, Goal, SubGoals)  :−
              member(Theory, (Goal  :− SubGoals)).
 4.  reduce(solve, Theory, Goal, true)  :−
              member(Theory, (Goal  :− SubGoals)),
              solve(Theory, SubGoals).
 5.  reduce(_, Theory, not(Goal), true)  :−
              notsolve(Theory, SubGoals).
 6.  reduce(_, Theory, Goal, true)  :−
              system(Goal),
              call(Goal).

 7.  select(_, Goal, Goal, true, true, solve)  :−
              Goal ≠ (_, _), !.
 8.  select(Theory, Goals, Goal, true, Rest, solve)  :−
              uniqs(Theory, Goals, Uniqs),
              Uniqs ≠ true,
              least_cost(Theory, Uniqs, Goal),
              remove(Goal, Goals, Rest), !.
 9.  select(Theory, Goals, Goal, Left, Right, expand)  :−
              split_at_member(Goal, Goals, Left, Right),
              uniquely_matchable(Theory, Goal), !.
10.  select(_, Goals, Goal, true, Rest, solve).
```

Figure 17.4: Goal ordering interpreter

by normal P.E., it is clearly unsatisfiable, and hence can be reduced to *false*. We thus propose that simple propositional consistency checking be performed on the suspended groundness conditions on each branch; as soon as inconsistency is detected, the branch is pruned (R_{16}).

We unfold the clauses that survive for *uniqs* into the branch for *select*; the next $\neq$ subgoal may prune one of the new branches. The *least_cost* and *remove* subgoals are totally evaluated on each branch (the cost estimates only depend on the predicate), and the cut is suspended. We would still produce many new clauses for *select*, but, since there are only n_i subgoals to choose, merging of clauses with identical heads (R_2) will leave at most n_i.

Clause 9   The *split_at_member* subgoal causes branching n_i ways. The procedure for *uniquely_matchable* uses a failure-driven loop with *assert/retract* to check if there is at most one matching clause for a goal. Hence, the *uniquely_matchable* call leads to suspended conditions. Hence, this clause for *select* will lead to n_i new clauses, each containing suspended conditions from *uniquely_matchable* followed by a cut.

Clause 10   This will lead to a single unit clause for the *select* call.

Thus, we end up with between $n_i + 1$ and $2 \cdot n_i + 1$ clauses from the *select* call. We unfold these clauses into the branch for *solve(rules, <body_i>)*, by rule R_{14} above, despite their cuts. The new branches for *solve(rules, < body_i >)* therefore contain suspended cuts. On each such branch, the next subgoal is *reduce(expand, rules, Goal, SubGoals)* or *reduce(solve, rules, Goal, SubGoals)*, depending on which clause for *select* gave rise to the branch. In the first case, the call can be P.E.'d to a single unit clause (because *Goal* is uniquely matchable); the *combine* subgoal which follows is also totally evaluated, leaving a single call to *solve* on a new goal list on the branch. In the second case, the *reduce* call leads to a subgoal pair *member(rules, (<goal> :− Subs)), solve(rules, Subs)*. We suspend this pair, even though they do not match the normal suspension condition (R_{17}) — the alternative would be an explosion in new clauses. The *combine* subgoal is then totally evaluated, leaving a call *solve(rules, <rest>)* on the branch, where *<rest>* is the list of subgoals which were not chosen in the preceding *select* call.

Hence, in either case, we end up with multiple branches for *solve(rules, < body_i>)*, each containing some suspended conditions, a cut and one non-suspended call, *solve(rules, <list>)*, where *<list>* is another goal list. P.E. is then called on *solve(rules, <list>)*, and the pattern above is repeated. At each stage, the *select* call leads to a multiplication of branches. The process bottoms out when there is just one subgoal in *< list >*, which leads to another suspended pair *member(rules, (<goal> : − Subs)), solve(rules, Subs)* (R_{17}). The clauses produced for *solve(rules, <list>)* cannot be unfolded because of the suspended cut (R_8), so an auxiliary call is created.

Therefore, the clauses which are finally produced for $solve(rules, <body_i>)$ are of the form $solve(rules, <body_i>) :- <cond>, !, f(<goal>), aux$, where $f(<goal>)$ is shorthand for the suspended subgoal pair, and aux is a call to an auxiliary predicate, which will have defining clauses of the same form, with more auxiliary predicates, and so on. These are unfolded into the branch for

$$reduce(solve, rules, p(X, Y), Subs);$$

the resulting clauses are, in turn, unfolded into the branch for the original goal $solve(rules, p(X, Y))$. We will have a huge proliferation of new clauses, at least $(n_i + 1)!$ arising from the ith clause for p, and generally exponentially more than this, which will make P.E. impractical, unless we can prune further.

Clause 9 for *select* multiplies the branches at each stage by the number of goals in $<list>$ — this alone is enough to make P.E. prohibitive. The problem is that the suspension of the conditions from *uniquely_matchable* prevents any filtering of possibilities. The hand-written transformer, which did not produce an unmanageably large theory, was unfaithful to the interpreter with respect to the *uniquely_matchable* goals — it effectively evaluated them prematurely. We propose that the same be done during P.E.. While unsound for general Prolog programs, this retains soundness and completeness *with respect to the object theory* (because it only affects the choice of subgoal). Hence, while it is undesirable to change the behaviour of an interpreter during P.E., it may be the only way of allowing P.E. to proceed successfully. We assume that *uniquely_matchable* is evaluated prematurely (R_{18}). Then, if it succeeds for any of the subgoals in $<body>$, we can evaluate the following cut to prune all subsequent clauses for *select* (R_{15}). Now, clauses 9 and 10 will, together, produce exactly one new clause.

Even with this done, the branching produced by clause 8 will still probably be prohibitive. However we can make use of the following three facts to allow the consistency checker to prune most of the branches (R_{16}):

1. if a "variable" is ground at some point in a clause, it is ground at all subsequent points;

2. if a "variable" is not ground at some point, it is also not ground at a later point, as long as it does not occur in any intervening and previous goals (apart from *ground* goals);

3. if a "variable" occurs in a call to the topological rules theory (i.e. one of the $f(<goal>)$ goals), it will be ground at all later points in the clause.

The first two facts are true for all object theories; the third happens to be true of the topological rules, since calls bottom out on protein theories which are ground unit clauses. These facts enable the state of many variables to be inferred from suspended conditions earlier in a branch (we assume the information is passed down through auxiliary calls). This will enable the consistency checker to prune the great majority of branches from clause 8, and will lead to a transformed theory of comparable size to that produced by the hand transformer.

The suspended $f(<goal>)$ goals, which remain in the new theory, will prevent PDMA from proceeding in the normal way. We therefore replace $f(<goal>)$ by $solve(rules, <goal>)$ (R_{19}); this will allow PDMA. Most of the clauses in the new theory will be of the form

$$p(X^i, Y^i) :- <cond>, !, <subgoal>, <aux\_call>$$

where $<cond>$ is a groundness condition, $<subgoal>$ is (usually) a goal from the body of the ith clause for p, and $<aux\_call>$ is a call to an auxiliary procedure, which will have defining clauses of the same form.

The new theory is comparable in size to that produced by the hand transformer, but different in form — the hand transformer produces clauses of the form

$$p(X, Y) :- p_i(X, Y).$$
$$p(X, Y) :- <conds>, !, q(X, Y), r(Y), \ldots.$$

The main difference is that the groundness conditions are collected together and followed by a cut — no further auxiliary predicates are used. We believe that the hand transformed version will be slightly faster. Using yet more special purpose rules, P.E. could produce an isomorphic theory (there is not enough space to go into this).

Special purpose rules

R_{15}: **Evaluation of cuts** Sometimes, a cut can be evaluated at P.E. time to prune other branches: if there are no suspended conditions on the branch, and the call is bound to match with the current instantiation of the head (verifying this may require mode analysis), the cut can be evaluated to prune all subsequent branches. [3] contains a rule with similar intent, but stated wrongly.

R_{16}: **Consistency checking** This is applicable, in principle, to pure Prolog, but is vital here to deal with suspended meta-logical conditions. To maximise the effect of the checking, we have seen that it is necessary to reason about the state of variables at different points in the evaluation of the body of a clause. This reasoning included the application of domain-specific meta-knowledge about the topological rules.

GPC [1] is able to perform such theorem proving during the course of P.E., but no Prolog P.E. systems can. This facility is vital to avoid an explosion in both theory size and in the time taken to perform P.E..

R_{17}: **Suspension condition** We are forced to suspend a pair of goals which do not match, but are equivalent to, the standard suspension condition. Furthermore, we replace the pair by the standard condition in order to PDMA. We have not found a general and valid form of this transformation — the same pair of subgoals occurred in P.E.'ing other interpreters, but the transformation would lead to a non-terminating procedure. However, the extra suspension condition is vital to the successful P.E. of the interpreter.

R_{18}: **Premature evaluation** We have found it necessary to break some of the rules for built-ins, in cases where this does not affect the soundness or completeness of the interpreter. In general, of course, this is unacceptable. In the context of P.E.'ing an interpreter, this amounts to allowing the P.E. system to alter the control strategy in order to P.E. effectively. While undesirable, this rule is, once again, vital.

17.7 Conclusion

We have seen that none of the P.E. systems reported in the literature are able to P.E. our interpreters effectively. We have numerous requirements and useful features for a P.E. system to be effective on our interpreters (in particular, to emulate the hand-written transformers). Few of these are offered by existing systems. We briefly summarise these:

- P.E. must be able to handle negation; the ability to *partially* evaluate a negation, as described in the introduction, is vital to the P.E. of the goal ordering interpreter. Most P.E. systems do not handle negation in the required way.

- P.E. must be restricted in the presence of non-logical features. However, we have seen that there are important exceptions which should be made. Note that a flexible P.E. system, which can perform all the operations described in the introduction, will be able to cope much better with restrictions, since some of its options will probably still be open.

- We have several special-purpose transformations which enable the removal of cuts.

- In some contexts, we must break some of the rules about built-ins, in order to continue P.E.. The context must ensure validity with respect to the object theory. While perhaps an unattractive recommendation, this may reflect a more general phenomenon — that the trade-offs in inference control procedures in the context of transformation will be different from those in the context of interpretation. We expect that similar issues will arise often as experience develops in specialising meta-interpreters.

- A consistency checker can be used to prune branches with unsatisfiable suspended conditions.

- An extra suspension condition must be used, together with an associated transformation, whose validity has not been established.

- Flexibility: flexibility in the (hypothetical) P.E. system has been crucial for dealing with the interpreters. In particular, the ability to make folding transformations as well as normal P.E. steps appears to be essential. Furthermore, we have seen that P.E. can benefit from flexibility in application of the possible moves. This flexibility includes choosing a folding transformation which will be re-usable elsewhere, and delaying commitment to a particular option as long as possible. Existing P.E. systems are "algorithmic" in nature, with decisions being taken locally; hence they do not offer the flexibility which we need.

We emphasise that most of the above are vital for the successful P.E. of our interpreters. We can, of course, always choose not to P.E. an interpreter. However, the hand transformers show that the interpreters are specialisable.

We should also note that the requirements have been produced from analysis of just four meta-interpreters. We expect that new interpreters will lead to additional requirements.

Given all the requirements, we have seen that P.E. can emulate the hand-written transformers in effectively specialising the interpreters with respect to the topological rules theory. This is a positive result: at the outset, it was not clear to the author that the necessary transformation could be described as P.E. at all.

References

[1] Y. Futamura and K. Nogi. Generalized partial computation. In *Proceedings of the Workshop on Partial Evaluation and Mixed Computation*, 1987.

[2] P. Kursawe. Pure partial evaluation and instantiation. In *Proceedings of the Workshop on Partial Evaluation and Mixed Computation, Denmark*, 1987.

[3] G. Levi and G. Sardu. Partial evaluation of metaprograms in a "multiple worlds" logic language. In *Proceedings of the Workshop on Partial Evaluation and Mixed Computation, Denmark*, 1987.

[4] J.W. Lloyd and J.C. Sheperdson. *Partial Evaluation in Logic Programming*. Technical Report CS-87-09, University of Bristol, 1987.

[5] R.A. O'Keefe. On the treatment of cuts in prolog source-level tools. In *Proceedings of the Symposium on Logic Programming*, 1985.

[6] S.G. Owen. *The Development of Explicit Interpreters and Transformers to Control Reasoning about Protein Topology*. Technical Memo IIPL-ISC-TM-88-015, Hewlett Packard Labs, 1988.

[7] S.G. Owen and R. Hull. *The Development of Explicit Interpreters to Control Reasoning about Protein Topology.* Technical Report, Hewlett Packard Labs, 1988.

[8] C.J. Rawlings, W.R. Taylor, J. Fox, and M.J.E. Sternberg. Reasoning about protein topology using the logic programming language prolog. *Journal of Molecular Graphics*, 3(4):151–157, December 1985.

[9] L. Sterling and R.D. Beer. *Meta-interpreters for Expert System Construction.* Technical Report CAISR TR 86-122, Case Western Reserve University, 1986.

[10] A. Takeuchi and K. Furukawa. Partial evaluation of prolog programs and its application to meta programming. In *Information Processing 86*, North-Holland, 1986.

[11] R. Venken and B. Demoen. A partial evaluation system for prolog: some practical considerations. In *Proceedings of the Workshop on Partial Evaluation and Mixed Computation, Denmark*, 1987.

Chapter 18

The Partial Evaluation of Imperative Programs Using Prolog

Brian J. Ross

The University of British Columbia[1]

Abstract

The feasibility of using Horn clauses as a means of describing and transforming imperative programs is explored. A logical semantics based in Horn clause logic is derived for a typical imperative language. The style of this semantics permits direct translations between the source language and semantic representations. This semantics is ideal as an intermediate representation in a program transformation environment because valid logical manipulations of the semantics result in correctness–preserving transformations of the source program. Given the use of Horn clauses in logic programming, the semantics is particularly useful since models of computation associated with logic programs can be applied to it. Treating the semantics as a pure Prolog program means that the source–to–source partial evaluation of imperative programs is easily performed.

18.1 Introduction

Imperative programming languages are those tailored to the architecture of von Neumann machines [Bac78]. Since the vast majority of computer applications still make use of imperative programming (engineers typically use FORTRAN, systems hackers use "C", many others use Pascal, ...), there is still a need to explore new techniques of program analysis for this class of programs.

Predicate logic continues to enjoy widespread use in the verification and transformation of imperative–style programs [LS84] [Hoa85]. With the advent of logic

[1]Current address: Department of Artificial Intelligence, University of Edinburgh, 80 South Bridge, Edinburgh, Scotland, EH1 1HN.

programming and other computational models for predicate logic there are increased opportunities to apply the logical analysis of programs in semi–automated environments. This paper explores the feasibility of using Horn clause logic to describe and transform imperative programs. Although declarative logic programming and imperative programming represent opposite stylistic philosophies, we will demonstrate that logic programming offers interesting possibilities as a tool for analysing its "imperative ancestor".

Section 2 introduces the concept of logical semantics. Section 3 discusses a logical semantics for a typical imperative language. Section 4 illustrates the ease with which imperative programs can be partially evaluated using our semantics. Section 5 outlines reasons why Prolog qualifies as Ershov's ideal systems programming language, and outlines some related work. Section 6 states some areas of work worth further study. For a more detailed presentation of the work in this paper, see [Ros88].

18.2   Logical Semantics

There are four major methodologies used in the formal description of programming languages: denotational semantics, logical semantics, operational semantics, and more recently, algebraic semantics. Logical semantics – the methodology we will use – can be traced back to work by [Bur69] [Flo67] [Hoa69]. In logical semantics, the behavior of programs and programming languages is described and analysed using first–order predicate calculus. Logical semantics have been particularly useful in program verification, since the derivation of proofs of program properties is equivalent to deriving logical proofs in a particular theory – a process which is made semi–automated through the use of user–guided deduction systems.

Predicative programming, a term introduced in [Bib75], is a programming paradigm in which programs are created from logical specifications though the use of formal logic. Hehner uses the term in a similar sense, with the additional perspective that it is possible to freely intersperse imperative program code with logic during program analysis and synthesis if one treats syntactic constructs of the programming language as predicates [Heh84] [HGM86]. Each construct in a language has a semantic defined for it which can be (i) composed in first–order predicate logic, (ii) defined in terms of subsidiary language constructs, which are likewise logically defined, or (iii) a combination of language constructs and logic. In a mixture of program code and logic, the code portions represent implementable parts of the computation, while the logic represents semantic descriptions. Using predicative programming, the transformation and analysis of code is assured of being logically sound. In addition, predicative programming provides a degree of elegance in merging these two different formal languages into one analytical framework.

We shall employ logical semantics in the source–to–source transformation of imperative programs, and will use the predicative programming paradigm as a means of translating the source language and predicate logic into one another. Our strategy is as follows. An imperative program, which is assumed complete and correct, is input. A predicative meaning is derived for the program by inspection of the program's syntax. The predicate is then optimised. Finally, through predicative programming, the predicate is re-mapped to the source language, resulting in a transformed, optimised program.

18.3   An imperative language and its semantics

We now introduce a generic imperative language called *Bruce*[2]. Section 3.1 outlines the Bruce syntax. An operational semantics for Bruce is presented in section 3.2. Using the operational semantics, a Horn clause or pure Prolog semantics is created for Bruce in section 3.3. Section 3.4 discusses an implemented Bruce-Prolog translation system.

18.3.1   Syntax

Environment:
$$E ::= \cup P$$

Programs:
$$P ::= \quad Progname_i(\bar{a}, \bar{e}) : [local\ \bar{x}]\ \{\ Q\ \}$$
where $Progname_i$ and each variable name $v \in \{\bar{a}, \bar{e}, \bar{x}\}$
is unique in E

Chains:
$$Q ::= \quad [label_i :]\ S\ \mid\ [label_i :]\ S; Q$$
where each label $label_i$ is unique in E

Statements:
$$S ::= \quad skip\ \mid\ v := e\ \mid\ if\ (b)\ then\ \{\ Q\ \}\ else\ \{\ Q'\ \}\ \mid$$
$$if\ (b)\ then\ \{\ Q\ \}\ \mid\ call\ p_i(\bar{v}, \bar{e})\ \mid\ while\ (b)\ \{\ Q\ \}\ \mid$$
$$repeat\ \{\ Q\ \}\ until\ (b)\ \mid\ goto\ label_i$$
where $b \in BoolExpr$, $e \in Expr$, $v \in variable\ names$,
$p_i \in Programs$

Figure 18.1: Bruce syntax

[2]Brian Ross's Unfriendly Computational Environment

Bruce has a Pascal–like syntax. Figure 18.1 describes the syntax of Bruce programs. Items enclosed in brackets, such as statement labels, are optional. An environment E contains all the programs to be executed. A program P is a conventional program or subprogram. A chain Q is a sequence of statements. Finally, a statement S represents a basic program construct. Bruce provides typical loop constructs, as well as local branches and procedure invocation. We assume that common boolean and mathematical expressions in assignments and tests are accounted for.

18.3.2   Operational Semantics

1. $Comp \ll E, P, \ S \gg \sigma \quad = \quad Comp \ll E, P, \ S; skip \gg \sigma$

2. $Comp \ll E, P, \ skip \gg \sigma \quad = \quad < \sigma >$

3. $Comp \ll E, P, \ skip; Q \gg \sigma \quad = \quad < \sigma > \star Comp \ll E, P, \ Q \gg \sigma$

4. $Comp \ll E, P, \ x := e; Q \gg \sigma \quad = \quad < \sigma[\mathcal{V} \ll e \gg \sigma / x] \equiv \sigma' >$
   $\star \ Comp \ll E, P, \ Q \gg \sigma'$

5. $Comp \ll E, P, call \ P_i(\bar{v}, \bar{e}); Q \gg \sigma \quad = \quad < \sigma > \star (Comp \ll E, P_i, Q^i \gg \sigma' \equiv \Sigma^i)$
   $\star \ Comp \ll E, P, Q \gg (\mathcal{K}(\Sigma^i))$
   where $P_i(\bar{x}, \bar{y}) : \{Q^i\} \in E,$
   $(\sigma[\bar{v}/\bar{x}])[\bar{e}/\bar{y}] \equiv \sigma'$

6. $Comp \ll E, P, \ if(b)then\{Q_1\}$
   $else\{Q_2\}; Q_3 \gg \sigma \quad = \quad \begin{cases} Comp \ll E, P, \ Q_1; Q_3 \gg \sigma \\ Comp \ll E, P, \ Q_2; Q_3 \gg \sigma \end{cases}$
   $\text{if } \mathcal{W} \ll b \gg \text{ is } true \text{ or } false$

7. $Comp \ll E, P, \ if(b)then\{Q_1\}; Q_2 \gg \sigma \quad = \quad Comp \ll E, P, \ if(b)then\{Q_1\}$
   $else\{skip\}; Q_2 \gg \sigma$

8. $Comp \ll E, P, \ while(b)\{Q_1\}; Q_2 \gg \sigma \quad = \quad Comp \ll E, P, if(b)\{Q_1;$
   $while(b)\{Q_1\}\}; Q_2 \gg \sigma$

9. $Comp \ll E, P, repeat\{Q_1\}until(b); Q_2 \gg \sigma \quad = \quad Comp \ll E, P, Q_1; if(\neg b)\{$
   $repeat\{Q_1\}until(b)\}; Q_2 \gg \sigma$

10. $Comp \ll E, P, goto \ l_i; Q \gg \sigma \quad = \quad < \sigma > \star Comp \ll E, P, Q' \gg \sigma$
    where $Q' = Buildenv(P, Q_i)$
    and $l_i : Q_i \in P$

Figure 18.2: Definition of $Comp$

Establishing an operational semantics involves the definition of an abstract machine or interpreter. The style of this operational semantics is based on those in [dB81] and [Coo78].

We will characterize a computation by its effect on the store, and in particular, the effect on the values of the program variables. A *state* is a static representation of the computer store during an instant in time of the computation. A state σ is defined as a function which maps program variables to their current values in the domain space *Domain*:

$$\sigma : Var \rightarrow Domain$$

$$Buildenv(P,Q) = \begin{cases} \ll Q \gg & \text{if } P : \{Q';Q\} \\ \ll Q;while(b)\{Q';Q\}; & \\ \quad Buildenv(P,Q^*) \gg & \text{if } Q \text{ belongs to a } while \\ \ll Q;if(\neg b)\{repeat & \text{if } Q \text{ belongs to a } repeat \\ \quad \{Q';Q\}until(b)\}; Buildenv(P,Q^*) \gg & \\ \ll Q; Buildenv(P,Q^*) \gg & \text{if } Q \text{ belongs to an } if \end{cases}$$

where $S\{Q';Q\};Q^*$,

ie. S is the parent statement containing Q, and Q^* is the chain following S

Figure 18.3: Definition of *Buildenv*

A variant $\sigma[e/v]$ of a state σ is a state σ' in which σ' differs from σ only in the mapping of variable v, which is mapped to e. $\sigma[\bar{e}/\bar{v}]$ represents the multiple application of a variant to a vector of elements. A computation sequence, denoted Σ, is an ordered list of successive states produced during the execution of a program:

$$\Sigma =< \sigma_1, \sigma_2, ..., \sigma_k, ... >$$

A function $\mathcal{K}$ is defined as:

$$\mathcal{K}(\Sigma) = \begin{cases} \bot & \text{if } \Sigma \text{ does not terminate} \\ \sigma_k & \text{if } \Sigma^i =< \sigma_0, ..., \sigma_k > \end{cases}$$

$\mathcal{K}$ simply returns the final result state of terminating computation sequences.

A concatenation operator $\star$ will be used to construct computation sequences from other sequences. If $\Sigma^1 =< \sigma_a, ..., \sigma_b >$ and $\Sigma^2 =< \sigma_y, ..., \sigma_z >$, then

$$\Sigma^1 \star \Sigma^2 =< \sigma_a, ..., \sigma_b, \sigma_y, ..., \sigma_z >$$

The first step in establishing the operational semantics for Bruce is to provide a means of interpreting expressions. Two functions, $\mathcal{V}$ and $\mathcal{W}$, respectively evaluate arithmetic and boolean expressions "in the usual way":

$$\mathcal{V} : Exp \rightarrow \sigma \rightarrow Domain$$
$$\mathcal{W} : BoolExp \rightarrow \sigma \rightarrow \{true, false\}$$

A function *Comp* is used to build Σ (figure 18.2). The state sequence Σ for a terminating computation starts at an initial state σ_0, and ends at a state σ_n. *Comp* takes as its arguments the environment E, a program P, a chain Q, and a state σ. E is a source where all available program definitions may be found – a necessity when processing subprogram calls. P defines which labels may be used as branch destinations. The chain Q is the program code currently being processed. σ is the current state of the store.

When processing branches, *Comp* makes use of an auxiliary function *Buildenv* (figure 18.3). The branch itself results in no change to the state, and the chain following the branch is ignored, which reflects the destructive nature branches have on command sequencing. Following the branch is the computation of the chain of code at *label*$_i$. Using *Buildenv*, the control context normally found at the branch destination is recreated. *Buildenv* creates a chain of program code by taking the chain at the destination label and appending appropriate control code for successive parent constructs, resulting in a chain of code which has an appropriate control context.

Finally, $\mathcal{M}$ is the *meaning* function of a program:

$$\mathcal{M} \ll P \gg \sigma = \mathcal{K}(Comp \ll E, Q, Q \gg \sigma)$$

where $P : \{Q\} \in E$. This initialises *Comp*'s evaluation of the program.

The Bruce abstract machine executes by code manipulation (*Comp*), expression evaluation ($\mathcal{V}$ and $\mathcal{W}$), and writing values into the store (state variants). The feature of this operational semantics worth special attention is the way control is processed by *Comp*. During execution, the contents of *Comp*'s chain argument contains an ever-changing chain of program instructions. This chain reflects the control context of the program at any particular moment in the computation. This somewhat parallels the way people "hand compute" programs, in that tracing a program's flow of control involves the implicit textual context of statements, in particular, the constructs in which they are nested and the code textually following them. The Bruce machine does this by explicitly constructing this context.

18.3.3   Basic Logical Semantics of Bruce

Hehner provides some logical semantics for typical imperative languages in [Heh84] and [HGM86]. We propose a logical semantics for Bruce which share many of the basic features of Hehner's semantics. Since our purpose is to use the semantics for program transformation, we simplify the semantics somewhat by assuming that any program input for analysis is (i) correct and (ii) terminates. We thus ignore logical semantics pertaining to such features as type checking, expression evaluation, and the termination of mechanisms. In addition, we choose to explicitly represent each syntactic entity of a program with a uniquely named predicate. Another key difference is that we will use a subset of first–order predicate calculus – Horn clauses – as our semantic formalism.

The goal of the logical semantics is to describe all the relevant behavior of a computational mechanism – in our case, the changes to program variables. Program constructs are thus represented by input–output relations over the store. We consider the entire computational environment to be described by a set of logical axioms. A mechanism such as a program or loop may be described by one or more axioms, each axiom describing an aspect of computation. If the axioms for a program (the *program predicate*) are logically satisfiable, then that program

Programs:

$Progname(\bar{a}, \bar{e}) : local\ \bar{x}\ \{\ Q\ \} \overset{\text{def}}{=} \models Progname(<\bar{a}_i, \bar{e}_i>, <\bar{a}_f, \bar{e}_i>) \Leftarrow$
$$Q(<\bar{a}_i, \bar{e}_i, \bar{x}_i>, <\bar{a}_f, \bar{e}_f, \bar{x}_f>)$$

Chains:

$Q \equiv S_1; S_2; ...; S_k \overset{\text{def}}{=} \models Q(\bar{v}_i, \bar{v}_f) \equiv S_1(\bar{v}_i, \bar{v}_2) \wedge S_2(\bar{v}_2, \bar{v}_2) \wedge ... \wedge S_k(\bar{v}_k, \bar{v}_f)$

Null operation:

$skip \overset{\text{def}}{=} true$

Assignment:

$x := e \overset{\text{def}}{=} \models asgn(\bar{v}_i, v_x, e, \bar{v}_f)$

Program invocation:

$call\ P(<v_1, ..., v_j>, <e_1, ..., e_k>) \overset{\text{def}}{=} \models callasgn(\bar{v}, x_1, e_1)$
$$\wedge ... \wedge callasgn(\bar{v}, x_k, e_k)$$
$$\wedge P(<v_1, ..., v_j, x_1, ..., x_k>, \bar{v}_f)$$

Tests:

$if\ (b)\ then\ \{\ Q_1\ \} \overset{\text{def}}{=} \models if_i(\bar{v}_i, \bar{v}_f) \Leftarrow b \wedge Q_1(\bar{v}_i, \bar{v}_f)$
$\quad\quad else\ \{\ Q_2\ \} \quad\quad \wedge if_i(\bar{v}_i, \bar{v}_f) \Leftarrow \neg b \wedge Q_2(\bar{v}_i, \bar{v}_f)$

$if\ (b)\ then\ \{\ Q_1\ \} \overset{\text{def}}{=} \models if_i(\bar{v}_i, \bar{v}_f) \Leftarrow b \wedge Q_1(\bar{v}_i, \bar{v}_f)$
$$\wedge if_i(\bar{v}_i, \bar{v}_i) \Leftarrow \neg b$$

While loops:

$while\ (b)\ \{\ Q\ \} \overset{\text{def}}{=} \models while_i(\bar{v}_i, \bar{v}_f) \Leftarrow b \wedge Q(\bar{v}_i, \bar{v}_2) \wedge while_i(\bar{v}_2, \bar{v}_f)$
$$\wedge while_i(\bar{v}_i, \bar{v}_i) \Leftarrow \neg b$$

Repeat loops:

$repeat\ \{\ Q\ \}\ until\ (b) \overset{\text{def}}{=} \models repeat_i(\bar{v}_i, \bar{v}_f) \Leftarrow Q(\bar{v}_i, \bar{v}_2) \wedge \neg b \wedge repeat_i(\bar{v}_2, \bar{v}_f)$
$$\wedge repeat_i(\bar{v}_i, \bar{v}_f) \Leftarrow Q(\bar{v}_i, \bar{v}_f) \wedge b$$

Figure 18.4: Logical semantics of Bruce constructs (no branching)

is implementable. An unsatisfiable program predicate is unimplementable or underspecified. A consequence of this convention is that the logical values *true* and *false* are themselves program specifications – the universally satisfiable and unsatisfiable program specifications respectively.

So, given a program P, we define for it a set of Horn clauses which define the input–output behavior of P and its constituent parts. This set of clauses has a logic program interpretation [CM81], and has both a procedural and declarative semantics [vEK76]. Thus, through the logic programming paradigm, the complete logical semantics of a program can be treated as a logic program, and can be executed using SLDNF resolution.

A program P is defined by a clause composed of a conjunction of relations, each representing a statement of the main program chain:

$$P : \{S_1; ...; S_k\} \overset{\text{def}}{=} \models \forall \bar{v}.P(\bar{v}_i, \bar{v}_f) \Leftarrow S_1(\bar{v}_i, \bar{v}_1) \wedge S_2(\bar{v}_1, \bar{v}_2) \wedge ... \wedge S_k(\bar{v}_{k-1}, \bar{v}_f)$$

The declarative meaning of this expression is: for all store values, if the input–output relations S_i all hold for some particular memory states, then P holds. Constructs which are elementary (eg. assignments) defined by atomic relations. More complex constructs require their own predicative definitions. Subsequent constructs within them are defined similarly. A program predicate thus has the form:

$$\models (P \Leftarrow S_1 \wedge ... \wedge S_k) \wedge (S_1 \Leftarrow T_1 \wedge ... \wedge T_m) ... \wedge (T_j \Leftarrow W_1 \wedge ...) \wedge ...$$

where the S_i's, T_i's, and W_i's are input–output relations.

Each $\bar{v}_j$ above is an input or output vector representing the state σ of the computation at a particular moment in time. Each variable parameter, value parameter, and local variable is represented by an element of the vector. The elements of the vector are logical variables whose scope is the clause within which they are used. Each element represents the value of a particular program parameter or local variable at an instant of the computation.

A *goal clause* represents an invocation of the program:

$$\models P(\bar{v}_i, \bar{v}_f)$$

The input parameters to P are appropriately set in the $\bar{v}_i$ input vector.

Figure 18.4 presents the basic semantics for Bruce constructs without branching. The semantics define the behavior of *Comp*. Features worth noting are:

- Vector elements are mapped to their Bruce objects by their position in the vector: $P(\bar{a}, \bar{e}) : local[\bar{x}]\{...\}$ would use the input–output vector format $< \bar{a}, \bar{e}, \bar{x} >$ throughout the body of the program.

- Each test and loop in a program is represented by a uniquely named predicate.

- Composition of statements (chains) involves a conjunction of relations representing each statement in the chain. Intermediate input–output vectors are used to "pass" the value of the store among the relations.

- $asgn(\bar{v}_i, v, e, \bar{v}_f)$ is an atom which represents a state variant. $\bar{v}_f$ is the state which results after substituting the value of the logical variable v in $\bar{v}_f$ with the value of expression e in the context of input state $\bar{v}_i$. $asgn$ uses the expression evaluator $\mathcal{V}$.

- Boolean tests are atomic relations. They implicitly use the input vector appropriate to the context of the test, and use the boolean expression evaluator $\mathcal{W}$.

- Subprogram invocation requires the evaluation of value parameters. $callasgn(\bar{v}, x, e)$ is a relation which represents the use of $\mathcal{V}$ to equate the value of expression e in the context of the current state $\bar{v}$ with a logical variable x. This valuation of the expression is then passed to the subprogram.

18.3.4 Handling Branches

Branches add a dimension of complexity to the semantics of Bruce. A program branch has consequences on the composition of commands, as it destroys statement sequencing. In addition, branching can alter the logical semantics of constructs. For example, a branch can be used to jump out of one or more nested loops – a phenomena which dramatically corrupts their normal semantics.

Handling branches in Bruce is a two step process. First, the meaning of a branch destination is defined. Our treatment of branches makes use of *continuations* [CII72] [Sto77] [Ten81] [Mal]. In a language with branching, a continuation for a statement is the expected result of all the program execution which will temporally follow the statement's execution. The meaning of a branch is therefore the direct effect on the store (which is none), plus the effect of the continuation which, in the case of branches, is the effect of executing the code at the statement label. Fortunately, using predicative programming methodology, this is easily handled. We treat a branch as a call to the *label program* identified by the branch destination label:

$$goto\ label_i \stackrel{\text{def}}{=} label_i(\bar{v}_i, \bar{v}_f)$$

Here, $\bar{v}_f$ represents the final state of the store for the rest of the mechanism's execution. The definition of the label program is simply the predicative meaning of the code generated by the *Buildenv* function used in Bruce's operational semantics.

The next step in processing branches is to account for disruptions in sequencing and control caused by branches. Our approach is to transform a predicate with a branch so that all the instances of code whose sequencing are affected by it are restructured. This restructuring is needed so that the axioms directly reflect the effects of branches on control. For example,

$$goto\ label_i; S \quad \equiv \quad label_i(\bar{v}_i, \bar{v}_f)$$
$$\neg \equiv \quad label_i(\bar{v}_i, \bar{v}_2) \wedge S(\bar{v}_2, \bar{v}_f)$$

The net effect of the restructuring is to "pre–compile" the effects of branches on sequencing into the predicate. Without this, meta–evaluation of branches is required (as in [Mos81]). The restructuring process is easily automated:

1. Expand statements by their semantic definitions until a branch is revealed.

2. Distribute the chains of code over the *or* ($\vee$) connective until we get a disjunction of terms.

3. Remove chains of code which sequentially follow the branch.

4. Replace the branch by a call to its label program.

5. (Optional) Simplify the disjunction by factoring common terms using distributivity.

Figure 18.5 shows a program where a branch removes control out of two nested loops, and figure 18.6 shows the corresponding logical treatment (relations are abbreviated). One expansion of each loop (step (iii)) is required to reveal the chain containing the branch. In step (iv), the chains are distributed through the internal disjunctions, creating a single disjunction of chains. Finally, step (v) shows the removal of the chain following the branch, and the replacement of the branch with a call to the label program (see first disjunct).

$$
\begin{array}{l}
P : \{ \\
\quad while(b_1)\{ \\
\quad\quad while(b_2)\{ \\
\quad\quad\quad goto\ end \\
\quad\quad \} \\
\quad \}; \\
\quad end : S \\
\}
\end{array}
$$

Figure 18.5: Branching out of two loops

$$(i)P \quad \Leftarrow \quad while(b_1)\{while(b_2)\{goto\ end\}\}; end : S$$
$$(ii) \quad \Leftarrow \quad (b_1 \wedge while(b_2)\{goto\ end\}; while(b_1)$$
$$\vee \neg b_1); end : S$$
$$(iii) \quad \Leftarrow \quad (b_1 \wedge (b_2 \wedge goto\ end; while(b_2)$$
$$\vee \neg b_2); while(b_1) \vee \neg b_1); end : S$$
$$(iv) \quad \Leftarrow \quad b_1 \wedge b_2 \wedge goto\ end; while(b_2); while(b_1); end : S$$
$$\vee\ b_1 \wedge \neg b_2 \wedge while(b_1); end : S$$
$$\vee\ \neg b_1 \wedge end : S$$
$$(v) \quad \Leftarrow \quad b_1 \wedge b_2 \wedge end(\bar{v}_i, \bar{v}_f)$$
$$\vee\ b_1 \wedge \neg b_2 \wedge while(b_1); end : S$$
$$\vee\ \neg b_1 \wedge end : S$$

$$where\ end(\bar{v}_i, \bar{v}_f) \Leftarrow S(\bar{v}_i, \bar{v}_f)$$

Figure 18.6: Logically handling of branch

18.3.5 Compiling Logic to Bruce

Once a program is defined in terms of the preceding semantics, its semantic representation can be transformed and analyzed using the laws of first–order predicate logic. In a program transformation environment, the intent is for the semantics to be manipulated to produce a result which yields greater efficiency or some other desired quality not found in the original source program. This optimized representation should then be transformed back into the source language using predicative programming.

Compiling a logical representation back into Bruce is the inverse of generating the logic from Bruce. Pattern matching is performed on the axioms of a semantic representation to search for a match with the logical definition corresponding to a Bruce construct. This matching may require some logical manipulation of the axioms, for example, factoring out common terms and unfolding predicate definitions. Depending on the nature of the transformations on the program predicate, it may also be necessary to order the goals in clauses with respect to the dataflow of the input–output vectors to ensure that Bruce statements are sequenced correctly. There is often more than one Bruce implementation derivable for a given set of axioms.

18.3.6 A Bruce–Logic Translation System

A Bruce–Logic translation system has been implemented in Prolog. This system represents the front–end (logic generator) and back–end (Bruce generator, *Brucifier*) of a Bruce transformation system discussed in section 4.

$$prog([y,n],[\,]) \; : \; local\;[x,eof]\;\{$$
$$\quad n := 0;$$
$$\quad while1 : \; if\;(true)\;\{$$
$$\quad\quad call\;read([x],[\,]);$$
$$\quad\quad n := n+1;$$
$$\quad\quad if\;(eof =:= true)\;\{$$
$$\quad\quad\quad n := n-1$$
$$\quad\quad\}$$
$$\quad\quad else\;\{$$
$$\quad\quad\quad y := y+x;$$
$$\quad\quad\quad goto\;while1$$
$$\quad\quad\}$$
$$\quad\}$$
$$\quad else\;\{$$
$$\quad\quad n := n-1$$
$$\quad\}$$
$$\}$$

$$prog([y,n],[\,]) \; : \; local\;[x,eof]\;\{$$
$$\quad n := 0;$$
$$\quad while\;(true)\;\{$$
$$\quad\quad call\;read([x],[\,]);$$
$$\quad\quad n := n+1;$$
$$\quad\quad if\;(eof =:= true)\;\{$$
$$\quad\quad\quad goto\;end$$
$$\quad\quad\};$$
$$\quad\quad y := y+x$$
$$\quad\};$$
$$\quad end : \; n := n-1$$
$$\}$$

$$\Longrightarrow$$

Figure 18.7: End of file control scheme (initial and final)

The logic generator reads a Bruce program and generates its logical equivalent. It operates in three stages:

1. A Bruce program is read and parsed using a definite clause translation grammar (DCTG) [Abr84]. Then, an initial semantics is created directly from the parse tree of the DCTG. This semantics is complete and adequate in the case when no branching exists in the program, and pointedly illustrates the semantic clarity of structured, branchless programming.

2. Should branching be found in the program, label program definitions are created for all the labelled code in the program.

3. Again, in the case of branches, the semantics are restructured to reflect the effect of branches on program control.

Some bookkeeping, such as saving the names of Bruce variables, is done to ease re-compilation into Bruce later. In addition, some features of Prolog itself are exploited, such as the ability to represent input–output vectors as Prolog lists, and the use of builtin arithmetic and relational operators to ease the evaluation of expressions.

A translation example is now given. The left program in figure 18.7 uses a common control strategy for exiting loops based on an end-of-file condition. The reference to *eof* represents a system call which signals the end of the input stream. Figure 18.8 has the logical equivalent of the source. The program derived from

$prog([Y1, N1], [Y2, N2]) :-$
  $asgn([Y1, N1, X3, Eof3], N4, 0, [Y1, N4, X3, Eof3]),$
  $while1([Y1, N4, X3, Eof3], [Y2, N2, X7, Eof7]).$

$while1([Y1, N1, X1, Eof1], [Y2, N2, X2, Eof2]) :-$
  $true,$
  $read([X1], [X4]),$
  $asgn([Y1, N1, X4, Eof1], N6, N1 + 1, [Y1, N6, X4, Eof1]),$
  $test1([Y1, N6, X4, Eof1], [Y2, N2, X2, Eof2]).$

$while1([Y1, N1, X1, Eof1], [Y1, N2, X1, Eof1]) :-$
  $\neg true,$
  $asgn([Y1, N1, X1, Eof1], N2, N1 - 1, [Y1, N2, X1, Eof1]).$

$test1([Y1, N1, X1, Eof1], [Y2, N2, X2, Eof2]) :-$
  $Eof1 =:= true,$
  $end([Y1, N1, X1, Eof1], [Y2, N2, X2, Eof2]).$

$test1([Y1, N1, X1, Eof1], [Y2, N2, X2, Eof2]) :-$
  $\neg Eof1 =:= true,$
  $asgn([Y1, N1, X1, Eof1], Y4, Y1 + X1, [Y4, N1, X1, Eof1]),$
  $while1([Y4, N1, X1, Eof1], [Y2, N2, X2, Eof2]).$

$end([Y1, N1, X1, Eof1], [Y1, N2, X1, Eof1]) :-$
  $asgn([Y1, N1, X1, Eof1], N2, N1 - 1, [Y1, N2, X1, Eof1]).$

Figure 18.8: Logical form

this predicate (figure 18.7) outlines the control which was implicit in the original source. The old loop structure is lost, as it never represented a true while loop. Note that it would have been possible to simplify the program predicate (eg. the tests *true* and ¬*true*) before generating the final program.

18.4   The Partial Evaluation of Bruce Programs

Once a program is translated into its logical representation, many types of transformations are possible. Deductive transformations and term rewriting are two possibilities which would likely incorporate a mixture of heuristics and user control in order to be practical. We chose partial evaluation as our program transformation scheme, as it is easily automated. The partial evaluation of pure Prolog programs has also been shown to be totally correct (under certain conditions) [LS87]. Lastly, partial evaluation most clearly illustrates the utility of a logical semantics which has inherent within it a model of computation.

Partial evaluation (or mixed computation) is a computational model which distinguishes executable, or *permissible*, code from non–executable, or *suspendable*, code [Ers82] [Ers85]. In imperative programs, permissible code is that which has all the necessary store values defined in order to evaluate an expression or test. Suspendable code is that in which a needed value is undefined. Typically, when such an undefined value arises, all the code which depends on this data is consequently made suspendable. Input parameters to the program are set so that the partial evaluator specializes the program with respect to that input. Partial evaluation then entails executing all permissible code, during which all suspendable code is retained as a partially evaluated program. This *residual* program is often more efficient than the original. In the best case (when all input parameters are defined) it is the *most* efficient implementation of the program with respect to the given parameter values.

The partial evaluation of *definite* logic programs (those not using the negation operator) has been proven to be correct and complete under certain conditions [LS87]. The Horn clause semantics of a program in our system can be treated as a definite logic program, as the negation operator used in negated goals only operates on closed boolean expressions in which resolution is never used. The partial evaluation of our semantics is sound because the partial evaluation of all definite logic programs is sound. The partial evaluation of definite logic programs is not necessarily complete, since the residual program may contain predicative references which are unsatisfiable. We maintain completeness by supplementing the residual program with generalized predicates from the original pre–interpreted program. Whenever a clause contains a reference to a relation which is more general than what can be currently satisfied by the residual program, the original predicate is added to the residual program to make that goal satisfiable. Thus, the partial evaluation of our semantics is totally correct.

Our partial evaluator takes the form of a meta–interpreter written in CProlog, and is based on implementations in [Ven85], [TF85], and [PS87]. Once a Bruce program is translated into logic, its representation is asserted into the Prolog environment, and the partial evaluator is applied to it with respect to given parameter settings. A residual program is eventually created. This resulting program is then given to the Brucifier, and a corresponding Bruce program is generated.

The most difficult problem faced when partially evaluating a program is determining when to inhibit the partial evaluation process. Our system provides both automatic and user–controlled goal inhibition. One automatic inhibition feature involves the detection of loops during goal resolution by the meta–interpreter. Another automatic feature checks that the variables used in a loop test are ground before that loop is unfolded. The user is allowed to enforce his or her own inhibition schemes. This is required when the program contains complex looping mechanisms caused by the use of branches. The user may also override any automatic inhibition strategy.

```
power([y], [x, n]) : {
    y := 1;
    while (n > 0) {
        while (n//2 * 2 =:= n) {
            n := n//2;
            x := x * x
        };
        n := n - 1;
        y := y * x
    }
}
```

Figure 18.9: Binary powers

Figure 18.9 has a Bruce program *power* which computes integral powers using a binary power algorithm (from [Ers82]), and figure 18.10 has its Horn clause equivalent. When *power* is partially evaluated with respect to $n = 5$, partial evaluation yields the residual logic program and Bruce program in figure 18.11. Note that a side effect of partial evaluation is that some vector values become ground. When converting such a relation back into Bruce, the ground terms implicitly represent assignments of constants to variables. Partially evaluating *power* with both $x = 2$ and $n = 5$ produces a program which simply sets the output parameter to the result (figure 18.12). Partially evaluating *power* with only x set results in the original program.

An example of code simplification is the binary gcd program of figure 18.13 (from [Knu81]). We assert goal inhibition clauses specifying that u must be ground before the label programs $b1$ and $b2$ are unfolded, and t must be ground before $b4$ is

$power([Y1, X1, N1], [Y2, X1, N1]) :-$
   $asgn([Y1, X1, N1], Y3, 1, [Y3, X1, N1]),$
   $while2([Y3, X1, N1], [Y2, X2, N2]).$

$while1([Y1, X1, N1], [Y2, X2, N2]) :-$
   $N1//2 * 2 =:= N1,$
   $asgn([Y1, X1, N1], N3, N1//2, [Y1, X1, N3]),$
   $asgn([Y1, X1, N4], X3, X1 * X1, [Y1, X3, N3]),$
   $while1([Y1, X3, N3], [Y2, X2, N2]).$

$while1([Y1, X1, N1], [Y1, X1, N1]) :-$
   $\neg N1//2 * 2 =:= N1.$

$while2([Y1, X1, N1], [Y2, X2, N2]) :-$
   $N1 > 0,$
   $while1([Y1, X1, N1], [Y3, X3, N3]),$
   $asgn([Y3, X3, N3], N4, N3 - 1, [Y3, X3, N4]),$
   $asgn([Y3, X3, N4], Y4, Y3 * X3, [Y4, X3, N4]),$
   $while2([Y4, X3, N4], [Y2, X2, N2]).$

$while2([Y1, X1, N1], [Y1, X1, N1]) :-$
   $\neg N1 > 0.$

$varinst(while1, [f, f, i]).$
$varinst(while2, [f, f, i]).$

Figure 18.10: Logical semantics of binary powers

$power([Y1, X1, 5], [Y2, X1, 5]) :-$
   $asgn([1, X1, 4], Y3, 1 * X1, [Y3, X1, 4]),$
   $asgn([Y3, X1, 2], X2, X1 * X1, [Y3, X2, 2]),$
   $asgn([Y3, X2, 1], X3, X2 * X2, [Y3, X3, 1]),$
   $asgn([Y3, X3, 0], Y2, Y4 * X3, [Y2, X3, 0]).$

$\Longleftrightarrow$

```
power2([y], [x, n]) : {
    y := 1 * x;
    x := x * x;
    x := x * x;
    y := y * x
}
```

Figure 18.11: Residual programs ($n = 5$)

$power([Y1, 2, 5], [32, 2, 5]).$ $\Longleftrightarrow$

```
power3([y], [x, n]) : {
    y := 32
}
```

Figure 18.12: Residual programs ($x = 2, n = 5$)

unfolded. Evaluating the program with $u = 7$ results in a residual program which is somewhat simpler than the original, though not a great deal more efficient.

18.5   Related Work

Ershov presents a transformation system which he uses to symbolically process imperative programs in order to partially evaluate them [Ers82] [Ers85]. The meta–interpretation of our logical semantics in fact parallels the transformations used by his system. Analogies between the transformation system presented in [Ers85] and SLDNF resolution of Horn clause semantics are as follows. (i) *Term reduction:* Ershov reduces expressions by replacing a term by its domain value. In our system, this occurs when an *asgn, callasgn* or boolean test is resolved and the expression value obtained is carried forward in the computation by the input–output vectors in relations. (ii) *Variable reduction:* Ershov uses variable reduction to carry an assigned value of a variable to other statements using that variable. In our system, Prolog's unification automatically "passes" the value of a variable among goals in a clause, and resolvents of a goal. (iii) *Assignment reduction:* Ershov removes any assignment whose variable value has been distributed throughout the code. Under SLDNF resolution, assignments (as with all goals) automatically "disappear" once they are resolved. (iv)*If and while–loop reduction:* These reductions are used to simulate the control of tests and loops. Again, SLDNF interpretation parallels these operations. In fact, the traces of program transformations given by Ershov are very analogous to goal traces obtained when executing our semantics in Prolog. The main difference between his transformations and ours is that he does symbolic computation directly on the program text, whereas we transform a program by performing logically valid transformations on the program predicate.

Logic elegantly handles *polyvariant computational schemes*, which entail partially evaluating the bodies of tests and loops whose tests have been suspended. Ershov handles this by explicitly maintaining memory states of alternate computations [Ers85]. In logic, this is naturally handled by unfolding the suspended test's defining clauses, and retaining the suspended test expression as a goal. Figure 18.14 shows a Bruce program with a suspended test (assume x is undefined). Figure 18.15 shows the mixed logic result for $c1 = 3$ and $c2 = 5$, along with its Bruce realisation.

We think that pure Prolog is a strong candidate for Ershov's systems programming language (SPL) [Ers82]. First and foremost, pure Prolog has a strong underlying mathematical model, namely, first–order predicate logic. This means that transformations of the program can be formally proved to preserve correctness. For example, we treat partial evaluation strictly as a logical manipulation of the program predicate, a formal treatment of which can be found in [LS87]. Another advantage of using Horn clauses as a transformation language is that, using the predicative programming paradigm, there is a strong and natural relationship

$bingcd([gcd], [u, v]) : \ local \ [k, p, t]\{$
  $k := 0;$
$b1 : \ if \ (((u//2) * 2) = \backslash = u) \ \{$
    $goto \ b2$
  $\};$
  $if \ (((v//2) * 2) = \backslash = v) \ \{$
    $goto \ b2$
  $\};$
  $k := k + 1;$
  $u := u//2;$
  $v := v//2;$
  $goto \ b1;$
$b2 : \ if \ (((u//2) * 2) = \backslash = u) \ \{$
    $t := 0 - v;$
    $goto \ b4$
  $\};$
  $t := u;$
$b3 : \ t := t//2;$
$b4 : \ if \ (((t//2) * 2) =:= t) \ \{$
    $goto \ b3$
  $\};$
  $if \ (t > 0) \ \{$
    $u := t$
  $\}$
  $else \ \{$
    $v := 0 - t$
  $\};$
  $t := u - v;$
  $if \ (t = \backslash = 0) \ \{$
    $goto \ b3$
  $\};$
  $call \ power([p], [2, k]);$
  $gcd := u * p$
$\}$

$\Longrightarrow$

$bingcd([gcd], [u, v]) :$
$local \ [k, p, t] \ \{$
  $t := 0 - v;$
  $u := 7;$
  $k := 0;$
$test4 : \ if \ (((t//2) * 2) =:= t) \ \{$
$b3 : \quad t := t//2;$
      $goto \ test4$
  $\}$
  $else \ \{$
    $if \ (t > 0) \ \{$
      $u := t$
    $\}$
    $else \ \{$
      $v := 0 - t$
    $\};$
    $t := u - v;$
    $if \ (t = \backslash = 0) \ \{$
      $goto \ b3$
    $\}$
    $else \ \{$
      $call \ power([p], [2, k]);$
      $gcd := u * p$
    $\}$
  $\}$
$\}$

Figure 18.13: Binary gcd $(u = 7)$

$$p([y, z], [x, c1, c2]) : \ local \ [r1, r2] \ \{$$
$$\quad if \ (x > z) \ \{$$
$$\quad\quad r1 := c1 + 1;$$
$$\quad\quad r2 := c1 - 1$$
$$\quad \}$$
$$\quad else \ \{$$
$$\quad\quad r1 := c\dot{2} - 1;$$
$$\quad\quad r2 := c2 + 1$$
$$\quad \};$$
$$\quad y := y + r1;$$
$$\quad z := z + r2$$
$$\}$$

Figure 18.14: A suspended test

to the semantics of a language and its syntactic realisation. Finally, Prolog has already proven its applicability in many systems programming applications (for example [ACRW88] [Sha83]).

Our semantics are based on those in [Heh84] and [HGM86], which are in turn similar in spirit to ones used in formal program verification [Bur69] [Flo67] [Hoa69]. This paper reformulates these existing styles of logical semantics into conventional logic program notation, and implements them as declarative representations of deterministic, imperative computations.

Moss has developed a similar methodology in which Horn clauses are used to formally describe languages [Mos81] [Mos82]. His semantic formalism is more robust than ours, as the complete semantics for a language in his system take the form of a sophisticated interpreter for the language. A program's semantics in our system can also be considered as a low–level interpreter for the program. However, there is a substantial difference between the two approaches. Taken as a logical theory for a particular language, the domain of discourse of his logical axioms are all the programs possible in the language, along with their abstract operational components. A theory in our system describes the computational behavior of a single program. The axioms describe the functionality of the program, and the domain of discourse is over the store values and expressions. Thus there is a much closer semantic proximity between the logic and programming language, a feature which enables us to map between the two notations.

[CvE81] have used Horn clauses for verifying flowcharts, which can be interpreted as representations of simple imperative computations. The style of their semantics is very similar to ours, though they make no attempt at mapping between Horn clauses and programming languages.

$$p([Y1, Z1, X1, 3, 5], [Y2, Z2, X1, 3, 5]) : -$$
$$X1 > Z1,$$
$$asgn([Y1, Z1, X1, 3, 5, 4, 2], Y2, Y1 + 4, [Y2, Z1, X1, 3, 5, 4, 2]),$$
$$asgn([Y2, Z1, X1, 3, 5, 4, 2], Z2, Z1 + 2, [Y2, Z2, X1, 3, 5, 4, 2]).$$

$$p([Y1, Z1, X1, 3, 5], [Y2, Z2, X1, 3, 5]) : -$$
$$\neg X1 > Z1,$$
$$asgn([Y1, Z1, X1, 3, 5, 4, 6], Y2, Y1 + 4, [Y2, Z1, X1, 3, 5, 4, 6]),$$
$$asgn([Y2, Z1, X1, 3, 5, 4, 6], Z2, Z1 + 6, [Y2, Z2, X1, 3, 5, 4, 6]).$$

$$\Updownarrow$$

```
p2([y, z], [x, c1, c2]) : local [r1, r2] {
    if (x > z) {
        y := y + 4;
        z := z + 2
    }
    else {
        y := y + 4;
        z := z + 6
    }
}
```

Figure 18.15: Polyvariant results

18.6   Conclusion

We have illustrated the applicability of Horn clause logic as a tool for transforming imperative programs. We described the semantics of a non–trivial imperative language using a relatively economical set of logical axioms. Using the notion of predicative programming, direct translation between semantical representations and the source language is possible. The main strength of our program transformation methodology is that *valid logical manipulations of a program's logical semantics result in correctness–preserving transformations of the program's source.* Our semantics, having Prolog's execution model, is also ideally suited to many types of transformations, one example being partial evaluation.

It would be interesting to extend the semantics to handle more complex imperative constructs. The inclusion of complex data types would be a relatively straight–forward extension, and would be especially useful given the preponderance of programs using arrays and other data structures. A real test would be to derive a Horn clause semantics in the style of this work for an existing language such as Pascal. Given that we use the entire computational environment throughout our axioms, programs with large resource usages may require a more clever and economical representation of the environment. A first step is to simplify the predicates to use the portion of the environment of computational relevance to them.

This work offers some insight into alternation trees and *and/or* models of programming [Har80], which form the foundation of models of parallel execution of logic programs. Casting an imperative program in terms of a pure Prolog equivalent means that an *and/or* tree is immediately definable for it. This might be a convenient base from which to derive a parallel execution scheme for the program. However, some data flow analyses of the Prolog representation would likely be necessary.

Further work in controlling the partial evaluation of imperative programs is needed. Inhibiting recursion on polyvariant computations is difficult in our system. This can be overcome to some extent by partially evaluating each clause in the program predicate individually. However, it is not obvious how constant values can be elegantly propagated to these clauses using this scheme.

Acknowledgements: Special thanks to Harvey Abramson for his encouragement and advice – many of his ideas are used in this paper. Thanks also to Wolfgang Bibel, Paul Voda, Matthew Crocker, Doug Westcott; the UBC Dept. of Computer Science for support and facilities; and my parents, Jack and Marlene Ross.

References

[Abr84]   H. Abramson. Definite Clause Translation Grammars. In *Proc. Logic Programming Symp.*, IEEE, Atlantic City, New Jersey, February 1984.

[ACRW88] H. Abramson, M. Crocker, B. Ross, and D. Westcott. A Fifth Generation Translator Writing System: Towards an Expert System for Compiler Development. In *International Workshop on Programming Language Implementation and Logic Programming*, INRIA, Orleans, France, 1988.

[Bac78]   John Backus. Can Programming Be Liberated from the von Neumann Style? *CACM*, 21(8):613–641, August 1978.

[Bib75]   W. Bibel. Pradikatives programmieren. In *GI - 2. Fachtagung uber Automatentheorie und Formale Sprachen*, pages 274–283, Springer, 1975.

[Bur69]   R.M. Burstall. Formal Description of Program Structure and Semantics in First Order Logic. In Meltzer and Michie, editors, *Machine Intelligence 5*, Elsevier, 1969.

[CH72]   M. Clint and C.A.R. Hoare. Programming Proving: Jumps and Functions. *Acta Informatica*, 1:214–224, 1972.

[CM81]   W.F. Clocksin and C.S. Mellish. *Programming in Prolog*. Springer-Verlag, 1981.

[Coo78]   S.A. Cook. Soundness and completeness of an axiom system for program verification. *SIAM Journal of Computing*, 7(1):70–90, 1978.

[CvE81]   K.L. Clark and M.H. van Emden. Consequence Verification of Flowcharts. *IEEE Transactions on Software Engineering*, SE-7(1):52–60, January 1981.

[dB81]   A. de Bruin. Goto Statements: Semantics and Deduction Systems. *Acta Informatica*, 15:385–424, 1981.

[Ers82]   A.P. Ershov. Mixed Computation: Potential Applications and Problems for Study. *Theoretical Computer Science 18*, 18:41–67, 1982.

[Ers85]   A.P. Ershov. On Mixed Computation: Informal Account of the Strict and Polyvariant Computational Schemes. In M. Broy, editor, *Control Flow and Data Flow: Concepts of Distributed Programming*, Springer-Verlag, 1985.

[Flo67]   R.W. Floyd. Assigning Meanings to Programs. In *Proc. Symp. Appl. Math.*, pages 19–32, Amer. Math. Soc., 1967.

[Har80]   D. Harel. Ans/Or Programs: A New Approach to Structured Programming. *ACM Transactions on Programming Languages and Systems*, 2(1):1–17, January 1980.

[Heh84]   E.C.R. Hehner. Predicative Programming Part I. *CACM*, 27(2):134–143, February 1984.

[HGM86]   E.C.R. Hehner, L.E. Gupta, and A.J. Malton. Predicative Methodology. *Acta Informatica*, 23:487–505, 1986.

[Hoa69]   C.A.R. Hoare. An Axiomatic Basis for Computer Programming. *CACM*, 12(10):576–583, October 1969.

[Hoa85]   C.A.R. Hoare. Programs are Predicates. In C.A.R. Hoare and J.C. Shepherdson, editors, *Mathematical Logic and Programming Languages*, pages 141–155, Prentice-Hall, 1985.

[Knu81]   D.E. Knuth. *Seminumerical Algorithms*. Addison-Wesley, 2nd edition, 1981.

[LS84]   J. Loeckx and K. Sieber. *The Foundations of Program Verification.* Wiley-Teubner, 1984.

[LS87]   J.W. Lloyd and J.C. Shepherdson. *Partial Evaluation in Logic Programming.* Technical Report CS-87-09, University of Bristol, December 1987.

[Mal]   Andrew J. Malton. Personal communication.

[Mos81] C.D.S. Moss. *The Formal Description of Programming Languages using Predicate Logic.* PhD thesis, Imperial College, London, U.K., July 1981.

[Mos82] C.D.S. Moss. How to Define a Language Using Prolog. In *Conference Record of the 1982 ACM Symposium on Lisp and Functional Programming*, ACM, 1982.

[PS87]   F.C.N. Pereira and S.M. Shieber. *Prolog and Natural-Language Analysis.* Volume 10 of *CSLI Lecture Notes*, CSLI, 1987.

[Ros88] B.J. Ross. *The Semantics and Transformation of Imperative Programs Using Horn Clauses.* Master's thesis, University of British Columbia, Vancouver, B.C., Canada, 1988.

[Sha83] E.Y. Shapiro. *Systems Programming in Concurrent Prolog.* Technical Report TR-034, ICOT, Tokyo, Japan, November 1983.

[Sto77] J. Stoy. *Denotational Semantics.* MIT Press, 1977.

[Ten81] R.D. Tennent. *Principles of Programming Languages.* Prentice-Hall, 1981.

[TF85]   A. Takeuchi and K. Furukawa. *Partial Evaluation of Prolog Programs and its Application to Meta Programming.* Technical Report TR-126, ICOT, Tokyo, Japan, July 1985.

[vEK76] M.H. van Emden and R.A. Kowalski. The Semantics of Predicate Logic as a Programming Language. *JACM*, 23(4):733–742, October 1976.

[Ven85] R. Venken. A Prolog Meta-Interpreter for Partial Evaluation and its Application to Source to Source Transformation and Query Optimisation. In T.O'Shea, editor, *Advances in Artificial Intelligence*, Elsevier Science Publishers B.V. (North Holland), 1985.

Chapter 19

Prolog Meta-Programming with Soft Databases

Paul Tarau†   Michel Boyer‡

†*Departement de Mathematique, Physique et Informatique,*
Universite de Moncton,
Moncton, CANADA, E1A 3E9
tarau@iro.umontreal.ca
(or taraup@udem.bitnet)
‡*Departement d'Informatique et de Recherche Operationnelle*
Universite de Montreal
C.P. 6128, Succ "A"
Montreal, CANADA, H3C 3J7
boyer@iro.umontreal.ca

Abstract

This paper introduces the notion of soft databases as a tool to model hypothetical meta-reasoning. They can be dynamically expanded or shrunk with the use of backtrackable and logically sound (hence "soft") counterparts to assert and retract namely "assume" and "forget".

Their content can be used either as data or as dynamic Prolog code.

Soft databases can be (and are) implemented on top of a very reduced kernel language (pure Prolog, the if-then-else construct and DCG expansion) by a meta-circular evaluation mechanism, with a surprisingly minimal overhead.

We give the Prolog code of the meta-circular evaluator and examples of its application to problem solving and automated induction.

Keywords: backtrackable logical databases, hypothetical reasoning, Prolog tools for meta-programming, DCG program transformation

19.1   Introduction

It is difficult to do realistic A.I. programming without opening the system to external knowledge sources. In the logic programming paradigm this interaction means updating in some way our axioms. This can obviously invalidate the current proof, depriving it of some result it took for granted. It can also contradict any theorem that had previously been added (explicitly or not) to the knowledge base. This is exactly what happens in Prolog when we use any member of the *assert* and *retract* family of impure extensions.

It is not surprising that these semantic difficulties led to various inconsistent implementations (see [MO86]). It is also well known that *assert* and *retract* suffer from efficiency drawbacks and last-call-optimization problems. Although sophisticated time-stamping techniques were invented (see [LK87]) to cure the last-call-optimization problem, the efficiency and memory management of dynamic code is still far behind compiled Prolog.

In spite of those drawbacks, *assert* and *retract* have been used extensively in theorem provers (to get the equivalent of lemmas), in state-related problems, and a number of object oriented extensions to Prolog, to mention just a few.

In logic programs, states can be represented in basically two ways:

- as a recursive argument passed through procedure calls or

- as a dynamic modification of the database.

The first one implies the usual term based representation of data structures and gives programs which look like the following:

```
process(<OldState>)←
    transform(<OldState>,<NewState>),
    process(<NewState>)
```

where <OldState> and <NewState> represent sequences of state variables.

The second one implies an assertional or relational representation as outlined in [KO79] and [IIO84]. Using this kind of representation an ordered set of elements can be represented by facts of the form:

```
element(NameOfSet,Position,Value).
```

But if implemented by using assert and retract, legitimate meta-logical manipulations would be affected by the semantic difficulties of the destructive assignment.

On the other hand, the use of recursive arguments to store state information let manifest an implicit form of the frame problem: if only one member of this set of recursive arguments changes at a given step, why should one pass all the others, bothering about their order, name and meaning?

Suppose that state information is stored as a sequence of recursive arguments. Then we would like to say: a given argument keeps its value, unless explicitly specified as changing. On the other hand, what is the logical meaning of passing a complex compound term that basically works as a permanent storage for changing information? What one implicitly wants to do in this case is to update the relations describing the considered state information. And putting their term representations on the argument list is only one possible way (not necessarily the best) to assimilate them as logical truth.

Therefore, what we really need is a backtrackable and logically behaving form of dynamic code. The soft databases we introduce, have the logical soundness of the recursive-argument solution, without the frame-problem related drawbacks.

One can consider soft databases as a form of reversible, short time memory, as opposed to the traditional dynamic database which models one-way transitions in the state of the world.

Our technique follows [WA82] and enforces the idea that higher order extensions to Prolog may be obtained through relatively simple program transformations. As an interesting example, we will show how strong constructs like the "all-solutions" predicate, can be obtained in (an almost) pure Prolog.

Our key conjecture at this point is that assimilating new knowledge remains within logic as far as the meta-level updating operations are hypothetical.

As dynamic modification of the database is an important issue in meta-logical programming (see [BK82],[BO85]), temporal and hypothetical reasoning (see [KS86],[GR84]) and truth-maintenance systems (see [MK84]), we hope that our implementation will be useful in applications related to these topics.

We start with a prototype example which contains also the basic hint to an efficient implementation.

19.2 Parsing as a Form of Hypothetical Reasoning

Consider what happens when a DCG parses an input sentence, say

$$S = [T_1, T_2, \ldots, T_n].$$

Basically, as rules are applied, consecutive symbols of the input sentence are consumed. If rules are unsuccessful, backtracking puts symbols back on the input-list.

We may give an equivalent, assertional representation of the input sentence as an (ordered) database containing the clauses $to\_analyze(T_k)$, for each term T_k.

Parsing can be described as a sequence of attempts to delete these assertions, provided that backtracking puts them back if erroneous rules are applied.

If parsing is combined with code generation, then code can be added to the database, (as ordered clauses of the predicate $emit/1$, for example), but it has to be (eventually) removed by the same backtracking mechanism.

We can notice that DCG parsing is a form of hypothetical reasoning which attempts to transform the database containing (a representation of) the input sentence into a new database containing (a representation of) the emitted code.

The following implementation extends this interpretation of grammars, to an arbitrary soft database.

19.3   A Specification of Soft Databases as an Abstract Data-Type

Soft databases are sets of Prolog clauses having their modifications undone on backtracking synchronously with the proof procedure.

They can be dynamically expanded or shrunk with the use of backtrackable or "soft" counterparts to the assert and retract family of predicates.

One can think about them in terms of an ordinary Prolog data structure, as a difference list or a binary tree, containing Prolog clauses usable as code and/or data.

Each one-argument operation on a soft-database is mapped in a three-argument meta-logical operation using the following transformation:

$$operation(SoftClause) \Rightarrow operation(SoftClause, OldDb, NewDb)$$

The meaning of the one-argument operation is defined as the meaning of the three-argument operation, in the context of the transformed logic program (see [VK76]).

Among the set of operations we will put forward, we will find *assume* and *forget*, that will take care of updates, and *assumed* and *wake_up*, that will access soft database contents. When failure occurs, successive states of soft databases are treated as ordinary logical variables.

Basically, once a clause is assumed in the soft database, we can retrieve it as a data object (extensional use), or execute it as a piece of code (intensional use). Intensional use is in fact a form of bilevel meta-programming. The program is partitioned into a read-only meta-level and a "writable" (and backtrackable) object level. Communication between levels is done by explicit calls.

Notice that in the case of a ground fact, extensional and intensional uses are operationally equivalent.

Assume, assume_last and *forget* are the soft relatives of *asserta, assertz* and *retract*.

Assumed works like *clause*, excepting that bindings generated by unification remain in the database. It implements the extensional use of assumed clauses.

On the other hand, *wake_up* uses the content of the reversible database in the same way as *call* uses the underlying Prolog database. It implements the intensional use of assumed clauses.

As one expects there is an important semantic difference between *assumed* and *wake_up*. The first uses its argument unevaluated while the second treats it as the head of a Prolog goal, attempting to prove it from the hypothetical axioms already assumed.

Assumed works on its argument itself, while *wake_up* works on a copy of its argument, with fresh variables.

These operations must be backtrackable even if they figure in embedded recursive calls. The following problem can be used as an "acid test" that can filter out incorrect implementations.

Input: an ordered set of facts, each of which is represented as a soft assertion of the form:

$$to\_permute(Element).$$

Output: any permutation of this set of facts.

```
permute →
    \+ assumed(to_permute(_))
permute →
    forget(to_permute(X)),
    permute,
    assume(to_permute(X)).
```

Obviously, the equivalent Prolog program obtained by replacing *assumed* by *clause*, *forget* by *retract*, *assume* by *assert* and → by ←, fails the test.

The program must also work if *assumed* is replaced by *wake_up*.

Two more operations have to be discussed here:

1. *getdb(CurrentDatabase)*, which gets the current database as a whole and

2. *setdb(NewDatabase)*, which replaces the current database as a whole with a new database.

The predicates *getdb(CurrentDatabase)* and *setdb(NewDatabase)* can be used to switch between databases or theories to efficiently implement meta-prolog extensions like those of [BO85] and [BA87], within existing Prolog systems.

The use of soft databases can partially free the programmer from choosing specific Prolog data structures.

As a consequence the code is completely independent of the underlying data structure, which implements the soft data base operations. The same code can be supported by alternative run-time libraries, giving different implementations for *assume*, *forget*, etc.

Moreover, the programmer is not concerned with argument passing and complex term unification.

Depending on the program solving context, the system and/or the programmer can decide the more suitable data structures for the concrete implementation of the soft database.

For example, recursive intensional calls to the soft database can be highly optimized by a splay-tree implementation as this ensures the migration to the top of frequently accessed clauses, while queuing mechanisms, as those used in Concurrent Prolog, can benefit from a difference list or priority heap implementation.

19.4 Implementation

The code is written using Quintus-Prolog on a Sun-3 work-station.

The basic idea is to meta-evaluate our bilevel program by a source-to-source transformation of most of the operations on the soft database, using a DCG driven term-expansion. The only overhead paid by predicates that do not access of modify soft databases is (at most) the burden of two variables.

In the source file clauses which use the soft database operations are represented by the functor $\rightarrow$ as in usual DCG rules. This means that two additional arguments, say $Db1$ and $Db2$, are appended at the end of each predicate-term. They can be viewed as the state of the database before and after the call. However, if the predicate-term is a variable, say X, it gives

$$phrase(X, Db1, Db2)$$

which means (in Quintus Prolog) that X will be only expanded at run-time, when it becomes instantiated.

The $\rightarrow$ functor may be interpreted declaratively as a grammar based specification of the problem, or procedurally as a description of soft data-base transformations.

The meta-circular evaluation mechanism works by chaining successive states of the soft database. This database is modified by *assume*, *forget*, etc. Previously assumed code in the database can be activated by using *wake_up*.

The "{}" escape mechanism provides a call to Prolog without term-expansion. The predicates *demo* and *wake_up* implement a meta-circular evaluation mechanism:

```
wake_up(H) -->
    assumed(T),{copy_term(T,C)},
    ( {C = (H :- B)} -> demo(B)
    ; {C = H}).

demo(C) -->
    (  {C=(P,Q)}    -> (demo(P),demo(Q))
    ;  {C=(I->T;E)} -> (demo(I) -> demo(T) ; demo(E))
    ;  {C=(P;Q)}    -> (demo(P);demo(Q))    ;  C).
```

This mechanism works as if it were a conventional meta-interpreter ([SS86]), but is far more efficient, since only a limited amount of interpretation is done (when compiled code explicitly uses *wake_up*).

In this case, the soft database is searched by *assumed* for a matching clause, then *demo* is called and the body of the current clause is traversed recursively, until a callable compiled predicate-term is reached. Then control is transferred to compiled code, which works as fast as it can.

If one of the predicates which interact with the database is called, it effectively uses the 2 hidden arguments corresponding to the state of the database.

Suppose, for example that in the source code *assume(C)* is called.

The DCG expansion done at compile time insures that *assume(C,Db1,Db2)* is executed, and if *Db1* is the state of the database before, then *Db2* will be the state of the database after assuming *C*.

That evaluation mechanism deserves to be called "meta-circular" because it handles correctly its own code. It is not strictly speaking a meta-circular "interpreter" since it interleaves interpreted and compiled code.

Since clauses in soft databases are stack-allocated, they allow a potentially faster storage management than traditional, heap-allocated dynamic clauses, and can be easily garbage-collected.

Moreover, the underlying Prolog machine can be simplified as there is practically no need to implement dynamic clauses, if one accepts to use only soft databases.

On systems like Quintus Prolog with a very fast *copy_term* primitive, compiled intensional soft predicates are almost as fast as interpreted extensional ones.

The most appealing feature of this implementation (see the complete source code in Appendix 1), is that a wise choice between extensional and intensional uses, allows the programmer to write programs with virtually no overhead.

As an example of the power of soft databases, we give the definition of an "all-solutions" predicate, which shows that some higher-order features may be easily expressed in this framework (see Appendix 1).

All the implementation is done in a cut-free, meta-circular kernel, consisting of pure Prolog and the "if-then-else" construct (basically equivalent to negation as failure, but more convenient).

Notice, however, the following alternative to the previous approach, based on an interesting idea of R.A. O'Keefe exposed in the (electronic) Prolog Digest (Vol. 2 No. 34). This implementation supposes the presence of the primitive *subgoal_of*, which finds an ancestor of the current goal, matching a given term.

O'Keefe's idea was to use ancestor calls to implement the equivalent of "global variables" in Prolog. Why not then use them to store soft databases? That can indeed be done as follows:

```
ancestor_based_demo(G,_) ← call(G).
```

wake_up_ancestor(H) ←
    subgoal_of(ancestor_based_demo(_,Db0)),
    member((H0←B0),Db0),
    copy_term((H0←B0),(H←B)),
    call(B).

works_like_append(A,B,C)← ancestor_based_demo(
    wake_up_ancestor(local_append(A,B,C)),
        [(local_append([],Y,Y)←true),
        (local_append([X—L],M,[X—R]) ←
        wake_up_ancestor(local_append(L,M,R)))
    ]).

A goal like

$$works\_like\_append([a, b, c], [d, e], L),$$

gives $L = [a, b, c, d, e]$.

The predicate *ancestor_based_demo* is used to store the local database (as its anonymous variable). The predicate *wake_up_ancestor* locates the database in the body of *ancestor_based_demo*, (one of its ancestors given by *subgoal_of*). By using $Db0$ as a difference list or binary search tree of successive states of the database, one can implement (although more expensively) an evaluation mechanism equivalent in power to the previous DCG based one.

However, most Prologs allow (for good reasons) *subgoal_of* only in interpreted code and therefore this approach can not really benefit from compilation. Moreover, in the case of a deep recursive embedding or a perpetual process, the ancestor may be very expensive or practically impossible to access.

In fact, our DCG based implementation provides direct access to soft databases and is easier to understand.

19.5 Hypothetical Reasoning and Automated Induction

Problem solving and especially the generate and test paradigm can be seen as special case of hypothetical reasoning. First, generated relations are assumed as hypotheses. Then testing simply means that some constraints must be provable from the static and/or the soft database. As soft databases are backtrackable, useless hypotheses are cleaned up automatically. This makes programming more declarative and more explicit, by partially replacing term representation of data structures, with an assertional representation.

Although the well-known duality between term representation and assertional representation of data-structures was pointed out by Kowalski in [KO79], logic programmers prefer data structures, because in Prolog, modifications of data structures are backtrackable and "logical", while asserting and retracting are not.

As soft databases circumvent this difficulty, we emphasize in the following example an almost purely "assertional" problem solving style. As an example, let us consider the following solution to the N-queens problem:

```
queens(N) -->
    make_free_positions(N),place(N),print_solution,{fail}
; {true}.
```

```
% makes a pool of free positions
```

```
make_free_positions(P) -->
    {P>0} -> assume(free(P)),{P1 is P-1},make_free_positions(P1)
; {true} .
```

```
% try to place the queen Q
```

```
place(Q) -->
    {Q>0} -> forget(free(P)),{S is Q+P, D is Q-P},% generate
            not_under_attack(S,D),                % test
            {NewQ is Q-1},place(NewQ)
; {true}.
```

```
% tests if on diagonals S and D the queen is not under attack and
% assimilates the proposed position as the intersection
% of two diagonals
```

```
not_under_attack(S,D) -->
    assumed(on_diagonals(S1,D1)),{S=S1;D=D1} -> {fail}
; assume(on_diagonals(S,D)).
```

```
% calculates the position of each queen and prints it
```

```
print_solution -->
    assumed(on_diagonals(S,D)),{P is (S-D)//2,write(P),fail}
; {nl}.
```

Notice the extensional use of assumed facts about previously placed queens. As the term *on_diagonals(S,D)* never contains free variables, it is possible to use the extensional:

$$assumed(on\_diagonals(S, D))$$

instead of the intensional:

$$wake\_up(on\_diagonals(S, D)),$$

which is semantically more appropriate but has an overhead factor due to clause "cloning".

Our program is shorter and (arguably) easier to conceive than a standard Prolog solution as can be found in textbooks (see [SS86], prog.14.3). It finds the 92 solutions for the 8-queens problem in less then 3s. There is virtually no overhead compared to the standard solution.

In Appendix 2 we show an application to automated induction, with intensional uses of soft predicates. A universe of static concepts is defined, with 'yes' and 'no' instances in the soft database. The concepts are not necessarily extensional, but their defining clauses are expected to generate all their elements in finite time. We want to induce a new concept, expressed as a conjunction of the existing ones, which subsumes the 'yes' instances and does not intersect the 'no' instances.

The program generates candidate clauses, assume them as hypotheses, then test them. Backtracking cleans up failed hypotheses. The program stops if a correct clause is synthesized or the set of hypotheses is exhausted.

19.6   Conclusions

Soft databases have a simple, logic based specification, allowing a DCG based efficient compilation and as they generate practically pure Prolog code, they are easily eligible for algorithmic program debugging.

Soft databases can be used to give fast implementations to systems like N-Prolog (see [GR84]) with very interesting logical and epistemological properties.

A very interesting form of "soft database" can be implemented in a system supporting logic continuations and "lateral control transfer" see ([IIA87]). In this case Prolog's trail is generalized to a tree structure called state-space.

This allows one to go back to previously rejected branches in the proof tree and therefore to an alternate, eventually competing state of the soft database.

Finally, soft databases are far more compatible with committed-choice concurrent programming languages, than an assert and retract based dynamic database, as they give more "locality of reference" and may be more easily distributed between processors.

This suggests the use of soft databases as a basis to implement object-oriented programming and parallel meta-interpreters in standard sequential Prolog.

There have been constant attempts in many object-oriented extensions to Prolog, to implement states of objects without using assert and retract based side-effects, as the command-stream approach of Shapiro and Takeuchi [ST83].

We believe that soft databases can be used to simplify this kind of elegant although relatively complex, approach.

References

[BA87] II.Bacha, "Meta-Level Programming: A Compiled Approach", in in J.L Lassez (ed.), Logic Programming: Proceedings of the Fourth International Conference, The MIT Press, 1987, p.394-410.

[BO85] K.A Bowen, "Meta-Level Programming and Knowledge Representation" New Generation Computing, No.2, 1985.

[BK82] K.A.Bowen, R.A.Kowalski, "Amalgamating language and metalanguage in logic programming", Logic Programming, K.L.Clark, S.A.Tarnlund (eds.), Academic Press, 1982.

[GR84] D.M Gabbay, U.Reyle, N-Prolog: An Extension of Prolog with Hypothetical Implications, The Journal of Logic Programming, No. 4, 1984, p.319-355.

[HA87] C.T. IIaynes, Logic continuations, The Journal of Logic Programming, No. 4, 1987, p.157-176.

[LK87] T. Lindholm, R.A. O'Keefe, "Efficient implementation of a Defensible Semantics for Dynamic PROLOG Code, in J.L Lassez (ed.), Logic Programming: Proceedings of the Fourth International Conference, The MIT Press, 1987, p.21-39.

[IIO84] C.J. IIogger, "Introduction to logic programming",Academic Press,1984.

[KO79] R.A.Kowalski, "Logic for problem solving", Elsevier North-IIolland, 1979.

[KS86] R.A.Kowalski, M.Sergot, "A Logic-based Calculus of Events", New Generation Computing, No.4, 1986.

[KU87] P.Kursawe, "IIow to Invent a Prolog Machine", New Generation Computing, No.5, 1987.

[MK84] T. Miyachi, S. Kunifuji, II. Kitakami, K. Furukawa, A. Takeuchi and II. Yokota, "A Knowledge Assimilation Method for Logic Databases", New Generation Computing, No.2, 1984.

[MO86] C.Moss, "Cut and Paste - defining the impure primitives of Prolog", in E.Shapiro (ed.) Lecture Notes in Computer Science No. 225, Third International Conference on Logic Programming, pp. 686-694.

[SS86] L.Sterling, E.Shapiro, The Art of Prolog, MIT Press,1986.

[ST83] E.Shapiro, A.Takeuchi, Object-oriented Programming in Concurrent Prolog, New Generation Computing, No.1, 1983.

[VK76] M.H. van Emden, R.A.Kowalski, The semantics of predicate logics as a programming language, Journal of the A.C.M, 23(4), 733-742.

[WA82] D.H.D Warren, Higher order extensions to PROLOG: are they needed, in Machine Intelligence 10, Ellis Horwood, 1982.

Appendix 1

```
% Source code of the meta-circular evaluation mechanism

% definition of soft database operations

make_empty_database(_,Db):-new(Db).      % the old database
                                         % may be lost


assume(C)-->add_front(C).                % like 'asserta'


assume_last(C)-->add_end(C).             % like 'assertz'


forget(C)-->remove(C). % like retract,
                       % potentially non-monotonic operation

% extensional retrieve

assumed(C,D,D):-find(C,D).        % like 'clause', but does not copy

% intensional retrieve

wake_up(H) -->                    % works like 'call'
  assumed(T),{copy_term(T,C)},
  ( {C = (H :- B)} -> demo(B)     % match a clause with a body
  ; {C = H}                       % match a fact
  ).

% meta-circular interpreter

demo(C) -->
  ( {C=(P,Q)}    -> (demo(P),demo(Q))
  ; {C=(I->T;E)} -> (demo(I) -> demo(T) ; demo(E))
  ; {C=(P;Q)}    -> (demo(P);demo(Q))
  ; C
  ).
```

```
% hack for 'demo' to handle {} when evaluating itself
{C} --> {call(C)}.

% other (optional) operations on soft databases

% gets all solutions (style findall - for simplicity)
% this predicate implements a conservative semantics:
% side-effects during the construction of the solutions
% are discarded

all_solutions(Pattern,Goal,Solutions) -->
    getdb(Db),                      % gets a 'reified' database
    make_empty_database,
    all(Pattern,Goal,Db),
    db_list(L)->{Solutions=L},      % collects solutions
    setdb(Db).

all(X0,H0,Db) -->
    {copy_term((X0,H0),(X,H))},     % makes a fresh copy
    {demo(H,Db,_)},                 % evaluates
    ( assumed(X) -> {fail}          % insures it is a new solution
    ; assume_last(X)                % accumulates the solution
    ) -> all(X0,H0,Db)              % repeat until there are
  ; {true}.                         % no more solutions

% builds a list from a database

db_list(L) -->
  {L=[C|Cs]},forget(C) -> db_list(Cs)
; {L=[]}.

% extends \+ to the expanded terms

\+ C -->
    demo(C) -> {fail}
  ; {true}.

% ensures that failure in C will not destroy the soft database

commit(C) -->
    demo(C) -> {true}
  ; {true}.
```

```
% clears all terms matching C0

cleardb(C0) -->
    forget(C),{copy_term(C0,C)} -> cleardb(C0)
  ; {true}.

% bridge between the "soft" and the "hard" database

hard_assert(C) -->
    assumed(C),{expand_term(C,Cls),assert(Cls),fail}
  ; cleardb(C).

% gets the soft data base as a term

getdb(D,D,D).

% destructively changes the whole soft database

setdb(NewD,_,NewD).

% failure driven printing of the assumed clauses

showdb -->
    {write('Soft database:'),nl},getdb(Db),{numbervars(Db,0,_)},
    assumed(C),{write(C),write('.'),nl,fail}
  ; {true}.

% simple read-eval loop

readloop -->
  {nl,write('<READ LOOP>'),nl,write('| ?- '),read(X)},
  ( X -> {write('Yes.')}
  ; {write('No.')}
  ), {nl},readloop.

% main predicate

go :- make_empty_database(_,Db),readloop(Db,_).

% definition of soft database operations

% difference list based implementation of
% soft database manipulation tools
```

```
% makes a new difference list

new(H:H).

% adds to the front of a difference list

add_front(X,H:T,[X|H]:T).

% adds to the end of a difference list

add_end(X,H:[X|T],H:T).

% finds an element of the difference list

find(X,H:T):- H\==T,
  ( H=[X|_]
  ; H=[_|H1],H1\==T,
    find(X,H1:T)
  ).

% removes an element of the difference list

remove(X,L1:T,R1:T):- L1\==T,
  ( L1=[X|R1]
  ; L1=[Y|L2],L2\==T,R1=[Y|R2],
    remove(X,L2:T,R2:T)
  ).
```

Appendix 2

```
% An example of automatic concept formation

% generates integers from Min to Max

int(Min,_,Min).
int(Min,Max,X):-Min<Max,
  Min1 is Min+1,
  int(Min1,Max,X).

% known concepts
```

```
even(X):-int(0,9,X),0 is X mod 2.
odd(X):-int(0,9,X),1 is X mod 2.
small(X):-int(0,4,X).
big(X):-int(5,9,X).

% data

concepts([big(X),small(X),odd(X),even(X)],
         yes_instance(X),
         no_instance(X),
         nice(X)
       ).

% generates conjunctions of known concepts

generate([],true).
generate([X|Xs1],Ys):-
  ( Ys=Ys1
  ; Ys=(X,Ys1)
  ),
  generate(Xs1,Ys1).

% tests a candidate new concept

test(Yes,No,New) -->
    \+ (assumed(Yes), \+ wake_up(New)), % Yes implies New
    \+ (wake_up(New),assumed(No)).      % New and No are disjoint

% this predicate builds a new concept represented as
% a conjunction of known concepts and synthesizes it
% as an intensional soft clause
% which is implied by its "yes" instances and
% disjoint from its "no" instances

induce -->
  make_empty_database,
  assume(yes_instance(2)),assume(yes_instance(4)),
  assume(no_instance(3)),assume(no_instance(8)),
  {concepts(Cs,Yes,No,New)},
  {generate(Cs,Hypo)},
  assume((New:-{Hypo})),
  test(Yes,No,New).
```

```
% The following terminal session shows the successful
% induction of a new concept from its "yes" and "no" instances.

<READ LOOP>
| ?- induce,showdb.
Soft database:
nice(A):-{small(A),even(A),true}.
no_instance(8).
no_instance(3).
yes_instance(4).
yes_instance(2).
Yes.

% and the intensional use of the new concept

<READ LOOP>
| ?- wake_up(nice(X)),{write(X),nl,fail}.
0
2
4
No.
```

Chapter 20

What Is a Meta-variable in Prolog?

Jonas Barklund

UPMAIL — Uppsala University

Abstract

We present a naming scheme for Prolog formulas and terms as Prolog terms to create a practical and logically appealing language for reasoning about terms, programs, proofs, provability, and other metalogical relationships. This could be used, e.g., to partially compute Prolog programs. The view attempts to make explicit as much as possible of the structure of names and it is compared to other approaches in the field. Examples are given and an realization is outlined.

20.1 Introduction

The main objective of this paper is to define a view on terms and meta-terms which we believe is practical when writing programs that reason about programs, relations, and proofs. Examples of such programs are compilers, (meta-) interpreters, and partial evaluators, but "intelligent" software should also belong to this class. We will proceed to give a few examples of the programs and, finally, we will suggest an realization. We will compare our view to others which have been put forward.

We wish to stay within a logical framework, but our way of reasoning will usually be from a practical point of view, rather than a philosophical. We will concentrate on names in a meta-language for terms and formulas and mostly ignore questions about various axiomatizations of provability.

When we refer to Prolog primitives, we mean primitives of 'Edinburgh' Prolog (Bowen, 1981, Clocksin and Mellish, 1987).

20.2   What is a meta-level in Prolog?

Suppose we were to write a program which analyzed modes of Prolog programs. Such a program would like the variables in the analyzed program to behave as constants, to be able to tell whether two terms are identical, by unification. Otherwise, a variable in the program might become instantiated by accident, and the program changed. Instead of somehow changing the behaviour of variables in the program, we could instead work with a ground name of the program.

In general, to reason about things, it is necessary to have names for the objects under consideration. When programming in Prolog, it is customary to let all terms serve as names for themselves. This usually works when reasoning about ground terms, but causes problems with variables. This is exemplified by the fact that unification cannot be used to tell whether two non-ground terms are really the same. Since such reasoning is necessary for certain programs, such as compilers, or the mode-analysis program above, Prolog contains primitives such as ==/2 which partially fulfills the need; given two terms A and B one can tell if they have the same name by A == B. Using the predicate var/1 it is possible to check whether a term at a particular time happens to be an uninstantiated variable. These predicates are logically impure, since they may be true at one time and false at another, e.g., in var(X), X=42, var(X). As has been noted by many researchers, the use of these 'impure' predicates is one of the reasons that program transformation techniques, such as partial computation, has so far had little success with real programs.

The solution cannot be to ban the applications, and not even the style of programming which leads to usage of these primitives, but rather to see which tools should be provided instead. We think the cue is 'name'. All predicates in the impure family which also contains atom/1, functor/3, name/2, nonvar/1, and others, are there to inspect names of terms. If names for terms were made different from the terms themselves, the logical status of the predicates above could be restored. This of course extends to names for programs and control structures. Prolog is said to have 'equivalence of programs and data.' This claim usually refers to either (i) that a database can be implemented in Prolog as clauses of a predicate, or (ii) that programs and data are in the same format, so a term can be given as argument to call/1 and interpreted as a formula. Let us take a closer look at the second meaning of this statement. The property of being able to construct a term which is later executed definitely adds strength to the language, if not in terms of computability, then at least in brevity of expression. But we do not think that the 'equivalence' should be misinterpreted to imply that terms, names of terms and names of formulas should all look the same.

Assuming that we want to define a meta-language for Prolog terms and formulas, there are several ways to do it. First of all, the meta-language need not have any similarity whatsoever to Prolog. But there are good reasons to use

Prolog terms for names, because programs manipulating the names can then be written in Prolog, and consequently programs can work on names of themselves. The latter property is important for partial computation, since it is assumed to be important for performance that a partial evaluator can partially compute (a name of) itself with respect to (a name of) itself.

In this context, what is a 'meta-program'? Traditionally it means a program whose data is (names of) programs, relations, proofs, etc. But if the name of a program is a Prolog term, suppose we created lists of such names and concatenated them. Would not the list concatenation program then be a meta-program? If we want to distinguish between programs and meta-programs we would then need two identical versions of the list concatenation program. And if we consider a program which did something with (the name of) the list concatenation meta-program we would have a meta-meta-program. Our conclusion is that we should not try to classify programs into meta-levels. The list concatenation program concatenates lists of Prolog terms and whether these terms happen to be names of other terms or programs does not make any difference whatsoever to it. What we mean is that if we fix the languages to be the same, at all meta-levels, there could be predicates with the same definition at each level.

As any term could very well serve as a name in a meta-language for another term, we challenge the traditional view that there should be an 'object level', which is a fixed lowest level, a 'meta level' which manipulates object-level programs, a 'meta-meta-level' and so on. We instead propose a more dynamic view. From a philosophical point of view, meta-levels could stretch infinitely above and below a given meta-level. There is no lowest level, because the terms of any selected object domain could be interpreted as names of terms and formulas in another language. From a practical point of view, there is a fixed highest level, which is the top-level of the Prolog system, which interprets the user's commands. The user may, e.g., call a compiler, which translates (the name of) a program to data, which are instructions for some machine. There would then be an object-meta relationship between the compiler and the compiled program, but there is no need to assign the compiler program as such to any particular meta-level, it is the *call* of the compiler which occurs at some particular level. In this case that level is immediately below the top-level. Because this view in a way turns the traditional view of meta-levels upside-down, we could refer to these levels (counted from the top-level) as 'atem levels'. Let us now see how this interacts with the way to assign names to terms.

As was indicated above, the major problem when manipulating terms and formulas is the variables. This has fuelled reasearch along lines where terms still serve as names of themselves, but where a new class of terms have been added to the language to serve as names for variables. There are a few variants on this theme. Rayner and Barklund (1984) distinguished variables ranging over different meta-levels by allowing the syntax of variables to change dynamically.

The normal syntax of variables in LM-Prolog (Carlsson, 1984) is like constants whose first character is '?'. During meta-level execution, the variable syntax would be temporarily changed to something else (e.g., atoms whose first character is '%'), thereby making the ordinary variables behave as constants. In particular, two different variables would not unify, because they would behave as different constants. Consequently, this has some desirable properties, but many things just do not work with this simple approach, and the semantic implications of dynamically partitioning variables and constants are unclear, to say the least.

Nakashima *et al.* (1984) introduce predicates to dynamically 'freeze' and 'melt' variables. A frozen variable acts almost like a name for the variable, so their built-in predicate `freeze/2` returns a frozen copy of a term, while `melt/2` returns the unfrozen term. We say 'almost like a name', because the way their predicate `melt/2` works is counter-intuitive to us. This is because they want melting a frozen term to return *the same* term, i.e.,

$$\texttt{freeze(X,Y), melt(Y,Z), X==Z}$$

holds. They also have a predicate `melt_new/2` which given a frozen term returns a *variant* of the original term, i.e., a copy with different variables. So

$$\texttt{freeze(X,Y), melt\_new(Y,Z), X=Z}$$

holds, while

$$\texttt{freeze(X,Y), melt\_new(Y,Z), X==Z}$$

does not. We understand why they want this functionality because they give examples, e.g., in a debugger it is desirable to be able to print the values of variables. We do not think this is the only way to achieve this functionality, and we do not even think this is the easiest way. For a simpler solution to their original problem, see the appendix.

Unlike Nakashima *et al.*, we do not believe that the name of a term (in particular a variable) should be universally unique to that term, but only to the equivalence class of all variants of the term. This is because all variables in the term should be considered to be universally quantified and the names of quantified variables do not really matter (Robinson, 1971). E.g.,

$$\texttt{compound(foo,[var(0)])}$$

could be a name for the compound terms `foo(X)`, `foo(Y)`, or any other unary term whose functor is `foo` and whose argument is an uninstantiated variable.

$$\texttt{compound(foo,[var(1)])}$$

could also be a name of these terms. What is important to notice here is that we *cannot* expect that building a name from two other names will generally work. E.g., putting together the name above for `foo(X)` with the name for `foo(Y)` giving

$$\texttt{compound(bar,[compound(foo,[var(0)]),compound(foo,[var(0)])])}$$

does not give a name for `bar(foo(X),foo(Y))`. This is a consequence of our note above about variables being universally quantified; putting together two terms from inside two different quantifications does not work, unless the variable names are standardized apart. E.g., in a list concatenation program written in the Prolog-10 syntax

```
append(A.X,Y,A.Z) :- append(X,Y,Z).
append([],X,X).
```

the fact that there is a variable named `X` in both the first and the second clause should be immaterial, since they differ in quantification (every variable in each clause is universally quantified) (Robinson, 1971). Therefore, a term must be named relative to a dictionary of names of variables in the current scope. If names of the terms `foo(X)` and `foo(Y)` above were computed relative to the same dictionary, different names would be assigned to the variables `X` and `Y`, and it would be possible to build the name of `bar(foo(X),foo(Y))` from these names. Our point can be summarized by stating that putting together names from different quantifications will normally produce meaningless results. To solve problems like these we will allow the 'dictionary' of quantified variables to be explicit when constructing names for terms.

20.3   Representation of Terms and Formulas

Let us now propose a convention for assigning names to Prolog terms and variables, following Tarski (1956). Tarski proposes two ways of giving names for sentences: *quotation-mark names*, and *structural-descriptive names*. The language LISP uses quotation-mark names. To get a name for a term T (which is an S-expression) we form the S-expression (`quote` T). Using the same approach for Prolog does not work so well. Suppose that the name of a Prolog formula F is formed as the term `quote(`F`)`. Consider now the term `quote(p(X))`. Is this a name for the formula $p(X)$ or is it an insufficiently instantiated name for some atomic formula with predicate name p? Structural-descriptive names need not suffer from this problem, because when describing the structure of a term we can make explicit what kind of term is referred to.

We therefore propose that the name of a term or formula should always be a ground term. A non-ground term can thus never be a name for a term, but it may be instantiated to become a name for some term. Also, not every ground term is a name of some term.

These properties becomes even more important when considering meta-programming in languages such as GHC (Ueda, 1985) or its flat niece KL1 (Kimura and Chikayama, 1987, Uchida, 1987), where it is not possible to test if a term is a variable.

We do not claim our naming scheme to be particularly original or definitive, e.g., Bowen and Kowalski mention a similar scheme (1982), but we wish to make it explicit here, so it can be discussed.

- The name of a constant X is the compound term `constant(X)`. For example, the name of the constant `frob` is `constant(frob)`.

- The name of a compound term whose functor is F and whose arguments are A1 to Am is `compound(F,[N1,...,Nm])`, where N1 to Nm are names of the arguments A1 to Am, respectively. E.g., the name of `foo(bar,baz)` is `compound(foo,[constant(bar),constant(baz)])`.

- A name of a variable X is a term `var(I)` where I is any positive integer, such that the same integer I is used for every occurrence of X in all terms under consideration, and that all distinct variables in these terms are assigned different names. E.g., one name of `fie(X,Y)` is `compound(fie,[var(0), var(1)])`, and another name for it is `compound(fie,[var(42),var(56)])`.

(It is probably practical but not necessary to assign successive numbers beginning with zero to the variables contained in the terms to be named, just the way the Prolog predicate `numbervars/3` is normally used.) Programs and formulas should also be assigned names.

- The name of a clause `H:-B` is a term `clause(Nh,Nb)`, where Nh is a name for the head of the clause, and Nb is a name for its body.

- The name of a directive `:-G` is a term `directive(Ng)`, where Ng is a name for the goal G.

- The name of a conjunction `G1,G2` is a term `conj(N1,N2)`, where N1 and N2 are names for G1 and G2 respectively.

- The name of a disjunction `G1,G2` is a term `disj(N1,N2)`, where N1 and N2 are names for G1 and G2 respectively.

- The name of a cut `!` is the constant `cut` (but see section 20.6 for an alternative).

- The name of a conditional `G1->G2;G3` is a term `if(N1,N2,N3)`, where N1, N2, and N3 are names for G1, G2, and G3 respectively.

- The name of an atomic formula whose predicate symbol is P and whose arguments are A1 to Am is `atom(P,[N1,...,Nm])`, where N1 to Nm are names of the arguments A1 to Am, respectively. For example, a name of the atom `append(A.X,Y,A.Z)` is

      atom(append,[compound('.',[var(0),var(1)]),var(2),
                       compound('.',[var(0),var(3)])]).

It is possible to add names for other program constructs. There should be a name for any construct recognized by the Prolog interpreter, or more precisely, the meta-interpreter which is supposed to represent derivability. The reason for distinguishing between names for `append(A.X,Y,A.Z)` when it occurs as a term and when it occurs as an atom in a formula is mainly that the operations one usually performs when reasoning about terms (e.g., unification and substitutions) are different from those on programs (e.g., compilation and interpretation).

We have also considered the possibility to let the name of a constant X contain a list of the characters making up the printed representation of X, rather than X itself. E.g., the name of the constant `frob` could be `constant([102,114,111,98])`, instead of `constant(frob)`. This has the practical advantage that names can be taken apart conveniently, but on the other hand, names for terms become larger. Nothing in this paper depends on this decision.

Finally, we compare our approach to that of Blomberg *et al.* (1987). They introduce the concept of a 'source variable,' corresponding to a frozen variable. The main difference is that a source variable can be at different 'quote levels.' A source variable at quote level zero is an ordinary variable. A source variable at quote level 1 corresponds to a frozen variable of Nakashima *et al.*, or a name of the variable in our approach. A source variable at quote level 2 corresponds to a name of a name of the variable, and so on for higher quote levels. Terms other than variables still serve as names for themselves. The functionality they want to implement corresponds to the 'macro' facility of LISP (Allen, 1978), which is a way to introduce new control structures, or to increase efficiency by doing part of the computation at compile-time. We believe that our names of terms and formulas can also serve this purpose, although we have not attempted it.

The macro processing facility of Kondoh and Chikayama (1988) uses Prolog as the meta-language for itself using terms as names for themselves. They can quote a term by prefixing it with one or two back quotes, e.g., `'(X+1)` or `''(X+1)`, but this is only to prohibit macro expansion.

20.4 An example: DCG expansion

As an example of what a program which manipulates another program would look like, we present an expander for definite clause grammar (DCG) rules (Pereira and Warren, 1980). The reader is assumed to know how DCG rules are expanded.

We assume that names for grammar rules have been added to the other names of programs above.

- The name of a grammar rule `H-->B` is a term `grammar_rule(Nh,Nb)`, where Nh is a name for the left hand side H of the rule, and Nb is a name for its right hand side B.

- The name of an empty list of terminals is a term [].

- The name of a non-empty list of terminals T.L is a term Nt.Nl, where Nt is a name for the term T and Nl is a name for the list of terminals L.

- The name for a condition {G} is a term {N}, where N is a name of the goal G.

Each clause corresponds to the name of a valid formula occurring in the right half of a grammar rule. The predicate variables/2 takes a name (of a formula or term) and returns a list of names for variables occurring in it. The predicate new_variable/2 takes a list of names of variables and returns the name of a variable not in the list. Programming these predicates is trivial (see section 20.7).

This program does not try to be clever to minimize the number of new variables and unifications. Some notes about the predicate translate_dcg/6: the first argument is the name of a DCG rule body. The second argument is the output translation of the first argument and is a name of a clause body. The third and fourth arguments are the names of the terms to be added as new arguments. Finally, the fifth and sixth arguments are lists of names of the variables occurring in the first and second arguments, respectively.

Perhaps this program is not a very good demonstration of our statements in section 20.2, since the transformation is very simple. The corresponding Prolog program for expanding DCG rules does not need the list of variables, since variables serve as names for themselves and a new uninstantiated variable can be created anytime. However, our program compiles to very neat code on a WAM-based machine (Warren, 1983), since indexing will cause it to be deterministic without any cuts.

```
dcg_expansion(grammar_rule(H,B), clause(H1,B1)) :-
    variables(grammar_rule(H,B), V0),
    new_variable(V0, S0), new_variable(S0.V0, S),
    translate_dcg_left(H, H1, S0, S),
    translate_dcg(B, B1, S0, S, S1.S0.V0, _).

translate_dcg_left(conj(atom(P,A),L), atom(P,A1), S0, S) :-
    translate_dcg_atom(A, A1, S0, X), dlist(L, X, S).
translate_dcg_left(atom(P,A), atom(P,A1), S0, S) :-
    translate_dcg_atom(A, A1, S0, S).

translate_dcg(conj(X,Y), conj(X1,Y1), S0, S, V0, V) :-
    new_variable(V0, S1, V1),
    translate_dcg(X, X1, S0, S1, V1, V2),
    translate_dcg(Y, Y1, S1, S, V2, V).
translate_dcg(disj(X,Y), disj(X1,Y1), S0, S, V0, V) :-
    translate_dcg(X, X1, S0, S, V0, V1),
    translate_dcg(Y, Y1, S0, S, V1, V).
```

```
translate_dcg(□, atom(=,[S0,S]), S0, S, V, V).
translate_dcg(X.Y, atom(=,[S0,X]), S0, S, V, V) :-
   dlist(X.Y, X, S).
translate_dcg({G}, conj(atom(=,[S0,S]),G), S0, S, V, V).
translate_dcg(atom(P,A), atom(P,A1), S0, S, V, V) :-
   translate_dcg_atom(A, A1, S0, S).

translate_dcg_atom(A, A1, S0, S) :- append(A, [S0,S], A1).

dlist([], L, L).
dlist(A.X, A.L1, L) :- dlist(X, L1, L).
```

The program is a much simplified version of a DCG translation program the author wrote as part of a compiler for KL1 (Sekita *et al.*, 1988). In committed choice languages such as KL1, where suspension is implicit, variables cannot serve as names for themselves, because it is not possible to test if a term is a variable. Current implementations sometimes use terms '$VAR'(I) as names for variables (the same terms as created by numbervars/3 in Prolog). The problem is, however, that program manipulating programs, such as the compiler, get deep in trouble when trying to operate on themselves.)

20.5   Partial Computation and Abstract Interpretation

Partial computation is related to meta-programming in two ways: firstly, partial evaluators are examples of meta-programs, and secondly, it is expected that partial computation of meta-interpreters with respect to a program will make execution by meta-interpreters computationally feasible.

Futamura has suggested that partial evaluation be generalized so that a program is partially computed with respect to information about the operating environment (Futamura, 1988). This is more powerful than partial computation with respect to the known value of a parameter. We believe that the information about the operating environment (u-information) can be implemented as formulas containing names of terms and fragments of the program being partially computed. The underlying logic can then be implemented as an interpreter for these formulas.

The u-information would contain at least two kinds of information; (i) bound variables, and (ii) the truth value of built-in predicates with respect to terms in the program. An example of the former is that after we have folded a goal atom(f,[var(4)]) with a clause clause(atom(f,[var(12)]),...) we would add something like bound(var(4),var(12)) in the current u-information.

An example of the latter is partial computation of a conjunction

$$conj(atom(>,[var(2),constant(3)]),\ldots),$$

in which case a formula similar to true(atom(>,[var(2),constant(3)])) (and possibly also true(atom(integer,[var(2)]))) is added to the u-information when partially computing the right half of the conjunction.

Partial computation is related to abstract interpretation of programs, at least in the sense that a partial evaluator does an abstract interpretation of a program with some initial information about the goal, where abstract interpretation as such could start with only a program. Therefore, what we have said above about partial computation should hold for abstract interpretation as well.

We believe that using names of terms in partial computation and abstract interpretation rather than the terms themselves will start to pay off when more complicated analysis of the program is being made, e.g., aliasing information and compile time garbage collection (Bruynooghe *et al.*, 1987, Mellish, 1986).

20.6   Partial Computation and Cut

Let us take up a subject somewhat related to the preceding section; a proposal for handling cut in partial evaluators. We will first describe an implementation of cut (Carlsson, 1986, Barklund and Millroth, 1986). Suppose that there are built-in predicates '$choice'/1 and '$cut'/1, such that '$choice'(X) instantiates X to some term representing the current choice point and '$cut'(X) sets the current choice point to the choice point represented by X. We will show how a Prolog compiler could implement cut, using these primitives, by an example. Suppose the predicate p/2 has one or more clauses containing cuts in its definition and let one of these be

$$p(A,C) \; :- \; q(A,B), \; !, \; r(B,C).$$

The compiler would then translate this clause (and by analogy all other clauses for p/2) to

$$p(A,C,X) \; :- \; q(A,B), \; '\$cut'(X), \; r(B,C)$$

and replace every occurrence of an atom p(S,T) in the program with a conjunction '$choice'(X),p(S,T,X). (This is somewhat simplified; one really wants two variants of '$cut'/1, and the calls to '$choice'/1 would be placed first in the code for p/2 rather than at every occurrence of p/2.)

For partial computation (or abstract interpretation) doing this transformation removes all cuts. The choice points to which they would cut are instead identified by variables, whose values are produced by '$choice'/1 and consumed by '$cut'/1. Now, suppose that we would fold the atom p(S,T,X) above, with respect to its definition. If there were more than one clause for p/2, then the resulting goal would in general be something like

$$'\$choice'(X), \; (\ldots \; ; \; q(A,B), \; '\$cut'(X), \; r(B,C) \; ; \; \ldots).$$

Now the partial evaluator could go on as usual and, among other things, it could use its knowledge about the operating environment to try to eliminate the occurrence of '$cut'/1 completely.

We also speculate that one could write a meta-interpreter for Prolog, using names for terms and formulas, whose state (represented as extra arguments) made the environment, the data base, the choice point stack, etc. explicit. Writing such a meta-interpreter should be possible (Fuchi, 1984). Suppose that this interpreter recognized '$choice'/1 and '$cut'/1. If the interpreter were successfully partially computed with respect to a program, the result should be a *deterministic* program. Potential but unexplored solutions would probably be represented in the resulting program by a new argument, containing a term which corresponds to the explicit choice point stack of the meta-interpreter.

20.7 Built-in predicates

It is clear that it would be convenient to have some built-in predicates which operate on names of terms, although many predicates corresponding to meta-predicates of Prolog could be defined by the user. E.g., one could define

```
var(var(X)).
```

```
functor(constant(C), constant(C), 0).
functor(compound(F,L), constant(F), N) :- length(L, N).
```

The predicate ==/2 would be obsolete and replaced by unification of names. For example, in the DCG expansion example we used the predicates variables/2 and new_variable/2. They could be defined by

```
variables(var(I), [var(I)]).
variables(constant(C), []).
variables(compound(F,L), V) :-
    var_list(L, U), sort(U, V).
var_list([], []).
var_list(A.X, V) :-
    variables(A, T), var_list(X, U), append(T, U, V).
```

```
new_variable(V, var(I)) :- max_var(V, I), J is I+1.
max_var([], -1).
max_var(var(I).X, K) :- max_var(X,J), max(I, J, K).
```

with the obvious meaning for sort/2, append/3, and max/3, although these definitions are not very efficient. A predicate with a dubious status is name_of/2, relating a term to a name for the term, so name_of(N,T) holds if N is a name for T. The question is how to interpret uninstantiated variables occurring in T or N, whichever serves as input. Bowen mentions this predicate (1985), but we are not convinced that the iteration process to which he refers gives a practical answer to the question. Nakashima *et al.* have two predicates for this; freeze/2 and melt/2. Blomberg *et al.* have the corresponding predicates to_ground/2 and from_ground/2. Reflection rules (Weyhrauch, 1980) link the derivability of theorems to assertions in its meta-language. They do not seem to require an explicit relation between objects and names for the objects in their meta-language, so predicates such as name_of/2 should not be necessary. However, they may still be of enough practical value when used carefully (in the same way that the meta-logical predicates of ordinary Prolog are useful) that they should be provided.

The actual choice of built-in primitives must be based on experience of what is most convenient to use and what can become significantly more efficient when provided as a primitive.

20.8   Assert & Retract

assert/1 and retract/1 etc. are usually assumed to have a side-effect on a global database. In a meta-logical framework, they can rather be seen as theories, and in meta-programming we will see them as sets of names for clauses. Bowen suggests the predicates add_to/3 and drop_from/3 to be defined over such theories (1985). Both predicates state that two databases are the same, except that one contains a clause which the other does not contain, they differ only in their modes and order of arguments. He also suggests an implementation of them, such that the theory returned by either of these predicates becomes the most efficient to access. Barklund and Millroth propose a similar scheme (1987 a).

Since a name of a clause is a ground term, there are no particular implementation problems in making them persistent to backtracking. Nakashima *et al.* have studied this and propose a separation of assert/1 into two primitive operations: freeze/2 and assert*/1. They do corresponding separations of retract/1, clause/2, read/1 and write/1. This may be useful and works just as well when working with names instead of frozen terms, and theories instead of a global database.

Providing theories explicitly in e.g., a meta-interpreter, also has an advantage in partial computation: a program which does not contain assert/1 or retract/1 cannot modify itself. The value of this property should be obvious. Furthermore, we believe that programs (i.e., theories) whose control are distributed over several layers of meta-interpreters do not need to modify themselves.[1] If the domain theory changes, it is because the meta-interpreter constituting the method level adds or removes a clause from it.

---

[1] Sterling, e.g., proposes three levels: the domain, method and planning levels (1984).

20.9 Realization

The ideas above are currently only partially implemented and will be the subject of further research. We therefore give only a brief explanation of the ideas. Barklund and Millroth have investigated the use of multiple internal representations of logical terms (1987 b). This realization of names continues in that direction.

A compact internal representation for the name of a term is a copy of the term, where the variables have been replaced by scalar objects with some new tag $MVR. Different variables are identified by their objects having different integer values. To indicate that this term is really the compact representation of a name for itself, it may only be referred to from an object with another new tag $FRZ. Below we will write an object whose tag is $FRZ and whose address is i as <$FRZ,$i$>, and similarly for $MVR-objects.

E.g., let us look at a name for the term α:

$$foo(X,bar,Y),$$

whose internal representation is shown in figure 20.1.

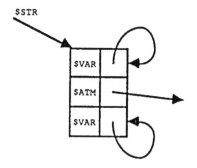

Figure 20.1: Internal representation of α.

One name for this term according to section 20.3 is β:

$$compound(foo,[var(0),constant(bar),var(1)]),$$

which can be implemented by the term γ:

$$<\$FRZ,foo(<\$MVR,0>,bar,<\$MVR,1>)>,$$

whose internal representation is shown in figure 20.2.

It is important that γ behaves in every respect as the term β.

To be able to efficiently represent names for names, the value of $MVR-terms should contain a naming level, besides the identification number. The naming level corresponds to source variables' quote levels by Blomberg *et al.*

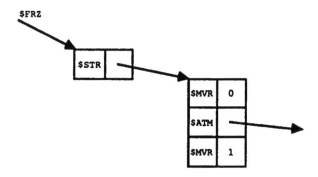

Figure 20.2: Internal representation of γ.

To allow efficient representation of some terms which can be instantiated to names, it would be possible to implement the inverse of $FRZ-terms. Let the tag of such a term be $MLT and its value be the address of a term. If a $MLT-term occurred somewhere inside a $FRZ-term, its subterm would appear to unification as itself. I.e., $MLT cancels the effect of $FRZ. A $MLT-term may contain variables. E.g., the term δ:

compound(foo,[X,constant(bar),var(1)]),

which becomes a name of a term when X is instantiated to the name of a term can have the internal representation shown in figure 20.3.

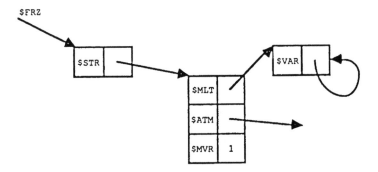

Figure 20.3: Internal representation of δ.

$FRZ and $MLT are analogous to '@' and '~' of Blomberg *et al.*, but they are not identical since they use '@' to get quotation-mark names rather than structural-descriptive names.

To be able to efficiently create a term from the efficient representation of the name of a term it turns out that it is useful to have two variants of $MVR-terms, one for the first occurrence of the variable (in a pre-order traversal of the term) and one for subsequent occurrences (in analogy with internal source terms of LM-Prolog and *_variable/*_value instructions of WAM).

With this implementation, creating a name from a term of size n, or creating a term from a name, takes $O(n)$ time. This is also the case for freeze/2 and melt_new/2 of Nakashima *et al.*

20.10 Conclusions and Future Work

We have presented an approach to meta-programming where we have tried to make the representation of terms and formulas as explicit as possible, to make a clear distinction between terms and names of terms. We believe that this explicitness is necessary for programs manipulating other programs, reasoning programs, etc. We have compared this approach to others and given examples of programs using our ideas. We want to try our approach empirically and implement it using the methods described in section 20.9, or further improvements of these methods. Several researchers at UPMAIL are working with partial computation, abstract interpretation, program transformation, and program synthesis; we expect to receive much feedback from them concerning the practicality or our ideas. We are also interested in programming multilevel problem solvers, possibly in combination with frames implemented as theories.

Acknowledgments

The author would like to thank Håkan Millroth for his contributions to this work, Marianne Ahrne for finding all the linguistic errors (all remaining erorrs have been added after her examination), Sten-Åke Tärnlund for providing the research environment at UPMAIL, and Åke Hansson whose comments on the paper have improved its clarity significantly. Thanks also to the other members of UPMAIL for valuable discussions and tea breaks. Last, but not least, without the continuous support from his wife and his daughter, this author's work would be impossible.

References

Allen, J., *Anatomy of LISP* (New York: McGraw-Hill, 1978).

Barklund, J., and H. Millroth, "Garbage Cut for Garbage Collection of Iterative Prolog Programs," *Proc. 1986 Symp. on Logic Programming*, ed. R. Keller (Washington, D.C.: IEEE Comp. Soc. Press, 1986), 276–83.

Barklund, J., and H. Millroth, "Hash Tables in Logic Programming," *Proc. 4th Intl. Conf. on Logic Programming*, ed. J-L. Lassez (Cambridge: MIT Press, 1987), 411–27.

Barklund, J., and H. Millroth, "Integrating Complex Data Structures in Prolog," *Proc. 1987 Symp. on Logic Programming*, ed. S. Haridi (Washington, D.C.: IEEE Comp. Soc. Press, 1987), 415–25.

Barklund, J., and H. Millroth, *The Basic Tricia Prolog Manual*, version 0.7 (Uppsala: Uppsala Univ., 1988).

Blomberg, G., B. Danielsson, and T. A. Larsson, *Macros and Source Variables in Z-Prolog*, draft (Stockholm: ZYX AB, 1987).

Bowen, D. L., *DECsystem-10 Prolog User's Manual* (Edinburgh: Univ. of Edinburgh, 1981).

Bowen, K. A., and R. A. Kowalski, "Amalgamating Language and Metalanguage in Logic Programming," *Logic Programming*, ed. K. Clark and S.-Å. Tärnlund (London: Academic Press, 1982), 153–72.

Bowen, K. A., "Meta-Level Programming and Knowledge Representation," *New Generation Computing* 3 (1985): 359–83.

Bruynooghe, M., G. Janssens, A. Callebaut, and B. Demoen, "Abstract Interpretation: Towards the Global Optimisation of Prolog Programs," *Proc. 1987 Symp. on Logic Programming*, ed. S. Haridi (Washington, D.C.: IEEE Comp. Soc. Press, 1987), 192–204.

Chapter 21

Meta-Programming in Prolog Through Direct Introspection:
A Comparison with Meta-Interpretation Techniques

Marco Cavalieri   Evelina Lamma   Paola Mello
Antonio Natali

DEIS-Universita' di Bologna
Viale Risorgimento 2
40136 Bologna - ITALY
boari%bodeis.infnet@icineca2.bitnet

Abstract

In this paper two different techniques to exploit meta-programming in logic programming systems are discussed and compared. The first is the well-known meta-interpretation technique. The second, less investigated, consists of the direct access to the run-time state of the underlying machine by means of reflection mechanisms and will be referred to as direct introspection. The paper is mainly devoted to practical considerations. Both techniques will be compared on the basis of their flexibility, elegance and, especially, performance. Performance comparisons have been made in three different cases: interpretation, partial evaluation and compilation. The results show that direct introspection is more brief, readable and efficient. Nevertheless, meta- interpretation is more flexible and general.

21.1   Introduction

It is widely recognized that meta-programming (see [Bow82], [Bow85]) is a very expressive and powerful technique to overcome some limitations of logic programming languages such as Prolog [Clo81] and to broaden their application area towards the Artificial Intelligence field. As stated in [Riv87], through meta-level programming some inaccessible aspects of the underlying object-level system can be made explicit and treated as first-class objects.

An interesting subclass of meta-programming systems is constituted by the introspective systems (see [Bat83], [Smi82]). In this case, the system has a description of its structure and behaviour explicitly available.

In order to make a system introspective, the supporting machine has to be able to dynamically construct an explicit representation (model) of the program being executed, on the basis of which the program itself may be reasoned, and actions on it supported.

Of course, the model a program has of itself in an introspecive system determines the computation of interest it can perform about itself and the modifications of interest it can carry out on itself.

In fact, whatever program model is adopted, there are always issues of program representation that remain implicit, thus not modifiable.

If evaluated following this line of reasoning, a standard Prolog machine can be considered a poor introspective system. In fact, the model of the program that can be accessed and manipulated is represented only by the set of clauses composing it. The overall dynamic computational state of the Prolog machine is completely hidden. For this reason, when a more detailed model of the program is necessary, the most common technique used in the Prolog community is to design meta-interpreters [Saf86].

In general, meta-interpreters use direct access to the program internal representation through the built-in predicate 'clause/2', and then have to reproduce the overall interpretation cycle at Prolog level.

We argue that a less extreme solution can be adopted in some cases if the underlying machine supports a more detailed program model. This solution consists in avoiding, if possible, reproduction at meta-level of the interpreter behaviour. Some parts of the computational state of the underlying Prolog machine can be directly accessed and manipulated through reflection mechanisms [Wey80].

This approach —referred to in the following as "direct introspection" — is not new (see [Fri84]), but has been less investigated in the logic programming community and is still poorly understood.

The aim of the paper is to explore the main features of direct introspection in comparison with full meta-interpretation techniques. The coordinates along which the comparison is done are:

1. flexibility and generality;

2. clarity, elegance, conciseness and readability;

3. performance.

The paper focuses mainly on performance considerations. One of the main drawbacks of meta-programming techniques is, in fact, the overhead they introduce. Efficiency improvement is necessary to make meta-programming a useful technique to implement real systems based on the logic programming paradigm.

Since we believe that a lot of experience has to be accumulated to implement and apply direct introspection to logic programming, the paper is mainly devoted to practical considerations. A case study has been selected: extending a Prolog machine supporting separate Prolog databases (Modular Prolog Machine - MPM) with mechanisms for dynamic context handling [Cav88b].

Depending on the program model adopted in the MPM, two different solutions have been investigated:

1. If the MPM is conceived as a very poor introspective system where only access to the internal clause representation is possible (Closed-MPM), context extension is implemented by a meta-interpreter.

2. If the MPM is designed as an introspective system with a richer program execution model (Open-MPM), context extension is implemented by direct introspection.

Open-MPM is based on a program model suitable for the case study selected. Nevertheless, Open-MPM has been profitably applied to other problems not discussed here (see [Mel87]).

The paper is organized as follows. In the first section the case study is presented. In the second section solution 1 is discussed. In the third section solution 2 is presented. In the fourth section the two solutions are compared. With regard to performance, the comparison is made by considering three different cases: interpretation, partial evaluation [Ven84] and compilation on a Warren Abstract Machine (WAM) [War83].

21.2 The Case Study

In standard Prolog a unique database is present, but several Prolog extensions already provide the notion of separate databases (see Prolog/KR [Nak84], MProlog [MPr85], ESP [Chi84], etc.) to increase Prolog expressive power and broaden its application area. The extended Prolog machine — called Modular Prolog Machine (MPM) — considered here, supports separate Prolog databases (units). Each unit is treated as a first-class object univocally identified by a name (a Prolog constant) and is composed of a set of Horn clauses. Clauses having head with same arity and functor, but belonging to different units are considered as separate procedures. The MPM tries to solve every (sub-)goal by considering only the clauses belonging to a particular unit (the current unit). Goals can have different results if invoked in different units.

Since it seems impossible to reach universal agreement on the best mechanism to dynamically combine units, it might be a good choice to allow the programmer to explicitly express rules for the sharing of knowledge between different units. For this purpose, in the basic MPM no policy for static or dynamic unit combination is present. Unit combination, in fact, can be better conceived as a meta-level specification on object-level goal demonstration. Being able to express unit combination by means of meta-programming techniques can be very suitable for prototyping different, flexible knowledge-based systems.

Let us suppose as a case study that a user, starting from the MPM, wants to implement a particular dynamic unit combination policy (called context extension) in Prolog by means of meta-programming techniques.

A new concept unknown to basic MPM, has to be defined and implemented: goals are always solved in a particular "context" [Cav88b]. A context represents a sort of current line of reasoning and is expressed as an ordered list of units that varies during execution, depending on user needs.

In other words, rather than evaluate a goal g simply in a particular unit u (i.e. $u \vdash g$) the user can dynamically choose to evaluate g in the union of different units (e.g. $u_1 \cup u_2 \cup \ldots u_N \vdash g$).

The MPM extended with context handling, supports the following operations:

1. Setting a new context C to solve a goal G (switch-context operator: $C \rightarrow G$). Switch is a non-monotonic operator, the context is set to a new list C on which the demonstration of goal G is activated. If switch fails, G is also considered failed and backtracking is activated in the previous context. If the new context is simply a one-element list, the "$\rightarrow$" operator can be considered similar to an external call to a different unit.

2. Solving a goal G by extending the current context with a new unit U (merge operator: $U adda G$). In Prolog the order of clauses has a great influence upon goal demonstration. $U adda G$ adds U clauses on the top of the current context. This operator can be very useful to handle hypothetical reasoning and multiple viewpoints and is embedded, in an *ad hoc* way, in logic-based systems (see for example [Nak84]).

In the following we will show and discuss two different solutions to the case study depending on the introspection capabilities and program model adopted in basic MPM.

21.3 Extending Closed-MPM with Context Handling

21.3.1 Closed-MPM

Suppose that — once a particular unit u has been specified — the only introspective capability supported by MPM is access to the internal clause representation in u. This is the case of a poor introspective system — as Prolog is — in which the computational state of the underlying machine remains implicit. In the following this system will be called Closed-MPM.

```
solve(true,_) :- !.
solve((A,B),C) :- !,solve(A,C),solve(B,C).
solve((C -> G),_) :- !,solve(G,C).
solve(adda(U,G),C) :- !,solve(G,[U|C]).
solve(G,C) :- member(U,C),clause(U,G,B),solve(B,C).

member(X,[X|_]).
member(X,[_|T]) :- member(X,T).
```

Figure 21.1: A pure meta-interpreter for context handling (PMI)

In Closed-MPM, direct access to the program internal representation is obtained via the built-in predicate *clause(<unit>,<head>,<body>)*, where *<unit>* represents the name of the unit in which a clause with head *<head>* has to be searched. If the search succeeds, *<body>* represents the clause body.

Therefore, the program model of a Closed-MPM consists only of an explicit representation — like Prolog structures — of different sets of clauses.

21.3.2   Context Implementation in Closed-MPM

In Closed-MPM, context handling can be supported only through traditional meta-interpretation techniques. The Prolog machine main loop, together with the computational rule, must be reproduced. A new "register" is added to the context handling machine as a meta-interpreter parameter.

A pure (i.e. not supporting built-in predicates) meta-interpreter able to solve context handling operators is sketched in figure 21.1. The first argument of predicate *solve/2* represents the goal to be solved, while the second represents the current context where the goal has to be proved. The meta-interpreter above (called PMI , i.e. Pure Meta-Interpreter) is able to solve the switch-context and merge operators, as well as goal conjunctions. Note that no extra-logical Prolog predicates are supported in PMI.

Writing a full meta-interpreter (called FMI) supporting standard Prolog (cut included) and context handling is not a trivial task: the FMI code becomes cumbersome and complex (see figure 21.2). The first and second arguments of *solve/3* still represent the current goal and context. The third argument is needed to deal with the *cut* operator. FMI handles both context operators and the complete set of Prolog built-in predicates.

```
solve(G,C) :- solve(G,C,R), R==true.

solve(true,_,true) :- !.
solve(!,_,R) :- !,(R=true; R=cut).
solve((A,B),C,R) :- !,solve(A,C,R1),
                       ( R1==true, solve(B,C,R2),
                          ( R2==true, R=true;
                            R2==cut, !, R=cut);
                          R1==cut, !, R=cut).
solve((A;B),C,R) :- !, (
                       solve(A,C,R1), (
                                        R1==true, R=tru;
                                        R1==cut, !, R=cut);
                       solve(B,C,R1), (
                                        R1==true, R=true;
                                        R1==cut, !, R=cut)).
solve(call(A),C,true) :- !,solve(A,C,true).
solve(not(A),C,_) - solve(A,C,R),R=true,!,fail.
solve(not(_),C,true) - !.
solve(A,C,true) :- system(A),!,call(A).
solve((C -> G),_,R) :- !,solve(G,C,true).
solve(adda(U,G),C,R) :- !,solve(G,[U|C],true).
solve(G,C,R) :- member(U,C),
                solve_local_cut(U,G,C,R).
solve_local_cut(U,G,C,R) :- clause(U,G,B),
                            solve(B,C,R1),
                            ( R1==true, R=true;
                              R1==cut, !, fail ).

member(X,[X|_]).
member(X,[_|T]) :- member(X,T).
```

Figure 21.2: A full meta-interpreter for context handling (FMI)

21.4 Extending Open-MPM with Context Handling

21.4.1 Open-MPM

The basic MPM on which to implement the case study (Open-MPM) is now more powerful. The main power of Open-MPM consists in its introspection capabilities: a more detailed description of the structure and behaviour of itself is explicit, and can be directly accessed and handled during computations. Computations accessing and modifying the program model are conceptually "meta-level" computations.

The program model in Open-MPM is enriched with the following dynamic informations [Mel86]:

$$\{Aux, CU, CG\}$$

where:

- *Aux* is bound to a generic data structure with no a *priori* semantics for Open-MPM. The meaning of this data structure is, in fact, established by the meta-level computation to define, in logic, new abstractions. The Open-MPM guarantees the consistency of *Aux* at each resolution step. In other words, *Aux* is as a new, generic register of the Open-MPM machine saved in the current environment on the local stack and restored when needed (see [Bru82]).

- *CU* is bound to a constant representing the current Prolog unit, i.e. the set of clauses currently used.

- *CG* is bound to the data structure representing the next (sub-)goal to be demonstrated.

At meta-level, *Aux*, *CU* and *CG* data structures exist as first-class objects in the sense that they can be values of (meta-) variables. In Open-MPM, reflection mechanisms have been provided to trigger the computation from the domain (object-) level to the introspective (meta-) level ("upward reflection") and *vice versa* ("downward reflection") [Aie86].

Object- and meta-computations can be separated in different units to introduce more structure into programs. In particular, when the built-in predicate *connect(mu)* is executed with success in a unit, *u*, unit *mu* becomes the meta-unit of *u*. In *mu* one can access and manipulate the program model of the object-level computation. Object-level and meta- level units have the same representation and computation capabilities such that introspection can recur.

If an (object-)unit *u* is connected to a (meta-)unit *mu*, Open-MPM automatically reflects in *mu* ("upward reflection") the moment at which a selected (sub-)goal *g* of *u* is going to be demonstrated. This applies only if *g* is not a system predicate. Otherwise *g* is directly executed at object-level. To perform upward reflection, Open-MPM "reifies" the current program model into meta-variables, and tries to demonstrate the goal *reflect_up(Aux,CU,CG)* in the corresponding meta-unit *mu*, where *CU* is bound to *u* and *CG* to *g*. When the meta-computation ends — i.e. the *reflect_up/3* demonstration terminates — Open-MPM will continue computation of the level below after reflecting the *reflect_up/3* results. In particular, if *reflect_up/3* succeeds, the resulting program model — where some variables in *CG* can be bound — is reflected (using a sort of implicit downward reflection) again in the actual object-level and *CG* succeeds in *CU*. If *reflect_up/3* fails, its failure is propagated to the connected object-level computation.

Downward reflection can be explicitly forced by the meta-level computation by calling the built-in predicate *reflect_down(Aux,CU,CG)*. If this is the case, a resolution step is activated at object-level starting from the program model specified in the *reflect_down/3* current arguments. If the *CG* demonstration terminates successfully, *reflect_down/3* too is considered demonstrated and some variables in the meta-level environment can be bound (using a sort of implicit upward reflection), otherwise *reflect_down/3* fails.

Since the (meta-)variable arguments of *reflect_up/3* and *reflect_down/3* predicates range over *CU*, *CG*, and *Aux* values respectively, the program model can be easily inspected and, if needed, modified.

Moreover, the causal connection problem [Bat83] is consistently solved: any modification in the program model at meta-level causes a corresponding modification in the structure and run-time environment of the object-level system and vice-versa.

21.4.2   Context Implementation in Open-MPM

In Open-MPM, context handling can be expressed without the need for a full meta-interpreter, but simply by direct introspection (DI). Three meta-rules (written in the unit *meta_context* and reported in figure 21.3) are sufficient to implement context handling.

Each object-unit connected with *meta_context* will be able to support context handling. When the switch operator is called (rule mr1.), the new context is set to *NewContext*. When the *adda* operator is called (rule mr2.), the new context is obtained by "stacking" *U*1 clauses on top of *C*. Since the operators discussed above can be nested, they have been implemented by means of a recursive call to *reflect_up/3*. Rule mr3. can be interpreted as a sort of high-level specification of context implementation. The first meta-rule parameter expresses the new information (*Aux* register) that has to be recorded in the stack for each resolution step. This information represents the context in which demonstration of the (sub-)goal *G* of the unit *U* has to be tried. The rule body states the new actions performed at each resolution step to support contexts. In particular, an element, *U*1, is extracted from the list *Context* (*member/2* predicate) and the demonstration is performed in it (*reflect_down/3*).

In this way, context implementation is performed by a simple form of 'generate-

```
unit(meta_context).

mr1. reflect_up(OldContext,U,NewContext->G):- !,
                    reflect_up(NewContext,U,G).

mr2. reflect_up(C,U,U1 adda G):-!,
                    reflect_up([U1|C],U,G).

mr3. reflect_up(Context,U,G):-
                    member(U1,Context),
                    reflect_down(Context,U1,G).

    member(X,[X|_]).
    member(X,[_|T]) :- member(X,T).
```

Figure 21.3: Direct Introspection to implement context handling (DI)

and-test', and backtracking on unit union is automatically supported by the underlying machine.

21.5 Comparing the Two Approaches

By using the reflection mechanisms and the program model of Open-MPM, the case study is easily solved without the need for a full meta-interpreter. In fact, built-in Prolog predicates (cut included) are not automatically reflected at meta-level, but directly supported by the underlying machine.

Changes can be directly made to the run-time environment of the basic interpreter by upward and downward reflection mechanisms.

For this reason the solution is more elegant, understandable and brief. The *Aux* register proved very useful in implementing context handling. This register is very general: it can be bound to any Prolog term and handled only at meta-level, but its consistency (e.g. its correct treatment during backtracking) is directly guaranteed by the underlying machine.

Of course, in spite of the generality of the *Aux* register, the program model present in the Open-MPM is very suitable only for a particular problem category (to which the case study belongs), but it becomes unsatisfactory if applied to different, more general problems. In fact, there is no general, optimal program model. For example, if one wants to change the Prolog computational rule [Llo84], the program model of Open-MPM is too superficial since the goal selection is implicit. If this is the case, the more flexible, full meta-interpreter approach has to be followed to avoid direct intervention on the low-level code of the underlying

```
unit(u0).
nrev([],[]).
nrev([A|X],Y) :- nrev(X,Z),append(Z,[A],Y).

unit(u1).
append([],X,X).

unit(u2).
append([T|C],Y,[T|Z]) :- append(C,Y,Z).
```

Figure 21.4: The program on which performance comparisons have been made

machine.

21.5.1   Performance Comparison

One of the main problems in using meta-programming techniques to build real systems is the overhead introduced by the presence of multiple computational levels. For this reason comparison of Closed- and Open-MPM here reported focuses on performance evaluations.

Performance comparisons have been made by considering the code of figure 21.1 (PMI), figure 21.2 (FMI) and figure 21.3 (DI). PMI and FMI run on Closed-MPM, while DI runs on Open-MPM. The comparisons have been performed in three different cases: interpretation, partial evaluation and compilation on a Warren Abstract Machine (WAM). The results have been normalized with respect to the DI solution.

The test is based on the object-level Modular Prolog program in figure 21.4 and is performed with the goals:

$$? - solve([u0, u1, u2] \rightarrow nrev([1, 2, ..., 20], X), \_)$$

for PMI and FMI,

$$? - [u0, u1, u2] \rightarrow nrev([1, 2, ..., 20], X)$$

for DI.

As will be clear in the following, the Modular Prolog program above favours FMI performance results compared to DI and PMI ones. In fact, in the program of figure 21.4, cuts and built-in predicates are not used.

Moreover, since there is not a great number of conjunctions in clause bodies, some overheads due to meta-interpretation are not made evident by the test.

DI	PMI	FMI
1	1.90	3.09

Table 21.1: Intepretation performance results normalized with respect to DI

Interpretation

Following the interpretation approach, Closed- and Open-MPM have been implemented by extending a Prolog interpreter (i.e. a C-Prolog interpreter [CPr87] running on a SUN workstation).

To implement the Closed-MPM, the C-Prolog clause representation has been modified to support separate Prolog databases. Moreover a new register (called CU and referring to the current unit) has been added and the unification algorithm has been partially modified. In particular, the value of the CU register is used at each resolution step to select the right clause for unification.

To implement the program model in Open-MPM, the new register Aux has been introduced in addition to the CU register. At each resolution step, if the current unit is connected to a meta-unit, the interpreter makes the program model explicit and reflects it at meta-level. To implement the *reflect_down/3* built-in predicate, the interpreter has to force *reflect_down/3* arguments into the Aux, CU and CG (i.e. the register referring to the current goal) registers and resume an object-level demonstration.

The test execution has given the results shown in table 21.1

Let us note that direct introspection is more efficient than meta- interpretation. In particular, the solution based on Open-MPM and direct introspection is about twice as fast as that based on Closed-MPM and the pure meta-interpreter (PMI). This ratio notably increases if the full meta-interpreter (FMI) is taken into account.

The overhead of Closed-MPM solutions is mainly due to the following reasons:

1. The computation rule is reproduced at meta-level. This overhead increases with the number of goal conjunctions in the clause body;

2. The explicit execution of the *clause/3* built-in predicate is slower than the equivalent operation in Open-MPM due to the need to handle clauses as data structures;

3. A greater number of unifications is necessary to find the solution;

4. A greater number of shallow backtrackings is performed since many alternatives for the *solve/3* predicate are present.

Moreover, system predicates in FMI are executed considerably more slowly than in DI. In fact, system predicates are directly solved at object-level, while in FMI

DI	PMI	FMI
6.16	13.18	6.71

Table 21.2: Partial Evaluation vs. Interpretation

they are handled by the meta-interpreter, that implies a greater numebr of shallow backtrackings and an additional test (*system/1*). This overhead does not appear in the case study, since system predicates are not used in the program of figure 21.4.

Partial Evaluation

In the comparison, partial evaluation techniques could not be ignored. In fact, partial evaluation [Ven84] [Tak86] is considered as one of the most promising techniques to reduce the meta-programming overhead.

Since tests are based on extended Prolog machines, a partial evaluator for standard Prolog [Cav88a] has been modified accordingly. In particular the partial evaluator for Closed-MPM deals with modularity, while the partial evaluator for Open-MPM deals with modularity and reflection.

In the case of DI, the extended partial evaluator is able to treat reflection mechanisms when a connection between object- and meta-level units is established. If this is the case, for each object-level sub-goal, the partial evaluator tries to unfold the corresponding *reflect_up/3* predicate in the meta-level unit. When the *reflect_down/3* predicate is reached, the partial evaluator tries to unfold the goal (specified as third argument of *reflect_down/3*) with object-level clauses. Moreover, the partial evaluator has to maintain, in a consistent way, two variables simulating the *Aux* and *CU* registers.

The PMI and FMI solutions have been partially evaluated with respect to the program of figure 21.4 and the goal:

$$? - solve([u0, u1, u2] \rightarrow nrev(Z, X), \_).$$

The DI solution has been partially evaluated with respect to the program of figure 21.4 and the goal:

$$? - [u0, u1, u2] \rightarrow nrev(Z, X).$$

Of course efficiency increases when partial evaluation is applied, as table 21.2 shows.

This table reports the ratio between execution times of the original code and the partial evaluated code for the test under examination. FMI has a lower performance increase because of the difficulties introduced by dealing with the cut.

DI	PMI	FMI
1	0.88	2.84

Table 21.3: Partial Evaluation test results normalized with respect to DI

The execution of the test has given the results in table 21.3 when normalized with respect to DI.

Let us note that direct introspection is still more efficient than full meta-interpretation, but the difference is significantly reduced. This is due to the fact that most of the Closed-MPM overhead (see section 21.5.1) is eliminated thanks to partial evaluation. For example, the *clause/3* predicate is no longer executed, the need for shallow backtracking is greatly reduced and a lot of unifications are eliminated. The optimized code of DI and PMI are similar in structure. Nevertheless the DI version is a bit slower than the PMI one. This is due to the fact that the DI *reflect_up/3* predicate has one more argument than the corresponding *solve/2* predicate in PMI. This argument represents the current unit that is not significant in the case study but, of course, the partial evaluator cannot omit it.

Compilation Based on the WAM

Comparisons have been done by implementing Closed-MPM and Open-MPM on the basis of a Warren Abstract Machine (WAM) [War83]. The performance results based on the WAM have to be considered subject to confirmation. In fact, they have been obtained by using a WAM emulator, written in C language, that has to be further improved.

Compiling programs for Closed-MPM in WAM code does not present any new significant features. Since predicates with the same head functor and arity defined in separate units are considered different procedures, separate codes are produced for them.

The main problem has been the implementation of the *clause/3* built-in predicate, not supported in the standard WAM instruction set. Since no decompilation technique is supported, *clause/3* requires clauses explicitly represented as data structures. To implement *clause/3*, a set of new instructions has been added to find the explicit clause representation.

With reference to the case study, it was necessary to compile only the meta-interpreter code. The object-level code, in fact, is used only as a data structure by the meta-interpreter, accessed through the *clause/3* predicate. It is never directly executed.

The compilation of programs for Open-MPM requires a major extension of WAM. In particular, the *Aux* machine register has been introduced together with instructions to handle it. Compilation of the case study has been done by statically

DI	PMI	FMI
1	2.10	5.44

Table 21.4: Compilation performance results normalized with respect to DI

fixing the connection between the object-level units *u0*, *u1*, *u2* and the meta-unit *meta_context*. To implement the upward reflection, the compiled code of each object-level procedure f/n in a unit *u* includes as header a sequence of WAM instructions. This sequence builds an explicit representation of the current goal, i.e. a structure with functor f and arity n. The arguments of this structure are unified with the n argument registers received by f/n. Then, after loading the content of *Aux* in *A0* WAM register, the unit name *u* in *A1* WAM register and a reference to the current goal in *A2* WAM register, a call to the *reflect_up/3* procedure in the unit *meta_context* is executed.

Downward reflection is implemented by forcing the *Aux* register to the value specified in the first argument of *reflect_down/3*, and then by executing the compiled code associated with the goal specified as the third argument. The right code is found by executing a two-level indexing, first on the unit, then on the goal structure. Since an object-level demonstration has now to be performed, the header code of the object procedure is skipped.

The test execution has given the following results shown in table 21.4 when normalized with respect to DI:

Let us note that direct introspection is considerably more efficient than meta-interpretation. This is due to the fact that the object-level program is compiled as well. In fact, in Open-MPM, the object-level program is not a data structure, but an executable code.

This avoids some sources of overhead which are, instead, present in the program compiled for Closed-MPM. Overhead sources for PMI and FMI in this case are the same as those pointed out in section 21.5.1.

Since the implementation of *clause/3* might be improved, we suppose the ratio between PMI/FMI and DI for compiled programs might decrease and become similar to that for interpreted programs. The ratio between execution times of the interpreted and compiled code for the test under examination is about 3.5. Nevertheless, we do not consider this value very significant because the WAM emulator is not optimized and might be considerably improved in the near future.

21.6   Conclusions

The paper has pointed out the power of meta-programming techniques in logic programming with particular emphasis on direct introspection. The main advantage of direct introspection is that the writing of full meta- interpreters can be avoided in some cases, depending on the visibility of the underlying machine. As can be inferred from performance results, direct introspection allows a better trade-off between efficiency and extensibility. Only partial evaluation techniques can make direct introspection and meta-interpretation comparable. In addition, direct introspection makes meta-programs more concise and readable.

The main problem in designing machines supporting direct introspection is to fit the program model for a particular class of applications. Open-MPM has a program model adequate to handle different policies for dynamic unit combinations of which context handling is only a particular example. However, Open-MPM cannot be suitable for implementing extensions or modifications of the standard Prolog control strategy through direct introspection. This is due to the insufficiency of the program model adopted. Therefore a lot of work has still to be done in this area.

Since no tool yet implemented and suitable for our performance comparisons existed, we had to implement from scratch interpreters, partial evaluators and extended WAM emulators. Since our implementations are not optimized, we apologize if the test results are not very reliable, especially with regard to absolute performance times and the compilation approach.

Of course we are aware that the case study is limited and reduces the value of performance comparisons. In the future we intend to execute quantitative comparisons between the two approaches in the case of more significant problems.

Acknowledgements

The paper has been partially supported by ENIDATA S.p.a, ALPES Esprit Project n. 973 and C.N.R..

References

[Aie86] L.Aiello, C.Cecchi, D.Sartini: "Representation and Use of Metaknowledge", Proc. of the IEEE, Vol. 74, No. 10, October 1986.

[Bat83] J.Batali: "Computational Introspection", MIT, Artificial Intelligence Laboratory, Memo 701, Cambridge, Massachusetts, Febraury 1983.

[Bow82] K.Bowen, R.Kowalski: "Amalgamating language and metalanguage in logic programming", in Logic Programming, eds. K.L.Clark and S.A.Tarnlund , Academic Press, 1982.

[Bow85] K.Bowen: "Meta-level Programming and Knowledge Representation", New Generation Computing, Vol. 3, No. 4, 1985.

[Bru82] M.Bruynooghe: "The Memory Management of Prolog Implementation", in Logic Programming, Clark and Tarnlund eds., Academic Press, 1982.

[Cav88a] M.Cavalieri et alii: "A Partial Evaluator to Optimize ADES Expert System", (in Italian), in Proc. 3rd Congress on Logic Programming, Rome, Italy, May 1988.

[Cav88b] M.Cavalieri, E.Lamma, P.Mello: "An Extended Prolog Machine for Dynamic Context Handling", in Proc. of ECAI-88, Pitman Publishing, Munich, August 1988.

[Chi84] T.Chikayama: "ESP Reference Manual", ICOT Report, February 1984.

[Clo81] W. F. Clocksin, C.S. Mellish: "Programming in Prolog" Springer- Verlag, New-York, 1981.

[CPr87] "C-Prolog User's Manual", ed. F.Pereira, SRI International, Menlo Park, Ca, USA, February 1987.

[Fri84] D. Friedman, M.Wand: "Reification: Reflection without meta-physic", Conf. Rec. 1984 ACM Symp. on LISP and Functional Programming, Austin, Aug. 1984.

[Llo84] J. W. Lloyd: "Foundations of Logic Programming", Springer-Verlag, 1984.

[Mel86] P. Mello, A.Natali: "Programs as Collections of Communicating Prolog Units" In: ESOP-86 and LNCS No.213, Springer-Verlag, March 1986.

[Mel87] P. Mello, A.Natali: "Objects as Communicating Prolog Units", in Proc. ECOOP'87 and LNCS No.276, Springer-Verlag, 1987.

[MPr85] "MProlog Language Reference Manual", — Logicware Inc., Toronto, Canada, September 1985.

[Nak84] K. Nakashima: "Knowledge Representation in Prolog/KR", International Symposium on Logic Programming, Atlantic City, February 1984.

[Riv87] J. des Rivieres: "Meta-Level Facilities in Logic-Based Computational Systems", in Proc. Conference on Meta-Level Architectures and Reflection, Alghero, Italy, 1987.

[Saf86] S. Safra, E.Shapiro: "Meta-interpreters for Real", in Proc. of IFIP-86, H-G-Kugler eds., Elsevier Science Publisher, 1986.

[Smi82] B. C. Smith: "Reflection and Semantics in LISP", Stanford CSLI Report No. CSLI-84-8, 1984.

[Tak86] A. Takeuchi, K. Furakawa: "Partial Evaluation of Prolog Programs and its Application to Meta-Programming", in: Proc. of IFIP-86, Elsevier Science Publisher, 1986.

[Ven84] R. Venken: "A Prolog Meta-Interpreter for Partial Evaluation and its Application to Source to Source Transformation and Query- Optimization", in Proc. of ECAI-84, North Holland, 1984.

[War83] D. H. D. Warren: "An Abstract Prolog Instruction Set", SRI Technical Note 309, SRI International, October 1983.

[Wey80] R. Weyhrauch: "Prolegomena to a Theory of Mechanized Formal Reasoning", Artificial Intelligence, Vol.13, n.1,2. North Holland.

Chapter 22

Design and Implementation of An Abstract MetaProlog Engine for MetaProlog

Ilyas Cicekli

Syracuse University

Abstract

Most of the meta-level systems are implemented last decade are meta-level interpreters which introduce extra interpretation layers which slow down the execution. The MetaProlog system described in this paper is a compiler-based meta-level system for the MetaProlog programming language. Since MetaProlog is an extension of Prolog, the Warren Abstract Machine (WAM) is extended to the Abstract MetaProlog Engine (AMPE) to get an efficient implementation for MetaProlog. Moreover, a MetaProlog program can be directly compiled into the instructions of the AMPE. The first class objects, theories and proofs, of MetaProlog and their representations in the MetaProlog system are also the main concern of this paper.

22.1 Introduction

Meta-level facilities in logic programming languages are sought by many researchers [2,3,4,7,10]. These meta-level facilities provide explicit representation of meta-level objects such as databases (theories), goals, and proofs in logic programming languages. When these meta-level objects are made explicit, they can be manipulated as other data structures in the system. For example, theories and proofs are first class objects in the MetaProlog programming language. A new theory can be created from an old theory, and a variable can be bound to that theory, so that it can be passed around as any other data structure in the MetaProlog system.

MetaProlog [2,3,4] contains all the features of Prolog, and cures shortcomings of Prolog in the handling dynamic databases. In Prolog, there is a single database, and when there is a need to update this database, assert/retract builtins, which are ad hoc extensions to the basic logic programming paradigm, are used to create the new version of this database by destroying the old version in the favor of the new version. On the other hand, there can be many theories in MetaProlog, and a new theory can be created from an old theory without destroying the old theory. Both the new theory and the old theory can be accessed in MetaProlog.

The provability relation between a goal and a theory is explicitly represented in MetaProlog by a two argument predicate *demo*. The relation *demo(Theory, Goal)* holds precisely when *Goal* is provable in *Theory*. Similarly, the relation *demo(Theory, Goal, Proof)* holds when *Proof* is the proof of *Goal* based on the axioms of *Theory*. When one of these provability relations is encountered, the underlying theorem prover tries to prove the given goal with respect to the given theory.

Many researchers in the logic programming area worked on the implementations of meta-level systems [8,10]. But, according to our knowledge, these systems are meta-level interpreters which introduce extra interpretation layers which slow down the execution. The MetaProlog system presented in this paper is a compiler-based system where MetaProlog programs are directly compiled into the instructions of the Abstract MetaProlog Engine (AMPE), an extension of the Warren Abstract Machine (WAM) designed for MetaProlog.

Theories, the most important objects in MetaProlog, and their representations in the MetaProlog system are described Section 22.2. Although there is also another way to handle theories in the MetaProlog system [1], only the non-default theory approach is discussed in that section. After theories are addressed in Section 22.2, the core part of the AMPE, which can only handle multiple databases and the two argument provability relation, is presented in Section 22.3. The AMPE presented in Section 22.3 cannot handle proofs and the three argument provability relation. Finally, proofs and the required extensions to the core part of the AMPE to implement proofs are discussed in Section 22.4.

22.2   MetaProlog Theories

In Prolog, there is only one theory, and all goals are proved with respect to this theory. On the other hand, there can be more than one theory in MetaProlog at a certain time, so that a goal can be proved with respect to one of them. When the predicate *demo(Theory, Goal)* is submitted as a goal, the MetaProlog system tries to to prove *Goal* with respect to *Theory*. The same goal can be also proved with respect to a different theory.

Theories of the MetaProlog system are organized in a tree whose root is a distinguished theory, the base theory. The base theory consists of all builtin predicates, and all other theories in the system are its descendants; i.e., all builtins in the base theory can be accessed from all other theories in the system.

A new theory is created from an old theory by adding some clauses or dropping them. The new theory inherits all the procedures of the old theory except for procedures explicitly modified during its creation. The system can still access both the new theory and the old theory. For example, the following builtin predicates create new theories.

addto(OldTheory, Clauses, NewTheory)
dropfrom(OldTheory, Clauses, NewTheory)

The given clauses **Clauses** are added to (dropped from) the given old theory **OldTheory** to create a new theory **NewTheory** by the predicate **addto** (**dropfrom**). The variable **NewTheory** is bound to the internal representation of the new theory after the execution of one of these commands. The new theory exists in the system as long as the variable **NewTheory** is accessible. When the variable **NewTheory** is not accessible, the theory will be discarded the same as for any other variable in the system.

22.2.1   Permanent Theories

After a new theory is created in the MetaProlog system from an old theory which already exists in the system, normally a variable is bound to the internal representation of this theory. We can access this theory by using this variable, and this variable should be passed to places where that theory can be accessed. Sometimes, passing this variable to many places is not very practical. For this reason, some theories in the MetaProlog system have names, and they can be referred by using their names at any place of the program.

Theories with names, called *permanent theories*, are always present in the system, and can be accessed via their names. On the other hand, *temporary theories*, theories without names, are created during the execution of a goal, and they are discarded after the execution of that goal. They are only accessible in the environments where the variables bound to the internal representation of them exist.

A *permanent theory* can be created by using the built-in predicate **consult**, or a *temporary theory* can be converted into a *permanent theory* by using the built-in predicate **nameof**. For example, when the goal **consult(FileName,TheoryName)** is executed, a new theory which contains all the predicates in the given file is created, and the name **TheoryName** is assigned as its name. The builtin **nameof(Theory,TheoryName)** can convert the temporary theory designated by **Theory** into a permanent theory, and assigns **TheoryName** as its name. Afterwards, this permanent theory can be accessed via its name at any time.

22.2.2   Non-Default Theories

Every theory in the MetaProlog system possesses a default theory except for the base theory. The default theory of a theory is the theory where we search for a procedure if the given theory doesn't know anything about that procedure. In other words, if we try to access a procedure in a theory T and cannot find it there, we search for the procedure in the default theory of the theory T. This search through default theories continues recursively until the procedure is found or the base theory is reached. In other words, the search starts from a node of a tree and proceeds with default theories along a certain branch until the procedure is found or the root of the tree is reached.

Theories in the MetaProlog system are classified into two groups: *default theories*, and *non-default theories*. A *non-default theory* is a theory that carries complete information about all procedures that underwent modifications in the ancestor theories between this theory and its default theory. Access to these procedures is very fast, at the expense of copying some references when the non-default theory is created. The default theory of a theory is the first ancestor theory that is a *default theory*. A *default theory* is a theory whose descendants don't carry any information about the procedures occurring in that theory. In other words, the default theory stops further the propagation of information about earlier procedures. If only default theories are used, access to a given procedure in a given theory may require a search through all its ancestor theories. In this case, access to a procedure may be slow, but no copying of references is needed. Depending on the problem, the system tries to use one or the other approach, or a combination of both to achieve a balance between speed of access and space overhead.

When a new theory T is created from a non-default theory N, the default theory of T will be its father's default theory; i.e., T's default theory will be N's default theory. But if a new theory is created from a default theory, its default theory will be its father. In the first case, the new theory will be at its father's level in the tree. In the second case, the new theory will be at one level above its father level. Thus we don't increment the depth of the tree when a new theory is created from a non-default theory.

The *naive approach* is to have all the theories in the system as default theories. In this case, the default theory relation between theories is same as the father relation[1] between them. This situation can be seen in Figure 22.1. The dotted arrows indicate the father relation and the solid arrows indicate the default theory relation between theories. In this approach, when a new theory is created, it will be at one level above its father's level because all theories are default theories. In this case, the theory tree can get very deep which explains why a search for a procedure can be expensive. For example, to reach the procedure "p" from

---

[1]Internally, there is no father relation in the system. Only the default theory relation between theories is represented in the system.

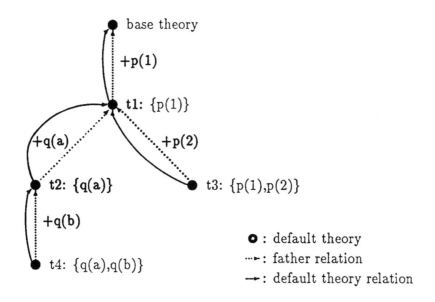

base theory

+p(1)

t1: {p(1)}

+q(a)

+p(2)

t2: {q(a)}

t3: {p(1),p(2)}

+q(b)

t4: {q(a),q(b)}

● : default theory
⋯►: father relation
─►: default theory relation

Figure 22.1: A Theory Tree in The Naive Approach

theory t4, first it is searched for in theory t4 where it doesn't exist. Then it is searched for in theory t2, and finally it is found in theory t1. Thus, to access to the procedure "p" from theory t4, we had to search for it in three theories.

To shorten the depth of the theory tree, we introduce non-default theories. If there is at least one non-default theory in the system, this situation is called the **non-default theory approach**. In this approach, the default theory of a given theory can be one of its remote ancestors instead of its father. In fact, when a new theory T2 is created from a non-default theory T1, the father of T2 will be different from the default theory for T2. The default theory of theory T2 will be its first ancestor theory which is a default theory. If no theory is created from any non-default theory, the theory tree will be same as the theory tree in the naive approach. The advantage of the non-default theory approach starts when we start to create theories from non-default theories. At that time, the depth of the tree won't grow fast, and the search for procedures will generally be shorter.

Figure 22.2 shows the tree of theories from Figure 22.1 in the non-default theory approach. We assume that only the base theory is a default theory and theories t1, t2, t3 and t4 are non-default theories. In this tree, reaching a procedure is much faster than reaching the same procedure in the tree in the naive approach. For example, to access to the procedure "p" in theory t4, only theory t4 is searched since the procedure "p" exists there. We have to search three

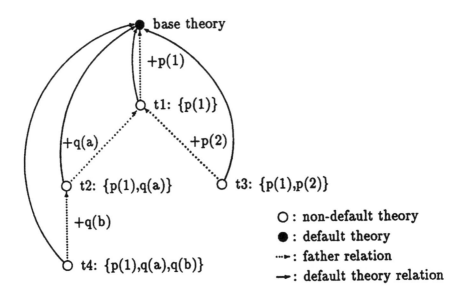

Figure 22.2: A Theory Tree In The Non-Default Theory Approach

theories to access same procedure in the naive approach.

The price we paid for fast access to procedures in the non-default theory approach is that we have to copy procedures of non-default theories into their descendants. In our example, we copied the procedure "p" of theory t1 into theories t2 and t4. Because we copy only a reference for each procedure into the new theory, this copying operation doesn't cost too much.

The system should decide which theories ought to be default theories and which ones ought to be non-default theories. To get the best performance from this approach, the theories with many procedures should be default theories and the theories with few procedures should be non-default theories. The decisions of the system depend on this observation. The system assumes that a theory T is a default theory if it contains more procedures than a certain number of procedures. In other cases, the system assumes that theory T is a default theory.

22.2.3   Context Switching

Since multiple theories are allowed in MetaProlog, we have to know at any time which context the system is in, and how to switch to the another context at a certain time. The MetaProlog system always runs in a certain context, also called the current theory, and all the goals are proved with respect to this current theory.

To prove a goal with respect to a certain theory T, first the context is switched to T, then the goal is proved with respect to the current theory.

In the MetaProlog system, there are two ways to switch context from one theory to the another. The first one, called *temporary context switching*, is the context switching operation done by the predicate demo. The command **demo(Theory,Goal)** switches the context **Theory**, and then **Goal** is proved with respect to the current theory. After the execution of this command, the context is automatically reswitched to the previous context. The predicate demo can be defined in Prolog as follows:

```
demo(Theory,Goal) :-
    context(PreviousContext),
    switch_context(Theory),
    call(Goal),
    switch_context(PreviousContext).
```

where "switch_context" is a low level system predicate which switches the context to the given theory, and the "context" predicate gets the current theory in which the system runs.

The second one, called *permanent context switching*, is the context switching operation done by the setcontext predicate. The command **setcontext(TheoryName)**, which is normally given from the top level to define the context of the top level of the MetaProlog system, switches the context to the theory designated by **TheoryName**. After the execution of this command, the context isn't reswitched to the previous context. Of course, the context can switched to the another theory by submitting one of commands above again. The setcontext predicate can be only used with permanent theories, theories with names.

At the implementation level, the context of the system is held by the *theory register*. Since this theory register is simply updated to switch context, the context switching operation is very fast in the MetaProlog system. This theory register is also saved in choice points, so that the context can be restored during backtracking.

22.3   Abstract MetaProlog Engine

Our main goal in this project is to get an efficient implementation of MetaProlog. Since MetaProlog is an extension of Prolog, the best starting point was the Warren Abstract Machine (WAM). For this purpose, we decided to extend the WAM to the Abstract MetaProlog Engine (AMPE). Along the way, we created our own WAM-based Prolog system [5], and then extended it to the current MetaProlog system.

The AMPE can run in two different modes. The first one is the simple mode in which the system runs when a two argument predicate *demo(Theory, Goal)* is encountered; i.e., the system only proves *Goal* with respect to *Theory*. On the other hand, the system not only can prove a goal with respect to a theory, it can also collect the proof when it runs in the proof mode. The system runs in the proof mode when a three argument demo is encountered. The core part of the AMPE described in this section is used in both modes. But there are also extra features of the AMPE which are only used when it is in the proof mode. Proofs and their implementation are explained in Section 22.4.

The AMPE performs most of the functions of the WAM, but it also has some extra features to handle multiple theories of MetaProlog. These extra features of the AMPE are :

1. Extra registers to handle theories in MetaProlog.
2. A different memory organization which is more suitable to handle compiled procedures and theories as data objects of the system.
3. The functions of the procedural instructions in the AMPE differ from their functions in the WAM.

In the following four subsections, the basic structure of the AMPE is discussed. In this discussion, the AMPE is widely compared with the WAM to explain similarities and differences between them. We assume the familiarity with the WAM [9].

22.3.1   Machine Registers

The AMPE has the same registers the WAM has and two extra registers to handle theories of MetaProlog. The registers which are same as the WAM registers perform the same functions in the AMPE. For example, the program counter (P in the WAM) still points to the instruction to be executed, and the last choice point register (B in the WAM) still points the last choice point in the local stack.

The first new register is the *theory register* which holds a pointer to the internal representation of the current theory of the system. The current theory of the system is the theory in which a procedure is searched for when a call to that procedure is encountered.

The value of the *theory register* is changed when the context of the system is switched to the another context by the predicate "demo" or "setcontext". The *theory register* is also saved in choice points such that it can be restored from the value saved in the last choice point during backtracking.

The second register, the *theory counter register*, is a simply a counter which holds the next available theory-id which is an integer. The function of the *theory counter register* is to produce a unique theory-id for each theory in the system. When a new theory is created, this register is automatically incremented to hold the next available theory-id.

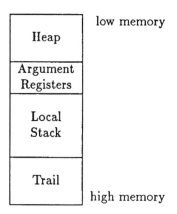

Figure 22.3: Memory Organization of The AMPE

22.3.2 Memory Organization of The AMPE

The memory of the AMPE is divided into the four consecutive areas (Figure 22.3). The heap and the local stack grow from the low memory to the high memory, and the trail grows from the high memory to the low memory. A certain number of memory locations (maximum 256) are reserved for the argument registers.

The function of the local stack, the trail and the argument registers is same as their function in the WAM except that choice points carry extra information. Every choice point carries extra locations to store the *theory register*, and the mode of the system when the choice point is created. Choice points and environments which are created when the system in the proof mode also carry extra information about proofs. The implementation of proofs is explained in Section 22.4.

The AMPE doesn't have a separate code area to store code as the WAM does. The code area and the heap in the AMPE are integrated as a single data area to handle compiled procedures as data objects of MetaProlog. Theory descriptors and compiled procedures can be created on fly, and they can be discarded after the need for them is gone. So, the heap also holds compiled procedures and theory descriptors in addition to structures and lists. Compiled procedures and theory descriptors are represented by *boxes* which are explained in Section 22.3.4.

Since the builtins **addto** and **dropfrom** are backtrackable, the space held by the code created by these builtins should be reclaimed during their failure. For example, the command **addto(T1,[p(1),p(2)],T2)** creates theory T2 by adding two clauses, namely p(1) and p(2), to theory T1. So, it creates a new theory descriptor for T2, two compiled clauses, and an indexing block for the procedure p/1 on the heap. If backtracking occurs, theory T2 will be discarded, and all the space used will be reclaimed if the space is not protected by another data structure in the heap. If the space is protected, it can be collected during garbage collection [6]. In other words, all unused space (held by theory descriptors, compiled procedures or other data structures) in the heap can be reclaimed during backtracking or garbage collection.

22.3.3   Procedural Instructions

A MetaProlog program is directly compiled into the instructions of the AMPE. The instruction set of the AMPE is the same as the instruction set of the WAM except that the functions of the procedural instructions differ from their functions in the WAM. Since each procedure in the WAM can be uniquely determined by its name and its arity, its address can be directly found when a *call* or an *execute* is executed. On the other hand, when a *call* or an *execute* instruction is executed in the AMPE, the procedure is searched for in the current theory which lives in the *theory register*. If the procedure is not found in the current theory, it is searched for in the default theory of the current theory which is one of ancestors of the current theory. This search continues recursively through default theories until the procedure is found or backtracking occurs if it cannot be found.

Although only the functions of the procedural instructions are different from their functions in the WAM when the system runs in the simple mode, the functions of some other instructions are also different from their functions in the WAM when the system runs in the proof mode. In fact, the functions of the procedural instructions in the proof mode also differ their functions in the simple mode. The functions of those instructions in the proof mode are presented in Section 22.4.

22.3.4   Data Types

Data types in the AMPE are similar to Warren's data types in the WAM [9] except that we have one extra data structure to hold untagged data such as compiled clauses or theory descriptors. Untagged data in the AMPE are sealed between two tagged words called a *box*.

Each object in the AMPE is represented by one or more 32-bit words. The low two, four or eight bits of a word can be used as a tag. Two-bit tags are used to represent pointer data types such as references, structure (or box) addresses, and list addresses. An unbound variable is represented by a reference to itself. Four-bit tags are used to represent non-pointer one-word objects such as integers and functors. Eight-bit tags are used to represent objects consisting of more than one word; these are *boxes*. The low four bits of an eight-bit tag indicates that the object is a box, and the next four bits of the tag indicates the type of that box.

Boxes are used to represent objects consisting of more than one word such as compiled clauses and theory descriptors in the system. A *box* consists of consecutive words of memory such that the first and last words are box headers. Words between these box headers are untagged, and their formats depend on the type of the box in question. Although the interior part of a box normally holds untagged words, it can also hold tagged words. Those tagged words should be located at word boundaries, and their positions in the box should be determined by the type of the box. A *box header* is a word in the following format:

size of box	box size	box tag

The box tag shows that the word is a box header, and box type shows the type of that box. The rest of the box header holds the size of that box in words. The format of the interior part of a box depends on the type of the box. But all untagged words of a box will lie between two box headers which are tagged words. For example, a box which represents a compiled clause is as follows:

size of compiled clause	compiled clause	box tag
WAM Instructions for the clause		
size of compiled clause	compiled clause	box tag

The box headers at the beginning and at the end of the box above show that it is a box for a compiled clause. The untagged part of that box contains WAM instructions for the clause, including indexing instructions such as *try_me_else*, *retry_me_else*, or *trust_me_else* as first instruction of the clause.

Similarly, theory descriptors, index blocks, try-retry-trust blocks, and floating point numbers are represented by boxes. Of course, the formats of their untagged portions are different from each other.

A theory descriptor contains a theory-id which uniquely identifies that theory, and a pointer to a default theory which is one of ancestors of that theory. We search for a procedure in the default theory if we cannot find the procedure in the original theory.

A try-retry-trust block is a box whose untagged portion consists of a sequence of *try*, *retry*, and *trust* instructions. The untagged portion of an index block contains a *switch_on_term* instruction together with sequences of *try*, *retry*, and *trust* instructions.

The box header at the beginning of a box is used to determine the type of the box. The box header at the end of a box may appear unnecessary to the reader, but it plays an important role during garbage collection [6]. It helps to identify the box when the heap is searched from top to bottom during garbage collection.

22.4   Proofs

Theories discussed in Section 22.2 are one of the first class objects in MetaProlog. In this section, I will explain proofs, the other meta-level object in MetaProlog, and their implementation. In MetaProlog, goals can not only be proved with respect to different theories, but their proofs can also be collected for future use. After the command *demo(Theory, Goal, Proof)* is executed, the variable *Proof* is bound to the proof of *Goal* in *Theory*.

Proofs are one of meta-level objects which have many applications in Artificial Intelligence. For example, they can be used to produce explanations in an expert system. Let *carexpert* be an expert program written in MetaProlog which can find out troubles in a given car. To find the problem in a given car, the following goal is submitted.

demo(carexpert, find_trouble(Car, Problem))

The variable *Car* is an input theory which contains information about a specific car, or asks questions to the user to get information about that car. The procedure *find_trouble* of the theory *carexpert*, finds the problem in the given car and returns *Problem* as an output. The two argument demo predicate above can find the trouble in the car, but it cannot explain how it finds the trouble. For this purpose, there is a three argument *demo* in MetaProlog. To get the proof about how *carexpert* finds the trouble, the following goal should be submitted:

demo(carexpert, find_trouble(Car, Problem), Proof)

After the execution of the goal above, the variable *Proof* will be bound to the proof of the predicate *find_trouble* in the theory *carexpert*. Later, the explanation can be given for how *carexpert* finds the trouble in the given car by examining *Proof*. We get this proof without updating the expert program *carexpert*.

In the example above, *Proof* is a variable which is bound to the proof of the predicate *find_trouble* after the execution of the three argument *demo*. But *Proof* can be also partially instantiated to a proof before the goal is submitted. For example, assume that the procedure *find_trouble* can find out any kind of trouble in a given car. But we only want to find out troubles about its cooling system. To do this, we can instantiate *Proof* to a partial proof which forces the system to only look for troubles in the cooling system. In this case, we still don't change anything in the expert program *carexpert*, but we forced the system to look for certain kind of problems by giving a partial proof.

22.4.1 Structure of Proofs

The proof of a goal G in MetaProlog is a list whose head is an instance of G, and whose tail is a list of proofs of subgoals. For example, let the theory *carexpert* contains the following clauses:

```
repair_suggestion(Suggestion) :-
    find_trouble(Problem),
    repair_suggestion(Problem, Suggestion).

repair_suggestion(water_leak(Source), change(Source)).

find_trouble(Problem) :-
    is_leaking(water),
    check_cooling_system(Problem).

find_trouble(Problem) :-
    is_leaking(oil),
    check_oil_system(Problem).

check_cooling_system(water_leak(Source)) :-
    water_leaking_from(Source).

is_leaking(water).

water_leaking_from(radiator_hose).
```

After the execution of *demo(carexpert, repair_suggestion(Suggestion), Proof)*, the variable *Proof* is bound to the following term:

[repair_suggestion(change(radiator_hose)),
  [find_trouble(water_leak(radiator_hose)),
    [is_leaking(water)],
    [check_cooling_system(water_leak(radiator_hose)),
      [water_leaking_from(radiator_hose)]]]
  [repair_suggestion(water_leak(radiator_hose),
                                    change(radiator_hose)]]

The head of the proof list above is an instance of our original goal *repair_suggestion(Suggestion)*, and its tail is a list which contains proofs of subgoals *find_trouble(Problem)* and *repair_suggestion(Problem,Suggestion)*.

We can also submit the goal above with a partial proof as follows :

demo(carexpert,repair_suggestion(Suggestion),
  [repair_suggestion(Suggestion),
    [find_trouble(Problem),
      SubProof, [check_oil_system(Problem) | SubSubProof]],
    RestofProof]]).

In this case, the third argument of the goal is a partial proof which forces the system to only look for the trouble in the oil system. After the execution of that goal, the partial proof is completed by the system.

22.4.2   Implementation of Proofs

The AMPE discussed in Section 22.3 represents only one mode of the actual Abstract MetaProlog Engine. It is the basic core of the system which is used when a two argument demo is submitted as a goal. The actual AMPE (I will call the AMPE after this point) runs in two different modes. When a two argument demo is submitted as a goal, the simple mode of the AMPE discussed in Section 22.3 is used. In the simple mode, the system proves the given goal with respect to the given theory. When a three argument demo is submitted as a goal, the system switches from the simple mode to the proof mode. In the proof mode, the system not only proves the given goal with respect to the given theory, it also collects its proof at the same time.

The system uses a global flag to determine in which mode it is running. This global flag is set to the proof mode when a three argument demo is encountered, and to the simple mode when a two argument demo is encountered. This global flag is saved in choice points; so that the system can switch from one mode to the another during backtracking. The general overhead of these two modes in the system is that the mode flag should be saved in choice points in both modes. The failure routine also should be able to switch from one mode to the another from the saved mode flag in the last choice point during backtracking.

Two new registers which are only used in the proof mode are used to collect proofs. The first one, *proof register*, points at the part of the proof being collected by the system. The second one, the *proof continuation register*, points at the part of the proof which will be collected by the system after the part of the proof pointed by the *proof register* is collected. In fact, there is a very close analogy between *proof register* and *program counter* (register P in WAM), and between *proof continuation register* and *program continuation register* (register CP in WAM).

These two new registers are saved in choice points when the system is in the proof mode. In other words, choice points created in the proof mode differ from choice points created in the simple mode. The type of a choice point can be determined by the saved mode flag in each choice point.

When a *call* for a procedure p/n is executed, the content of the *proof register* is unified with a list whose head is the proof list of this procedure. A pointer to the tail of this list, a part of the proof of the procedure calling the procedure p/n, is put into the *proof continuation register*. The head of the proof list is the term $p(A_1, ..., A_n)$; i.e. i^{th} argument of the term is unified with i^{th} argument register. The tail of this proof list is an unbound variable which will be bound the proof of this procedure. Finally, a pointer to the tail of this proof list is put into the *proof register*; so that, it can be bound to the proof of this procedure.

On the other hand, when an *execute* for the procedure p/n is executed, the content of the *proof register* is unified with a singleton list whose only element is the proof list of the procedure. The tail of the proof list is moved into the *proof register*. The *execute* doesn't update the *proof continuation* register.

When a *proceed* instruction is executed, the content of the *proof register* is unified with the empty list, and the content of the *proof continuation register* is moved into the *proof register*.

The *proof continuation register* is saved in environments by *allocate* instructions, and restored by *deallocate* instructions in the proof mode. The environment created in the proof mode is marked by a bit to show that it is created in the proof mode. Although there is a mark bit in environments, this doesn't lead any overhead in the simple mode. That bit is only used in the proof mode or during the garbage collection [6].

22.5   Conclusion

The MetaProlog system presented in this paper, according to our knowledge, is the first compiler-based meta-level system. We believe that this system can be used as a programming tool for many artificial applications where meta-level knowledge is necessary. For example, the explicit proof representation of MetaProlog can be very useful in explanation facilities of expert systems. Moreover, the inheritance mechanism in MetaProlog theories can find many applications in the frame problem in artificial intelligence [4].

The core part of the MetaProlog system provides explicit representations of theories and goals, and the explicit representation of the provability relation between them. The provability relation between a theory and a goal is represented by the two argument predicate *demo*. When a two argument *demo* predicate is submitted as a goal, the underlying theorem prover proves the given goal with respect to the given theory. In this case, we don't have much control on the execution of this goal. The extra control in the MetaProlog system is provided by extended provability relations. For example, in the current version of the system, a partial proof in a three argument *demo* can force the system to make certain selections among possible proofs of the given goal. In the future, more extended versions of the *demo* predicate will be implemented to provide extra control on the execution of a goal such as the depth of the proof.

Acknowledgements

This work is supported in part by US Air Force contract F30602-81-C-0169 and by US Air Force grant AFOSR-82-0292. The author is very grateful to Kenneth A. Bowen for his role in guiding this research and the following people for numerous valuable conversations on the topics of this paper: Hamid Bacha, Kevin Buettner, Keith Hughes, Andrew Turk, and Chris White.

References

[1] Bacha, H., *Meta-level Programming: A Compiled Approach*, Proc. of 4th Int. Conf. on Logic Programming, Melbourne, 1986.

[2] Bowen, K.A., and Kowalski, R.A., *Amalgamating Language and Metalanguage in Logic Programming*, in Logic Programming, ed. K. Clark, and S.-A Tarnlund, 1982.

[3] Bowen, K.A., and Weingber, T., *A Meta-level Extension of Prolog*, Proc. of 1985 Int. Symp. on Logic Programming, Boston, 1985.

[4] Bowen, K.A., *Meta-level Programming and Knowledge Representation*, New Generation Computing, Vol 3, 1985.

[5] Bowen, K.A., Buettner, K.A., Cicekli, I., and Turk, A., *A Fast Incremental Portable Prolog Compiler*, Proc. of 3rd Int. Conf. on Logic Programming, London, 1986.

[6] Cicekli, I., *A Garbage Collector For The MetaProlog System (or: Collecting All The Garbage In Prolog Systems)*, Logic Programming Research Group Technical Report LPRG-TR-88-2, Syracuse, 1988.

[7] des Reveiere, J., *Meta-Level Facilities in Logic-Based Computational Systems*, The Workshop on Meta-Level Architectures and Reflection, Alghro-Sardinia, Italy, 1986.

[8] Safra, S., and Shapiro., E., *Meta Interpreters for Real*, Technical Report from The Wiezmann Institute in Isreal, 1986.

[9] Warren, D.H.D., *An Abstract Prolog Instruction Set*, SRI Technical Report 309, 1983.

[10] Weyhrauch, R.W., *Prolegomena to A Theory of Mechanized Formal Reasoning*, Artificial Intelligence, Vol 13, 1980.

Chapter 23

Qu-Prolog: an Extended Prolog for Meta Level Programming

J. Staples   P.J. Robinson   R.A. Paterson
R.A. Hagen   A.J. Craddock   P.C. Wallis

*Department of Computer Science, University of Queensland
St. Lucia, Queensland 4067, Australia.*

Abstract

This paper describes the design and implementation of a language, Qu-Prolog, which extends Prolog to support computation on object level languages which include object level variables and object level quantifier (binder) notations. A particular motivation is to provide a convenient, high-level implementation language for interactive verification systems.

The main features of Qu-Prolog syntax and semantics are introduced, its use is demonstrated by a simple implementation of a lambda calculus interpreter and a summary is given of the conceptual basis of the Qu-Prolog unification algorithm. This unification algorithm finds a meta level substitution to unify two schemes of object level terms, in the following sense. Two object level terms are unified if they are equivalent up to changes of bound variables (alpha equivalent).

23.1   Introduction

In this paper meta level programming means programming in which object level languages and theories are prominent data types.

Few programming languages have strong support for meta level programming. A key area in which deficiencies occur is support for quantifier (binder) notations, and notations for object level substitutions. An example is metaProlog, developed by Bowen and others (a recent paper is [1]). Numerous functional languages, and some logic programming languages (a recent example is λProlog [3]) support the use of quantifier notations in programming. Typically such languages have roots in the lambda calculus, and we shall refer to such languages as lambda languages. The use of quantifier notations in lambda language programming is conceptually quite different from meta level programming, whose algorithms operate on quantifier notations as data. The meta level approach has more flexibility, since it can both perform genuinely meta level transformations, and can also emulate the lambda language approach when required. As a simple example of both capabilities, we shall give a trivial Qu-Prolog program which implements a lambda calculus interpreter.

It is possible to merge the concepts of lambda language and meta level programming language by supporting quantifier notations both at the meta level and at the object level. It is however interesting and instructive that free variable logic programming notations can support a nontrivial meta level language. We argue that in this paper. A preliminary account of Qu-Prolog which appeared in [6] is superseded by this paper.

To introduce our approach we review ordinary pure Prolog from the viewpoint of open world logic programming. Our interest in open world logic programming is partly because of its practical importance for open world data bases of all sorts, and more specifically because the closed world approach is not compatible either with the applications we have in mind (to powerful object level languages such as set theory) or with the incomplete inference algorithms we use. This review is not intended to be a comprehensive account of open world logic programming.

23.1.1   An open world semantics for pure Prolog

A pure Prolog program defines a theory whose **terms** and **atomic formulas** are defined relative to the vocabulary of the program, as usual. The **axioms** of the theory are the program facts, together with an equation $X = X$. Inference in the theory is defined by the following recursive definition of its **theorems**.

(i) All instances of axioms are theorems.

(ii) For all $k \geq 0$, all theorems $T_1, \ldots, T_k$ and all rule instances

$$T \text{ :- } T_1, \ldots, T_k,$$

T is a theorem.

A **query** in this theory is an atomic formula. An **answer** to a query Q is a substitution σ such that σQ is a theorem. Given an interpreter I, that is an algorithm which attempts to find answers to queries, a **computed answer** (relative to I) is an answer found by I.

Note that in this open world view, the only assumptions made about the intended interpretations of a pure Prolog program are the assumptions stated in the program itself. In particular, no assumption is made that the theory refers to Herbrand objects.

Our open world approach makes it natural to consider reasoning about objects whose structure is richer than that of Herbrand objects. Here we consider object languages whose syntactic structure is as rich as that of the terms and formulas of full first order predicate calculus, with quantifiers.

23.1.2 Object level terms

Object level terms are defined recursively as follows, given a finite set of quantifiers and a finite set of function symbols, where each function symbol may have a finite number of arities. Each arity is a nonnegative number defining a legal length for an argument list. An infinite set of object variables is also assumed given.

(i) Each object function symbol of arity 0 is an object term.

(ii) Each object variable is an object term.

(iii) For each $k \geq 0$, each function symbol f of arity k, and each k-tuple $t_1, \ldots, t_k$ of object terms, $f(t_1, \ldots, t_k)$ is an object term.

(iv) For each quantifier q, each object variable x, and each object term t, $q \, x \, t$ is an object term.

A language based on such terms can be more expressive than Herbrand objects. Such languages are perhaps the simplest object level vocabularies which allow substantial exploration of practical meta level programming.

It is acknowledged that various extensions of this object level vocabulary are of great practical importance. A prime example is support for type structure in the object level language. Another is support for more general quantifier notations. Both these extensions will be supported in later versions.

23.2 Qu-Prolog syntax

It should be clearly understood that Qu-Prolog syntax does not include *any* object level syntax. Some Qu-Prolog constants are intended to *name* specific items in the object language, but the constants themselves are at the meta level. This explains why Qu-Prolog syntax is not spattered with quotation marks.

To organise our description we classify Qu-Prolog terms into various meta level **types**. These types are used only in our description. They are not part of the formal syntax of the current version of Qu-Prolog, which follows Prolog in requiring a minimum of declaration and typing.

Each Qu-Prolog term has one of the types: object-function-symbol; object-quantifier; object-var; substitution-item; substitution; object-term; system.

To give a brief overview of Qu-Prolog syntax we give the following context-free grammar for pure Qu-Prolog, in which nonterminals are in italics, terminals are quoted, and some low-level nonterminals, discussed informally later, are left undefined.

$$
\begin{array}{ll}
program & ::= (clause)^* \\
clause & ::= fact \mid rule \\
fact & ::= head \\
rule & ::= head \text{ `:-' } body \\
head & ::= atomic - formula \\
body & ::= subgoal \text{ (`,' } subgoal)^* \\
subgoal & ::= atomic - formula \\
atomic - formula & ::= proc - name \mid proc - name \text{ `(' } arg - terms \text{ `)'} \\
arg - terms & ::= arg - term \text{ (`,' } arg - term)^* \\
arg - term & ::= object - term \\
& \mid object - var \\
& \mid object - function - symbol \\
& \mid object - quantifier \\
& \mid system - term \\
object - term & ::= object - constant \\
& \mid object - var \\
& \mid object - term - variable \\
& \mid object - function - symbol \text{ `(' } object - terms \text{ `)'} \\
& \mid object - quantifier\ object - var\ object - term \\
& \mid substitution\ object - term \\
object - terms & ::= object - term \text{ (`,' } object - term)^* \\
substitution & ::= \text{ `<<' } substitution - items \text{ `>>'} \\
substitution - items & ::= substitution - item \text{ (`,' } substitution - item)^* \\
substitution - item & ::= object - term \text{ `/' } object - var
\end{array}
$$

The syntactic structure of each type of term is as follows.

23.2.1   Object-function-symbols

In the current version of Qu-Prolog, each object-function-symbol term is a Qu-Prolog constant. In other words, it is a meta level function symbol of arity zero. It is however intended to name an object level function symbol, which may have a finite set of arities. Accordingly each object-function-symbol has associated with it a finite set of numbers which are intended to represent the arities of the object it names. We may refer to these numbers as **object arities**. An object function symbol which has 0 as one of its object arities may be called an object constant.

Lexically different object-function-symbol constants are assumed to denote distinct symbols of the object level theory.

The current version of Qu-Prolog has no variables of object-function-symbol type. The choice of object-function-symbol constants is user programmable. They have the same lexical structure as Prolog atoms. They are declared implicitly by their appearance in Qu-Prolog programs. The object arities of an object-function-symbol constant f are implicitly declared by the uses which are made of f in the Qu-Prolog program.

23.2.2   Object-vars

In the current version of Qu-Prolog, each object-var term is a Qu-Prolog variable. We may loosely refer to an object-var variable as an object variable. This abuse turns out to be very convenient, but it should be clearly understood that object-var variables are meta level variables. This version of Qu-Prolog does not name any specific variables in the object theory.

Each object-var variable is intended to range over object level variables. For technical reasons we divide object level variables into two classes, each infinite. The variables in one of these classes are called **local**. Likewise, object-var variables are classified as either local or not, and are intended to range over the corresponding class of object level variables. Intuitively, local object-var variables are used only for Qu-Prolog's internal calculations, and are excluded from instantiations of answer variables.

A key reason for using object-var variables rather than object-var constants is to achieve separation of occurrences of object-var variables in distinct copies of Qu-Prolog clauses. It also emphasises that lexically distinct object-var variables may denote the same variable in the object theory, and allows the Prolog instantiation mechanism to record that. There are also occasions when we wish to record that lexically distinct object-var variables denote distinct variables of the object theory. The conceptual basis for that is described later.

Object-var variable names are user programmable. They have the same lexical structure as Prolog atoms. As in Prolog, execution creates variant names, by subscripting. An object-var variable x may be declared explicitly, by executing

```
?- object_var(x).
```

as the first reference to the identifier x. Alternatively, if the first appearance of x in a Qu-Prolog program is in a position of object-var type, that serves as an implicit declaration of x as an object-var variable.

23.2.3   Object-quantifiers

In the current version of Qu-Prolog, each object-quantifier term is a Qu-Prolog constant. It may be loosely referred to as an object quantifier, but that is an abuse. Each object-quantifier constant is a meta level constant, intended to refer to a quantifier of the object language. We use the traditional prefix notation for quantified object level terms; that is, $q\ x\ t$, where q is an object quantifier, x is an object variable and t is an object term. Each object-quantifier constant q has an associated Prolog-style precedence which is used, when parsing $q\ x\ t$, as the precedence of t.

The names used for object-quantifier constants are user programmable. They have the same lexical structure as Prolog atoms. Lexically distinct object-quantifiers are assumed to denote distinct object quantifiers. Each object-quantifier constant q used in a Qu-Prolog program must be declared explicitly, by executing

$$?- \text{op}(precedence, \text{quant}, q).$$

as the first reference to the identifier q.

23.2.4 Substitution-items

In the current version of Qu-Prolog, the only terms of substitution-item type are those constructed by the use of a two-place function symbol whose result type is substitution-item. The infix notation / is used for this function symbol. The first place of this function symbol has type object-term, and the second place has type object-var. In view of the restricted opportunities for using terms of this sort, a precedence of this infix operator notation is not needed and is left undefined.

   To avoid any confusion with integer division, Qu-Prolog uses the name div for integer division.

23.2.5 Substitutions

In the current version of Qu-Prolog the only substitution terms are nonempty lists of substitution-items, in which the object-var variables of the several substitution items are lexically distinct. We shall also require that they denote distinct object level variables, as discussed later.

   For visual emphasis, Qu-Prolog uses a non-standard list notation for substitutions, of the form

$$<\!<t_1/x_1, \ldots, t_n/x_n>\!>$$

Each such substitution term is intended to denote the operation of parallel substitution of t_i for x_i, $i = 1, \ldots, n$. Here we mean correct parallel substitution, in which bound variables within the term being operated on are changed to avoid capture of variables.

23.2.6 Object-terms

The only constants in the object-term type are those object-function-symbol constants which have zero amongst their object arities. Object-var terms are also terms of object-term type. Further, there is a separate class of object-term variables, which are intended to range over arbitrary terms of the object language. Object-term terms can also be constructed using function symbols which have object-term result type, as indicated below.

Names for object-term variables are user programmable and, as in Prolog, execution can create variant names by subscripting. The lexical structure of object-term variables is the same as for Prolog variables. In the current version of Qu-Prolog, object-term variables are declared implicitly by their appearance in the program.

In the current version of Qu-Prolog, function symbols of positive arity and object-term result type are *not* user programmable. That facility would be useful — for example it would support natural programming of algorithms involving weakest precondition notations. It will be supported by future versions of Qu-Prolog. At present only the following, system-defined function symbols are supported.

Apply.

This function symbol has arity two. Its first argument has type object-function-symbol, and its second is a list of object-terms. When the first argument is f and the second is $t_1, \ldots, t_k$, the Qu-Prolog syntax for the result is $f(t_1, \ldots, t_k)$.

Substitute.

This function symbol has arity two. Its first argument is a substitution and its second argument has type object-term. When the first argument is b and the second argument is t, the Qu-Prolog syntax for the result is $b\ t$.

Quantify.

This function symbol has arity three. Its argument types are respectively object-quantifier, object-variable and object-term. When q, x and t are three such arguments, the Qu-Prolog syntax for the result is $q\ x\ t$.

It is required to exclude local variables from instantiations of object-term variables. This is implemented by a **local-occurs** check which is applied at the time of instantiation to the value of each object-term variable. This check is delayed as required for correctness.

23.2.7 System terms

Terms of the Qu-Prolog system type are those terms which do not refer to the vocabulary of an object theory, but which are concerned with other aspects of the Qu-Prolog universe of discourse. Examples are notations for integers and integer operations, which are not necessarily part of the object language, but which serve a useful purpose in algorithms which transform the object language.

System terms do not include quantifier or substitution notations. The syntax of system terms is the same as for ordinary Prolog terms. In the current implementation of Qu-Prolog, terms of system type are confused with object-term terms. That defect will be removed in future versions.

23.2.8   Qu-Prolog atomic formulas, clauses, predicates, programs, queries and answers

These constructs are defined in the same way as for ordinary pure Prolog. In particular, except where modified by operator declarations, Qu-Prolog atomic formulas have the form

$$p(t_1,\ldots,t_n)$$

where p is a predicate name as in Prolog and $t_1,\ldots,t_n$ are terms. The current version of Qu-Prolog does not declare types for the arguments of predicates. Neither does it support using substitution items, or substitutions, as arguments to predicates.

Primitive predicates play a key role in any version of Prolog. We review here two Qu-Prolog primitive predicates, which are used in the following example.

Equality

In Qu-Prolog the equality symbol '=' is overloaded so that it refers to equalities of all types which can be arguments to procedures. We consider the implementation of equality of object-term terms.

Correct implementation of equality in ordinary Prolog requires an occurs check in the unification algorithm. References to Prolog unification below assume this occurs check is done.

As in Prolog, Qu-Prolog equality is implemented by a unification algorithm, but this algorithm differs from Prolog unification in three major ways, as follows. These differences implement the intuition that the interpretation of equality of object-term terms is equivalence of object level terms, up to changes of bound variable. This equivalence is often called alpha equivalence.

First, since substitution notations do not appear in the object language, Qu-Prolog unification evaluates substitution notations.

The second variation from elementary unification is that unification subproblems which cannot be solved without introducing incompleteness or branching are delayed, perhaps beyond the end of the current unification call, in the hope that other instantiations may make the delayed subproblem easier to solve. Examples of situations where that may occur are subgoals of the form $b\,A = t$ and $b\,x = t$, where b is a substitution, A is an object-term variable, x is an object-var variable and t is an object-term. The technique of delaying unification subproblems was used by Huet [2] in the context of resolution theorem proving, and is formalised for lambda unification in [5]. Delays are discussed further below.

The third variation from ordinary Prolog unification arises in the unification of object-term terms

$$q\,x_1\,t_1 \text{ and } q\,x_2\,t_2.$$

To capture the requirement that equality should permit changes of bound variable, such a unification problem is regarded as equivalent to, and is simplified to, the unification of

$$\ll \nu/x_1 \gg t_1 \text{ and } \ll \nu/x_2 \gg t_2$$

where ν is a 'new' object-var variable.

This sort of transformation of the unification problem has no counterpart in elementary unification, and neither does the newness requirement. Strictly, the newness requirement is imposed at the object level. The meta level calculations of Qu-Prolog must manage this object level requirement correctly.

In particular it is not enough simply to create a new object-var variable ν, since then the object level requirement could be frustrated, in either of the following two ways. First, unifying ν with some existing object-var variable would frustrate the newness requirement. Second, object-var variables can generally occur free in answer substitutions. That is not appropriate for such a ν, since it does not occur free or bound in any query or clause copy. Intuitively, ν is created after the time at which the possible answers to queries are defined. These new variables are the local variables introduced previously.

The predicate ob_var

We have already described a predicate `object_var` for explicitly declaring object-var variables. The predicate `ob_var(1)` is used to test whether a given object-term term has been explicitly or implicitly declared to be an object-var variable. Execution of this predicate delays if the object-term term is an object-term variable or substituted object-term variable, until that variable is instantiated.

23.3   Example: a lambda calculus interpreter

We first indicate the class of terms being interpreted, by defining a predicate which recognises them.

Since the traditional notation $(t\ u)$ for lambda application is not available in Prolog, we exploit Qu-Prolog list notation and write $[t,\ u]$ instead. We declare a quantifier name `lambda`.

```
op(600, quant, lambda).
object_var x.

lambda_term(x).
lambda_term([T, U]) :-
lambda_term(T),
lambda_term(U).
lambda_term(lambda x T) :- lambda_term(T).
```

Note the close correspondence of this formal definition with the ordinary informal definitions of lambda terms.

To define a lambda interpreter, we implement leftmost-outermost lambda reduction by the following procedure =>*.

```
A =>* C :- A => B, B =>* C.
A =>* A.
```

where the single step relation => is:

```
[lambda x T, U] => <<U/x>> T.
lambda x T => lambda x U :- T => U.
[T, U] => [V, U] :- T => V.
[T, U] => [T, V] :- U => V.
```

Note again the close correspondence between these Qu-Prolog clauses and the clauses of the traditional informal definition.

It is instructive to extend this example by adding the lambda calculus 'eta' rule: when a lambda term t has no free occurrence of the variable x, then $\lambda x\,(t\,x)$ can be contracted to t. To capture this rule we need a way of saying in Qu-Prolog that an object variable x does not occur free in a term t. We do that by saying

$$<<y/x>>t = t,$$

where y is an object variable distinct from x. For the sake of readability we introduce a binary infix procedure name not_free_in as follows.

```
object_var(y).
op(600, xfx, not_free_in).
x not_free_in A :- <<y/x >>A = A.
```

As explained below, this predicate definition automatically ensures that x and y denote distinct object variables.

Now we extend the definition of => by appending the clause

```
lambda x [A, x] => A :- x not_free_in A.
```

Here are some examples of how Qu-Prolog executes queries on the procedure =>.

(a) `[lambda y y, z] => Result.`

Unification of this goal with the first clause of => recognises that the binding of y in the goal corresponds to a binding of x in the clause, and so instantiates T to x. Then U instantiates to z, and finally Result to z. The query then succeeds, reporting the instantiation of Result.

(b) `Term => y.`

First `Term` is instantiated to `[lambda x T, U]`. Then an attempt is made to unify `<<U/x>>T` with `y`.

The attempted unification delays, in the hope that the problem will simplify by instantiation of `Result`, in later processing of the query. No such instantiation occurs, so the delayed problem remains at the end of query processing. According to a preset user option, query processing then either aborts the query, fails the query or reports the delayed subproblems together with the computed answer. In the latter cases the query will succeed on backtracking at the eta rule, by instantiating `Term` to `lambda x [y, x]`.

(c) `?- lambda w [lambda y lambda z y, w] => lambda u lambda z u.`

Unification with the head of (a copy of) the second clause of `=>` succeeds, by instantiating `T` to `[lambda y lambda z y, x]`, then `U` to `lambda z x`. The remaining subgoal is then

`[lambda y lambda z y, x] => lambda z x.`

That unifies with the head of (a copy of) the first clause. Say the copy is

`[lambda x1 T1, U1] => [U1/x1] T1.`

The unification instantiates `T1` to `lambda z x1`, then `U1` to `x`, and succeeds.

23.4 Apartness of object-var variables

Symbolic computation with quantified terms often depends on knowing whether two object variables are lexically distinct or not. Qu-Prolog must manage this information correctly from its meta level. To explain how that it done, it will be useful to review the delaying of subgoals in Prolog execution.

As mentioned above, the Qu-Prolog interpreter creates delayed subgoals, including delayed unification subproblems. Delayed subproblems are found in several Prolog implementations, and are often considered as modifying the order in which subgoals are solved. Delayed subproblems can however be considered as constraints in their own right, in the same way as the body of a Prolog rule constrains the assumption that the head of the rule is true. Delayed subgoals which remain at the end of query processing can be reported, as constraints on the answer.

In Prolog execution delayed subgoals are generally exceptional occurrences, and it is generally considered unfortunate if any remain at the end of query processing. In Qu-Prolog however, there are some special classes of subgoal whose normal condition is to be delayed; for example, subgoals of the form $x \neq y$, where

x and y are object-vars. We call them **apartness** subgoals. When $x \neq y$ is present as an apartness subgoal we say that x and y are **apart**.

Apartness subgoals are very common; so common that Qu-Prolog uses a special convention to avoid stating them all explicitly. This convention is that whenever two lexically distinct object-vars x and y appear in the same clause copy or query, it is implied that x and y are apart. The same convention applies to answers returned by Qu-Prolog. In particular, this means that the object-vars which appear as substituted variables in a parallel substitution, which must be lexically distinct on syntactic grounds, consequently must also represent distinct object variables.

In Prolog implementations of delayed subgoals, a delayed subgoal generally has no influence on query processing until it is awoken, by a relevant variable instantiation. That is not appropriate for the management of apartness subgoals, since they encode information which is needed for substitution evaluation. For example, evaluation of $<<a/x>>y$ should be to y in the case when x and y are apart.

Evaluation of $<<a/x>>y$ cannot proceed until the question $x = y$ is resolved. In this situation Qu-Prolog delays the subgoal in which this problem arises, until $x = y$ is resolved. It may be resolved either by unification of x and y, or by encountering the apartness subgoal $x \neq y$.

Because of the key role played by apartness subgoals in substitution evaluation, and therefore in Qu-Prolog unification and query processing, apartness subgoals are managed in a special way which gives access to the information they encode. An apartness relation is implemented. It is true of object-vars x and y whenever x and y are recorded as apart. That is the only storage of apartness subgoals, which are never woken in the usual sense.

Local variables are apart from all other object-var variables, including other local variables.

23.5 Overview of Qu-Prolog unification

We shall indicate the unification of Qu-Prolog object-terms within a general framework. This framework is a development of the approach of [5]. It is described in more detail in [4].

23.5.1 A general unification framework

We assume a set of objects **O**, and a set of terms **T**, including a set of variables **V**. **T** and **O** will have some structure which serves to define restricted classes of functions **T** → **T** and **T** → **O**, called **homomorphisms**. **T** will also be a free construction over the variables **V**, in the sense that every homomorphism **T** → **T** or **T** → **O**, is uniquely determined by the values it takes on **V**. A homomorphism **T** → **O** is called a **valuation**.

A **substitution** is a homomorphism $\mathbf{T} \rightarrow \mathbf{T}$ in which only finitely many variables are not mapped to themselves. A convenient representation of a substitution is a set of (term, variable) pairs, written $[t_1/X_1, \ldots, t_n/X_n]$. The identity substitution is denoted by id.

In the application to Qu-Prolog these substitutions will be meta level instantiations of object-term variables and object-var variables.

A **constraint item** has the form $P(t_1, \ldots, t_n)$, where P is an n-ary predicate. A **constraint** is a set of constraint items, written $c_1 \, \& \, \ldots \, \& \, c_n$. The empty constraint is written *succeed*. Valuations and substitutions extend to constraint items and constraints in the normal way.

A **problem** is a set of (substitution, constraint) pairs, written

$$(\sigma_1, C_1) \mid \ldots \mid (\sigma_n, C_n). \tag{23.1}$$

The empty problem is written **fail**. A singleton problem may be confused with its unique element.

Notation. The problem (id, C) may be abbreviated as C.

In a unification context, each element of a problem represents a branch in the solution of a unification problem. The substitution contains the instantiations made so far, while the constraint contains the sub-goals yet to be satisfied. The alternative elements of a problem define all possible branches of a general solution.

Each n-ary predicate symbol P is given meaning by a corresponding n-ary relation P_O at the object level. The set of **solutions** of a problem p is

$$\{ \, v \circ \sigma \mid v \text{ is a valuation}, (\sigma, C) \text{ is in } p \text{ and } vC \text{ is true} \, \}$$

For any problems p, p', we write $p \rightarrow p'$ to assert that every solution of p is a solution of p'. We write $p \leftrightarrow p'$ to assert that $p \rightarrow p'$ and $p' \rightarrow p$.

One of the predicates will be equality, with $=_O$ being identity. An immediate consequence is the following:

PROPOSITION **23.5.1.** *(Replacement Rule)*
    Let t and t' be terms, X a variable, and c a constraint item. If C is a constraint such that $C \rightarrow t = t'$, then $C \, \& \, [t/X]c \leftrightarrow C \, \& \, [t'/X]c$.

The composition operation is extended to problems as follows:

$$(\sigma, C) \circ (\sigma', C') = (\sigma \circ \sigma', C \, \& \, \sigma C')$$

$$(p_1 \mid p_2) \circ p_3 = (p_1 \circ p_3) \mid (p_2 \circ p_3)$$

$$p_1 \circ (p_2 \mid p_3) = (p_1 \circ p_2) \mid (p_1 \circ p_3)$$

The following property of composition will be useful:

THEOREM **23.5.2.** *For all problems p, p' and p'', if $p \rightarrow p'$ then $p \circ p'' \rightarrow p' \circ p''$.*

Proof: Each element of $p \circ p''$ has the form $(\sigma \circ \sigma'', C \, \& \, \sigma C'')$ for some (σ, C) in p and (σ'', C'') in p''. Thus each solution of $p \circ p''$ will have the form $v \circ \sigma \circ \sigma''$, for some valuation v and choice of (σ, C) and (σ'', C'') such that $v(C \, \& \, \sigma C'')$ is true. Then vC and $v \circ \sigma \, C''$ are true. Since $p \to p'$, there is a (σ', C') in p' and a valuation v' such that $v'C'$ is true and $v \circ \sigma = v' \circ \sigma'$. It follows that $v'(C' \, \& \, \sigma' C'')$ is true and $v \circ \sigma \circ \sigma'' = v' \circ \sigma' \circ \sigma''$. Thus $v \circ \sigma \circ \sigma''$ is a solution of $p' \circ p''$.

For a particular theory, one supplies theorems of the form $C \leftrightarrow p$, enabling a simple constraint C to be transformed into an equivalent problem p. Such theorems can also be deduced using the replacement rule. The following result allows these transformations to be applied in any context:

COROLLARY 23.5.3.   *If a constraint C and a problem p satisfy $C \leftrightarrow p$, then for all problems p' and p'', $(C \circ p') \mid p'' \leftrightarrow (p \circ p') \mid p''$.*

A non-deterministic unification algorithm is defined by selecting theorems of the forms $C \to t = t'$ and $C \leftrightarrow p$. Theorems of the first kind define replacements, which are intended to simplify terms, while theorems of the second kind define transformations of problems. Unification proceeds by identifying constraints in context, to which these transformations can be applied. The non-determinism arises because the order in which constraints are solved is not prescribed.

23.5.2   Unification of Qu-Prolog object-terms

Here we apply the unification mechanism of the previous sub-section to Qu-Prolog meta level notations for object level terms. From here on, the substitutions mentioned in the previous sub-section will be referred to as instantiations, to avoid any confusion with Qu-Prolog's notations for object level substitution.

Recall that there are two classes of variable, object-term variables and object-var variables. While an object-term variable may be instantiated to any object-term, object-var variables can be instantiated only to other object-var variables. In what follows, b, b' denote object-level substitutions, while v, v' denote local variables.

Qu-Prolog object level terms have been defined earlier. More precisely, the objects we consider are the α-equivalence classes of object level terms, where α-equivalence is equivalence up to changes of bound variables. We may confuse equivalence classes with representative elements. Qu-Prolog valuations map non-local object-var variables to non-local object-level variables, local object-var variables to local object variables, and object-term variables to object level terms with no free occurrences of local variables.

The following types of constraint items occur:

(i) $t_1 = t_2$ — a delayed unification problem.

(ii) loc t — a delayed local occurs check on the term t.

(iii) $x \neq y$ — an apartness subgoal.

The predicate **loc** is interpreted by a relation **loc** $_O$, which is satisfied by terms with no free occurrences of local variables. The relation $\neq_O$ holds for all pairs of distinct object variables.

If X is a set of object-var variables, we write *separate*(X) for a constraint which includes $x \neq y$ for each distinct pair of object-var variables x and y in X.

When performing an occurs check for a variable A in a sub-term like $[A/x]C$ of a proposed instantiation for A, it may not be obvious whether, on subsequent instantiation of C, the sub-term will actually contain an instance of A. Similar problems occur when checking for occurrences of local variables; both can cause delays. We define two restricted notions of occurrence for use in the later work:

- A variable A **directly occurs** in a term t if

  (i) t is A, or

  (ii) t is $f(t_1, \ldots t_n)$ and A directly occurs in one of $t_1, \ldots t_n$, or

  (iii) t is $q\ x\ t'$ and A directly occurs in t', or

  (iv) t is $b\ t'$ and A directly occurs in t'.

- A variable A **statically occurs** in a term t if

  (i) t is A, or

  (ii) t is $f(t_1, \ldots t_n)$ and A statically occurs in one of $t_1, \ldots t_n$, or

  (iii) t is $q\ x\ t'$ and A statically occurs in t', or

  (iv) t is $<<t_1/x_1, \ldots, t_n/x_n>>\ t'$ and A statically occurs in t' or $t_1, \ldots t_n$.

In principle, each simplification step is an equivalence $p \leftrightarrow p'$, suggesting the replacement of the problem p by the problem p'. Here we state only simple equivalences, which generate other equivalences using the above Corollary. Each of the implications $C \to t = t'$ in the next two lemmas generates equivalences using the replacement rule.

LEMMA **23.5.4.** *(Substitutions)*

(i) **succeed** $\to b\ f(t_1, \ldots t_n) = f(b\ t_1, \ldots, b\ t_n)$

(ii) **succeed** $\to b\ q\ y\ t = q\ \nu\ b\ <<\nu/y>>t$

(iii) **succeed** $\to b\ A = A$, *if the domain of b consists only of local variables.*

(iv) *separate*$(\ x_1, \ldots, x_n\ ) \to <<t_1/x_1, \ldots, t_n/x_n>>x_i = t_i$

(v) *separate*$(\ x_1, \ldots, x_n, y\ ) \to <<t_1/x_1, \ldots, t_n/x_n>>y = y$

LEMMA **23.5.5**. *(Combining Substitutions)*
    Let b and b' be the following object-level substitutions:

$$b = <<u_1/x_1, \ldots, u_n/x_n>>$$

$$b' = <<t_1/y_1, \ldots, t_m/y_m>>$$

Then for all terms t,

$$C \to b\; b'\; t = b <<t_1/y_1, \ldots, b\; t_m/y_m, others>>\; t$$

where C is separate($\{x_1, \ldots, x_n\} \cup \{y_1, \ldots, y_m\}$), and *others* is the list of all the
pairs u_i/x_i for which x_i is not one of $y_1, \ldots, y_m$.

The remaining lemmas state simple equivalences.

LEMMA **23.5.6**. *(Failure Conditions)*
    The following constraint items have no solutions (i.e. are equivalent to fail):

  (i) $f(t_1, \ldots t_n) = g(t_1, \ldots, t_m)$, if f, g are distinct.

  (ii) $q\; x\; t = q'\; y\; t'$, if q, q' are distinct.

  (iii) $x = f(t_1, \ldots t_n)$

  (iv) $f(t_1, \ldots t_n) = q\; x\; t$

  (v) $q\; x\; t = y$

  (vi) $A = t$, if A directly occurs in t, and t is not $b_1 \ldots b_n\; A$.

  (vii) $x \neq x$

(viii) **loc** ν, if ν is a local variable.

LEMMA **23.5.7**. *(Success Conditions)*
    **The following constraint items have all instantiations as solutions (i.e. are
equivalent to succeed):**

  (i) **loc** t, if no local variable statically occurs in t.

  (ii) $x \neq \nu$, where x is a non-local variable and ν is a local variable.

  (iii) $\nu \neq \nu'$, where ν and ν' are distinct local variables.

LEMMA **23.5.8**. *(Branching)*
    succeed $\leftrightarrow x = y \mid x \neq y$

This branching step is used to permit substitutions to be simplified using the reductions defined above. The current version of Qu-Prolog uses this step only when one branch can be immediately reduced to **fail**.

LEMMA **23.5.9.** *(Simplifications)*

(i) $f(t_1, \ldots t_n) = f(t_1, \ldots, t_n) \leftrightarrow t_1 = t_1' \ \& \ \ldots \ \& \ t_n = t_n'$

(ii) $q \ x \ t = q \ y \ t' \leftrightarrow <\!<\!v/x\!>\!>t = <\!<\!v/y\!>\!>t'$

(iii) $bA = t \leftrightarrow A = b^{-1}b \uparrow t$, *if b renames distinct non-local object variables to distinct local variables, where b^{-1} is the inverse of b and $b \uparrow$ renames all the non-local variables of b to new local variables.*

(iv) $\mathrm{loc} \ f(t_1, \ldots t_n) \leftrightarrow \mathrm{loc} \ t_1 \ \& \ \ldots \ \& \ \mathrm{loc} \ t_n$

(v) $\mathrm{loc} \ q \ x \ t \leftrightarrow \mathrm{loc} <\!<\!y/x\!>\!>t$, *if y is a new non-local object variable.*

LEMMA **23.5.10.** *(Instantiations)*

(i) $x = y \leftrightarrow ([y/x], \mathrm{succeed})$

(ii) $A = t \leftrightarrow ([t/A], \mathrm{loc} \ t)$, *if A does not statically occur in t.*

23.6 Acknowledgements

The first author thanks Alan Bundy for hospitality at the Department of Artificial Intelligence, University of Edinburgh, during preliminary work for this paper. Thanks also to Alan Robinson for helpful criticism.

This work was supported in part by a University of Queensland Special Research Grant, and in part by the Australian Research Council.

23.7 References

1. Bacha, H., Meta-level programming: a compiled approach, in *Proc. Fourth Int'l Conf. on Logic Programming*, ed. J.-L. Lassez, MIT Press, 1986, 394–410.

2. Huet, G.P., A mechanization of type theory, in *Proc. 3rd IJCAI* (1973) 139–146.

3. Miller, D. and Nadathur, G., A logic programming approach to manipulating formulas and programs, in *Proc. IEEE Fourth Symposium on Logic Programming*, San Francisco, 1987.

4. Paterson, R.A. and Staples, J., A general theory of unification and constraint solving, University of Queensland Dept of Computer Science Tech. Report No. 90 (1988).

5. Staples, J., Delaying unification algorithms for lambda calculi, *Theor Comput Sci* **56** (1988) 277–288.

6. Staples, J., Robinson, P.J. and Hagen, R.A., Qu-Prolog - an extended Prolog for symbolic computation, *Austral. Comp. Sci. Communications* **10** (1988) 194–203.

Chapter 24

A Meta-Logic for Functional Programming

John Hannan   Dale Miller

The University of Pennsylvania

Abstract

We define a meta-logic to serve as a formal framework in which meta-programming tasks for a simple functional language can be elegantly specified. Highlighting the relationships among meta-programming, logic programming and natural deduction, we consider both practical and theoretical concerns of program analysis and thus motivate our methods. Then, using techniques inspired by structural operational semantics and natural semantics, we investigate how, in a natural deduction setting, we can specify a wide variety of tasks that manipulate functional programs as data objects. Specifications of this sort are presented as sets of inference rules and are encoded as clauses in a higher-order, intuitionistic meta-logic. Program properties are then proved by constructing proofs in this meta-logic. We argue that the meta-logic provides clear and concise specifications that suggest intuitive descriptions of the properties or operations being described. In particular, the rich structure of functional programs, including a variety of binding and scoping mechanisms, can be naturally represented and analyzed. We support this claim by providing three example specifications for simple meta-programming tasks. From a practical standpoint, the meta-logic can be implemented naturally in a logic programming language and thus we can produce experimental implementations of the specifications. We expect that our efforts will provide new perspectives and insights for program manipulation tasks.

24.1   Introduction

Meta-programming, in its most general setting, is any programming task in which programs are treated as data objects. We typically distinguish between the meta-language, in which we write the meta-programs, and the object-language, in which the programs being manipulated are written. These two languages may in fact be the same language (giving rise to meta-circular interpreters, for example) but in general they can be two unrelated languages. Considering this definition of meta-programming we observe that many common programs or procedures can be classified as meta-programs: (*i*) editors treat programs as objects that are to be modified; most editors do not treat object programs as a special data type (distinct from arbitrary text), though some recent programming systems include editors in which they are [27]; (*ii*) compilers treat programs as the source and target objects of a translation process; (*iii*) interpreters treat programs as input data and produce as output the result of executing the program. A more narrow definition of meta-programming includes only meta-interpreters providing extensions to languages and program transformers, e.g., partial evaluators and abstract interpreters. In this chapter we assume the former, more encompassing, definition of meta-programming. This choice does not greatly affect the issues that arise in this study, but merely enlarges the set of examples from which we can select.

The focal point of this work is the definition and examination of a meta-logic for specifying meta-programming tasks over functional programs. We cannot hope to be completely general in this goal as we must make certain choices during our investigations: the choice of the functional programming language that we consider and the range of meta-programming tasks to be considered. We will use a small subset of Standard ML as our object language. Although we hope that the methods we present will accommodate a wide range of meta-programming tasks, we do not expect to define formally the limits of our methods.

The main purpose of this work is to demonstrate how, with the proper meta-logic, a natural deduction paradigm provides a suitable framework for manipulating and analyzing functional programs. Previous work has used inference rules to specify the dynamic semantics and other properties of programs [5, 25], but their emphasis has typically been more towards software engineering issues and less towards a study of the resulting proof system. We are concerned with defining and characterizing a formal meta-language via proof-theoretic methods and with understanding the nature of proofs that can be constructed in this language. From a practical standpoint this work finds immediate application in the development of programming languages and programming language environments. Such tasks require development tools that are both expressive and extensible (as well as other qualities as described below). The methods pursued in this work seem to be well suited in both regards.

An expectation of this work is that with a single meta-language, we can specify a wide variety of tasks that treat programs as objects. We have considered specifications for tasks such as evaluation, type inferencing and compilation, each presented by a set of inference rules. Additional work has considered strictness analysis and mixed evaluation. By describing these apparently disparate tasks in a unified framework we hope to gain insight into the similarities and differences among these tasks. From a practical standpoint, this uniform treatment of tasks suggests the possibility of integrating various tools. From a theoretical standpoint, a detailed analysis of a variety of tools can be performed using uniform techniques. Thus the same (meta-theoretic) analysis techniques used on the static semantics of a language could apply to a compiler for the language.

Another expectation of this work concerns an analysis of the proof-theoretic tools we describe. By exploiting our foundations in proof theory we hope to reason about meta-theoretic properties via proof transformations and manipulations. For example, we can show that certain program transformers have a correctness-preserving property by demonstrating an equivalence between certain classes of proof trees. Thus, using some well-established methods of proof theory we can express and prove important (meta-)properties of our meta-programs.

Finally, an important aspect of this work is its operational characteristic. We can interpret the meta-programming specifications as defining an operational semantics in the sense of [25]. Thus we provide an operational description, that we claim is natural and intuitive, of a variety of program analysis tasks. Such descriptions facilitate our understanding of these tasks.

The remainder of the chapter is organized as follows. In Section 24.2 we present some general background material on meta-programming, natural deduction and logic programming. We discuss the relationships between these concepts and motivate some of our decisions. In Section 24.3 we describe the issues involved in manipulating programs as first-class objects. In Section 24.4 we describe a general framework for our proof systems and the methods used to encode functional programs as terms. We outline how program properties can be denoted by propositions in a suitable logic. In Section 24.5 we describe a simple functional language E and then in Sections 24.6 and 24.7 we specify a static semantics (for type inferencing) and a standard evaluation semantics for E.

24.2 Meta-Programming, Natural Deduction and Logic Programming

To help motivate our particular methods we consider several perspectives of meta-programming, both practical and theoretical. Our first point is to distinguish between meta-logic and meta-programming. Meta-programming implicitly implies some programming language is used to manipulate object programs, but it does not stipulate the properties of this meta-language. One could choose languages such as Lisp or Prolog to implement all of the meta-programming tasks that we have in mind. We are, however, concerned with the formal properties of such implementations and so we are concerned with a logic for meta-programming, which we refer to as a meta-logic. Our approach is to first define a logic (including terms, propositional formulas and methods for constructing proofs) suitable for describing manipulations and analyses on simple functional programs. Then we shall describe an implementation for this logic.

Above we described a class of programming tasks operating on programs as data and labeled these as meta-programming. This viewpoint provides one aspect to this work, that of the "high-level" tasks involved and their motivations. Equally important are two orthogonal issues: logical formalism and implementation. Logical formalism refers to the logic upon which our methods or solutions are based. From this viewpoint we expect to provide a formal basis from which we can reason about the tasks involved. We choose a natural deduction system to provide the formal or logical basis of our methods. We also wish to provide practical implementations of the meta-programs and so we must consider the perspective of implementation. We choose a logic programming paradigm to provide an implementation vehicle. The justification for these two choices is given by the intimate relationship among them and meta-programming.

24.2.1   Natural Deduction and Meta-Programming

In a natural deduction theorem prover, one thinks of constructing proofs of propositions according to a prescribed set of inference rules. These propositions are typically defined in some formal logic, e.g., first-order predicate calculus. The inference rules are typically characterized as being either introduction or elimination rules according to whether a logical connective is introduced or eliminated in the conclusion. For our application, the atomic propositions will denote statements about object programs. These statements may either be statements concerning a program property (*"program P is well-typed"*) or concerning an operation on the program (*"program P evaluates to value V"*). The inference rules for our purposes will correspond roughly to the inference rules of Gentzen's *NJ* (natural deduction for intuitionistic logic). The particular choice of terms, propositional formulas and inference rules is largely based on the object language that we consider, though the kind of program property or operation that we consider, also matters.

This connection between natural deduction and meta-programming largely originated with the work on structural operational semantics [25] and later natural semantics [4, 16]. The current work is closely related to the application of the LF (Logical Framework) system to operational semantics [3] and grew out of an effort to extend the methods of natural semantics [11]. While natural semantics provides methods for specifying many meta-programming tasks, we feel that its use of strictly first-order terms and limited types of inference figures makes the formal properties of their meta-program harder to determine. We shall represent programs instead as simply typed λ-terms and shall also extend the underlying reasoning mechanism of natural semantics with two kinds of introduction and discharge rules. We argue that this extension yields a higher-level description of many program manipulations and provides a more natural specification of these tasks. Many low-level routines for manipulating program code, such as substitutions for free variables, changing bound variable names, maintaining a context, *etc.*, are essentially moved to the meta-language and need not be written into the specification.

24.2.2 Natural Deduction and Logic Programming

The connection between natural deduction and logic programming has already been exploited in the work of natural semantics where the specifications are compiled into Prolog. In general, logic programming languages provide many features that make them suitable implementation languages for natural deduction theorem provers [6]. A brief examination of these features makes this connection obvious. A foremost aspect of computation in logic programming is the search operation. Taking a procedural view of logic programming we can describe the execution of a logic program by describing a search process through a space defined by the program. Search is also an important component of natural deduction theorem proving. The task of constructing a proof can be described as the exploration of a search space. Unification is a second characteristic feature of logic programming. It provides a mechanism for matching two terms. More specifically, we can specify "generic" clauses in a program and then use these clauses in specific instances via unification. A similar mechanism plays an important role in constructing proofs in natural deduction. A natural deduction system can be specified by a set of inference rules. These rules are typically given by rule templates, i.e., ones that contain free variables. Proofs will contain only closed instances of these rules and so some matching or unification process is required to produce the required instances of these rules. Finally, most logic programming languages are constructed from clauses of the general form "*Body* ⊃ *Head*" with the intuitive reading "if *Body* is true then *Head* is true." Thus the inference rules used to specify a natural deduction system should have a natural translation into clauses of this form. The head and body of a clause will denote the consequent and the antecedent of an inference rule. This straightforward translation into clauses together with the declarative style of logic programming suggests that using logic programs can provide perspicuous implementations of natural deduction theorem provers.

24.2.3 Meta-Programming and Logic Programming

As discussed above, the characteristic feature of meta-programming is the manipulation of programs as data objects. Thus we require a language that is equipped with terms suitable for representing programs as first-class objects and with mechanisms for analyzing these terms. We will argue that an encoding of programs into simply typed λ-terms provides a convenient representation for manipulating functional programs as objects. A characteristic feature of logic programming is unification of terms and we will make a use of a particular kind unification to provide an appropriate mechanism for analyzing terms representing programs. We will also make a simple use of β-conversion for manipulating λ-terms in useful ways.

A common presentation of meta-programming is in terms of some kind of conditional rules. For example, a program transformation system, in which an input program is manipulated into another program, is typically given by a set of rules. Each rule contains conditions describing the applicability of the rule and these conditions may be in the form of tests or procedures to be performed on the incoming program. Such rules can be naturally encoded as clauses in a logic programming paradigm.

A third point considers again the search paradigm of logic programming. Meta-programming, too, is often reduced to a problem of search. In fact, part of the complexity of many meta-programming tasks is their lack of a simple deterministic algorithm. Rather, a search must be conducted, as in the case of program transformation where many rules may be applicable for a given program.

24.2.4   Natural Deduction and Sequent Systems

In his seminal paper on logical deduction Gentzen presented two intuitionistic proof systems, LJ and NJ [7]. In the system LJ, sequents of the form $\Gamma \longrightarrow A$, where Γ is a sequence of formulas and A is a formula, form the basic propositions. The sequent $\Gamma \longrightarrow A$ denotes the proposition: from the formulas in Γ, the formula A follows. In contrast, the basic proposition in the proof system NJ is a single formula: the context by which that formula is proved is left implicit. A common distinction made between the two systems is that the more notationally explicit LJ system is more suitable for machine implementation while the less explicit NJ is more suitable for human understanding.

A similar distinction between styles of operational semantics can be made. The work on natural semantics is built essentially on a sequent style proof system where sequents are of the form $\Gamma \vdash \mathcal{P}(P)$ in which $\mathcal{P}(P)$ is a predicate over program P and Γ is a set of assumptions about the identifiers (free variables) of P. The work in this paper is built essentially on natural deduction proof systems. In a sense, the difference between the two approaches is insignificant: for the examples presented in this paper a simple translation from one style to the other is possible. Each method does have certain advantages over the other, however. For example, by being more explicit, the sequent style is more closely tied to conventional implementations of functional programming languages. The set Γ often acts as a mapping from identifiers to values and such mappings can be efficiently implemented. While the natural deduction style systems, which rely on introduction and discharge rules, seem further removed from efficient implementations, they are often more easily manipulated in a formal setting. See [10] for an examples where the formal manipulation of a natural deduction style proof system was much more convenient than its corresponding sequential specification.

24.3 Programs as First-Class Objects

At the heart of meta-programming is the issue of representing programs as first-class objects and manipulating these objects. The static structure of programs, however, is inherently complex, with structure arising from a variety of binding constructs and scoping rules. Hence a meta-logic (or meta-programming language) should be suitably equipped with appropriate data structures and operations to facilitate the task of effectively representing these objects. In this section we attempt to characterize an effective representation for the kind of program analyses that we would like to specify in our meta-logic. In what follows we assume the reader to be familiar with the notion of lexical scoping.

If we consider Standard ML [13] as the prototypical functional programming language then we can immediately observe several kinds of binding operations occurring in simple programming examples. The example program in Figure 24.1 contains four different kinds of bindings. The datatype definition introduces two new identifiers: the type name MYPAIR and the constructor pair. The scope for these two identifiers is assumed to be "global" in that the definition has been added to the top-level environment. Next we have the definition of functions that introduce the identifiers swap, fst and snd, all denoting (function) values. The scope of the identifier swap is, like the two above, global, while the scope of both fst and snd is local to the definition of swap. Finally, each of the three function definitions introduces identifiers as formal parameters with a scope local to the associated definition: p is local to the definition of swap; instances of x and y are local to the definitions of both fst and snd.

As this small example plainly illustrates, even a simple programming language can incorporate a number of binding constraints. Here we have four, over type names, constructors, function names and formal parameters. The notion of global scope is really only one of convenience and does not need to be considered as a special case. Note that in each case above what was introduced was simply an identifier, regardless of whether it denotes a value, type, etc. Thus our meta-logic may only need a single mechanism for providing a scoping for identifiers over (a representation of) expressions to capture a wide variety of binding operations in the object language.

Consider using Standard ML itself as the meta-language for just this simple example. We could naturally define (at the meta-level) datatypes for representing expressions, declarations and bindings, as was done in the Standard ML of New Jersey compiler [1]. (In this compiler, the datatype declaration for bindings alone contains the union of nine different kinds of bindings!) In this compiler the binding information is managed via an explicit environment that performs binding, lookup and scope management functions. For the particular application of compilation, this treatment of bindings is perhaps optimal as it is efficient and easily implemented. So one conclusion possible from the experience with the Standard ML compiler is that Standard ML provides suitable facilities for representing itself

```
datatype MYPAIR = pair of int * int;

fun swap p =
  let fun fst(pair(x,y)) = x;
      fun snd(pair(x,y)) = y
  in
      pair(snd(p), fst(p))
  end;
```

Figure 24.1: Examples of Bindings in Standard ML

as data objects. Compilation, however, is only one of several meta-programming
tasks we would like to consider.

Consider, then, the possible analysis or manipulation facilities that Standard
ML could provide. At the primitive level of the language, only simple pattern
matching is provided to decompose terms. As a simple example of how this level
of sophistication is inadequate for some purposes, consider the following two expressions:

```
fun fst(pair(x,y)) = x;          fun snd(pair(y,x)) = y
```

and suppose we wish to determine if these two expressions denote the same expression. A simple check for syntactic identity would report that these two programs
are different. A more sophisticated program could, of course, be written that
would check for the alphabetic variants in bound variable names and conclude
that these two fragments are equal. Note, however, that the two instances of
the identifier **pair** could refer to different constructors (e.g., one defined over
pairs of integers and one over pairs of reals), depending on the contexts in which
each function was defined. The problem encountered with this example is that
equality between λ-terms is typically considered modulo λ-conversion. This notion of equality is a much more complex operation than the simple syntactic
equality provided naturally by pattern matching. In particular, using this notion
of equality, a λ-term is equal to any alphabetic variant of itself (α-equivalence).
Meta-programming equality modulo λ-conversion is a particularly appealing idea:
λ-terms provide the essential de-sugared elements of functional programming, dis-
pensing with the need for keeping tract of bound variable names.

To provide further analysis capabilities we consider unification of simply typed
λ-terms as described in [14]. If the only method for manipulating λ-terms is via
normalization and unification then it is impossible to distinguish between two
programs which are equal modulo λ-conversion. Furthermore, unification is a
sophisticated mechanism that can be used to probe the structure of programs,
respecting congruence classes modulo λ-conversion. The use of λ-terms and λ-
term unification to implement program manipulation systems has been proposed
by various people. Huet and Lang in [15] employed second-order matching (a

decidable subcase of λ-term unification) to express certain restricted, "template" program transformations. Miller and Nadathur in [18] extended their approach by adding to their scheme the flexibility of Horn clause programming and richer forms of unification. In [11] we argued that if the Prolog component of the TYPOL system [2] were enriched with higher-order features, logic programming could play a stronger role as a specification language for various kinds of interpreters and compilers.

With these ideas in mind we shall define an abstract syntax for programs and types of the object language based on the simply typed λ-calculus. We shall represent programs as simply typed terms by introducing an appropriate set of constants to a calculus from which we can construct terms denoting programs. In general, for each programming language construct we introduce a new constant which is used to build a term representing this construct. And for each construct that introduces a binding (of an identifier), we use a λ-abstraction where the abstracted variable denotes the bound identifier and the expression over which it is abstracted defines the scope of the binding. This uniform treatment of bindings provides a natural specification of many programming language constructs. We also define new base types (or sorts) corresponding to the different categories of the object language. For example, a simple functional language might require two sorts, one for object-level terms and one for object-level types. We provide an example of such an abstract syntax in Section 24.5.

While we are only concerned in the current work with the simply typed λ-calculus, richer and more flexible λ-calculi have been proposed as a suitable representation system for programs. For example, Pfenning and Elliot in [23] have extended the simply typed λ-calculus to include simple product types. They also discuss in depth the role of *higher-order abstract syntax, i.e.*, the representation of programs as λ-terms, in the construction of flexible and general program manipulation systems. The LF specification language [12] uses a λ-calculus with a strong typing mechanism to specify various components of proof systems: much of this specification language could profitably be used in the context we are concerned with here [3].

Similar advantages of the blend of higher-order unification and logic programming have been exploited in systems that manipulate formulas and proofs of logical systems. Felty and Miller in [6] discuss the use of a higher-order logic programming language to specify and implement theorem provers and proofs systems. Here again, λ-terms and higher-order unification are used to represent and manipulate formulas and proofs. The Isabelle theorem prover of Paulson [22] also makes use of these features to implement flexible theorem provers.

24.4 The Meta-Logic

Having settled on the representation of programs as λ-terms we now define the propositional formulas of our logic and a core of "primitive" inference figures.

These inference figures will correspond to a subset of the inference figures of Gentzen's *NJ* system. For a specific specification (of some meta-programming task), additional inference figures will be added.

Propositions in our meta-logic are either atomic or compound, and are given the type o. The atomic propositions of our meta-logic will be constructed from a finite set of n-ary propositional symbols (typically with $n = 2$), each with a given type. Given a propositional symbol p of type (in curried form) $(\sigma_1 \rightarrow \sigma_2 \rightarrow \cdots \sigma_n \rightarrow o)$ and typed λ-terms $t_1{:}\sigma_1, t_2{:}\sigma_2, \ldots t_n{:}\sigma_n$, then $p(t_1, t_2, \ldots t_n)$ is a proposition of type o. Compound propositions are constructed with the logical connectives $\&{:}(o \rightarrow o \rightarrow o)$, $\Rightarrow{:}(o \rightarrow o \rightarrow o)$ and $\forall{:}((\sigma \rightarrow o) \rightarrow o)$. Here, $\forall$ is polymorphic in the type variable σ. So, for example, if A_1 and A_2 are propositions then so are $(A_1 \& A_2)$, $(A_1 \Rightarrow A_2)$ and $(\forall \lambda x.A_2)$. We shall typically write $(\forall \lambda x.A)$ as $(\forall x\ A)$.

To manipulate such propositions, particularly the compound ones, the meta-logic comes equipped with four primitive inference figures, given in Figure 24.2. The first one, $(\beta\eta)$ is applicable when the λ-terms representing the propositions in A_0 and A_1 are $\beta\eta$-convertible. By virtue of this rule, we generally think of any two λ-terms as equal if they are $\beta\eta$-convertible. For example an instance of this rule is

$$\frac{type(1,\ \ int)}{type((\lambda x.x\ \ 1),\ \ int)}$$

where *type* is some non-logical predicate constant.

The second inference figure, $(\& I)$, is called *conjunction introduction*. When using this inference rule to construct proofs we interpret it in the following backward fashion: to establish the proposition in $A_1 \& A_2$, establish the two separate propositions found in A_1 and A_2.

The remaining two rules deal with introduction and discharge. To specify the introduction and discharge of assumptions needed to prove hypothetical propositions we use the inference figure $(\Rightarrow I)$. That is, to prove $A_1 \Rightarrow A_2$, first assume that there is a proof of A_1 and attempt to build a proof for A_2 from it. If such a proof is found, then the implication is justified and the proof of this implication is the result of discharging the assumption about A_1. This rule is called *implication introduction*. Proving a universally quantified proposition has a similar structure, suggesting the inference figure labeled $(\forall I)$. Here, to prove a universal instance, a new parameter (c) must be introduced and the resulting generic instance of the quantified formula must be proved. Of course, after that instance is proved, the parameter must be discharged, in the sense that c cannot occur free in A or in any undischarged hypotheses. This rule is called *universal introduction*. The corresponding discharge or elimination rules are also included in the meta-logic but are not used in any of the examples presented.

These two rules, implication and universal introduction, are not typically found in other presentations of operational semantics. We shall use these two together in the following way. For a particular meta-programming task we shall

$$\frac{A_1}{A_0} \ (\beta\eta) \qquad\qquad \frac{A_1 \quad A_2}{A_1 \ \& \ A_2} \ (\& I)$$

$$
\begin{array}{c}
(A_1) \\
\vdots \\
\underline{\quad A_2 \quad} \\
A_1 \Rightarrow A_2
\end{array} \ (\Rightarrow I)
\qquad\qquad
\frac{A[x \mapsto c]}{(\forall x)A} \ (\forall I)
$$

Figure 24.2: Primitive Inference Figures

introduce a new inference figure whose premise is of the form

$$\forall c(A_1(c) \ \Rightarrow \ A_2(c))$$

which we can describe operationally as follows:

> Introduce some new constant c, not occurring in A_1, A_2 or any current hypothesis; then assume property A_1 about c. From this assumption attempt to prove property A_2 for c. If such a proof can be found then discharge the assumption $A_1(c)$ and the parameter c.

We shall see how this kind of reasoning provides a powerful and natural way of describing aspects of meta-programming tasks, particularly when dealing with object-level bound variables.

A specification of a meta-level program will be a collection of atomic propositions which will denote axioms and a collection of inference figures, none of which introduce the symbols $\&, \Rightarrow, \forall$. Of course, the premises to user supplied inference figures can contain instances of these symbols. Following the convention of specifying proof systems, we interpret these inference figures as schemas, in that the inference figures may contain free variables that get instantiated to specific instances. (We assume all capitalized identifiers denote variables.) Thus we take the universal closure of each inference figure. When providing examples of inference figures later in this chapter, we shall drop references to the connective $\&$ in premises. Inference figures of the form

$$\frac{A_1 \ \& \ A_2}{A_0} \quad \text{will simply be written as} \quad \frac{A_1 \quad A_2}{A_0} \ .$$

Notice that we have not explicitly included the corresponding elimination rules $((\& E), (\Rightarrow E)$ and $(\forall E))$. For all the examples in this paper, the inclusion of these rules is not necessary.

A proof in this language will be understood in the standard sense of proofs in natural deduction. For more information on natural deduction and its terminology (both of which are used in this chapter) see [7, 26].

We shall view the construction of a proof of a proposition as a kind of computation. Rarely shall we be particularly interested in the actual proof constructed, but rather in some instantiation of existentially quantified variables. This is accomplished by starting with propositions containing free variables and assuming that they are existentially quantified. For example, we may have a proposition of the form $type(1, T)$ which can be interpreted as the query *"what is type type of 1?"* Constructing a proof of this proposition should result in the instantiation of the existentially quantified variable T to some ground term, e.g., *int*.

Following the observation described in [16] that natural semantics has an intimate connection to logic programming, we show how the preceding four inference figures are related to logic programming. First-order Horn clauses, however, are not strong enough to directly implement these inference rules. First, the notion of equality between terms would be that of simple tree equality, not that of $\beta\eta$-conversion. Horn clauses also do not provide a mechanism for directly implementing the introduction and discharge of parameters and assumptions. It is not difficult to modify our proof system so that the explicit references to introducing and discharging assumptions could be eliminated in favor of treating basic propositions as essentially sequents. That is, a proposition *Prop* would be replaced by a proposition $\Gamma \rightarrow Prop$, in which Γ is used to store assumptions. This is, for example, used in natural semantics to handle contexts. A more serious challenge to Horn clauses is that they cannot naturally implement the universally quantified proposition.

There is, however, a generalization of Horn clauses which adds both implications and universal quantifiers to the body of clauses and permits quantification over higher-order variables. This extension, called *higher-order hereditary Harrop formulas* [19] has (partially) been implemented in the λProlog system [21]. λProlog does, in fact, provide a natural implementation language for these inference rules. For example, the user can specify inference rules by directly writing program clauses containing conjunction, implication, and universal quantifiers, since these are understood on a primitive level of λProlog. For example, clauses of the form

$$A_0 \; :- \; A_1 \; \& \; (\forall x)(A_2 \Rightarrow A_3).$$

can be used to represent complex inference figures. Free (higher-order) variables here are assumed to be universally quantified over the scope of the full clause corresponding to the universal closure of inference schemas. Queries to construct proofs of propositions will become goals in λProlog, so the example query above becomes

$$?-type(1, T)$$

and a successful computation of this goal results in reporting the answer substitution: $T = int$. Instead of using the λProlog syntax to present example inference rules in later sections, we shall continue to use the more graphically oriented inference figures. All the examples presented here have been implemented and tested in a version of λProlog.

24.5 Abstract Syntax as Lambda Terms

Having defined our meta-logic, including its terms, propositional formulas and inference figures, we now describe how a simple functional programming language can be encoded as terms in our meta-logic. Of course, there may be many possible ways of representing programs as terms, but we want one that will allow us to make full use of the meta-logic. We distinguish between concrete syntax, which may provide a convenient representation for human understanding, and abstract syntax, which contains the essential information needed for program manipulation. In our introduction to handling binding information we have already hinted at what a good abstract representation should include. Here we make these ideas precise by starting with a simple language, namely the pure untyped λ-calculus (λ^u). Later we extend this language to into a more substantial subset of Standard ML. This presentation demonstrates how an abstract syntax for a functional language can be constructed using simply typed lambda terms and how this abstract syntax captures the binding and scoping constructs found in functional programming languages. We take care in making the distinction between terms and types at the object (λ^u) level and terms and types at the meta-level. We refer to the latter as meta-terms and meta-types.

Suppose that the concrete syntax for λ^u is given by the following grammar:

$$U \quad ::= \quad x \mid \lambda x.U \mid (U\ U).$$

(We must be careful here because we shall overload the use of the symbol λ.) We introduce a new meta-type tm for representing (at the meta-level) terms of λ^u. Now there is a standard way of encoding untyped terms into the simply typed λ-calculus ($\lambda^\rightarrow$) and this is described in [17]. The idea is to introduce two new constants into the typed calculus ($\lambda^\rightarrow$):

$$\Psi \quad : \quad (tm \rightarrow tm) \rightarrow tm$$
$$\Phi \quad : \quad tm \rightarrow (tm \rightarrow tm)$$

We can then define a simple mapping $(\cdot)^* : \lambda^u \longrightarrow \lambda^\rightarrow$ as follows:

DEFINITION 1 $((\cdot)^*)$. *For any* $M \in \lambda^u$ *let* $(M)^*$ *be*

$$
\begin{aligned}
(x)^* &= x^*{:}tm \quad \text{for } x \text{ a variable.} \\
(MN)^* &= \Phi M^* N^* \\
(\lambda x.M)^* &= \Psi(\lambda x^*{:}tm.M^*)
\end{aligned}
$$

$$
\begin{array}{ll}
C & tm \\
if & tm \to tm \to tm \to tm \\
@ & tm \to (tm \to tm) \\
lamb & (tm \to tm) \to tm \\
let & (tm \to tm) \to tm \to tm \\
fix & (tm \to tm) \to tm
\end{array}
\qquad
\begin{array}{lll}
int & : & tp \\
bool & : & tp \\
\to & : & tp \to tp \to tp
\end{array}
$$

Figure 24.3: Signature for Terms and Types of E

We assume that $(\cdot)^*$ defines a bijective mapping of untyped variables to typed variables (of type tm). For a more complete discussion of this encoding, including soundness and completeness results, see [8]. As an example of this encoding, consider the untyped term $\lambda x \lambda y(xy)$. Via this encoding its corresponding typed term is $\Psi(\lambda x(\Psi(\lambda y(\Phi x\, y))))$. Note that this is a term of type tm. Thus we have a simple way of representing any pure untyped λ-term as a simply typed term of uniform type. This is important because in the task of type inference, to be discussed in the next section, we must be able to handle terms that are both well-typed and untypable.

We now consider a slightly larger programming language. Let E be the functional language whose concrete syntax is defined by the following grammar:

$$
\begin{aligned}
E \ ::= \ & \mathbf{C} \ | \ \mathbf{x} \ | \ \text{if } E \text{ then } E \text{ else } E \ | \ (E\,E) \ | \\
& \lambda \mathbf{x}.E \ | \ \text{let } \mathbf{x} = E \text{ in } E \ | \ \text{fix } \mathbf{x}.E
\end{aligned}
$$

Here, x ranges over variables and $\mathbf{C}$ ranges over primitive constants, typically including the integers and booleans and a set of primitive operations to manipulate them.

To define our abstract syntax for E we follow an approach similar to the above one for λ^u and in the same spirit as [23]. We begin by giving a signature for some meta-terms that we use to construct terms and types at the object level. (See Figure 24.3.) Notice that the constants $lamb$, let and fix are higher-order, that is, they each require a functional argument of type $tm \to tm$. In the examples that follow M will be used as a higher-order (meta-)variable of this meta-type. '$\to$' is the function space constructors for tp. We have overloaded the symbol '$\to$', using it at both the object and meta levels; its use, however, should always be clear from context. The object types we consider are only monotypes (in the sense of [20] as we do allow type variables). In the next section we present a separate discussion of manipulating polytypes.

Using the signature of Figure 24.3 we can build up λ-terms forming an abstract syntax for E as follows. For constants and variables in the concrete syntax we just introduce associated constants and variables of type tm to the abstract syntax.

For the **if** statement we introduce the new constant *if* such that given three terms $e_1, e_2, e_3 : tm$, then $(if\ e_1\ e_2\ e_3) : tm$. Application is made explicit with the infix operator '@' so that $e_1@e_2$ represents the expression denoted by the term e_1 applied to e_2. For lambda abstraction we introduce the constructor *lamb* that takes a meta-level abstraction of the form $\lambda x.e$, in which x and e are of meta-type tm, and produces a term of type tm. For example the concrete syntax for lambda abstraction is **λx.E** and its abstract syntax is $(lamb\ \lambda x.e)$ (for e the λ-term corresponding to E). Similar to *lamb*, the *let* construct uses a meta-term M of the form $\lambda x.e$ to represent the binding of an identifier. Thus the concrete syntax **let x** $= E_1$ **in** E_2 is given by the abstract term $(let\ \lambda x.e_2\ e_1)$ in which e_1 and e_2 are the (abstract) terms denoting the expressions E_1 and E_2, respectively. To represent the recursive **fix** construct we introduce the *fix* constant which again uses an explicit abstraction to capture the binding. An example of this construction is given below.

Throughout most of this chapter we will avoid discussing primitive operations such as $+$, $-$, *etc.* They are, of course, important to have in the full language but including them here is neither difficult nor illuminating. We shall typically assume, for the sake of examples, that we at least have some basic set of list operations. In the following and subsequent examples we systematically drop the apply "@" operator in order to make examples more readable.

Consider the following expression that defines the append function and then applies it to two lists.

let app = (fix f.λk.λl.(if empty(k) then l else cons(hd(k) f(tl(k) l))))
in (app [1] [2]).

The corresponding term in the abstract syntax is

$(let\ \lambda app.(app\ (cons\ 1\ nil)\ (cons\ 2\ nil))$
$\quad (fix\ \lambda f(lamb\ \lambda k(lamb\ \lambda l(if\ (empty\ k)\ l\ (cons\ (hd\ k)\ (f\ (tl\ k)\ l))))))))$.

Note how the four bindings in the concrete syntax (**app, f, k, l**) are translated into explicit λ-abstractions in the abstract syntax.

Before presenting some example specifications we recall the distinction we made earlier between natural deduction and sequent style systems. Now that our abstract syntax has been defined further comment concerning the difference between our method and typical approaches to natural or operational semantics is appropriate. This distinction concerns the treatment of identifiers. The typical approach to programs analysis uses an environment (or context) to denote a finite mapping from identifiers to some domain (e.g., types or terms). When analyzing an abstraction, the bound variable is stripped from the abstraction and the identifier which names that bound variable is added to the context. The meaning of such an identifier within the body of the abstraction is then determined by "looking up" the value associated with the identifier in the current environment.

We refer to this technique as the environment approach.

Given our commitment to representing program abstractions using abstractions with λ-terms and to equating such terms when they are βη-convertible, it is impossible to access the bound variable name of a λ-term at the meta-level, since such an operation would return different answers on equal terms. A combination of the ∀ and ⇒ propositions, as suggested earlier, can provide a very simple solution to this problem. When an abstraction is encountered, typically within *lamb*, *let* and *fix* constructions, a ∀ judgement is used to introduce a new parameter. That parameter is then substituted into the abstraction using β-conversion. The value or type to be associated with this new parameter is then introduced as an assumed proposition. In this way, the newly introduced identifier is used to stand for the name of the bound variable.

This relation between the environment approach and our technique is similar to an observation by Plotkin about evaluations in the SECD machine [24]. There two different evaluation functions were defined: the awkward *Eval* function defined in terms of closures and the simpler *eval* defined using substitution (β-conversion, here). While these two functions were shown to be equivalent, introducing the simpler definition for evaluation allowed properties of the SECD machine to be described much more naturally than with the first, more cumbersome, definition. Similarly, we believe that the use of abstractions and substitution in our meta-language will often produce this kind of advantage over programs using the environment approach.

In the following two sections we present some meta-programming examples using our abstract syntax.

24.6   Static Semantics

Static semantics refers to a class of program analyses that provide information about programs based on their static structure (i.e., not considering their behavior during some form of evaluation). One common example of a static semantics is type inferencing. An example of this kind of analysis is given below. Other kinds of static analysis include type checking, certain kinds of flow analysis and possibly complexity analysis.

24.6.1   Type Inference

We introduced the language E as an implicitly typed functional language, in the same vein as Standard ML. Thus an important static operation on E programs is type inference. More specifically, we only wish to admit programs generated by the given grammer for E that are "well-typed." By this we mean that a type can be given to the program according to some laws. The idea of using inference rules to specify type inference is not new. Most recently Tofte has given a thorough treatment of polymorphic type inference in an operational semantics style [28].

$$c \xrightarrow{ty} \mathcal{C}(c) \qquad \frac{e_1 \xrightarrow{ty} bool \qquad e_2 \xrightarrow{ty} \tau \qquad e_3 \xrightarrow{ty} \tau}{(if \ e_1 \ e_2 \ e_3) \xrightarrow{ty} \tau} \qquad (1,2)$$

$$\frac{(\forall c) \ (c \xrightarrow{ty} \tau_1 \ \Rightarrow \ (M \ c) \xrightarrow{ty} \tau_2)}{(lamb \ M) \xrightarrow{ty} (\tau_1 \rightarrow \tau_2)} \qquad \frac{e_1 \xrightarrow{ty} (\tau_1 \rightarrow \tau_2) \qquad e_2 \xrightarrow{ty} \tau_1}{(e_1 @ e_2) \xrightarrow{ty} \tau_2} \qquad (3,4)$$

$$\frac{e_2 \xrightarrow{ty} \tau_2 \qquad (M \ e_2) \xrightarrow{ty} \tau_1}{(let \ M \ e_2) \xrightarrow{ty} \tau_1} \qquad \frac{(\forall c) \ (c \xrightarrow{ty} \tau \ \Rightarrow \ (M \ c) \xrightarrow{ty} \tau)}{(fix \ M) \xrightarrow{ty} \tau} \qquad (5,6)$$

Figure 24.4: Type Inference for E

The specification for type inference in E is given in Figure 24.4. We introduce the infix propositional symbol $\xrightarrow{ty}$: $tm \rightarrow tp \rightarrow o$ and construct propositions of the form $e \xrightarrow{ty} \tau$ where τ is a λ-term built up from the constants int, $bool$, etc. and $\rightarrow$. The proposition $e \xrightarrow{ty} \tau$, in which e is a closed term denoting the abstract syntax of functional program E and τ is a closed term denoting the abstract syntax of a type, states that e has type τ. We assume that we have a fixed map $\mathcal{C}$ from the abstract constants to types, such that for each base constant c of the abstract syntax, $\mathcal{C}(c) = \tau$. Clause 1 of the specification types the constants using the map $\mathcal{C}$. The next clause 2 gives the typing for the conditional statement. Clause 3 is the typing rule for lambda abstraction and it is a bit different from the usual typing rule using environments [28]. In the environment approach, typing the term $(\lambda \ x.E)$ would first require adding the type assignment $x : \tau_1$ to the environment, then computing the type of E in this new environment to be τ_2, and then finally inferring the type of the original term to be $\tau_1 \rightarrow \tau_2$. Our rule uses β-reduction and operationally works as follows. Given the term $(lamb \ M)$ we first pick a new constant c and assume it has type τ_1 (i.e., we introduce the assumption $c \xrightarrow{ty} \tau_1$). Under this assumption we then type (the $\beta\eta$-normal form of) the term $(M \ c)$. If M is of the form $\lambda x.e$ then the β-reduction is, in this case, equivalent to the substitution $e[x \mapsto c]$. If we infer the type τ_2 for this term then we infer the type of the original term to be $\tau_1 \rightarrow \tau_2$. Informally, this infers the correct type because every occurrence of x bound by this abstraction has been replaced by a term c whose type will be inferred to be τ_1. Although this is in many ways similar to the environment approach, it avoids the need to access the names of bound variables.

Clause 4 is the usual typing rule for application. Clause 6 for fixed points uses the same technique as $lamb$, though in this case we know that M must be of type $\tau{\rightarrow}\tau$ for some τ. Clause 5 requires some explanation. The more standard implementation of type inference for *let* first infers a type for e_2, then generalizes that type with a universal quantifier over type variables, yielding a polytype. Later in the typing of the abstraction M, various universal instances of this polytype could be made for instances of the abstracted variable of M. Our meta-language, however, contains no method for generalizing a free variable into a bound variable, and so this kind of implementation is not possible here. Instead, we avoid inferring a polytype for e_2 explicitly. Clause 5 requires that e_2 have some type, but that type is then ignored. β-reduction is used to substitute e_2 into the abstraction M, and then the type of the result is inferred. If e_2 is placed into several different places in M, each of those instances will again have a type inferred for them; this time the types might be different. Therefore, e_2 could be polymorphic in that its occurrences in M might be at several different types.

We do not need a rule for typing identifiers because any identifier occurring in a term is replaced via β-reduction with either (*i*) a term explicitly typed via an assumption (*lamb*, *fix*) or (*ii*) a term whose type has already been inferred (*let*). (Recall that we are typing only closed expressions.) Note that the three clauses that make use of β-reduction correspond precisely to the three clauses in the environment approach that extend the environment. This is not surprising as these are the only three clauses that introduce identifiers and bindings.

We can view this proof system as a declarative specification for type checking problems. Given a *closed* proposition of the form $e\xrightarrow{ty}\tau$, finding a proof of this proposition asserts that the type of (the expression denoted by) e is τ. Of course we would like to have type inference algorithm to which we supply the open proposition $e\xrightarrow{ty}T$. Numerous works have shown that type inference can be accomplished by unification. We apply these ideas by exploiting our logic programming implementation for our meta-logic that comes equipped with unification. Thus by posing the query $?-\ e\xrightarrow{ty}T$, for some closed e, to the logic program corresponding to this specification, unification resolves all the type constraints imposed by the inference rules. Note that the resulting answer substitution θ may not be ground, i.e., $\theta(T)$ may contain free type variables. For example the result of the query

$$?-\ (lamb\ \lambda x.x)\xrightarrow{ty}T$$

would have T instantiated to $t{\rightarrow}t$ for some type variable t. We have no explicit rule for quantifying over type variables but we may implicitly assume the expression to denote the type $\forall t.t{\rightarrow}t$.

24.6.2   The Subsumes Relation for Polytypes

As a second example of using our meta-language to manipulate ML-like types, we present a proof system for the subsumes relation on polytypes [20]. For this purpose, we now introduce a higher-order constant for constructing ML types, namely the type quantifier *forall* which is of meta-type $(tp{\to}tp){\to}tp$. Any term of type tp which does not contain an instance of this constant is a monotype. A term of type tp in which all of occurrences of *forall* are in its prefix (that is, no occurrence of *forall* is in the scope of $\to$) is called a *polytype* (a monotype is a polytype). It is possible to construct terms (of meta-type tp) that are neither monotypes nor polytypes, but these will not interest us here. In the following discussion, the greek letter τ will represent a monotype and σ a polytype. Before defining the subsumes relation we provide an auxiliary definition.

DEFINITION 2 (Instance of a Polytype). *τ is an instance of polytype (forall $\lambda t_1(\ldots(forall \ \lambda t_n(\tau'))\ldots))$ if there exists some substitution S of the variables $t_1,\ldots,t_n$ into monotypes such that $S(\tau') = \tau$.*

The subsumes relation on polytypes is then given by the following.

DEFINITION 3 (Subsumes). *Let σ_1 and σ_2 be two polytypes. σ_1 subsumes σ_2, written $\sigma_1 \sqsubseteq \sigma_2$, if every instance of σ_2 is also an instance of σ_1.*

For example, the polytype *(forall $\lambda t.t$)* subsumes all other polytypes. An informal operational description of this definition is the following. Given σ_1 and σ_2, erase the quantifiers of each yielding two monotypes, τ_1 and τ_2. Then $\sigma_1 \sqsubseteq \sigma_2$ iff there exists a substitution S such that $S(\tau_1) = \tau_2$. Since the erasure of bound variables is another operation not available in our meta-language, we need to approach the implementation of subsumes differently.

In our meta-language we can construct a simple proof system for the subsumes relation; it is given in Figure 24.5. The first clause states the obvious: any polytype subsumes itself. The second clause produces a 'canonical' instance of σ_2. This step is essentially like the process of erasing a type quantifier. The meta-level universal quantifier used in this clause ensures that, after removing the quantifiers on σ_2, revealing a monotype, any future substitution does not affect this monotype (its free variables are, in a sense, protected). The third clause is used to build an instance of the first type by stripping off a quantifier (replacing a bound (type) variable with a free one).

Notice that these three proof rules have a simple declarative reading. Assume that types are interpreted as sets of objects of that type, that *forall* is interpreted as intersection, and $\sqsubseteq$ as subset. The second clause states that a type is a subset of the intersection of a family of types if it is a subset of all members of the family. The third clauses similarly states that if some member of a family is a subset by a given type, then the intersection of that family is a subset of that type.

24.7 Dynamic Semantics

Dynamic semantics refers to a class of program analyses that provide information about programs based on a dynamic behavior, i.e., some set of evaluation

$$\sigma \sqsubseteq \sigma \qquad \frac{(\forall c)\ \sigma_1 \sqsubseteq (M\ c)}{\sigma_1 \sqsubseteq (forall\ M)} \qquad \frac{(M\ x) \sqsubseteq \sigma_2}{(forall\ M) \sqsubseteq \sigma_2}$$

Figure 24.5: Subsumes Relation for Polytypes

rules is assumed and the behavior of programs under these rules is considered. In this section we present a standard evaluation semantics that provides a declarative specification for an E interpreter. Other, non-standard semantics, including strictness analysis and mixed evaluation are also possible [9].

We would like to specify the evaluation of expressions in E, based on a simple interpreter for the language. (We say standard here to distinguish from a non-standard semantics.) Following [16] we refer to a formal specification of an evaluator for a language as the language's *dynamic semantics*. We characterize the dynamic semantics of an object language via judgements of the form $e \longrightarrow \alpha$ in which e is an expression of the object language and α is the result of evaluating e. Informally, the terms appearing to the left of $\longrightarrow$ denote expressions and the terms appearing to the right are the "values" or meanings of the expressions. By providing rules corresponding to the operational behavior of the language (with the general guideline of having one rule for each programming language construct) we can specify the declarative aspects of evaluators for the language, isolated from control issues. As mentioned previously this provides a convenient tool for analyzing and experimenting with new programming languages.

We now present a dynamic semantics for E, using the same abstract syntax as given in Section 24.5. As with the type inference specification we introduce a new infix propositional symbol $\xrightarrow{se} : tm \to tm \to o$. Propositions in our system are of the form $e \xrightarrow{se} \alpha$ in which e and α are expressions in E and α is the result of "evaluating" e. Proofs of these propositions are constructed from the proof system given in Figure 24.6. The first rule treats the constants of the language as just evaluating to themselves. The next two rules treat the *if* expression in a natural way: the conditional part, e_1 must evaluate to *true* or *false* for a proof to be found. Rule (3) states that an abstraction evaluates to itself. In the rule for application (4), meta-level β-reduction correctly captures the notion of function application (with a call-by-value semantics). Similar comments apply to our rule for *let* (5). In the rule for recursion (6) we introduce a fixed point operator with its intuitive operational semantics (i.e., unfolding). This again makes explicit use of meta-level β-reduction as the meta-term M is applied to the term $(fix\ M)$. The result of β-converting this expression substitutes the recursive call, namely $(fix\ M)$, within the body of the recursive program, given by M. Static scoping is ensured with this specification because β-reduction, as a means of propagating binding information, guarantees that the identifiers occurring free within a lambda abstraction are replaced (with their associated value) prior to manipulating the

$$c \xrightarrow{se} c \qquad\qquad (1)$$

$$\frac{e_1 \xrightarrow{se} true \qquad e_2 \xrightarrow{se} \alpha}{(if\ e_1\ e_2\ e_3) \xrightarrow{se} \alpha} \qquad\qquad \frac{e_1 \xrightarrow{se} false \qquad e_3 \xrightarrow{se} \alpha}{(if\ e_1\ e_2\ e_3) \xrightarrow{se} \alpha} \qquad (2a, 2b)$$

$$(lamb\ M) \xrightarrow{se} (lamb\ M) \qquad\qquad (3)$$

$$\frac{e_1 \xrightarrow{se} (lamb\ M) \qquad e_2 \xrightarrow{se} \alpha_2 \qquad (M\ \alpha_2) \xrightarrow{se} \alpha}{(e_1 @ e_2) \xrightarrow{se} \alpha} \qquad (4)$$

$$\frac{e_2 \xrightarrow{se} \alpha_2 \qquad (M\ \alpha_2) \xrightarrow{se} \alpha}{(let\ M\ e_2) \xrightarrow{se} \alpha} \qquad\qquad \frac{(M\ (fix\ M)) \xrightarrow{se} \alpha}{(fix\ M) \xrightarrow{se} \alpha} \qquad (5, 6)$$

Figure 24.6: Standard Evaluation Semantics for E

abstraction.

The values implicitly defined by this specification (i.e., the set of terms that can appear to the right of $\xrightarrow{se}$) are just the set of constants, lambda abstractions and primitive constructors. In general, the set of values may not always be a subset of the language (as is the case in [16]). Now given some closed expression e we can think of evaluating e by finding some value α such that $e \xrightarrow{se} \alpha$ is provable. We assume some non-deterministic search procedure is used to find such an α and construct such a proof.

24.8 Summary

We have presented a meta-logic for the analysis and manipulation of functional programs. Using a higher-order, intuitionistic meta-logic we encoded axioms and inference rules as clauses in this logic. The expressive power of this logic provides us the ability to specify, in a natural and formal setting, a variety of program manipulation tasks (e.g., type inferencing, evaluation and compilation) as proof systems. This formal setting distinguishes our approach, as a meta-logic, from more ad hoc methods of meta-programming. Though not discussed here, existing methods from proof theory, as pertain to natural deduction, often provide a natural basis for performing meta-theoretic analyses of these proof systems.

We presented several examples to support our claim that this meta-logic permits a high-level and elegant specification of program manipulations. From the perspective of program specifications, we argued that the proof rules provided in this meta-logic were more perspicuous than, for example, a first-order logic, and we did not need to introduce any non-logical meta-level operations to implement all the examples considered. An important aspect of practical meta-programming systems is the compiling of the specifications (e.g., inference rules) into efficient programs. Although we see no reason to believe that the specifications given here could not be implemented efficiently, it seems probable that such compiling will be more involved than it is for compiling specifications written in a first-order meta-logic.

The ability of a meta-language to "scale-up" to richer languages is also important. The language that we considered was only a simple one providing a small subset of Standard ML. In particular, we did not include datatype definitions, exceptions, modules, etc. We have, however, used our meta-logic to represent and manipulate an enriched language containing datatype definitions (both concrete and abstract). The binding and scoping of the datatype constructors is handled in a manner similar to our treatment of bound variables: New (higher-order) constants are added to the abstract syntax for constructing terms denoting the introduction of data constructors and type names to expressions. For abstract datatypes, the concealment of the structure of the datatype is naturally handled using meta-level abstractions in λ-terms. Additional binding and scoping facilities exist in Standard ML (e.g., modules) and future work will explore the applicability of our methods to these.

Acknowledgements: We would like to thank Carl Gunter for first directing us towards the work on operational and natural semantics. We also like to thank Amy Felty, Elsa Gunter and Val Breazu-Tannen for several valuable discussions related to this paper.

The first author is supported in part by a fellowship from the Corporate Research and Architecture Group, Digital Equipment Corporation, Maynard, MA USA. Both authors are supported in part by grants NSF CCR-87-05596, ONR N00014-88-K-0633, and DARPA N00014-85-K-0018.

References

[1] A. Appel and D. MacQueen. A standard ML compiler. In G. Kahn, editor, *Proceedings of the Conference on Functional Programming and Computer Architecture*, Springer-Verlag LNCS, Vol. 274, 1987.

[2] P. Borras *et. al. CENTAUR: the System.* Technical Report 777, INRIA, December 1987.

[3] R. Burstall and Furio Honsell. A natural deduction treatment of operational semantics. In *Foundations of Software Technology and Theoretical Computer Science*, pages 250–269, Springer-Verlag LNCS, Vol. 338, 1988.

[4] D. Clément, J. Despeyroux, T. Despeyroux, and G. Kahn. A simple applicative language: mini-ML. In *Proceedings of the ACM Lisp and Functional Programming Conference*, pages 13–27, 1986.

[5] D. Clément, J. Despeyroux, L. Hascoët, and G. Kahn. *Natural Semantics on the Computer*. Research Report 416, INRIA, June 1985.

[6] A. Felty and D. Miller. Specifying theorem provers in a higher-order logic programming language. In *Proceedings of the Ninth International Conference on Automated Deduction*, 1988.

[7] G. Gentzen. Investigations into logical deduction. In M. Szabo, editor, *The Collected Papers of Gerhard Gentzen*, pages 68–131, North-Holland Publishing Co., 1969.

[8] J. Hannan. Notes on embedding the untyped λ-calculus in a simply typed λ-calculus. 1988. (Unpublished notes).

[9] J. Hannan. Proof theoretic methods for analysis of functional programs. December 1988. Dissertation Proposal, University of Pennsylvania, Technical Report MS-CIS-89-07.

[10] J. Hannan and D. Miller. Deriving mixed evaluation from standard evaluation for a simple functional language. In *Proceedings of the International Conference on Mathmatics of Program Construction*, Springer-Verlag, 1989. (to appear).

[11] J. Hannan and D. Miller. *Enriching a Meta-Language with Higher-Order Features*. Technical Report MS-CIS-88-45, University of Pennsylvania, June 1988.

[12] R. Harper, F. Honsell, and G. Plotkin. A framework for defining logics. In *Symposium on Logic in Computer Science*, pages 194–204, 1987.

[13] R. Harper, R. Milner, and M Tofte. *The Semantics of Standard ML, Version 2*. Technical Report, Edinburgh University, 1988.

[14] G. Huet. A unification algorithm for typed λ-calculus. *Theoretical Computer Science*, 1:27–57, 1975.

[15] G. Huet and B. Lang. Proving and applying program transformations expressed with second-order logic. *Acta Informatica*, 11:31–55, 1978.

[16] G. Kahn. Natural semantics. In *Proceedings of the Symposium on Theoretical Aspects of Computer Science*, pages 22–39, Springer-Verlag LNCS, Vol. 247, 1987.

[17] A. Meyer. What is a model of the lambda calculus? *Information and Control*, 52(1):87–122, 1981.

[18] D. Miller and G. Nadathur. A logic programming approach to manipulating formulas and programs. In *Proceedings of the IEEE Fourth Symposium on Logic Programming*, IEEE Press, 1987.

[19] D. Miller, G. Nadathur, and A. Scedrov. Hereditary Harrop formulas and uniform proof systems. In *Symposium on Logic in Computer Science*, pages 98–105, ACM Press, 1987.

[20] J. Mitchell and B. Harper. The essence of ML. In *Proceedings of the ACM Conference on Principles of Programming Languages*, pages 28–46, 1988.

[21] G. Nadathur and D. Miller. An overview of λProlog. In K. Bowen and R. Kowalski, editors, *Fifth International Conference and Symposium on Logic Programming*, MIT Press, 1988.

[22] L. Paulson. The foundation of a generic theorem prover. (To appear in the *Journal of Automated Reasoning*).

[23] F. Pfenning and C. Elliot. Higher-order abstract syntax. In *Proceedings of the ACM-SIGPLAN Conference on Programming Language Design and Implementation*, 1988.

[24] G. Plotkin. Call-by-name, call-by-value and the λ-calculus. *Theoretical Computer Science*, 1(1):125–159, 1976.

[25] G. Plotkin. *A Structural Approach to Operational Semantics*. DAIMI FN-19, Aarhus University, Aarhus, Denmark, September 1981.

[26] Dag Prawitz. *Natural Deduction*. Almqvist & Wiksell, Uppsala, 1965.

[27] T. Reps. *Generating Language-Based Environments*. MIT Press, 1985.

[28] M. Tofte. *Operational Semantics and Polymorphic Type Inference*. PhD thesis, University of Edinburgh, 1987.

Chapter 25
Meta Logic Programming for Epistemic Notions

Yue Jun Jiang†   Nader Azarmi‡

†Cambridge University, Cambridge, U.K.
‡University of Essex, Colchester, U.K.

Abstract

Current meta logic programming paradigms are mostly concerned with a *first order representation* of meta-level concepts. A consequence is that the *semantic aspect* of the concepts is generally handled in an *indirect syntactical encoding* of a first order theory. In particular, the meta concept of epistemic notions is treated as a relationship between a syntactical predicate BEL/Prove and a sentence. In this paper however, we introduce a *possible-worlds semantics* based meta logic programming paradigm for epistemic notions. Such a paradigm is intended to *directly* represent and reason what beliefs we (introspectively) have and do not have; and what beliefs we think other agents to have and not to have. For this purpose, a *computational* Horn clausal logic of *quantified* epistemic notions with an *epistemic SLD-like resolution* proof procedure is presented. In particular, the logic is augmented with a formal intensional scheme to handle the *intensional imputation* of epistemic notions that is often overlooked in current meta logic programming paradigms of epistemic notions.

25.1   Introduction

25.1.1   Motivations

An object-level formalism is concerned with the representation of the world (or domain of application); while a metalevel formalism is concerned with the representation of the object-level formalization such as inference mechanism and theories. There are many aspects of meta knowledge such as syntax [Genesereth & Nilsson 87], provability [Bowen & Kowalski 82], proofs [Bowen 85], controls

[Galliare & Lasserre 82] and KR-structures [Nakashima 84]. However in this paper, we are only concerned with a particular semantic aspect of meta concepts - the epistemic notions.

Epistemic notions are important because our representation of the world is generally *incomplete* and *subjective* (or we subjectively think it is objective). This means that an effective logic programming paradigm should attempt to solve a problem on the basis of what it knows and what it does not, rather than to wait for the complete state of the world which may never be obtained. This requirement is more crucial for distributed problem solving systems where communication and cooperation are essential. In this case, a system is further required to rely on its knowledge (or beliefs) about other systems's knowledge (or beliefs) in order to make a proper decision.

The importance of epistemic notions is also well-recognized in both computer science in general [Fagin, Halpern & Vardi 84] (eg. distributed systems [Halpern & Moses 84]) and in artificial intelligence in particular [Moore 85] (eg. multi-agent planning [Konolige 81, Morgenstern 86]). Thus the introduction of epistemic notions into a meta programming paradigm is both conceptually enriching and practically useful. In particular, such an introduction will additionally grant us the ability of introspective reasoning [Maes 87] of our own knowledge and meta-reasoning of other people's knowledge.

However it should be noted that epistemic notions could be formulated in many existing meta logic programming paradigms [eg. Simi & Motta 88]. Nevertheless, a *framework* that is capable of encoding concepts should not be confused from a *theory* that reasons about these concepts. It is the theory of epistemic notions that is lacking in most current meta logic programming paradigms (eg. [Bowen & Kowalski 82]). In the case that such a theory does exist in some paradigms (eg. [Perlis 87, Attardi & Simi 84]), a common trend is that a *syntactic* approach (eg. virtually all papers in [Maes & Nardi 88]) to beliefs is usually adopted due to the first order logic foundation of these paradigms.

In this approach, beliefs are treated as a set of syntactic formulae [Eberle 74]. However in order to reason about such beliefs, the approach normally has to identify beliefs with a proof theory of some logic. Usually a first order proof theory is assumed [Konolige 85]. In a first order setting, this entails to encode beliefs as meta terms [eg. Moore 85]) or godelized formula (either in quotation [eg. Perlis 87]) or godel labelling [eg. Jiang 88c]). In a meta-architectural setting [Genesereth 83], a base set of beliefs is assumed which can be successively examined by a meta system [Konolige 85a]. In both cases, introspection is normally obtained by examing the current level of representation using techniques such as *reflection* [Smith 82], *meta-agents* [Doyle 80] or *impasse activation* [Laird etal 84].

While the syntactical approach does have many appealing features to formalize beliefs (eg. regarding logic omniscience and higher-order concepts etc. [Perlis 87, Morgenstern 86, Moore & Hendrix 79, Jiang 88d, Weyhrauch 80]), it however generally suffers the following main problems

1. Since the syntactic approach to beliefs/knowledge is usually a simulation of our intuitive understanding, unlike a semantic approach, it is difficult to analyze the set of epistemic axioms used [Halpern & Moses 85]. In particular, the approach is too *fine grain* [Levesque 84] in the sense that it distinguishes too much. For example, $A\&B$ will be different from $B\&A$ in the syntactic approach unless proper axioms are introduced.

2. The use of quotations or godelizations in the place of formulae (eg. [Perlis 85], [Morgenstern 86]) although has the advantage of allowing variable sentences, it nevertheless complicates the first order proof theory involved (eg. involving non-trivial string operations or godelization mapping), especially in the case of nested quantify-in beliefs (also see [Rivieres & Levesque 86] for more enlightment on this subject).

3. Although a first order quotation-like representation allows an infinite level of self-referential (or meta) expressiveness (eg. FOL [Weyhrauch 80]), this however could also introduce paradoxes as a result of epistemic reasoning. For example, if a system C receives the message from B "Do whatever A tells you to do" and the message from A "Do not do whatever B tells you to do", then a paradox would arise in System C's reasoning.

Although there are solutions to this problem [Gilmore 74, Kripke 75, Perlis 87, Herzberger 82], they tend to dismantle the simplicity of standard first order logic with the introduction of a possibly large set of truth axioms. In particular as shown by Turner [88], though externally two valued, the internal logics of these systems are essentially three valued based on either [Kleene 52] or [Luckasiewicz 30]. A consequence is that many of the (intuitively correct) principles in standard Tarskian truth definition become invalid (eg. the excluded-middle principle $P \vee \neg p$ fails in [Kripke 75]; the meta excluded-middle principle $\text{TRUE}(p) \vee \text{TRUE}(\neg p)$ fails in [Perlis 87]).

4. Perhaps the most serious defect of the first order syntactical approach to beliefs is its inability to reason about beliefs *directly*. First order Hilbert style systems of beliefs are usually used (eg. [Morgenstern 87]), however no serious proofs exist to automate them [Geissler & Konolige 86]. As an alternative, McCarthy etal [78] and Moore [85] proposed a first order axiomatization of possible-worlds semantics at the expense of quantification over beliefs. This has been shown by Sakakibara [87] to be implementable in Prolog. This approach nevertheless is still very inefficient because it involves reasoning about possible worlds and other objects of semantic domains, rather than manipulating beliefs *directly*.

25.1.2   The semantical approach to beliefs and problems

In this paper, we thus propose a *semantical* approach to beliefs in an epistemic meta logic programming paradigm. In this approach, beliefs are characterized by a set of possible worlds [Hintikka 62] in the semantics of Kripke structures [Kripke 63]. A Kripke's structure is a tuple $(S, \pi, p_1, \ldots, p_m)$ where S is a set of possible worlds/states, π is an assignment of truth values to the primitive propositions for each state $s \in S$, and p_i is agent i's *accessibility* relation. Intuitively, $(s, t) \in p_i$ if agent i cannot distinguish state s from state t (so that if s is the actual state of the world, agent i would consider t a possible state of the world). Thus in Kripke's possible-worlds semantics of beliefs, if an agent believes p, then p is true in all the worlds he thinks to be possible.

One important advantage of the semantical approach is that by slight modifications (eg. reflexive, symmetric, transitive, serial, euclidean etc) of the accessibility relations between possible worlds, we can obtain various axiomatic modal logics (eg. K, D, T, S4, S5) of beliefs that can be useful in various applications. These logics are both important as an analytic tool in analyzing systems, and as a means of endowing artificial agents with the ability to reason about the knowledge and belief of other agents [Halpern & Moses 85].

One important problem of possible-worlds formalization of epistemic notions is *logical omniscience* which entails that every agent believes the consequential closure of his explicit beliefs and every agent knows all the axioms; ie. every agent has the same level of general procedure. Although there are solutions to this problem in [Levesque 84], [Fagin & Halpern 85], we however omit it in this paper due to space limit. Detailed solutions can be found in [Jiang 88b].

Another important problem in epistemic formalisms is the so called *intensional imputation* as defined by Barnden [86] which is often overlooked in a first order meta languages (eg. in [Perlis 87]). It is concerned with the generation of unwarranted inferences of concepts as a failure to capture the intensional meanings of the concepts in epistemic formalisms. One simple case of intensional imputation in epistemic formalisms is that a *rigid designator* or *standard naming scheme* is usually assumed so that a name always identifies the same objects. For example, the term *John's father* in "Simon knows that John's father likes Mary" and "Tom knows that John's father dislikes Mary" denotes the same individual even Tom may be referring a particular individual who happens to be John's father; while Simon may be talking about John's father without even knowing who he is. Since the meaning of terms is important in many AI applications, eg. natural language understanding and planning, a proper remedy of the problem is thus quite crucial.

A third and most important problem in formalizing epistemic notions in modal logics is their computer automation. Clearly, the Hilbert style systems (eg. [Gabbay etal 80, Wolper 80]) would be very inefficient. Thus normally, the decision methods are restricted at the propositional level [Halpern&Moses 85]. Otherwise the introduction of quantified modal logic often requires much creative help from a user or give rise to long proofs [Abadi&Manna 86].

Farinas del Cerro [83] proposed imitating classical clausal resolution [Robinson 65] in some modal logics (eg. temporal logics). The proposed method can be incorporated in a very efficient Prolog environment [Farinas del Cerro 86], but fails to treat many epistemic notions under consideration. In particular, quantifying-in beliefs are not allowed. Another classical approach to modal logic is taken by [Abadi & Manna 87]. Their system however is mainly concerned with (extended Horn clausal) temporal logics. Thus the problems of intensional imputation and epistemic reasoning are not addressed. A similar approach is also taken by Fujita *et al* [86] based on Moszkowski's temporal *interval* logic [83] (rather than *points* as opposed to Abadi & Manna 87).

A non-classical automation was taken by Abadi&Manna [86] who introduce non-clausal resolution rules for modal logics. This has the virtue of added clarity, since formulae do not need to be rephrased in unnatural and sometimes long clausal forms. However the resulting system involves many simplification rules and deduction rules which could significantly compromise the efficiency and the transparency of the system. This problem is particularly serious when dealing with quantifiers and flexible symbols which additionally require complex constraints to be satisfied to ensure the *soundness* of first order modal resolutions rules.

Despite the possibly unnatural form of clauses, clause-based resolution still remains as an important proof strategy for quantified epistemic logics. In [Konolige 86], Konolige thus introduced a clausal resolution based proof theory called *B-resolution* for quantified epistemic notions. In his approach, he first developed an intensional scheme to solve the quantifying-in variables. Then a technique based on *semantic attachment* [Weyhrauch 80] [1] was presented. However their mechanization is lack of control of search space and involve inefficient recursive procedure calls in resolving epistemic formulae [Jackson and Reichgelt 87].

Nevertheless, B-resolution appears to provide a foundation for mechanizing epistemic logics in the same spirit as Robinson's resolution for first order logic. Like Robinson's resolution, unrestricted B-resolution would also inevitably generate a huge search space. This has been demonstrated in an earlier work [Jiang 88a]. However the logic used is full clausal form of logic which is still rather inefficient as a logic programming paradigm.

In this paper, we thus try to develop a SLD-like [Lloyd 84] B-resolution for a Horn clausal epistemic logic. This logic is intended as the theoretical basis of an epistemic logic programming paradigm in the same spirit as a Horn clausal logic [Kowalski 83] to Prolog-like paradigms [Clocksin & Mellish 81]. In other words, we want to write down epistemic formulae as a program whose execution is *directly* based on the proof theory of the epistemic logic.

---

[1] The idea of showing validity or unsatisfiability of a predication by means of a computation that reflects the intended meaning of the predicate is called semantic attachment.

The paper is organized as follows. In section 25.2, we introduce a powerful but simple intensional scheme to to enhance the expressive power of representing the meaning of terms in epistemic context. We will define its formal semantics. In section 25.3, we will show how the intensional scheme can be used to obtain a satisfiability-preserving skolemized quantifier free epistemic formulae. We then show how an intensionalized epistemic formulae can be transformed into a satisfiability-preserving clausal form of epistemic logics. In Section 25.4, we first introduce B-resolution and analyze its problems. We then show how a sound and complete set-of-support strategy and a linear refutation strategy can be applied to B-resolution for a restricted logic of belief.

25.2   A formal intensional scheme

Partial solutions to the *intensional imputation* problem have been proposed by several people. On the semantic front, Konolige [86] has introduced a bullet operator to quantifying-in variables/terms. Thus in the formula $\exists x p(x) \& B(q(\bullet x))$, the bullet operator would enable the quantifying-in variable x to denote a rigid term in the actual world, no matter what the context of interpretation. On the syntactic front, McCarthy [79] has introduced a two level intensional scheme *(de ref* and *de dicto)* denoted by lower case and upper case strings respectively in his first order formalization of concepts.

Both approaches however fail to capture the intensional imputation that could arise from implicitly quantifying-in terms (eg. constants, function terms etc) in nested beliefs. For example, "John's father" is not distinguished in the following two sentences "Simon knows that John's father likes Mary" and "Tom knows that Simon knows that John's father likes Mary", even though Simon may be referring a particular individual that happens to be John's father; while Tom may be referring John's father without even knowing him.

In recognizing this problem, Abadi&Manna [86] introduced some new equations and some new universal variables for (implicitly/explicitly) quantifying-in terms in nested beliefs. For example, in their logic, the formula that contains an explicitly quantifying term,

$$B(a, \exists x(p(x)\&B(b, q(x))))$$

can be represented by the following skolemized formulae where c is a flexible skolem constant:

$$B(a, \forall x(x = c) \rightarrow (p(x)\&B(b, q(x)))).$$

This approach however is very inefficient due to the introduction of equations which gets particularly messy in deep nested beliefs.

The intensional imputation problem was also addressed in Wilks & Ballim [87] when they are concerned with the ascription of atypical beliefs. Their solutions uses a variation of McCarthy's lambda formulae [see Wilks 1986] to represent the relationships between values of terms (expressed in lambda formulae) and agents. However the introduction of lambda expressions could significantly compromise the efficiency of the proof theory. It is also not clear what the semantics of such formulation is. In particular, there does not seem to be a coherent way of reasoning about these lambda formula.

To solve these problems, we propose a *levelled intensional scheme* that does not assume the rigid designator assumption nor constant domain assumption. For the purpose of this paper, we restrict ourselves to a constant domain of possible worlds (ie. the Barcan formula $\forall x B(p(x)) \leftrightarrow B(\forall x p(x))$ holds).

Since the intensionality of a quantifying-in (implicit/explicit) term is possible-world dependent and the nestness of agents characterizes the nestness of accessibility relations between possible worlds, we can thus use the nested agents as a measure of the intensional *flexibility* of a quantifying-in term in a nested beliefs. This is indicated at the syntactic level by a pair structure consisting of the term and an *ordered* list of nested agents with defaults denoting the outmost (or actual world) quantifying-in terms. For example, we could represent the statement "Simon believes that Tom believes that Venus likes Mars" as

$$B(S, B(T, L((V, < S, T >), (M, < S >)))),$$

if Venus denotes a concept in what Simon believes to be in Tom's mind; and Mars denotes a concept in Simon's mind. Semantically, Mars is a flexible constant in all the worlds Simon thinks to be possible; ie. it can denote different entities in different Simon's worlds. However for each entity in each of Simon's possible worlds, it will be rigid with respect to Tom's possible worlds from the perspective of Simon's world; ie; it denotes the same entity in all Tom's possible worlds in Simon's view. On the other hand, Venus will be flexible in Tom's worlds from the perspective of a Simon's possible world.

It is also possible to refer to entities in other agent's mind in an agent's beliefs [Jiang 88d]. However due to the complexity of their semantics, in this paper, we will not allow cross-references between agents. In other words, we restrict ourselves to the case that the intensionality of a term in a formula only be measured against the agents that contain the term in the formula.

In this case, the structure of a nested list of agents simply indicates the level of B modal scope, we could replace the structures with numbers ranging from zero onwards. The default level which denotes a rigid objects in the actual world is zero. In this way, the above example can be simplified as follows:

$$B(S, B(T, L((V, 2), (M, 1)))).$$

For clarity reason, we will use subscripts to indicate the levels of intension of a term in the future, eg. $Venus_2$ for $(Venus, 2)$ or

$$B(S, B(T, L(V_2, M_1))).$$

Because of the introduction of levels, existential quantifiers of different intensional scopes can be distinguished through levels. Thus instead of having a bullet operator which cannot represent intensional terms in nested beliefs, we use levels to indicate the flexibility scope of existential quantifiers. For example, the intensional forms of the following two formulae:

$$\forall x B(a, \exists y B(b, p(x, y)))$$
$$B(a, \forall x B(b, \exists y p(x, y)))$$

can be represented respectively as follows:

$$\forall x B(a, \exists y_1 B(b, p(x, y_1)))$$
$$B(a, \forall x B(b, \exists y_2 p(x, y_2)))$$

It may be noted that the level of intension of an explicitly quantifying-in variable need not be explicitly represented at all. This is because such level corresponds to the position of the existential quantifiers within the scope of nested B operators. Nevertheless, we explicitly keep the levels here for reason of skolemization as shown in the next section.

Because of the assumption of Barcan formulae, the variables of universal polarity in each intensional scope (or B-operator) always have the same intensionality. We use the symbol "_" to denote the levels of intension of these variables, meaning that such a level is unifiable with any other levels (see later regarding unification).

To see how function terms may be intensionally represented, we use the following different interpretations of "John's father" in the sentence "Simon believes that Tom believes that John's father likes Mary" as an illustration.

1. $B(s, B(t, l(f(j), m)))$

   In this formula, Simon is simply referring an individual in the actual world who happens to be John's father.

2. $B(s, B(t, l(f(j)_1, m)))$

   In this formula, Simon is referring John's father whom he believes Tom to know although he may not know John's father himself.

3. $B(s, B(t, l(f(j)_2, m)))$

   In this formula, Simon is referring John's father whom he himself may not know and whom he may not think Tom to know either.

We can now extend the possible-worlds semantics to include the concept of intensions of terms (denoted by integer levels of intension) as follows. We define the following Kripke like model structure $M = (W, D, p_j, F, g)$ where

1. W is a non-empty set of possible worlds with $w0$ as the actual world;

2. D is a constant universe of discourse for all possible worlds;

3. p_j is the accessibility relation for each agent j;

4. F is a function which assigns to each pair consisting of a n-place function symbol and an element w of W, a function from D^n to D, and which assigns to each pair consisting of a n-place predicate symbol and an element w of W, a set of tuples of D^n;

5. g is a assignment function which assigns an element of a domain of a world to an individual constant.

Given the above semantic structure M, we can define the following satisfiability relation $\models_M$ recursively between a possible world and a belief as follows. Unlike standard possible worlds semantics, we use a sequence of possible worlds $< w0, ..., w_i >= ws$ to denote a possible world w_i from the perspective of w_{i-1} which eventually comes from the perspective of $w0$.

1. $ws \models_M p(a1_{ag1}, ..., an_{agn})$ iff $< Val(a1_{ag1}, ws, g), ..., Val(an_{agn}, ws, g) > \in F(p, w_i)$

   where $Val(t_{ag1}, ws, g) = g(t, \Pi(ag1, ws))$ if t is a constant,

   $Val(f(t1, ..tn)_{ag1}, ws, g) = g(F(f, w)(< Val(t1, ws, g), ..., Val(tn, ws, g) >), w)$

   where $w = \Pi(ag1, ws))$

   where Π is a function from an integer j and a sequence of possible worlds to the jth world of the sequence; ie.

$$II(j, ws) = ws[j]$$

2. $ws \models_M B(a, p)$ iff for all $w1$ such that $(w_i, w1) \in p_a$, $ws\|w1 \models_M p$ where $< w0, .., w_i > \|w =< w0, ..., w_i, w >$

3. $ws \models_M \neg p$ iff $\neg(ws \models_M p)$

4. $ws \models_M p \vee q$ iff $ws \models_M p$ or $ws \models_M q$

5. $ws \models_M p\&q$ iff $ws \models_M p$ and $ws \models_M q$

6. $ws \models_M p \to q$ iff $ws \models_M \neg p$ or $ws \models_M q$

7. $ws \models_M \forall x\, p(x)$ iff for all $d \in D$ $ws \models_M p(d)$ where $p(d)$ is obtained by replacing all x in the formula p by d.

8. $ws \models_M \exists x_{ag}\, p(x_{ag})$ iff $\Pi(ag, ws) = w_i$ and there exists a $d \in D$ $ws \models_M p(d)$ where $p(d)$ is obtained by replacing all x in the formula p by d.

Now Konolige [86] has shown that Herbrand's theorem *A set of a first order formulae is unsatisfiable iff a finite subset of its ground instances is* which sanctions the *lifting* of proofs over ground sentences to those with universal variables, is not true for modal logics with standard Kripke's semantics as shown by the following example.

$$p(m(c))$$
$$\neg B(s, p(m(c)))$$
$$\forall x(p(x) \rightarrow B(s, p(x)))$$

It is easy to confirm that although all the sentences are satisfied, the substitution of $m(c)$ in the last sentence will cause the resulting set unsatisfiable. The reason for that is, although x must refer to the same individual, the substituted expression $m(c)$ need not. Konolige's solution is to redefine the meaning of instance by introducing a bullet operator • mentioned earlier whenever there is a substitution for variables inside the context of modal operators.

In contrast, Herbrand's theorem is still *naturally* valid in our logic. The reason is that, the second formula in our logic would be in the form of $\neg B(s, p(m(c)_1))$. In this case, $m(c)_1$ would denote a flexible entity in the domains of the set of possible worlds which Simon thinks to be possible; while $m(c)$ if substituted in the last sentence would denote an entity in the domain of the actual world. Thus the derived $B(s, p(m(c)))$ from the first and the third sentence would not contradict the second sentence; ie. consistency is maintained. The proof of Herbrand's theorem can be done in parallel with Konolige [86]. On the other hand, if "$m(c)$" in the second formulae has a zero intensional level (a point appears to be overlooked in [Konolige 86]), the set of formulae would be inconsistent. Thus instead of using syntactical notations to take quantifying-in variables outside B operators, our intensional scheme attemps the other way around by specifying notions for terms meant to be in the intensional scopes of B operators. This gives us a natural way of representing nested levels of intension as shown above.

Another advantage of our intensional scheme is that Lebinitz's principle of equality substitution can still be valid, provided that the equal terms have the same level of intension. Consider the earlier example that involves the functional term "John's father", if John's father is Jim in the actual world, then we can inter-substitute these two expressions in the first formula but not the others. On the other hand, if Simon believes John's father is Jim, then we can inter-substitute these expressions in the second formula but not the others.

Finally, it may be concluded that Barnden's imputation problem can be solved in our logic. It may also be noted that our intensional scheme is similar to Creary's concept formation scheme [79] that is used in Barnden's solution [86]. The difference is that we develop our scheme on a model-theoretic basis which has well-founded proof theories.

25.3 Skolemization and clausalization of epistemic formulae

25.3.1 A global skolemization scheme

Now it is widely known that skolemized forms of logic can be manipulated more efficiently and conveniently than otherwise (eg. admitted in the non-clausal approach of [Abadi&Manna 86]). However classical first order skolemization rules would fail in modal formulae because quantified variables in this case can be bound to an intensional scope. In other words, quantifiers cannot be moved outside the modal operators to yield a prenex normal form. Konolige's solution is to apply a local skolemization outside B-operators each time a recursive application of B-resolution is invoked. Our solution is to achieve a global skolemization throughout B-operators. This is possible because the levels of quantifiers indicate the position of the quantifier with respect to the modal scope/B-operators in our levelled intensional scheme.

The basic idea is that skolemization can be processed in the normal way provided proper levels of intension of quantified variables and polarity are carried forward to the skolemized term. For example, the following formulae

$$\forall x\, B(a, \exists y\, B(b, l(x, y)))$$
$$B(a, \forall x\, B(b, \exists y\, l(x, y)))$$

can be skolemized into the following forms in our logic respectively,

$$B(a, B(b, l(x, f(x)_1))).$$
$$B(a, B(b, l(x, f(x)_2))).$$

In parallel with Konolige [86], the skolemization rule preserves unsatisfiability.

Theorem: A sentence of our epistemic logic is unsatisfiable iff its skolemized form is.

To see how nested beliefs can be modelled in a skolemized form, we illustrate with the following example:

$$
\begin{array}{ll}
1. & \exists x\, B(S, B(J, U(x))) \\
2. & B(S, \exists x\, B(J, U(x))) \\
3. & B(S, B(J, \exists x\, U(x)))
\end{array}
$$

which can be skolemized into:

$$
\begin{array}{ll}
1. & B(S, B(J, U(a_0))) \\
2. & B(S, B(J, U(b_1))) \\
3. & B(S, B(J, U(c_2)))
\end{array}
$$

where a, b, c are skolem constants.

25.3.2   A clausal form of epistemic logic

As shown in the last section, our intensional scheme can be used to obtain a
satisfiability-preserving skolemized form of logic. In this section, we will take a
step further to produce a clausal form of logic.

Now the problem is that a general (standard) clausal form cannot be obtained
for modal formulae. Our solution is to introduce clausalization only in each intensional scope of the belief operator. We first define the following definitions.

Definition: An epistemic formula is in an epistemic conjunctive normal form
iff it is of the form:

$$A_1 \& A_2 \& \ldots \& A_n$$

where each A is an epistemic clause.

Definition: An epistemic literal is either a standard first order literal, ie. of the
form p or ¬p where p is an atom; or it is of the form $B(a, p)$ or $\neg B(a, p)$ where p
is an epistemic clause.

Definition: An epistemic clause is a disjunction of epistemic literals, ie.

$$C_1 \vee C_2 \vee \ldots \vee C_n$$

where each C is an epistemic literal.

For example, the formula $B(a, p \vee q) \& \neg B(b, p \vee q)$ is an epistemic conjunctive
normal if p and q are epistemic literals. On the other hand the formula $B(a, p\&q)$
is not a conjunctive normal form. By applying the standard clausal transformation
rules (such as $a \vee (b\&c) = (a \vee b)\&(a \vee c)$, $(a \rightarrow b) = (\neg a \vee b)$, $\neg(a\&b) = \neg a \vee \neg b$
) and the modal transformation rule $B(a, p\&q) = B(a, p)\&B(a, q)$ in the scope
of each B-operator, we can prove the following theorem with induction on the
nestness of modal (similar to [Cavalli&Del Cerro 83]) operators:

Theorem: There is an effective procedure which can transform every epistemic
formula into a satisfiability-preserving formula in an epistemic conjunctive normal
form.

Now because $A\&B$ are equivalent to A and B, we will use a set of epistemic
clauses to replace an epistemic conjunctive normal form. As a complex example,
the following formula or statement "for any two persons, John believes that if they
are married and love each other, then they must believe that they like something
in common",

$$\forall x \forall y (B(j, (m(x, y)\&l(x, y))$$
$$\rightarrow (B(x, \forall z lk(x, z)\&lk(y, z))$$
$$\& B(y, \exists w lk(x, w)\&lk(y, w))))$$

can be converted into the following set of clauses:

$$B(j, \neg m(x,y) \vee \neg l(x,y) \vee B(x, lk(x, f(x,y)_2)))$$
$$B(j, \neg m(x,y) \vee \neg l(x,y) \vee B(x, lk(y, f(x,y)_2)))$$
$$B(j, \neg m(x,y) \vee \neg l(x,y) \vee B(y, lk(x, g(x,y)_2)))$$
$$B(j, \neg m(x,y) \vee \neg l(x,y) \vee B(y, lk(y, g(x,y)_2)))$$

25.4 B-resolution, set-of-support and linear resolution

25.4.1 The B-resolution proof system

In [Konolige 86], Konolige has proved a set of epistemic resolution rules called *B-resolution* rules to be sound and complete for the corresponding class of logics. We can define B-resolution for a set of epistemic logics as follows.

B-resolution: Let $\Gamma = \{\gamma_1, \gamma_2 \ldots\}$, $\Sigma = \{\sigma_1, \sigma_2, \ldots\}$ and $\Delta = \{\delta_1, \delta_2 \ldots\}$ be finite sets of formulae.

In the case of ground clauses, given the following clauses (omiting the agents and intensionality of terms),

$$A_1 \vee B\gamma_1$$
$$A_2 \vee B\gamma_2$$

$$\vdots$$

$$AA_1 \vee \neg B\delta_1$$
$$AA_2 \vee \neg B\delta_2$$

$$\vdots$$

$$AB_1 \vee \sigma_1$$
$$AB_2 \vee \sigma_2$$

We can derive the following resolvent,

$$A_1 \vee A_2 \vee \ldots \vee AA_1 \vee AA_2 \vee \ldots \vee AB_1 \vee AB_2 \vee \ldots$$

where

1. $\{\Gamma, \neg\delta_1\}$ is unsatisfiable for K, T epistemic logic;

2. $\{\Gamma, B\Gamma, \neg\delta_1\}$ for K4, S4 epistemic logic;

3. $\{\Gamma, B\Gamma, \neg\delta_1, \neg B\Delta\}$ for K45 epistemic logic;

4. $\{\Gamma, B\Gamma, \neg\delta_1, \neg B\Delta, \neg B\neg\Sigma\}$ for S5 epistemic logic.

In addition, in the case of T, S4 and S5 epistemic logics, we also need to add the following *knowledge rule of inference:*

$$B\Phi \vee A$$

$$\overline{}$$

$$\Phi \vee A$$

Because the Herbrand theorem remains to be true if bullet operator is introduced for quantifying-in terms, the above ground rule will be complete if we are allowed to perform unifications among literals. However there are two problems with B-resolution. The first is that there may be no "most general" unifier as shown by the following example where there are two substitution ($x = a$ and $x = b$):

$$B(p(a)\&p(b))$$

$$\neg Bp(x)$$

The second problem is that the resolution rule is not an effective decision procedure because the search space is exponential in the number of modal literals. In order to be complete in general theory resolution [Stickel 85], rules must be applied to a minimal set of unsatisfied literals.

Geissler&Konolige's solution [86] is to apply the *semantic attachment* technique (mentioned earlier) to recursively checking the unsatisfiability condition. Suppose, each time a negative B-literal participates in a B-resolution, another refutation procedure (or a view which is similar to Kripke's device of auxiliary tableaux [59]) is invoked (or opened) using the indicated sets of sentences. Then the execution of deductions in the main refutation proof is intermixed with execution in the subsidiary ones being used to check unsatisfiability. If at some point a subsidiary refutation succeeds, we can construct a resolvent with bindings returned to a disjunction of auxiliary remainder literals in the main refutation. This allows free variables (eg. the above example) to perform a schematic refutation.

Nevertheless, B-resolution is still very inefficient because it involves recursion and lacks of control. The recursion problem is particularly severed by the need to clausalize the arbitrary forms of literals within B-operators each time a new (recursive) view is opened. The clausalization process can be exponential to the size of the literals in concern [Lakemayer 87]. The control problem on the other hand is compounded by the inability of doing set-of support and/or linear resolution.

25.4.2   A BLS-resolution proof system for an epistemic Horn clausal logic

Now our solution is to extend Konolige's resolution-based proof system to solve (or reduce the complexity of) its problems mentioned in the last section (We only show this for the simplest K logic here). Firstly, it has been shown in Section 25.2 that we have provided a more powerful intensional scheme than Konolige's bullet approach to deal with the intensional imputation problem. In this case, the unification in our logic will be defined as follows: *two terms are unifiable iff they have the same/unifiable level of intensions and they are unifiable in the standard sense.* Note here that a *variable of universal polarity* always has a unifiable level of intension with any other terms. The symbol that denotes such a level, ie. "_" has the same kind of function as the symbol "_" in Prolog. Namely, it denotes a dummy variable. Since a levelled term is itself a term, thus there is no need to change the standard unification algorithm.

Secondly, we have also *partially* solved the clausalization problem because our intensional scheme allows a global clausalization within each B operator.

Now like Robinson's general resolution principle, unrestricted use of B-resolution can also generate a plethora of redundant and irrelevant information. To use computers effectively for mechanically proving theorems, it is necessary to find strategies which will materially impede the generation of irrelevant inferences. However unlike ordinary resolution, a major problem of B-resolution is its inability to enforce a set-of-support strategy of [Wos&Robinson 65] which involves carrying out only such resolutions in which at least one of the parent clauses has ancestry traceable back to a clause in the original set-of-support.

We illustrate the problem by the following example.

query: $\neg B(a, p)$

Refuted query: $B(a, p)$

Database:

$B(a, \neg p \vee q)$

$\neg B(a, q)$

If we use the refuted query as the set-of-support, because the B-clause is positive, we cannot apply the B-resolution rule of inference (or open a view). On the other hand, the theorem/query would be proved in a general B-resolution-based system by opening a view for the negative B-clause $\neg B(a, q)$. Thus B-resolution with set-of-support will not be complete.

To solve this problem, we propose a *semi-set-of-supports* strategy for each view. The basic idea is to define a set-of-support for each view by navigations of set-of-support from a parent view in a hierarchical view structure. Initially, the refuted query is started as the set-of-support of the initial view. In any view, if the set of support is a negative B-literal $\neg B(a, p)$, we open a subview for the agent a with $\neg p$ as its set of support; on the other hand if it is a positive B-literal $B(a, p)$, we look for a negative B-literal $\neg B(a, q)$ in the view to open a subview for the agent a with p as the set-of-support of the view.

Now for the set-of-support strategy for non-modal clauses, Wos&Robinson have proven the following completeness theorem:

Theorem (completeness): If S is a finite unsatisfiable set of clauses and if $T \subseteq S$ is such that $S - T$ is satisfiable, then there exists a proof D with T as set-of-support.

To extend the theorems to B-resolution with the query as a semi-set-of-support, we must assume that the set of sentences against which the theorem to be proved, is satisfiable in our logic to maintain completeness result. The soundness follows from Konolige's B-resolution principle. For completeness, we can prove the following theorem in parallel with Wos&Robinson's result inductively on the modal depth.

Theorem (completeness): If $S + T$ is unsatisfiable and S is satisfiable in our logic, then there exists a B-resolution proof D with T as the semi set-of-support for the initial view of $S + T$.

Because linear resolution [2] is compatible with set of support for a consistent set of sentences, we can thus combine linear resolution with set of support in each view of B-resolution. Unlike ordinary set of support resolution which has a fixed set of support throughout a proof, B-resolution with set of support however can generate exponential size of set of support in a view structure of B-resolution proof. This is because, a negative B-literal of the form $\neg B(a, p \vee q \vee \ldots)$ would generate an explosive set of support $\{\neg, \neg q, \ldots\}$ for the view opened by the literal.

To solve this problem, a restricted subset of the logic which only admits *epistemic Horn clauses* is proposed. We define the following definitions.

Definition: An epistemic Horn clause is a disjunction of H-literals in which there is at most a positive H-literal.

Definitions: A H-literal is either (1) a standard first order literal; (2) a B-literal with positive polarity in a clause such that the formula in the B-operator is an epistemic Horn clause; (3) a B-literal with negative polarity in a clause such that the formula in the B-operator is a conjunction of H-literals in which there is at most a negative H-literal.

Definitions: A B-literal $B(a, p)$ has positive (or negative) polarity in a clause if there is an even (or odd) number of negation operators that contains the literal in the clause.

Now the interesting thing about Horn restriction is that the set of support for each view in our proof system will always be a single Horn clause. This is because a positive B-literal $B(a, p)$ will contain p as a Horn clause; while a negative B-literal $\neg B(a, p)$ will convert p into a Horn clause when negation is passed through the B-operator if a view is opened by the B-literal.

Since each view contains only Horn clauses and its set of support is a single Horn clause, we can thus have a sound and complete linear input B-resolution

[2]This is developed by Loveland [69] and Kowalski&Kuehner [71]

strategy with set-of-support (which we call the BLS proof procedure) for a consistent set of Horn epistemic formulae. In other words, epistemic reasoning can be performed by applying recursively a SLD-like procedure in each view.

Theorem: The BLS proof system is sound and complete for a consistent set of epistemic Horn clauses.

We can now illustrate BLS resolution proof system in the following example (omitting unification):

Query: $r \& \neg B(a, p)$

Database:

1. $\neg B(a, q)$
2. $B(a, \neg p \vee q)$
3. r

Refuted query:

0. $\neg r \vee B(a, p)$:set-of-support

Now use the refuted query as the set-of-support for the initial view, and resolve away non-modal literals first (in a linear input resolution with set-of-support similar to a SLD), we obtain:

4. $B(a, p)$

Since the literal left is a positive B-literal, we then choose a negative literal of the same agent (ie. a) to open a view with p as the set-of-support of the new view. In this case, clause 1 is chosen to open a new view, ie.

View a,

---

5. $\neg q$
6. p :set-of-support
7. $\neg p \vee q$

Again we can use a linear resolution with clause 6 as the set-of-support of the view:

resolve 6 with 7, yield:

8. q

resolve 8 with 5, yield:

9. empty

Proof is completed.

Finally, it is also possible to extend the BLS proof system to include equalities. Since terms are intensionally levelled, paramodulation thus can still be applied in the same way as before. In this case, only equal terms with same intension levels can participate in an epistemic paramodulation (details omitted here).

25.5 Conclusion

In this paper, we have presented a *computational* logic of quantified epistemic notions as the theoretical foundation of a particular type of meta logic programming — *epistemic logic programming*. It is computational because it has been indicated that it is implementable in every stage of the proof mechanization of the logic. In particular, we have addressed the following problems in the logic.

- We have developed an intensional scheme with enhanced expressive features (such as no rigid designator assumption etc.) in representing the subtle meanings of terms. In particular, we have extended the standard Kripke semantics of epistemic logics to accommodate the intensional scheme.

- We have introduced a global skolemization rule for epistemic formulae. In particular, we have shown that a clausal form of logic of belief can be obtained globally throughout epistemic formulae.

- We have shown how Konolige's B-resolution can be argumented with a linear resolution strategy with set of support as a *sound* and *complete* proof system for a Horn clausal form of epistemic logic

One serious defect of our epistemic logic is that it cannot handle quantification over beliefs; while a first order quotation-like encoding of beliefs [(eg. Morgenstern 87]) can. Nor can the logic handle quantification over predicates. For the former case for example, we cannot represent such information as "John knows what Mary knows" in our logic. For the latter case for example, we cannot represent such information as "I know what John did to Mary" (eg. John beat Mary) in our logic. It appears that some kind of higher oder epistemic logics need to be introduced to solve these problems. Unfortunately, a high order modal logic is incomplete and inconsistent for paradoxes [Rivieres & Levesque 86, Perlis 85]. For this reason, a first order syntactical view of epistemic notions is taken in [Jiang 88c]. Ongoing research is to apply a similar solution as that of Miller & Nadathur [87] for a higher-order epistemic logic that allows quantification over beliefs.

Another serious defect of our logic is that there is no effective proof theory that can handle common beliefs (by adding common belief modal operator) which are essential in distributed knowledge based systems [Halpern & Moses 84]. This is also being studied.

In summary, by ascending to epistemic resolution, Horn clausal logic programming can be naturally extended to deal with epistemic meta notions without much compromise on the existing implementations. Nevertheless, it can be seen from the paper that we have only described the theoretical framework of a logic programming paradigm. There is no indication of a Prolog implementation. Afterall Prolog is not equal to logic programming [Kowalski 83].

Acknowledgements

We like to thank Professor S.H. Lavington, Prof. R. Turner (Essex), Dr P. Aczel (Manchester), Prof. D. Warren (Bristol), for their helpful discussions. Special thanks must also be given to Dr J. Barnden (Indiana), Dr D. Perlis (Maryland) for taking up their valuable time to discuss some of the works reported in this paper.

References

M. Abadi & Z. Manna (1986), Modal theorem proving, 8th Int. Conf. on automated deduction, LNCS No 230, pp.173-189.

M. Abadi & Z. Manna (1987), Temporal Logic Programming, IEEE Inter. Symp. on logic programming, San. Francisco, pp.4-16.

L. Aiello & G. Levi (1984), The use of meta knowledge in AI systems, ECAI 84, Pisa, Italy.

A. Anderson & N. Belnap (1975), Entailment:The logic of relevance and necessity. Vol.1 Princeton Univ. Press.

G. Attardi & M. Simi (1984), Metalanguage and reasoning across viewpoints, ECAI 84, pp.315-323.

J. Barnden (1986), Interpreting propositional attitude reports: towards greater freedom and control, Proc. 7th European Conf. on AI, July, 1986.

J. Barwise & J. Perry (1983), Situations and attitudes. MIT Press.

K. Bowen & Kowalski (1982), Amalgamating language and meta-language in logic programming, Logic programming, Clark,K.L., and Tarnlund, S.-A (eds) 153-172, Academic Press, New York.

K. Bowen (1985), Meta-level programming and knowledge representation, New Generation Computing 3, pp.359-383.

K. Bowen & T. Weinberg (1985), A meta-level extension of Prolog, IEEE 1985 Sym. on Logic programming, pp.48-53.

A.R. Cavalli & L. Farinas Del Cerro (1983), A decision method for linear temporal logic, IJCAI 83.

W.F. Clocksin and C.S Mellish (1981), Programming in Prolog. Springer Verlag.

L.G. Creary (1979), Propositional attitude: Fregean representation and simulative reasoning. Proc. of 6th IJCAI. Tokyo, Japan, August.

M.J. Cresswell (1972), Intensional logics and logical truth, in J. of Phil. logic 1, 1972, pp.2-15.

J. Doyle (1980), A model for deliberation, action, introspection, MIT TR 581, Cam. Massachusetts.

R. Eberle (1974), A logic of believing, knowing and inferring, Synthese 26, 1974, pp.356-382.

H. Enderton (1972), A mathematical introduction to logic, Academic Press, 1972.

L. Farinas del Cerro (1983), Temporal reasoning and termination of programs. IJCAI, Karlsruhe, West Germany, pp.926-929.

L.Farino del Cerro (1986), MOLOG: A system that extends Prolog with modal logic. New Gen. Computing 4 pp.35-50.

R. Fagin, J.Y. Halpern & M.Y. Vardi (1984), A model theoretic analysis of knowledge, 25th IEEE Symp. on Foundations of Comp. Science., pp.268-278.

R. Fagin & J.Y. Halpern (1985), Belief, awareness, and limited reasoning. IJCAI 85, pp.491-501.

Fujita etal (1986), Logic programming based on temporal logic and its compilation to Prolog, 3rd International Conf. on Logic programming 86, London, July, 1986.

D. Gabbay, A. Pnueli etal (1980), The temporal analysis of fairness, 7th ACM Sym. on Principles of programming language, pp.163-173, 1980.

H. Galliare & C. Lasserre (1982), Metalevel control for logic programs, in logic programming (eds. CLark & Tarland), Plenum Press, pp.173-185.

Geissler&Konolige (1986), A resolution method for quantified modal logic, in Proc. theory of knowledge, ed. Y. Halpern.

M. Genesereth & N. Nilsson (1987), Logical foundations of AI. Morgan Kaufmann, 1987.

M. Genesereth (1983), A overview of meta-level architecture, in AAAI-83., Maryland.

P. Gilmore (1974), The consistency of partial set theory without extensionality, ed. J. Tech. in Axiomatic set theory, Amer. Math. Society, Prov. RI, 1974.

J. Hintikka (1962), Knowledge and belief. Ithaca, New York, Cornell Univ. Press.

J.Y. Halpern, Y. Moses (1984), Knowledge and common knowledge in a distributed environment. 3rd ACM Conf. on principles of distributed computing, pp.50-61.

Y.J. Halpern, Y. Moses (1985), A guide to the modal logics of knowledge and belief: preliminary draft. IJCAI 85, Vol.1

J.Y. Halpern (1986), Reasoning about knowledge - an overview, Proc. on the theorectical aspects of knowledge, eds. J.Y. Halpern.

H. Herzberger (1982), Notes on naive semantics, J.Phil. logic, Vol. 11, No.1, 1982.

G. Hughes & M. Cresswell (1984), An introduction to modal logic, The Chaucer Press, 1984.

P. Jackson, Reichqelt, H (1987), A general proof method for first order modal logic. IJCAI-10, pp. 942-944.

Y.J. Jiang (1988a), An epistemic model of logic programming, revised script for New Generation Computing, 1988.

Y.J. Jiang (1988b), Intension, quantified beliefs and epistemic resolution, IM-SIM 3, Torino, Italy, Oct., 1988.

Y.J. Jiang (1988c), A self-referential data model of knowledge, IFIP 88 on the role of AI in database and information systems, Canton, China, July, 1988.

Y.J. Jiang (1988d), A computational model of belief, J. of Computer and Artificial Intelligence, June, VEDA, Bratislava, 1988.

S. Kleene (1952), Introduction to metamathematics. Van Nostrand.

K. Konolige (1981), A first order theory of knowledge and action, Machine Intelligence 10.

K. Konolige (1985), Belief and incompleteness. in Formal theories of the commonsense world, Ed. J.R. Hobbes, R.C.Moore. Ablex Pub. Corp. 1985. pp.359-403.

K. Konolige (1985a), A theory of introspection, IJCAI 85.

K. Konolige (1986), Resolution and quantified epistemic logics. 8th Int. Conf. on automated deduction, LNCS No 230, pp.199-208.

R. Kowalski & D. Kuehner (1971), Linear resolution with selection function, AI. 2, pp.227-60, 1971.

R. Kowalski (1983), Logic Programming. IFIP 83, pp.133-145.

S.A. Kripke (1959), A completeness theorem in modal logic, J. of Symbolic Logic 24, pp.1-14.

S.A. Kripke (1963), Semantic considerations on modal logic, Acta Philosophica Hennica 16 pp.83-84.

J. Laird, P. Rosenbloom & A. Newell (1984), Towards chunking as a general learning mechanism, AAAI 84, Aus. Texas.

G. Lakemayer (1986), Steps towards a first-order logic of explicit and implicit belief, Proc. on theory of knowledge, ed. J. Halpern, 1986.

G. Lakemayer (1987), Tractable Meta-reasoning in propositional logics of belief, IJCAI 87.

H.J. Levesque (1984), A logic of implicit and explicit belief. Proc. National Conf. on Artificial Intelligence. pp.198-202.

H.J. Levesque (1984a), The logic of incomplete knowledge bases. On Conceptual Modelling, eds M.Brodie, J.Mylopouos&J.Schmidt, Springer-Verlag, 1984, pp.165-187.

J.W. Lloyd (1984), Foundations of logic programming, Spring-Verlag, 1984.

D. Loveland (1969), A simplified format for the model elimination theorem proving procedure, JACM 16, pp.349-363.

J. Lukasiewicz (1930), On 3-valued logic, in McCall, S. Polish Logic, Oxford, U.P. 1967.

P. Maes (1987), Introspection in knowledge representation, AISB 87, Edinburgh.

P. Maes & D. Nardi eds. (1988), Meta level architectures and Reflection, Elservier Science Publishers, North Holland, 1988.

J. McCarthy & P. Hayes (1969), Some philosophical problems from the standpoint of artificial intelligence, Machine Intelligence 4, pp463-505.

J. McCarthy et al (1978), On the model theory of knowledge, Memo AIM-312, Stanford Univ.

J. McCarthy (1979), First order theories of individual concepts and propositions. Machine Intel. 9, Eds, J.Hayes, D.Michie, L. Mikulich, Ellis Horwood.

D. Miller & G. Nadathur (1986), Higher-order logic programming, 3rd Int. Conf. on logic programming" London, LNCS 225, pp.448-462.

R. Moore & G. Hendrix (1979), On the computational semantics of belief sentences. SRI Technical Note 187, Menlo Park CA.

R. C. Moore (1985), A formal theory of knowledge and action. in Formal theories of the commonsense world, Ed. J.R. Hobbes, R.C.Moore. Ablex Pub. Corp. 1984.

L. Morgenstern (1986), A first order theory of planning, knowledge and action, Proc. of theory of knowledge, 1986.

B. Moszkowski & Z. Manna (1983), Reasoning in Interval temporal logic, LNCS 164, Logic of programs, pp.370-382.

II. Nakashima (1984), Knowledge representation in Prolog/KR, IEEE international symp. on logic programming, pp.126-130, Washington, 1984.

D. Perlis (1985), Language with self-reference I: foundations, AI 25, pp.301-322.

D. Perlis (1987), Languages with self-reference II: Knowledge, Belief and Modality. UMIACS TR 1987, also a shorter version in IJCAI 86.

J.D. Rivieres & H.J. Levesque (1986), The consistency of syntactical treatments of knowledge, Proc. of theory of knowledge, 1986.

J.A. Robinson (1965), A machine oriented logic based on the resolution principle. in JACM, Vol 12, pp.23-41.

Y. Sakakibara (1987), Programming in modal logic: An extension of Prolog based on modal logic, Logic programming 87, Japan, pp.81-91.

B. Smith (1982), Reflection and semantics in a procedural language, MIT, TR.272, Cam. Massachusetts.

M. Stickle (1985), Automated deduction by theory resolution, 9th IJCAI, 1985.

M. Simi & E. Motta (1988), Omega: an integrated reflective framework, in P. Maes etal eds. 1988 above. pp.209-227.

R. Turner (1988), Logics of Truth, unpublished manuscript, also to appear as tutorial in ECAI 88, Munich.

M.Y. Vardi (1986), On epistemic logic and logical omniscience. Proc. of the theory of knowledge, 1986.

R. Weyhrauch (1980), Prolegomenta to a theory of mechanized formal reasoning, in AI Journal Vol. 13, No. 12. North Holland. Amsterdam. The netherlands.

Y. Wilks & A. Ballim (1987), Multiple agents and the heuristic ascription of belief, IJCAI 87.

Y. Wilks (1986), CRL work on belief and computation, Workshop on the foundations of AI, Univ. of Naples, Italy, 1986.

P. Wolper (1981), Temporal logic can be more expressive, IEEE Foundation of computer science, 1981, pp.340-348.

L. Wos & A. Robinson (1965), Efficiency and completeness of the set of support strategy in theorem proving, in JACM 12, pp.536-541.

Chapter 26

Algorithmic Debugging with Assertions

Włodek Drabent ⋆   *Simin Nadjm-Tehrani*
Jan Małuszyński

⋆ *Institute of Computer Science, Polish Academy of Sciences*
Dept. of Computer and Information Science, Linköping University

Abstract

Algorithmic debugging, as presented by Shapiro, is an interactive process where the debugging system acquires knowledge about the expected meaning of a program being debugged and uses it to localize errors. This paper suggests a generalization of the language used to communicate with the debugger. In addition to the usual "yes" and "no" answers, formal specifications of some properties of the intended model are allowed. The specifications are logic programs. They employ library procedures and are developed interactively in the debugging process. An experimental debugging system incorporating this idea has been implemented. In contrast to some other systems, its diagnosis algorithms do not require instantiation of unsolved goals by the oracle. This is achieved by generalization of the oracle in the incorrectness algorithm, and by adopting a new approach in the insufficiency algorithm. A formal proof of correctness and completeness of the new insufficiency algorithm is presented. Extensions for some Prolog features are discussed.

26.1   Introduction

This paper deals with diagnosis of logic programs and extends the pioneering work of Shapiro (Shapiro 1983) by studying a way of partial automating of the oracle by means of assertions. The paper also includes extensions of the approach for some Prolog features. Implementation issues and preliminary experimental results are reported in Drabent et al. (1988b).

Logical foundations of algorithmic debugging can be found in Ferrand (1987) and Lloyd (1987). Our basic notions, though slightly different, have been strongly influenced by these papers. (For discussion of the differences see Section 26.6).

Every (pure) logic program P has a model (see e.g. (Lloyd 1987)). P is often considered to be the specification of the least Herbrand model M_P. On the other hand, the program should properly reflect the intentions of the user. These can be thought of as the "intended model" and can be viewed as a subset I_P of the Herbrand base. If I_P differs from M_P the program is erroneous.

The program P is said to be

- incorrect iff $M_P - I_P \neq \emptyset$, i.e. iff it specifies some element which is not in the intended model, and

- insufficient iff $I_P - M_P \neq \emptyset$, i.e. iff some elements of the intended model are not specified by the program.

In this paper we do not deal with the termination aspect; we concentrate on tracing incorrectness and insufficiency of a logic program. The objective of debugging is to find a cause of an error in the program.

In the case of incorrectness it is a clause which "produces" elements not in I_P. More precisely, it is a clause whose body is valid in I_P and whose head is not valid in I_P. Such a clause will be called *incorrect*. It has a ground instance, such that all atoms of its body are in I_P and its head is not in I_P.

In the case of insufficiency it is a predicate p for which some atom $p(t_1, \ldots, t_n)$ valid in I_P cannot be produced by the clauses defining p. More precisely, there is no ground instance $H \leftarrow B_1, \ldots, B_m$ $(m \geq 0)$ of a clause of P such that H is an instance of $p(t_1, \ldots, t_n)$ and $B_1, \ldots, B_m$ are in I_P. The atom $p(t_1, \ldots, t_n)$ is called *uncovered*.

The elements of M_P can be computed using SLD-resolution. To discover an error and to localize its cause in the program one has to compare the results of computations, including failures, with the intended model. However, the latter is generally not formalized. To solve this problem Shapiro introduces the concept of oracle (Shapiro 1983). The *ground oracle* decides whether an atom is in the intended model. The *existential oracle* decides whether there is a solution to a given goal and is capable of producing elements of the intended model which are instances of the given goal. In practice, it is the user who answers the questions concerning the intended model.

Shapiro's debugging system acquires knowledge about the intended model through necessary interactions with the oracle. This knowledge consists of:

1. a finite subset of the intended model — YES answers of the ground oracle and the solutions produced by the existential oracle;

2. a subset of the complement of the intended model — NO answers of the ground oracle;

3. a finite set of atoms satisfiable in the intended model — YES answers of the existential oracle;

4. a finite set of atoms unsatisfiable in the intended model — NO answers of the existential oracle.

The language of the oracles does not allow to specify infinite subsets of the intended model nor infinite sets of atoms satisfiable in the intended model. The negative answers of the existential oracle are not used for tracing incorrectness although they specify infinite subsets of the complement of the intended model. This language is rather low level — the knowledge about the intended model is communicated in form of examples. There may therefore exist many queries concerning similar atoms.

Shapiro pointed out that incorporation of "constraints and partial specifications" into the algorithmic debugging scheme may reduce the number of interactions with the user (Shapiro 1983, p.79). This paper develops and formalizes this idea. In the approach presented the user is allowed to provide the system with formal specifications of some properties of the intended model. These formal specifications may be developed interactively in the debugging process. The diagnosis system uses its actual knowledge about the intended model to localize errors. Whenever this is not sufficient for evaluation of results of the computation the system queries the user. The answer augments system knowledge about the intended model. This scheme includes as special cases the answers used in Shapiro's system. But generally the language of answers is more powerful. If the user is able to provide the system with some general properties of the intended model, the number of interactions decreases dramatically.

Another aspect of our debugging methodology is the relative ease with which the user can interact with the system. As it is unlikely that the complete specification of the model is conveniently provided by the user, there will be a number of interactions between the system and the user. Our insufficiency diagnoser, in contrast to Shapiro's, will not require the user to provide instances of unsolved goals. Instead, the user is expected to recognize the solutions to a goal and to identify a case where some answer is missing.

The rest of the paper is organized as follows. In Section 26.2 a language of assertions is introduced as a natural generalization of the language of the oracle and the use of assertions for algorithmic debugging is discussed. Section 26.3 describes the necessary oracle interactions. In section 26.4 debugging algorithms based on assertions are presented. The section also includes a formal proof of correctness and completeness of our insufficiency diagnosis algorithm. Extensions for some Prolog features are discussed in section 26.5 and comparisons with related work are presented in section 26.6. Sections 26.7 and 26.8 contain conclusions and topics for future research.

26.2   Assertions

We suggest to extend the communication language of the algorithmic debugger. In addition to the simple YES and NO answers we want to provide the user with a possibility to describe some properties of the intended model. For this we introduce assertions as a device to specify (not necessarily finite) sets of (not necessarily ground) atoms of the object language. An obvious choice is to use logic programs to provide executable specifications of such sets using, as much as possible, existing library procedures.

Let S be a set of (not necessarily ground) atoms in the language L of a given logic program P. The objective is thus to construct a logic program Q with a unary predicate s "specifying" the set S. The clauses of Q beginning with the symbol s will be called assertions (for S).

More precisely, there should be a one-to-one correspondence between set S and the set of all ground atoms of the form $s(\ldots)$ that are logical consequences of Q. In other words, each atom A of L should be coded as a ground term A' of the language M of the program Q. We adopt the following coding scheme:

> if A is an atom and $X_1, \ldots, X_n$ are variables occurring in A, the image of A is $A' = A\{X_1/var(1), \ldots, X_n/var(n)\}$ $(1 \leq i \leq n)$

where var is a functor not used in the object language. (To obtain uniqueness it may be assumed that $X_1, \ldots, X_n$ are ordered according to their first occurrences in A).

This is a ground representation in terms of (Hill and Lloyd 1988). Notice that all the predicate symbols and functors of L become functors of M. Atoms which are not the same up to variable renaming have different images.

One may argue that assertions can be used for full specification of the intended model. This would amount to giving an alternative correct version of the buggy program (Dershowitz and Lee 1987). Such a solution is completely unrealistic in most cases.

It is often suggested that while developing a new version of an existing program the existing version can be used as an oracle (e.g. (Sterling and Shapiro 1986)). Taken literally, this idea is also unrealistic because it requires that every procedure of the new program has its counterpart with the same intended meaning in the old program. Sterling and Shapiro (1986, p. 323) mention *permutation_sort* and *quicksort* (Sterling and Shapiro 1986 - p.55,56) as an example. However, *quicksort* contains procedures *partition* and *append* that are not specified by the *permutation_sort* program.

We suggest to employ four properties of the intended model I_P in our debugging framework. They generalize the four types of answers given by the oracles as discussed in section 26.1. The properties are specified in the above-mentioned sense by four fixed predicate symbols in a program $As(I_P)$. This gives rise to four types of assertions. The ways the debugging algorithms use $As(I_P)$ are described in section 26.3.

We now give definitions of the 4 types of assertions.

> *Positive assertions.* These are used to define sets of (not necessarily ground) atoms valid in the intended model. We specify positive assertions using the predicate symbol *true*. If $true(A')$ is a logical consequence of $As(I_P)$ and A' is the image of A then for all substitutions θ, $A\theta \in I_P$ provided $A\theta$ is ground.

Example 1.

Consider the intended relation *insert* as in Shapiro (1983). It includes (as a proper subset) all triples (X, Y, Z) such that X is an integer, Y is a sorted list of integers and Z is a sorted list whose elements are X and all elements of Y. This property can be formalized as the following assertion:

$$true(insert(X, Y, Z)) \leftarrow$$
$$\quad integer(X),$$
$$\quad sorted\_integer\_list(Y),$$
$$\quad sorted\_integer\_list(Z),$$
$$\quad permutation([X \mid Y], Z).$$

(It is assumed that $As(I_P)$ contains procedures with the obvious meaning for the predicate symbols of the body.)

> *Negative assertions.* These are used to specify sets of atoms not valid in the intended model. We specify negative assertions using the predicate symbol *false*. If $false(A')$ is a logical consequence of $As(I_P)$ and A' is the image of A then there exists a substitution θ, such that $A\theta$ is ground and $A\theta \notin I_P$.

Example 2.

Consider the intended relation *sort* where the arguments are integer lists and the second one is a sorted permutation of the first. The following assertion characterizes an infinite set of atoms not valid in the intended model:

$$false(sort(X, Y)) \leftarrow$$
$$\quad member(var(N), Y),$$
$$\quad not\_member(var(N), X).$$

(If there is a variable that is a member of the second list but not a member of the first then the atom has a ground instance outside the intended model.)

Note that YES and NO answers to questions asked by the ground oracle can be seen as singleton positive and negative assertions respectively.

Positive existential assertions. These are used to specify sets of atoms satisfiable in the intended model. We define positive existential assertions using the predicate symbol *posex*. If $posex(A')$ is a logical consequence of $As(I_P)$ and A' is the image of A then there exists a substitution θ such that $A\theta \in I_P$.

Example 3.

The intended *isort* predicate of Shapiro (1983) has the property that whenever it is called with the first argument being a list of integers and the second argument being an uninstantiated variable then there exists an instance of this call which is in the intended model. This can be formalized as the following assertion:

$$posex(isort(X, var(Y))) \leftarrow integer\_list(X).$$

The positive existential assertions generalize YES answers of the existential oracle.

Negative existential assertions. These are used to specify sets of atoms unsatisfiable in the intended model. We define negative existential assertions using the predicate symbol *negex*. If $negex(A')$ is a logical consequence of $As(I_P)$ and A' is the image of A then for all substitutions $\theta, A\theta \notin I_P$.

Example 4.

The intended *isort* predicate of Shapiro (1983) has the property that none of its success instances have an unsorted list as the second argument. In the language of assertions this can be formalized as follows:

$$negex(isort(X, Y)) \leftarrow$$
$$\quad integer\_list(Y),$$
$$\quad not\_sorted(Y).$$

The negative existential assertions generalize NO answers to existential queries. It is worth noticing that various notions of types for logic programs discussed in the literature e.g. (Zobel 1987), (Mycroft and O'Keefe 1984), (Nilsson 1983), can be related to negative existential assertions (if an argument in an atom is of a wrong type then the atom should be unsatisfiable).

At every stage of development the program $As(I_P)$ should describe the intended model. A necessary condition for that is that it describes some model. This is not the case if, for example, both $true(A')$ and $false(A')$ are logical consequences of $As(I_P)$. That corresponds to A being both valid and not valid in I_P. The responsibility for providing consistent assertions is on the user. In the next section it is described how (partial) consistency checking of $As(I_P)$ is performed. Notice, that even the basic Shapiro algorithms are not free of the danger of inconsistent answers. Let A be an atom with variables and B its ground instance. When tracing incorrectness the answer concerning B may be YES, i.e. B is in I_P. Independently, when tracing insufficiency the answer concerning A may be NO, i.e. there is no instance of A in I_P.

26.3   Oracle interactions

In order to show how the assertions are used, we set out the questions that are posed by the diagnosis algorithms and the way they are answered. The basic idea is that a question is first attempted to be answered with the help of $As(I_P)$. Only if this attempt fails, the user is queried. She may either answer with YES/NO or specify a relevant property of I_P by adding new clauses to $As(I_P)$.

The ground image of atom A in the coding scheme used by assertions is denoted by A'.

(1) Universal questions:

This type of question is asked by the incorrectness diagnoser:

"Is the atomic formula A valid in the intended model?" (i.e. are all its ground instances members of I_P?)

The insufficiency diagnoser requires answers to two additional types of questions:

(2) Existential questions:

"Is A satisfiable in the intended model?" (i.e. is there a ground instance of A which is a member of I_P?)

(3) Incompleteness questions:

The algorithm needs the information whether certain solved goals have produced all the expected answers in the intended model. This is obtained by asking:

"For the atom A, is there an instance $A\theta \in I_P$ such that $A\theta$ is not an instance of some member of the set $\{A\theta_1, \dots, A\theta_n\}$?" (Substitutions $\theta_1, \dots, \theta_n$ are (all the) computed answer substitutions for $\leftarrow A$ and P).

The system uses the knowledge explicitly represented in $As(I_P)$ for answering the above questions before querying the user. Moreover, some queries to the user may be avoided by exploiting the information that is implicit in the assertions. For instance, it may happen that $true(A')$ is a logical consequence of $As(I_P)$ but $posex(A')$ is not. However, in this case the answer to the existential question for A is YES and querying the user is unnecessary.

Let A be an atom and B its instance. The following properties hold:
(1) If A is valid in I_P then it is also satisfiable in I_P.
(2) If A is unsatisfiable in I_P then it is not valid in I_P.
(3,4) If atom A is valid (unsatisfiable) in I_P then B is also valid (unsatisfiable) in I_P.

(5,6) If B is not valid (satisfiable) in I_P then A is not valid (satisfiable) in I_P.
(7) A ground atom is satisfiable iff it is valid.

The procedure for answering *universal* questions employs properties (2), (6) and (7). For atom A:

- If $true(A')$ is a logical consequence of $As(I_P)$ then the answer to this question is YES.

- If A is ground and $posex(A')$ is a logical consequence of $As(I_P)$ then the answer is YES.

- If $false(B')$ or $negex(B')$ is a logical consequence of $As(I_P)$ for some B being an instance of A then the answer to this question is NO.

- Otherwise the user is queried.

The procedure for answering *existential* questions employs properties (1),(5) and (7). For atom A:

- If $posex(B')$ or $true(B')$ is a logical consequence of $As(I_P)$ for some B being an instance of A then the answer to this question is YES.

- If $negex(A')$ is a logical consequence of $As(I_P)$ then the answer to this question is NO.

- If A is ground and $false(A')$ is a logical consequence of $As(I_P)$ then the answer is NO.

- Otherwise the user is queried.

The properties (3) and (4) are not used by the answering procedures due to implementation difficulties. However, if the decoded set of atoms defined by $true$ (resp. $negex$) is closed under substitution then employing properties (3) and (4) does not change anything. In practice, these two sets are closed under substitution in every reasonable $As(I_P)$.

The YES/NO answers to the incompleteness questions are to be provided by the user.

Let $Assertion$ be any of the predicate letters $true, false, posex, negex$. The answering procedures require checking whether there exists an instance B of a given atom A such that $Assertion(B')$ is a logical consequence of $As(I_P)$. To do this, program $As(I_P)$ is queried with the goal $\leftarrow Assertion(A)$ (note: not coded A). This is because the coded image of any instance of A is also an instance of A and if the coded image of a term is an instance of A then the term is an instance of A.

Consider a universal (or an existential) question to be answered by the system. The answering procedures may sometimes be able to give both YES and NO answers to this question. In this case $As(I_P)$ is inconsistent and debugging is aborted.

To accumulate the knowledge implied by user YES/NO answers to universal and existential queries, new assertions can be added to $As(I_P)$ by the system. If the user answer to the *universal* query for A is NO then assertion $false(A') \leftarrow$ is added. If the user answer to the *universal* query for A is YES then any instance of A is valid in I_P. So assertion $true(A) \leftarrow$ is added. Now for any instance B of A, $true(B')$ is logical consequence of $As(I_P)$ (since coded image of any instance of A is also an instance of A and vice versa).

If the user answer to the *existential* query for A is YES then assertion $posex(A') \leftarrow$ is added. If the user answer to the *existential* query for A is NO then the assertion $negex(A) \leftarrow$ is added (since any instance of A is unsatisfiable in the intended model).

User answers to incompleteness questions can also be recorded. If the answer is NO then unary clause $complete\_solutions(A) \leftarrow$ is recorded. Then a success of $\leftarrow complete\_solutions(B')$ implies a NO answer to the incompleteness question concerning B since the answer is NO for any instance of A. (It turns out that recording of YES answers is unnecessary.)

26.4 Diagnosis algorithms

(1) Incorrectness diagnosis

If the SLD-refutation procedure of a goal $\leftarrow A$ with program P produces a substitution θ such that $A\theta$ is not valid in I_P, then an incorrect clause instance has to be found.

The original algorithm (Shapiro 1983) finds an incorrect clause by systematic traversal of a ground proof tree whose root is not in I_P. In actual computations of logic programs the proof trees constructed need not be ground. The idea can be extended for non-ground trees in two different ways. The suggestion of (Shapiro 1986, p.325) is that the oracle should instantiate the visited node, if possible to an instance not included in the intended model, otherwise to any instance. The solution used in this paper is to require that the oracle decides whether the visited node is *valid* in the intended model or not. (This is a generalization of the original *ground oracle* since validity of a ground atom in I_P means that it is an element of I_P.)

We use the top down version of Shapiro's basic algorithm as presented in (Sterling and Shapiro 1986) with this generalization. The queries posed by the algorithm are dealt with in the manner described above. The input to the algorithm is an atom A for which the program gives a wrong answer (this means a success instance of A which is not valid in I_P). The algorithm returns a (not necessarily ground) instance of a clause in P such that the atoms in the body of the clause are valid in I_P and the head is not.

The algorithm is sound because it always returns an incorrect clause instance. It is also complete in the sense that it terminates and returns such an answer for any input that satisfies the input condition stated above.

(2) Insufficiency diagnosis

We will say that program P is *insufficient* for $\leftarrow A$ if there exists θ such that $A\theta \in I_P$ and no answer more general than θ is a computed answer substitution for $\leftarrow A$ and P. An atom A is *completely covered* by program P if for every θ such that $A\theta \in I_P$, P contains a clause which has an instance where $A\theta$ is the head and all the atoms in its body are in I_P. (Hence A is not completely covered if there exists θ such that $A\theta \in I_P$ and there is no clause instance of P with the head $A\theta$ and the body atoms in I_P.)

If a program P is insufficient for a goal $\leftarrow A$ then the insufficiency diagnoser is called to identify an atomic formula C not completely covered by the program P. The algorithm is based on the assumption that Prolog computation rule is used in the resolution.

Before describing the algorithm we introduce the following definition:

The **search forest** for A consists of a tree for each non-unary clause of P whose head is unifiable with A. Let $H \leftarrow B_1, \dots, B_n \ \ (n > 0)$ be a variant of such a clause.
Then

> (B_1, γ), where γ is an mgu of H and A, is the root of the corresponding
> tree

and
if (B_i, θ) is a node of the tree, and program P gives $\{\sigma_1, \dots, \sigma_m\} \ \ (m \geq 0)$ as computed answer substitutions to goal $B_i\theta$

> then $(B_{i+1}, \theta\sigma_j)$ for $j = 1, \dots, m$ is a child of this node if $i < n$
> and $(\square, \theta\sigma_j)$ for $j = 1, \dots, m$ is a child of this node if $i = n$.

Note that (B_i, θ) is a node in the forest iff B_i instantiated to $B_i\theta$ is a selected goal (on the top level) in the computation for A. Note also that $(\square, \dots)$ leaves correspond to successes of $\leftarrow A$. If $(\square, \theta)$ is a leaf in the forest then goal $\leftarrow A$ succeeds with computed answer substitution $\theta \mid variables(A)$ (where $variables(A)$ stands for the set of variables occurring in A and $\theta \mid S$ stands for the restriction of θ to the elements of S). For a given A, the search forest is unique up to variable renaming.

The Algorithm

The input to the algorithm is an atomic formula A for which the program is insufficient and the computation for $\leftarrow A$ is finite (under Prolog computation rule); the output is a *not completely covered* atom.

The insufficiency diagnoser asks questions about the nodes of the search forest for A. The types of questions asked have been discussed in section 26.3. (The order of visiting the nodes is irrelevant to the correctness of the algorithm).

For (B, θ) being a leaf of the forest, $B \neq \square$, the existential question is asked about $B\theta$. If the answer is YES then the algorithm is recursively called with $B\theta$. (No questions are asked about a success leaf.)

For (B, θ) being an internal node with children $(C, \theta\sigma_1), \dots, (C, \theta\sigma_m)$ (where C is an atomic formula or $\square$), the incompleteness question is asked about the set $\{B\theta\sigma_1, \dots, B\theta\sigma_m\}$ and the goal $B\theta$. If the answer is YES then the insufficiency diagnoser is called recursively on $B\theta$.

If for all nodes of the forest the answers for all the questions are NO, then A is returned as a not completely covered atom and the algorithm terminates. Otherwise, a not completely covered atom is found by the recursive call(s) of the algorithm.

Correctness and completeness of the algorithm

Lemma

Consider program P and a search forest for atom C.

If

> for every node in the forest the answer to the question asked by the algorithm is NO and
>
> C is completely covered by P

then

> P is sufficient for $\leftarrow C$.

Proof

Assume that the premises of the lemma hold. Let $C\gamma \in I_P$ (without loss of generality it may be assumed that the domain of γ is $variables(C)$). We show that there exists a computed answer substitution for $\leftarrow C$ that is more general than γ. As C is completely covered by P, there exists

$$A \leftarrow B_1, \dots, B_n \qquad\qquad (*)$$

which is a variant of a clause of P and there exists a substitution δ such that

$$C\gamma = C\delta = A\delta,$$

$$B_1\delta, \dots, B_n\delta \in I_P.$$

If $n = 0$ then an mgu of C and A (restricted to $variables(C)$) is the required computed answer substitution. Assume $n > 0$. We show that in the search forest for C, in the tree corresponding to $(*)$ there exists a leaf $(\Box, \theta)$ such that θ is more general than δ. Assume that this does not hold. Note that for the root (B_1, θ_1) substitution θ_1 is more general that δ. Let i be the greatest number for which there exists a node (B_i, θ) in the tree where θ is more general than δ. Then $B_i \delta$ is an instance of $B_i \theta$. Two cases are possible.

1. (B_i, θ) is a leaf of the tree. The answer to the existential question about $B_i \theta$ is YES (as $B_i \delta \in I_P$). Hence contradiction.

2. (B_i, θ) has sons $(C, \theta\sigma_1), \ldots, (C, \theta\sigma_m)$ where $C = B_{i+1}$ or $C = \Box$. As the answer to the incompleteness question about $B_i \theta$ is NO, for some substitution j, $\theta\sigma_j$ is more general than δ. Contradiction.

Now, the computed answer substitution corresponding to $(\Box, \theta)$ is $\theta \,|\, variables(C)$. This solution is more general than $\delta \,|\, variables(C) = \gamma$. This concludes the proof.

$\Box$

As the algorithm is (recursively) called for atom C only if P is insufficient for C, it follows by the Lemma that the atom returned by the algorithm is not completely covered by P. Hence the algorithm is correct.

Note that each search forest is finite. So is the recursion depth of the algorithm (otherwise the computation for $\leftarrow A$ would be infinite). Thus the algorithm always returns an answer. So the algorithm is complete, in the sense that it returns a correct answer for any atom satisfying the input conditions of the algorithm. This notion of completeness is weaker than the usual one (where a diagnoser answer is required even for goals that loop). However, the difference is insignificant if the program in question is run under the Prolog computation rule. This is because the insufficiency diagnoser is not used for a goal for which the program loops (under this computation rule). It should be mentioned that all practical insufficiency diagnosing algorithms are incomplete with respect to this stronger completeness (Naish 1988).

It remains to discuss a situation where a program is both incorrect and insufficient. An example is a program giving a wrong answer and missing a correct one. In such cases it is more convenient to perform incorrectness diagnosis first. The incorrectness diagnoser usually searches a smaller search space, does not ask incompleteness questions and produces more informative answers: an incorrect clause instance refers to a wrong clause while a not completely covered atom refers to a whole procedure.

A particular case is when one of the atoms displayed by an incompleteness question is not valid in I_P. Then it is convenient to interrupt the insufficiency diagnosis and start diagnosing incorrectness with such an atom. This usually leads to a faster and more informative result.

26.5 Extensions

In this section extensions of the method for some Prolog features are discussed. The approach presented above is declarative: the intended meaning of a logic program is its intended model (and the actual meaning is its least Herbrand model). Extensions of the method will be discussed within the same framework. This excludes programs with side effects: those using input-output or *assert-retract*.

26.5.1 Built-in predicates

Many Prolog built-in predicates can be treated declaratively since they can be specified by the relations they define (over the Herbrand universe). Programs employing such built-ins can be treated as logic programs by including unary clause $p(t)$ for any built-in p and any term tuple t in the relation corresponding to p. This includes predicates such as *functor, arg, integer* etc., $= .. (univ), =, \backslash=$ and Prolog arithmetic (since uninstantiated arguments to arithmetic procedures are detected as run-time errors). No questions are posed by the debugging algorithms about such built-ins. They are assumed to be implemented correctly.

The built-in predicates $var, nonvar, ==$ (exact equality) and $\backslash==$ (exact inequality) cannot be described by the declarative semantics. They will be referred to here as *extralogical predicates*. Operationally, their role is to succeed without binding their arguments or to fail. This may be seen as (conditional) pruning of a part of a search tree.

Programs using such predicates can be dealt with by our method if the programmer knows the intended model of the program with extralogical predicates removed. Such a model provides an approximation of the expected behaviour which is inexpressible in a declarative way. Obviously, only those bugs that lead to insufficiency or incorrectness with respect to this model can be found by the diagnoser. In such a setting, an extralogical predicate call can be a reason for insufficiency but not for incorrectness. The insufficiency diagnoser returns an atom and the error is in the procedure corresponding to this atom. Either the reason for insufficiency is an extralogical call in this procedure or the atom is not completely covered with respect to the procedure with extralogical calls removed. In the first case the programmer has to decide whether the behaviour of the procedure is actually erroneous.

26.5.2 Cut

Here we discuss introducing *cut* into our debugging framework. As the framework is declarative, cut should be treated declaratively. This means that its role is understood as cutting away part of the search space. If inserting a cut removes some program's answers then this cut is called red. Otherwise it is called green (van Emden 1982). Obviously, the declarative semantics is no longer valid for programs with red cuts. However, the declarative debugging approach is still able to provide meaningful information about bugs in such programs, as shown below.

For incorrectness diagnosis the same algorithm is used. It analyses a proof tree that lead to a wrong answer. As a result an incorrect instance of a program clause, say $p(T) \leftarrow B$, is obtained. Now, wrong clauses are allowed in correct programs provided the clauses are protected by (red) cuts. The user has to decide whether the error has to be treated as a wrong clause or as a wrong usage of the cut. In the second case the reason is a not activated cut. It can be either a cut missing (or misplaced) in the program text or a cut not executed due to a failure of preceding calls. The inactivated cut should occur in the clauses of procedure p since p succeeds with a goal instance $p(T)$ not in I_P (and all the goals in B gave correct answers).

A possible treatment at this stage is to search for insufficiency that could lead to a cut not being executed. A search forest is built for the preceding clauses of procedure p that contain cuts. Incompleteness and existential questions are then asked about its nodes as in the insufficiency diagnoser. If there is a YES answer then some answers to the corresponding subgoal are missing. The insufficiency diagnoser has to be called for this subgoal. If all the answers are NO then procedure p has to be corrected.

This is similar to a suggestion of (Huntbach 1987) (with a modification that non-failing subgoals also have to be examined) and to the approach of (Pereira and Calejo 1988). A similar procedure is performed by a programmer in the examples of (Takahashi and Shibayama 1985). The difference is that in our approach the user is guided towards a declaratively correct program. A construction "red cut + incorrect clause" is accepted by a debugger only after an explicit decision of the user.

For insufficiency diagnosis, a variant of the algorithm of section 26.4 is used. Only the goals that actually occurred during the computation are represented in the search forest. (This means a node (B_i, θ) has sons $(B_{i+1}, \theta\sigma_1), \dots, (B_{i+1}, \theta\sigma_j)$ only if during the actual computation $B_i\theta$ succeeded j times (with answer substitutions $\sigma_1, \dots, \sigma_j$); j may be less than the number of answers of the program to goal $B_i\theta$ due to interruption of backtracking by a cut.) For leaves of the form $(B, \theta), B \neq \square$, the existential questions are asked as in the basic algorithm. Incompleteness questions are asked only about those internal nodes (B, θ) for which it is known that the corresponding goal $\leftarrow B\theta$ produced all the answers (in other words it eventually failed). A recursive call of the algorithm is made for a node for which the answer is YES. The algorithm returns an atom A for which all questions in the related search forest were answered NO. Either A is not completely covered (in the sense of section 26.4) or the reason for insufficiency is a cut in procedure p, where $A = p(\dots)$. More precisely, the cut is either misplaced or is unnecessarily executed due to an incorrect success of the preceding procedure calls of the same clause. In the last case, the incorrectness diagnoser can be used to find an actual bug.

To assist the user, she is informed

1. which clauses with a head matching A were not used in the computation and

2. for which nodes (B, θ) in the search forest there exists a missing answer to $B\theta$ (together with a list of answers obtained for each such node).

Note that giving lists of answers missing due to cut may be informative but it may also lead to infinite computations for some programs.

If a cut is the reason for insufficiency then the information given to the user provides a compacted version of a trace of the procedure execution. It allows her to localize clauses and cut(s) executed and shows a history of backtracking in the clause containing this cut (these cuts). This makes it possible to decide whether a cut is misplaced and to localize a possible incorrect success.

26.5.3   Negation

For programs with negation (Lloyd 1987), the intended model I_P is a model of the completion of a correct program. For a sound implementation of negation it is necessary that computation of the program is safe or weakly safe (Lloyd 1987). This means that whenever $\neg A$ is selected and fails, A succeeds with an empty answer substitution. This requirement should be checked by the debugging system.

To incorporate negation, the algorithms of section 26.4 are extended in an obvious way suggested by McCabe (Shapiro 1983) (Lloyd 1987). If the incorrectness diagnoser, instead of an incorrect clause instance, finds a literal $\neg A$ that incorrectly succeeds then the insufficiency diagnoser is called with A. Whenever the answer to a question posed by the insufficiency diagnoser about a literal $\neg B$ is YES, the incorrectness diagnoser is called with input B (YES means missing solutions). The insufficiency diagnoser does not ask incompleteness questions about successful negative literals because there cannot be any missing solutions (negative literals succeed with empty substitutions).

Answering questions about negative literals refers to the property that $\neg A$ is valid (satisfiable) in I iff A is unsatisfiable (not valid) in I. Hence to answer the universal (existential) question about $\neg A$ the existential (universal) question about A is answered as described in section 26.3 and the answer is negated.

The diagnoser obtained by composing the extended incorrectness and insufficiency diagnosers in this way, is *sound* in the sense that for any atom satisfying the respective input conditions, the result (if any) is either an incorrect clause instance or a not completely covered atom. The definitions of these notions are obvious extensions of those for definite programs. The input condition is either that for the incorrectness diagnoser or that for the insufficiency diagnoser of section 26.4. The proof of soundness is a straightforward modification of the proofs for the definite program diagnosers.

The diagnoser is also *complete* in the sense that it returns an answer for any atom satisfying the relevant input condition. An outline of a proof is given below.

The Prolog computation rule is assumed. Let the diagnoser be called with an atom A as an input. From the input conditions it follows that there exists a finite computation D of the given object program P with goal $\leftarrow A$ such that D results in an incorrect answer or searches the whole search space.

The computation of the composed diagnoser can be seen as a sequence of mutual calls of the incorrectness and insufficiency diagnosers. The argument passed at such a call is an instance of an atom that actually occurred as a selected subgoal in D. The sequence of these atoms is a subsequence of the sequence of selected goals of D. Hence the number of mutual calls is finite.

The computation corresponding to a single call to the incorrectness diagnoser is finite since it is a search of a finite tree. By an argument analogous to that of section 26.4, the computation corresponding to a single call to the insufficiency diagnoser is finite. Hence the whole computation is finite.

26.6   Comparisons with related work

The types of assertions introduced originate from the analysis of the logical nature of answers given by the oracles of Shapiro. They also have their counterparts in the algorithms of Ferrand (1987) and Lloyd (1987) where the oracles are represented by the predicates *valid* and *unsatisfiable* (and to a certain extent *impossible* (Ferrand 1987)). But the oracles have complete knowledge of the intended model while the assertions only approximate it. For example the assertions *true* and *false* provide incomplete information about validity of a given atom in the intended model. The first of them specifies a set of atoms valid in the intended model, the other a set of atoms non-valid in the intended model. A given atom may belong to none of the sets while the validity oracles of Ferrand and Lloyd can always decide its validity. However, the oracles are outside the system, while the assertions constitute a part of the system (which is incrementally developed during the external interactions). External interactions are necessary in our system only if the actual assertions cannot produce the required answer. In this case the external interaction provides an increment for the existing assertions so that the question can be answered.

The only work known to us that uses a concept similar to our approximate specification is a recent paper by Lichtenstein and Shapiro (1988). It deals with debugging of concurrent programs and introduces an additional *abstract oracle*. The abstract oracle specifies a superset of the intended behaviour of a program while the concrete oracle specifies the intended behaviour exactly. The intention of introducing abstract oracle is to ask questions that are simpler to answer by a programmer, whereas the role of assertions in our approach is to automatically answer some of the questions. Assertions can specify not only supersets but also subsets of the set of interest. (The set of interest is either I_P or the set of atoms satisfiable in I_P.) For a given debugger, it is fixed which (super-) sets can be specified by the abstract oracle, while assertions can specify any set.

The algorithms of (Shapiro 1983) (Sterling and Shapiro 1986), Ferrand (1987) and Lloyd (1987) require that the oracle is able to deliver elements of the intended model. If the oracle is the user, this type of interaction may create difficulties or even lead to wrong answers. One of our objectives has been to free the user from this burden.

A new algorithm for insufficiency diagnosis presented in this paper automatically generates answers for atomic subgoals. Instead of generating bindings the user is (sometimes) asked whether the set of generated answers is complete. A similar approach is presented by Pereira (1986). However that work seems to rely on the procedural semantics of Prolog, while ours has a clean logical foundation and our algorithm is proved correct and complete.

Clearly, the bindings provided by the user can speed-up the diagnosis process. However, the decision whether a binding is to be given or not should be left to the user. Our algorithms can be easily extended with that option.

There are some differences in basic definitions used in this paper and the papers by Ferrand and Lloyd which give logical foundations for declarative debugging. We follow Lloyd in that our intended model is a ground Herbrand model in contrast to the nonground term model of Ferrand.

Another difference concerns the results produced by the debugger. Since we do not force the user to produce bindings during the debugging process, the final result may come out less instantiated than in the other systems. To be more precise, consider separately the form of our results in diagnosing incorrectness and insufficiency.

For incorrectness, the result returned is an incorrect instance of a program clause, that is $H \leftarrow B$ such that B is valid in I and H is non-valid in I. This is similar to Ferrand's definition of incorrectness ((Ferrand 1987) Definition 4). However, his debugger returns such $H \leftarrow B$ that B is valid and H is unsatisfiable. The results produced by the debugger of Lloyd also have this property. In the case of Ferrand (1987) this is due to representing variables of the program by variables of the debugger. (The diagnoser is a logic program, if it returns $H \leftarrow B$ then it is also able to return any instance of $H \leftarrow B$; hence H has to be unsatisfiable for the diagnoser to be sound.) The approaches are equivalent, since any incorrect clause (in our terminology) has an instance where the head is unsatisfiable and the body valid.

For insufficiency diagnosis the situation is similar. The results produced by our debugger are atoms which are not completely covered while Lloyd's debugger produces uncovered atoms (An atom A is called uncovered if A is valid in I_P and none of its instances is in $T_P(I_P)$; A is completely covered iff $A\theta \in I_P$ implies $A\theta \in T_P(I_P)$). Comparing the definitions one can see that every not completely covered atom has an instance which is uncovered. This instance is not produced by our system. This is because we do not force the user to produce bindings for subgoals during the debugging process. Ferrand's notion of insufficiency is a counterpart of Lloyd's uncovered atom but it is weaker than the latter (A is an insufficiency if A is valid in I_P and not all its ground instances are in $T_P(I_P)$). However, the answers really produced by Ferrand's algorithm are similar to those of Lloyd. More precisely, in both cases the result of insufficiency diagnosis is an uncovered atom.

Another difference to be mentioned concerns inputs for insufficiency diagnosis. Usually it is supposed to be a finitely failed goal which is satisfiable in the intended model. However, the finite failure of this goal may be caused by the fact that some subgoal of the computation does not fail but produces an insufficient number of answers. In most systems this situation is handled by asking the oracle to provide all intended answers for the subgoal. The answer not produced by the insufficient program will cause its failure and eventual localization of insufficiency. Our system does not require the user to provide correct subgoal instances. This also results in extending the allowed inputs for the diagnoser: the input is a goal whose computation terminates and delivers an incomplete set of computed answers.

A different debugging approach is presented in Pereira (1986), and Pereira and Calejo (1988). That approach is not declarative but operational. It does not refer to an intended model but to the intended *behaviour* of the program. A program is understood through its operational properties and not through the logical ones.

In addition to incorrectness and insufficiency, a third kind of program error is introduced in Pereira (1986), and Pereira and Calejo (1988), namely inadmissible call pattern. An example of such an error is violation of a mode declaration. The following is not made explicit there but is important from our point of view. Inadmissibility is related to an additional specification saying which call patterns are allowed during program computation. Inadmissibility is not related to the declarative semantics: a program P may be correct (that means $M_P = I_P$) but manifest inadmissible call pattern(s).

An earlier work using assertions within logic programming is (Drabent and Małuszynsński 1987). Here assertions are used to prescribe predicate call and success patterns. Preassertions in this sense describe all the predicate calls that are possible: those which succeed and those which fail. The described form of procedure calls is not expressible in terms of declarative semantics and is therefore, in general, not related to the assertions introduced in this paper. Nevertheless, it is possible to make use of such assertions in the debugging process by detecting inadmissible call patterns. We believe that this can be a generalization of Pereira's queries relating to admissibility of a goal (Pereira 1986), (Pereira and Calejo 1988).

In this paper we are interested in logic programming as a declarative programming paradigm. Thus we do not include inadmissibility into our debugging framework.

26.7   Conclusions

The main contribution of this paper is the formalization of the concept of assertion for algorithmic debugging. Assertions provide a formal description of some properties of the intended model, thus "approximating" it. They give a flexible framework for its formal description. On one end of the spectrum the yes/no oracle answers provide rudimentary but easy to produce information about the intended model. On the other end the full formal specification of the intended model can be used, if so desired. Assertions can be seen as generalizations of the simple oracle answers and include them as special cases.

It is worth noticing that the concept of assertion is orthogonal to the concept of debugging algorithm: any debugging algorithm based on oracle interactions can also use appropriate assertions.

A prototype debugger using assertions has been implemented. Algorithms which do not require correct instantiations of atoms by the user are incorporated in the implementation. Our experiments show a reduction in the debugging effort through the use of rather simple assertions and the improved algorithms. A more detailed account of experiments performed can be found in Drabent et al. (1988a) (1988b).

Modifications of the initial assertions may be preserved from session to session. In this way the debugging process gives as a side effect an interactively developed formal description of some properties of the intended model.

26.8   Future work

In practice it often happens that the intended model is not known to the programmer. Instead, she knows a set J_P of atoms that should be in M_P and a set K_P of atoms that should be in $B_P - M_P$ (where B_P is the Herbrand base). The rest, $B_P - J_P - K_P$, is irrelevant to program's specification. An interesting task is a declarative debugging methodology based on such an approximation of the intended model.

Further experiments with debugging of Prolog programs are needed to understand the debugging process better, to evaluate the presented approach and to develop pragmatics of declarative debugging with assertions.

Another subject of future work is to discuss testing of logic programs and correcting of errors. The objective would be a testing-diagnosing-correcting methodology. It should be based on declarative features of existing logic programming languages and may be a complement to methods of systematic construction and verification of programs. Although proving programs correct seems to be a more important target, programs still need debugging and providing sound methods and tools for this is a significant research task.

Acknowledgements

This work has been partially supported by the National Swedish Board for Technical Development, project number: 87-02926P, and a grant by The Royal Swedish Academy of Engineering Sciences (IVA). The first author was also supported by Polish Academy of Sciences. The editors of FGCS'88 proceedings (©ICOT, Tokyo 1988) kindly permitted us to use fragments of Drabent et al. (1988b) in this paper.

References

Dershowitz, N., and Lee, Y., Deductive Debugging, *Proceedings of the IEEE Symposium on Logic Programming* - San Francisco 1987 : 298-306.

Drabent, W., and Małuszyński, J., Inductive Assertion Method for Logic Programs, *Proceedings of the International Conference on Theory and Practice of Software Development* (TAPSOFT) 1987, LNCS 250, Springer Verlag : 167-181.

Drabent, W., Nadjm-Tehrani, S., and Małuszyński, J., (1988a) Algorithmic Debugging with Assertions, Research Report LiTH-IDA-R-88-04, Linköping University, March 88.

Drabent, W., Nadjm-Tehrani, S., and Małuszyński, J., (1988b) The Use of Assertions in Algorithmic Debugging, *Proceedings of the FGCS conference* - Tokyo, November 88 : 573-581.

van Emden, M., Warren's Doctrine on the slash, Logic Programming Newsletter, December 1982.

Ferrand, G., Error Diagnosis in Logic Programming, an Adaptation of E.Y. Shapiro's Method, *Journal of Logic Programming* 1987(4): 177-198.

Hill, P.M., Lloyd, J.W., Analysis of Meta-Programs, *Proceedings of the workshop on Meta-Programming in Logic Programming*, Bristol, 1988: 27-42.

Huntbach, M., Algorithmic PARLOG debugging, *Proceedings of the IEEE Symposium on Logic Programming* - San Francisco, 1987 : 288-297.

Lloyd, J.W., *Foundations of Logic Programming*, Springer Verlag, Second edition, 1987.

Lichtenstein Y., Shapiro E., Abstract Algorithmic Debugging, *Proceedings of the fifth International Conference and Symposium on Logic Programming* - Seattle, 1988: 512:531.

Mycroft, A., O'Keefe, R.A., A Polymorphic Type System for Prolog, *Artificial Intelligence 23* , 1984 : 295-307.

Naish, L., Declarative Diagnosis of Missing Answers, Department of Computer Science, University of Melbourne, Technical report 88/9.

Nilsson, J.F., On the Compilation of a Domain-based Prolog, in: Mason, R.E.A. (ed), *Information Processing 83*, North Holland 1983 : 293-298.

Pereira, L. M. and Calejo, M., A Framework for Prolog Debugging, *Proceedings of the fifth International Conference and Symposium on Logic Programming - Seattle*, 1988: 481:495.

Pereira, L. M., Rational Debugging in Logic Programming, *Proceedings of the 3rd International Conference on Logic Programming*, LNCS 225, Springer Verlag, 1986 : 203-210.

Takahashi, H. and Shibayama, E., PRESET- A Debugging Environment for Prolog, *Proceedings of the fourth Logic Programming Conference - Tokyo*, 1985: LNCS 221, Springer Verlag: 90-99.

Shapiro, E.Y., *Algorithmic Program Debugging*, MIT Press, 1983.

Sterling, L. and Shapiro, E.Y., *The Art of Prolog*, MIT Press 1986.

Zobel, J., Derivation of Polymorphic Types for Prolog Programs, in: Lassez, J.L.,(ed), *Proceedings of the Fourth International Conference on Logic Programming*, Melbourne 1987 : 817-838.

Chapter 27

The Logical Reconstruction of Cuts as One Solution Operators

Paul J. Voda

Complete Logic Systems Inc.
741 Blueridge Ave.,
N. Vancouver, B.C. V7R 2J5 Canada

Abstract

Cuts are used in Prolog to control the search for a proof of a query. Hence cuts are meta-theoretical concepts without a direct meaning in the object theories of Prolog programs.

Very often only one solution to a formula is needed by a program. So after the solution has been found choice points set in the formula are removed by a cut and the program continues using the result.

We describe in this paper the logical semantics of the one solution construct implemented in the logic programming language Trilogy. The meaning is obtained by arithmetizing the meta-theoretic notion of a search path within the formal theory of Trilogy programs.

The paper also discusses the conditions under which the one solution construct of Trilogy can be introduced in a sound way into Prolog.

27.1 Introduction

The cut operator of Prolog is a meta-theoretic device controlling backtracking, i.e. the search for proofs. Thus, it is a proof-theoretic (syntactic) concept not directly explainable by the semantics of object theory.

There are two main uses of cuts in Prolog [7]:

- as a substitute for the if-the-else construct, and

- as a method of disabling backtracking in situations where we are interested only in one solution.

In this paper we are concerned with the second use of cuts. Operators like Unfortunately, neither of these constructs achieves our goal of communicating the results outside of the formula cut and remains sound at the same time.

If the goal of a cut does not contain free variables, then there is no problem:

```
C(x) :- R(x,y), !.
```

Once the goal $C(a)$ with a closed (ground) term a succeeds, there is no need to backtrack to it again. If the term a contains free variables then in the best case we lose some of the solutions. For instance, the query $Q(x$ with the predicate Q defined as follows:

```
Q(1) :-
Q(2).
```

does not return the solution $x = 2$. In the worst case, we can get a wrong result. The query

$$all(x, Q(x), r)$$

should logically return the list $r = 1, 2, Nil$ and not $r = 1, Nil$.

From our experience with practical programs we feel that there is a genuine need for cuts of the second kind in situations where we have free variables through which we communicate one solution and we are not interested in additional ones. The implementation of such cuts is straightforward: all choice points set within the cut formula are removed.

The logical explanation is something else. Essentially we have to embody the meta-theoretic notion of the first proof found within the semantics of computed predicates.

In this paper we describe the solution we have adopted in the logic programming language Trilogy [10,11,9,2,4]. The solution requires a quite extensive data flow analysis. We will show that unless a similar analysis is done in Prolog, the cuts will remain extralogical.

The cut operator '!' of Prolog is a positional one depending on the context of its use. We shall instead explicate the construct

$$one\ x_1, x_2, \ldots, x_n A$$

Here one solution satisfying the formula A is communicated to the outside through the variables $x_1, x_2, \ldots, x_n$.

27.2   The Object Language

The reader has surely noticed that in the preceding section we have slightly abused the syntax of Prolog. We have started the predicate names with capital letters and the variables with the lower case ones. This is a convention used in logic and also in Trilogy. The discussion of the one solution construct will be carried out in a subset of Trilogy. This is because we need the explicit connective of disjunction '|' instead of implicit disjunction of Horn clauses.

The terms of Trilogy simplified for the purpose of this presentation The atomic formulas are either predicate applications (calls) or identity formulas of the form $a = b$. The non-atomic formulas are composed from the atomic ones by the connectives of conjunction '&' and disjunction '|'.

Trilogy uses the if-and-only-if notation for predicates. The notation is known as the completed form of Prolog predicates [5]. The translation from Prolog to the iff setting of Trilogy is straightforward. The above predicate Q (without the cut) has the following definition:

```
Q(x) iff x = 1 | x = 2
```

The Prolog predicate Append

```
append(nil,X,X).
append((H.T),X,(H.Y)) :- append(T,X,Y).
```

is coded in Trilogy as follows:

```
Append(x,y,z) iff
    x = Nil & z = y | x = h,t & Append(t,y,z1) & z = h,z1
```

The local variables $h,t,z1$ are implicitly existentially quantified in the body (the right-hand-side formula) of *Append*.

Instead of placing the cut inside the predicate Q we use the cut formula *one* $x\, Q(x)$ which is equivalent to the formula *one* $x\,(x = 1\,|\,x = 2)$.

27.3   First Attempt at Explication of One Solution Operator

Since the one solution operator gives a solution, we think first of the Hilbert's non-determinate epsilon operator [3]. The term $\epsilon x A(x)$ denotes a certain object x satisfying the formula $A(x)$, if there is such an object; a distinguished but unspecified object otherwise. The semantics of the epsilon operator is given by a choice function assigning to each non-empty subset of the universe one of its elements. The choice function assigns a distinguished element to the empty set.

We might hope that the one solution formula can be explained as follows:

$$one\, x\, A(x)$$

Unfortunately, this is not the case. Since the choice function always assigns the same object to the same set the following holds:

$$\epsilon x(x = 1 \lor x = 2) = \epsilon x(x = 2 \lor x = 1)$$

Thus the one solution operator would have to return the same solution for all equivalent formulas. The solution would have to be distinguishable from the others. The minimal element (in a given linear ordering of the universe) satisfying a formula comes as a natural candidate for the one solution:

$$one\ x\ A(x) \leftrightarrow A(x) \wedge \forall y(A(y) \rightarrow x \leq y)$$

This is perfectly acceptable from the logical point of view but it is quite expensive to compute. Triology actually offers a minimization construct $min\ x\ A(x)$ with the above semantics. Trilogy implements the minimization operator as the all solutions construct, returning the smallest solution found.

The minimization operator is useful when needed but, in addition to being expensive to compute, it does not capture the essence of a cut: Find the first solution in the sequential order of searching for the proof.

27.4   Expressing the Meta Theoretic Search in the Theory

A cut is actually a meta-theoretic minimization operator: Find the first proof in the sequence of proofs considered. We can employ the idea of Gödel when he arithmetized the meta-theoretic notion of provability within the object theory of Peano Arithmetic, see for instance [3,8]. Actually, arithmetization was already used in the framework of logic programming to explicate some meta-theoretic notions within object theory [1]. One can define the provability predicate, called Demo in [1], to capture the sequential search.

Although this approach works, we think it rather heavy-handed for the task of explaining cuts. We are going to explicate the cuts by adjoining to every defined predicate P an adjunct predicate P' containing one additional argument. The additional argument will encode (will be the Gödel number of) the path in the search tree leading to the solution. We want to have the following property of the adjunct predicate:

$$P(x_1,\ldots,x_n) \leftrightarrow \exists p\, P'(p, x_1,\ldots,x_n) \tag{27.1}$$

i.e. $P(x_1,\ldots,x_n)$ holds iff there is a path in the search tree encoded by p leading to the solution. A path is a list composed of the atoms L and R describing the left or right branch of an or node of the search tree. For the predicates Q and *Append* the adjunct predicates are defined as follows:

```
Q'(p,x) iff
      x = 1 & p = L,Nil | x = 2 & p = R,Nil

Append'(p,x,y,z) iff
      x = Nil & z = y & p = L,Nil |
      x = h,t & Append'(pp,t,y,z1) & z = h,z1 & p = R,pp
```

To every solution there is a path leading to it. For instance:

$$Append'((R, R, L, Nil), x, y, (1, 2, 3, Nil)) \leftrightarrow x = 1, 2, Nil \land y = 3, Nil$$

We can linearly order the paths in the lexicographic way to satisfy the following:

$$L, x < R, y$$
$$p, x < p, y \leftrightarrow x < y$$
$$Nil < p, x$$

The cut is then explained as the operator minimizing the search path. **For instance:**

$$one\ x\ Q(x) \leftrightarrow \exists p(Q'(p, x) \land \forall q, x(Q'(q, x) \to p \le q)) \leftrightarrow x = 1$$

We hasten to note here that although one formulas obtain their semantics via minimization of earch paths, the implementation of one formulas is without any explicit computation of paths since the search strategy guarantees that the first proof found, minimizes the search path.

27.5   The Semantics of One Formulas

We shall use the boldfaced notation for the vectors of variables. For instance, the variable $\mathbf{x}$ in the formula $A(\mathbf{x})$ stands for a vector of variables $x_1, x_2, \ldots, x_n$.

For each formula $A(\mathbf{x})$ of our language, we define its adjunct formula $A'(p, \mathbf{x})$ as follows:

- If $A(\mathbf{x}) \equiv P(\mathbf{x})$ then $A'(p, \mathbf{x}) \equiv P'(p, \mathbf{x})$,

- If $A(\mathbf{x}) \equiv a(\mathbf{x}) = b(\mathbf{x})$ then $A'(p, \mathbf{x}) \equiv a(\mathbf{x}) = b(\mathbf{x}) \land p = Nil$,

- If $A(\mathbf{x}) \equiv B(\mathbf{x}) \lor C(\mathbf{x})$ then $A'(p, \mathbf{x}) \equiv B'(q, \mathbf{x}) \land p = L, q \lor C'(q, \mathbf{x}) \land p = R, q$,

- If $A(\mathbf{x}) \equiv B(\mathbf{x}) \land C(\mathbf{x})$ then $A'(p, \mathbf{x}) \equiv B'(q, \mathbf{x}) \land C'(r, \mathbf{x}) \land Append(q, r, p)$,

- If $A(\mathbf{x}) \equiv one\ \mathbf{y}\ B(\mathbf{x}, \mathbf{y})$ then $A'(p, \mathbf{x}) \equiv one\ \mathbf{y}\ B(\mathbf{x}, \mathbf{y}) \land p = Nil$.

The last case is necessary since we have added the *one* formulas to our language. Note that similarly as the path for identity formulas $a = b$, the path for one formulas is Nil. This is because both constructs are deterministic without any backtracking into them.

For a predicate declaration

```
P(x1,...,xn) iff A(x1,...,xn)
```

the adjunct predicate $P'(p, x1, ...xn)$ is defined as follows:

```
P'(p,x1,...,xn) iff A'(p,x1,...,xn)
```

Note that our definition of adjuncts satisfies the formula 27.1.

Let us consider now a formula $A(\mathbf{x}, \mathbf{y}, \mathbf{z})$ with three vectors of variables. We want to give the semantics to the formula *one* $\mathbf{x}\, A(\mathbf{x}, \mathbf{y}, \mathbf{z})$ where the variables $\mathbf{x}$ communicate the solution with the minimal path, the variables $\mathbf{y}$ are local to the *one* formula and the variables $\mathbf{z}$ are non-local parameters. The semantics is defined to satisfy the following:

$$one\ \mathbf{x}\, A(\mathbf{x}, \mathbf{y}, \mathbf{z}) \leftrightarrow \exists p, y(A'(p, \mathbf{x}, \mathbf{y}, \mathbf{z}) \wedge \forall q, \mathbf{v}, \mathbf{w}(A'(q, \mathbf{v}, \mathbf{w}, \mathbf{z}) \rightarrow p \leq q)) \quad (27.2)$$

This is the semantics of the one solution operator in Trilogy, the implementation is, of course, the standard one by means of a cut.

The logical explication of one solution construct does not automatically carry over to the cut of Prolog. There are two reasons for this: Using the terminology of Trilogy, the variables $\mathbf{x}$ are output variables, i.e. their values are fully determined by the one formula whereas the variables $\mathbf{z}$ are input variables with the values fully known before the one formula is entered. Let us now investigate why the Trilogy system insists on the restrictions.

The Prolog query $x = 2, Q(x)$ does not behave identically to the Trilogy query $x = 2\, \&\, one\ x\, Q(x)$. The Prolog query succeeds, whereas in Trilogy we have

$$one\ x\, Q(x) \leftrightarrow x = 1$$

so the query fails. Note that this is what we want because the logically equivalent Prolog query $Q(x), x = 2$ fails just like Trilogy's query $one\ x\, Q(x)\, \&\, x = 2$.

The problem with the cuts of Prolog is that their behaviour is determined by the current bindings of variables in the cut formulas. The notion of current bindings is a purely operational one depending on the order of execution. This goes contrary to the standard semantics of logic where the meaning of a closed formula is indpendent of its context and the meaning of an open formula is relative only to the assignment of values to its free variables. A formula with an unassigned free variable does not have a meaning.

Independence from the bindings of variables $\mathbf{x}$ is expressed by the universal quantifier on $\mathbf{v}$ in the definition 27.2.

One formulas can contain parameters (non-local variables). As can be seen from the definition 27.2, the parameters $\mathbf{z}$ are not bound by any quantifiers and the results $\mathbf{x}$ generally depend on the parameters. We have seen that it is essential that during the execution of a *one* formula, the result variables $\mathbf{x}$ do not have any bindings (that they are output). The following example demonstrates why it is essential that the parameters are fully known (that they are input) before the execution of the one formula starts. Consider the Prolog definition:

```
T(z,x) :- z = 0, x = 2, !.
T(z,x) :- z = 1, x = 3.
```

The query $z = 1, T(z, x)$ succeeds with $z = 1, x = 3$ whereas the logically equivalent query $T(z, x), z = 1$ fails. This is because the behaviour of cuts in Prolog depends on the operational notion of the current binding of the parameter z.

The situation in Trilogy is as follows:

```
T(z,x) iff z = 0 & x = 2   z = 1 & x = 3
```

The query $z = 1 \,\&\, one\, x\, T(z, x)$ succeeds with the same results as in Prolog. The query $one\, T(z, x) \,\&\, z = 1$ is rejected by the system because the parameter z must have a value before the one formula is entered.

27.6   Conclusion

The conclusion is that because of their operational behaviour, the cuts of Prolog are unexplainable in the classical predicate calculus. The sitution can be improved only by a mode and data flow analysis performed by Prolog processors. Since modes are not an integral part of Prolog, there is little hope that the situation can be corrected.

Yet, the idea of finding and taking the first solution is a sensible one and it is quite extensively neededin practical programs. Moreover, the implementation is inexpensive and consists of removing all choice points set by the one formula. This is why we have implemented *one* formulas in Trilogy. We have escaped non-logical behaviour because Trilogy has the modes built-in and the Trilogy processor performs a quite extensive data-flow analysis before it accepts a formula.

References

[1]   Bowen, K., Kowalski, R.A., Amalgamating Language and Metalanguage in Logic Programming, Dept. of Computing, Imperial College, London, 1981.

[2]   Grogono, P., More Versatility with Pascal-like Trilogy, Computer Language, April 1988.

[3]   Hilbert, D., Bernays, P., Grundlagen der Mathematik, Springer, 1970.

[4]   Lane, A., Trilogy: A New Approach to Logic Programming, Byte, March 1988.

[5]   Lloyd, J.W., Foundations of Logic Programming, Springer, 1984.

[6]   Naish, L., Negation and Quantifiers in Nu-Prolog, Proceedings of the Third ICLP London, Springer, 1986.

[7]   O'Keefe, R.A., On the Treatment of Cuts in Prolog Source-Level Tools, Proceedings of the 2nd IEEE SLP, Boston, July 1985.

[8] Shoenfield, J.R., Mathematical Logic, Addison-Wesley, 1967.

[9] Trilogy - Programming Manuel, CLS Vancouver, 1987.

[10] Voda, P.J., The Constraint Language Trilogy - Semantics and Computations, submitted to the Fifth ICLP, Seattle 1988.

[11] Voda, P.J., Types of Trilogy, submitted to the Fifth ICLP, Seattle 1988.

Chapter 28

Hypergraph Grammars and Networks of Constraints versus Logic Programming and Metaprogramming

Francesca Rossi
MCC
3500 W. Balcones Dr.
Austin, TX 78759

Ugo Montanari
Dip. di Informatica
Corso Italia 40
56100 Pisa, Italy

Abstract

In this work we aim to show how different objects as hypergraphs, context-free hypergraph grammars and networks of constraints can be expressed within the unique framework of logic programming. Moreover, we will show that while networks of constraints can be completely described at the object level, the computation in the context-free hypergraph grammar context needs a metalevel description. The two notion of networks and grammars can then be used together to show that our approach may be not only elegant, but also very efficient.

28.1 Introduction

Hypergraphs and networks of constraints can be represented using a very similar formulation, and also context-free hypergraph grammars can be seen as a technique for generating particular classes of networks of constraints. Moreover, all these objects can be easily expressed by using logic programming.

In order to understand the connection among these three fields (hypergraphs, networks and logic programs), let us first describe informally the objects we will deal with from a syntactical point of view:

- a hypergraph is a set of nodes plus a set of hyperarcs, each of which connects an ordered subset of the nodes;

- a context-free hypergraph production replaces a hyperarc with a hypergraph;

- a context-free hypergraph grammar is a set of productions plus an initial symbol;

- a structured hypergraph is the description of a hypergraph through the sequence of productions necessary to generate it;

- a network of constraints is a hypergraph where nodes are variables and each hyperarc connecting k nodes is labelled with a set of k-tuples of values (this is the definition of the constraint among the k variables); the solution of a network is an instantiation of all its variables which satisfies all its constraints;

- a structured network is a structured hypergraph where the hyperarcs of the generated hypergraph are labelled by relations.

From a semantical point of view: the semantics of a hypergraph grammar is its language, i.e. the set of hypergraphs which can be generated using its productions, while the semantics of a network of constraints is the set of its solutions.

Our idea is first to define, from the syntactical point of view, the subclasses of logic programs corresponding to the above described objects, and then to study also the semantical correspondence.

The syntactical mapping is very easy: a node is represented by a variable, a hyperarc by an atom, a connection hypergraph by a rule, a network by a rule plus a set of ground facts (network program), a context-free hypergraph production by a rule, a contex t-free hypergraph grammar by a set of rules (grammar logic program), a structured hypergraph by a set of nonrecursive rules (structured logic program), a structured network by a set of nonrecursive rules plus a set of ground facts (structured network prog ram).

Going to the semantic side, the situation is easy for networks of constraints: the standard semantics of a network program coincides with that one of the given network (its solutions). On the contrary, if we consider hypergraph grammars, this corresponden ce disappears. In fact, grammar logic programs contain no facts; thus, their standard semantics is empty even if the semantics of the given hypergraph grammar is not. But we may note that the difference between the operational semantics of context-free hy pergraph grammars and of grammar logic programs is not enormous. In fact, the basic mechanism is the same and thus a simple metainterpreter may simulate grammar behaviour.

As an example, let us consider a class of networks of constraints whose topology is described by the structured hypergraphs generated by some context-free hypergraph grammar. According to a previous results of the authors ([6]), each network in this class can be solved by a very efficient solution algorithm which utilizes the structured description of the network to achieve a time complexity linear in the number of used productions. In the logic programming field, such networks c an be syntactically represented by structured network programs where the rules correspond to the productions used for generating the hypergraph, while the ground facts define the constraints. A simple metainterpreter which elaborates these programs using a bottom-up technique is enough for implementing this linear solution algorithm.

Section 28.2 defines hypergraphs and context-free hypergraph grammars, while section 28.3 defines networks of constraints. Then, section 28.4 (resp. 28.5) gives the syntactical and semantical correspondence between hypergraph grammars (resp. networks) and logic programs. In section 28.6 we show a case where expressing grammars and networks in logic programmi ng is very efficient. Section 28.7 concludes the paper summarizing its results.

28.2   Hypergraphs and context-free hypergraph grammars

As it can be intuitively understood, a hypergraph is a natural generalization of a graph where arcs (now called hyperarcs) connecting more than two nodes are allowed. Now, a connection hypergraph is a hypergraph plus the selection of one of its hyperarcs. A labelled connection hypergraph is a connection hypergraph where each hyperarc is labelled with a symbol of a ranked label set L. A (context-free hypergraph) grammar is as a simple method for incrementally generating labelled connection hypergraphs. An introduction to graph grammars can be found in [1]. The semantics of a grammar is its language, i.e. the set of all terminal connection hypergraphs generable using its productions. A syntactic tree is the hystory of the generation of one of these hypergraphs. The formal definitions follow.

DEFINITION 1.   *A hypergraph* $G =< N, A, c >$ *consists of*

- *a set of nodes N;*

- *a set of hyperarcs A; $A = \bigcup_k A_k$ is a ranked set, i.e. $a \in A_k$ implies that a is a hyperarc connected to k nodes and that a has rank k;*

- *a connection function $c : \bigcup_k (A_k \to N^k)$, where $c(a) = (x_1, \ldots, x_k)$ is the tuple of nodes connected to a.∎*

DEFINITION 2.   *A connection hypergraph is a hypergraph plus a tuple of its nodes, i.e. a quadruple $CG =< N, A, c, a >$, where $a \in A$. If $a \in A_k$, then CG is called a k-connection hypergraph.∎*

DEFINITION 3.   *A labelled connection hypergraph $F =< N, A, c, l, a >$ is a connection hypergraph $< N, A, c, a >$ plus a labelling function l such that $l : \bigcup_k (A_k \to L_k)$, where $L = \bigcup_k L_k$ is a ranked set of labels.∎*

DEFINITION 4. *Given a nonterminal ranked alphabet NT and a terminal ranked alphabet T, a* **context-free hypergraph production** *p of rank k is a k-connec-/tion hypergraph $F = < N, A, c, l, a >$, where $l(h) \in T \cup NT$ for all h in A.∎*

DEFINITION 5. *Given a k-connection hypergraph $F_1 = < N_1, A_1, c_1, l_1, a_1 >$, a production $p = F = < N, A, c, l, a >$ which is an i-connection hypergraph and a hyperarc h in F_1 such that $l(a) = l(h)$, p* **replaces** *F for h in F_1 and thus derives a new k-connection hypergraph $F_2 = < N_2, A_2, c_2, l_2, a_2 >$ such that, if F' is a fresh copy of F, we have:*

- *$N_2 = N_1 \cup N'$ (with the exception that the nodes in $c(h)$ are merged with the nodes in $c(a)$);*

- *$A_2 = A_1 \cup A'$ (with the exception that h and a are merged);*

- *$c_2 = c$ on A' and $= c_1$ on A_1;*

- *$l_2 = l$ on A' and $= l_1$ on A_1.*

We will write $F_2 = F_1[F'/h]$.∎

DEFINITION 6. *A* **context-free hypergraph grammar** *GG is a quadruple $GG = < V, T, \tilde{S}, P >$, where V is the ranked set of the symbols, $T \subseteq V$ is the ranked terminal alphabet ($V - T$ is the nonterminal alphabet), $\tilde{S} = < N_S, A_S, c_S, l_S, a_S >$, where $c(a) = < x_1, \ldots, x_k >$ for some k, $N_S = x_1, \ldots, x_k$, $A_S = a_S$, $l_S(a_S) = S \in V - T$, is the distinct initial hypergraph and P is a finite ranked set of productions.∎*

While defining a grammar, an approach different from ours consists in allowing the initial symbol to be a general hypergraph (with more than one hyperarcs). However, our approach is not restrictive, because any grammar of the other kind can be easily tran sformed into a grammar satisfying our definition (we only have to add a new production representing that general hypergraph). Moreover, we think that starting from a single hyperarc is more elegant and natural.

DEFINITION 7. *Given a grammar $GG = < V, T, \tilde{S}, P >$, where S has rank k, a* **syntactic tree** *for GG is a connection hypergraph $T = < N_T, A_T, c_T, l_T, a_T >$ which can be constructed with the following rules:*

- *$\tilde{S}$ is a syntactic tree for GG;*

- *given a syntactic tree T for GG, a production $p = F = < N, A, c, l, a >$, and a hyperarc $b \in A_T$ such that $b \neq a$, $l(b) \in V - T$, and $rank(b) = rank(a)$, then $T' = T[F/b]$ is a syntactic tree for GG.∎*

In general, in the following, a connection hypergraph written in the form $F = \tilde{S}[F_1/b_1][F_2/b_2]\ldots[F_n/b_n]$ will be called a structured hypergraph. Note that $b_i \in \bigcup_{k=1,\ldots,i-1} F_k$.

DEFINITION 8. *A* **structured hypergraph** *is a connection hypergraph F which can be written as* $F = \tilde{S}[F_1/b_1][F_2/b_2]\dots[F_n/b_n]$. ∎

Given a syntactic tree T for GG, T represents the generation of a particular connection hypergraph. More precisely, if

$$T = < N_T, A_T, c_T, l_T, a_T > = \tilde{S}[F_1/b_1][F_2/b_2]\dots[F_n/b_n],$$

the generated connection hypergraph is $F = < N_T, A_T - \{b_1, \dots, b_n\}, c_T, l_T, a_T >$.

DEFINITION 9. *Given a grammar* $GG = < V, T, \tilde{S}, P >$, *its* **language** $L(GG)$ *is the set of all connection hypergraphs labelled on T corresponding to all the syntactic trees for GG.* ∎

28.3 Networks of constraints

A network of constraints is a declarative knowledge representation model, useful for describing problems in terms of objects (represented by variables) and relations (constraints) among them. A solution of the represented problem is an instantiation of al l (or only some) variables such that all constraints are satisfied (a constraint is satisfied when the values of the variables it connects form a tuple belonging to the constraint). A detailed description of networks of constraints and their properties ca n be found in [4, 5].

A network of constraints is here defined as a particular case of labelled (connection) hypergraph, where each hyperarc connecting k nodes (variables) is labelled by a set of k-tuples of values of a finite universe. Thus, the label set is now the powerset of the chosen universe.

DEFINITION 10. *A* **network of constraints** $H = < N, A, c, l >$ *is a labelled hypergraph where nodes are called variables, hyperarcs are called constraints, and the ranked label set L is such that* $L_k = \wp(U^k)$, *where U is a finite set of values for the variables in N (and $\wp$ denotes the powerset). A solution of a network of constraints* $H = < N, A, c, l >$ *is an assignment on U of all the variables in N such that all constraints in A are satisfied.* ∎

Sometimes, we may find it useful to represent a problem through a network of constraints, but we are interested, from the solution point of view, only to a subset of the variables. This means that a solution of our problem is an instantiation of only the selected variables such that all constraints are satisfied (not only the constraints connecting subsets of the selected variables). This situation can be described with a so called connection network, which is a network of constraints plus a selected con straint.

DEFINITION 11. *A* **connection network** *is a network of constraints plus a selected hyperarc, i.e. a quintuple* $C = < N, A, c, l, a >$. *It can also be seen as* *a labelled connection hypergraph. If $c(a)$ contains k variables, it is called a k-connection network. A solution of a connection network $C = <N, A, c, l, a>$ is a tuple of values obtained restricting a solution of the network $<N, A, c, l>$ to the variables in $c(a)$.*∎

In the following we will deal only with connection networks, because this formalism includes that one of networks of constraints.

Sometimes a connection hypergraph can be described, as we have seen in the previous section, both in the usual way (definition 2) and in a structured way (definition 8). Thus, we can also define structured networks as connection networks whose underlying hypergraphs have a structured description.

DEFINITION 12. *A **structured network** is a connection network C which can be written as $C = \tilde{S}[F_1/b_1][F_2/b_2]\ldots[F_n/b_n]$, where F_i is a connection network for $i = 1, \ldots, n$, and $\tilde{S}$ is a connection network consisting of only one hyperarc and the nodes it connects.*∎

28.4   Hypergraphs and context-free hypergraph grammars in logic programming

In this section we describe how to express both hypergraphs and context-free hypergraph grammars in logic programming (for a complete introduction to the syntax and the semantics of logic programming, see [3]). The first subsection gives the syntac tical mapping, while the second one deals with the semantical correspondence.

28.4.1   Syntax

In this section we will see how to write different and well studied objects such as hypergraphs and context-free hypergraph grammars within the unique formalism of logic programming.

This syntactical mapping is straightforward. We associate a k-arity predicate p to each labelled hyperarc of rank k. The predicate symbol of p is the label of the hyperarc and its arguments are k (non necessarely distinct) variables representing the nodes connected by the hyperarc.

DEFINITION 13. *Given a hyperarc h such that $c(h) = <x_1, \ldots, x_k>$ and $l(h) = lab$, the corresponding **atom** is $lab(x_1, \ldots, x_k)$.*∎

Following the approach of the above definition, an entire labelled hypergraph is represented by a set of atoms, as many as the number of its hyperarcs, and a labelled connection hypergraph is represented by a rule where the body represents the hypergraph and the head the selected hyperarc.

DEFINITION 14. *Given a labelled connection hypergraph*

$$F = < N, A, c, l, a >,$$

where $c(a) = < x_1, \ldots, x_k >$, $l(a) = l_a$, *the corresponding* **rule** *is:*
$l_a(x_1, \ldots, x_k) \leftarrow \bigwedge \{l_i(x_{i1}, \ldots, x_{ih(i)})$ *for all* a_i *in* A, *if* $c(a_i) = < x_{i1}, \ldots, x_{ih(i)} >$
and $l(a_i) = l_i\}$. ∎

Productions are labelled connection hypergraphs, thus definition 14 works also for
them. In this way an entire grammar is represented by a logic program, from now
on called a grammar logic program (denoted by $P(GG)$ if it corresponds to the
grammar GG), with as many rules as the number of productions in the grammar,
pl us an atomic goal corresponding to the initial hypergraph $\tilde{S}$.

Note that no fact is generated during the construction of this logic program,
and that the arguments in the rules are all variables.

A structured hypergraph, and so also a syntactic tree, is represented by a logic
program very similar to a grammar logic program, but always nonrecursive and,
moreover, deterministic.

DEFINITION 15. *Given a grammar* $GG = < V, T, \tilde{S}, P >$, *the corresponding*
grammar logic program $P(GG)$ *contains all the rules corresponding to the
productions in* P *plus the goal* $\leftarrow S(x_1, \ldots, x_k)$, *if* $\tilde{S}$ *contains only one hyperarc
labelled* S *which connects* k *variables.* ∎

DEFINITION 16. *Given a structured hypergraph* $F = \tilde{S}[F_1/b_1][F_2/b_2] \ldots$-
$[F_n/b_n]$, *the corresponding* **structured logic program** *contains all the rules
corresponding to the productions* $p_1, \ldots, p_n$, *where, for all* $i = 1, \ldots, n$, p_i *is a fresh
copy of* $(F_i)\theta_i$ *and* θ_i *is the substitution* $\{a_i = b_i\}$, *plus the goal* $\leftarrow S(x_1, \ldots, x_k)$,
if $\tilde{S}$ *contains only one hyperarc, labelled* S, *which connects* k *variables.* ∎

28.4.2 Semantics

While studying the semantical correspondence between context-free hypergraph
grammars and grammar logic programs, let us remember that the semantics of a
context-free hypergraph grammar is its language (i.e. a set of labelled connection
hypergraphs), whil e the standard semantics of a logic program is a set of ground
atoms (all the possible instantiations of the variables of the goal). Thus, the
standard semantics of logic programs is not useful for grammar logic programs.

Let us note that both grammars and their semantics (the generable connection
hypergraphs) can be represented as logic programs. This means that the kind of
computation that a grammar logic program must do to completely represent (also
from a semantical po int of view) a grammar is a meta-computation, because it can
be considered as a logic program whose execution returns another logic program.

Moreover, we may note that the semantics of a grammar (its language) can be
obtained in an operational way using as basic step essentially the same mechanism

used in the standard operational semantics of logic programs. In fact, on one side we have the ap plication of a production which rewrites a hyperarc into a set of hyperarcs, on the other side a selected goal (among a collection of goals) is turned to a set of goals by using a clause of the program. The real difference between the operational semantic s of a grammar and that one of a logic program is in the termination condition: in the language theory we stop the sequence when we have only terminal hyperarcs (all the nonterminals have been rewritten), while in logic there is no distinction between ter minals and nonterminals and so we halt only when all predicates have been rewritten (i.e. the empty clause is obtained).

These considerations imply that grammar logic programs must have, as results, not ground atoms (as in standard semantics), but rules (the correspondents of connection hypergraphs). In another way, each result of a grammar logic program is another logic p rogram (a single rule), thus the semantics of grammar logic programs can be obtained only using a metainterpreter.

In reality, as usual in these cases, another approach is possible: instead of using a metainterpreter, we can equivalently change the definition of the semantics of logic programs, in order to distinguish between terminal and nonterminal atoms and to obta in rules instead of ground atoms. This approach has been investigated for a new definition of both the operational and the fixpoint semantics of logic programs ([2]), and turned out to be very interesting and fundamental. Nevertheless, we think that the metainterpreter approach is more elegant, besides the fact that it can be directly used in the standard logic programming systems implementing the usual definition of semantics.

Note that the real difference between the two approaches is where the metalevel, always necessary for expressing the behaviour of grammars in logic programing, is added. In fact, in the metainterpreter approach it is put into the language, while in the ne w semantics approach it is in the interpretation of the language.

A simple metainterpreter which is able to express the computation necessary to generate a hypergraph is the following one (it can be applied to any grammar logic program where facts are added to define the terminal hyperarcs).

$$R(in, l) \leftarrow G(in, l).$$

$$G(a, a) \leftarrow clause(a, true).$$

$$G((a_1, a_2), (l_1, l_2)) \leftarrow G(a_1, l_1), G(a_2, l_2).$$

$$G(a, l) \leftarrow clause(a, b), G(b, l).$$

The goal is $\leftarrow R(S(x_1, \ldots, x_k), l)$.

Predicate G solves the input goal "in" (i.e. $S(x_1, \ldots, x_k)$)) as in standard semantics but stores in a list the generated terminal atoms. In this way, the result of an execution of the given grammar logic program is an atom whose predicate name is the label of the selected hyperarc in the initial hyperarc of the grammar, plus a collection of atoms describing the generated hypergraph. Thus we obtain, as output, an implicit rule with only variables $(S(x_1, \ldots, x_k) \leftarrow l.)$ which corresponds to a connection hypergraph in the language of the given grammar.

A simple modification of this metainterpreter allows us to obtain not the rule corresponding to the generated hypergraph, but the related syntactic tree, i.e. a structured hypergraph (in the form of the sequence of productions applied). This new metainter preter is as follows.

$R(in, l) \leftarrow G(in, l).$

$G(a, [\,]) \leftarrow clause(a, true).$

$G((a_1, a_2), (l_1, l_2)) \leftarrow G(a_1, l_1), G(a_2, l_2).$

$G(a, l) \leftarrow clause(a, b), G(b, l_1), compose(a, b, l_1, l).$

$compose(a, b, [\,], [(a, b)]) \leftarrow .$

$compose(a, b, l_1, [(a, b) \mid l_1]) \leftarrow .$

The goal is $\leftarrow R(S(x_1, \ldots, x_k), l).$

This metainterpreter can be applied to any grammar logic program and returns the list (l) of productions used to generate one of the hypergraphs in the language of the given grammar. Predicate G solves the input goal "in" as in standard semantics but records, at each step, the production used, i.e. the rewritten nonterminal atom and the generated conjunction of atoms. In this way, the result of an execution of the given grammar logic program is a list of implicit rules representing the used production s.

28.5 Networks of constraints in logic programming

As hypergraphs and context-free hypergraph grammars, also connection networks can be easily represented in logic programming.

28.5.1 Syntax

In this subsection we follow the same approach of section 28.4.1, except for the new problem of representing the definitions of constraints in logic programming. This problem is easily solved mapping each relation into a set of facts. In each one of the se facts, the predicate name is a new name associated to the hyperarc and the arguments are one of the tuples belonging to the considered relation.

DEFINITION 17. *Given a connection network* $C = < N, A, c, l, a >$, *where* $c(a) = < x_1, \ldots, x_k >$ *and* $l(a) = l_a$, *the corresponding* **network program** $P(C)$ *consists of*

- *a rule*
  $l_a(x_1, \ldots, x_k) \leftarrow \{l_i'(x_{i1}, \ldots, x_{ih(i)}), \text{ for all } a_i \text{ in } A \text{ such that } l(a_i) = l_i \text{ and } c(a_i) = < x_{i1}, \ldots, x_{ih(i)} > (l_i' \neq l_j' \text{ for all } i, j)\}$, *plus*

- *a set of ground facts*
  $\{l_i'(c_{i1}, \ldots, c_{ih(i)}) \leftarrow \cdot, \text{ for all } a_i \text{ in } A \text{ such that } l(a_i) = l_i \text{ and } < c_{i1}, \ldots, c_{ih(i)} > \text{ is in } l(a_i)\}$.
  The goal for a network program is
  $\leftarrow l_a(x_1, \ldots, x_k). \blacksquare$

A structured network, i.e. a network whose underlying hypergraph is a structured hypergraph, can be represented by a logic program composed by as many rules as the number of productions used to generate the hypergraph, plus a set of facts for defining the terminal hyperarcs.

DEFINITION 18. *Given a* **structured network** $C = \tilde{S}[F_1/b_1][F_2/b_2] \ldots [F_n/b_n]$, *the corresponding* **structured network program** *contains the structured logic program corresponding to C (definition 16 works well, with the exception that the predicate names related to the terminal hyperarcs must be new, for ex ample l_i if the label is the relation r_i), plus a set of facts $\{l_i(c_{i1}, \ldots, c_{ih(i)}) \leftarrow \cdot, \text{ for all } r_i \text{ in } T \text{ such that } r_i = l(a_i), < c_{i1}, \ldots, c_{ih(i)} > \text{ in } l(a_i)\}$. The goal is $\leftarrow S(x_1, \ldots, x_k)$, if S connects k variables.* $\blacksquare$

28.5.2   Semantics

A network program is trivially equivalent to the corresponding connection network, in the sense that the solution of the connection network coincides with the standard semantics of the network program.

THEOREM 1. *Given a connection network* $C = < N, A, c, l, a >$, *its solution coincides with the standard semantics of the corresponding network program* $P(C)$. $\blacksquare$

The following theorem shows that also the standard semantics of a structured network program coincides with the solution of the corresponding structured network (better, the solution of the network generable applying the productions in the given structur ed network).

THEOREM 2. *Given a structured network* $C = \tilde{S}[F_1/b_1][F_2/b_2] \ldots [F_n/b_n]$, *its solution coincides with the standard semantics of the corresponding structured network program.* $\blacksquare$

As we see, using logic programming for representing networks of constraints allows us to remain on a declarative level. In fact, if we want to solve a network, we only have to write the network program (or the structured network program) representing it, because the standard solution algorithm (i.e the backtrack search) is directly implemented by the standard interpreter.

28.6 Networks and grammars together in logic programming lead to an efficient solution algorithm

Networks of constraints and context-free hypergraph grammars represent two well studied classes of objects which have always been treated separately. In this work they are brought nearer from the fact that networks are defined as labelled hypergraphs and, moreover, from the fact that they are both representable as logic programs. Here we will show that these two conditions are enough for characterizing a particular class of networks which are represented by logic programs with a very efficient execution.

In section 28.5.2 we have shown that the standard semantics of a network program coincides with the solution of the corresponding network. Let us now make some complexity considerations.

The technique used by the standard interpreter is the backtrack search. This means that the worst case time complexity for finding all (or even one of) the solutions of the given network can be exponential in its size, i.e. it is $O(U^n)$, where U is the universe where the variables are instantiated and n is the number of variables of the network. This fact is not dramatic. In fact, the problem of solving a network of constraints has been shown to be NP-complete, thus it is obvious to find such a worst case time complexity.

We will show now that, introducing context-free hypergraph grammars in the field of networks of constraints can help us to identify the family of all classes of networks which have a very efficient solution algorithm. They are the classes of the structure d networks of constraints (remember that the underlying hypergraph of a structured network of constraints is generated by a context-free hypergraph grammar and is described by the sequence of productions used in its derivation).

As we know, the standard semantics of a structured network program coincides with the solution of the corresponding structured network. As before, if we execute it using the standard interpreter, the worst case time complexity for obtaining a solution of the given network can be exponential in its size. However, now we have the possibility of applying the bottom-up execution technique, which is much more efficient, because it stresses the deterministic and nonrecursive nature of the set of rules in a stru ctured network program. This execution results linear in the number of rules and, for each rule, exponential in the size of this rule (a bounded quantity). Moreover, this technique allows us to obtain the whole set of the solutions of the network as the r esult of a unique execution of the logic program (and not to obtain one solution at a time).

A simple metainterpreter which implements the bottom-up execution technique of a structured network program is the following. It receives as input the goal (the initial symbol of the grammar from which the structured hypergraph is generated) and the list of the productions (in the form of pairs) used for generating the hypergraph, and returns as output a list of instantiations of the goal which is the solution of the structured network. Naturally, this list is obtained using the bottom-up technique, i.e. elaborating each production from the last to the first.

$R(in, l, sol) \leftarrow H(l), G'(in, sol).$

$H([\,]) \leftarrow .$

$H([h \mid t]) \leftarrow H(t), Dem(h).$

$Dem(a, b) \leftarrow Dem'(b), assertz(newterm(a)), fail.$

$Dem(\_, \_) \leftarrow .$

$Dem'((a, b)) \leftarrow Dem'(a), Dem'(b).$

$Dem'(b) \leftarrow clause(b, true).$

$Dem'(b) \leftarrow newterm(b).$

$G'(in, [in1 \mid sol]) \leftarrow G''(in, in1), G'(in, sol).$

$G'(in, [\,]) \leftarrow .$

$G''(in, in1) \leftarrow dupl(in, in1), retract(newterm(in1)).$

$dupl(x, x) \leftarrow .$

The goal is $\leftarrow R(S(x_1, \ldots, x_n), [p_1, \ldots, p_n], sol).$

Predicate H scans the list l (of productions) from the first to the last element in order to elaborate them in the reverse order, while predicate Dem takes a production (a, b) (representing the rule $a \leftarrow b$), proves the truth of the collection of atoms b (through predicate Dem') in all the possible ways and, for each one of these proofs, asserts the corresponding ground instantiation of the atom a. Predicate Dem' differs from the usual proof of a collections of atoms for its third clause, which is necessary for distinguishing terminal predicates from those nonterminal predicates previously defined (asserting a set of facts) by a call of Dem. Predicate G' puts all the obtained instantiations of the goal (in) into the list sol to be returned as output.

Putting together the metainterpreter above and the second metainterpreter of section 28.4.2 (remember that it takes a grammar and returns the structured representation of one of the hypergraphs in its language), we obtain a metainterpreter which takes a grammar and returns one of the hypergraphs in its language (in a structured description) plus the solution of the network which has this hypergraph as topology and the definition of the terminals of the grammar as constraints. This last metainterpreter follows.

$$R(in, l, sol) \leftarrow G(in, l), R'(in, l, sol).$$

$$G(a, [\,]) \leftarrow clause(a, true).$$

$$G((a_1, a_2), (l_1, l_2)) \leftarrow G(a_1, l_1), G(a_2, l_2).$$

$$G(a, l) \leftarrow clause(a, b), G(b, l_1), compose(a, b, l_1, l).$$

$$compose(a, b, [\,], [(a, b)]) \leftarrow .$$

$$compose(a, b, l_1, [(a, b) \mid l_1]) \leftarrow .$$

$$R'(in, l, sol) \leftarrow H(l), G'(in, sol).$$

$$H([\,]) \leftarrow .$$

$$H([h \mid t]) \leftarrow H(t), Dem(h).$$

$$Dem(a, b) \leftarrow Dem'(b), assertz(newterm(a)), fail.$$

$$Dem(\_, \_) \leftarrow .$$

$$Dem'((a, b)) \leftarrow Dem'(a), Dem'(b).$$

$$Dem'(b) \leftarrow clause(b, true).$$

$$Dem'(b) \leftarrow newterm(b).$$

$$G'(in, [in1 \mid sol]) \leftarrow G''(in, in1), G'(in, sol).$$

$$G'(in, [\,]) \leftarrow .$$

$$G''(in, in1) \leftarrow dupl(in, in1), retract(newterm(in1)).$$

$$dupl(x, x) \leftarrow .$$

The goal is $\leftarrow R(S(x_1, \ldots, x_n), l, sol).$

28.7   Conclusions

We have shown how logic programming can be used for expressing such different objects as hypergraphs, context-free hypergraph grammars and networks of constraints.

From the syntactical point of view, the situation is easy, because each one of these objects corresponds to a particular subclass of logic programs.

From the semantical point of view, we had to represent in logic programming the computation technique used, respectively, for generating a hypergraph and for solving a network. In the network field, the standard interpreter suffices; for context-free hype rgraph grammars, due to their metalevel position in logic programming, it is necessary a kind of symbolic computation which can be implemented by a simple metainterpreter.

In addition to that, we have described a particular case in which the use of logic programming for defining both grammars and networks is not only elegant and natural, but also efficient.

Acknowledgments

Francesca Rossi has been supported by a grant from the Italian National Reseach Council. Furthermore, she would like to thank Antonio Brogi for useful discussions about earier versions of the paper.

References

[1] Ehrig II., Nagl M., Rozenberg G. eds., "Proc 2nd International Workshop on Graph-Grammars and Their Application to Computer Science", 1982, *LNCS 153*, Springer-Verlag.

[2] Falaschi M., Levi G., Martelli M., Palamidessi C., "Declarative Modeling of the Operational Behaviour of Logic Languages", *Tech. Report 10-88*, Computer Science Dept., University of Pisa, Italy.

[3] Lloyd J.W., *Foundation of logic programming*, 1984, Springer-Verlag.

[4] Montanari U., "Networks of constraints: fundamental properties and application to picture processing", *Information Science 7*, 1974, pp. 95-132.

[5] Montanari U., Rossi F., "Fundamental properties of networks of constraints: a new formulation", on *Search and A.I.*, Kanal L. and Kumar V. eds., Springer-Verlag, 1988.

[6] Montanari U., Rossi F., "An efficient algorithm for the solution of hierarchical networks of constraints", Proc. International Workshop on Graph-Grammars and Their Application to Computer Science, 1986, *LNCS 291*, Springer-Verlag.

The MIT Press, with Peter Denning, general consulting editor, and Brian Randall, European consulting editor, publishes computer science books in the following series:

ACM Doctoral Dissertation Award and Distinguished Dissertation Series

Artificial Intelligence, Patrick Henry Winston and J. Michael Brady founding editors; J. Michael Brady, Daniel G. Bobrow, and Randall Davis, current editors

Charles Babbage Institute Reprint Series for the History of Computing, Martin Campbell-Kelly, editor

Computer Systems, Herb Schwetman, editor

Exploring with Logo, E. Paul Goldenberg, editor

Foundations of Computing, Michael Garey and Albert Meyer, editors

History of Computing, I. Bernard Cohen and William Aspray, editors

Information Systems, Michael Lesk, editor

Logic Programming, Ehud Shapiro, editor; Fernando Pereira, Koichi Furukawa, and D. H. D. Warren, associate editors

The MIT Electrical Engineering and Computer Science Series

Research Monographs in Parallel and Distributed Processing, Christopher Jesshope and David Klappholz, editors

Scientific Computation, Dennis Gannon, editor

Technical Communication, Edward Barrett, editor